ALIEN AGENDA

ALSO BY JIM MARRS

Crossfire

INVESTIGATING THE
EXTRATERRESTRIAL PRESENCE
AMONG US

ALIEN AGENDA

JIM MARRS

HarperCollinsPublishers

HarperCollins books may be purchased for educational, business, or sales promotional use. For information please write: Special Markets Department, HarperCollins Publishers, Inc., 10 East 53rd Street, New York, NY 10022.

FIRST EDITION

Designed by Alma Hochhauser Orenstein

Library of Congress Cataloging-in-Publication Data

Marrs, Jim.
    Alien agenda : investigating the extraterrestrial presence among us / Jim Marrs. — 1st ed.
        p.   cm.
    Includes bibliographical references and index.
    ISBN 0-06-018642-9
    1. Unidentified flying object—Sightings and encounters.   2. Life on other planets.   3. Human-alien encounters.   I. Title.
    TL789.M264   1997
    001.942—dc21   96-52017

97 98 99 00 01 ❖/RRD 10 9 8 7 6 5 4 3 2 1

C O N T E N T S

Photographs follow page 194.

ACKNOWLEDGMENTS

It should be acknowledged that our current understanding of UFOs and the alien agenda is the result of many hours of hard work by dedicated and courageous individuals, too often the objects of ridicule, dismissal, or worse. These investigators—from well-known authors and researchers to unheralded private citizens—are too numerous to list here. But their combined efforts have contributed to our knowledge and understanding. Likewise, any attempt to enumerate the many people who have contributed to this work would prove excessively long and most likely overlook someone. Suffice it to say, "None of us is as smart as all of us."

INTRODUCTION

The controversy over the existence of UFOs is over.

UFOs are real.

Only those persons whose outlook prevents them from dealing honestly with the massive amount of documentation and reports collected over the past five decades still cling to the idea that nothing soars in the skies of Earth but man's imagination. Evidence accumulated over the past half-century clearly indicates that UFOs represent real and tangible objects exhibiting traits unlike anything that man can yet produced.

Of course, arguments and protestations will continue. There are, after all, some few folks who still refuse to believe that the world is round.

But, whether you believe in them or not, UFOs are now part of our reality. Gather more than a half-dozen persons in a room and odds are at least one of them has either had a personal UFO experience or knows someone who has. UFO sighting stories permeate our society—from migrant farm workers to former presidents. We are surrounded by UFOs. They're with us in books, comics, advertising, movies, and television; on posters, T-shirts, billboards, trinkets, caps, and bumper stickers.

There are those who still prefer to ignore the phenomenon, hoping it will simply go away and stop intruding on their comfortable world-view. Others are deeply fascinated by what the reality of UFOs might portend. UFO researchers, organizations, and conventions continue to grow throughout the world.

The questions now are "What are they?" and "What do they want?" What is the alien agenda?

The answers may be found by taking an overview of the total UFO experience, a wide-ranging investigation through the maze of UFO literature—much of it sensational, contradictory, distorted, disjointed, and deficient in one way or another, although certain common themes can be discerned.

This confusion is compounded by documented government deceit and duplicity aided by the reluctance of conventional science to publicly address the evidence. For few people—particularly among the smug scientific and political intelligentsia—are willing to give any public credence to the subject. By failing to publicly take notice of the phenomenon, these bastions of conformity and conservatism have left the field open to a wide array of private researchers, who range from serious and dedicated investigators to the wildest of charlatans and profiteers. This situation has meant that any serious and unbiased look at UFOs immediately opened the researcher to a barrage of ridicule and arrogant dismissal by those who have some reason to ignore the subject.

So this is not really a book about UFOs. It is more a book about mind-set.

Mind-set involves what you know and, perhaps more important, how you know it. From the moment of birth we are continuously imprinted by our experiences, our parents, the people and places around us, and our social conditioning—the most dominant of which are public education and religion. This conditioning continues through life, aided principally by the print and broadcast media.

While the media obviously cannot dictate how we are to think, they certainly set the agenda on what we are to think about. Who has time for tedious stories of government conspiracies and financial manipulations when the newspapers and airwaves are filled with crime, accidents, and celebrities? Who bothers to notice when a prime-time TV network "news break" contains nothing but sports scores?

For most people—perhaps the majority—UFOs represent an issue to be avoided. So they bury their minds in the safe, conventional world of the local newspaper and their favorite anchorperson who nightly tells them everything is really okay—just after delivering the day's litany of death and sorrow. These people then assure themselves they are well informed.

Added to this self-assurance is the regular media infusion of conventional thinking by various experts, most of whom owe their livelihood to government in one way or another. Most yield to the immense pressure of the status quo and say nothing publicly that might cause controversy. Those who do are usually branded as kooks or profit seekers.

A clear illustration can be found in comparing two UFO authors with widely divergent opinions. Maj. Donald E. Keyhoe, an Annapolis graduate, Marine pilot, and associate of Charles Lindbergh, began a study of the UFO issue almost from its inception in 1947. During his career, Keyhoe developed close relationships with many high-ranking military and government officials. Keyhoe wrote in *Aliens from Space*, "During my long investigation of these strange objects I have seen many reports verified by AF Intelligence, detailed accounts by AF pilots, radar operators and other trained observers proving the UFOs are high-speed craft superior to anything built on Earth. Before the censorship tightened I also was given the secret conclusions by AF scientists and Air Technical Intelligence officers." In 1957, Keyhoe was named director of the National Investigations Committee on Aerial Phenomena, one of the first private UFO research organizations.

In 1968, noted U.S. meteorologist Dr. James E. McDonald told a congressional committee, "I must stress that much checking on my part has convinced me that Keyhoe's reportorial accuracy was uniformly high . . . his reliability must be recognized as impressive." Major Keyhoe would seem to be a well-connected and credible commentator on UFOs who, after careful study of the data, came to the conclusion that the phenomenon represented extraterrestrial visitation.

A more recent author, Curtis Peebles, also presented impressive credentials. In 1995, Peebles saw the paperback publication of his UFO book, *Watch the Skies!* The title is deceptive because Peebles, after presenting a well-organized and documented overview of UFOs, concluded the whole issue constitutes some sort of mass psychosis—a myth with no objective reality. So why look up? According to Alex Doster, editor in chief of the Smithsonian Institution Press, which originally published Peebles's work, his conclusion that UFOs don't exist represents "generally the views of the Smithsonian."

Now consider how Peebles, who followed in the footsteps of UFO debunkers like Philip J. Klass and Dr. Donald H. Menzel, treated Keyhoe. First, he made the undocumented statement that "by early 1949, Keyhoe was having problems making ends meet and was looking for ideas," implying that Keyhoe probably would write anything to make a buck. Next, Peebles related how Keyhoe was assigned to study UFOs by Ken Purdy, editor of *True* magazine, and stated, "One thing stands out from Keyhoe's meeting with Purdy. From the very start, both were convinced that flying saucers were real, and that the Air Force knew it and was covering it up. . . . Every comment, every action, every rumor was fitted into this preexisting belief." In other words, Keyhoe's conclusion that UFOs represent extraterrestrial visitors was wrong because he built his case based on a preconception.

But what about Peebles? In the introduction to his book, he blatantly admitted to his own preconception when he wrote, "I am a skeptic. I believe flying saucer reports are misinterpretations of conventional objects, phenomena, and experiences. I do not believe the evidence indicates the Earth is under massive surveillance by disk-shaped alien spaceships." Hasn't he too operated from a preconceived idea—his mind-set that there's nothing there? This colors his interpretation of all subsequent UFO issues, as evidenced by his flippant remark about "massive" surveillance of Earth by "disk-shaped alien spaceships." Not all UFO researchers would agree to either "massive," "disk-shaped," "alien," or "spaceships" as a true depiction of the phenomenon.

Peebles and others of his ilk are not true skeptics. They are debunkers—determined to defend their mind-set against UFOs at all cost—and will be referred to as such in these pages.

The truly skeptical must evaluate experts—particularly government experts—in the same manner they would any individual: Has this source proven trustworthy in the past? Unfortunately, the government's track record in veracity is shameful. UN ambassador Adlai Stevenson, based on information given him by government sources, assured the world that the United States had absolutely no connection with the ill-fated Bay of Pigs invasion in 1961. The public was told there was "light at the end of the tunnel" in Vietnam just prior to the 1968 communist Tet offensive. President Richard Nixon said he was not a crook just before he resigned to avoid impeachment. In 1975, the public was told there was a serious shortage of gasoline, yet storage tanks in Texas were filled to the brim. In 1980, President Ronald Reagan gained office by promising to balance the federal budget, then ran up a $2 trillion deficit. President Bill Clinton admitted he smoked marijuana but declared he never inhaled. The list is endless. If the U.S. government were an individual, no one would have anything to do with him.

To get beyond such a restrictive mind-set, one must be open to all possibilities—to seriously consider alternative theories and explanations. One must look past the media pundits who narrowly define the issues and paradigms of the day. One must seek truth in whatever form it may appear—whether in alternative publications, video documentaries, newsletters, or even comic books. Only after absorbing as much information on UFOs as possible, from as widely divergent sources as possible, can the thoughtful individual begin to gain the overview necessary to determine the realities of the phenomenon.

With the proliferation of inexpensive video and automatic cameras, hardly a month goes by without yet another UFO captured on film or tape. Add to this growing photographic evidence ever-increasing personal accounts as portrayed in both the print and broadcast media.

While admittedly the UFO mystery is seriously deepened by the lack of hard physical evidence, anyone who can state unequivocally that UFOs do not exist either has neglected to study the massive amount of literature now available or is in a state of denial that no amount of evidence will penetrate. "If you bet against UFOs, you'd be betting against a sure thing," stated U.S. astronaut John W. Young. "There are so many stars that it's mathematically improbable that there aren't other life sources in the universe."

Many knowledgeable and visionary scientists have spoken seriously about UFOs. German Professor Hermann Oberth, who pioneered rocket technology, wrote, "It is my thesis that flying saucers are real and that they are space ships from another solar system. I think that they are probably manned by intelligent observers who are members of a race that may have been investigating our Earth for centuries." One of Oberth's former pupils and another famous rocket scientist, Wernher von Braun, noted, "Professor Oberth has always been 20 to 40 years ahead of the rest of us."

Today the entire UFO issue has become a multifaceted phenomenon involving much more than spaceship hardware. Peripheral issues involving physics, history, evolution, spatial dimensions, and time enter into the discussion, as do spiritual and psychic matters. Yet a tangible reality exists within these various aspects.

At least this is what the vast amount of material now available on the subject suggests to me. And "me" is the key word here. So much of the belief in UFOs and the weight placed on the evidence is subjective.

Does one uncritically accept every report of a UFO sighting or abduction? Or does one automatically discount such reports? Can one give unquestioned credence to government reports and experts, or are they all suspect? Lacking personal experience, who does one believe and who does one disbelieve?

It's a genuine problem. I had heard of mud raining from the sky, but until I experienced such a thing while living in West Texas, I considered it just another of the Lone Star State's notorious tall tales. Since one's beliefs are inextricably tied to one's life experiences, I feel it is necessary to step into this journalist narrative for a short time and present a personal introduction to the subject.

A Silent Bright Light

To the best of my knowledge I have never seen a UFO. The only possible exception occurred when I was nine years old. The year was 1952 and my family was living in a suburb of Jackson, Mississippi. It was Christmas Eve. Filled with the excitement and expectation of the holiday, I was unable to sleep. Well past midnight I lay tossing and turning in my bed when, on a whim, I got to my knees and looked out the window. The neighborhood of moderate frame homes was bathed in moonlight and especially quiet. Not even the usual barking dogs could be heard.

As I stared out the window contemplating the activities of the coming day, I became aware of a bright light in the sky moving from my left to right. It passed low over the house next to ours. I saw no colored lights and nothing blinking. It was a steady and very bright light that I immediately thought must be an aircraft's landing light. I decided an airplane must be coming in for a landing.

But then two thoughts struck me. One, there was no airport anywhere in the vicinity, and secondly, there was no sound. I listened intently. Like many young boys of that time, I was fascinated with aircraft and could recite names and specs at will. The P-51 Mustang and the P-38 Lightning, two World War II workhorses, were still flying and among my favorites. The reliable C-47, known in its civilian role as a Douglas DC-3, was still widely in use. And, thanks to the Korean War, I and my friends were familiar with the F-86 Sabre and MiG military jets. The ever-present threat of nuclear annihilation made the big B-52 and Soviet Bison bombers only too well known to us. Even at that tender age, I was no babe in the woods when it came to aircraft.

Yet, I could hear no sound from the bright light passing over my neighbor's house. No piston engine sounds. No scream of a jet. I was perplexed, yet I was not amazed. I was not well read enough to be aware of the flap over "flying saucers." I thought perhaps I was upwind and the engine sound blew away from me. Or perhaps it was a meteor. I went back to bed and finally fell asleep. But the incident stuck in my mind, and as I grew older and learned about UFOs, I have often wondered about that bright, noiseless light.

Many people have had a similar experience or know someone who has. Fast-moving lights in the sky, bright flashing illuminations that hover in midair are common experiences. My own father-in-law once described a most unusual-acting shining object he observed off the east coast of Mexico. This man had a responsible lifelong career with Braniff Airlines. He was not given to daydreams and wild imaginings.

Yet such episodes prove nothing. My own experience could have been a low-flying aircraft or a spaceship from Alpha Centauri. After the event, there is simply no objective way of determining for certain. Unimaginative debunkers would probably say I saw only Venus or, like Ebenezer Scrooge, it was only the product of undigested beef. And they might be right.

So one must take a longer view of the UFO issue. Consider all the facts, including the human anecdotes. After all, we are all the sum total of not only what we have personally experienced in life but also of what we have heard along the way.

My Mississippi experience piqued my curiosity in the unusual and I began reading science fiction. Authors such as Ray Bradbury, Isaac Asimov, Robert Heinlein, and Arthur C. Clarke broadened my horizons and stimulated my imagination as well as increasing my scientific knowledge of the universe.

My mother, a devout Southern Baptist, complained that I was cluttering my mind with nonsense. After all, as she patiently explained, everyone knew that there was nothing outside our own planet and the idea of space flight and orbiting satellites was preposterous.

But on October 4, 1957, she stopped saying such things.

I can still recall the confounded expression on my mother's face when I showed her the headlines proclaiming that the Russians had placed *Sputnik I* in orbit around the earth. I too learned something from *Sputnik*. I learned that just because authority figures say something is impossible does not make it so.

One authority figure who appeared to think nothing was impossible was President John F. Kennedy. On May 25, 1961, shortly after taking office, he committed the United States to placing humans on the moon within the decade when he stated, "Now is the time to take longer strides, time for a great new American enterprise, time for this nation to take a clearly leading role in space achievement, which in many ways may hold the key to our future on Earth."

The year after Kennedy spoke those words I was in college and had a most disquieting conversation with one of my roommates. By this time I had read much about UFOs and was thoroughly confused on the subject. Many credible people claimed they were real and that they were craft from other worlds, but the U.S. government, to include the United States Air Force, had more mundane explanations.

One evening I was discussing the subject with my current roommate, whose father was an air force colonel stationed in the Pentagon. Doug grew quite serious and told this story: Only a few years back Doug and his father, whom he saw only infrequently due to military assignments, took a fishing trip together. Late at night, around the campfire and after several beers, the topic of UFOs came up. Doug asked his father what he thought about the subject, and his father began to describe how he was part of a military team that had made contact with an alien craft that landed at a military installation on the West Coast. His father began to describe the craft's occupants when he suddenly broke off the conversation, saying he had said too much. Despite Doug's pleadings, he refused to say another word on the subject.

Here was a story that might or might not be true. Doug could have been ribbing me, but I don't think so. He was too serious about the matter and his story clearly brought out the strained relationship with his father, a subject I doubt he would treat lightly. It was obvious that Doug believed the story. So perhaps the air force colonel was joking with his son. But, if so, why confound his son by refusing to elaborate or even finish his account? I was also struck by the credentials of Doug's father. He was no jokester, but a ranking air force officer. Why tell something so outrageous if he was only joking with his son? And why not admit to the joke later? Instead, Doug said he was later instructed by his father never to repeat what he had been told.

Unfortunately, at this late date I have no way of checking on this story. I have long since lost contact with Doug and I can't remember if I ever knew his father's name. But it is a story that typifies many I have heard through the years as a journalist covering aviation, police, government, and the military.

I have heard extraordinary reports from police officers, pilots, military officers, air traffic controllers, and many others. While some possibly were misinterpretations of explainable occurrences or the product of an unbalanced mind, most came from credible sources who were sincere in what they reported. But while these stories have remained with me, few can now be substantiated. Other stories regarding now-famous UFO cases stuck with me.

For example, in the mid-1960s while working for the *Lubbock Avalanche-Journal* I met many people who clearly recalled the "Lubbock Lights" of 1951. They remembered how the U.S. Air Force concluded the lights were the underside of ducks reflecting streetlights. They hooted in derision, certain that what they had seen could not be explained as "duck butts."

Later, working as a news reporter for the *Fort Worth Star-Telegram* during the late 1960s and 1970s, on three separate occasions I met former air force personnel who claimed they were stationed at Fort Worth's Carswell Air Force Base in 1947 when the infamous Roswell UFO crash allegedly took place. All three said pieces of the crashed object were brought through Carswell, and two of the men claimed to have actually seen the debris. None of the three believed it to be a weather balloon. Only one of these men claimed to have knowledge of alien bodies. This man said that while he had not seen the bodies himself, an air force buddy had guarded them and told him about them. He was adamant that the story of recovered aliens was true. Unfortunately, I made no notes as to names, dates, and places or, if I did, they are long since lost.

More recently I was interviewing a man with documented close ties to secret government defense work. He suddenly began recounting an amazing tale.

At the request of a supersecret UFO unit connected to the government, he was asked to join an expedition to a small lake in the Northwest that was being regularly visited by a UFO. Determined to study the craft, a group, including my storyteller, stood watch until a three-dimensional diamond-shaped craft faded into existence above the lake where it hovered in midair, apparently drawing up water. Suddenly, a bright beam of light shot out from the craft, blasting nearby dirt and rocks. The men, including tough Special Forces types, fled like frightened children.

My source laughed loudly recounting this display of military fortitude but nevertheless gained my pledge not to reveal his identity.

I picked up these stories during work on other assignments. But such accounts remained with me. Since I cannot document names or other details, you'll not find these stories in this book. But these along with many other stories I heard during my reporting years spurred my interest in the UFO phenomenon.

But don't get the idea that I buy into every weird story that comes my way. In 1969, I was the first reporter to tell the story of a "man-goat" monster that terrorized folks at Lake Worth just northwest of Fort Worth. This beastie came to be known as the "Lake Worth Monster" and became somewhat of a legend in the area. As recently as October 1992, the Lake Worth Monster story was repeated in an issue of *Fate* magazine. Consulting Editor Mark Chorvinsky wrote, "Some believe that the monster is still on the loose, roaming Greer Island [at Lake Worth] and the environs. . . ."

While I hesitate to dampen a good yarn with the facts, I tracked the Lake Worth Monster story for nearly two years when, as duly noted by Chorvinsky, I finally determined the entire monster scare was initiated by some students from nearby Brewer High School using an old gorilla suit and a clear plastic mask. I interviewed the students who had confessed their prank to police on the promise that there would be no prosecution or publicity. The early reports were genuine—people had encountered something—but in the end it was all a big hoax. Yet, because it involved minors whom I could not identify, the resolution of the story was never published, leaving the Lake Worth Monster free to roam through accounts of the strange and bizarre.

Then in 1973, I got to investigate a genuine mystery. It concerned a UFO crash that occurred only a few miles from where I now live. It was an investigation illustrative of the problems and issues involved in attempting to solve the UFO mystery. To tell the whole story again requires a personal narrative.

The Aurora Crash of 1897

April 17, 1897, dawned clear and cool in North Texas when out of the south came a large, silver, cigar-shaped object dropping lower and lower as it approached the small hamlet of Aurora, Texas, less than twenty miles northwest of Fort Worth. There it struck a windmill and exploded, scattering debris—and at least one body—in all directions.

Or did it?

Despite straight-faced coverage in the local newspapers at the time, the Aurora crash continues to be a source of controversy. Here's what I know:

In the spring of 1973, Bill Case, aviation writer for the now-defunct *Dallas Times Herald*, wrote a series of articles about the Aurora crash after being told the story by Hayden Hewes of the International UFO Bureau. Case immediately looked up the April 19, 1897, article in his newspaper's microfilm library.

The story stated:

> About six o'clock this morning the early risers of Aurora were astonished at the sudden appearance of the airship which has been sailing throughout the country. It was traveling due north, and much nearer the earth than before. Evidently some of the machinery was out of order, for it was making a speed of only ten or twelve miles and hour and gradually settling toward the earth. It sailed over the public square and when it reached the north part of town collided with the tower of Judge Proctor's windmill and went to pieces with a terrific explosion, scattering debris over several acres of ground, wrecking the windmill and water tank and destroying the judge's flower garden. The pilot of the ship is supposed to have been the only one aboard, and while his remains are badly disfigured, enough of the original has been picked up to show that he was not an inhabitant of this world.
>
> Mr. T. J. Weems, the U.S. Signal Service officer at this place and an authority on astronomy, gives it his opinion that he was a native of the planet Mars. Papers found on his person—evidently the

records of his travels—are written in some unknown hieroglyphics and cannot be deciphered. This ship was too badly wrecked to form any conclusion as to its construction or motive power. It was built of an unknown metal, resembling somewhat a mixture of aluminum and silver, and it must have weighed several tons. The town today is full of people who are viewing the wreckage and gathering specimens of strange metal from the debris. The pilot's funeral will take place at noon tomorrow. Signed: E. E. Hayden.

A similar story was published in the *Fort Worth Register*, but in this account, it did not mention the hieroglyphics and stated simply, "The pilot, who was not an inhabitant of this world, was given Christian burial in the Aurora Cemetery."

The similarities between the Aurora account and modern UFO cases—silver, metallic, cigar-shaped object, small humanoid occupant, unreadable hieroglyphs—were striking and argued against the hoax thesis.

At the time I was an aviation/aerospace writer for the *Fort Worth Star-Telegram* and decided to follow the Aurora story. I contacted Bill Case and found him to be exactly what one would expect of an aviation writer. He was a practical man who was highly knowledgeable of the aircraft industry and, like most people in that field, very precise and technical in his approach to issues.

Case told me he had spoken to some of the old-timers in Aurora and was convinced that something had indeed occurred there in 1897. I arranged to meet Case at the Aurora cemetery, where he showed me what he said was the airship's pilot's grave. The grave was not full size. It was obviously the grave of a child or very small man. At the head of the grave was a crude rock headstone. It appeared that half of the marker had broken off and was missing. On the remaining half was etched a design that resembled a large *V* lying on one side. Inside the *V* shape were three small circles. The entire design indeed resembled one end of a saucer-shaped structure, and the small circles seemed to be portholes. I was acquainted with the old cemeteries in the area, many containing the graves of early settlers and the Maltese cross markers of Confederate soldiers. This was a very unusual and intriguing marker.

Case told me that he had used a metal detector on the grave site and it indicated at least three large pieces of metal in the grave. While Case set out to find someone to analyze whatever might be retrieved from the grave, I began researching the 1897 period, trying to put the Aurora story in perspective. What I discovered was astounding. The Aurora story was not an isolated incident. The microfilm editions of area newspapers of the period were filled with various accounts of flying objects and even contacts with their crews.

It was the Great Airship Mystery of 1896–97, which all started in the fall of 1896 when a large airship was seen in California on the evening of November 17, 1896, by several hundred residents of Sacramento. Observers were able to discern a definite oblong shape behind the light and said it was moving purposely against the prevailing wind.

From California, sightings of the Great Airship began moving across the country. Tens of thousands reported seeing the ship, or ships, and estimates of its speed ranged from five miles per hour to more than two hundred miles per hour. The reported high speeds are noteworthy. I recall reading an article in the 1897 papers in which prominent scientists asserted with authority that humans could not survive speeds greater than forty miles per hour. Therefore, considering that the fastest transportation of the day—trains—crawled along at speeds no greater than thirty-five miles per hour, to claim something moved at greater than one hundred miles per hour meant it was traveling faster than anything known.

It should be noted that in 1878, a Denison, Texas, farmer named John Martin saw a dark flying disk high in the sky. According to the *Denison Daily News*, Martin described his UFO as a "saucer," thus first coining a term that would not come into common usage for nearly a hundred years.

There were hoaxes associated with the flap. In the 1960s, an aging railroad telegrapher confessed that the entire airship story was just a joke concocted by railroad men in Iowa. He said when the joke spread to Texas, railroad worker Joseph "Truthful" Scully was selected to initiate the tale. Pranksters in Iowa admitted they made luminescent hot-air balloons out of tissue paper and candles, provoking sightings across the southern portions of the state on April 10, 1897.

Yet hoaxes could not account for all the sightings. It was clear that something was flying through the air in 1897. If that something was a man-made dirigible, no one ever came forward to take credit. The first recorded dirigible flight in the United States was in 1904 when Thomas Balwin's "California Arrow" lifted off from Oakland, California.

It was also clear that the Great Airship Mystery did not end in Aurora. Reports of the craft continued for days after the reported crash. Author Philip J. Klass wrote, "During a five-day period between April 15 and April 19, 1897, *The Dallas Morning News* reported sightings from 21 different towns in Texas. During the next nine days the *Houston Post* carried nine others."

Debunker Klass, after reviewing reports of the airship, concluded, "The events demonstrate that when the public has been conditioned by the news media to believe that there are strange objects in the skies, many people will report having seen such objects—even when the objects do not really exist." While Klass's thesis undoubtedly is sometimes true, it does not hold up when considering the slow transportation and communication of 1897. Radio was nonexistent and newspapers took days, even weeks, to be delivered. Many of the airship witnesses in small Texas towns could not have heard of the other far-flung sightings.

After reviewing the airship literature, I could not draw any firm conclusion, so I began interviewing people in Aurora.

The population of the little hamlet in 1973 was less than five hundred. They seemed almost evenly divided in their beliefs concerning the crash—half claimed it really happened, while the other half claimed it was merely a hoax perpetrated by Hayden, a "stringer" for local newspapers who had previously written several satirical pieces.

I learned that Etta Pegues, a "stringer" for the *Fort Worth Star-Telegram* in 1973, was a major source for the news media regarding the crash. "It's all a hoax," she said flatly. "I have talked to people who were alive then. They all said Judge Proctor had no windmill." Her primary source of information was Robbie Hanson.

Robbie Reynolds Hanson said, "They're still trying to bring up the hoax about the spaceship." She was twelve years old on the day of the crash, her family lived outside of town, and no one knew anything about it until a man rode by several days later and told the story. "I remember my father remarked that the judge outdid himself that time," she recalled. Wise County Historical Commission chairwoman Rosalie Gregg has consistently decried the Aurora story as a hoax. Her primary source of information was Etta Pegues.

Brawley and Etta Oates bought Judge Proctor's property in 1945 and lived there for years. Brawley died about the time the 1973 publicity about Aurora broke. "I heard the story for years," said Mrs. Oates, adding, "Nothing grew for years in that one spot in the field where that spaceship is supposed to have hit." The Oates family all suffered serious health problems, including cysts and goiters, which they told me were caused by drinking water from the old well where the crash occurred. "I've been told it's radioactive," Mrs. Oates confided.

By 1973, there were only three people still living who may have had direct knowledge of the crash. One was Robbie Hanson, who admitted she had no personal knowledge. Another living witness was Mary Evans, then almost ninety-two years old. She said, "I was only fifteen at the time and had all but forgotten the incident until it appeared in the papers recently. We were living in Aurora at the time, but my mother and father wouldn't let me go with them when they went up to the crash site at Judge Proctor's well. When they returned home they told me how the airship had exploded. The pilot was torn up and killed in the crash. The men of the town who gathered his remains said he was a 'small man' and buried him that same day in Aurora cemetery. That crash certainly caused a lot of excitement. Many people were frightened. They didn't know what to expect. That was years before we had any regular airplanes or other kinds of airships."

Of these two elderly women, neither had any direct knowledge and one said it happened because her parents told her about it, while the other said it was a hoax because that's what her father said. Pro and con, you could take your pick.

Then there was Charlie C. Stephens. He was eighty-three in 1973 and, although somewhat physically enfeebled, appeared to retain a clear mind. Speaking through the screen door of a relative's house, he told me that he had always declined to talk to reporters about the crash because he "didn't want to get involved." Finally, after some neighborly conversation—in my part of the country they call it "visiting"—Stephens loosened up and gave this account.

As a boy less than ten years old, he was with his father putting some cattle out to pasture on the morning of April 19, 1897, when the pair saw a cigar-shaped object with a bright light pass overhead. The craft was very low and moved straight ahead toward Aurora about three miles to the north. The pair then heard what seemed to be an explosion, and a fire lit up the northern sky for several minutes. "I wanted to go immediately and see what had happened," Stephens recalled, "but my daddy said we had to finish our chores."

Stephens said his father rode a horse into town the next day. Returning to the family farm, he described a mass of torn metal and burned rubble. He made no mention of the pilot. This struck me as a credible detail. According to the contemporary accounts, the pilot was buried the same day as the crash. So when Stephens's father was in town, there was no body to view and, being a conservative farmer type, he declined to talk about anything he had not personally seen. But the elder Stephens had no trouble talking about the crash.

"During the years I was growing up he told me the story many times," recalled Stephens, adding he was almost twenty years old before he heard about the dead pilot.

A chart of the Masonic Cemetery showed no unidentified graves. However, Mrs. Isla Finlayson, a resident of nearby Rhome who cared for the cemetery in the 1960s and 1970s, said many people were buried without headstones and that early maps did not list all burials. "There are a lot of people out there we don't know about," she told a reporter.

On it went. For every claim, there was a counterclaim. All I was left with was one witness, Stephens, some bits of metal gathered from the crash site, and the grave. Hardly convincing evidence.

Then the story took an intriguing twist. After analyzing some of the metal from the Aurora crash site, physicist Dr. Tom Gray of the University of North Texas in Denton stated in a news release that at least one fragment was "puzzling." Gray said three of four samples he studied using "highly sensitive" equipment had "properties and content common to metals of this area." But the fourth "may require more investigation," he said. The fourth fragment appeared melted and looked as if it had been "splattered on the ground." Gray said the most intriguing aspect of the fragment was that, although it was made up primarily of iron, it displayed no magnetic properties. He added that the piece was shiny and malleable instead of dull and brittle like iron. The piece was determined to contain 75 percent iron and 25 percent zinc with "a few trace elements." Yet it was not magnetic like stainless steel, which contains only 15 percent iron.

Debunker Klass later wrote, "Subsequent analysis of the fragments by scientists at the National Aeronautical Establishment of Canada reportedly showed the metal fragments to be commonplace, without unusual composition or structural characteristics." However, Klass offered no citation for this statement, and I have remained unaware of this development. Anyone with a suspicious mind might asked if the Canadian study actually took place and if so, did they receive all of the original fragments or just the commonplace ones? As will be seen, there is a reason for my suspicions.

While the fragments were being studied, Bill Case and I had written further on the Aurora story and had generated some interest in exhuming the small grave. I was excited. An exhumation might settle the matter once and for all. But it was not to be.

Despite the fact that no legal action had been taken to seek an exhumation, several Aurora residents, including cemetery directors, stood guard at the cemetery to prevent any unauthorized digging and threatened to seek a restraining order against anyone who tried. "They are afraid you'll dig up Grandma," explained Decatur attorney Bill Nobles. H. R. "Pig" Idell, then Aurora's city marshal, "rode shotgun" on the cemetery for about two weeks to prevent any digging. "We didn't call out the National Guard," Idell recalled. "There was me, the sheriff, and a couple of deputies. That was enough." The night after the patrols stopped, the strange headstone was stolen.

Vandals, souvenir hunters, anyone could have taken the head-stone. More unexplainable was the fate of the metal in the grave. A few months after the exhumation furor had died away, Bill Case met me at the Aurora graveyard, saying there was something he wanted to show me. When he ran his metal detector over the small grave, there were no readings. He knelt down and showed me three small holes that had been drilled in the exact location of the metal. "They took it away," he said cryptically. "Who do you think did this?" I asked. Case looked me in the eye and replied, "The government." Case died about a year later.

With the headstone and grave metal missing, an exhumation impossible, and even the old-timers squabbling over the truth of the crash, excitement over the Aurora story quickly faded. Displaying an obvious lack of understanding about the crudeness of life in nine-teenth-century rural Texas, debunker Curtis Peebles summed up the Aurora crash thusly: "In retrospect, it is clear there is nothing to back up the story of the Aurora 'crash' except the single newspaper article. There were no follow-up articles, no photos, no police reports, no let-ters or diaries mentioning the crash, no samples of the wreckage, nor were the spaceman's papers ever published. The other airship stories in the *Dallas Morning News* were all 'tall tales.' There is no evidence the newspaper or its readers ever believed it was more than that."

I continue to be undecided. I have tried to convince myself there was nothing to the story, but there were too many oddities—the context of the Great Airship Mystery, the small grave containing sig-nificant bits of metal, the "puzzling" fragment, the deformities of the Oates family, the recollection of Charlie Stephens. And, if the story was merely a hoax, why would anyone use sophisticated equipment to surreptitiously remove the metal from the grave?

To compound the puzzle, years later my wife, who was teaching school in the area, was told in all seriousness by Pig Idell's son, James Idell, that his grandfather had helped bury the pilot, described as "a three-foot-tall, big-headed spaceman." The son also said his father knew who took the headstone but wouldn't elaborate, indicating some kind of official secrecy.

The Aurora crash story underscores the problems and issues involved in seeking the truth about UFOs. The problem of unreliable witnesses on all sides is magnified by what appears to be official complic-ity in the maddening lack of physical evidence. Here's another example.

The Thing in the Pond

On Monday, January 10, 1977, following one of the harshest blizzards of that winter, William McCarthy of Wakefield, New Hampshire, discovered a three-foot-diameter hole in the center of an iced-over duck pond he had dug five years previously. The overnight appearance of the hole seemed strange to McCarthy, as the remainder of the pond was covered with thick ice. It was as if something had fallen down from the sky. Puzzling over the hole most of the day, McCarthy finally called police and the saga began.

I became aware of the story the next day when the Associated Press wire machine at the newspaper where I worked received a twelve-paragraph dispatch with the lead, "National Guard and state Civil Defense authorities were dispatched today to a small New Hampshire farm where a mysterious object broke a hole in the ice of a pond." The story stated that New Hampshire deputy attorney general Thomas Rath said tests had been made on the object, which was still in the pond. It also quoted a spokesman for the North American Air Defense Command, who stated, "No artificial satellites have fallen into the area."

Within just a few hours, the AP again transmitted the story but had added two paragraphs reading, "In Washington, meanwhile, Air Force officials said today that tests conducted at the scene revealed no radioactivity. Major John Duemmel, an Air Force information officer, said reports of radioactivity have been 'over-stressed.' In Concord, an Air National Guard source who asked not to be identified, said the last reports he has seen show 'no nuclear activity.'" Since the first report had not mentioned radioactivity, I was intrigued by the sudden disclaimers and continued to monitor the wire machine.

Within a few more hours came a new story stating, "State officials who converged on a small farm pond because of reports that a possibly radioactive object had fallen through the ice have found no object and no radioactivity, a spokesman for Gov. Meldrim Thomson said today."

This story was followed by a lengthy piece by Associated Press writer George Esper, who wrote, "Wakefield, N.H.—The Great Ice Caper has melted into thin air. But it stirred up a lot of excitement while it lasted in this normally serene, picturesque community of white frame houses, snow-covered trees and 1,400 people on the Maine–New Hampshire border." Esper's story described the entire affair as a "comedy of errors" and went on to say that early reports of high radioactivity were superseded by more sophisticated equipment. He wrote, "A second reading 12 hours later was negative." Remember that twelve-hour time factor.

That was the end of that story, at least as far as the news media was concerned. The initial story and the retractions hit the wires so rapidly that most news outlets, including my own newspaper, did not even carry the story at all. But I was not satisfied that the whole story had been told. My journalistic instincts were aroused. So I began telephonically checking out the story of the thing in the pond. Here's what I learned:

A few days after the incident I got an account from Mrs. McCarthy, who told me her husband was still outside trying to clean up the mess left by officials and the news media.

She said McCarthy discovered the hole on Monday, January 10, after a particularly heavy snow, which made it all the more conspicuous. Peering into the hole, McCarthy saw what appeared to be a black cube resting on the bottom of the pond. Growing more curious, he probed the bottom of the pond with a six-foot-long piece of wood. "He couldn't feel anything and since the pond is only about three feet deep, he thought that was curious," said his wife. "In fact, he couldn't really tell if he was hitting bottom. It felt like it was all squishy, which was strange because the bottom of that pond is like rock."

She said later that day, her husband notified the local police, who came out and checked the pond with a small Geiger counter. "They came running back up to the house saying they had found high radioactivity," she recalled. About 2:00 A.M. Tuesday morning, she said the police returned accompanied by a Civil Defense official. "They wanted to know if they could make some tests, so we said, 'Sure,' and went back to sleep. We didn't hear any more until morning."

Later on Tuesday, according to Mrs. McCarthy, the governor's office called and wanted permission to conduct further tests, which they granted. After waiting for some time, the McCarthys left to run some errands. "When we came back home, the state people were there," she said. "They were walking all around and then they interviewed my husband. Then this assistant to the attorney general went off to make a phone call. I thought that was strange. I don't understand why he didn't call from our house."

Mrs. McCarthy said both the state authorities and the local police told her and her husband not to say anything to anyone about the object in the pond. By Wednesday, everyone had left and the McCarthys thought the incident was over. But about 4:00 P.M. she said they received the first of more than five hundred phone calls inquiring about the object, mostly from the news media. Later that evening the local police called to inform the McCarthys that state officials would be at their home on Thursday to drain the pond and retrieve the object.

Early Thursday morning the local road maintenance engineer arrived and said the state had ordered him to plow snow from the field around the pond so a pump truck could be brought in. He said they told him to be at the McCarthy farm at 6:00 A.M. "[That's] like the middle of the night here," commented Mrs. McCarthy. As the morning wore on people started arriving at the farm. "They were miserable and cold and their cars were stacked all the way down our little drive," recalled Mrs. McCarthy. "I could have made a fortune selling hot coffee. Then the police evacuated the area. They would not let the reporters get near. This drove the news media up the wall."

With the media held at a distance, the authorities continued their work until one official told them it was too difficult to drain the pond and work ceased. "I saw them carry away some plastic bags. I don't know what was in those bags. Mud off the bottom of the pond, I guess," said Mrs. McCarthy.

Suddenly the officials all left, and shortly the news media poured in and stayed until late in the evening. Phone inquiries were coming from as far away as Canada and Hawaii. "Since the officials left with those plastic bags, no one in authority has contacted us," Mrs. McCarthy said. "I really don't understand it."

McCarthy in the initial wire story was quoted as saying he had been ordered not to discuss the object. He added the thought that "all the attention given to the hole in the ice is ridiculous." In later stories there was no mention of the gag order and he was quoted as simply saying "ridiculous," leaving the impression that the whole story was unfounded.

Making further telephone inquiries, I learned:

- Governor's spokesman Roland Jenkins said, "The entire matter was caused by false preliminary instrument readings" on equipment that turned out to be "faulty." He added that "those who reported seeing an object apparently were misled by shadows across the cracked ice."
- The Wakefield Police Department denied knowing anything about the incident. The officer I spoke with said it must have happened someplace else.
- The Wakefield police chief, who initially told several persons he had seen the object and confirmed the high radiation readings, later denied saying any such thing. "No comment," he told me.
- A United Press International reporter who was at the scene was asked if the initial wire stories were true or the result of sloppy reporting. "Well, I can tell you it was not sloppy reporting," he replied. However, he would not elaborate on what knowledge he had about the incident.
- Two McCarthy neighbors, Mrs. Ernest Bellow and Mrs. Frederick Fisher, told me they understood that an object

about eighteen inches in diameter was recovered from the pond.

- The Wakefield town clerk said he thought the entire affair was "damn foolishness" but admitted he had not been to the McCarthy farm.
- Wakefield selectman William Tomley told me he too had been ordered by state authorities not to discuss the object. He did confirm that there were "suspicious readings" initially on radiation equipment but that later there were no more readings.

Was there anything in the pond? Was there radiation? Was the object sneaked away in the middle of the night? Or was it taken away by officials in those plastic bags? Or was there never anything there in the first place? If there was, could it have been a meteorite? A secret weapon? A piece of a satellite? A part from a UFO? A child's toy? Your guess is as good as mine.

But the Wakefield story clearly illustrates how the news media can be manipulated and how authorities can bypass what is supposed to be an open and democratic system. Almost no one knew of this story when it happened and no one remembers it today. How many other stories like this one have been swept under the rug? And what became of the black cube, if there was one? Could it be sitting next to the Ark of the Covenant in that government warehouse depicted by Steven Spielberg?

The sum total of my experiences has left me open and receptive to all information—no matter the source—but likewise, skeptical of all, particularly official pronouncements. The black cube story and many others like it engendered in me a deep distrust for the facile and self-serving explanations of officialdom.

Has the government obtained solid evidence of UFO activity? I can't say yes or no with any confidence. But based on my experience, I can say with considerable confidence that there are persons within the government who know a lot more about UFOs than they will publicly admit. I am not alone in that belief. A 1995 poll by Scripps-Howard News Service and Ohio University asked the question whether or not it is likely that the federal government is covering up the existence of UFOs. Forty-three percent responded it was "unlikely," but a full 50 percent replied such a cover-up was likely and 7 percent were uncertain.

As long as there is official reticence to address the issue of UFOs, it will remain a matter of personal belief and conjecture based on mind-set. And the question of belief is compounded by the undeniable fact of a concerted effort on the part of certain authorities to conceal the reality of the subject. This effort amplifies a natural and innate desire to deny their existence to ourselves. We all fervently wish to preserve our belief systems about our world and the universe. Most telling is the established fact that the government has denied the existence of UFOs and any interest in the issue, while internal documents made public through the years show that a very real and serious interest has—and continues—to exist.

This documented interest supports the confident statement that UFOs represent a real phenomenon. They are not simply will-o'-the-wisps or hallucinations. They are real.

But what is their agenda? In the following chapters, the many issues surrounding the UFO mystery will be addressed. Veteran students of UFO literature will be reminded of classic cases and controversies. Their inclusion is necessary to present the full spectrum of the UFO experience. But there are also many unpublicized or forgotten issues along with some new accounts. Hopefully everyone will gain some new knowledge or insight along the way.

I have sought out what I believe to be the most authoritative sources, although this does not necessarily always mean the mainstream corporate media. I also have relied on sources that over time have proven to be credible in both facts and assertions. A world-renowned physicist undoubtedly is more susceptible to government pressure than a private citizen who has quietly made his own in-depth study of UFOs over many years. Therefore, scrutiny should be given more to the information and its source rather than the person who presents it. In this work, the emphasis will be on issues rather than personalities. Information is where you find it. The trick is to study it all, looking for consistencies and agreement. The overview usually yields discernible lines of truth.

So dropping back into a more formal journalistic style, let us seek the alien agenda.

—Jim Marrs

CHAPTER 1

THE GREATEST UFO?

One particularly bright, circular object has been observed moving through Earth's skies since the beginning of human history. Every person on the planet has seen this object. We call it the moon.

Although this object is identified—at least we have a name for it and we know it's there—the moon cannot be hastily disqualified as a UFO. Despite six visits by U.S. astronauts between 1969 and 1972, the moon remains a riddle to scientists in many regards. The solutions to these riddles could indicate an alien aspect of our familiar moon.

Before the Apollo missions, lunar scientists longed for the time when humans could walk on the moon's surface. By studying the makeup of our satellite, they hoped to resolve some of the mysteries of how our planet and solar system came into existence. Well-known space expert and the first chairman of the National Aeronautics and Space Administration's (NASA) Lunar Exploration Committee Dr. Robert Jastrow has stated, "The moon is the Rosetta stone of the planets."

Six moon landings later, the public perception was that we had learned all we needed to about the moon. However, those same lunar scientists were no closer to agreement on how to answer even the most basic questions—such as how the moon was created. Despite the return of some 842 pounds of rocks and soil samples, photos and videotape, and the placement of five nuclear-powered scientific stations on the lunar surface, there are still no clear-cut solutions to the moon's mysteries.

Quite the reverse: what we have learned about the moon in the wake of the Apollo missions has only raised more questions. Science writer Earl Ubell declared, "The lunar Rosetta stone remains a mystery. The moon is more complicated than anyone expected; it is not simply a kind of billiard ball frozen in space and time, as many scientists had believed. Few of the fundamental questions have been answered, but the Apollo rocks and recordings have spawned a score of mysteries, a few truly breath-stopping."

Consider some of these "breath-stopping" mysteries, or anomalies, as scientists prefer to call them:

The moon is far older than previously imagined, perhaps even much older than the earth and sun. By examining tracks burned into moon rocks by cosmic rays, scientists have dated them as billions of years old. Some have been dated back 4.5 billion years, far older than the earth and "nearly as old as the solar system," according to Jastrow. The oldest rocks ever found on Earth only date back 3.5 billion years. It is accepted by scientists today that the earth is about 4.6 billion years old. Harvard's respected astronomy journal, *Sky and Telescope*, reported that at the Lunar Conference of 1973, it was revealed that one moon rock was dated at 5.3 billion years old, which would make it almost a billion years older than our planet. This puzzle was compounded by the fact that the lunar dust in which the rocks were found proved to be a billion years older than the rocks themselves. Chemical analysis showed that the moon rocks were of a completely different composition from the soil around them. Since dusty soil is usually produced by the weathering and breakup of surrounding rocks, the lunar rocks must have come from someplace other than where they were found. But where?

The moon has at least three distinct layers of rocks. Contrary to the idea that heavier objects sink, the heavier rocks are found on the surface. Stated Don Wilson, "The abundance of refractory elements like titanium in the surface areas is so pronounced that several geochemists proposed that refractory compounds were brought to the moon's surface in great quantity in some unknown way. They don't know how, but that it was done cannot be questioned. These rich materials that are usually concentrated in the interior of a world are now on the outside." Ubell, a former science editor for CBS television, acknowledged this mystery, saying, "The first [layer], 20 miles deep, consists of lavalike material similar to lava flows on Earth. The second, extending down to 50 miles, is made up of somewhat denser rock. The third, continuing to a depth of at least 80 miles and probably below, appears to be of a heavy material similar to the Earth's mantle. . . ." Ubell asked, "If the Earth and moon were created at the same time, near each other, why has one body got all the iron and the other [the moon] not much? The differences suggest that Earth and moon came into being far from each other, an idea that stumbles over the inability of astro-physicists to explain how exactly the moon became a satellite of the Earth."

The moon is extremely dry and does not appear to have ever had water in any substantial amounts. None of the moon rocks, regardless of location found, contained free water or even water molecules bound into the minerals. Yet instruments left behind by Apollo missions sent a signal to Earth on March 7, 1971, indicating a "wind" of water had crossed the moon's surface. Since any water on the airless moon surface vaporizes and behaves like the wind on Earth, the question became, where did this water originate? The vapor cloud eruptions lasted fourteen hours and covered an area of some one hundred square miles, prompting Rice University physicists Dr. John Freeman Jr. and Dr. H. Ken Hills to pronounce the event one of "the most exciting discoveries yet" indicating water within the moon. The two physicists claimed the water vapor came from deep inside the moon, apparently released during a moonquake. NASA officials offered a more mundane, and questionable, explanation. They speculated that two tanks on Apollo descent stages containing between sixty and one hundred pounds of water became stressed and ruptured, releasing their contents. Freeman and Hills declined to accept this explanation, pointing out that the two tanks—from *Apollo 12* and *14*—were some 180 kilometers apart, yet the water vapor was detected with the same flux at both sites, although the instruments faced in opposite directions. Skeptics also have understandably questioned the odds of two separate tanks breaking simultaneously and how such a small quantity of water could produce a hundred square miles of vapor. Additionally, *Apollo 16* astronauts found moon rocks that contained bits of rusted iron. Since oxidation requires oxygen and free hydrogen, this rust indicates there must be water somewhere on the moon.

Moon rocks were found to be magnetized—not strong enough to pick up a paper clip, but magnetic nevertheless. What makes this so odd is that there is no magnetic field on the moon itself. So where did the magnetism come from? The argument that perhaps the moon picked up its magnetism from close contact with the earth collapses when one considers that if the moon got close enough to pick up a magnetic field, it was close enough to be ripped apart by the earth's gravitational pull.

The presence of maria, or large seas of smooth, solidified molten rock, on the moon indicates nothing less than a vast outpouring of lava at some distant time. It has now been confirmed that some of the moon's craters are of internal origin. Yet there is no indication that the moon has ever been hot enough to produce volcanic eruptions. Stated Ubell, "The relative cool of the lunar interior (about 1,800 degree Fahrenheit as compared with the Earth's interior temperature of between 3,600 and 9,000 degrees) suggests that the moon was pretty cool to begin with and that the interior contains less radioactivity than the Earth or the surface of the moon." Jastrow tried to explain this conundrum by stating that the moon was volcanically active some billions of years ago but, being a small world, rapidly lost its heat. "Those ancient lava flows look as though they had happened yesterday," he wrote. "This fact misled the hot-moon scientists into believing that the moon had been volcanically active during much of its history." There are certain areas of the moon that remain "hot" during both eclipse and daytime conditions, indicating internal heat. Another puzzle is that almost all—four-fifths—of the maria are located on the moon's earthside hemisphere. Few maria mark the far side of the moon, often erroneously referred to as the "dark side." Yet the far side contains many more craters and mountainous areas. In comparison to the rest of the moon, the maria are relatively free of craters, suggesting that craters were covered by lava flow. Adding to this mystery are the mascons—large, dense, circular masses lying twenty to forty miles below the center of the moon's maria. The mascons were discovered because their density distorted the orbits of our spacecraft flying over or near them. One scientist proposed that the mascons are heavy iron meteorites that plunged deep into the moon while it was in a soft, formable stage. This theory has been discounted, since meteorites strike with such high velocities, they would vaporize on contact. Another mundane explanation is that the mascons are nothing more than lava-filled caverns, but skeptics say there isn't enough lava present to accomplish this. Since the maria appear to have been formed by hot lava, why did these heavy mascons not sink to the bottom? "What they are is a major moon mystery," wrote Wilson. "It now appears that the mascons are broad disk-shaped objects that could be possibly some kind of artificial construction. For huge circular disks are not likely to be beneath each huge maria, centered like bull's-eyes in the middle of each, by coincidence or accident."

During the Apollo missions seismographic equipment was placed at six separate sites on the moon. Between 1969 and 1977, when this equipment ceased operating, up to three thousand "moonquakes" were detected during each year of operation. Most of the vibrations were quite small and were caused by meteorite strikes or falling booster rockets. But many other quakes were detected deep inside the moon. This internal creaking is believed to be caused by the gravitational pull of our planet, as most moonquakes occur when the moon is closest to the earth. However, an event occurred in 1958 in the moon's Alphonsus crater that shook the idea that all internal moonquake activity was simply settling rocks. In November of that year, Soviet astronomer Nikolay A. Kozyrev of the Crimean Astrophysical Observatory set the scientific world on its ear by photographing the first recorded gaseous eruption on the moon near the crater's peak. Kozyrev attributed this to escaping fluorescent gases. He also detected a reddish glow characteristic of carbon compounds, which "seemed to move and disappeared after an hour." Some scientists refused to accept Kozyrev's findings. However, astronomers at the Lowell Observatory also saw reddish glows on the crests of ridges in the Aristarchus region in 1963. Days later colored lights lasting more than an hour were reported at two separate observatories. Something was going on inside the volcanically dead moon. And whatever it is, it occurs the same way at the same time. As the moon moves closer to the earth, seismic signals from different stations on the lunar surface detect identical vibrations. Could internal shifting inside the moon always occur the exact same way? Hardly likely. *New York Times* writer Walter Sullivan wrote, "It is as though the ups and downs of the stock market repeated themselves precisely for each period of fluctuation." The question of identical vibrations prompted Wilson to conclude that "it is hard to understand how this could be a natural phenomenon. However, something artificially constructed could produce the same identical seismic result, which could occur over and over." For example, a broken hull plate could shift exactly the same way each time the moon passed near the earth.

There are many indications that the moon may be hollow. The moon's mean density—about 3.34 grams per cubic centimeter, or 3.34

times as much as an equal volume of water—is significantly different from the 5.5 gram density of the earth's mantle. Studies of moon rocks indicate that the moon's interior differs from the earth's mantle in ways suggesting a very small, or even no, core. As far back as 1962, NASA scientist Dr. Gordon MacDonald stated, "If the astronomical data are reduced, it is found that the data require that the interior of the moon be less dense than the outer parts. Indeed, it would seem that the moon is more like a hollow than a homogeneous sphere." Unwilling to believe the moon hollow, MacDonald believed his data may have been faulty. However, other studies tended to confirm his findings. Nobel chemist Dr. Harold Urey has suggested that the density question may be answered by what he termed "negative mascons," or large areas inside the moon where "there is either matter much less dense than the rest of the moon or simply a cavity." MIT's Dr. Sean C. Solomon wrote, "The Lunar Orbiter experiments vastly improved our knowledge of the moon's gravitational field . . . indicating the frightening possibility that the moon might be hollow." Why frightening? The significance was stated by astronomer Carl Sagan way back in his 1966 work *Intelligent Life in the Universe:* "A natural satellite cannot be a hollow object."

The most startling evidence that the moon could be hollow came on November 20, 1969, when the *Apollo 12* crew, after returning to their command ship, sent the lunar module (LM) ascent stage crashing back onto the moon, creating an artificial moonquake. The LM struck the surface about forty miles from the *Apollo 12* landing site, where ultrasensitive seismic equipment recorded something both unexpected and astounding—the moon reverberated like a bell for more than an hour. The vibration wave took almost eight minutes to reach a peak, then decreased in intensity. At a news conference that day, one of the codirectors of the seismic experiment, Maurice Ewing, told reporters scientists were at a loss to explain the ringing. "As for the meaning of it, I'd rather not make an interpretation right now. But it is as though someone had struck a bell, say, in the belfry of a church a single blow and found that the reverberation from it continued for 30 minutes." Dr. Frank Press of MIT added, "None of us have seen anything like this on Earth. In all our experience, it is quite an extraordinary event. That this rather small impact . . . produced a signal which lasted 30 minutes is quite beyond the range of our experience." Later it was established that small vibrations had continued on the moon for more than an hour. Dr. Press later attempted to explain the phenomenon by saying the LM crash may have set off "a cascade of avalanches and collapses over a very large area." However, this idea failed to explain why the seismic data showed long, sustained readings following the impact. The phenomenon was repeated when the *Apollo 13*'s third stage was sent crashing onto the moon by radio command, striking with the equivalent of eleven tons of TNT. According to NASA, this time the moon "reacted like a gong." Although seismic equipment was more than 108 miles from the crash site, recordings showed reverberations lasted for three hours and twenty minutes and traveled to a depth of twenty-two to twenty-five miles. Subsequent studies of man-made crashes on the moon yielded similar results. After one impact the moon reverberated for four hours. This ringing coupled with the density problem on the moon led some to conclude the moon may have an unusually light—or even no—core. They hoped to record the impact of a meteor large enough to send shock waves to the moon's core and back and settle the issue. That opportunity came on May 13, 1972, when a large meteor stuck the moon with the equivalent force of two hundred tons of TNT. After sending shock waves deep into the interior of the moon, scientists were baffled to find that none returned, confirming that there is something unusual about the moon's core. According to author Wilson, one NASA scientist has admitted that the U.S. government has conducted experiments "which were not publicly announced" to determine if the moon is hollow or contains large cavities. Dr. Farouk El Baz was quoted as saying, "There are many undiscovered caverns suspected to exist beneath the surface of the moon. Several experiments have been flown to the moon to see if there actually were such caverns." The results of these experiments have not been made public.

It seems apparent that the moon has a tough, hard outer shell and a light or nonexistent interior. The moon's shell contains dark minerals such as titanium, used on Earth in the construction of aircraft and space vehicles. Many people still recall watching our astronauts on TV as they vainly tried to drill through the crust of a moon maria. Their specially designed drills could penetrate only a few inches. The puzzle of the moon's hard surface was compounded by the discovery of what appeared to be processed metals. Experts were surprised to find lunar rocks bearing brass, mica, and amphibole in addition to the near-pure titanium. They conclude it is the large amount of titanium in the black mineral illeminite that gives the dark tone to the lunar seas. Uranium 236 and neptunium 237—elements not previously found in nature—were discovered in moon rocks, according to the Argone National Laboratory. While still trying to explain the presence of these materials, scientists were further startled to learn of rustproof iron particles in a soil sample from the Sea of Crisis. In 1976, the Associated Press reported that the Soviets had announced the discovery of iron particles that "do not rust" in samples brought back by an unmanned moon mission in 1970. Iron that does not rust is unknown in nature and well beyond present earth technology.

Undoubtedly the greatest mystery concerning our moon is how it came to be there in the first place. Prior to the Apollo missions, one serious theory as to the moon's origin was that it broke off of the earth eons ago, although no one could positively locate where on Earth it originated. This idea was discarded when it was found that there is little similarity between the composition of our world and the moon. A more recent theory had the moon created out of space debris left over from the creation of the earth. This concept proved untenable in light of current gravitational theory, which indicates that one large object will accumulate all loose material, leaving none for the formation of another large body. It is now generally accepted that the moon originated elsewhere and entered the earth's gravitational field at some point in the distant past. Here theories diverge—one stating that the moon was originally a planet that collided with the earth, creating debris that combined to form the moon, while another states that the moon, while wandering through our solar system, was captured and pulled into orbit by Earth's gravity. Neither of these theories is especially compelling because of the lack of evidence that either the earth or the moon has been physically disrupted by a past close encounter. There is no debris in space indicating a past collision, and it does not appear that the earth and the moon developed during the same time period. A current encyclopedia states that "there seems to be a record of lunar magmatic [molten rock] processes in operation long before any processes that can be deduced directly by terrestrial geological studies." As for the "capture" theory, even scientist Isaac Asimov, so well known for his works of fiction, has written, "It's too big to have been captured by the Earth. The chances of such a capture having been effected and the moon then having taken up nearly circular orbit around our Earth are too small to make such an eventuality credible." Asimov was right to consider the moon's orbit—it is not only nearly a perfect circle but stationary, one side always facing the earth with only the slightest variation. As far as we know, it's the only natural satellite with such an orbit. This circular orbit is especially odd considering that the moon's center of mass lies more than a mile closer to the earth than its geometric center. This fact alone should produce an unstable, wobbly orbit, much as a ball with its mass off center will not roll in a straight line. Additionally, almost all of the other satellites in our solar system orbit in the plane of their planet's equator. Not so the moon, whose orbit lies strangely nearer the earth's orbit around the sun or inclined to the earth's ecliptic by more than five degrees. Add to this the fact that the moon's bulge—located on the side facing away from Earth, thus negating the idea that it was caused by the earth's gravitational pull—makes for an off-balanced world. It seems impossible that such an oddity could naturally fall into such a precise and circular orbit. It is a fascinating conundrum, as articulated by science writer William Roy Shelton, who wrote, "It is important to remember that something had to put the moon at or near its present circular pattern around the Earth. Just as an Apollo spacecraft circling the Earth every 90 minutes while 100 miles high has to have a velocity of roughly 18,000 miles per hour to stay in orbit, so something had to give the moon the precisely required velocity for its weight and altitude. . . . The point—and it is one seldom noted in considering the origin of the moon—is that it is extremely unlikely that any object would just stumble into the right combination of factors required to stay in orbit. 'Something' had to put the moon at its altitude, on its course and at its speed. The question is: what was that 'something'?" If the precise and stationary orbit of the moon is seen as sheer coincidence, is it also coincidence that the moon is at just the right distance from the earth to completely cover the sun during an eclipse? While the diameter of the moon is a mere 2,160 miles against the sun's gigantic 864,000 miles, it is nevertheless in just the proper position to block out all but the sun's flaming corona when it moves between the sun and the earth. Asimov explains, "There is no astronomical reason why the moon and the sun should fit so well. It is the sheerest of coincidences, and only the Earth among all the planets is blessed in this fashion."

How does one explain these and many other moon mysteries? Scientists are a conservative lot who all too often tend to ignore any data not pertaining to their own particular area of expertise. They are as lost at explaining our nearest satellite as they are at explaining tektites—small glassy extraterrestrial blobs found at only a few sites on Earth. For years scientists believed tektites were blown to Earth by meteorite strikes on the moon. However, this theory was overturned when the Apollo missions failed to find anything comparable on the moon.

In July 1970, two Russian scientists offered a bizarre theory of the origin of the moon—but one that provided an answer to all the mysteries.

The Spaceship Moon Theory

Little notice was taken when Michael Vasin and Alexander Shcherbakov published an article in the Soviet journal *Sputnik* entitled

"Is the Moon the Creation of Alien Intelligence?" After all, who could take seriously such an outrageous concept?

They advanced the theory that the moon is not a completely natural world but a planetoid that was hollowed out eons ago in the far reaches of space by intelligent beings possessing a technology far superior to ours. Huge machines were used to melt rock and form large cavities within the moon, spewing the molten refuse onto the surface. Protected by a hull-like inner shell plus a reconstructed outer shell of metallic rocky junk, this gigantic craft was steered through the cosmos and finally parked in orbit around the earth.

In their article Vasin and Shcherbakov wrote, "Abandoning the traditional paths of 'common sense,' we have plunged into what may at first sight seem to be unbridled and irresponsible fantasy. But the more minutely we go into all the information gathered by man about the moon, the more we are convinced that there is not a single fact to rule out our supposition. Not only that, but many things so far considered to be lunar enigmas are explainable in the light of this new hypothesis."

The Spaceship Moon theory was revitalized in 1975 with the publication of *Our Mysterious Spaceship Moon* by Don Wilson, who collected an impressive array of supporting facts. Wilson urged the scientists of the world to take the Vasin-Shcherbakov theory seriously, stating, "Too many pieces of evidence seem to fit to reject the 'wild' theory without investigation."

Wilson said he rejected the theory at first as "unbelievable" but changed his attitude in light of the information gained through the Apollo missions. "Scientists themselves are continuing to uncover bewildering and baffling scientific facts that indicate the moon is not what it seems, but a world that may not be entirely natural," he wrote.

Outrageous as the spaceship moon theory might first appear, consider how all of the mysteries of the moon are reconciled by this model:

It would explain why the moon gives evidence of being much older than the earth and perhaps even our solar system.

It explains why there are three distinct layers within the moon, with the most dense materials in the outside layer. This is exactly the type of "hull" one would expect to find on a spacecraft.

This theory could explain why no sign of water has been found on the moon's surface, yet there is evidence it exists deep inside.

It also would explain the magnetism found in moon rocks. These rocks were magnetized as the mooncraft passed by planets and suns on its journey through space.

The strange maria, or moon seas, are explained as dumping pools for molten rock blasted from the moon's interior. The mascons—those dense masses located just below the center of each maria—may be the remnants of the machinery used to hollow out the moon.

An artificial satellite could explain the odd, rhythmic "moon-quakes" as artificial constructs reacting the same way during periods of stress from the earth's pull. And artificial equipment beneath the moon's surface might be the source of the gas clouds that have been observed.

The "terraforming" of the moon could prove the solution to the argument between "hot moon" and "cold moon" scientists—they are both right! The moon originally was a cold world that was transformed into a spacecraft by artificially heating and expelling vast quantities of its interior.

This theory also could explain the seeming contradictions over the question of a hollow moon. If the moon originally was a solid world that was artificially hollowed out, there would be evidence of both phases—exactly what we have with current moon knowledge.

An artificially hollowed-out moon would explain why the satellite rings like a bell for hours after struck and why specimens of tough, refractory metals such as titanium, chromium, and circonium, as well as "rustproof" iron, uranium 236, and neptunium 237 have been found there.

Finally, the Spaceship Moon theory may come closer than any other in reconciling the questions over the origin and amazing orbit of the moon.

There is even tantalizing evidence that in the dim recesses of human memory there have been recollections of a time before the arrival of the moon.

Aristotle told of a people called the Proselenes who lived in Arcadia, a mountainous region in central Greece, long before the coming of the Greeks. The name Selene—the Greek goddess of the moon—has come to refer to the moon itself, and the term Proselenes means "before the moon." According to ancient legend, the Proselenes held claim to Arcadia because they lived there "before there was a moon in the heavens." The Greek writer Plutarch also referred to "prelunar people" in Arcadia, and the Roman author Ovid stated that the Arcadian "folk is older than the moon." The Roman Apollonius Rhodius wrote that the Arcadians "dwelt on the mountains and fed on acorns, before there was a moon." In Tibetan texts, there are references to a people on a lost continent named *Gondwana*, said to be civilized before the moon shone in the night sky.

Iconoclast Immanuel Velikovsky also has written about an early time before there was a moon. "The traditions of diverse people offer corroborative testimony to the effect that in a very early age, but still in the memory of mankind, no moon accompanied the earth," he said. Velikovsky quotes from the Finnish epic poem *Kalevala* regarding a time "when the moon was placed in orbit."

Legends and sacred writings across the world indicate that the moon was once much closer to the earth. Marine sediment found in the Andes mountains reaching twelve thousand feet higher than present sea levels adds evidence that the moon may have been much closer and exerted tidal pull thousands of years ago. However, British astronomer John D. Barron pointed out that the study of coral growth rings in the Bahamas indicated that 350 million years ago an earth day was only 21.9 hours long. He attributed this to the pull of the moon, which has lengthened the day by about two-thousandths of a second every century, thus suggesting the moon has been in place for millions of years.

In the Bolivian city of Tiahuanaco is a large courtyard called the Kalasasaya, constructed by people who lived there long before the Incas. This ancient calendar presents accurate descriptions of the equinoxes, solstices, the astronomical seasons, and even the movement of the moon, which takes into account the orbit of the earth. Based on astronomical and solar alignments presented on the walls of the Kalasasaya, author Graham Hancock concluded that the edifice was originally constructed more than seventeen thousand years ago, long before recorded history. Some researchers even claim that symbols on the nearby Great Idol indicate knowledge of a round earth and the moon arriving in its orbit. Undeterred by the coral study, authors H. S. Bellamy and Dr. P. Allen wrote, "The symbols of the idol record that the satellite came into orbit around the Earth 11,500 to 13,000 years ago."

Such fragments of legend provide provocative speculation but no real proof of the Spaceship Moon theory. Whether or not the moon may eventually be shown to be a hollow "spaceship," there remains ample evidence that it harbors many anomalies.

Moon Lights and Monuments

Several thousand sightings of gaseous clouds, colored mists, and bright moving lights on the lunar surface have been reported worldwide for many years, many by prestigious astronomers and institutions. In 1968, a year before U.S. astronauts landed on the moon, NASA published Technical Report R-277 entitled *Chronological Catalogue of Reported Lunar Events*, which listed more than 570 moon anomalies from 1540 to 1967.

Some of the more intriguing events in this study included:

A "star" was seen within the body of a crescent moon "directly between the points of her horns" on March 5, 1587.

A small white "cloud" was seen on the moon on November 12, 1671, by French astronomer Gian Domenico Cassini, who was director of the Paris Observatory.

Flashes of light seen on the moon on May 18, 1787, by two astronomers were explained as "lightning," although lightning could not occur on an airless world.

During March and April 1787, Britain's Sir Frederick William Herschel, a pioneer of the reflecting telescope and the discoverer of Uranus, claimed to have sighted three "bright spots," four "volcanoes," and lights moving "above the moon."

In July 1821, a German astronomer reported sighting "brilliant flashing light spots." His was one of numerous reports of flashing or blinking lights seen on the moon.

In February 1877, a line or streak of light was seen stretching across Eudoxus Crater. This light was observed for about an hour, ruling out the possibility that it was merely a meteorite striking the lunar surface with a flash.

On April 24, 1882, moving shadows were seen in the moon's Aristotle area.

A beam of light was sighted in the crater Clavius on April 23, 1915.

Two streaks of medium-intensity light were recorded on June 14, 1940, in the crater Plato, a location where reports of lights have numbered in the thousands.

"Glitter" similar to an electrical discharge was seen near the moon's south pole on May 24, 1955.

On September 13, 1959, something blocked the view of the Littrow area, and on June 21, 1964, something dark moved across the moon's surface near the Ross D. area. This mysterious dark mass was observed for more than two hours.

A "black cloud surrounded by violet color" was seen in the Sea of Tranquility by Canadian astronomers on September 11, 1967.

Such Lunar Transient Phenomena (LTP) are well known among veteran astronomers. Bright and blinking lights, colorful displays, clouds, or mists have been reported in many lunar craters, especially those of Aristarchus, Plato, Eratosthenes, Biela, Rabbi Levi, and Posidonius.

Author Don Wilson pointed out that NASA must have been impressed with the lunar events study, "for soon thereafter NASA carried out Operation Moon Blink, a search for unexplainable lights and 'happenings' taking place on the moon. It was done in conjunction with cooperating observatories around the world, and in a short time Operation Moon Blink reported ten more such inexplicable lunar phenomena, three of which were confirmed independently and separately by observers outside the program. In fact, by August, 1966, 10 Moon Blink stations had detected 28 lunar events."

Modern computer imaging technology has increased the ability to scrutinize the lunar surface, but has yet to explain what can be clearly seen in photographs.

For example, *New York Herald Tribune* science editor John J. O'Neill on July 29, 1953, claimed to have seen a twelve-mile-long "bridge" straddling the Mare Crisium crater. After reporting his find to the Association of Lunar and Planetary Observers, O'Neill was scorned by astronomers. However, a month later the "bridge" was confirmed by British astronomer Dr. H. P. Wilkens, who told the BBC, "It looks artificial. It's almost incredible that such a thing could have been formed in the first instance, or if it was formed, could have lasted during the ages in which the moon has been in existence." Further confirmation came from Patrick Moore of the British Astronomical Association, who declared the "bridge" had "popped up" almost overnight.

Another most amazing structure is known as the "Shard" located in the Ukert area of the moon, which is at a point nearest the earth. The Shard was photographed by *Orbiter 3* in preparation for the Apollo missions. This odd monument towers up a mile and a half from the moon's surface. Dr. Bruce Cornet, an independent geologist who has studied photos of the Shard at length, said, "No known natural process can explain such a structure."

Perhaps even more amazing is a huge upright structure in the Sinus Medii region dubbed the "Tower." Dr. Cornet said, "The Tower represents an enigma of the highest magnitude, because it rises more than five miles above the surface of the moon, and has been photographed from five different angles and two different altitudes. In all four photographs the same structure is visible and can be viewed from two different sides. The Tower exists in front of and to the left of the Shard in the Lunar Orbiter III-84M photograph. The top of the Tower has a very cubic geometry and appears to be composed of regular cubes joined together to form a very large cube with an estimated width of over one mile!"

Private researcher George H. Leonard came to a startling conclusion regarding activity and structures on the moon. In 1977, after years of "haunting" NASA photo files, Leonard claimed to have found enough evidence to convince him that "the moon is occupied by an intelligent race or races which probably moved in from outside the solar system." "The moon is firmly in the possession of these occupants," he added. "Evidence of their presence is everywhere: on the surface, on the near side and the hidden side, in the craters, on the maria, and in the highlands. They are changing its face. Suspicion or recognition of that triggered the U.S. and Soviet moon programs—which may not really be so much a race as a desperate cooperation."

Leonard published a book in 1977 entitled *Somebody Else Is on the Moon* in which he discussed more than two dozen NASA photos. While many of these photos were indistinct to the untrained eye and might have shown almost anything, some were indeed curious. Some seem to show "bridges" across lunar chasms, evidence of "stitching" connecting surface splits, domed-shaped objects in the center of lit craters, and lengthy "tracks" in the moon dust. "The professionals choose to ignore these signs. They do not fit into the orthodoxy," wrote Leonard, adding that an unnamed NASA scientist confided to him that "discoveries" had been made but not announced to the public.

After studying hundreds of lunar photos, Leonard concluded that whoever is on the moon is doing at least two things: mining for minerals—or perhaps water and oxygen—and repairing damage to the moon's surface.

Leonard is not alone in his beliefs. Some researchers claim that moon photos show a series of transparent domes under which can be seen orderly lines indicating the possible ruins of cities or large stations.

Add to these anomalies the fact that several distinct pyramids have been reported sighted on the moon, especially in the Sea of Tranquility Apollo landing site. In November 1966, *Lunar Orbiter II* took photos from twenty-nine miles above the sea showing what appear to be several slender pyramids or obelisks similar to Central Park's Cleopatra's Needle, some as high as a fifteen-story building. Predictably, NASA denied that the *Orbiter* photos disclosed anything unusual on the moon, even as they released some of the pictures. Since there was no official confirmation, most news outlets did not cover the story. One that did was the *Washington Post*, which on November 22, 1966, carried the story on the front page with the headline, "Six Mysterious Statuesque Shadows Photographed on the Moon by Orbiter."

Some scientists, such as Dr. William Blair of the Boeing Institute of Biotechnology, have claimed that these structures are geometrically positioned, forming a right-handed coordinate system resulting in six isosceles triangles and two axes of three points each. Russian space engineer Alexander Abramov added to the mystery by stating, "The distribution of these lunar objects is similar to the plan of the Egyptian pyramids constructed by Pharaohs Cheops, Chephren and Menkaura at Gizeh, near Cairo. The centers of the spires in this lunar 'abaka' are arranged in precisely the same way as the apices of the three great pyramids."

If these structures are pyramids and if they do match the layout of the Egyptian pyramids, they might connect to the pyramid-shaped structures photographed by a Viking probe of Mars in 1976. Objects that appear to be pyramids, along with the controversial "face on Mars," were seen in pictures taken of the Cydonia area. Some researchers have wondered if these monuments might represent some grand marking system.

"It is the eerie similarity between the pyramidal structures that have come to stand for 'Egypt' and those lying—empty and abandoned—at Cydonia, that almost scream of some 'connection,'" wrote Richard C. Hoagland, a science writer who has publicized the theory of artificial structures on both Mars and the moon.

Hoagland suggested that perhaps the Apollo missions had an

unstated agenda of seeking the truth of these anomalies. He and other suspicious-minded UFO researchers have publicly wondered if the destinations of some of the Apollo moon missions—such as the Sea of Tranquility for *Apollo 11* and the Taurus-Littrow area for *Apollo 17*—were selected because of the high incidence of abnormal sightings in those locations. If they were, nobody in NASA officially is talking about it.

In March 1996, Hoagland, along with several men connected to NASA or space engineering, held a press conference at the National Press Club in Washington, D.C., for the avowed purpose of alerting the American public to space photographs and films that they said proved the existence of alien artifacts on the moon. A media release stated, "These official mission films—analyzed over a period of four years via scientific techniques and computer technologies literally unavailable even to NASA 30 years ago when the original photographs were taken—now provide compelling scientific evidence for the presence of ancient artificial structures on the moon. Further, it is now apparent that the entire purpose of President John F. Kennedy's sudden, all-out Apollo Program to land Americans on the moon within 10 years was to send American astronauts directly to these ruins, to record them on film, and to bring back physical evidence—including manufactured artifacts—for analysis on Earth." At the news conference, speakers presented analysis and photographs to support their arguments.

Although more than a hundred news media representatives were present to see and hear this evidence, little or no coverage was given the news conference by media outlets throughout the country. What little mention was made was usually done in a flippant manner, such as one reporter who wrote, "My son's *Barney* videotape jammed this morning, too. Is Barney part of this conspiracy? What is Barney's planet of origin?"

But the questions raised in Washington deserve serious answers. Many prominent scientists including Karl Gauss, Charles Cros, and Joseph Johanne von Littrow have stated that the best way to alert someone in outer space that intelligent beings inhabit this planet would be to build huge artifacts such as canals, towers, and geometric shapes formed from rock or forests. "Patterns. Geometricities. Straight lines. It is assumed that a triangle . . . will reveal the existence of our brains, and it will," wrote author George Leonard. "But then we turn around and ignore exactly this and a thousand even more convincing patterns on the Moon. This is science?"

Anomalies such as lights, odd structures, and moving shadows are provocative, but hardly firm proof that someone other than the

Apollo astronauts has been—or still is—on the moon. What, then, do the astronauts have to say about their space experiences? Again, it's hard to determine the truth because of official denial and obfuscation.

NASA Means Never a Straight Answer

As a whole the U.S. astronauts appear to have maintained a united front, stoutly denying than any valid UFO encounters have taken place. Following the Hoagland news conference in March 1996, astronaut Alan Bean told the media, "It's not true. No one, certainly not me and Pete Conrad, who I was with the whole time, saw anything that suggested ancient civilizations." NASA spokesman Brian Welch added, "Everything we found, we made public."

On December 29, 1986, Neil Armstrong, the first man to step onto the moon, told author Timothy Good, "There were no objects reported, found, or seen on *Apollo 11* or any other Apollo flight other than of natural origin. All observations on all Apollo flights were fully reported to the public."

However, rumors have persisted for years that the astronauts—nearly all military officers susceptible to being silenced under orders—may have seen something more on the moon than rocks and dust. According to transcripts of the technical debriefing following the *Apollo 11* mission, astronauts Armstrong, Edwin "Buzz" Aldrin, and Michael Collins told of an encounter with a large cylindrical UFO even before reaching the moon. Aldrin said, "The first unusual thing that we saw I guess was one day out or pretty close to the moon. It had a sizable dimension to it. . . ." Aldrin said the Apollo crew at first thought the object was the Saturn 4 booster rocket (S-IVB) but added, "We called the ground and were told the S-IVB was 6,000 miles away." Aldrin described the UFO as a cylinder, while Armstrong said it was "really two rings. Two connected rings." Collins also said it appeared to be a hollow cylinder that was tumbling. He added, "It was a hollow cylinder. But then you could change the focus on the sextant and it would be replaced by this open-book shape. It was really weird."

Two astronauts who appear to have broken ranks are Dr. Edgar Mitchell and Gordon Cooper. On an Oprah Winfrey show on July 19, 1991, Mitchell hinted that all information regarding UFOs has not been released, saying, "I do believe that there is a lot more known about extraterrestrial investigation than is available to the public right now [and] has been for a long time. . . . It's a long, long story. It goes back to World War II when all of that happened, and is highly classified stuff."

On *Dateline NBC* in 1996, Mitchell was even more candid. "I have no firsthand experience, but I have had the opportunity to meet with people from three countries who in the course of their official duties claim to have had personal firsthand encounter experiences . . . with extraterrestrials," he said. Asked if he thought extraterrestrials have already visited the earth, Mitchell replied, "From what I now understand and have experienced and seen the evidence for, I think the evidence is very strong, and large portions of it are classified . . . by governments."

Cooper, who retired as a colonel from the U.S. Air Force in 1970, has been even more vocal. In 1978, during a meeting at the United Nations to discuss UFOs, a letter from Cooper was read, stating: "I believe that these extraterrestrial vehicles and their crews are visiting this planet from other planets, which are obviously a little more advanced than we are here on Earth."

Also that year, Cooper wrote a letter to the ambassador of the mission of Grenada to the United Nations supporting a UN initiative to study UFOs. In his letter, which has since been made public, Cooper stated that astronauts "are very reluctant to even discuss UFOs due to the great numbers of people who have indiscriminately sold fake stories and forged documents abusing their names and reputations without hesitation. Those few astronauts who have continued to participate in the UFO field have had to do so very cautiously. There are several of us who do believe in UFOs and who have had occasion to see a UFO on the ground, or from an airplane."

Cooper's mention of a "UFO on the ground" apparently was a reference to his own experience at Edwards Air Force Base on May 2, 1957. In 1993, Cooper reportedly gave this account to German documentary producer Michael Hesemann: "I had a crew that was filming an installation of a precision landing system we were installing out on the dry lake bed, and they were there with stills and movies and filmed the whole installation and they came running in to tell me that this UFO, a little saucer, had come down right over them, put down three gear, and landed about 50 yards from them, and as they proceeded to go on over to get a closer shot of it, it lifted up, put the gear in, and disappeared in a rapid rate of speed. . . . I had to look up the regulations on who I was to call to report this, which I did, and they ordered me to immediately have the film developed, put it in a pouch, and send them by the commanding general's plane to Washington, which I did. And that was the last I've ever heard of the film."

It is interesting to note that, despite the continued protests that there is no government secrecy regarding UFOs, there is no public report on this incident. Although the event was listed in the Project Blue Book index, a full report and clear photos are suspiciously absent.

Yet Cooper, who claimed to have reported the UFO landing, was selected as a Mercury astronaut only two years later. In a 1996 interview, Cooper said he discounts any conventional explanation for his experience. Asked his thoughts on UFOs, the astronaut said, "Well, I figured it was somebody coming from some distant place to visit us."

One account of how the astronauts were muzzled came from ex-NASA space program member Otto Binder, who accused his former employer of censoring transmissions from *Apollo 11* and other missions by switching to radio channels unknown to the public. He claimed that unnamed ham radio enthusiasts monitored *Apollo 11* transmissions after the astronauts landed in the Sea of Tranquility and overheard one of the astronauts exclaim, "These babies are huge, sir . . . enormous. . . . Oh, God, you wouldn't believe it! I'm telling you there are other spacecraft out there . . . lined up on the far side of the crater edge . . . they're on the moon watching us. . . ."

Binder's account of an unexpected Welcome Wagon on the moon was dismissed out of hand by all but the most credulous UFO researchers. However, a variation on this story was repeated by Maurice Chatelain in his 1978 book, *Our Ancestors Came from Outer Space*. Chatelain wrote, "When *Apollo 11* made the first landing on the Sea of Tranquility and, only moments before Armstrong stepped down the ladder to set foot on the moon, two UFOs hovered overhead." He added, "The astronauts were not limited to equipment troubles. They saw things during their missions that could not be discussed with anybody outside NASA. It is very difficult to obtain any specific information from NASA, which still exercises a very strict control over any disclosure of these events."

It would be easy to dismiss Chatelain as quickly as Binder except for the man's credentials. Chatelain had every opportunity to know what he was talking about, since he was in charge of designing and building the Apollo communication and data-processing system for NASA. Since coming to the United States from French Morocco in 1955, Chatelain established a reputable career in the aerospace industry. He was in charge of engineering new radar and communications systems for Ryan Electronics in the late 1950s, receiving eleven patents, including an automatic radar landing system used in the Ranger and Surveyor moon flights. He began working on the Apollo project after joining North American Aviation

Chatelain acknowledged that NASA had the capability to hide secret Apollo transmissions among a wide variety of radio channels. "When Apollo arrived within proximity of the moon, the communications carriers previously used could not reach that far so all communications went through one single, very powerful, transmitter with a directional antenna in the S band, between 2,106 and 2,287 MHz [megahertz], with a great number of channels, each transmitting several signals at the same time through multiplexing. For instance, there were seven channels to feed medical information about the physical condition of the astronauts, nine to retransmit the stored telemetry data from the passage behind the moon that could not be beamed directly," he stated.

Further evidence of NASA's willingness to hide information from the public came from Representative Howard Wolpe of Michigan, who in the early 1990s reported that congressional investigators discovered a two-page set of instructions to NASA administrators advising how to avoid disclosing "controversial" information. According to Wolpe, "This NASA document instructs government employees to: 1. rewrite and even destroy documents 'to minimize adverse impact'; 2. mix up documents and camouflage handwriting so that the document's significance would be 'less meaningful'; and 3. take steps to 'enhance the utility' of various FOIA (Freedom of Information Act) exemptions." A NASA official, unsurprisingly, said the document was a "misrepresentation" of NASA's policy of openness.

The space agency not only had the capability to suppress UFO information but used it, according to Dr. Garry Henderson, a General Dynamics researcher who worked with NASA. He said astronauts are under strict orders not to discuss UFO sightings with anyone.

Add to this the power of secret intelligence agencies, some with much more clout than even the CIA. As Don Ecker, research director for *UFO* magazine, pointed out, "Sitting behind all this is the National Security Agency (NSA), which monitors all transmissions and screens all footage taken on missions."

The refrain of censorship was recently joined by Brian O'Leary, a scientist-astronaut during the Apollo program and deputy team leader of the *Mariner 10* Venus-Mercury television science group. "During the late 1960s while I was a NASA astronaut, I had no knowledge of astronauts' UFO sightings," O'Leary later wrote. "My enduring friendship with one of the astronauts who had been reported to have had a sighting did not seem to matter when I asked him about whether he had: He was conspicuously evasive. Have the astronauts been sworn to secrecy? Was this the main reason why all of us astronauts—civilians included—had to have top secret clearances? If so, this situation has put the UFO observers into the hot seat with respect to the Government—not an enviable position." O'Leary revealed his sentiments, however, by repeating the story of a ham radio operator who reportedly picked up this transmission from a space shuttle flight in March 1989: "Houston, this is *Discovery*. We still have alien spacecraft under observance."

In answer to the question of why NASA and the government would hide away evidence of extraterrestrial life, several researchers, including Richard Hoagland, pointed to a NASA report done by the Brookings Institution in 1960. Entitled "Proposed Studies on the Implications of Peaceful Space Activities for Human Affairs," the report stated, "While face-to-face meetings with [extraterrestrial life] will not occur within the next 20 years—unless its technology is more advanced than ours, qualifying it to visit Earth—artifacts left at some point in time by these life forms might possibly be discovered through our space activities on the Moon, Mars, or Venus."

The report added, "Anthropological files contain many examples of societies, sure of their place in the universe, which have disintegrated when they had to associate with previously unfamiliar societies espousing different ideas and different life ways; others that survived such an experience usually did so by paying the price of changes in values and attitudes and behavior." This caution was picked up by writers for the *New York Times*, which carried a headline crying, "Brookings Institution Report Says Earth's Civilization Might Topple If Faced by a Race of Superior Beings."

The idea seemed to be that the public should be protected from the startling news of extraterrestrial life to avoid panic and chaos. Over the years it must have become more and more difficult for the people in power to admit that they had mounted a cover-up. It was the old "one lie begets another" syndrome.

Interestingly, perhaps some of the most convincing evidence of UFOs to date came from NASA itself—video made from the space shuttle *Discovery* in 1991.

Maneuvers in Outer Space

On September 15, 1991, a camera aboard the *Discovery* was taping the curvature of the earth during mission STS-48 and transmitting images to a NASA select channel cable television network. Donald Ratsch, a Maryland space researcher, managed to tape the NASA feed and was astounded to discover what appeared to be moving objects maneuvering some miles from the space shuttle.

His find soon made the rounds of the UFO community, and many others believed the tape showed UFOs in space. Soon a quality copy of the *Discovery* tape was obtained from NASA files and analyzed. The STS-48 story, while discussed on several broadcast programs, still is largely unknown to the general public.

In the dramatic four-minute tape segment, several bright objects were seen moving at various speeds to the far right of the shuttle. One object appeared to exit the earth's atmosphere, then proceeded to fly parallel to the planet's curvature until a bright flash was recorded by the shuttle camera. At that moment, the object abruptly changed course by almost 120 degrees and accelerated into space. A second object that appeared stationary before the flash also accelerated in the same direction as the first object. Meanwhile, in the right bottom portion of the picture, two more bright objects moved parallel to each other toward the top of the picture. Other objects were seen moving in a variety of directions.

With the tape in the hands of the public, NASA was forced to respond. A spokesman stated that the bright moving objects were merely frozen droplets of water reflecting sunlight floating near the shuttle. UFO researchers were unconvinced, since the shiny objects obviously were accelerating, decelerating, and changing course—an absolute impossibility for any natural floating object.

The issue became even more contentious when Dr. Jack Kasher, a physicist at the University of Nebraska and a NASA consultant since 1991, determined to prove once and for all that the moving objects were indeed ice particles as NASA claimed. Dr. Kasher carried impressive credentials, having worked from 1975 through 1992 at the Lawrence Livermore National Laboratory in connection with the Strategic Defense Initiative (SDI) "Star Wars" program. However, after careful study of the STS-48 tape and working through the mathematics, Dr. Kasher was forced to conclude that NASA's statement of ice particles was a "completely untenable position."

In a 1994 taped interview, Dr. Kasher said he determined that the *Discovery's* camera was focused on "infinity" when taping, which made it impossible to record small ice particles near the shuttle. He said the objects in the tape were about twenty miles from the shuttle. Dr. Kasher said nearly a half-dozen separate pieces of evidence proved conclusively the objects were not ice particles. "And once the idea of ice particles has been discarded," he said, "there aren't many options left. . . . These objects are clearly above the air glow, the atmosphere, maneuvering in outer space. Therefore, they are some sort of spacecraft.

"The only viable alternative [to the ice particle theory]," stated Dr. Kasher, "is that these anomalous glowing objects are intelligently directed spacecraft that clearly are accelerating and maneuvering above the Earth's atmosphere." Despite Dr. Kasher's findings and the movement plainly seen in the STS-48 tape, NASA continued to support the ice particle idea.

Adding more fuel to the fire of rumors that NASA covered up many encounters between astronauts and UFOs, former space worker

Maurice Chatelain claimed, "It seems that all Apollo and Gemini flights were followed, both at a distance and sometimes also quite closely, by space vehicles of extraterrestrial origin—flying saucers, or UFOs (unidentified flying objects), if you want to call them by that name. Every time it occurred, the astronauts informed Mission Control, who then ordered absolute silence." Chatelain went to far as to state that rumors within NASA were that *Apollo 13* carried a small nuclear charge to be set off on the moon for seismic testing but barely managed to return to Earth after being disabled by a UFO apparently protecting "some moon base established by extraterrestrials."

For years it has been the topic of discussion among UFO researchers why the moon missions came to a complete halt after *Apollo 17*. An obviously disheartened Chatelain wrote, "The program, which had started in the 1960s with so much enthusiasm, ended amid growing indifference and even some hostility from many Americans, who were shocked to find out how high the cost of landing on the moon really was. Some even complained that the live TV coverage of the moon missions had pre-empted their cherished football games."

Many people, including most scientists, bemoaned the end of the moon missions when new mysteries remained begging for solutions and were dubious of the official explanation—lack of funding. "It's like buying a Rolls-Royce and then not driving it because you want to save money on the gasoline," groused Dr. Thomas Gold, professor of astronomy at Cornell University.

Others offered a more sinister explanation. "For years, rumors abounded that we were 'asked' to leave early on—by the much-speculated 'somebody else on the moon'—but that would have caused massive questioning and perhaps panic if we suddenly stopped, so we completed the program and then went into hiatus . . . this idea is pure speculation and rumor," wrote UFO researcher Don Ecker.

Author Timothy Good, generally respected as a diligent journalist, added to this rumor when he published an unattributed report on a conversation involving astronaut Neil Armstrong. According to Good, an unnamed personal friend overheard Armstrong at a NASA symposium say, "It was incredible . . . the fact is, we were warned off. There was never any question then of a space station or a moon city. . . . I can't go into details, except to say that their ships were far superior to ours both in size and technology—boy, were they big! . . . and menacing." Armstrong reportedly explained that the final Apollo missions were completed because "NASA was committed at that time and couldn't risk a panic on Earth."

Moon researcher George Leonard noted that prior to the lunar landings there was much media speculation on the profitable aspects of a colony and mining operations on the moon. All such talk ended abruptly after the Apollo missions were canceled. "We put enough billions into [the U.S. space program] to pull all the major cities of America out of debt, and then some. And after the successful Ranger and Surveyor and Orbiter and Apollo flights, we dropped manned lunar exploration like a hot potato," he noted.

More recent space failures—the Challenger shuttle disaster, several satellite washouts including the *Titan 4*, *Landsat 6*, and Hubble telescope, plus the loss of both Soviet (*Phobos II*) and American (Mars *Observer*) Mars probes, as well as the Russian Mars '96—have prompted more thoughtful consideration of the concept of an alien quarantine of Earth.

An early case was reported by Dr. Robert Jacobs of the University of Wisconsin, who in the early 1960s was a first lieutenant in the air force. Dr. Jacobs stated that on September 15, 1964, he was in charge of filming missile tests at Vandenberg AFB, California, and photographed the launch of an Atlas rocket. A few days later, reviewing the film with his superior, Maj. Florenz J. Mansmann, and two unidentified plainclothes men from Washington, Jacobs was astounded to notice "a UFO swim into the picture" as the Atlas reached an altitude of about sixty miles. "It flew right up to our missile and emitted a vivid flash of light," Jacobs recalled. "Then it altered course, and hovered briefly over our missile . . . and then there came a second vivid flash of light. Then the UFO flew around the missile twice and set off two more flashes from different angles, and then it vanished. A few seconds later, our missile was malfunctioning and tumbling out of control into the Pacific Ocean, hundreds of miles short of its scheduled target." Asked for his assessment of the object in the film, Jacobs said it was a UFO. Major Mansmann then told him, "You are to say nothing about this footage. As far as you and I are concerned, it never happened!" Jacobs said the two unnamed men, believed to be CIA agents, took the film and it has never been seen since. "It's been 17 years since that incident," said Jacobs recounting his story in 1982, "and I've told nobody about it until now. I have been afraid of what might happen to me. But the truth is too important for it to be concealed any longer. The UFOs are real. I know they they're real. The Air Force knows they're real. And the U.S. government knows they're real. I reckon it's high time that the American public knows it too."

A recent example of failed attempts to probe beyond our planet is the spacecraft *Clementine*, a joint NASA–Department of Defense project to return newly developed sophisticated photographic equipment to the moon. Launched in January 1994, hopes were high that the $75 million *Clementine* might transmit photos that could resolve many moon mysteries. But control over the craft failed after a motor reportedly misfired and yet another space probe with military connections was lost. In early 1996, hope was renewed that contact with the *Clementine* might be restored.

It is reasonable to conclude that if indeed someone is tampering with our space probes, our moon would be a logical base of operations. The evidence suggests that someone has been there for a long time. As an artificial world created billions of years ago to travel through space containing timeworn ruins on or under the lunar surface, the moon presents indications of activity obviously predating man's history—perhaps even man himself.

Since man has made such a tremendous effort to send astronauts to the moon—thought by most to be a lifeless world—it must be considered that someone might have made a similar effort to send their astronauts to Earth. This could be happening today or it may have taken place in man's dim early history, leaving evidence that led to the present widespread belief in ancient astronauts.

CHAPTER 2

ANCIENT
ASTRONAUTS

Until well into the twentieth century scientists believed that both the earth's history and man's were marked by gradual, evolutionary change.

This idea was set on its ear by the theories of a Russian Jew named Immanuel Velikovsky. A practicing physician and psychiatrist, Velikovsky traveled to the United States in 1939 intending to write about the historical figures of Moses, Oedipus, and Akhenaten in connection with the psychological concepts of Sigmund Freud. However, in the course of his studies he discovered evidence leading to his theory that the cultures of the world all describe sudden and violent cataclysms in man's early history. Velikovsky theorized that these upheavals were caused by the near miss of a comet that caused global disasters and later moved into orbit around the sun, becoming the planet Venus. Besides threatening the gradual-evolution theory of his day, Velikovsky's work was seen as a radical departure from the traditions of religion, cosmology, geology, archeology, sociology, and psychology.

In a discussion of new or alternative theories, it is instructive to consider the reaction to Velikovsky's ideas. After failing to interest the scientific community in his theories, Velikovsky finally published his ideas in the book *Worlds in Collision*, released in 1950 to great popular interest. "What followed was a modern classic case of academic demagoguery," commented researcher Arthur Bloch. "Scientists and scholars who supported Velikovsky's thesis—and even those who simply defended his right to be heard—were shouted down. Some, like the astronomer Gordon Atwater and Macmillan editor James Putnam, were summarily dismissed from their positions. Favorable reviews of the book were killed before their publication, to be replaced by fervent attacks on 'irresponsibility' in the publishing industry. All too frequently, these attacks were written by scientists who admitted they had not read *Worlds in Collision*, while those who had read the book grossly misrepresented the author's position and ignored or distorted his evidence." There was even an attempt to create a scientific "theory-censoring board" to prevent publication of the "wrong kinds of scientific books." Since then, many of Velikovsky's theories have been proven correct, and today the theory of planetary upheavals, such as Noah's flood and the sudden extinction of the dinosaurs, is generally accepted as fact.

Playing off Velikovsky's thesis that early legends had some basis in fact, Swiss author Erich von Däniken advanced the notion that ancient astronauts may have visited Earth centuries ago. In the 1970 American publication of his book *Chariots of the Gods?*, von Däniken boldly stated, "I claim that our forefathers received visits from the universe in the remote past even though I do not yet know who these extraterrestrial intelligences were or from which planet they came. I nevertheless proclaim that these 'strangers' annihilated part of mankind existing at the time and produced a new, perhaps the first, *homo sapiens*."

Like Velikovsky's, von Däniken's theories were greeted by great interest on the part of the public but were savagely attacked by traditionalists, who accused him of both sloppy research and writing. Even British author Colin Wilson, himself a collector of occult and supernatural lore, chastised von Däniken for "absurd guesses" and "distortion of fact." Wilson pointed to von Däniken's description of space flight and a loudspeaker in the Assyrian *Epic of Gilgamesh*, saying, "In fact, a careful perusal of the [epic] reveals that these events do not occur." He even accused von Däniken of deliberate deceit in a later book in which he described his visit to a cave system in Ecuador but later admitted he had never been there. According to Wilson, von Däniken excused this lapse of journalistic integrity by explaining that writers such as himself are permitted to "embroider their facts."

Another critic named Wilson was Clifford Wilson, a former lecturer with Australia's Melbourne Bible Institute, who attacked von Däniken based on theological beliefs. In a 1972 book whose cover was modeled after *Chariots of the Gods?* and entitled *Crash Go the Chariots*, Wilson asserted, "Von Däniken is not the first—nor will he be the last—who has foundered when he presumed to attack that impregnable Rock of Holy Scripture." His arguments against the ancient astronaut theories, usually based on the premise that those who believe the Bible simply knew better, were generally as weak as some of von Däniken's stretches of logic.

Von Däniken found himself attacked from all sides—from the scientific establishment to religious conservatives. "The result of all this," commented Colin Wilson, "is that Däniken has now been totally discredited and that the 'ancient astronaut' theory associated with his name has few serious supporters. This is a pity, for there is far more convincing evidence than that presented by Däniken."

Indeed, many other serious writers, among them Andrew Tomas, Maurice Chatelain, Zecharia Sitchen, Harold T. Wilkins, Peter Kolosimo, Serge Hutin, W. Raymond Drake, and Jacques Vallee have presented compelling evidence for the appearance of UFOs in man's early history. "There is, in short, no way around von Däniken," wrote science writer Richard C. Hoagland, who found himself at the center of controversy with his theories of alien artifacts on the moon and the Cydonia region of Mars. "In order to look for the shadow of Cydonia on Earth—however faint the shadow—I must turn to the Monuments of Egypt. In order to suggest transport between worlds, I must invoke images of 'humanoid' astronauts and giant starships. As soon as I do, they will find their way into blond, white space explorers and—possibly—anti-gravity machines . . . Chariots of the Gods."

Striking evidence connecting cultures from opposite sides of the earth came in September 1996, when Han Ping Chen, an authority on the ancient Chinese Shang dynasty, confirmed that markings found on Central American figures dated to more than three thousand years ago were clearly Chinese characters. The figures were from the Olmecs, forerunners of the Aztec and Mayan civilizations, and were discovered in Mexico in 1955. Smithsonian archeologist Betty Meggers supported Chen's analysis, stating, "Writing systems are too arbitrary and complex. They cannot be independently reinvented."

Furthermore, a close study of mythology from around the world reveals striking similarities. Legends from different peoples living in all corners of the earth seem to tell the same essential story—that in the dim distant past certain individuals with "godlike" powers molded mankind into a civilized state following a period of cataclysmic upheaval.

The great teacher of the Aztecs was known as Viracocha, to the Mayans as Quetzalcoatl, and to the ancient Egyptians as the Sun God

Ra. Sargon, the first great leader of the Akkadian dynasty, which succeeded the Sumerians, attributed his knowledge to the god Anu, while the Babylonian king Hammurabi was said to have gained power through Marduk.

In India, it is believed that man is descended from gods who flew in fiery craft. The Teutons point to ancestors in flying "Wanen." The ancient Mayans thought their predecessors came from the Pleiades, while the Incas said simply they were the "sons of the sun." Native Americans claim to be the sons and daughters of the great "Thunderbird." Chinese texts tell of long-lived rulers from the heavens who sailed through the skies in "fire-breathing dragons."

One common denominator of these ancient gods was their ability to fly through the air. Interestingly, these gods did not just appear or disappear as one would expect of a god, but were constrained to fly through the use of devices—flaming wheels, chariots, bright globes, and the like.

Scholars have always faced two choices in dealing such ancient texts and legends—assume they are allegorical fantasy or take them literally. For too long, they wrote off the old stories as myth. But in the modern world, with recent advances in geology, archeology, and even spaceflight, a whole new view of our past is taking shape.

It was once thought that the Greek poet Homer's accounts of the Trojan Wars were sheer fiction until Troy's ruins were located by Charles McLaren in 1822. Even then, it was not until the extensive excavations of Heinrich Schliemann in 1870 that the reality of Troy was accepted. Likewise, the ancient Mesopotamian city of Ur was thought to be largely myth until it was discovered and excavated by Leonard Woolley following World War I.

Author Zecharia Sitchen, who has made an extensive study of ancient documents in their original language, stated, "Archeological finds and the deciphering of Sumerian, Babylonian, Assyrian, Hittite, Canaanite and other ancient texts and epic tales increasingly confirm the accuracy of the biblical references to the kingdoms, cities, rulers, places, temples, trade routes, artifacts, tools and customs of antiquity."

If the Bible is now being more and more accepted as containing historical accuracy, perhaps other ancient writings deserve more serious inspection.

For example, three important Hindu texts—the *Bhagavata-Purana*, *Mahabharata*, and *Ramayana* scriptures—date back to at least 3000 B.C. They are among the oldest writings known to man. These works speak extensively about flying machines called *vimanas* that could travel not only through the air but also to other worlds. Richard L. Thompson, an expert on India's Vedic culture who has worked on

NASA-funded satellite remote sensing, stated the Hindu *vimanas* "could be grossly physical machines, or they could be made of two other kinds of energy, which we can call subtle energy and transcendental energy. Humans of this Earth generally did not manufacture such machines, although they did sometimes acquire them from more technically advanced beings."

Vedic writings speak of gods from other planetary systems called Devas who act as administrators for a hierarchical universal government, tell how the human soul—our sentient energy—inhabits a succession of physical bodies, and how the ancient Vedic people were regularly visited by the Devas, often in flying machines. "There is much material in Vedic texts that is practically unknown to Western people who do not have an explicit interest in Indian culture. Some of this material shows parallels with commonly reported features of the appearance and behavior of UFOs and UFO entities," said Thompson. Explaining why the UFO connection within the Vedas has not been seen before, Thompson said, "Some meanings may differ so strongly from what a person is accustomed to thinking that he will fail to grasp them for a long time. He will tend to take words out of the context understood by the author and force them into a context dictated by his own cultural conditioning. This may cause him to reject the text as absurd, and such rejection can create an impediment to true understanding." This explanation could also apply in dealing with any writings of antiquity.

Thompson related how the Tenth Canto of the *Bhagavata-Purana* described an incident that seemed to describe an aerial attack. It spoke of a certain King Salva who asked his god, Lord Pasupati, to provide him with an impregnable flying vehicle that could go anywhere he wished and terrify his enemies. Thus a "flying iron city" was constructed and presented to King Salva. This "whirling firebrand" was used by Salva to besiege an enemy city. A description from the canto reads, "From his excellent airship he threw down a torrent of weapons, including stones, tree trunks, thunderbolts, snakes and hailstones. A fierce whirlwind arose and blanketed all directions with dust."

Many other attributes were given to the mysterious flying *vimanas* of Hindu legend, such as the ability to become invisible (stealth technology?), to hear and see at great distances (radio and television?), to ascertain the course of enemies (radar?), and to destroy enemy craft.

One description of these fabulous machines stated:

These verily wondrous, red of hue,
Speed on their course with a roar

over the ridges of the sky . . .
And spread themselves with beams of light . . .
Bright, celestial, with lightning in their hands
and helmets of gold upon their heads.

Within the context of UFO sightings, the meaning of this stanza seems self-evident.

Nor was such imagery confined to the Hindu Vedas. The *Popol Vuh*, the hallowed book of the Mayan Indians of Central America, described their ancestors as "admirable men . . . able to know all, and they examined the four corners, the four points of the arch of the sky, and the round face of the earth." These Indians knew the earth was round centuries before the Europeans, indicating they gained such knowledge from someone able to view the earth from high above.

As in the Vedas, Mayan legends contained a close connection with the heavens. The *Popol Vuh* mentioned that several gods, including Hunahpu, Xbalanque, and the great god-king Quetzalcoatl, returned to the stars after their life on Earth ended.

Italian author Peter Kolosimo made an in-depth study of Quetzalcoatl, described as the son of the sky-god Mixcoatl, and concluded, "In the opinion of many scholars, this legend may be interpreted as follows. Upon Atlantis there descended one day a race of beings so advanced that they seemed like gods—*Mixcoatl*—in the eyes of the primitive earth-dwellers. They were borne on a slender spaceship—the cloud-serpent—and mingled with the people of Earth—*Chipalman*—whom they raised to a high level of civilization."

Across the world in Tibet, a book entitled the *Kantyua*, meaning "the translated word of Buddha," tells of flying "pearls in the sky" and transparent spheres containing gods who come to visit men. A book reportedly written by Tibetan lama T. Lobsang Rampa put forth these ideas from ancient writings: "We [Tibetans] believe, firmly, that we are reborn time after time. But not merely to this Earth. There are millions of worlds and we know that most of them are inhabited. Those inhabitants may be in very different forms to those we know, they may be superior to humans. We in Tibet have never subscribed to the view that Man is the highest and most noble form of evolution. We believe that much higher forms are to be found elsewhere, and they do not drop atom bombs. In Tibet I have seen records of strange craft in the skies. 'The Chariots of the Gods,' most people call them. The Lama Mingyar Dondup told me that a group of lamas had established communication with these 'gods,' who said that they were watching Earth, apparently in much the same way as humans watch wild and dangerous animals in a zoo." The "Royal Pedigrees of Tibetan Kings," a document dating back to the seventh century, states that the first seven Tibetan kings came from the stars to which they eventually returned.

In Babylonia some 4,700 years ago a poem entitled the "Flight of Etana" was written. It seems to be a lucid account of an ascent into space, much as a modern astronaut might describe:

> Etana looked down and saw that the earth had become like a hill and the sea like a well. And so they flew for another hour, and once again Etana looked down: the earth was now like a grinding stone and the sea like a pot. After the third hour the earth was only a speck of dust, and the sea no longer seen.

One of the strangest stories dealing with ancient visitors began in 1938 when archeologist Chi Pu Tei discovered regularly aligned rows of graves in the Baian Kara Ula mountains near the Sino-Tibetan border. Beneath cave drawings of beings wearing helmets along with depictions of the stars, sun, and moon, small frail skeletons with unusually large skulls were found. Chi Pu Tei theorized that the skeletons belonged to an extinct species of mountain ape and that the drawings were left in the caves later by human tribes. Since the graves were in systematic rows, his theory was laughed at and forgotten until 1962, when stone plates found among the graves were translated by Professor Tsum Um Nui of the Academy of Prehistoric Research in Beijing.

The translation told an eerie story of a group of beings who crash-landed on the third planet of this star system about twelve thousand years ago. Unable to repair their craft, this group attempted to make friends with the mountain tribes but were hunted down and killed due to their nonhuman features. Since this account was not compatible with the Western world-view, it too was dismissed.

But surprising support for the idea of men walking the earth far longer than presently acknowledged came in 1959. According to author Serge Hutin, that year a joint Soviet-Chinese paleontological expedition headed by Dr. Chu Ming Chen discovered a stone in the Gobi Desert that proved to be about a million years old; embedded in it was "the perfectly recognizable imprint of a shoe sole." In 1920, according to author Peter Kolosimo, a Professor Julio Tello found vases on the Peruvian coast depicting llamas with five toes instead of the usual two. Tello went on to find prehistoric llama skeletons that indeed had five toes. "The skeletons of five-toed llamas excavated by Tello proved, contrary to the general view, than mankind already existed and, in some parts of the world, had reached quite a high degree of civilization, at the time when the first mammals made their appearance and giant saurians were not yet extinct," concluded Kolosimo.

Many other physical oddities all across the globe attest to superior knowledge gained through aerial observation in the dim past.

The most well known of these are the pictographs and lines on the plateau of Nazca in southern Peru. Scraped into the black volcanic surface and preserved since prehistory due to lack of rainfall are hundreds of different figures, from simple geometric designs to intricate pictures of animals and birds—a whale, heron, hummingbird, condor, pelican, spider, and monkey. All of these designs can be seen only from high in the air. Until the advent of commercial aviation in the 1930s, no one realized that this panorama of ancient artwork existed at Nazca. Peruvian oral tradition claimed the markings on the desert plateau were connected to legends of the "Viracochas," bearded white strangers who brought civilization following a great cataclysm. These facts, plus several lengthy straight lines, both parallel and intersecting, have caused some writers to speculate that Nazca was an ancient spaceship landing site.

Author Graham Hancock discounts this idea, questioning why extraterrestrials who could travel through interstellar space would need landing strips. "Surely such beings would have mastered the technology of setting their flying saucers down vertically," he stated, obviously believing that such beings would be far advanced of our own space technology, which still requires a lengthy landing strip for space shuttles. Yet he conceded to puzzlement over the Nazca lines. "The truth is that no one knows their purpose, just as no one really knows their age; they are a genuine mystery of the past."

Author Peter Kolosimo quoted Pennsylvania University professor J. Alden Mason as saying that the lines "doubtless . . . were made to be seen by celestial deities." "There are said to be many other sites of this kind in Peru and parts of Chile," wrote Kolosimo, "but the Indians who know of them cannot explain their purpose, though they related stories which suggest that the figures were intended to guide the course of navigators from outer space who established bases on Earth." Von Däniken speculated that in the distant past "unknown intelligences" landed at Nazca and laid down two runways before departing. Pre-Inca tribesmen witnessed their arrival and later extended the two runways plus added several of their own to induce the "gods" to return.

Should this prove the case, it may have been the world's first "cargo cult," which is still practiced today in certain areas of Melanesia in the Pacific. Cultists believed for years that the sky gods would bring them manufactured goods (cargo) in "big birds." They thought this belief was fulfilled during World War II when American planes dropped food and materiel in the jungles for advancing Allied troops. After the war, the natives built mock airstrips and even bamboo "radios" in an effort to prepare for a return of the "gods." "Throughout all these childish beliefs there were some bases in reality," wrote author Andrew Tomas. "In like manner the ancient legends of the 'gods descending upon Earth' and an era when 'men and gods' mixed could be a folk memory of an epoch when sky ships of a different technology were seen in our atmosphere."

Another amazing pattern found only by aerial observation was described by NASA official Maurice Chatelain. He discovered that drawing a circle on a map and connecting the venerated Greek island of Delos to thirteen geographical sites—"sacred places marked by temple ruins constructed over even more ancient ruins from time immemorial"—within a radius of 450 miles produced the perfect figure of a Maltese cross, an ancient holy sign worn on the shields of the Crusaders. Delos was considered one of ancient Greece's most holy sites, although no one has ever known exactly why. Wrote Chatelain, "What interests us now is how and why such a gigantic pattern was marked on the Aegean and surrounding lands. I do not believe that even today's land surveyors could so precisely mark such a gigantic figure of over 360 miles jumping from island to island and stretching over sea and mountains. Except from high up in the air this Maltese cross would not be visible. To measure and mark all the salient points, two very modern tools of mapping are an absolute necessity. First, a fixed-position space satellite. . . . Then, to keep the capsule stationary over Delos, one of our newest devices that was perfected only a short time ago—a navigation and distance-measuring ground radar."

Biblical UFOs

In the Bible, the foundation of Western thought and philosophy, there are many accounts that seem to describe events with decidedly UFO characteristics.

The Book of Genesis describes how Jacob, founder of the twelve tribes of Israel, camped while on a journey from Beersheba to Haran. After bedding down for the night, Jacob dreamed he saw a "ladder set up on the earth, and the top of it reached to heaven" and he saw "the angels of God ascending and descending on it." At the top of the ladder stood a being who proclaimed himself "Jehovah, the God of Abraham," who told Jacob his descendants would proliferate and spread to the four corners of the earth like "dust." While most Bible scholars see this story as an allegorical dream, some believe Jacob may have seen ancient astronauts exiting a UFO.

The beginning of Psalm 104 seems to be an account of flight, stating, "O Lord my God . . . Who coverest thyself with light as with a garment; who stretchest out the heavens like a curtain: Who layeth the beams of his chambers in the waters; who maketh the clouds his chariot: who walketh upon the wings of the wind . . . "

Zechariah 6:1–7 (Living Bible) also can be interpreted as an observation of flying machines on a reconnaissance mission when it states, "Then I looked up again and saw four chariots coming from between what looked like two mountains made of brass. The first chariot was pulled by red horses, the second by black ones, the third by white horses and the fourth by dappled-greys. 'And what are these?' I asked the angel. He replies, 'These are the four heavenly spirits who stand before the Lord of all the earth; they are going out to do his work. The chariot pulled by the black horses will go north, and the one pulled by white horses will follow it there, while the dappled-greys will go south.' The red horses were impatient to be off, to patrol back and forth across the earth, so the Lord said, 'Go. Begin your patrol.' So they left at once."

Another familiar Bible story with UFO-visitor overtones concerns the destruction of the cities of Sodom and Gomorrah in the year 2024 B.C. Some progressive Bible scholars tend to explain the fire and brimstone destruction of the twin cities as the result of some natural disaster such as a volcanic eruption or earthquake that was interpreted as an act of God. But the evidence denies this view.

The biblical account is quite clear that the devastation was known in advance, since Abraham, a direct descendant of Noah and the first Hebrew patriarch, was warned and even managed to bargain with his God, revising the number of righteous persons for which the cities might be spared down from fifty to ten.

According to the story, Abraham's nephew Lot met two men at Sodom's gate, whom he somehow recognized as being very special, for he bowed down to them. The Bible calls them "angels," although the original Hebrew word *Mal'akhim* actually means "emissaries." This pair apparently appeared quite human, since Lot brought them to his home and fed them fresh bread. Later that night when a crowd of Sodomites demanded that the pair be given to them for sexual pleasure, Lot protected them, even offering his own virgin daughters in exchange. Undeterred, the men attempted to force their way into the house only to be temporarily blinded by the two strangers.

Following this incident, the strangers revealed to Abraham that the cities would soon be destroyed. Lot tried to warn his neighbors, but none would listen. The next day, the two strangers told Lot it was urgent that he and his family leave immediately, indicating that a specific time frame for the destruction was in motion. "Escape for thy life," Lot was told. "Look not behind thee, neither stay thou in all the plain; escape to the mountain, lest thee be consumed."

The two strangers then accepted Lot's proposal that he flee only as far as the small nearby city of Zoar rather than the mountains. Once Lot was in Zoar, "Then the Lord rained upon Sodom and upon Gomorrah brimstone and fire from the Lord out of heaven. And he overthrew those cities, and all the plain, and all the inhabitants of the cities, and that which grew upon the ground. But Lot's wife looked back from behind him, and she became a pillar of salt." Ancient document scholar Zecharia Sitchen argues that the literal meaning of the term *Netsiv melah* (pillar of salt) should be "pillar of vapor." Thus, Lot's wife was vaporized by the explosive destruction of the cities, seen miles away by Abraham as "columns of smoke and fumes, as from a furnace, rising from the cities there."

As some writers have pointed out, this account sounds eerily like those of the Hiroshima and Nagasaki atomic bombings. But is there anything to support this idea? According to Sitchen, archeologists have found evidence that communities near the southern end of the Dead Sea—thought to be the site of Sodom and Gomorrah—were suddenly abandoned in the twenty-first century B.C. and not reoccupied for several centuries. Furthermore, one report claimed that water in the area was found to be contaminated with harmful amounts of radioactivity. This, plus the claim of a Soviet scientist that fused silicone or glassy sand was discovered in the region, indicates an atomic blast may well have leveled Sodom and Gomorrah.

Is this story of grand destruction simply a fanciful tale concerning the consequences of immorality, or were the cities destroyed by nuclear fire? Was it a deliberate act by or the result of warfare between ancient astronauts? Or could it have been a crippled UFO whose nuclear power went critical and exploded?

Another biblical story often connected with UFOs is the account of Ezekiel and the fiery wheel. Again, most Bible scholars believe Ezekiel, a sixth-century B.C. prophet during the Babylonian exile of the Israelites, presented his messages in allegorical stories derived from visions. However, a close study of the Old Testament book indicates that Ezekiel was more a precise journalist than a starry-eyed visionary.

In opening his book, Ezekiel does not merely state that one day he had a vision. He is very detailed in giving the time frame of his experience. "Now it came to pass in the thirtieth year, in the fourth month, in the fifth day of the month, as I was among the captives by the river Chebar, that the heavens were opened, and I saw visions of God," he wrote. If he was this precise with his dating, the remainder of his book should be considered a literal account of his experiences.

Much confusion has stemmed from the semantics of the various biblical translations. For example in the King James Version, Ezekiel speaks of seeing "visions of God," indicating he saw something that he could only describe as a vision of something God-like, beyond his experience. This idea is reinforced in subsequent verses in which Ezekiel states that the "visions of God" carried him to a city on a very high mountain (Ezekiel 40:2); that the "spirit" of God took him up accompanied by a "great rushing" noise (Ezekiel 3:12); and that the "Glory of God" appeared out of the east with a sound "like the roar of rushing waters and the whole landscape lighted up" (Ezekiel 43:1–2). It seems plain enough that Ezekiel was attempting to described a material object that he both saw and heard and that later even carried him into the air.

Yet in recent translations, such as the Living Bible, Ezekiel 1:1 reads, "One day late in June, when I was 30 years old, the heavens were suddenly opened to me and I saw visions from God." "Visions from God" implies a holy hallucination, a small but very critical departure from "visions of God," implying a tangible object for which Ezekiel has no word of description. Where the King James Version says "In the visions of God brought he me into the land of Israel" (Ezekiel 40:2), the Living Bible states, "and in a vision he took me to the land of Israel." With such slight, but significant, differences in translation—compounded over the centuries by changes due to editing, copying, and interpretation—it is easy to see why there is such confusion over the meaning of biblical verses.

It is clear that Ezekiel seems to be trying hard to describe the "vision of God." "I looked, and I saw a windstorm coming out of the north—an immense cloud with flashing lightning and surrounded by brilliant light. The center of the fire looked like glowing metal and in the fire was what looked like four living creatures. In appearance their form was like a man but each of them had four faces and four wings. . . . As I looked at the living creatures, I saw a wheel on the ground beside each creature with its four faces. This was the appearance and structure of the wheels; they sparkled like chrysolite [a yellow or greenish gem] and all four looked alike. Each appeared to be made like a wheel intersecting a wheel. As they moved, they would go in any one of the four directions the creatures faced; the wheels did not turn about as the creatures went. Their rims were high and awesome, and all four rims were full of eyes all around. When the living creatures moved, the wheels beside them moved, and when the living creatures rose from the ground, the wheels also rose. . . . Above the expanse over their heads was what looked like a throne of sapphire, and high above on the throne was a figure like that of a man." Later in the book, Ezekiel has two more encounters with the same "vision of God," stating in Ezekiel 43:3, ". . . and the visions were like the vision that I saw by the river Chebar; and I fell upon my face."

Von Däniken and others saw in these accounts the plausible depiction of UFO encounters, with Ezekiel trying his best to describe something totally foreign to him. One of Von Däniken's readers was NASA official Josef F. Blumrich, who said, "I began to read von Däniken with the condescending attitude of someone who knows beforehand that the conclusions presented can by no means be correct. However, von Däniken quotes, among other things, passages from the Book of Ezekiel, whose vague technical information he thinks is a description of a spacecraft. With that he touches on a field very familiar to me, since I have spent the greater part of my professional life with design and analysis of aircraft and rockets. So I decided to use the statements of the prophet to refute von Däniken and to prove the fallacy of his allegations. Seldom has a total defeat been so rewarding, so fascinating, and so delightful!"

Blumrich, after an exhaustive study allowing for the fact that the Book of Ezekiel was fragmentary and written by someone other than Ezekiel many years after the events, nevertheless concluded that not only was the craft described by Ezekiel "technically feasible" but "very well designed to fulfill its functions and purpose." He said such a craft is within today's technological capabilities. "Moreover," added Blumrich, "the results indicate a spaceship operated in conjunction with a mother spacecraft orbiting the earth."

"I want to say that I have carried it out from the viewpoint of an engineer, out of technical curiosity, so to speak. My interest was primarily focused on those parts of the Book of Ezekiel that contain statements describing shapes and procedures relevant to my professional area of activity. These parts, incidentally, are almost without exception clearly distinct from the prophetic content," Blumrich explained. "At all times we must remember that Ezekiel does not interpret what he sees, because he cannot interpret it. What he does is describe to the best of his ability the optical and acoustical impression."

Blumrich proceeds to depict a subspace landing module drawn from Ezekiel's account, which seems to be a cross between a space capsule and a helicopter. He said the craft is "superbly suited" for tip-first entry into the earth's atmosphere, where it then could extend four helicopter blades to support the main body in a gentle landfall. He further sees known and tested space technology in Ezekiel's description of the landing. The appearance of "glowing coals" could alternatively refer to heating due to entry into the atmosphere or perhaps a nuclear power plant; "two pairs of wings" may refer to helicopter blades that allow the craft to fly through the atmosphere; and "a wheel in the middle of a wheel" is an accurate description of modern omnidirectional wheels such as the casters on a chair, which can move in any direction, a feat quite unknown in Ezekiel's time.

Other explanations of Ezekiel's experiences include the phrase "the hand of the Lord God was there upon me," which Blumrich states could refer to the feeling of weight due to the pull of gravity while flying. When Ezekiel states he was taken upward "by the lock of my head," he could mean that static electricity caused his hair to stand on end. His description of the craft's commander sitting on a throne cannot help but prompt a comparison with the padded, high-backed seats in modern airliners.

"Moreover, with the exception of some misplaced Verses, Ezekiel describes all the parts he saw in the order that corresponds to the phases of the landing process," said Blumrich. "Ezekiel begins with the fire and the clouds of the braking phase; then he describes the helicopters during the aerodynamic flight, and the radiator of the reactor and the control rockets as the spaceship is hovering; then he observes the functioning of the wheels and the rolling on the ground. Thus, the wheels appear in the text at the very place where they become necessary from a functional point of view. This sequence is an additional confirmation that the wheels were retractable, and further proof of the accuracy of the description."

Whether Blumrich's interpretation is correct or not, it is ironic that the most severe opposition to his theory comes not from scientists but from Christian fundamentalists who claim to believe in the inerrancy of the Bible on the one hand while rejecting Ezekiel's story as a truthful account of a real event on the other. "In the very first verse of his prophesy Ezekiel says that he saw 'visions from God,'" stated Clifford Wilson, who proclaimed "strong Christian beliefs" and "acceptance of the Bible as the revealed Word of God." "'Visions' are not necessarily literal phenomena, and in fact the descriptions that follow cannot all be taken literally in our physical sense," Wilson concluded.

The biblical stories suggesting flight more than two thousand years before our time are mirrored by similar accounts on the opposite side of the world. Chinese tradition tells of Hou Yih, an engineer for the Emperor Yao, who described a flight to the moon in the year

2309 B.C. in a craft "mounting the current of luminous air." Once high above the earth, Hou Yih said "he did not perceive the rotary movement of the sun," an accurate description that can be made only from outside the earth's atmosphere. Both Hou Yih and his wife claimed to have visited the moon, which was described as "a luminous sphere, shining like glass, of enormous size and very cold; the light of the moon has its birth in the sun." This is a most accurate depiction of the moon's hard, cold surface, which reflects sunlight.

But if accounts of ancient astronauts and fabulous flying machines are accurate, why have there not been many more detailed stories handed down over the centuries? Wouldn't additional and even more descriptive documents be available today?

The answer is a simple "no" thanks to the destructive nature of man. Only some of Homer's epic poems survived the destruction of the collected works of the Greek tyrant Pisistratus in Athens. Nothing survived the destruction of the Egyptian library in the Temple of Ptah in Memphis. Likewise, an estimated two hundred thousand volumes of priceless works disappeared with the destruction of the library of Pergamus in Asia Minor. When the Romans leveled the city of Carthage, they destroyed a library said to contain more than five hundred thousand volumes. Next came Julius Caesar, whose war against Egypt resulted in the loss of the library at Alexandria, considered the greatest collection of books in antiquity. With the loss of the *Serapeum* and the *Bruchion*, a total of some seven hundred thousand volumes of accumulated knowledge went up in flames. What little survived was destroyed by Christians in 391. European libraries also suffered under the Romans and later from zealous Christians. Between the sacking of Constantinople and the Inquisition during the Middle Ages, an inestimable number of ancient works were irretrievably lost. Collections in Asia fared little better, as the Chinese emperor Tsin Shi Hwang-ti ordered wholesale book burning in 213 B.C.

"Because of these tragedies we have to depend on disconnected fragments, casual passages, and meager accounts," wrote researcher Andrew Tomas. "Our distant past is a vacuum filled at random with tablets, parchments, statues, paintings, and various artifacts. The history of science would appear totally different were the book collection of Alexandria intact today."

We are left with fragmentary writings mostly from oral traditions to inform us of our distant past. Yet these stories are filled with strange and inexplicable accounts that continue to intrigue modern researchers. But compelling as these stories may be, they hardly constitute documentation of ancient visitations. Does any tangible proof exist today to support the idea of high technology in the distant past?

The answer would seem to be a clear "yes" after considering some of the world's known mysteries.

Ancient Artifacts

In 1900, Greek sponge divers discovered an ancient ship lying in waters near Antikythera, a small island off the coast of Crete. After much work and a second trip to the site later that year, the divers managed to retrieve several bronze and marble statues from the wreck, which were taken to the National Archeological Museum in Athens, Greece.

Awed by both the quality and quantity of the statues, observers initially gave little notice to some lumps of corroded bronze among the find. When finally studied by archeologist Spyridon Stais in May 1902, it was discovered the lumps contained complex cogwheels and gears. There was an immediate dispute as to what this mechanism represented. One thought was that it may have been an astrolabe used for measuring the elevation of heavenly bodies.

Only one thing seemed certain: Based on inscriptions found on the mechanism's case, its date of manufacture was about 80 B.C.

The Antikythera Mechanism, as it came to be called, remained an enigma until 1958, when British scientist Dr. Derek J. de Solla Price pronounced the device a predecessor to our modern computer. "It appears that this was, indeed, a computing machine that could work out and exhibit the motions of the sun and moon and probably also the planets," he wrote in 1962. Price was amazed by the piece, stating, "Nothing like this instrument is preserved elsewhere," he wrote. "Nothing comparable to it is known from any ancient scientific text or literary allusion. On the contrary, from all that we know of science and technology in the Hellenistic Age we should have felt that such a device could not exist."

The device consists of dials set into a wooden box containing at least twenty wheel gears plus an astounding system of differential gears, not known to exist prior to clocks made in the late 1500s. In 1971, X-ray photographs showed a full array of meshing gears inside the machine far more complicated than even the earliest known clockworks. The sophistication of the device prompted Price in 1959 to state, "Finding a thing like this is like finding a jet plane in the tomb of King Tutankhamen."

Despite the fact that the Antikythera Mechanism has been described as "one of the greatest basic mechanical inventions of all time," most modern Americans are unaware of its existence, and even those who are have never considered it as evidence that someone with technological superiority may have visited the earth nearly two thousand years ago. Scientist and acclaimed science fiction writer Arthur C. Clarke admitted, "Looking at this extraordinary relic is a most disturbing experience." However, Clarke cannot allow himself to view it as evidence of extraterrestrial visitation, instead commenting, "We can be absolutely certain that the Antikythera computer is the product of human skill; but if there is anywhere one might expect to find crashed spaceships or other alien artifacts, it would be in the oceans that cover three-quarters of our world." Clarke may have rebutted his own argument when he wrote, "If the insight of the Greeks had matched their ingenuity, the Industrial Revolution might have begun a thousand years before Columbus. By this time we would not merely be pottering around on the moon; we could have reached the nearer stars." Since man has not yet reached the stars, couldn't this be evidence that the Antikythera Mechanism was given to humans or perhaps copied from one of nonhuman origin?

Giving credence to the idea that our forefathers may have used electricity, an energy source we are taught was only discovered by Italian anatomist Luigi Galvani about 1786, is a series of vessels discovered in Iraq that can only be ancient batteries. In 1936, a German scientist named Wilhelm König was working in the Iraq Museum when he found several odd pieces, including a clay vase containing a copper cylinder held by asphalt. In the center of this was a protruding iron rod tipped by oxidized lead. "After all the parts had been brought together and then examined in their separate parts, it became evident that it could only have been an electrical element. It was only necessary to add an acid or an alkaline liquid to complete the element," König wrote.

Naturally, König's conclusions were hotly contested by traditional scientists, but became muted after another German scientist, Egyptologist Dr. Arne Eggebrecht, came across yet another pot and tube device among treasures on tour from Iraq. Testing his theory, Eggebrecht poured freshly pressed grape juice into the copper cylinder, which promptly caused an attached voltmeter to register half a volt of electricity. Eggebrecht has stated that the electric current produced by the "Baghdad battery" may have been used to electroplate gilded statuary more than a hundred years before the birth of Christ.

Many other mysterious objects support the concept of either unknown early civilizations or visits by technologically advanced travelers. The so-called Skull of Doom is especially perplexing. A near life-size human skull, this intricate artifact is carved from pure quartz crystal and is believed by some to be the remnant of a lost South American civilization. Despite the fact that it cannot be accurately dated and some controversy swirls around its discovery, it remains a genuine enigma compounded by the existence of a second crystal skull on display in the Museum of Mankind, a part of the British Museum. The museum has no idea as to the origin of its skull, which was bought from New York's Tiffany's jewelers in 1898.

Yet a study of the two skulls in 1936 prompted scientists at the British Museum to state, "It is safe to conclude that they are representations of the same human skull, though one may have been copied from the other." The concept of copying appears strong since the museum skull is much cruder and is one piece compared to the craftsmanship and separate jaw of the "Skull of Doom."

The latter skull belonged to Anna Mitchell-Hedges, who claimed to have discovered it herself in 1927 while excavating the Mayan city of Lubaantum in British Honduras with her father, explorer F. A. Mitchell-Hedges. Her father declined to detail the circumstances of the find, saying only that "I have reason for not revealing." This reticence, of course, led to controversy over the skull, with some claiming it is more likely of Aztec origin than Mayan. All apparently agree that the age of the skulls goes back more than three thousand years.

Controversies aside, there can be no doubt of the existence of the skulls, and exactly who made them and how remains a mystery to modern scientists. Mitchell-Hedges himself speculated that the skull carving "must have taken 150 years, generation after generation working all the days of their lives, patiently rubbing down with sand an immense block of rock crystal until the perfect skull emerged." To add to the mystery, when the British Museum Laboratory examined the museum skull recently, they discovered evidence that a "powered cutter" may have been used in its creation. Is this evidence of a hoax or of technology predating man's history?

Oddities from different times and cultures provide support for the presence of technology long before we would expect it. In 1869, miners near Treasure City, Nevada, unearthed a fist-sized piece of feldspar, a silicate mineral, containing a two-inch-long metal screw. Its taper and threads were clearly visible. The stone in which the screw was embedded has been estimated as much older than mankind. Tom Kenny of Plateau Valley, Colorado, was digging a cellar in 1936 when at a depth of ten feet he uncovered a smooth, level pavement composed of mortared tiles five inches square. The mortar used to cement the tiles was of a composition of material not found anywhere near Plateau Valley, and scientists estimated the date of the pavement's origin as almost a million years ago, since the fossil of a three-toed Miocene horse was found in the same geological stratum of earth. This discovery was closely duplicated when workmen in Blue Lick, Kentucky, discovered a broad pavement of well-cut and neatly fitted stone slabs beneath the bones of a prehistoric mastodon. The perfectly symmetrical giant round balls—some eight feet in diameter weighing more than sixteen tons—found in the Diquis Delta of Costa Rica represent a technology not known until modern times.

Alan Landsburg produced such impressive television programs as *The Undersea World of Jacques Cousteau*, *The March of Time*, and *The National Geographic Series* in the 1960s and 1970s. Not given to flights of imagination, Landsburg nevertheless became intrigued with historical anomalies around the world. His 1974 book, *In Search of Ancient Mysteries*, included these intriguing items:

Ornaments formed from molten platinum found by anthropologist J. Alden Mason in Peru. Since platinum's melting temperature is 1,730 degrees, it is unclear how early primitives could have generated such heat.

Landsburg himself found a gold object in Colombia that "was a clear model of a delta-winged jet fighter and it was thought to be 2,000 years old."

Former British Naval Intelligence officer Ivan Sanderson discovered a manufactured gold chain in a Pennsylvania coal deposit believed to be at least a million years old.

In the mid-1800s, about sixty stone cubes were found in Ireland containing inscriptions found to be "a very ancient class of Chinese characters."

Ancient concave mirrors—identical to modern parabolic optical reflectors—were uncovered near La Venta, Mexico.

Cuneiform tablets from Babylon in the British Museum described an outer planet that could not have been seen in ancient Babylon without the aid of modern telescopes.

The list goes on. Individually, such cases might be explained away as hoaxes or misinterpretation of data. Much harder to explain is the existence today of ancient maps that depict an accurate knowledge of both prehistoric geography and astronomy.

Mystifying Maps

The Greek geographer Strabo, who lived during the time of Jesus, wrote that there were people living in the temperate zone north of the parallel passing by Athens and west of the Atlantic Ocean. Lucius Annaeus Seneca, the Roman tragedian, wrote in *Medea*, "Another Tiphys shall disclose new worlds, and lands shall be seen beyond Thule." This was a clear reference to North America, as Tiphys referred to the pilot of the legendary ship *Argos* and Thule has been identified as Iceland.

Even the sacred Hindu text *Vishnu-Purana* speaks of a continent composed of two lands lying south of the North Pole, a fitting enough description of North and South America. A timeworn chart found in Tibet was deciphered by the Soviet philologist Bronislav Kouznetsov in 1969 as a map referring to the ancient nations of Bactria, Babylonia, Persia, and locations including the Persian city of Pasargady, Jerusalem, Alexandria, and the Caspian Sea. This map provided some of the first hard evidence to support the idea that prehistoric Tibetans had links with Persia and Egypt centuries ago.

Researcher Graham Hancock told of a Chinese map copied from an earlier one onto a stone pillar in 1137, which indicated sophisticated concepts of longitude and spherical trigonometry. "Indeed, on close examination, it shares so many features with the European and Middle Eastern maps that only one explanation seems adequate: it and they must have stemmed from a common source," he wrote.

But one of the most compelling bits of evidence indicating a prehistoric knowledge of the world's geography is found in the two surviving maps of the sixteenth-century Turkish cartographer Admiral Piri Reis. Under the translated title *Book of the Seas*, Piri Reis published 210 well-drawn maps. One of his maps, still in the possession of the National Museum of Turkey, is dated 1513 and depicts the western coast of Africa, the eastern coast of South America, and the northern coast of Antarctica. In a letter dated July 6, 1960, Air Force Colonel Harold Z. Ohlmeyer of the 8th Reconnaissance Tactical Squadron of the Strategic Air Command stated, "The geographic detail shown in the lower part of the [Piri Reis] map agrees very remarkably with the results of the seismic profile made across the top of the ice-cap by the Swedish-British Antarctic Expedition of 1949. This indicates the coastline had been mapped before it was covered by the ice-cap."

The English explorer Captain James Cook attempted the first scientific visit to Antarctica in 1773 but returned thinking the entire area was nothing but frozen ocean. Mainland Antarctica was first sighted by the American sea captain Nathaniel Palmer in 1820. Exploration of the Antarctic region continued well into the twentieth century. It was once believed that the southernmost continent had been covered by thick ice since its creation. However, the discovery of ice-encased Cenozoic unicellular algae in 1983 indicated that Antarctica may have been at least partly free of ice as late as three million years ago. The discovery of meteorites in the ice sheets has allowed testing, which indicates some sheets formed as recently as ten thousand years ago. The late Professor Charles Hapgood, who taught the history of science at Keene College in New Hampshire, advanced the theory in 1953 that Antarctica may have moved further south by some two thousand miles due to "Earth-crust displacement" and therefore could have been partially free of ice until as late as 4000 B.C. This is still a thousand years before traditional academicians believe that the first true civilizations of Egypt and Sumer with their seafaring explorers began.

So the puzzle is how Piri Reis could have accurately drawn the contours of Antarctica, since it was not discovered until some three hundred years after he drew his map and is covered with an ice sheet more than six thousand feet deep and at least six thousand years old.

Fortunately, Piri Reis was helpful. He left behind notes telling how he acquired the information used in his maps. Piri Reis said that in the year 1501, when he was thirty-one years old, he joined an uncle in fighting against Spain. Following a naval battle, maps were found on a Spanish sailor who claimed to have sailed with Columbus. The captive said he had obtained the maps from Columbus, who had made them after reading an old book dating from the time of Alexander the Great. However, Piri Reis said the Columbus map was not his sole source of information. In a marginal note to his map, he wrote, "In preparing this map I made use of about 20 old charts and eight Mappa Mundis, i.e. of the charts called *Jaferiye* by the Arabs and prepared at the time of Alexander the Great, in which the whole inhabited world was shown." It is known that Piri Reis had access to the Imperial Library in Constantinople, where many ancient manuscripts were kept. Obviously, Piri Reis was making use of charts and maps drawn farther back than ancient Greece, whose intellectuals admittedly drew from even older Egyptian and Sumerian sources.

But the idea that someone had accurately mapped an ice-free Antarctica in prehistoric times paled beside the fact that Piri Reis's 1513 map also depicted the correct position of the Falkland Islands, not discovered until 1592, and the rivers of South America—the Orinoco, Amazon, Parana, Uruguay, and others not fully charted until the advent of satellites.

And the Piri Reis maps were not simply flukes. Perhaps drawing on the same sources as Piri Reis, mapmakers Gerard Kremer, known as Mercator (1569), Oronteus Finaeus (1531), and Philippe Buache (1737) also produced maps of the Antarctic topography that are still in existence.

Studying this issue prompted Professor Hapgood to comment, "The evidence presented by the ancient maps appears to suggest the existence in remote times, before the rise of any of the known cultures, of a true civilization, of a comparatively advanced sort, which either was localized in one area but had worldwide commerce, or was, in a real sense, a worldwide culture."

Hapgood based this speculation on knowing that whoever produced the antique maps of an ice-free Antarctica must have traveled there thousands of years before our known history. The same could be said for the mapping of the South American rivers—unless both achievements were accomplished by aerial mapping. Von Däniken saw evidence of this due to slight distortions of the South American coast on the Piri Reis map. He claimed this same type of distortion is noticeable on satellite photos in which corners of pictures warp due to the curve of the earth's surface. Von Däniken concluded that Piri Reis's source documents may have been drawn from aerial photographs. Of course, the thought that someone may have flown over Antarctica and South America prior to 4000 B.C. cannot be seriously considered within the context of traditional history.

Therefore, both Hapgood and his student, author Graham Hancock, have concluded that a previously unknown human civilization, with very advanced technology, existed in prehistoric times. Neither man appeared willing to publicly postulate that such a civilization might have been the result of extraterrestrial contact. Yet the evidence for this theory continues to grow.

In 1912, a New York antiquarian named Wilford Voynich discovered an old manuscript inside a locked chest in an ancient castle near Rome. Despite several serious attempts—including the experts who cracked the Japanese and German codes of World War II—no one has been able to decipher the manuscript, which has been dated before 1500. Drawings in the document depict cross sections of leaves and roots that could only have been produced with the aid of a microscope. But even more telling is a drawing of a spiral with eight legs and a cloudy mass of what appears to be stars in the center. A partially translated caption reading "by the navel of Pegasus, the girdle of Andromeda and the head of Cassiopeia" may indicate a reference to the Andromeda galaxy, which would have been invisible without a modern telescope.

In fact, some of the most substantial artifacts found in the world all seem to have a connection with the heavens. One ancient wonder is the stone megaliths of Stonehenge built upon Salisbury Plain in south-ern England. Its most notable features include concentric rings of stone slabs surrounding an upright horseshoe of stone and a solitary vertical slab known as the Heel Stone. It is generally accepted that Stonehenge was built toward the end of the Stone Age, between 1900 and 1400 B.C., as both a religious center and an observatory.

Stonehenge is only the most famous of about a thousand stone circles in England and northern France, all of which remain a total mystery as to who built them or why. Centuries ago, writers attributed these megalithic circles to the Druids, mystical Celtic priests who studied astronomy, because they were mentioned by Julius Caesar. However, there is no evidence directly linking Stonehenge to the Druids and, in fact, the Druids seemed to have flourished more than a thousand years after their creation.

Some of the giant stones used in Stonehenge come from more than two hundred miles away in southwest Wales with at least three rivers intervening. Yet scientists today have focused on the speculation that ancient Stone Age Celts quarried these stones, floated them across rivers, and rolled them on logs before pulling them upright into their present positions. Some of the stones weigh up to sixty tons. In 1938, it took twelve men five days of work using steel cables to restore a small eight-ton stone to its original position. We are told the ancients' tools consisted of handmade rope, stone axes, and picks made from discarded deer antlers. This concept prompted one author to comment, "Our remote ancestors must have been strange people; they liked making things difficult for themselves and always built their statues in the most impossible places. Was it just because they liked a hard life?"

Scientists were disconcerted to discover that hardly any of the stone circles were actually circular. There was clear evidence that who-ever built them intentionally made them in odd elliptical shapes, which indicated some premeditated purpose. That purpose connects to the stars.

Following a detailed computer study of Stonehenge, Boston University astronomer Gerald Hawkins concluded that the stone circle was nothing less than an astronomical computer. The builders of Stonehenge revealed knowledge of the fifty-six-year cycle of lunar eclipses. Reporting on his own study, NASA official Maurice Chatelain reached the same conclusion. In 1978 he wrote: "The scientific skill and astronomical knowledge of Stonehenge is rooted in the 56 Aubrey holes, in which at different dates of the year were placed wooden poles of different height, giving an astounding variety of precise alignments with the celestial bodies. It made Stonehenge a huge, cleverly and skillfully executed calculator."

The theory that Stonehenge and other stone circles were used to calculate the movement of the stars was confirmed in the 1960s with the restoration of the Newgrange Tumulus tomb located near Drogheda, Ireland. Professor Michael O'Kelly of University College in Cork discovered that a small quartz "shutter" above the tomb's five-ton stone entryway illuminated the tomb on precisely midwinter sunrise each year. Another monument clearly designed on astronomical knowledge is the Maes Howe tomb in the Orkney Isles north of Scotland, which aligns with a monolith each winter solstice. Teacher Magnus Spence, who first recorded the connection in 1893, wrote, "The alignment formed with this long passage of Maes Howe and the Standing Stone of Barnhouse indicates directions too remarkable to be merely accidental."

More remarkable than simple celestial alignments is the theory that Stonehenge is an energy transmitter. Support for this concept came in 1979 when a scientist-led team detected ultrasonic energy pulses emanating from the Rollright Stones, a circle of seventy-seven stones near Oxfordshire.

The greatest astronomical calculator of them all—and another structure claimed to contain powerful energy—is the Great Pyramid of Cheops. The last surviving member of the Seven Wonders of the World, the Great Pyramid has been a source of mystery and controversy throughout man's history.

The Amazing Pyramids

In the fifth century, the historian Herodotus was told by guides that the major Egyptian pyramids were built by Cheops, his son, and brother. Herodotus repeated this hearsay in the earliest known account of the pyramids. "All other commentators, up to the present, continued uncritically to follow in the Greek historian's footsteps," stated author Graham Hancock.

Although its creation is popularly attributed to the pharaoh Cheops, there is no indisputable evidence of this idea. In fact, the best evidence points to the existence of the pyramid thousands of years prior to the Egyptian empires. This evidence is the obvious vertical erosion found principally on the nearby Sphinx, but to some degree on the Great Pyramid.

John Anthony West, the author of both travel guides and serious scholarship, claimed vertical erosion can come only from continuous downpours of rain over long periods of time. Since the Sphinx is supposed to have been built by Cheops's son, Khafre, its creation has been placed around 2500 B.C. West pointed out that no significant rainfall has occurred on the Giza plateau—site of both the Sphinx and the Great Pyramid—since before 10,000 B.C. This can only mean that both structures were built more than seven thousand years prior to the Egyptians, a conclusion conveniently ignored by traditional Egyptologists.

West took the initiative from French scientist R. A. Schwaller de Lubicz, who, after making a study of the Luxor Temple during the 1940s, claimed to have found mathematical evidence that early Egyptian science was much more advanced than previously thought. Schwaller also mentioned that Egypt was subjected to devastating rains and floods more than twelve thousand years ago. After verifying these claims by his own studies, West said the fact of vertical rain erosion is "ironclad evidence for the existence of a previously unidentified high civilization of distant antiquity."

While the ancient Egyptians undoubtedly mimicked the Great Pyramid by building much smaller and fragile pyramids, most of which have long ago fallen into ruin, the origin of the prototype remains a mystery. Its sheer physical size provokes awe in everyone with knowledge of construction techniques. Rising nearly five hundred feet in the air, the Great Pyramid covers thirteen acres of land at its base and is built of stones with an average weight of two and a half tons. Some stone blocks weigh almost a hundred tons yet are so well crafted that a single piece of paper cannot be slipped between them.

At the nearby Valley Temple of Khafre hundreds of stone blocks weigh more than two hundred tons. According to Hancock, "At present there are only two land-based cranes in the world that could lift weights of this magnitude. . . . In other words, modern builders with all the advantages of high-tech engineering at their disposal, can barely hoist weights of 200 tons. Was it not, therefore, somewhat surprising that the builders at Giza had hoisted such weights on an almost routine basis?"

Commenting on the technology needed to construct the pyramid, I. E. S. Edwards of the Egyptian Department of the British Museum wrote, "Cheops, who may have been a megalomaniac, could never, during the reign of 23 years, have erected a building of the size and durability of the Great Pyramid if technical advances had not enabled his masons to handle stones of considerable weight and dimension."

Another oddity is the lack of written history for the Great Pyramid. The only mention of Pharaoh Cheops, alternately called Khufu, in the pyramid is in markings found in 1837 by Col. Howard Vyse. However, the Vyse find has been called into question, as it is known he was in desperate need of justification for his expenses; no other mention of Cheops has ever been found; the lack of any other inscriptions and the fact that the markings contained mistakes in both spelling and grammar. In fact, Vyse and his assistants were caught in one hoax concerning a wooden coffin and human remains reported discovered by Vyse in a smaller pyramid. Author Zecharia Sitchen reported, "The fact, however—known to scholars for some time now but for some reason still hardly publicized—is that neither the wooden coffin nor the skeletal remains were authentic. Someone—undoubtedly that Colonel Vyse and his cronies—had brought into the pyramid a coffin . . . and bones from the even much later Christian times, and put the two together in an unabashed archeological fraud."

Other Egyptian documents, such as the Inventory Stela, made it plain that the Great Pyramid was already built prior to Cheops's rule. These, however, have been ignored or dismissed by traditional Egyptologists. It is also interesting to note that the Bible, which, theology aside, is a detailed history of the Hebrew people, never mentions work on the pyramid, although they were the slaves of the Egyptians for many years.

The questions concerning the purpose of the Great Pyramid equal that of its construction. Traditionally, it was thought to have been the tomb of Cheops. However, no inscriptions or funeral regalia have been found. In fact, as Graham Hancock pointed out, "Not a single one of these monuments had ever been found to contain the body of a pharaoh, or any signs whatsoever of a royal burial." So what was its purpose?

While theories abound, the most credible involve a connection to the stars. In the 1930s, American architect James A. Kane presented a detailed study that he saw as proof that the three Giza pyramids were built according to geometrical and surveying principles connected to astronomical observations. The idea that the pyramids' design was based on the stars has been supported by Egyptologist I. E. S. Edwards and archeologist Martin Isler. R. O. Faulkner, a translator of the Pyramid Texts, wrote: "It is well known that the Ancient Egyptians took great interest in the stars . . . inscribing star-maps and tables in their coffins and tombs . . . in which the stars were regarded as gods or as the souls of the blessed dead."

A look at the orientation of the Great Pyramid confirms its well-planned and sophisticated design. Each of its four sides precisely face the four points of the compass with only a one-twelfth degree of variation, which has been explained by the gradual movement of the earth's axis rather than any mistake on the part of its designer. Also, although there are slight differences due to damage by both man and nature, the height of the Great Pyramid is proportional to the radius of the earth and the perimeter to the circumference. Measurements of the two base halves yield the numbers 365.256 and 365.259, the exact number of days it takes for the earth to compete its orbit of the sun and the time it takes to return to its starting point in the elliptical orbit. More astounding is the fact that during the International Geophysical Year (1957–58) satellite technology established that the earth's mean polar radius was 150,265,030.4 British inches. One ten-millionth of this distance would be 25,0265 British inches—the exact figure found in three separate measurements inside the Great Pyramid. The number 25,000 also happens to be the distance from the earth to the sun and the number of years in the precessional cycle, the time it takes for the earth to pass through the twelve zodiacal constellations.

These amazing facts go far beyond any chance of coincidence or lucky guesswork. They tend to confirm the idea that whoever built the Great Pyramid was in possession of astronomical and geophysical knowledge unsurpassed even today. Author Peter Lemesurier described the Great Pyramid as "an architectural symbol for the planet Earth itself."

Using the North and South Poles, the equator, and the earth's center as reference points, the pyramid accurately sections the entire planet into a three-dimensional grid of thirty, sixty, and ninety degrees. Utilizing these grids, any aircraft can successfully navigate from the pyramid to any location on Earth with only a minor deviation. When first built, the Great Pyramid was covered with a reflective casing of fine white limestone, making it highly visible—an excellent aerial navigation marker. In fact, several researchers have determined geometric patterns with the pyramid as the center that they said could indicate ancient flight paths.

Furthermore, it is known that the faces of the Great Pyramid are not flat but slightly concave. "The most astonishing result of this arrangement is that it pushes back the two half bases of the pyramid by a quarter degree so that the two halves form an angle of $\frac{1}{2}$ degree. This results in a difference of two minutes of solar clock time and could have served the ancient astronomers to set their water clocks or hourglasses to the exact solar time," wrote Maurice Chatelain, who concluded that the Great Pyramid is a keeper of time among other things.

Chatelain said the pyramid also functions as a solar calendar. He produced complicated mathematical formulae based on the Egyptian calendar that he claimed showed clear correlations to the amazing Antikythera Mechanism. Chatelain also saw the Great Pyramid as an astronomical observatory.

Authors Robert Bauval and Adrian Gilbert believe they may

have found the secret astronomical reference point for the Great Pyramid. In studying ancient religious writings found in Fifth and Sixth Dynasty pyramids known as the Pyramid Texts, they found continual references to Osiris, including a passage stating, "O Horus, these kings are Osiris, these pyramids are Osiris, these constructions of theirs are Osiris. . . ." Osiris was the ancient Egyptian god of the underworld with life-giving powers connected to the constellation Orion.

After extensive study, Bauval determined that the configuration of the three Giza pyramids—two in line while the third is offset— indeed match that of Orion. Furthermore, one of the small tunnels inside the Great Pyramid long described as an "air shaft" indeed aligned with the star cluster of Orion's Belt.

But to their astonishment they realized that the arrangement of the Giza pyramids reflected the position of Orion as it would have only appeared about the year 10,450 B.C.—a date more nearly matching the growing body of evidence confirming a prehistoric genesis for the Great Pyramid.

Just as strange energy readings were found at the ancient Rollright Stones in England, similar results have been found in Egypt's pyramids, leading to tales of mystic magic and psychic power. Although largely discredited in the public mind, the sensational stories of "pyramid power" carry elements of truth. Many studies indicate that razor blades stay sharp longer and fruit ripens slower when placed within a properly oriented pyramid.

In the late 1960s, Nobel Prize winner Dr. Luis W. Alvarez, with the full cooperation of the Egyptian government and Ein Shams University of Cairo, devised an investigation of the Khafre pyramid—the second largest—utilizing cosmic rays. Since such rays would register higher intensity in hollow spaces, it was hoped that any hidden rooms or passageways would be revealed. But, according to the *London Times*, nothing worked properly. Instrument readings differed from one day to the next. Computer analysis of the readings produced "garbled nonsense" so that not even the direction the instruments were being aimed could be determined. The equipment was rechecked. It worked fine except within the pyramid. Frustrated, Dr. Alvarez returned to America.

"As impossible and improbable as it may seem," commented Chatelain, "apparently the ancient Egyptians must have been capable of predicting the future and set up radiation barriers against us, impenetrable even to electronic scouting. It looks as if somebody or something thousands of years ago had installed electromagnetic radiation sources in at least one of the pyramids or their vicinity just to prevent the electronic devices of later generations from discovering their hidden secrets."

The mysteries of the Egyptian pyramids do not represent some fluke of the ancient world.

The pyramids of Mexico and Central America are just as astonishing and just as mysterious. One of the artifacts left by the Olmec civilization of Mexico is a large pyramid remarkably similar to those found in Egypt. The Olmecs are believed to be the ancestors of the Mayans, who also built pyramids, including some that had a limestone facing like the Great Pyramid.

As the similarities of widely spread cultures continue to be appreciated, a pattern of common worldwide connections is emerging. Egyptian legends tell of *Tep Zepi*, or the First Time, an age when sky gods came down to Earth, raised the land up from under mud and water, flew through the air in flying "boats," and gave man laws and wisdom through a royal line of pharaohs. It is intriguing to note that these ancient gods displayed very human attributes. They required food and clothing. They liked to imbibe wine and were not above consorting with comely young ladies. Likewise, South American legends tell of the white, bearded "Viracochas" who lifted indigenous natives out of ignorance and taught them civilization, producing intricate highways and other wonders. They too lived among the native peoples for a time, eating, bathing, and conducting themselves in a very human way.

"A . . . global influence clearly existed more than a millennium ago as evidenced by the remarkable similarities between ancient Mayan and Egyptian cultures," wrote author William Bramley, adding, "One thing that remained consistent was the building of pyramids." Researcher Graham Hancock concurred, writing that "a global legacy must have been handed down—a legacy of inestimable value, in all probability incorporating much more than sophisticated geographical knowledge." He added that "certain mysterious structures scattered around the world were built to preserve and transmit the knowledge of an advanced civilization of remote antiquity which was destroyed by a terrifying upheaval."

There are many Japanese traditions that include UFOs. Earthen statues dating back more than three thousand years have been found that depict humanoids eerily similar to the descriptions of modern UFO witnesses—creatures with long arms and large heads that appear to be wearing one-piece suits along with helmets bearing air filters and goggles.

In light of so many strange and unexplained ancient monuments, artifacts, and similarities of cultures, the presence of a prehistorical technological society appears almost certain. This gave renewed credence to the legends of Atlantis—that great Atlantic Ocean island that many people believe was the progenitor of all the early civilizations. The question now is whether such a civilization was a strictly human one that evolved naturally, then mysteriously vanished, leaving few traces, or if such a civilization, perhaps in some ways technologically superior to our own, was the result of extraterrestrial contact. The latter idea cannot be summarily dismissed due to the numerous and obvious connections between the ancients and advanced astronomical knowledge. Furthermore, almost all of the world's cultures tell of "gods" coming from the heavens in antiquity.

Zecharia Sitchen, a New York author who made a detailed study of ancient literature for more than thirty years, often reading from the original texts, has written a series of books entitled *The Earth Chronicles*, which present his interpretation of many early writings—principally from Babylonian and Sumerian sources. Sitchen recounted how man's early history was shaped by visitors from a twelfth planet in our solar system called Nibiru by the ancient Sumerians and Marduk by the Babylonians. This planet reportedly is on a thirty-degree inclined orbit to the parallax of our solar system, which takes it far into space, preventing viewing today. It comes close to the earth every 3,600 years and is due back between the years 2060 and 2065.

Incredibly enough, in 1983—twelve years after publication of Sitchen's first Earth Chronicles book, *The 12th Planet*—the *Washington Post* News Service reported, "A heavenly body possibly as large as the giant planet Jupiter and possibly so close to the earth that it would be part of this solar system has been found in the direction of the constellation Orion by an orbiting telescope called the Infrared Astronomical Observatory (IRAS)." For some astronomers, the discovery was no surprise. In 1981, astronomer Thomas Van Flandern reported to the American Astronomical Society that irregularities in the orbit of Pluto indicated that our solar system contained a tenth planet. The *Detroit News* commented, "If new evidence from the U.S. Naval Observatory of a 10th planet in the solar system is correct, it could prove that the Sumerians, an ancient eastern Mediterranean civilization, were far ahead of modern man in astronomy." Sitchen's idea of a twelfth planet and the discovery of a tenth planet are compatible, as Sitchen, like the ancient Sumerians, counted the sun and the moon as "bodies" in the solar system.

In an elaborate and compelling analysis of ancient literature, Russian-born Sitchen, one of fewer than two hundred persons who can read the Sumerian language, began with this new planet, which was said to have entered our solar system about four billion years ago and demolished a planet, creating the asteroid belt beyond Mars. His translations wove a story of alien civil war, personality clashes, and colonization efforts on Earth to include the creation of modern man.

In this account, a ruler named Alalu was overthrown and fled from the twelfth planet Nibiru, which was losing atmosphere and dying. Landing on Earth more than four hundred thousand years ago, he discovered that gold—one of the best conductors of heat and electricity—could be used to stabilize the atmosphere of Nibiru. As the quantity of gold was depleted, ground stations soon spread from the Middle East to Africa, where the hardship of the mining operations caused a revolt among the aliens, prompting their leaders to create modern man as slave workers by genetically manipulating early humans. This new race of *Homo sapiens* was taken to the Fertile Crescent in Mesopotamia about three hundred thousand years ago and allowed to multiply. Much to their fellow colonists' disgust, some aliens began to interbreed with the humans.

Sitchen claimed the offspring of these alien-human contacts are the Nephilim mentioned in Genesis 6:4, and indeed most Bible translators have concluded that the term Nephilim "designates ancient heroes who . . . are the products of sexual union of heavenly beings . . . and human women."

About thirteen thousand years ago, the aliens realized that the return of their home world—the twelfth planet—would cause widespread floods and tidal waves on Earth. They agreed not to share their knowledge with the humans but to allow the cataclysm to deplete their population. One alien, however, broke the agreement by warning the human Noah of the impending disaster.

Following the Great Flood of biblical times, years of wars and internal political unrest wrecked the alien expedition. Many were killed, while others returned to their home planet, leaving only ruins, legends, and vague bits of knowledge for the surviving humans, who began the ancient civilizations of Sumer, Babylon, and Egypt.

Sitchen's account is easy to dismiss—he even claimed the Great Pyramid at one time was equipped with instruments for guiding shuttle craft to a post-Diluvial "Spaceport" in the Sinai—until serious consideration is given to his depth of research. Drawing from records of our ancient civilizations, Sitchen's conclusions are coherent, internally consistent, and well supported.

A Crash Victim's Story

On August 13, 1947, just a little more than a month after the infamous Roswell incident, six Native Americans discovered a still-smoldering metallic object crashed in the New Mexico desert. Inside they found an alien creature who, though injured, was still alive.

Hearing the approach of military troops, the men decided to

keep the being from capture and care for him themselves. Taking him to their home, they found the being could communicate with them through a crystal device that conveyed images.

One of the rescuers was the now-deceased grandfather of Robert Morning Sky, a Native American of Hopi and Apache extraction, who today tells his ancestor's story and lectures on an alternative history of Earth as pieced together from the crash victim. His account of the being's rescue has been supported by other Native Americans who claimed they too have heard the story of the being called the "Star Elder."

Morning Sky said the basic message of the "Star Elder," whose name was Bak'Ti, was simple. "Star Beings have been here since Earth was a barren rock. They were here throughout evolution. In some cases their involvement was benevolent; in some cases it was not. Man has been guided . . . and he has been misled. The Star Beings have been our gods . . . and our devils. They have always been here, and they are still here now."

The story of man's history as recounted by Bak'Ti is strikingly similar to those of Sitchen and other sources. According to Morning Sky's work entitled "The Terra Papers," humans were created by DNA manipulation to provide labor for alien mining operations. The leader of these creator aliens was vying for control of Earth with his brother. To gain an edge, this leader placed some of his own DNA in the human gene pool, thus making them his own "children" after a fashion. Other alien DNA was contributed by a birdlike race that were "emotional and soulful." As humans began to breed and grow in numbers, two distinct groups came into being—one a docile bunch easily controlled by their alien overlords and the other an emotional and intelligent group that quickly developed independent will.

One faction of aliens, headed by the creator's ambitious brother, tried to destroy the willful humans by first casting them into the wilderness to die and later allowing a great flood to consume them. However, the creator leader managed to save a small group of humans.

This conflict over the stewardship of the human race continues today, according to Morning Sky, with one alien faction using elements of the U.S. government to hide their activities. Another faction has bases on the moon, which has been declared "off-limits" to humans.

"We do not realize the extent of alien influence behind the scenes of our world's political and economic systems, so we are easily manipulated in favor of alien agendas," wrote Karen Degenhart, who reported Morning Sky's story. "They use our planet's natural resources, they use our bodies for genetic material to continue their breeding experiments, and they use our government agencies, like NASA and the CIA, to maintain the UFO cover-up. The aliens don't want us to know they are here, or we might try to regain control of our planet."

According to Morning Sky, a later alien leader named Ra sought to destroy all evidence of man's real history to keep humans ignorant and controllable. But Ra lost power to an alien race descended from lizards, which today are known as the "greys." Today, the greys are reportedly involved with yet another alien race and are seeking to add specific human DNA to their own to enhance their well-developed intellect with the addition of human emotion and intuition.

Whether or not the accounts of Morning Sky, Sitchen, and others have any foundation in fact, the evidence for prehistoric technology is very compelling. But is it possible for a highly advanced civilization to disappear so thoroughly that even with modern scientific methods we cannot say with certainty it ever existed?

"I have asked this question myself and I think that I have found an answer," wrote Maurice Chatelain. "No material except solid rock, which is not easily transported, and maybe solid gold, can last for 12,000 years. Most other materials oxidize and turn to dust." He also pointed out that many objects now in museums are the unidentified remnants of an ancient society. Add to this the great destruction of antiquities done by the Romans, Christian crusaders, invading Turks, Conquistadors, and New World explorers and it is easy to appreciate why so little of our heritage remains.

Nothing in the known record precludes the idea of extraterrestrial contact in prehistoric times. In fact, considering the preceding information—which merely skims the surface of the subject—there is much to recommend it.

No serious researcher wants to follow the much-assailed path trod by von Däniken, but the issue of ancient astronauts refuses to go away as evidence of extraterrestrial contact in antiquity continues to grow, coupled with the recent controversies concerning the sightings of pyramids on both the moon and Mars.

If ancient astronauts operated on the earth in the distant past, they must not have vanished for good because UFO sightings have continued down through the centuries.

CHAPTER 3

MILITARY
OBSERVERS

Floyd Thompson was piloting his fighter-bomber on a bombing run over Italy during World War II when he noticed a light-colored oval object trailing behind his formation. After completing the mission, the bomber formation split up for safety's sake and began the harrowing trip home. Thompson noticed the strange metallic object was still there. But no one in his unit talked about it until they returned to base and were debriefed.

"Anyone see anything unusual during the mission?" the pilots were asked. Only then did several admit to seeing the strange orb, which seemed to be monitoring their flight. In light of reports such as this, most UFO researchers—or ufologists as they are often called—trace the advent of modern UFO sightings back to World War II.

Lights in the sky or strange flying craft had been reported throughout the ages, but it was during that period of global strife that the first unequivocal reports of unidentified flying objects came to public attention.

Prior to the war, strange aerial sightings were recorded throughout the centuries, even back to ancient civilizations. British author B. Le Poer Trench quoted from fragments of a papyrus of hieroglyphics believed to date back to Pharaoh Thutmose III, who ruled Egypt between about 1468 and 1436 B.C.: ". . . the scribes of the House of Life found it was a circle of fire that was coming in the sky . . . they went to the Pharaoh . . . to report it. . . . Now after some days had passed, these things became more numerous in the sky than ever. They shone more in the sky than the brightness of the sun, and extended to the limits of the four supports of the heavens. . . . Powerful was the position of the fire circles. The army of the Pharaoh looked on with him in their midst. It was after supper. Thereupon, those fire circles ascended higher in the sky towards the south. . . ."

Such reports were common through the time of the Roman Empire. While many were probably misinterpretations of comets or meteors, others obviously referred to something flying through the air. One Roman writer, Julius Obsequens, reported that in the year 212 B.C. "things like ships were seen in the sky." The respected historian Titus Livius wrote that the next year an "altar" was seen in the Italian sky accompanied by "the strange spectacle of men in white clothing." Roman scientist Pliny the Elder told how in 66 B.C. a "spark" fell to Earth, becoming as large as the moon before returning to the sky.

Reports of lights, strange craft, and even crosses in the sky continued throughout the Middle Ages. In 840, the archbishop of Lyons told of a "certain region called Magonia from whence come ships in the clouds" and how he prevented the stoning death of "three men and a woman who said they had fallen from these same ships."

W. R. Drake, author of an article entitled "Spacemen in the Middle Ages," recounted how a Christian church in England was saved from Saxons in 776 when craft bearing "the likeness of two large shields reddish in color" hovered overhead, scaring off the attackers.

While some of the hundreds of sightings during early European history undoubtedly can be explained as natural phenomena or even hoaxes, many show a definite correlation to modern UFO reports. In 1113, religious pilgrims in southwest England saw a fire-belching "dragon" emerge from the sea into the air. In January 1254, it was recorded that in Saint Albans, England, "in serene sky and clear air, with stars shining and the Moon eight days old, there suddenly appeared in the sky a kind of large ship elegantly shaped, well equipped and of marvelous color." One mealtime at Yorkshire's Byland Abbey in 1290, the friars were frightened by "a flat, round, shining, silvery object" flying overhead. There were even reports of a sky battle over Nuremberg, Germany, on April 4, 1561, supported by a woodcut depiction by artist Hans Glaser. Ball-shaped objects, disks, and crosses emerged from two large black cylindrical craft and seemed to fight each other. In 1566, a similar sight was seen over Basel, Switzerland. Most of these events were seen as "signs" from God.

By the 1800s, although descriptions of lights and objects in the sky continued, they were couched in more modern terminology. Objects were described as dirigibles or airships, and less religious connotations were placed on them. Such sightings continued well into the twentieth century but, with the exception of the previously mentioned Great Airship Mystery of 1896–97, received scant media attention.

Two great military conflagrations—World Wars I and II—overshadowed any concerns over flying objects. Unidentified artillery shells, mortar rounds, observation balloons, airplanes, and dirigibles were all too common, particularly near battle zones. The public had became accustomed to ever-advancing technology and lost interest. They were more concerned with personal safety and comfort. Whatever was in the skies seemed to be drawn primarily to military activity.

In the early and mid-1930s, there were reports of "ghost" aircraft passing over military installations in the United States, Britain, and Scandinavia. No one could identify them and no nation admitted responsibility. Most people dismissed these reports as secret reconnaissance missions by the Germans or Soviets. Yet there was definitely a strangeness to the reports. The flights often came in weather that would have grounded conventional aircraft. Reports stated the craft would cut power, yet circle several times. Their flight paths seemed to indicate a point of origin inside the Arctic Circle, and they often were accompanied by powerful searchlights and flashing colored lights, hardly advisable on secret missions. Others claimed Europeans were simply getting jumpy during this time when Adolf Hitler and Benito Mussolini were rearming their nations.

War nerves also were blamed for a never fully explained incident in wartime Los Angeles.

The Los Angeles Air Raid

By late February 1942, just three short months after the Japanese bombing of Pearl Harbor, tensions were high on the West Coast—with just cause. America had been attacked without warning and there was a fear of imminent invasion. Air raid drills had been conducted regularly since the attack, and on February 23, a Japanese submarine had shelled the Bankline Oil Company refinery in Goleta, just north of Santa Barbara.

At 2:25 A.M. on February 25, Los Angeles County residents were awakened by the wail of air raid sirens. Most believed it was simply another drill. They were blissfully unaware that one of America's most recent military secrets—radar—had picked up blips indicating a flight of approaching aircraft about 120 miles west of Los Angeles shortly after 2:00 A.M. According to a report on the incident sent to President Franklin Roosevelt the next day, 1,430 rounds of antiaircraft ammunition were fired at the incoming craft, yet no planes were shot down and no bombs were dropped. There were no casualties among American military forces and no army or navy planes were involved.

The firing, which went on for about an hour, caused considerable damage to several homes and public buildings. The city was littered with pieces of metal from exploded ordnance. At least six civilians died as the result of automobile accidents and heart attacks attributable to the gunfire. The all-clear signal did not come until 7:21 A.M., and traffic jams lasted well into the morning rush hour.

For all the commotion, there was no evidence that an enemy attack had taken place. Embarrassed military officials immediately began to downplay the incident. In Washington, Navy Secretary Frank Knox said "that as far as I know the whole raid was a false alarm and could be attributed to jittery nerves." But his reassuring statement was not supported by West Coast witnesses.

They told of fast-moving red or silver objects high in the sky accompanied by a large slower-paced—some said as slow as sixty miles per hour—object, which then hung motionless in midair for some time as antiaircraft shells burst all around it.

Peter Jenkins, who was on the staff of the *Los Angeles Evening Herald Examiner*, said, "I could clearly see the 'V' formation of about 25 silvery planes overhead moving slowly across the sky toward Long Beach." Long Beach police chief J. H. McClelland said he watched from the roof of Long Beach City Hall and gave this description: "An experienced Naval observer with me using powerful Carl Zeiss binoculars said he counted nine planes in the cone of a searchlight. He said they were silver in color. This group passed along from one battery of searchlights to another, and under fire from antiaircraft guns, flew from the direction of Redondo Beach and Inglewood on the land side of Fort MacArthur, and continued toward Santa Ana and Huntington Beach. Antiaircraft fire was so heavy, we could not hear the motors of the planes." Paul T. Collins, an employee of the Douglas Aircraft Company, observed the objects as he stood beside his car. He said he saw several "unidentified red objects . . . appearing from nowhere and then zigzagging from side to side." Collins said he and other observers estimated the objects' top speed "conservatively to be five miles per second."

With such witnesses running into the thousands and the damage done to the area, the official explanation of "jittery nerves" fell on suspicious ears. "There is a mysterious reticence about the whole affair," editorialized the *Long Beach Independent*, "and it appears some form of censorship is trying to halt discussion of the matter." In fact, prior to the 1974 release of the day-after report to Roosevelt, U.S. military authorities had claimed they had no record of the incident.

Some researchers have offered the opinion that the whole thing was caused by the ascent of meteorological balloons, one of which apparently indeed was released carrying a red flare by an antiaircraft unit in Santa Monica in response to the alarm. While this theory is supported by the fact that batteries were officially chastised for wasting ammunition on targets moving too slowly to be aircraft, it was shot down thanks to an Associated Press photo that showed one of the objects caught by converging searchlight beams and surrounded by bursting shells. This photo prompted one commentator to correctly conclude: "That it was not a balloon seems probable because the escape of no balloon has been reported as well as because it failed to collapse under intense and apparently accurate shell-fire."

Lost quickly amidst the reports of the battles and home-front campaigns of World War II, the Los Angeles Air Raid of 1942 has been all but forgotten except to those who lived through it. But toward the end of the Second World War, aerial warfare took on a new—and unexpected—aspect.

Foo-Fighters

In late 1944, Lt. Donald Meiers of Chicago was flying in a British-made twin-engined night fighter called a Beaufighter over Germany's Rhine Valley when what appeared to be flaming globes suddenly appeared and moved toward his plane. "I turned starboard and the balls of fire turned with me," Meiers recalled. "I turned to port side and they turned with me. We were doing 260 miles an hour and the balls were keeping right up with us. . . . When I first saw the things . . . I had the terrible thought that a German . . . was ready to press a button and explode them. . . . They just seemed to follow us like will-o'-the-wisps."

This was one of many such reports of circular objects chasing Allied aircraft. They became known as "foo-fighters." There has been some confusion regarding the origin of that name. Some have said "foo" is an adulteration of the French word for fire, *feu*, thus indicating a "fire fighter." However, author Paris Flammonde reasoned that since the term originated with young American flyers, it more probably came from a play on the term *Beaufighter* by using the words of a pre-war comic strip character named Smokey Stover, who frequently voiced the gag line "Where there's foo, there's fire."

Regardless of the origin of the name, "foo-fighters" soon caught the attention of the American news media. The *New York Herald Tribune* of January 2, 1945, reported, "Now, it seems, the Nazis have thrown something new into the night skies over Germany. It is the weird, mysterious *foo-fighter* balls that race alongside the wings of *Beaufighters* flying intruder missions over Germany. Pilots have been encountering this eerie weapon for more than a month in their night flights. No one apparently knows what this sky weapon is. The 'balls of fire' appear suddenly and accompany the planes for miles. They seem to be radio controlled from the ground, so official intelligence reports reveal . . . "

Lieutenant Meiers explained, "There are three kinds of these lights we call *foo-fighters*. One is red balls of fire which appear off our wing tips and [the second, which] fly in front of us, and the third is a group of about 15 lights which appear off in the distance—like a Christmas tree in the air—and flicker on and off."

Despite an extensive investigation by the U.S. Army's 8th Air Force, there was no conclusive solution to the mystery of the *foo-fighters*. Various explanations were offered—Saint Elmo's fire or ball lightning could have explained the lights dancing on wings and fuselage; the "Christmas tree" lights may have been flares or aluminum "window" strips tossed from Allied bombers to confuse German radar. One ingenious theory was that the lights were light reflections from ice crystals formed when interior air leaked into colder exterior air due to battle damage holes. Of course, "combat fatigue" hallucination was a ready catch-all explanation. And several sightings of a "ball of fire" thought to be a Japanese attack plane outfitted with a large searchlight reported by B-29s on their way to bomb Japan were explained away as an exceptionally bright Venus. But none of these proved satisfactory answers to all sightings.

For instance, on the night of December 22, 1944, Lt. David McFalls of the 415th Night Fighter Squadron was over Hagenau, Germany, when he observed two "huge, bright orange lights" climbing toward his plane. He quickly put his plane into a dive and banked hard, but the lights stayed with him for two minutes before peeling off and disappearing. Similar reports came in from the 415th dating back to September. A *London Daily Telegraph* story early in 1945 stated Royal Air Force pilots described their tormentors as "strange orange lights which follow their planes, sometimes flying in formation with them, and eventually peeling off and climbing."

As author W. A. Harbinson noted, "Most reports indicated that they appeared to be under some kind of control and were certainly not 'natural' phenomena."

Similar incidents were recorded in the Pacific theater of war. As early as 1943, pilots flying the "Burma hump" reported being buzzed by glittering objects that caused their instruments to fail. On August 10, 1944, on a bombing mission from Ceylon to Sumatra, Cpt. Alvah M. Reida of the 792nd Squadron, 486th Bomb Group, reported a most unusual encounter just after making a bombing run in his B-29. His report stated, "At about 20 or 30 minutes later the right gunner and copilot reported a strange object pacing us about 500 yards off our starboard wing. At that distance it appeared as a spherical object, probably 5 or 6 feet in diameter, of a very bright and intense red or orange in color. . . . It seemed to throb or vibrate constantly. Assuming it was some kind of radio-controlled object sent to pace us, I went into evasive action, changing direction constantly as much as 90 degrees and altitude at about 2,000 feet. It followed our every maneuver for about eight minutes, always holding a position 500 yards out and about two o'clock in relation to the plane. When it left, it made an abrupt 90-degree turn, and accelerated rapidly, disappearing in the overcast. . . ."

Adding to the mystery of the foo-fighters was the fact that captured enemy airmen—both German and Japanese—claimed they too had been followed by the fiery objects. They expressed the belief that the orbs were American or Russian secret weapons.

Of course the Allies believed they were Japanese or German secret weapons—and therein lies a fascinating and largely untold story that some people believe may shed light on the origin of at least some modern UFOs.

Saucers of the Reich

There is no question that the Germans produced a number of scientific breakthroughs in their quest for war technology during World War II. The V-1 buzz bombs—an ancestor of today's cruise missiles—and the V-2 rockets that terrorized London are two of the most famous examples, along with the Messerschmitt 262, the world's first operational jet fighter.

As respected British historian Barrie Pitt noted, "The Nazi war machine swung into action utilizing as much as it could of the most up-to-date scientific knowledge available, and as the war developed the list of further achievements grew to staggering proportions. From guns firing 'shells' of air to detailed discussions of flying saucers; from beams of sound that were fatal to a man at 50 yards, to guns that fired around corners and others that could 'see in the dark'—the list is awe-inspiring in its variety."

Pitt stated while some German technology was less developed

than imagined at the time, "some were dangerously near to a completion stage which could have reversed the war's outcome."

Secret German weapons nearing completion in 1945 included the Messerschmitt 163 *Komet* and the vertically launched *Natter* rocket fighters, the jet-powered flying wing Horten Ho-IX and the delta-winged Lippisch DM 1. Another secret weapon that might account for some of the "foo-fighter" reports was an antiradar, unmanned device called the *Feuerball,* or Fire Ball. Piloted by remote control, the Fire Ball was designed to interfere with the ignition systems and radar operation of Allied bombers. According to author Renato Vesco, the *Feuerball* was "a highly original flying machine . . . circular and armored, more or less resembling the shell of a tortoise, and was powered by a special turbojet engine, also flat and circular, whose principles of operation . . . generated a great halo of luminous flames. . . . Radio controlled at the moment of take-off, it then automatically followed enemy aircraft, attracted by their exhaust flames, and approached close enough without collision to wreck their radar gear."

Vesco claimed that the basic principles of the *Feuerball* were later applied to a "symmetrical circular aircraft" known as the *Kugelblitz,* or Ball Lightning, automatic fighter, which became an "authentic antecedent of the present-day flying saucers." He said this innovative craft was destroyed after a "single lucky wartime mission" by retreating SS (*Schutzstaffel,* or Defense Force) troops and later kept secret from the Americans and Russians by the British military, who captured plans for the craft.

Here the story of a Nazi saucer becomes more fragmentary and questionable. British author W. A. Harbinson wrote two novels based on the idea that the Nazis developed a flying saucer and secreted them away after the war in a hidden base in Antarctica. He claimed that he got his ideas after discovering postwar German articles concerning a former Luftwaffe engineer, Flugkapitan Rudolph Schriever. According to information gleaned from articles in *Der Spiegel, Bild am Sonntag, Luftfahrt International,* and other German publications, Harbinson learned that Schriever claimed to have designed a "flying top" prototype in 1941, which was actually test-flown in June 1942. In 1944, Schriever said he constructed a larger jet version of his circular craft with the help of scientists Klaus Habermohl, Otto Miethe, and an Italian, Dr. Giuseppe Belluzzo. Drawings of this saucer were published in the 1959 British book *German Secret Weapons of the Second World War* by Maj. Rudolph Lusar.

Lusar described the saucer as a ring of separate disks carrying adjustable jets rotating around a fixed cockpit. The entire craft had a height of 105 feet and could fly vertically or horizontally, depending on the positioning of the jets.

"Schriever claimed that his 'flying disc' had been ready for testing in early 1944," wrote Harbinson, "but with the advance of the Allies into Germany, the test had been canceled, the machine destroyed, and his designs either mislaid or stolen. His story was, however, contradicted by alleged eyewitness Georg Klein, who later stated to the German press that he had actually seen the test flight of the Schriever disc—or one similar—on February 14, 1945."

Schriever reportedly died in the late 1950s, and according to a 1975 issue of *Luftfahrt International*, notes and sketches concerning a large flying saucer were found in his effects. The periodical also stated that Schriever maintained until his death that his original saucer concept must have been made operational prior to war's end. This possibility is acknowledged by British author Brian Ford, who wrote, "There are supposed to have been 'flying saucers' too, which were near the final stages of development, and indeed it may be that some progress was made toward the construction of small, disc-like aircraft, but the results were destroyed, apparently before they fell into enemy hands."

Another candidate for inventor of a German UFO is the Austrian inventor Viktor Schauberger, who after being kidnapped by the Nazis reportedly designed a number of "flying discs" in 1940 using a flameless and smokeless form of electromagnetic propulsion called "diamagnetism." Schauberger reportedly worked for the U.S. government for a short time after the war before dying of natural causes. Shortly before his death, he was quoted as saying, "They took everything from me. Everything." No one ever knew for certain if he meant the Nazis or the Allies.

While a number of books and documentaries have suggested that the Nazi hierarchy dabbled in occult practices, there is no question that the Germans were experimenting with a variety of innovative aircraft and propulsion systems toward the end of the war and that they at least contemplated building a flying saucer. There are tantalizing bits of evidence that Nazi Germany indeed added a flying disc to its inventory of secret superweapons. But there is no indication what became of it.

The solution to this puzzle may be found by studying the man in charge of Germany's high-tech weapons programs—SS Obergruppenführer Dr. Hans Kammler. In mid-1943, SS chief Heinrich Himmler sent a letter to Germany's minister for armaments and munitions, Albert Speer. "With this letter, I inform you that I, as SS *Reichsführer* . . . do hereby take charge of the manufacture of the A-4 instrument," it read. The A-4 rocket was later designated by Hitler as the V-2—V for Vengeance weapon, the V-1 buzz bomb being the first. The V-2 was Germany's most secret high-tech weapons system. Himmler then placed Kammler in overall command of the rocket program.

According to Speer, Kammler insinuated his way into all phases of the V-2 program until Hitler finally put him in charge of all air armaments, including any possible secret saucer project. "Thus—just a few weeks before the end of the war—he had become commissioner general for all important weapons," wrote Speer, who bemoaned the fact that as the war drew to a close, Himmler's SS gradually assumed total control over Germany's weaponry production and research.

Working closely with Kammler on the V-2 project were Wernher von Braun, who after the war headed America's National Aeronautics and Space Administration, and his superior, Luftwaffe Maj. Gen. Walter Dornberger, who later became vice president of Bell Aircraft Company and of Bell Aerosystems Company in the United States.

Alarmed by progress on the V-2 rockets, Britain's Bomber Command sent 597 bombers on the night of August 16–17, 1943, to raid Peenemünde—Germany's top-secret rocket facility built on an island at the mouth of the Oder River near the border of Germany and Poland. Because so much of Peenemünde was underground or well camouflaged, much was left undamaged. Author Brian Ford described the results: "Even so, over 800 of the people on the island were killed. . . . After this, it was realized that some of the facility had better be dispersed throughout Germany; thus the theoretical development facility was moved to Garmisch-Partenkirchen, development went to Nordhausen and Bleicherode, and the main wind-tunnel and ancillary equipment went down to Kochel, some 24 miles south of Munich. This was christened *Wasserbau Versuchsanstalt* Kochelsee—experimental waterworks project—and gave rise to the most thorough research center for long-range rocket development that, at the time, could have been envisioned." It has been noted that a certain portion of top-secret Nazi weaponry development was moved to an area near Blizna, Poland—the same area where Allied air crews first encountered the "foo-fighters."

As Kammler, von Braun, Dornberger, and company worked feverishly to perfect the V-2s and other secret weapons, Himmler was taking steps to separate his SS from normal party and state control. "In the spring of 1944 Hitler approved Himmler's proposal to build an SS-owned industrial concern in order to make the SS permanently independent of the state budget," wrote Albert Speer.

In moves that were to be copied in later years by America's Central Intelligence Agency, SS leaders created a number of business fronts and other organizations—many using concentration-camp labor—with an eye toward producing revenue to support SS activities. These highly compartmentalized groups headed by young, ambitious SS officers neither required nor desired any connection with Germany's high-profile leaders. Their purpose was to continue Nazi goals long after the defeat of Germany.

Speer conceded that there were weapons developments he knew nothing about and even mentioned one SS scheme in 1944 for a secret weapon plant requiring 3,500 concentration-camp workers. "The Führer protocols make no mention whatsoever of this new weapon," Speer wrote. "[But] it was certainly not the 'flying saucers,' which extreme right-wing circles now claim were secretly produced by the SS toward the end of the war and concealed from me."

But with secret projects in the hands of the fanatical SS and with factories and research facilities scattered over—and under—the countryside, it is entirely conceivable that a UFO device could have been developed without the knowledge of anyone except Himmler, who committed suicide by poison capsule on May 23, 1945, after being caught trying to sneak through British lines disguised as an German army private. Perhaps after the war, certain right-wing circles with SS connections did know more about German saucers than Speer or other ranking Nazi leaders. Consider the fate of Hans Kammler.

As the war drew to a close, Kammler made no secret of the fact that he intended to use both the V-2 scientists and rockets under his control as leverage for a deal with the Allies. On April 2, 1945, on Kammler's orders, a special train carried rockets, five hundred technicians, and engineers escorted by a hundred SS troopers to an Alpine redoubt in Bavaria. According to von Braun and Dornberger, Kammler planned to "bargain with the Americans or one of the other Allies for his own life in exchange for the leading German rocket specialists."

Yet on April 4, 1945, when von Braun pressed Kammler for permission to resume rocket research, the SS officer quietly announced that he was about to disappear for "an indefinite length of time." True to his word, no one saw Kammler again. As everyone knows, von Braun, Dornberger, and other scientists—and many of the V-2 rockets—eventually made their way to the United States, becoming founding members of our modern space program.

Author Jean Michel, himself an inmate of concentration camp Dora, which provided slave labor for Kammler's rocket program, wrote of Kammler, "The chief of the SS secret weapon empire, the man in Himmler's confidence, disappeared without a trace. Even more disturbing is the fact that the architect of the concentration camps, builder of the gas chambers, executioner of Dora, overall chief of all the SS missiles has sunk into oblivion. There is the Bormann mystery, the Mengele enigma; as far as I know, no one, to this day, has taken much interest in the fate of *Obergruppenführer SS* Hans Kammler." Michel, along with others, wondered "why had the 'cold and brutal calculator' described by Speer so abruptly discarded the trump cards he had so patiently accumulated?" Did Kammler escape with weapons plans even more technologically advanced and secret than the V-2 rocket? Did the Reich, or an extension of it, have the capability to produce a UFO or the clout to deal from a position of strength with one of the Allied nations?

Information, principally from Dornberger, suggested that Kammler committed suicide when the Czech resistance overcame SS troops in Prague. However, there was no proof of this, and the issue is far from settled. As Michel mentioned, there was a long-standing controversy over the proclaimed deaths of Hitler's deputy Martin Bormann and the notorious SS Dr. Josef Mengele.

Mengele reportedly died in recent years after hiding in Argentina, Brazil, and Paraguay for decades. Another ranking SS official, Obersturmbannführer Adolf Eichmann, escaped to Argentina but was abducted to Israel in 1960, where he was tried for war crimes and executed.

But the biggest fish to get away was Reichsleiter Bormann. Rumors persisted for years that Bormann was living in South America and running a worldwide Nazi empire, which included the infamous organization to aid escaping Nazis, *Organization der Ehemaligen SS-Angehörigen* (ODESSA). In 1972, Munich bishop Johannes Neuhausler made public a church document stating that Bormann had escaped Berlin during the final days and gone to Spain by airplane. Later that year, Berlin workmen unearthed two skeletons near the ruins of the Lehrter railroad station and, in 1973, West German officials held a news conference proclaiming that one of the skeletons had been identified as Bormann and that he had died in 1945 trying to escape Berlin.

Bormann's identification was based on dental records prepared from memory in 1945 by Dr. Hugo Blaschke on orders of a U.S. Army investigation team. By 1973, Blaschke was dead and the actual identification was made by a Fritz Echtmann, a dental technician who claimed to have made fittings for Hitler, Eva Braun, and Bormann. The entire case for the Berlin death of Bormann rested on dental records prepared from memory by a dentist who had been a loyal Nazi for many years and the sole statement of a dental technician who had been imprisoned in Russia due to his proclaimed knowledge of Bormann's dental work. Adding to suspicions that Bormann's death announcement was a bit too convenient was the fact that Willy Brandt's government canceled all rewards and warrants for Bormann and instructed West German embassies and consulates to ignore any future sightings of the Reichsleiter. These suspicions were compounded by statements from several persons who claimed that the body found near the railroad station was placed there in 1945 by troops commanded by Waffen SS Gen. Heinrich "Gestapo" Mueller, who was known to have used decoy bodies on other occasions. Bormann's death notice did not convince Simon Wiesenthal of the Documentation Center in Vienna, who said, "Some doubts must remain whether the bones found in Berlin are really those of Bormann."

Was it possible that Bormann and other Nazis wielded enough power to misdirect West German investigations and silence foreign governments and news organizations? The simple answer appears to be yes. To understand, one must look at German business history and Bormann's activities beginning in mid-1944.

Operation Eagle Flight

By early August 1944, many top Nazi officials could see the writing on the wall. The French town of Saint-Lô, center of the German defense line facing the Normandy beachhead, had fallen on July 18, opening all of southern France to Allied armor and infantry. The German army hastened eastward toward the Fatherland, narrowly escaping total encirclement at Falaise. Only the Rhine River and overextended supply lines slowed the Allied advance in the west. With the Russians pressing ever deeper into the Reich on the eastern front, Nazi leaders knew the end of the war was only a matter of time.

Adolf Hitler, who according to captured medical records was on a roller-coaster ride of euphoria and depression due to large daily doses of amphetamines, increasingly lost contact with reality. However, the second most powerful man in the Reich, Hitler's deputy Martin Bormann, was not so incapacitated. On August 10, 1944, Bormann called together German business leaders and Nazi Party officials. They met in the Hotel Maison Rouge at Strasbourg. Bormann explained the purpose of the meeting to one attendee: "German industry must realize that the war cannot now be won, and must take steps to prepare for a postwar commercial campaign which will in time insure the economic resurgence of Germany."

These "steps" came to be known as "Aktion Adlerflug," or Operation Eagle Flight. It was nothing less than the perpetuation of Nazism through the massive flight of money, gold, stocks, bonds, patents, copyrights, and even technical specialists from Germany. As part of this plan, Bormann, aided by the black-clad SS, the central Deutsche Bank and the powerful I. G. Farben combine, created 750 foreign front corporations—58 in Portugal, 112 in Spain, 233 in Sweden, 214 in Switzerland, 35 in Turkey, and 98 in Argentina.

Bormann's efforts were substantially helped by close connections with foreign banks and businesses begun long before the war. As documented by former *New York Times* writer Charles Higham, America's International Telephone & Telegraph Corp. (ITT) sold Germany communication and war material, including as many as fifty thousand artillery fuses per month, more than three years after Pearl Harbor. Illustrating the interconnecting business associations of this time was ITT's German chairman Gerhardt Westrick, a close associate of John Foster Dulles, who would become U.S. secretary of state under President Dwight Eisenhower, and partner to Dr. Heinrich Albert, head of Ford Motor Co. in Germany until 1945. Two ITT directors were German banker Baron Kurt von Schroder and Walter Schellenberg, head of counterintelligence for the Nazi Gestapo.

Rockefeller-owned Standard Oil also came under investigation during World War II for a series of complex business deals that resulted in desperately needed gasoline reaching Nazi Germany. "None of these transactions was ever made public," reported Higham. "The details of them remained buried in classified files for over 40 years. However, it proved impossible for Ralph Gallagher and Walter Teagle (both Standard chairmen) . . . to conceal the fact that shipments of oil continued to fascist Spain throughout World War II, paid for by [Spanish dictator Francisco] Franco funds that had been unimpounded by the Federal Reserve Bank while Loyalist funds were sent to Nazi Germany from the vaults of the Bank of England, the Bank of France and the Bank for International Settlements. The shipments to Spain indirectly assisted the Axis through Spanish transferences to Hamburg. At the same time, there were desperate shortages in the United States, long lines at gas stations, and even petroleum rationing. While American civilians and the armed services suffered alike from restrictions, more gasoline went to Spain than it did to domestic customers." Questioned about this situation by the *New York Times*, a spokesman for U.S. Secretary of State Cordell Hull explained that the oil was coming from the Caribbean, not the United States. What was not explained was that Standard Oil, under the leadership of William Stamps Farish, had early on changed the country of registration for Standard's tanker fleet to Panama. Higham pointed out that both Standard chiefs Farish and Teagle were "mesmerized by Germany" and were close associates of I. G. Farben's Hermann Schmitz.

Such ties were buttressed by banking connections such as the

1936 partnership between the J. Henry Schroder Bank of New York and Rockefeller family members. According to Higham, "Schroder, Rockefeller and Company, Investment Bankers, was formed as part of an overall company that *Time* magazine disclosed as being 'the economic booster of the Rome-Berlin Axis.' The partners in Schroder, Rockefeller and Company included Avery Rockefeller, nephew of John D., Baron Bruno von Schroder in London, and Kurt von Schroder of the [Bank of International Settlements] and the Gestapo in Cologne. . . . Their lawyers were John Foster Dulles and Allen Dulles of Sullivan and Cromwell. Allen Dulles (later CIA director and Warren Commission member) was on the board of Schroder. Further connections linked the Paris branch of [the Rockefeller] Chase National Bank to Schroder as well as the pro-Nazi Worms Bank and Standard Oil of New Jersey in France. Standard Oil's Paris representatives were directors of the Banque de Paris et des Pays-Bas, which had intricate connections to the Nazis and to Chase."

It is interesting to note that throughout the war, Chase maintained its financial connections with the Nazis through its Paris bank and that I. G. Farben chief Hermann Schmitz served as Chase president for seven years prior to the war and eventually held as much stock in Standard Oil of New Jersey as the Rockefellers. "Schmitz's wealth—largely I. G. Farben bearer bonds converted to the Big Three successor firms, shares in Standard Oil of New Jersey . . . , General Motors, and other U.S. blue chip industrial stocks, and the 700 secret companies controlled in his time by I. G., as well as shares in the 750 corporations he helped Bormann establish during the last years of World War II—has increased in all segments of the modern industrial world. The Bormann organization in South America utilizes the voting power of the Schmitz trust along with their own assets to guide the multinationals they control, as they keep steady the economic course of the Fatherland," wrote investigator Paul Manning, who added, "The Bormann organization is not merely a group of ex-Nazis. It is a great economic power whose interests today supercede their ideology."

Further documentation of this unpublicized world power came in 1996 when the U.S. National Archives released declassified reports from a variety of intelligence agencies proving that Allied officials from the start had known all about the money relationship between top Nazis and their Swiss bankers. According to *The Guardian* of London, "The evidence . . . suggests that something on the order of 15 billion *Reichsmarks* was banked, invested, moved, and laundered through Swiss banks. That was the equivalent of three percent of America's gross domestic product (GDP) in 1944. To put this into today's terms, three percent of America's GDP is $200 billion, which is more than the entire GDP of Switzerland. Allow for interest, compounded over 50 years, and the value of the Nazi cache that went through Switzerland moves into the region of a trillion dollars."

These long-standing banking and business connections coupled with the Schmitz business network allowed Reichsleiter Bormann to forge a formidable Nazi-controlled organization for postwar activities. Author Jim Keith wrote, "In researching the shape of totalitarian control during this century, I saw that the plans of the Nazis manifestly did not die with the German loss of World War II. The ideology and many of the principal players survived and flourished after the war, and have had a profound impact on postwar history, and on events taking place today."

Orvis A. Schmidt, the U.S. Treasury Department's director of Foreign Funds Control, in 1945 offered this description of the Nazi flight-capital program: "The network of trade, industrial, and cartel organizations has been streamlined and intermeshed, not only organizationally but also by what has been officially described as 'personnel union.' Legal authority to operate this organizational machinery has been vested in the concerns that have majority capacity in the key industries such as those producing iron and steel, coal and basic chemicals. These concerns have been deliberately welded together by exchanges of stock to the point where a handful of men can make policy and other decisions that affect us all."

Could one of those "decisions" have been the creation of Nazi-developed UFOs? While this notion may superficially appear to be sheer nonsense, the public record offers compelling—if incomplete—evidence to support this idea.

There are two theories offered in this area. The first is that Bormann and other top Nazis escaped to South America or a secret base in Antarctica where they built UFOs so sophisticated that their secret Nazi empire has exerted significant control over world events and governments to this day. While there can be no question that the business and financial network created by Bormann wields a certain amount of power even today, evidence for the existence of a major Nazi base containing UFOs is virtually nonexistent, consisting primarily of the known exploration of Antarctica's Queen Maude Land—renamed Neuschwabenland by the Germans—in 1938 and some unverified statements. Reportedly, German navy grand admiral Karl Doenitz stated in 1943, "The German submarine fleet is proud of having built for the Führer in another part of the world a Shangri-la on land, an impregnable fortress." And it has been reported that U.S. Admiral Richard Byrd, upon his return from an expedition to Antarctica in 1947, stated it was "necessary for the USA to take defensive actions against enemy air fighters which come from the polar regions" and that America could be "attacked by fighters that are able to fly from one pole to the other with incredible speed."

Advancing the idea that the Nazis continually shipped men and matériel to the South Pole throughout the war years, Harbinson wrote, "Regarding the possibility of the Germans building self-sufficient underground research factories in the Antarctic, it has only to be pointed out that the underground research centers of Nazi Germany were gigantic feats of construction, containing wind tunnels, machine shops, assembly plants, launching pads, supply dumps and accommodation for all who worked there, including adjoining camps for slaves—and yet very few people knew that they existed."

But, while tales of a secret Nazi base in Antarctica may appear plausible to some, the idea that it has remained undiscovered and no one has escaped or deserted the place in more than fifty years stretches belief to the breaking point. It is more likely that Antarctica was merely a way station for Nazi leaders traveling on to their new homes in Argentina and Paraguay.

The second theory of Nazi UFOs—and a much more believable one—is that the German saucer program was used as bargaining leverage by the Nazis and secretly developed by one or more of the Allied nations after the war.

If this theory is correct, it could solve one of the postwar UFO mysteries—the "ghost rockets" of Sweden.

Ghost Rockets

Beginning in May 1946, strange objects spouting fire were seen over Sweden. By August, reports of the UFOs were coming in from all over Europe and even from the northern and eastern portions of the Mediterranean. On August 11, after investigation by a special committee of military and aviation officials, Swedish authorities acknowledged the phenomenon, stating, "Ghost rockets—mysterious spool-shaped objects with fiery tails—have become a common sight in Sweden." In addition to the description of the objects as metallic rocket-shaped devices, some with small fins, about thirty fragments reportedly fallen from the objects were studied. They were determined to be pieces of slag that did not seem to be part of any rocket. By December 1946, reports of the "rockets" waned and Swedish authorities claimed that 80 percent of the sightings had conventional explanations, leaving only 20 percent "unidentified." They seriously considered the idea that the craft were captured German V weapons being sent over Sweden by the Russians for purposes of intimidation.

British researcher Mark Birdsall, after an intensive study of Nazi secret weapons, concluded, "Without question, nearly all Foo-Fighter and Ghost Rocket reports can be categorized as advanced technology channeled from these various secret German WWII scientific facilities."

Authors Renato Vesco and David Hatcher Childress, citing Italian Ministry of Aeronautics documents dated September 16, 1946, claim the British may have been the originators of the devices. They reported that in August 1946, the BBC reported that a new aeronautical research center was to be built in Bedfordshire that would produce "machines that it is hoped will be able to reach at least 1,500 mph." The report added, "According to some experts, these planes have already been built and tested and it is probable that in the near future they will be flying over Great Britain. If necessary, such planes could fly nonstop around the world many times, because they need fuel only for takeoff and landing. Great Britain has already astonished the world with its excellent turbojet engines, but this new development of British scientists is the greatest step that aeronautics has taken since man began to fly."

Since no such craft were ever flown in England, Vesco and Childress concluded that testing must have been carried out elsewhere—namely in the wilds of southwest Canada.

They cited a report in the *Toronto Star*, in which Minister of Defense Production C. D. Howe told the House of Commons that a new type of aircraft was being built in a collaboration between the Royal Canadian Air Force and A. V. Roe Ltd. (AVRO) at facilities near Malton, Ontario. The newspaper commented that Howe's words were "adding weight to reports that AVRO is even now working on a mockup model of a 'flying saucer' capable of flying 1,500 miles per hour and climbing straight up in the air."

The United States may have shared in this new technology, as suggested by another Toronto news story that stated, "A mockup of the Canadian flying saucer, the highly secret aircraft in whose existence few believe, was yesterday shown to a group of 25 American experts, including military officers and scientists." This partnership was confirmed on October 25, 1953, when U.S. Air Force Secretary Donald Quarles released a statement advising, "We are now entering a period of aviation technology in which aircraft of unusual configuration and flight characteristics will begin to appear. . . . The Air Force will fly the first jet-powered vertical-rising airplane in a matter of days. We have another project under contract with AVRO Ltd. of Canada, which could result in disc-shaped aircraft somewhat similar to the popular concept of a flying saucer. . . . While some of these may take novel forms, such as the AVRO project, they are direct-line descendants of conventional aircraft and should not be regarded as supra-natural or mysterious. . . ." The AVRO saucers—there were at least two versions, the AV-9 and the AZ-9 "AVRO-Car"—were disc-shaped, jet-powered craft designed by John

Frost for AVRO Ltd., which reportedly were first flown in 1959.

When the United States began working with the Canadians, the idea of a circular aircraft was not new. It had produced its own flying saucer in 1942 when Charles H. Zimmerman designed the V-173 "Flying Flapjack" for the U.S. Navy. This experimental, disc-shaped craft was built and test-flown by Chance-Vought Corp. but reportedly was abandoned in 1947 as impractical. An original V-173 was on exhibit in the Smithsonian Institution for several years. Likewise, the AVRO-Car saucer project reportedly was termed a failure and canceled in 1960.

"However," wrote Harbinson in 1991, "while the Canadian and U.S. governments have insisted that they are no longer involved with flying saucer construction projects, there are many who believe that they are lying and that the Canadian, British, U.S., and even Soviet governments are continuing to work on highly advanced, saucer-shaped, supersonic aircraft based on the work done in Nazi Germany." Lending weight to this allegation was a CIA memorandum dated October 19, 1955, which stated, "[AVRO-Car designer] Mr. Frost is reported to have obtained his original idea for the flying machine from a group of Germans just after World War II. . . ."

A stranger variation of this charge came from former U.S. Air Force Lt. Col. George Edwards, who claimed he worked on the AVRO project and came to understand that it was a cover for testing a "real alien spacecraft." Edwards said, "The VZ-9 was to be a 'cover' so the Pentagon would have an explanation whenever people reported seeing a saucer in flight." This theme was taken up by writer Robert Dorr, an air force veteran who claimed to have learned of an alien saucer recovered from a crash on the East Coast in 1953. Dorr said use of the AVRO-Car as a "smoke screen" to shift public attention away from the real UFO answered many questions about the AVRO program—such as why the weapons system was never designed to be armed, why as the current aerospace leader the United States entered business with a secondary power like Canada, and why the AVRO was so publicized when first announced in 1955 but not publicized when test-flown in 1959.

It is intriguing to note that as will be seen shortly, America's first highly publicized UFO sightings took place in the northwest United States and, in both cases, the UFOs flew off toward Canada.

But before the first great UFO "flap" occurred, it should be mentioned that a literary endeavor may have built up both public reception and perception of the coming events.

In 1938, a Wisconsin-born hunchbacked dwarf named Raymond A. Palmer had been named editor of *Amazing Stories*, a pulp magazine targeting adolescent boys with tales combining heroic adventures, robots, science fiction, ghosts, and wartime patriotism. For example, one story in the March 1943 issue concerned "A new asteroid [which] came to the solar system and circled Earth—and became a base for Nazi bombers!" In January 1944, Palmer ran a letter from a Richard Sharpe Shaver, a worker in the Philadelphia shipyards, who claimed to hear "voices" coming from his welding equipment. Encouraged by having his letter published, Shaver sent Palmer a rambling manuscript penciled onto envelopes, sacks, bills, and other scraps of paper entitled, "A Warning to Future Man." Shaver said his writings were based on memories of life on the long-lost continent of Lemuria induced in him by "alien minds" who had come to Earth 150,000 years ago and were still living in vast caverns within the earth. Palmer expanded Shaver's manuscript threefold and published it in March 1945 as "I Remember Lemuria!"

Despite the outré nature of Shaver's narrative, Palmer published it as a true story, though in later years he admitted to being aware that Shaver had spent some years in a mental hospital. Magazine sales soared to more than 250,000 a month, and stories about spaceships and aliens increased. In mid-1946, Palmer wrote, "If you don't think space ships visit the Earth regularly . . . and if you think responsible parties in world governments are ignorant of the fact of space ships visiting the Earth, you just don't think the way we do."

Author Curtis Peebles commented, "One would be hard pressed to find a more concise summary of the flying saucer myth. Yet this was a year before the first widely publicized sighting." The stage was set for the first major UFO reports, with visiting extraterrestrials, flying craft with miraculous energy systems, and government secrecy already a part of the public lore.

Arnold and the Maury Island Mystery

The year 1947 proved pivotal, separating previous accounts of objects in the sky from modern UFO sightings. Most people believe this stemmed from one major case that year. In fact, there was an epidemic of UFO incidents that year. These continuing sightings were only mentioned in local newspapers and many have remained unknown until today.

The beginning of one widely publicized UFO event of the modern era occurred on June 21, 1947, on Maury Island in Washington State's Puget Sound. Harold A. Dahl, a harbor patrolman, reported that at 2:00 P.M. he—along with two crewmen, his teenage son, and his dog—had guided his boat into a Maury Island bay to escape bad weather when they saw six "doughnut-shaped" objects about two thousand feet in the air. Five appeared to be circling the sixth, which seemed to be in difficulty and was losing altitude. They were described as gold and silver metallic objects approximately one hundred feet wide with a hole in the center and what appeared to be portholes around the perimeter and a dark window underneath. Following a small "explosion," hot slag showered the area, killing the dog and slightly injuring the son's arm, Dahl said. Fearing the craft might crash, he beached his boat and started taking photos with a small camera. Soon the six UFOs rose and moved off to the northwest toward Canada and the Pacific. Dahl said he tried to radio a report, but his equipment was jammed with interference. Gathering up some of the fallen metal, Dahl and company returned to his Tacoma base, where he sent his son for treatment and gave the metal samples, his camera, and film to his superior, Fred Lee Crisman.

Crisman, angered over damage to the boat, disbelieved Dahl's story but agreed to investigate Maury Island and look at the reported "20 tons" of fallen debris. But the next day, before anyone had been informed of the events on the island, Dahl said a man dressed in black visited his home and told him, "Silence is the best thing for you and your family. You have seen what you ought not to have seen." The following day, June 23, Crisman visited Maury Island as promised. There he later reported finding glassy, dark material and shiny foil strewn along the beach. He said his inspection was interrupted by the appearance of one of the inner-tube-like UFOs, which silently passed overhead before disappearing into the clouds.

There the matter rested until after the most famous of the initial modern UFO sightings.

On June 24, 1947, thirty-two-year-old Kenneth Arnold, a successful Boise, Idaho, businessman, pilot, deputy federal marshal, and a member of the Idaho Search and Rescue Mercy Flyers, was flying home when he decided to help in the search for a Marine Curtiss C-46 transport plane believed to have crashed somewhere in the Cascade Mountains. A $5,000 reward was an added incentive. The sole occupant of a Callair private plane, Arnold had taken off from Chehalis, Washington, with a scheduled stop at Yakima, when he diverted from his flight path to search the Mount Rainier plateau for the missing transport. Sometime after 2:00 P.M., while he was cruising at an altitude of about 9,200 feet, a "tremendously bright flash lit up the surfaces" of his aircraft. Seeking the source of the flash, Arnold could see only a Douglas DC-4 airliner off to his left. As he was about to decide that the flash had been caused by the sun glinting off the wings of a rapidly passing military fighter, another flash drew his attention to the skies north of Mount Rainier.

"I observed far to my left and to the north, a formation of very bright objects coming from the vicinity of Mount Baker, flying very close to the mountain tops and traveling at a tremendous speed," Arnold later reported. "They didn't fly like any aircraft I had seen before . . . they flew in a definite formation, but erratically . . . like speed boats on rough water or similar to the tail of a Chinese kite that I once saw bobbing in the wind . . . they fluttered and sailed, tipping their wings alternately and emitting very bright blue-white flashes from their surfaces."

As the objects were moving almost directly across Arnold's flight path and passing behind some of the mountains, he had no trouble in calculating their speed. Arnold checked his watch as the first of the nine objects passed Mount Rainier and again as the last object passed the crest of Mount Adams. One minute and forty-two seconds had passed. Later, after checking the distance between the two peaks, Arnold determined the objects were flying close to 1,700 miles per hour—twice the speed of sound. No aircraft of that time had achieved speeds anywhere close to this.

After landing, Arnold related his experience to other pilots, many of them military veterans. The suspicion grew that he had encountered the secret testing of new military devices, either ours or the Soviets'. Arnold later wrote, "They were guided missiles, robotly [sic] controlled. I knew that speeds of this velocity the human body simply could not stand, particularly considering the flipping, erratic movements of these strange craft."

That evening after flying to Pendleton, Oregon, Arnold discussed his encounter with a staff member of the *East Oregonian* newspaper. He said the objects "flew like a saucer would if you skipped it across the water," describing not the appearance but the flight characteristics of the UFOs. News of Arnold's sighting reached the Associated Press, which called the UFOs "saucer-like objects" and wired the story all across America. The term "flying saucer" quickly become part of the language. "The significance of this," wrote John Spencer, vice chairman of the British UFO Research Association (BUFORA), "is that it shows the power of the media in influencing the public's perception of events and indeed it could be held that the media misrepresentation of Arnold's phrase has created part of the mythology around UFOs which is incorrect, and worse, masks the reality."

While Arnold's sighting certainly did not initiate the modern UFO age—with no supporting witnesses, no photos, and no radar confirmation, it was a rather weak case—it did ignite the first widespread media attention. And it was media attention that precipitated the next phase of the Maury Island story, which brought together Kenneth Arnold, editor Raymond Palmer, and the Maury Island witnesses—and a story filled with insoluble puzzles that presaged the current bewilderment over UFO cases.

A few weeks after his sighting, Arnold said he was visited by a

Cpt. William Davidson and Lt. Frank M. Brown, who said they were with Military Intelligence of the Fourth Air Force, Hamilton Field, California. The officers listened wide-eyed as Arnold recounted his experience, then returned to their base.

Meanwhile *Amazing Stories* editor Palmer was quick to direct his readers to the nationwide reports of flying saucers as proof of Richard Shaver's claims of unearthly visitors in spacecraft. He had received a letter from Dahl and Crisman relating the Maury Island story. Interestingly, Crisman had written to Palmer previously, claiming to have battled in a cave with a mutation created by one of Shaver's aliens. Later Palmer even said he recognized Crisman's voice as that of a man who had telephoned him at various times from different parts of the United States.

Having communicated with Kenneth Arnold regarding his Mount Rainier sighting, Palmer wrote again asking the pilot to investigate the Maury Island case.

Arnold, his curiosity piqued by the avalanche of saucer reports plus an advance of $200 from Palmer, agreed and flew to meet Dahl on July 29. Here the story began moving into the bizarre. Incredibly—and largely unknown even to serious UFO researchers—Arnold experienced a second UFO encounter on this trip. During a descent for refueling at LaGrand, Oregon, Arnold said about twenty-four small, brass-colored UFOs similar in configuration to those he had seen five weeks earlier passed rapidly within four hundred yards of his plane. But these objects appeared to be much smaller than the earlier ones, measuring only two or so feet in diameter. Arnold filmed this flight of UFOs, but due to the brevity of the encounter, his film only showed a few small dots and was not considered strong evidence.

Arriving in Tacoma for his meeting with Dahl, Arnold found there were no hotel rooms available. In a final attempt at accommodations, he tried the most expensive hotel in town and was shocked to learn there was a room reserved in his name, although no one was sure who had made the reservation. On July 30, Arnold met with Dahl, who said he was hesitant to speak after his experience with the man in black. At Arnold's insistence, Dahl relented and repeated his story but failed to produce the photographs of the UFOs, claiming Crisman had misplaced them. Dahl did provide Arnold with a specimen of what he said was UFO debris from Maury Island. Arnold was unimpressed, as the material appeared to be nothing more than volcanic rock.

Arnold was even more dumbfounded when Dahl told him about an anonymous letter he had received once word of the Maury Island incident got out. As later recounted by Arnold in a book with Raymond Palmer entitled *Coming of the Saucers*, the letter writer claimed that saucers were occupied by beings less dense than ourselves who had become visible to us only because of radiation released by atomic blasts and that they were here to protect humans from outside influences and enemies.

After interviewing Crisman, Arnold felt uncomfortable with the Maury Island story. He later said he felt Crisman was attempting to monopolize the story, diverting any real investigation, and was hiding his actual identity. Seeking help, Arnold contacted and was joined by United Airlines pilot Cpt. E. J. Smith. Both men reviewed the story and evidence and both felt the story indicated a hoax or a "dangerous" espionage plot. Their suspicions were heightened when they learned that someone had provided the United Press International office in Tacoma with verbatim transcripts of their interviews and conversations. Yet an extensive search of their hotel room revealed no bugging device. Author Paris Flammonde commented, "Arnold appears not to have connected the fact that when he arrived in Tacoma he could not get a room in several hotels, but found himself registered by an unknown benefactor and an unidentifiable clerk in a specific room of a pre-selected hotel. It would have been little problem for a professional intelligence operator, trained in electronic surveillance, to secrete a listening device in quarters into which Arnold would be channeled by a simple arrangement of circumstances."

Arnold and Smith were now highly suspicious, both of Crisman and because they could not interview Dahl's son—reportedly in the hospital for treatment of his arm—nor the other crewmen, who could not be located. Furthermore they could not verify that Dahl or Crisman actually were harbor patrolmen and their "launch" turned out to be little more than an ill-kept fishing boat. They examined pieces of metal given to them by Dahl and Crisman as UFO material and concluded the evidence was "fake." "We had seen hundreds of piles of this stuff in salvage dumps many places throughout the United States where surplus Army bombers had been junked," Arnold later wrote. However, he noted that the "stuff" did not match Dahl's earlier description of "extremely light white metal."

Arnold said he wanted to bring military intelligence into the case, a proposal that met with mixed reactions. Smith agreed without enthusiasm, Crisman seemed overjoyed by the prospect, while Dahl said he would refuse to speak to military men and seemed reluctant to continue with the investigation. Undaunted, Arnold telephoned Lieutenant Brown, who refused to accept his call at his base but soon returned the call from a public pay phone. Brown agreed to join the investigation. Before the day was over, both Brown and Captain Davidson had arrived to join Arnold and Smith.

Despite their rapid response, once on the scene both Brown and

Davidson seemed strangely unconcerned. "They gave me the impression they thought Smith and I were the victims of some silly hoax," Arnold wrote later. "When we offered them pieces of the [UFO] fragments . . . they were just not interested." Debunkers believe the two intelligence officers simply recognized both the story and the evidence as phony. The pair left Arnold and Smith near midnight, not even bothering to take the UFO fragments.

However, according to Arnold, as Brown and Davidson were departing for the airport, Crisman ran up to their automobile and handed them a carton thought to be UFO debris. Arnold said that as they loaded the carton in the trunk, he glimpsed the material, which "looked similar to the fragments we had in our room" but somehow "looked more rocky and less metallic."

The next morning the case took a more ominous turn. Arnold and Smith were stunned to learn that the B-25 carrying Brown and Davidson had crashed after takeoff, killing both men. Two enlisted men had parachuted to safety. The fatal crash could have been simply a tragic end to a hoax story. Instead it only added to the puzzle.

At the invitation of Tacoma's UPI chief Ted Morello, Arnold listened to a recorded interview with Master Sgt. Elmer L. Taff, one of the survivors of the B-25 crash. Taff said he had only hopped a ride home on the plane and did not know any of the other three occupants. He did say that he saw the two officers (Brown and Davidson) load a heavy carton on the plane just before takeoff. Taff said about twenty minutes after takeoff, the plane's left engine burst into flame and when one of the crewmen tried to activate the emergency fire-fighting equipment, it was inoperable. According to Taff, Lieutenant Brown came from the front of the plane and ordered the two enlisted men to don parachutes and jump. Taff recalled that it was approximately ten minutes between the time he jumped and the plane plunged to earth. He had no explanation why the two officers could not have parachuted themselves or radioed a distress call.

The air force said the crash was caused by a mechanical defect in the left engine that set the wing on fire, but others were not so sure. The August 1, 1947, issue of the *Tacoma Times* carried headlines reading "Sabotage Hinted in Crash of Army Bomber at Kelso" and "Plane May Hold Flying Disc Secret." An unidentified informant told newspaper staffers that the plane had been tampered with to prevent the UFO debris from reaching the officers' California base. The paper quoted a Maj. George Sander as confirming the plane carried "classified material." Author Curtis Peebles made no mention of the heavy carton and dismissed the "classified material" as "only a file of reports they had offered to take back to Hamilton; the reports had nothing to do with flying saucers."

Major Sander, after arriving on the scene, tried to convince Arnold and Smith they had been conned and that the UFO debris was only slag taken from the Tacoma Smelting Company. Yet, Sander was adamant that all of the material be turned over to him. "We don't want to overlook even one piece," Arnold quoted him as saying. It was definitely an odd demand from someone who plainly stated the entire episode was a hoax. Researcher Harold Wilkins claimed in a 1967 book that some of the slag was independently tested and found to contain an unusually high proportion of unoxidized calcium along with iron, zinc, and titanium, which indicated an unknown manufacturing process.

Saddened by the deaths and disgusted with the uncertainties of the investigation, Arnold decided to drop the whole affair. But before leaving Tacoma, he decided to pay one last visit to Dahl and Crisman—only to find that both men had disappeared without a trace.

While Crisman may have vanished from the Maury Island case, he did not disappear from the conspiracy stage. In yet another bizarre twist, Crisman in later years turned up in another major mystery—the assassination of President John F. Kennedy.

In 1968, Crisman was subpoenaed before a grand jury by New Orleans District Attorney Jim Garrison, who claimed to have uncovered a plot in his city to kill Kennedy. Garrison said the plot involved accused assassin Lee Harvey Oswald, New Orleans International Trade Mart director Clay Shaw, former FBI agent Guy Banister, CIA-Mafia agent David Ferrie, and others. In a press release dated October 31, 1968, Garrison stated, "Mr. Crisman has been engaged in undercover activity for a part of the industrial warfare complex for years. . . . Our information indicates that since the early 1960s he has made many trips to the New Orleans and Dallas areas in connection with his undercover work for that part of the warfare industry engaged in the manufacture of what is termed, in military language, 'hardware'— meaning those weapons sold to the U.S. Government which are uniquely large and expensive."

Crisman, for his part, stated from his home in Tacoma that he was willing to testify but knew nothing of an assassination plot, although he personally believed that Kennedy indeed was killed by a conspiracy. Crisman was connected to the Garrison case through New Orleans disc jockey Thomas Edward Beckman. Crisman told newsmen that Beckman was a "banker" for "Cuban freedom fighters," and apparently Garrison thought he might know something of importance regarding Beckman. According to Garrison's sources, Crisman also was closely connected to Clay Shaw and, in fact, was "the first man Clay called after being told he was in trouble."

Shaw's background added to the intrigue. According to his official biography, Shaw was an aide-de-camp to Gen. Charles O. Thrasher during World War II, an officer involved in the handling of top Nazi prisoners, many of whom were resettled in the United States under a highly classified program known as Project Paperclip. Shaw admitted to having been a member of the Office of Strategic Services (OSS), a forerunner of the CIA. He also was listed as a board member of Permindex, whose parent company, Centro Mondiale Commerciale (World Trade Centers), was considered by Italian authorities as an intelligence front headed by prominent fascists such as Benito Mussolini's undersecretary of agriculture, Prince Gutierrez di Spadaforo, whose daughter-in-law was related to former German minister of finance and Reichsbank president Hjalmar Horace Greeley Schacht, the man who had brought Hitler and wealthy German industrialists together.

According to CIA files, Crisman too was a member of the OSS during World War II, serving as a liaison officer with the British Royal Air Force. At the end of the war, Crisman, supposedly discharged from the military, entered a special OSS Internal Security School and was quietly transferred to the newly formed CIA, where he operated as an "extended agent," primarily as an internal security specialist in "disruption" activities. The files show Crisman was involved in a highly classified subsection of Internal Security known as 1Sece, Easy Section, a disruption planning unit whose very existence was denied by the CIA. The CIA documents detailed Crisman's activities over the years—including secret reports to the agency on military officers during the Korean War and company officials while working for Boeing in Seattle—but contained no mention of the Maury Island affair. They did state that "Crisman left the Rainier, Oregon, area and spent several months in New Orleans where he appears to have been very friendly with several political figures and he made the city of New Orleans a headquarters for several small disruption areas. . . . He was . . . later remembered by Garrison. Garrison did not know at this time that Crisman was a CIA agent or that he was in any way a federal employee."

Crisman testified before the New Orleans grand jury, divulging nothing useful and denying that he was any kind of agent. The public took little notice when he died on December 10, 1975.

In 1987, UFO author John Keel published the theory that Crisman may have been working on behalf of the fledgling Atomic Energy Commission (AEC) and, after hearing of the Kenneth Arnold experience, enlisted Dahl's help in fabricating the Maury Island UFO story to cover up illegal dumping of radioactive slag from the AEC's plutonium processing plant in Hanford, Washington.

Most UFO researchers today do not even mention the Maury Island affair in their writings, having written the whole thing off as a hoax. But in doing so, they have missed the deeper significance of what was behind the story. Did Dahl and Crisman actually have a brush with alien spacecraft? Were they pressured by intelligence operatives into covering up the event? Or was it truly a hoax? For what purpose? If it was to gain fame and fortune, neither man did. Was it a setup to discredit Kenneth Arnold? Was it to cover up illegal waste dumping by the AEC? Was the story obscured to protect the secrecy of Project Paperclip? Or was it to distract attention from the secret testing of Nazi saucer craft?

Debunker Curtis Peebles accepted the official air force report on the matter, which stated, "Both [Crisman and Dahl] admitted that the rock fragments had nothing to do with flying saucers. The whole thing was a hoax. . . ." Kenneth Arnold was not so certain. Writing in 1952, Arnold said, "Today it is still as big a mystery as to what actually took place in Tacoma as it was on August 3, 1947." Award-winning investigative journalist Anthony Kimery noted, "What is clear is that the intelligence community was deeply immersed in the very events that launched contemporary ufology." It also seemed clear that the Maury Island witnesses, particularly Crisman, knew much more than they were saying.

A couple of hoaxers is one thing, but this case obviously involved much more. If nothing else, it set the tone for many later UFO cases with its undocumented encounters, disappearing evidence, questionable witnesses, "men in black" issuing gag orders, and the involvement of intelligence agents.

It should be noted that hardly anyone at the time—except perhaps Raymond Palmer and the readers of *Fate*, a magazine he founded after departing as editor of *Amazing Stories*—seriously considered flying saucers to be extraterrestrial spacecraft. In fact it was the spring 1948 initial issue of *Fate* that carried a story by Kenneth Arnold in which he first stated that flying saucers might be from outer space. Most people believed them to be secret government weapons, either from the United States or Russia.

No one was more aware of the threat of advanced foreign aircraft than the Pentagon, where certain high-level military officials must have known about the AVRO-Car saucers and perhaps others. Although every branch of service proclaimed uninterest in such reports, by mid-1947, the involvement of the United States military in the UFO issue was well established.

THE ROAD TO RECOVERY

The year 1947 was a watershed for both UFOs and the United States military. The Kenneth Arnold and Maury Island stories were widely disseminated by the news media, and UFO reports began to pour in to authorities. The military, always concerned over new foreign technology, began to consider the possibility of recovering a crashed specimen—either by accident or design.

Media pundits wondered aloud if growing reports of flying saucers represented some new invasion of the skies or if UFOs had been there all along and were only just now being publicly acknowledged. In hindsight, it would appear to be the latter.

In the mid-1990s, Jan Aldrich, a retired U.S. Army Field Artillery noncommissioned officer, began his one-man Project 1947, an effort to cull North American and foreign newspapers published between June 24 and July 15, 1947, for UFO reports. Aldrich, who eventually enlisted other researchers in his project, discovered more than a thousand documented UFO incidents after screening more than 3,200 publications worldwide—and those were just the reports that found their way into print and were located. Aldrich said there were indications that thousands more cases might be uncovered with continued effort.

But one case in particular was to become the most publicized and mysterious UFO story of all time—it concerned the reported crash and recovery of a UFO in July 1947 in New Mexico.

The Roswell Crash

No UFO story has captured the imagination of the public as has the reported crash at Roswell, New Mexico. It remains one of the most well documented of UFO issues, yet there is no clear consensus even now on what actually happened.

To search for the truth, one should first consider a chronological account of the matter.

The story began on Tuesday, July 1, 1947, when radar installations in New Mexico started tracking an object that zigzagged across the state, exhibiting unconventional speeds and maneuvering ability. On Wednesday, an object was sighted over Roswell. On Thursday, some Washington officials flew in to observe the object.

Late Friday night, the object was lost on radar screens and believed crashed.

Saturday, July 5, Grady L. "Barney" Barnett claimed he, along with some archeologists who happened to be working north of Roswell, discovered wreckage and reported it. The Roswell Volunteer Fire Department was called to the scene, which was on a ranch thirty-five miles north of Roswell. The rancher, William "Mac" Brazel, found debris scattered over an area three-quarters of a mile long and several hundred feet wide—so much debris that his sheep refused to walk through it. On Sunday, July 6, Brazel drove to town and talked to the sheriff, who suggested that the military be notified. Soon, military units arrived and cordoned off the area. Later in the day, Brazel spoke with air intelligence officer Maj. Jesse A. Marcel and showed him a piece of the debris. Brazel returned to his base and notified higher authorities that something unusual had occurred. By Monday, July 7, a systematic examination of Brazel's field by the military began, including an air search.

Early on Tuesday morning Major Marcel stopped by his home as he returned to the airfield and showed unusual material to his wife and son. The military authorities must have felt the debris did not constitute a serious security problem, for later that morning the information officer of the 509th Bomb Group at Roswell Army Air Field—the only unit armed with atomic weapons at the time—was authorized to issue a press release announcing that the military had recovered a "flying disc." This stirred media interest all over the world. That afternoon, Major Marcel was ordered to fly with the debris to Carswell Air Force Base in Fort Worth, Texas.

Meanwhile in Washington, higher military authorities either learned of new developments—some researchers believe they had learned of the discovery of the main body of the UFO and alien bodies by military searchers—or had second thoughts about publicizing the debris. According to the Associated Press, Deputy Chief of the Army Air Forces Lt. Gen. Hoyt S. Vandenberg moved to take control of the news out of Roswell. On Tuesday evening, 8th Air Force commander Brig. Gen. Roger Ramey from his Carswell office told newsmen that Marcel and others had been mistaken and that the "flying disc" actually was nothing more than a weather balloon. Ramey's weather officer, Warrant Officer Irving Newton, was brought in and identified the debris he saw as belonging to a weather balloon. Photographers were allowed to take pictures of the "balloon" wreckage. Years later, researchers Kevin D. Randle and Donald R. Schmitt claimed the original debris was replaced by balloon wreckage in Ramey's office minutes before newsmen were ushered inside.

Following announcement of the balloon explanation, media interest quickly faded. In those security-conscious days following World War II, with fear of Russian attack becoming a way of life, no one thought to question the official version. There the matter rested until 1978, when Jesse Marcel broke his silence, telling UFO researchers Stanton Friedman and Leonard Stringfield that the object he recovered was not from the earth. Since then, the story of the Roswell crash has become a focal point of UFO research, spawning dozens of books, TV documentaries, and videos.

There can be no doubt that something dropped out of the skies near Roswell on July 4, 1947. The question is what. Once again, we encounter conflicting mind-sets. One mind-set accepts the official explanation that a secret military balloon crashed, somehow was mistaken for a spaceship by otherwise competent intelligence officers, and was hidden away for security's sake for almost a half-century. Another accepts that a downed spacecraft containing alien bodies was recovered by the military and hidden from the public.

Everyone agrees that no spaceship wreckage or alien bodies have been made public. Therefore, the truth seeker is left with only human testimony and official pronouncements. The basis for accepting the balloon version rests exclusively on government reports, which deny any unusual aspect to the Roswell case. A lengthy recitation of past official lies, disinformation, and deceit should not be necessary to establish that such pronouncements cannot be accepted at face value.

Some recent theories contend that the wreckage actually was a secret test of a ten-balloon cluster device under Project Mogul, which was launched July 3 from Alamagordo, New Mexico, or a secret navy "Skyhook" balloon. If it were either of these devices, competent intelligent officers should have been able to distinguished it from a flying saucer. Furthermore, if this theory is correct, a common weather balloon must have been substituted for the Mogul or Skyhook balloon for the news photographers in Fort Worth, substantiating claims that the air force deliberately deceived the news media and the public. And if they lied about one thing, it stands to reason they would lie about another.

According to several reports, both the debris and alien bodies were taken to Roswell's military hospital, then flown first to Andrews Air Force Base in Washington and on to Wright Field at Dayton, Ohio.

Debunker Curtis Peebles scarcely mentioned alien bodies in his book, concentrating instead on the debris as exhibited in Fort Worth. Peebles gave the accounts of only four witnesses, one of whom was Barney Barnett, whose story he correctly discounts, as Barnett's location of the crash site differed from most versions and since investigators in 1990 found that Barnett's 1947 diary contained no mention of the Roswell crash. Peebles was able to state that Barnett's story was "unsupported by any documentation or additional witnesses." After alluding to some of the more outrageous theories concerning the Roswell incident, Peebles smugly concluded, "If all these extraneous stories are removed, one is left only with a few fragments in a field."

On the other hand, consider these "additional witnesses" drawn from the well-documented book *The Truth About the UFO Crash at Roswell* by researchers Randle and Schmitt:

William Woody, watching the skies south of Roswell on July 4 with his father, saw a brilliantly glowing object with red streaks. Unlike other meteors he had seen, it was brighter, the wrong color, and took a long time to fall.

Mother Superior Mary Bernadette, from the roof of Roswell's St. Mary's Hospital, saw a bright light go to earth north of town and recorded the time as between 11:00 and 11:30 P.M. July 4, in a logbook.

Sister Capistrano, a Franciscan nun standing beside Mother Superior Bernadette at St. Mary's Hospital, also saw the object come down.

Cpl. E. L. Pyles, stationed south of Roswell Army Air Field, saw what he first thought was a large shooting star with an orange glow fall through the sky sometime between 11:00 P.M. and midnight.

James Ragsdale, a camper who saw a fiery object crash near his camp on the night of July 4. The next day, Ragsdale discovered a crashed circular craft and small bodies. He fled when the military arrived, thinking he might get in trouble.

Trudy Truelove, a camping companion with Ragsdale, confirmed his account, stating she also saw the craft and bodies.

Jason Ridgway (a pseudonym to protect the man's identity) saw the crashed object, identified it as a saucer craft, but refused to talk about it for many years. He was a friend of Mac Brazel, the rancher who owned the property.

C. Curry Holden, one of several field archeologists who stumbled upon the crash site, described a "fat fuselage" without wings. He also said he saw three bodies, two outside the craft, one partially visible inside.

Dr. C. Bertrand Schultz, a paleontologist working in the area, heard of the crash and bodies from Holden and encountered the military cordon thrown up around the site.

Maj. Jesse Marcel, the Roswell intelligence officer who was first on the scene and announced the crash of a "flying disc," took pieces of strange metal that would straighten out after bending home to show his family. Although Marcel did not contradict the balloon explanation at the time, in later years he said he was correct the first time about a craft from space and that he was muzzled by military authorities. "It was not anything from this Earth. That, I'm quite sure of," Marcel said. "Being in intelligence, I was familiar with all materials used in aircraft and in air travel. This was nothing like this. It could not have been."

Dr. Jesse Marcel Jr., Major Marcel's son and an Air National Guard flight surgeon, who clearly remembered markings on the metal brought home by his father as consisting of "different geometric shapes, leaves and circles" akin to hieroglyphics. His father told him the metal came from a flying saucer, then had to explain what a flying saucer was to young Marcel.

Col. William Blanchard, Roswell Army Air Field commander, visited the crash site and initially indicated to Marcel that the crash involved something highly unusual, perhaps a Soviet secret weapon. He immediately passed the entire matter up to his superiors. Nothing was said about a balloon.

Maj. Edwin Easley, Blanchard's provost marshal in charge of the military police who guarded the crash site, told researchers a large volume of crash debris was loaded onto trucks and taken to the Roswell base, where it was place on an airplane. In recent years, Easley said he promised the president he would not reveal what he saw, but indicated he believed it was an extraterrestrial craft.

Sgt. Thomas C. Gonzales, one of the guards at the site, later confirmed the recovery of "little men" with large heads and eyes.

Steve MacKenzie, stationed at Roswell, tracked the object on radar for almost twenty-four hours and then visited the crash site, where he said a major from Washington took charge of the dead bodies, described as small with large heads and eyes. MacKenzie said if the object he tracked had been a weather balloon, secret or not, his superiors would have ordered him to ignore it.

Lt. Col. Albert L. Duran, a member of MacKenzie's unit, has acknowledged seeing the small bodies.

Warrant Officer Robert Thomas flew to Roswell from Washington with a team of experts, including two photographers, early on July 4 after learning of the erratic path of the object. All were on hand at the crash site, according to MacKenzie.

Master Sgt. Bill Rickett, a counterintelligence corps agent, arrived late at the crash site but described what he saw as a curved craft with a batlike trailing edge that had struck front first into the side of a cliff, scattering a great deal of debris. Rickett was assigned to assist University of New Mexico scientist Dr. Lincoln La Paz. According to Rickett, La Paz, apparently unaware of the bodies, concluded the craft was an unmanned probe from another planet.

Sgt. Melvin E. Brown later told family members he helped transport alien bodies from the crash site to a Roswell hanger. He described them as smaller than humans with leathery skin like that of a reptile.

Frank Kaufmann of the 509th Bomb Group staff told of a single large crate that was placed in a cleared-out hanger at Roswell and protected by armed guards. He said he understood the crate contained bodies recovered at the crash site.

W. O. "Pappy" Henderson, a pilot with the 1st Air Transport Unit, flew the crate and debris in a C-54 transport plane to Andrews Air Field in Washington, then on to Wright Air Field in Ohio, according to Steve MacKenzie. Henderson's widow, Sappho, said he had described the debris as "weird" and nothing he had ever seen before. She added that, following a TV special in 1988, Henderson confirmed the descriptions of small recovered bodies.

Sarah Holcomb, who worked at Wright Field at the time, told researchers she heard from a crew member that a plane had landed with bodies from a flying saucer. Later the base commander came around and said there was no truth to the story but added that anyone mentioning the "rumor" would be subject to twenty years in jail and a $20,000 fine.

Helen Wachter also was at Wright Field and said she overheard the husband of a friend tell excitedly about the arrival of "alien bodies." At first, she thought he meant people from outside the country, but she quickly understood he was referring to extraterrestrials.

John Kromschroeder, a close friend of pilot Henderson with an interest in metallurgy, said he was given a piece of metal by Henderson, who said it was part of the interior of the crashed craft. Kromschroeder said the metal was gray and resembled aluminum but he was unable to cut it, even using a variety of tools.

Maj. Ellis Boldra, who may have studied the same piece of metal as Kromschroeder, told his family that the fragment was incredibly strong and did not melt when he subjected it to an acetylene torch but in some way dissipated heat.

Floyd and Loretta Proctor, nearest neighbors of rancher Mac Brazel, recalled that Brazel showed them pieces of the debris, which could not be cut or burned.

William Proctor, the Proctors' son, saw a large amount of debris and took some home. Later, according to family members, he was forced to turn it all in to the military.

William W. "Mac" Brazel, owner of the crash site, said he heard an explosion during a thunderstorm on the night of July 4 and the next day, along with William Proctor, found a field full of scattered debris and described many big pieces of dull gray metal that was unusually lightweight and could not be cut or burned. Four days later, after being held by military authorities and accompanied by military officers, Brazel told the Associated Press the debris was actually found on June 14 and consisted of string, paper, some tape, and bits of metal that covered no more than two hundred yards in diameter. Oddly enough, he ended this obvious description of some sort of kite or balloon by saying, "I am sure what I found was not any weather observation balloon."

Bill Brazel, Mac's son, said his father was held for eight days by the military and released only after swearing not to discuss the incident. He told his son he was better off not knowing about it but swore what he saw was not a balloon. Bill Brazel said his father was muzzled by military authorities. He also said he handled some of the debris found later on his father's ranch and that it resembled aluminum foil but when wadded into a ball, it would straighten itself out smooth. He too said it could not be cut or burned. The younger Brazel said he showed pieces of the metal to friends.

Sallye Tadolini, the daughter of another of Mac Brazel's neighbors, told researchers that she recalled Bill Brazel showing her a piece of dull-colored metal that he balled up into his fist and, when he opened his hand, returned to its original shape.

Frank Joyce, in 1947 a radio announcer for Roswell station KGFL, confirmed to researchers that Mac Brazel's story after being taken into military custody was "significantly" different from an initial interview. Joyce said that when he talked to Brazel privately, the rancher admitted that he had changed his story but said "he had been told to come in or else."

Glenn Dennis, then a mortician working for Ballard's Funeral Home in Roswell, said about 1:30 P.M. July 5, he received a call from the Roswell base mortuary officer asking if the funeral home could provide a number of small caskets that could be hermetically sealed. Dennis said he realized something strange had occurred when the officer called back and asked how to prepare a body that had been burned or left out in the elements for a time. Later that day, Dennis drove to Roswell Field to deliver an injured airman. At the base hospital he saw strange pieces of wreckage in the rear of an ambulance but soon was chased off by an officer, who told him not to talk or "somebody will be picking your bones out of the sand." A few days later, Dennis said a nurse friend told him she was called in to assist in the autopsy of three "foreign bodies" that gave off an overpowering odor. She said the bodies were small with large heads and hands with four fingers ending in pads that looked like suction cups.

E. M. Hall, former Roswell police chief, confirmed to researchers that he heard Dennis talking about the base requesting coffins for "the bodies from a flying saucer" within days of the incident.

George Bush, whose sister Mary worked as secretary to the base hospital administrator, told researchers he would never forget the day in July 1947 that she came home and told him she had seen a creature from another world.

Chaves County Sheriff George A. Wilcox kept a carton of crash debris left by Mac Brazel but was ordered to turn it over to the military. For some time, Wilcox complained how the military usurped his authority, even barring his deputies from the crash site. Worse yet, Wilcox and his wife, Inez, were told by military police that if he ever talked about the incident, his entire family would be killed.

Barbara Dugger, the granddaughter of George and Inez, said her grandmother quoted military police as saying if anything was ever said about the incident in any way, "not only would we be killed, but they would get the rest of the family." Years later, Inez Wilcox also confided to her granddaughter that a flying saucer had crashed near Roswell.

Frankie Rowe was the teenaged daughter of Dan Dwyer, a Roswell fireman who went to the scene on Saturday morning and later told his family he saw the wreckage of a flying craft, two small dead bodies, and "a very small being about the size of a 10-year-old child." According to Rowe, military authorities threatened her family, and one man told her if she talked about the incident, she would disappear into the desert and never be seen again.

Brig. Gen. Arthur E. Exon was a World War II combat pilot who spent time in a German POW camp and later was stationed with the Air Material Command at Wright-Patterson Air Force Base, as it was known after Wright Field and Patterson Field merged. In recent years, Exon became the highest ranking officer to confirm that a quantity of material from Roswell arrived at Wright Field for testing by a "special project" team of lab workers. He said the material was "unusual," looked like foil, but couldn't be dented even by hammers. He also said that he flew over the crash site and was able to see where the craft had come down. Exon added that bodies were found with the main portion of the craft, which ended up in a separate location from the debris.

Naturally, considering the clash of mind-sets, questions have been raised about both the competency and veracity of the Roswell witnesses. But even if half of these witnesses are discounted, the remainder should be more than enough to convince anyone with an open mind that something quite extraordinary occurred at Roswell in the summer of 1947. That the incident stayed on the minds of men in power is illustrated by a story related by William Pitts. A former military man who today is a lecturer for the Society of Manufacturing Engineers, Pitts is the head of Project Blue Book, a private organization sanctioned by the U.S. Air Force to investigate UFO sightings. He said that in early 1977 he and others, including J. Allen Hynek, were summoned to a meeting regarding UFOs by Dr. Frank Press, science adviser to newly elected President Jimmy Carter. "The first question," recalled Pitts, "was regarding Roswell. What did we know about Roswell? I turned it around and ask them what they knew about Roswell and they did not reply. They went on to something else." It was not until more than a year later that UFO researchers began to hear the saucer crash story from Jesse Marcel and interest in the Roswell case was revived.

Various theories have been advanced to explain what was recovered at Roswell. These include a Rawin Target weather balloon, a Japanese Fugo balloon bomb, or a V-2 nose cone containing monkeys. None of these theories can explain away all the evidence now available about this event, and if any of these theories are correct, it would still mean the air force deceived the public when the weather balloon story was announced.

Responding to a request by New Mexico Republican representative Steven Schiff, the U.S. General Accounting Office (GAO) conducted a document search on records pertaining to the Roswell incident, which only added to the mystery. In July 1995 the GAO reported, "RAAF (Roswell Army Air Field) administrative records (from March, 1945, through December, 1949) and RAAF outgoing messages (from October, 1946, through December, 1949) were destroyed." Schiff's press liaison, Barry Bitzer, stated, "Having spent 24 years in the military, [Schiff] did express some surprise that those records were destroyed, supposedly against regulations and without traceable authorization." Only two records were found, a unit history report stating that a "flying disc" turned out to be a radar tracking balloon and an FBI teletype stating that the military reported that a high-altitude weather balloon was recovered near Roswell. Of course, it was these two reports—official pronouncements produced only after the official version was conceived—which were used by debunkers to dismiss the Roswell crash story. The FBI teletype was especially odd, as it indicated the Bureau may have been monitoring Roswell base telephones and it clearly stated a "disc" was sent to Wright Field. The teletype read, "[name blanked out] further advised that the object found resembles a high-altitude weather balloon with a radar reflector, but that telephonic conversations between their office and Wright Field had not borne out this belief. Disc and balloon being transported to Wright Field by special plane for examination."

Adding to the confusion were claims that other disc-shaped craft may have been recovered at other times and in other locations. Saucers reportedly were recovered in Paradise Valley north of Phoenix, Arizona, in October 1947; near Aztec, New Mexico, in March 1948; and in Mexico near Laredo, Texas, later in 1948. Any one of the crash stories could have been real with the others acting as red herrings, or all the stories could be false. Information on these crashes is meager compared to Roswell and involved the familiar charges and countercharges of lies and hoaxes.

Even a purported autopsy film of an alien body recovered in 1947 has been offered as proof of the crash recovery. During 1995, Ray Santilli, owner of a small London video distribution company, caused a worldwide clamor by revealing what he claimed was authentic 1947 black-and-white movie film of the autopsy of an alien creature found in New Mexico. At first glance, the film—an "Alien Autopsy" complete with 1940s telephone, clock, and medical instruments and a "real" handheld shaky quality—seemed to offer objective evidence that alien bodies had indeed been recovered in New Mexico.

But the clash between mind-sets quickly engulfed this piece of evidence, along with other problems such as conflicting statements and foot-dragging by the film's owners. Debunkers swiftly went to work attacking the film, and scientists took a standoffish attitude. Dr. Chris Stringer of the Natural History Museum in London said he believed the body was a fake because "It's most improbable that aliens could have evolved to look so like humans."

Arguments raged back and forth about the legitimacy of the autopsy film until even many ufologists grew tired of the issue and it faded into the background—although no one was ever able to prove beyond question that it was a fake. Such is the fate of issues mired in the uncompromising battle between mind-sets.

Without resorting to convoluted speculation with little or no supporting evidence, it would appear that the most straightforward explanation of the Roswell story is that a very unusual craft crashed and the occupants—whether dead or alive—were taken into custody by the U.S. military, which then conducted a cover-up.

The military is the key here.

Certainly by the time of the "foo-fighters," ranking members of the military establishment must have known that something new and unusual was in the skies. Some researchers even contend that authorities became aware of UFOs prior to World War II. Contingency plans must have been drawn up with an eye toward the eventual capture or recovery of unusual aircraft. Such plans would have been activated after an examination of whatever was recovered at Roswell.

It is fact that this period marked a definite turn in the military's response to UFOs. Prior to Roswell, the military had been intensely interested in UFOs and open to the idea that they represented extraterrestrial visitation. But with the knowledge gained from the Roswell incident, the military became secretive and publicly offered every mundane explanation possible to account for UFO sightings. It may even be that the Maury Island affair was a military intelligence contingency plan to plant a discrediting UFO story in the public mind that was activated after the Roswell crash. Although the incident reportedly happened on June 21, 1947, there was only the word of Dahl and Crisman to substantiate that date, as it was not reported until after the time of the Roswell crash. And the intelligence background of Crisman added considerable weight to this consideration.

Whether Roswell played any role in subsequent events or not, it is a fact that on September 15—less than four months after Arnold saw discs soaring over Mount Rainier and only two months after the Roswell incident—President Harry S. Truman signed into law the National Security Act of 1947, which among other things created the National Security Council (NSC) and the air force as a separate branch of service, united the military branches under a Department of Defense, and created America's first peacetime civilian intelligence organization, the Central Intelligence Agency. According to unauthenticated documents—collectively known as the MJ-12 papers—a small, select group of prominent military officers and scientists answerable only to the president was created at this time to deal with UFOs.

Shortly after this establishment of our modern military and intelligence institutions, the U.S. military took its first official step to identify the source of the burgeoning UFO reports, although interest had been high since the first saucer sightings appeared in the media in mid-1947.

A View of the Projects

Shortly before the air force became a separate service, chief of staff of the Army Air Force, Brig. Gen. George Schulgen, requested information on UFOs. Lt. Gen. Nathan F. Twining, former chief of staff of the U.S. Army and at that time chief of the Air Material Command, Air Technical Intelligence Center, at Wright-Patterson Air Force Base in Dayton, responded with a letter stamped "secret" dated September 23, 1947.

In his letter, Twining began his conclusions by stating, "The phenomenon reported is something real and not visionary or fictitious." While Twining admitted that some UFO reports may have been caused by natural phenomena such as meteors, he said the reported operating characteristics of UFOs "lend belief to the possibility that some of the objects are controlled either manually, automatically or remotely." After giving a common description of UFOs, Twining stated that, while it may have been possible "within the present U.S. knowledge" to construct such a craft, it would be a costly and time-consuming process that would only draw resources from existing projects. He recommended that a permanent group be established to study UFOs.

Twining's letter also contained a sentence that would be used against those who argued that a crashed saucer was recovered at Roswell. One would expect an officer of Twining's position to be knowledgeable about a recovered disc. Yet more than two months after the Roswell incident, Twining said consideration must be given to "the lack of physical evidence in the shape of crashed recovered exhibits which would undeniably prove the existence of these objects." It is intriguing that he wrote about "crashed recovered exhibits," yet indicated that none existed. Was this simply wistful thinking or was it his way of saying something without saying something?

Since Twining's letter was marked "secret" and since any reference to a real UFO crash at Roswell undoubtedly would have been classified much higher, it is hardly surprising that Twining would obscure the fact. It should also be noted that if both the Roswell incident and UFOs were as clearly explained as some suggest—particularly if the issue involved some top-secret military balloon or aircraft tests—Twining certainly would not have recommended an intense study with reports to be passed along to the navy, the Atomic Energy

Commission, and several other agencies. Roswell authors Kevin Randle and Donald Schmitt suggested that Twining's letter sought further study of the UFO phenomenon on the one hand, while attempting to close off any discussion of a crashed vehicle on the other. Another item that may support the idea that Twining knew more than he was telling was found in a secret memo from General Schulgen's Air Intelligence Requirements Division dated October 28, 1947. Entitled "Draft of Collection Memorandum," the five-page document stated, "While there remains a possibility of Russian manufacture, based on the perspective thinking and actual accomplishments of the Germans, it is the considered opinion of some elements that the object may in fact represent an interplanetary craft of some kind." Materials mentioned for such a craft included "various combination of metals, metallic foils, plastics, and perhaps balsa wood or similar material . . . to achieve extreme light weight and structural stability." This description is very close to the material described by Maj. Jesse Marcel, indicating Schulgen may have been aware of the material recovered at Roswell.

As a direct result of Twining's recommendation, a UFO study group was formed within the air force, complete with a high national priority rating—2A, with only 1A being higher—yet with the lowest security classification, "restricted." It was designated Project Sign.

Some Sign members may have heard rumors of a saucer crash, for soon the officers found themselves sharply divided between those who believed UFOs were secret Soviet technology and those who believed UFOs represented something unearthly. "The division grew greater as it became increasingly clear that the 'ordinary' foreign technology explanation was untenable," wrote Dr. J. Allen Hynek, who joined Project Sign in early 1948 while director of Ohio State University's McMillin Observatory. While conceding that the original 237 reports studied by Sign members were not too convincing and did not support "visitors from space," Hynek nevertheless said the group moved closer toward accepting the extraterrestrial thesis. Author Peebles noted that at least a dozen reports remained "unidentified" even after every possible alternative explanation was considered.

Hynek began as a skeptic. "Before I began my association with the air force, I had joined my scientific colleagues in many a hearty guffaw at the 'psychological postwar craze' for flying saucers that seemed to be sweeping the country and at the naïveté and gullibility of our fellow human beings who were being taken in by such obvious 'nonsense,'" he wrote in later years. "It was thus almost in a sense of sport that I accepted the invitation to have a look at the flying saucer reports. . . . I also had a feeling that I might be doing a service by helping to clear away 'nonscience.' After all, wasn't this a golden opportunity to demonstrate to the public how the scientific method works, how the application of the impersonal and unbiased logic of the scientific method—I conveniently forgot my own bias for the moment—could be used to show that flying saucers were figments of the imagination?"

But over time, Hynek's attitudes began to change. "It was not until several years had passed and data of similar nature continued to flow not only from this country but from many others that I had occasion to feel that the phenomenon was indeed being proved: there were too many occurrences that couldn't be explained in 'ordinary' terms."

Others in Project Sign began to share Hynek's views, particularly after some decidedly odd UFO incidents.

One such incident involved what some researchers considered the first recorded human death attributed to a UFO.

On January 7, 1948, Kentucky Air National Guard Captain Thomas F. Mantell Jr. was piloting an F-51 (a postwar version of the famed P-51D Mustang) en route to Standiford Air Force Base, Kentucky, accompanied by three other Guard planes. Shortly after 1:30 P.M. Kentucky State Police reported that citizens were sighting a large circular object over Mansville, Kentucky. Similar reports soon came in from Irvington and Owensboro. It was seen from the control tower of Godman Air Force Base. The object, described as large, round, and white with a red light near the lower part, was slowly moving southward. About 2:40 P.M. Mantell's flight was asked to investigate. One pilot received permission to continue his flight, while Mantell and two others began climbing in an effort to intercept the UFO. With Mantell in the lead, the three Mustangs soon reached fifteen thousand feet, where Mantell radioed, "The object is directly ahead of and above me now, moving at about half my speed. . . . It appears to be a metallic object or possibly reflection of Sun from a metallic object, and it is of tremendous size. . . . I'm still climbing . . . I'm trying to close in for a better look."

Reaching twenty-two thousand feet, Mantell's two companions turned back, as the World War II fighters had not been equipped with oxygen. Mantell continued on and apparently passed out from lack of oxygen as his plane leveled off at about thirty thousand feet. It then plunged into a spiral dive, crashing to earth on the William J. Phillips farm near Franklin, Kentucky. According to the official accident report, Mantell's body was still strapped in the wreckage. His watch had stopped at 3:18 P.M.

By 3:50 P.M. the UFO had been lost from sight at Godman, but reports continued to come in from areas further south and even into Tennessee.

The cause of Mantell's death prompted immediate debate. Two days after the incident, the *New York Times* carried a story with the headlines "Flier Dies Chasing a 'Flying Saucer'" and "Plane Exploded over Kentucky As That and Near States Report Strange Object." Speculation that the UFO caused Mantell's death was quickly put to rest by the air force, which announced that the fighters were chasing Venus and Mantell crashed due to anoxia (oxygen deprivation). Both pilot and his engine simply ran out of oxygen at the higher altitudes and the craft fell to earth. But as with many UFO issues, nothing is as simple as it can be made to seem.

While anoxia is the most probable explanation of Mantell's death, it does not explain the report of a witness cited by the newspaper. Glen Mays, who lived near Franklin, said he saw the aircraft explode in midair. "The plane circled three times, like the pilot didn't know where he was going," reported Mays, "and then started down into a dive from about 20,000 feet. About halfway down there was a terrific explosion." Neither does it explain why Godman base commander Guy F. Hix, who told reporters he observed the "flying saucer" for almost an hour with binoculars, would confuse the object with the planet Venus.

Richard T. Miller, who would later record incredible communications from what he termed "space brothers," also objected to the official explanation. Miller said he was in the air force and standing in the operations room of Scott Air Force Base in Belleville, Illinois, during the time of the Mantell chase and heard the radio talk between the Godman tower operators and the pursuit planes. Miller claimed to have heard Mantell's last radio transmission, which was, "My God, I see people in this thing!" In a subsequent briefing he said that he learned that according to the crashed F-51's instruments, Mantell had flown for more than an hour after his fuel ran out. "No one could account for this," recalled Miller. He also said that farmer Mays did not specifically say he saw an explosion. "He said as the aircraft reached tree-top level, it was enveloped by a brilliant white flash of light. This light was so bright, it was like looking at the sun. The aircraft appeared to fall out of this light and pancake into the ground. Now whatever this brilliant light was, it brought the aircraft out of a spin, and slowed its rate of descent. . . . Some mysterious force had somehow interfered with the crash of this aircraft. When the plane hit the ground, Captain Mantell's shoulder straps broke, he flew forward over the control stick and it impaled him through the chest. That is how Captain Mantell died."

Miller said the morning after Mantell's crash, investigators had concluded that Mantell died "pursuing an intelligently controlled

unidentified flying object," but that by evening Air Technical Intelligence Center officers from Wright-Patterson AFB arrived and
ordered all personnel to turn over any materials relating to the crash.
"Then after we had turned it over to them, they said they had already
completed the investigation," he said. "I was no longer a skeptic. I had
been up to that time. Now I wondered why the government had gone
to all of the trouble of covering it up, to keep it away from the press
and the public."

Supporting Miller's version of Mantell's crash is the testimony
of Cpt. James F. Duesler, today living in retirement in England. In a
recent interview, Duesler stated that he was one of several military
observers who saw the UFO hovering over Godman Field in 1948. A
pilot and crash investigator, Duesler described the UFO as a "strange
gray-looking object" that looked like a rotating inverted ice cream
cone.

Duesler, who visited the crash site shortly after Mantell's body
had been removed, was puzzled by the wreckage. "The wings and tail
section had broken off on impact with the ground and were a short
distance from the plane," he recalled. "There was no damage to the
surrounding trees and it was obvious that there had been no forward
or sideways motion when the plane had come down. It just appeared to
have 'belly flopped' into the clearing. There was very little damage to
the fuselage, which was in one piece, and no signs of blood whatsoever
in the cockpit. There was no scratching on the body of the fuselage to
indicate any forward movement and the propeller blade bore no telltale scratch marks to show it had been rotating at the time of impact,
and one blade had been embedded into the ground. The damage pattern was not consistent with an aircraft of this type crashing at high
speed into the ground. Because of the large engine in the nose of the
plane, it would come down nose first and hit the ground at an angle.
Even if it had managed to glide in, it would have cut a swath through
the trees and a channel into the ground. None of these signs were
present. All indications were that it had just belly flopped into the
clearing. I must admit, I found this very strange." The official report
of the Mantell incident contained a "certified" statement by crash
investigator Duesler. However, Duesler said he never made such a
statement and the one presented in the official report was a "fake."

While it now appears likely that Mantell indeed passed out and
crashed from lack of oxygen, the question of what he was chasing
remains open, as does the question of the circumstances of his crash.

For some time the media were satisfied with the air force explanation that Mantell, an experienced World War II combat pilot, was
climbing past safe limits after Venus. Only his friends and family ques-

tioned this verdict. A friend and fellow pilot said, "The only thing I can think was that he was after something that he believed to be more important than his life or his family."

Soon after Mantell's death, UFO researchers were able to demonstrate that at the time of the incident Venus was only thirty-three degrees above the horizon, hardly in a position to be "above" Mantell, and it was at only half its maximum brightness, which would have made it nearly invisible, especially in midafternoon. Discomfited by these facts, the air force officers of Project Sign began to seek a more defensible explanation. They found one in the Office of Naval Research, which on September 25, 1947, began launching large "Sky-hook" balloons designed to test the atmosphere high above the limits of conventional aircraft. Until well into the 1970s, the navy launched an average of about a hundred Skyhook balloons a year. Thus, air intelligence officers were able to shift the object of Mantell's chase from Venus to a balloon, although they were unable to locate any records showing that such a balloon had been sent aloft during the time in question.

It was obvious, however, that the air force did not wholeheart-edly believe UFOs to be nonexistent. Immediately following the Mantell incident, Air Force Directorate of Intelligence Brig. Gen. Charles P. Cabell—who later would become deputy director of the CIA—sent a secret memo on February 12, 1948, to the director of Plans and Operations urging that all air force bases in the United States and Alaska provide a minimum of one fighter plane "or interceptor type aircraft" equipped with "gun camera and such armament as deemed advisable" to obtain data on "any reported and sighted unusual phenomena, of the 'flying disc' type, in the atmosphere." Although Cabell's request was turned down as impractical, the memo showed how concerned the air force had become to obtain further intelligence on UFOs.

It should be noted that Mantell's UFO—or another like it—was seen in the days following his death. On January 9, 1948, residents of Clinton, North Carolina, reported a red cone-shaped object with a green tail dancing through the sky at an amazing speed. It was so bright they could see its outline even behind clouds. On February 1, a metallic UFO emitting a bright orange light was sighted near the ground at Circleville, Ohio. By the end of February, strange sightings were reported as far north as Boise and Emmett, Idaho.

Another extraordinary incident—which has never been satisfactorily explained—occurred on October 1, 1948, and has been described as a dogfight or aerial duel between a plane and a UFO. George F. Gorman, a twenty-five-year-old construction company manager and a second lieutenant in the North Dakota Air National Guard, was at seven thousand feet preparing to land his P-51 at Fargo, North Dakota, about 9:00 P.M. when a bright object swept past his right wing. Occupants of a nearby Piper Cub also saw the object moving swiftly to the west. The Hector Airport Tower reported no other craft in the vicinity. To Gorman the object appeared to be heading for the airport tower, so he gave chase but realized his plane could not match the object's speed. Banking hard to his left, he attempted to head off the object, which then turned toward him. "Suddenly, the thing made a sharp turn right, and we were headed straight for each other!" Gorman stated. "Just as we are about to collide, I guess I got scared. I went into a dive and the light passed over my canopy at about 500 feet. Then the thing made a left circle about 1,000 feet above me, and I gave chase again." Gorman described the object as a clear white, perfectly round globe—only eight inches in diameter. Again it turned toward his plane. "When collision seemed imminent, the object shot straight up into the air. I climbed after it to a height of about 14,000 feet, when my plane went into a power stall. The thing now turned in a northwest-north heading, and vanished." Later, Gorman told authorities, "The object was not only able to out turn and out speed my aircraft . . . but was able to attain a far steeper climb and was able to maintain a constant rate of climb far in excess of my aircraft. . . . I am convinced that there was definite thought behind its maneuvers."

With this clear description of the encounter, supported by the occupants of the Piper Cub and the tower controllers plus an indication of unusually high radioactivity readings on Gorman's plane, Project Sign investigators issued an Estimate of the Situation report stating that something highly unusual had occurred. The report was rejected and ordered destroyed a few days later by Air Force Chief of Staff Vandenberg, citing insufficient evidence. By the end of 1948, the Gorman "dogfight" was explained as an encounter with a lighted weather balloon, its "maneuvers" simply an illusion of the light and lack of any reference point. The radioactivity was explained as the natural result of increased cosmic ray bombardment at higher altitudes.

This official rejection of UFOs as an unearthly phenomenon set the tone for Project Sign, which by the end of the year had explained away all but seven of the reports assigned to it. On February 11, 1949, the group's name was changed to Project Grudge after the news media became aware of their existence and erroneously dubbed the endeavor Project Saucer. "While I was still working on my report for Project Sign, it became Project Grudge, and the Pentagon began to treat the subject with subtle ridicule," Hynek wrote.

Where Project Sign members' conclusion that UFOs were real

and probably from another world was kept secret, Project Grudge officers began a public relations effort assuring the public that all UFO reports could be explained away. "The change to Project Grudge signaled the adoption of the strict brush-off attitude to the UFO problem," commented Hynek. "Now the public relations statements on specific UFO cases bore little resemblance to the facts of the case. If a case contained some of the elements possibly attributable to aircraft, a balloon, etc., it automatically became that object in the press release."

Air Force Cpt. Edward J. Ruppelt, who would later head another UFO project, stated, "This drastic change in official attitude is as difficult to explain as it was difficult for many people who knew what was going on inside Project Sign to believe. . . . Here were people deciding that there was nothing to this UFO business right at the time when the reports seemed to be getting better. From what I could see, if there were any mind-changing to be done, it should have been the other way. . . ."

This official lack of interest in and disdain for a phenomenon that was stirring the public imagination is indeed difficult to understand unless it played a part in another controversy in the UFO issue.

The MJ-12 Papers

On December 11, 1984, UFO researcher and TV producer Jaime Shandera heard his daily mail drop through the slot in his front door. He also heard his screen door shut. Opening the door, he found a brown envelope. It bore no return address but was stamped and bore a cancellation mark. Inside was a roll of thirty-five-millimeter Tri-X black-and-white film.

When Shandera and fellow researcher William Moore developed it, the film proved to contain photos of what purported to be eight pages from a November 18, 1952, "Briefing Document" prepared for President-elect Dwight D. Eisenhower concerning "Operation Majestic 12." Both the top and bottom of the pages were stamped TOP SECRET/MAJIC EYES ONLY.

The documents were extraordinary, to say the least. They listed twelve prominent men as members of Operation Majestic 12, "a TOP SECRET Research and Development/Intelligence operation responsible directly and only to the President of the United States" who were to deal with the UFO issue at the highest level. The papers went on to detail how a "secret operation" was begun on July 7, 1947, to recover the wreckage of a disc-shaped craft from a crash site "approximately 75 miles northwest of Roswell Army Air Base." Also, "four small human-like beings [who] had apparently ejected from the craft" were found dead about two miles east of the wreckage site. The document added, "Civilian and military witnesses in the area were debriefed, and news reporters were given the effective cover story that the object had been a misguided weather research balloon."

It was believed the dead beings, termed "Extra-Terrestrial Biological Entities or EBEs" in the documents, possibly came from Mars or even "another solar system entirely." It was stated that efforts to decipher "a form of writing" found in the wreckage and to determine the method of propulsion were unsuccessful, and added, "It is assumed that the propulsion unit was completely destroyed by the explosion which caused the crash." The documents explained that "a need for as much additional information as possible about these craft, their performance characteristics and their purpose" led to the creation of Air Force Projects Sign and Grudge. To assure security "only two individuals within the Intelligence Division of Air Material Command" passed along information from the projects to Majestic 12.

The "briefing" papers ended by stating, "Implications for the National Security are of continuing importance in that the motives and ultimate intentions of these visitors remain completely unknown. In addition, a significant upsurge in the surveillance activity of these craft beginning in May and continuing through the autumn of this year [1952] has caused considerable concern that new developments may be imminent. It is for these reasons, as well as the obvious international and technological considerations and the ultimate need to avoid a public panic at all costs, that the Majestic-12 Group remains of the unanimous opinion that imposition of the strictest security precautions should continue without interruption into the new administration."

As listed in the documents, Majestic-12 members included:

Adm. Roscoe H. Hillenkoetter, the third director of Central Intelligence who became the first director of the CIA upon its formation in September 1947, was a logical choice for a top-secret group. Hillenkoetter, after retirement from government, joined the private UFO group, the National Investigations Committee on Aerial Phenomena (NICAP), and stated publicly that UFOs were real and "through official secrecy and ridicule, many citizens are led to believe the unknown flying objects are nonsense."

Dr. Vannevar Bush, an eminent American scientist who in 1941 organized the National Defense Research Council and in 1943, the Office of Scientific Research and Development, which led to the production of the first atomic bomb, was another prime candidate for a high-level UFO group. In 1949, the U.S. Intelligence Board asked Bush to study ways of combing intelligence from all agencies. Bush's plan was initiated by James Forrestal, also listed as an MJ-12 member.

Secretary James V. Forrestal became secretary of defense in July 1947—the time of the Roswell incident—but resigned in March 1949, a month before he reportedly committed suicide at Bethesda Naval Hospital. According to a footnote in the MJ-12 documents, more than a year passed before his MJ-12 position was permanently filled by Gen. Walter Bedell Smith, Eisenhower's chief of staff and former U.S. ambassador to Moscow, who had replaced Hillenkoetter as director of Central Intelligence.

Gen. Nathan F. Twining, commander of the Air Material Command based at Wright-Patterson and a man already heavily involved in the UFO issue, in fact canceled a scheduled trip on July 8, 1947, "due to a very important and sudden matter." This was the day the Roswell Air Base press release regarding the recovery of a flying saucer was issued. UFO researcher William Moore claimed that Twining actually made a two-day trip to New Mexico. It was Twining's recommendation that resulted in the creation of the UFO study group, Project Sign.

Gen. Hoyt S. Vandenberg, air force chief of staff and a former director of Central Intelligence, had ordered the original Project Sign report that UFOs were real destroyed. Many UFO researchers believe Vanderberg's public posture was to maintain security for MJ-12.

Dr. Detlev Bronk, a physiologist and biophysicist with international credentials, chaired the National Research Council and was a member of the medical advisory board of the Atomic Energy Commission. Bronk also was on the Scientific Advisory Committee of the Brookhaven National Laboratory with Dr. Edward Condon, who later headed a major UFO study for the air force.

Dr. Jerome Hunsaker, an aircraft designer, chaired the Departments of Mechanical and Aeronautical Engineering at the Massachusetts Institute of Technology and the National Advisory Committee for Aeronautics.

Mr. Sidney W. Souers, a retired rear admiral who in 1946 was the first director of Central Intelligence, was executive secretary to the National Security Council in 1947 and remained a special consultant on security matters for a time after leaving that post.

Mr. Gordon Gray, assistant secretary of the army in 1947, became secretary of the army in 1949 and a year later was named a special assistant on national security affairs to President Truman. According to one source, Gray directed a psychological strategy board consulted by CIA director Walter B. Smith in regards to UFOs.

Dr. Donald Menzel, as a director of the Harvard College Observatory, was a respected astronomer. He also became a widely known debunker of UFOs after writing three books in which he explained away most reports and dismissed others, saying, "All non-explained sightings are from poor observers."

Gen. Robert M. Montegue was base commander at the Sandia Atomic Energy Commission facility in Albuquerque, New Mexico, from July 1947 to February 1951. Researchers believe Montegue undoubtedly would have known about any crashed saucer at Roswell.

Dr. Lloyd V. Berkner worked under Vannevar Bush as executive secretary of the Joint Research and Development Board in 1946 and headed a study that resulted in the creation of the Weapons Systems Evaluation Group. Berkner also was a member of the 1952 CIA-sponsored panel headed by Dr. H. P. Robertson that concluded that UFOs did not constitute any direct threat to national security.

These distinguished men appeared to have two things in common—they were all connected to the highest levels of the military and national security and they were all dead at the time the MJ-12 papers surfaced and thus unable to answer any questions about their role, if any, in such a group.

For more than a decade, various UFO researchers have tried to establish the authenticity of the MJ-12 documents. As debunker Philip Klass declared, "Either [the documents] are the biggest news story of the past two millennia or one of the biggest cons ever attempted against the public."

Any attempt to determine the validity of the MJ-12 documents must begin with a look at UFO researcher William L. Moore. In 1979, Moore, a former high school English teacher turned novelist, authored a book entitled *The Philadelphia Experiment* with Charles Berlitz, which for him began a serious interest in UFOs. In 1980 he and Berlitz published *The Roswell Incident*, one of the better investigative efforts on the story at that time and a popular success. While publicizing his book, Moore later claimed he was recruited as an operative by government agents. His primary contact was a man he would only identify as the Falcon. Falcon told Moore he represented a group within intelligence who wanted to get truth about UFOs to the public and offered to help Moore if he would help them. Moore agreed, hoping this contact would lead him to more solid UFO information. Soon Falcon put Moore in touch with Master Sgt. Richard C. Doty with the Air Force Office of Special Investigations (AFOSI) at Kirtland AFB in Albuquerque, and Moore was given his first undercover assignment.

It involved investigating the strange activities of Dr. Paul Bennewitz, a physicist who was president of a small Albuquerque electronics firm. Bennewitz previously had reported to the Aerial Phenomena Research Organization (APRO), of which Moore was a director, that he had monitored audio transmissions from UFOs with equipment he designed and even captured UFOs on film. Bennewitz said his studies—which he called "Project Beta"—had convinced him that aliens were controlling certain people by implanting tiny devices in their body during an abduction. Moore went to Albuquerque to meet with Bennewitz after the AFOSI asked him to evaluate the man's claims. Bennewitz maintained his UFO monitoring had disclosed that two types of extraterrestrials were active on Earth—peaceful "white" or "blond" aliens who wanted to help mankind and the more sinister "grey" aliens who were behind cattle mutilations and human abductions. He added that certain people within the U.S. government had met with the "greys" and had agreed to allow them to build an underground base in New Mexico in return for advanced space and weapons technology. Bennewitz said this relationship had deteriorated and that open warfare appeared imminent.

Reporting back to Falcon through Doty, Moore said he learned that for almost three years AFOSI agents had been conducting a "disinformation" campaign against Bennewitz. This involved giving Bennewitz "official" documents detailing the alleged alien-government contacts through a variety of sources. This was designed to "systematically confuse, discourage and discredit" Bennewitz, Moore said. Bennewitz was lured deeper into an investigation of underground bases and mind control that took him away from his surveillance of UFOs and their transmissions.

For four years, Moore watched as Bennewitz's mental and emotional state deteriorated until he was hospitalized with a breakdown. He may have even contributed to Bennewitz's decline, since it was Moore who in February 1981 gave Bennewitz a pre-Majestic-12 document known as the "Project Aquarius Telex."

This document purported to be a message from AFOSI headquarters in Washington to the Kirtland AFB office concerning UFO photos taken by Bennewitz. One sentence stated, "The official U.S. Government policy and results of Project Aquarius is still classified Top Secret with no dissemination outside official intelligence channels and with restricted access to 'MJ Twelve.'" It was the first mention of Project Aquarius and MJ-12. In 1982, Moore worked with reporter Robert Pratt in a plan to publish information concerning Project Aquarius as a novel.

Next came another incredible document, nine pages of a presidential "Executive Briefing" that stated, "This document was prepared by MJ12." Moore said he was allowed to photograph a copy of these documents after being summoned to Maryland by unnamed government agents. UFO researcher Linda Moulton Howe said she too was shown the document—or one very similar—on April 9, 1983, by Sergeant Doty in the Kirtland AFB AFOSI office.

According to these briefing papers:

Only MJ-12 has access to Project Aquarius.

Project Aquarius was created in 1959 by order of President Eisenhower and placed under the control of the National Security Council and MJ-12.

Project Aquarius was funded by nonappropriated confidential CIA money.

The purpose of the project was to "collect all scientific, technological, medical and intelligence information from UFO/IAC (Identified Alien Crafts) sightings, and contacts with Alien Life forms."

Information gained through Project Aquarius was used to advance the United States Space Program.

"In 1947 an aircraft of extraterrestrial origin crashed in the desert of New Mexico. The craft was recovered by the military, four Alien—non-homo-sapiens—bodies were recovered in the wreckage."

"In late 1949 another Alien aircraft crashed in the United States and was recovered partially intact by the military. One Alien of extraterrestrial origin survived the crash. The surviving Alien was male and called itself, 'EBE.' This being came from a planet in the Zeta Reticula star system, approximately 40 light years from Earth. EBE lived until June 18, 1952, when he died [due] to an unexplained illness.

During the time period EBE was alive, he provided valuable information regarding space technology, origins of the Universe, and exobiological matters."

Beginning in 1947, the U.S. Air Force began a series of programs to determine if these aliens posed a threat to national security. This program operated under the code names Sign, Grudge, and Blue Book. These programs determined that 90 percent of an estimated twelve thousand analyzed reports were considered hoaxes, explainable aerial phenomena, or natural astronomical objects with 10 percent considered "legitimate Alien sightings and/or incidents."

In 1953, President Eisenhower ordered a parallel reporting and study program begun under the name Project Gleem, which then became Project Aquarius in 1966.

In 1958, an abandoned but operational UFO was recovered in Utah that provided a large amount of technological data, only some of which scientists could understand.

In 1966, the United States established contact with aliens and "felt relatively sure the Aliens' exploration of Earth was non-aggressive and non-hostile . . . [and] did not directly threaten the security of the United States."

Project Blue Book was conducted to "satisfy public curiosity," and when it was closed in December 1969, "Project Aquarius continued operation under control of NSC/MJ12."

"MJ12 feels confident the Aliens are on an exploration of our solar system for peaceful purposes" but it was decided to "observe and track" the aliens in secret.

The living alien, EBE, stated "that 2,000 years ago his ancestors planted a human creature on Earth to assist the inhabitants of Earth in developing a civilization. This information was only vague and the exact identity or background information on this homo-sapien was not obtained. Doubtless, if this information was released to the public, it would cause worldwide panic."

A program was developed "for a gradual release of information over a period of time in order to condition the public for future disclosures."

Project BANDO was established in 1949 to collect and evaluate medical information provided by EBE and alien autopsies and to seek "certain answers to the evolution theory." It was ended in 1974.

Project SIGMA, originally part of Project Gleem, became a separate project in 1976 for the purpose of establishing communication with aliens. Primitive communication was begun in 1959, which led to a three-hour face-to-face meeting between two aliens and an air force intelligence officer on April 25, 1964.

Project SNOWBIRD was a program to test-fly recovered alien aircraft and is continuing today in Nevada.

Project POUNCE was established in 1968 and designed to evaluate all alien information pertaining to space technology.

Most UFO researchers believed these documents "too good to be true," and their suspicions were justified. In 1982, after air force officials declared the Aquarius Telex a forgery based on flaws in both style and format, Moore admitted that he had retyped the document and added a date stamp. Respected British UFO author Timothy Good proclaimed the document "an actual classified AFOSI message that had been skillfully doctored."

With questions raised about the authenticity of the Aquarius documents, researchers turned to the MJ-12 papers. Objections were immediately raised by several researchers, especially longtime debunker Philip Klass, who attacked the legitimacy of the documents with everything from the curious mixture of military and civilian date forms, to misspellings, to oddities of punctuation and style such as the use of the term "media," which did not come into vogue until the 1960s.

Klass argued that members of the MJ-12 group could not have had knowledge of crashed UFOs and bodies, since several spoke out publicly against the reality of UFOs. This argument totally ignored historical precedents showing that prominent men will often say the opposite of what they know to be true, particularly if they feel it is in the nation's best interest. Furthermore, Klass questioned why such a group would include a mere astronomer like Donald Menzel. His question was answered by respected UFO researcher Stanton Friedman, who learned that Menzel led a double life. After studying Menzel's unpublished autobiography and speaking with his widow, Friedman found the astronomer was a covert consultant for the CIA and the National Security Agency with a Top-Secret Ultra security clearance.

He was also involved with secret research programs for more than thirty companies and made frequent trips for the government to Washington and to New Mexico. Menzel also was closely associated with MJ-12 listees Bush, Bronk, and Berkner. Friedman was convinced that no hoaxer could have known of Menzel's secret connections to government intelligence, thus indicating the MJ-12 documents were legitimate.

But the arguments continued. What was needed was yet another official document that could substantiate the MJ-12 papers. Just such a document conveniently turned up in the National Archives in 1985—but its discoverer was none other than Moore again. He was at the archives with Jaime Shandera when they said they found an unsigned carbon copy of a memo to Gen. Nathan Twining from President Eisenhower's special assistant Robert Cutler. Dated July 14, 1954, and stamped "Top Secret Restricted Security Information," the memo's subject was "NSC/MJ-12 Special Studies Project." The text stated that the President had decided that a MJ-12 briefing should take place during an already scheduled White House meeting on July 16 rather than afterward as planned. Here was another document that substantiated the existence of the MJ-12 group—or did it?

Immediately, this document came under fire, with Klass arguing that the memo used a large pica type while the Eisenhower White House used a small elite type. Yet Friedman claimed to have found more than a dozen examples of the memo's typeface used on other White House messages. Furthermore, Friedman said, "In the case of the Cutler-Twining memo, we have the original paper, so you can see the watermark on the onion skin with the name of the company that made the paper. We contacted them to find out when they made this particular paper, and we were told between 1953 and 1973. That's good, it covers our time period."

However, critics pointed to the "Top Secret Restricted Security Information" classification, stating that the Eisenhower Library agreed that "Top Secret" and "Restricted" were two separate classifications never seen together on any other Eisenhower document. Furthermore, an official with the Freedom of Information Office of the National Security Council said the classification "Top Secret Restricted Information" did not come into use until the Nixon administration.

Next Klass attacked a memo signed by President Harry Truman that accompanied the MJ-12 documents, claiming that the president's signature was identical to one on a letter to Vannevar Bush, an impossibility for two separate signatures. Then he found a document expert who said the Truman memo was typed on a Smith-Corona typewriter first sold in 1963, fifteen years after the memo was supposedly produced.

To compound this controversy, yet another MJ-12 document recently surfaced—an April 1954 "Majestic-12 Group Special Operations Manual."

A member of the Fund for UFO Research, a group headed by former U.S. Navy physicist Dr. Bruce Maccabee that paid researcher Stanton Friedman $16,000 to investigate the initial MJ-12 documents, received the operations manual—also anonymously and also on a roll of thirty-five-millimeter film. The manual is incomplete but, according to Roswell author Kevin Randle, it "reveals that a great deal of work went into its preparation." "This was no simple, quick, and dirty job. It suggests someone who is familiar with the style of military manuals of recent decades. The cover is impressive, looks authentic, and even includes a 'seal' to add to the visual impact," Randle wrote.

According to the operations manual, "Operation Majestic-12" was created by a special classified presidential order on September 24, 1947, on the recommendation of Secretary of Defense James V. Forrestal and Dr. Vannevar Bush, chairman of the Joint Research and Development Board. Its purpose was to recover and study "all materials and devices of a foreign or extraterrestrial manufacture" as well as "entities or remains of entities not of terrestrial origin," establish "Special Teams" and facilities to accomplish this—all the while maintaining "absolute top secrecy." It also stated, "Several dead entities have been recovered along with a substantial amount of wreckage and devices from downed craft, all of which are now under study at various locations." The manual gives descriptions of various types of UFOs and occupants along with instructions on how to secure a crash site, prepare materials and bodies for shipment, and even how to present "false statements to preserve the security of the site." "Meteors, downed satellites, weather balloons and military aircraft are all acceptable alternative" explanations, it offered.

Numerous arguments were quickly presented against the authenticity of the manual, such as discrepancies in the classification codes, internal inconsistencies, possible anachronisms, and even reference to a "MJ Form 1-007." Randle concluded, "In short, the MJ-12 Operations Manual, like the rest of the MJ-12 documents, is a fake for these reasons: It does not conform to the regulations, it contains inaccurate information, and it is incomplete. We have no provenance for it, we can't find independent verification of it from other government agencies, and no evidence for its validity has ever been offered."

Richard Davis, director of national security analysis for the General Accounting Office, said there have been many FOIA requests made to various government agencies concerning the MJ-12 papers. In 1995 he wrote, "In each instance these agencies have stated that they have no knowledge of the documents and that there is no evidence that the Majestic 12 written material constitutes actual documents originally created in the executive branch. During our review for Congressman Schiff we could not find any evidence to contradict these statements."

The battle over the MJ-12 papers raged on, and UFO researchers took sides based on their individual mind-sets. Debunkers like Klass were joined by Randle and coauthor Donald Schmitt, who stated flatly that the MJ-12 documents were a hoax and hinted broadly that Moore may have had a hand in the fabrication. On the other side were Friedman and British author Timothy Good, who wrote in 1988, "My inquiries into the authenticity of the Majestic 12 story during research during a recent trip to the United States in 1986 have led me to believe that the group did indeed exist, and the document seems authentic enough. Unfortunately, all the members are now deceased and my questions addressed to a former director of the CIA, as well as two ex-Presidents, remain unanswered, which is hardly surprising." But by 1993, even Good was backtracking. Writing that "valid objections have now been raised," Good stated he believed the MJ-12 documents to be fraudulent but added that based on his own research "some information contained therein, at least, is essentially factual."

Charge and countercharge, undercover agents, "disinformation" campaigns, phony documents—the whole thing carried the odor of rotting fish. It was apparent that the MJ-12 documents were produced by someone with extensive knowledge and expertise in military documentation, as everyone agreed the papers presented the appearance of authenticity. So if the MJ-12 documents were fabrications, many researchers reasoned it signaled a sophisticated "disinformation" campaign on the part of someone within the U.S. military. Such a campaign would clearly show that the U.S. military—particularly the air force—had long taken a keener and deeper interest in both the UFO phenomenon and its investigators than previously imagined, a highly curious circumstance in light of the fact that the air force had long denied that there is anything going on in the first place.

So whether real or bogus, the MJ-12 and Project Aquarius documents and others would seem to establish beyond doubt that certain persons within the government were concealing their intense interest in UFOs. If they are genuine—a determination that does not appear to be within easy reach anytime soon—they would explain much in regard to continued government secrecy.

One simple test failed to establish fraud. By 1995, a researcher and aerospace worker named Lee Graham had decided that either the

MJ-12 documents were genuine or someone had committed a felony by fabricating and publicizing top-secret government papers. Graham worked for Aerojet, a firm that did contract work for the U.S. Air Force, and had signed a secret security agreement that stated, "If I am uncertain about the classification status of information, I am required to confirm from an authorized official that the information is unclassified before I may disclose it." Graham learned that any document bearing a top-secret classification stamp came under Department of Defense regulation 5200.1-R. Therefore, when Graham obtained a copy of the MJ-12 documents in 1987, he was obligated under regulations to report that top-secret material may have been compromised. On May 24, 1990, after he had written to then Vice President Dan Quayle, Graham received a letter from the Defense Investigative Service (DIS) that included a copy of his Quayle letter along with the MJ-12 documents, which Graham noted had been marked "Unclassified." In subsequent correspondence, DIS agent Dale Hartig stated that the MJ-12 papers were authentic. "Going by the lawful security procedures governing the handling and disposition of classified documents, there can only be two possible conclusions," Graham wrote, "the Briefing Document: Operation Majestic 12 is legitimate, or Dale Hartig should be charged with violating DoD Regulation 5200.1-R. There is no middle ground!" Graham noted that "in this instance, the security breach committed by Moore/Shandera was apparently ignored by all government agencies, including the presumed current MJ-12 group or their successors."

This ignoring of security violations was confirmed by an FBI investigation launched in the wake of the disclosure of the MJ-12 documents. Spurred by a letter from Philip Klass in 1987, the Bureau began an investigation of the MJ-12 documents, which, whether legitimate or a fabrication, would constitute a grave security violation. Bureau agents spent more than a year trying to determine if the MJ-12 papers were stolen government property or forgeries. Why would someone go to the trouble to fabricate the documents? they asked. Who had the knowledge and experience to concoct such an elaborate and credible hoax? If someone forged the papers, he would have had to know details of people and events more than almost fifty years ago plus the correct form of writing, dates, and security stamps. By the end of their investigation, FBI agents could not find any agency or individual willing to admit that the papers had been purloined from the government or make a formal complaint of forgery. Author Howard Blum wrote that one FBI agent involved in the MJ-12 investigation confided, "All we're finding out is that the government doesn't know what it knows. There are too many secret levels. You can't get a straight story. It wouldn't surprise me if we never know if the papers are genuine or not."

So today—and for the foreseeable future—questions over the authenticity of the papers continue to swirl in a cauldron of controversy, with heated arguments coming from all sides. Once again, it would seem to be a question, not of final proof, but of which mind-set one chooses to accept. Interestingly enough, there does appear to be a general agreement among UFO researchers matching Good's conclusion that, even if the documents are proven to be false, they still may contain elements of truth. For there is some legitimate documentary evidence indicating that an MJ-12 group—similar in operation if not in name—indeed existed and that UFO crash recoveries may indeed have taken place.

In the 1991 book *UFOs, MJ-12 and the Government: A Report on Government Involvement in UFO Crash Retrievals*, authors Grant Cameron and T. Scott Crain Jr. reported that Dr. Eric A. Walker, former executive secretary for the Defense Department's Research and Development Board, felt the publicized MJ-12 documents were not authentic. However, he admitted knowing about an MJ-12 group since its inception in 1947. Walker said MJ-12 was "a handful of elite, and they are not all Americans." Walker also admitted attending meetings at Wright-Patterson Air Force Base concerning recovered UFOs. Asked about UFO occupants, Walker replied that not much had been learned from them. "We are not working with them," he added, "only contact." "As to the existence of a special committee to oversee UFO crash retrieval operations—which may or may not have been named MJ-12—there is a wealth of data to support its reality," authors Cameron and Crain concluded.

For example, several government documents have become public mentioning MJ-12, including a pay record for Bob Lazar, a man who claimed to have worked with crashed UFOs, and a CIA document reporting on a crashed saucer and alien bodies mentioned by Marilyn Monroe. All such documents are branded fakes by debunkers, although none have been proven to be so and their number seems to be increasing.

One intriguing story regarding MJ-12 came from longtime UFO researcher Tommy Bland, who recalled that in 1990 he met a woman who seemed to know all about the secret group. "Margaret Fuller lived in the same apartment complex as we did. She was a widow and lived alone and one day I helped her move some things into her apartment. On the walls I saw framed photographs of her with President Truman and Allen Dulles and several other people I only knew from history. Some of them were ranking military officers that I knew from my research had been connected with the UFO issue. Over time I got to know Mrs. Fuller quite well and found out that since World War II she had been an executive secretary for several top-ranking Army generals. She finally showed me many files relating to her work and told me that there was a secret group in control of the UFO situation. She said it was not then called MJ-12 but it operated the same way that MJ-12 was described. She said this group was still in existence.

"According to Mrs. Fuller, most early UFO sightings involved aeronautical experimentation with captured Nazi technology. Later the issue grew to include psychological warfare and disinformation campaigns. However, she said that within all this was some real but unknown things bordering on magic. She said these things were classified at a much higher level. Some of the generals said there was a connection between the unknown UFOs and spiritualism.

"Mrs. Fuller said she had photographs of most of the original members of this UFO group and she was looking for them the same week she had a heart attack. As they were wheeling her out of her apartment, she grasped my arm and said, 'Tommy, don't let my family get those files.' They took her to a hospital in Nashville. She died while in the hospital. A relative told me that she saw a nurse give Mrs. Fuller medication which was not prescribed for her. Some people who claimed to be her family came, sacked up her files in plastic bags and took them away. It was all highly unusual."

But while anecdotes such as this might be easy for some to dismiss, other evidence that the government had laid its hands on real UFOs—if not alien bodies—is harder to disregard.

Official UFO Notice

There is an amazing FBI document that indicated that Director J. Edgar Hoover had knowledge of an early UFO recovery. This 1947 FBI memorandum recommended the Bureau not investigate UFO sightings, "it being noted that a great bulk of these alleged discs reported found have been pranks." At the bottom of the page assistant FBI director and Hoover's roommate Clyde Tolson added, "I think we should do this." Hoover added in his own handwriting, "I would do it but before agreeing to it we must insist upon full access to discs recovered. For instance in the [La?] case the Army grabbed it and wouldn't let us have it for cursory examination." Some researchers think the illegible "La" in the memo might stand for Los Alamos, where some wreckage from Roswell reportedly was taken, or it might refer to a reported saucer recovery in Louisiana. Regardless, this memo was strong support for the idea that a UFO was recovered and being studied within the government.

The FBI continued to receive UFO information. A March 22, 1950, office memorandum to Hoover from the special agent in charge of the FBI's Washington office reported, "An investigator for the Air Force stated that three so-called flying saucers had been recovered in New Mexico. They were described as being circular in shape with raised centers, approximately 50 feet in diameter. Each one was occupied by three bodies of human shape but only three feet tall, dressed in metallic cloth of a very fine texture. Each body was bandaged in a manner similar to the blackout suits used by speed flyers and test pilots."

More support came from a foreign source. In November 1950, Wilbert B. Smith, an official with the Canadian Department of Transport, wrote a secret memorandum to his superiors recommending that a UFO research project be created. Smith said he had learned from American scientist Dr. Robert Sarbacher that "flying saucers exist" and that the issue was considered to be of "tremendous significance" by U.S. authorities, who had classified the matter at a "rating higher even than the H-bomb." He also wrote that the study of UFOs by a "concentrated effort is being made by a small group headed by Doctor Vannevar Bush." The Canadian Department of Transport responded to Smith's recommendation by creating Project Magnet in December 1950, downplayed later as "a small program of investigation in the field of geomagnetics." Yet, another Smith report on August 10, 1953, stated, "It appears then, that we are faced with a substantial probability of the real existence of extraterrestrial vehicles. . . ."

Smith's source of information, Dr. Robert Sarbacher, was a respected scientist on the U.S. government's Research and Development Board as well as president and board chairman of the Washington Institute of Technology. On November 29, 1983, in response to queries from UFO author William Steinman, Sarbacher wrote a provocative letter, stating, "Relating to my own experiences regarding recovered flying saucers, I had no association with any of the people involved in the recovery and have no knowledge regarding the dates of the recoveries. . . . Dr. Vannevar Bush was definitely involved, and I think Dr. Robert Oppenheimer also. . . . I did receive some official reports when I was in my office at the Pentagon but all of these were left there as at the time we were never supposed to take them out of the office. . . . About the only thing I remember at this time is that certain materials reported to have come from flying saucer crashes were extremely light and very tough. I am sure our laboratories analyzed them very carefully. There were reports that instruments or people operating these machines were also of very light weight, sufficient to withstand the tremendous deceleration and acceleration associated with their machinery. I remember in talking to some of the people at the office that I got the impression these 'aliens' were constructed like certain insects we have observed on earth. . . . I still do not know why the high order of classification has been given and why the denial of the existence of these devices."

Author Good reported that in 1950 none other than Secretary of State for Foreign Affairs Gen. George C. Marshall admitted to a friend that there had been at least three UFO landings that "proved disastrous for the occupants."

Another fascinating story involved the late comedian Jackie Gleason. According to Gleason's second wife, Beverly McKittrick, he returned home visibly shaken one night in 1973. Gleason, who was known to have an avid interest in UFOs, said his friend President Richard Nixon had arranged for him to visit Homestead Air Force Base in Florida, where he viewed the remains of small alien beings under tight security. This story was confirmed by Larry Warren, who said Gleason met with him in May 1986 to hear Warren's account of a UFO experience in England. During their conversation, Gleason related the Nixon-aliens story and said the experience traumatized him for weeks. "You could tell that he was very sincere," said Warren. "He took the whole affair very seriously, and I could tell that he wanted to get the matter off his chest, and this was why he was telling me all of this." Before his death in 1987, Gleason was asked about this incident but declined to comment, a most interesting circumstance, since it was an opportunity to refute the story if it was false.

JFK, Marilyn, and the UFOs

An even more bizarre story concerned a UFO connection between President John F. Kennedy and Hollywood icon Marilyn Monroe—for years the subject of rumors linking the actress romantically with both John and Robert Kennedy.

In 1994, Los Angeles private investigator Milo Spiriglio, who wrote three books about Monroe's controversial death, obtained a poorly reproduced copy of what appeared to be a CIA report dated August 3, 1962—just two days before the actress died of a reported drug overdose. The report stated that, through a telephone wiretap, agents had listened in on a conversation between the renowned reporter Dorothy Kilgallen and a close friend in Hollywood. The friend talked about a breakup between Monroe and the Kennedys and said the actress was attending parties hosted by Hollywood's "inner circle," where she was threatening to hold a press conference and reveal "secrets" she had learned from both John and Robert Kennedy.

According to the report, these secrets included her knowledge of "bases" in Cuba—perhaps a reference to the Soviet missile sites that led to the crisis a few months later—and Kennedy's plans to kill Fidel Castro.

But the first listed "secret" was a "visit by the President at a secret air base for the purpose of inspecting things from outer space." Kilgallen did not seemed shocked by this statement. In fact, according to the CIA report, she replied that she might know the source of such a visit—a crash in New Mexico in the late 1940s. She stated that in the mid-1950s, she had learned from a British government official about a secret effort to identify the origin of crashed spacecraft and dead bodies.

Spiriglio, a court-certified document expert, declined to reveal the name of the person who provided the report, saying that at least two federal agencies were investigating the matter, although no official word has been forthcoming. But he added that several ex-CIA contacts had verified the document's contents. "It appears to be a summary designed to be transferred to other agencies," commented researcher Vic Golubic, who investigated the document for more than a year and still could neither confirm nor deny its authenticity. "I have checked with many people and 50 percent say it's authentic and 50 percent say it's not. Either it's a very clever hoax or it's legitimate."

The document appeared to be signed by none other than James Angleton, former chief of CIA counterintelligence. Adding to suspicions about the document's legitimacy was a reference to Project Moon Dust and a smudgy imprint at the bottom that appeared to read "MJ-12."

However, there is some intriguing support for the notion that the story might be true. First is an article by Dorothy Kilgallen published in 1955. Under the headline "'Flying Saucer' Wreckage Assures Britons of Reality," she wrote, "I can report Sunday on a story which is positively spooky, not to mention chilling. British scientists and airmen, after examining the wreckage of one mysterious flying ship, are convinced that these strange aerial objects are not optical illusions, but are actually flying saucers which originate on another planet. The source of my information is a British official of cabinet rank who prefers to remain unidentified. 'We believe, on the basis of our inquiries thus far, that the saucers were staffed by small men—probably under four feet tall,' my informant told me. 'It's frightening but there is no denying the flying saucers come from another planet.' This official quoted scientists as saying a flying ship of this type could not possibly have been constructed on Earth. The British government, I learned, is withholding an official report on the 'flying saucer' examination at this time, possibly because it does not wish to frighten the public. In the United States, all kinds of explanations have been advanced. But no responsible official of the U.S. Air Force has yet intimated the mysterious flying ships actually vaulted from outer space."

Considerable support for Kilgallen's story came during that same period, when British Air Chief Marshal Lord Dowding, commander in chief of RAF fighters during the Battle of Britain, told the *London Sunday Dispatch* knowingly, "I am convinced that these objects [UFOs] do exist and that they are not manufactured by any nation on Earth. . . . I think that we must resist the tendency to assume that they all come from the same planet, or that they are actuated by similar motives. It might be that the visitors from one planet wished to help us in our evolution from the basis of a higher level to which they had attained. Another planet might send an expedition to ascertain what have been those terrible explosions which they have observed, and to prevent us from discommoding other people besides ourselves by the new toys with which we are so light-heartedly playing. Other visitors might have come bent solely on scientific discovery and might regard us with the dispassionate aloofness which we might regard insects found beneath an upturned stone."

Further support for high-level knowledge on UFOs came from a former steward aboard *Air Force One* who told of a cryptic remark by President Kennedy. Bill Holden, who also served as loadmaster for *Air Force One*, traveled with Kennedy to Europe in the summer of 1963. He said a UFO conference in Bonn, Germany, prompted a discussion of the subject aboard the President's plane one morning.

Holden said he turned to Kennedy and asked, "What do you think about UFOs, Mr. President?" He said Kennedy became quite serious and thought for a moment before replying, "I'd like to tell the public about the alien situation, but my hands are tied."

Spurred on by such tantalizing bits of evidence, some researchers even claimed that Kennedy's assassination was to prevent him from revealing the news of extraterrestrial visitation to the public.

Not only do these accounts appear to provide some substantiation for the recovered saucers story, but recent government letters make it plain that Project Aquarius—the subject of the telex that started the whole document controversy—actually exists.

When a researcher sent a Freedom of Information request to the National Security Agency (NSA), Dennis Chadwick, chief of information policy, responded, "Please be advised that Project Aquarius does not deal with unidentified aerial objects." Chadwick added, "Since you indicate in your letter that you will not be paying the

$15,000.00 fee to search for records pertaining to Aquarius, this response completes our action on your request." Undaunted, the researcher inquired further and on April 15, 1986, received this intriguing reply from Julia Wetzel, the NSA's director of policy: "The document located in response to your request as stated in your 7 March letter has been reviewed by the Agency as required by the FOIA and has been found to be currently and properly classified . . . and remains TOP SECRET. . . . The document is classified because its disclosure could reasonably be expected to cause exceptionally grave damage to the national security. . . ." While confirming the existence of TOP SECRET Project Aquarius, the NSA gave no indication if it involved UFOs. Considering past government reliance on semantic ambiguity, some researchers believed the denial that the project concerned "unidentified aerial objects" left open the question of identified objects on the ground.

It was ironic that as the government's official line that UFOs simply don't exist hardened, such documentation as above along with official reports and anecdotes increased in both quality and quantity. Something definitely was going on, but the public would not find out what through official government channels.

PLAUSIBLE DENIABILITY

In the early 1950s, the shift of attitude toward denial of UFOs solidified within the highest levels of military and civilian leadership. Like a pebble in a pond, it rippled down through the lower levels of authority.

Project Grudge foundered, strapped by political, economic, and manpower problems. Edward J. Ruppelt, who soon would head the new official air force UFO investigation, said, "Project Grudge lapsed more and more into a period of almost complete inactivity." He termed it the "Dark Ages." One of the only reports to come out during this period was characterized by a newsman as "quite impressive, but only in its ambiguousness, illogical reasoning, and very apparent effort to write off all UFO reports at any cost . . . to cover up the real story." Ruppelt himself spoke of a "schizophrenic approach" at the Air Technical Intelligence Center (ATIC). "On the surface they sided with the belly-laughers on any saucer issue, but if you were alone with them and started to ridicule the subject, they defended it or at least took an active interest," he said.

This all changed in the fall of 1951 when ranking officers in the Pentagon, irritated that the public and news media would not drop the subject, ordered a reorganization of Project Grudge. On October 27, 1951, the new Project Grudge was officially established with Captain Ruppelt in charge.

UFO reports improved in quality, and the air force even issued orders to its pilots and air controllers on what procedures to follow should one be encountered. These instructions were known as Communication Instructions for Reporting Vital Intelligence Sightings (CIRVIS). The orders themselves caused problems for the military. Joint Army-Navy-Air Force Publication (JANAP) 146 directed pilots to report UFOs but keep the reports secret under penalties contained in the Communications Act of 1934 and espionage laws. Air Force Regulation (AFR) 200-2 limited the distribution of UFO reports to three air force intelligence groups.

Soon this censorship and secrecy was extended beyond the military. On February 17, 1954, air force officials met with representatives of the nation's major airlines. According to Scripps-Howard News Service, commercial pilots had been reporting between five and ten UFO sightings per night prior to this meeting. Pilots would notify the air force of their sightings through their companies after landing. To "get the reports in the quickest possible way," air force officers instructed pilots to radio such reports directly to Military Air Transport Service (MATS) intelligence in Washington or to the nearest air force base. According to one news account of the meeting, "Airline pilots are asked not to discuss their sightings publicly or give them to the newspapers."

This unsubtle muzzling of commercial pilots prompted one to tell news reporters, "[The air force policy is] a lesson in lying, intrigue and the 'Big Brother' attitude carried to the ultimate extreme." Nearly five hundred airline pilots signed a petition protesting this policy, but to no avail. Someone with a great deal of power was determined to close off public discussions of UFOs.

Researcher and author Maj. Donald Keyhoe pointed to the CIRVIS regulations as proof the air force was suppressing UFO information. "Because of JANAP 146 and AFR 200-2, hundreds of new, dramatic encounters have been kept under cover," he wrote, adding that the UFO secrecy policy was coming from an MJ-12-type clique of highly placed men he termed the "silence group."

Despite the official attitude that UFOs didn't exist, it was quite apparent that top officials were seeking as much information as possible. But still there were no hard-and-fast answers.

One good example is what came to be known as the "Lubbock Lights." Beginning on the evening of August 25, 1951, and lasting for several more nights, a strange line of bluish, glowing lights were seen flying swiftly over Lubbock in far West Texas. Four professors from Texas Technological College—a geologist, a physicist, a chemist, and a petroleum engineer—witnessed the lights on several successive nights. After careful study, the academicians decided they were under intelligent control. A college freshman named Carl Hart Jr. managed to take five photographs of the V-shaped formation of lights. The air force eventually decided the whole incident was caused by mercury vapor streetlights reflecting off the backsides of birds, first identified as plovers, then changed to ducks when it was pointed out that plovers usually traveled only in pairs. This explanation was not well received among the hundreds of Lubbock residents who witnessed the flyover.

Ruppelt, who personally investigated the Lubbock Lights, also was not convinced by the bird story. He stated the photographs could not be proven to be a hoax and discounted the streetlight reflection theory, since people far from the city also saw the formation. Furthermore, there were radar tracks and sightings as far away as Albuquerque to support the sightings. He stated that government scientists and intelligence officers "were convinced that some of the UFOs that were being reported were interplanetary spaceships and the Lubbock series was one of these reports." But in his 1956 book, Ruppelt finally stated that, after he received information from a source he could not identify, the lights were a "very commonplace and easily explainable natural phenomenon." It was a most unsatisfying conclusion.

Ruppelt generally brought a fresh and objective viewpoint to the air force investigation. He claimed to have dismissed three staffers for being either too skeptical or too accepting of the spaceship theory. And he quickly immersed himself in the quagmire of UFO reports. In January 1952, Ruppelt and a scientist met with employees of General Mills in Minneapolis, who claimed they had witnessed UFO sightings for more than a year. These people had a special place in the ranks of UFO witnesses. Ruppelt explained, "The Aeronautical Division of General Mills, Inc., of Wheaties and Betty Crocker fame, had launched and tracked every Skyhook balloon that had been launched prior to mid-1952. They knew what their balloons looked like under all lighting conditions and they also knew meteorology, aerodynamics, astronomy, and they knew UFOs. I talked to these people for the better part of a full day and every time I tried to infer that there might be some natural explanation for the UFOs I just about found myself in a fresh snowdrift." This set the theory that many—if not most—UFO sightings had been Skyhook balloons on its ear.

With new hopes of resolving the growing UFO phenomenon, the name Project Grudge was finally scrapped in March 1952. The air force investigation, now working closely with the Air Defense Command, became a separate organization officially called the Aerial Phenomena Group. This soon changed to Project Blue Book. Another change came due to Ruppelt's disgust that the term "flying saucer" had come to represent anything and everything decidedly strange and unworldly. He popularized the term Unidentified Flying Object, or UFO, in the belief that this more closely represented the object of the air force investigation.

Where the air force had been trying to discredit all UFO sightings, Ruppelt and Blue Book were trying to keep an open mind. However, they quickly dismissed any report that appeared to have a conventional explanation, which came to about 60 percent. They concentrated on the remainder.

Public perception was electrified when *Life* magazine published an article in April 7, 1952, entitled, "Have We Visitors from Space?" Not only did the article seem to substantiate the idea that aliens were here but, by citing certain high-placed sources, appeared to endorse the concept. Many people felt the air force was trying to leak truth in a nonthreatening manner. Ruppelt and author Peebles both concurred that the idea of interplanetary spacecraft was certainly the personal opinion of several Pentagon officers at the time. Both, however, stopped short of Major Keyhoe's belief that the *Life* article was part of a process approved at the highest levels to condition the public to the idea of extraterrestrial visitation. One thing was certain—the idea of aliens on Earth, while ridiculed at lower levels, apparently was taken quite seriously at higher ones.

Blue Book, engrossed with the effort to reorganize, was unprepared for the rash of sightings that began in the summer of 1952. Said Ruppelt, "By mid-July we were getting about 20 reports a day plus frantic calls from intelligence officers all over the United States as every Air Force installation in the U.S. was being swamped with reports." And this was only the beginning.

UFOs over Washington

The reality of UFOs became undeniable—at least to the population of Washington, D.C.—on July 19, 1952, when more than eight UFOs were tracked on radar at both Andrews Air Force Base and Washington National Airport. The objects would cruise along at low speeds of 100 to 130 miles per hour and then accelerate to "fantastically high speeds." The objects were observed by experienced pilots and air controllers as well as tracked by radar for several hours. Ominously, they were well within Washington's most restricted airspace—passing over both the Capitol and the White House.

Over the ensuing days, the UFOs reappeared, first here and then there. The sightings came as a surprise to the Blue Book staff, although, in hindsight, they shouldn't have. Ruppelt reported later there had been a steady buildup of sightings along the East Coast for some months.

When the sightings first began, news reporters and photographers pressed into the radar room at National Airport to watch the UFOs cavort. Quickly, however, the media were ordered out with the explanation that classified radio frequencies and procedures would be used to vector fighters to the UFOs. "I knew that this was absurd because any ham radio operator worth his salt could build equipment and listen in on any intercept," Ruppelt later wrote. He said he learned that the real reason for dismissing the media was to prevent them from learning the reality of the UFOs, should one be brought down.

F-94 military jets were sent aloft to intercept the bogies, which were flying through restricted airspace. But every time the jets would close in, the UFOs would accelerate and disappear. Radar positions would be given, but ground observers couldn't see anything. It was all very frustrating. And the news media had a ball. "Fiery Objects Outrun Jets over Capital—Investigation Veiled in Secrecy Following Vain Chase" and "Jets Alerted for Saucers—Interceptors Chase Lights in D.C. Skies" screamed the headlines.

Responding to the clamor, Maj. Gen. John Samford called a news conference for the afternoon of July 29. It was the largest and longest press conference convened by the air force since World War II. According to Ruppelt, General Samford hedged on some questions simply because he didn't have an answer. He finally passed the buck to an intelligence officer who speculated that the hubbub over Washington was caused by temperature inversions, a phenomenon creating pockets of warm air unable to rise due to similar temperature layers in the sky. Temperature inversions might reflect light and might be picked up on radar, it was explained. The news media then reported "Air Force Debunks Saucers as Just Natural Phenomena."

The Civilian Aeronautics Authority, forerunner of the Federal Aviation Administration, conducted a study and concluded that "temperature inversion had been indicated in almost every instance" of the Washington sightings. It was an explanation warmly embraced by debunker Peebles but systematically picked apart by Ruppelt. Blue Book's investigation determined that UFOs had been seen frequently over Washington—fifty targets were tracked on May 23 alone—and that each night there was a sighting the temperature inversions were never strong enough to affect radar. Ruppelt also found that while inversions occurred almost every night during June, July, and August, the "slow-moving, 'solid' radar targets appeared only on those few nights." "So the Washington National Airport Sightings are still unknowns," Ruppelt concluded.

The CIA Takes Control

Following the mid-1952 Washington saucer scare, the factions within Blue Book were beginning to agree on one thing—it was time to end the official secrecy regarding UFOs.

This idea was hurried along due to Secretary of the Navy Dan Kimball, who had his own UFO experience while flying to Hawaii in April 1952. Two disc-shaped craft, flying at speeds estimated at more than 1,500 miles per hours—an impossible speed in those days— zoomed in and circled Kimball's executive plane and another plane carrying Adm. Arthur Radford. Upon landing, Kimball radioed the air force with a report. Some time later, Kimball was outraged to learn that the air force had apparently not seriously investigated his case but would not even release to him what analysis they did prepare. He quickly ordered the navy to begin a parallel UFO investigation with the newly created air force. This action soon yielded one of the best documented UFO cases to that time.

On July 15, 1952, Navy Chief Warrant Officer Delbert C. Newhouse and his wife had just driven through Tremonton, Utah, just north of Salt Lake City, when they saw a group of twelve to fourteen bright shiny objects maneuvering in formation at high speeds. Stopping his car, Newhouse, a navy photographer for twenty-one years, grabbed his film camera and set the turret at the three-inch telephoto lens. He exposed about forty feet of film before the objects flew out of sight. Moments before disappearing, one of the objects split off from the main group and headed east. Later, Newhouse said the objects looked like "two pie pans, one inverted on the top of the other."

This time the film went to the Navy Photo Interpretation Laboratory near Washington, where analysts closely studied the objects and soon ruled out aircraft, balloons, and birds. Their final conclusion was "unknown objects under intelligent control."

With the navy entering the UFO picture with this startling film footage and with Ruppelt and the air force officers wanting to speak publicly about interplanetary spaceships, it appeared obvious from the standpoint of a person in highest authority that something had to be done. And it was.

Major Keyhoe, a man with considerable insider contacts, later reported that he learned that the CIA had been keeping tabs on the UFO situation and the air force investigation almost since its inception. "Admiral Hillenkoetter told me afterward, this had been going on since 1948, when he was CIA director," wrote Keyhoe. This was the same Hillenkoetter named in the dubious MJ-12 papers.

According to Keyhoe, the CIA managed to stall any meaningful action by Navy Secretary Kimball until after the November 1952 elections. With the election of Dwight Eisenhower, a Republican, Kimball became a lame duck and lost strength in his effort to break up UFO censorship. "Even though the Kimball threat seemed ended," Keyhoe wrote, "the CIA knew another Navy fight could erupt, and the AF had shown it was not tough enough to cope with such a danger. The only answer was to seize control of the AF investigation and insist on a hard-boiled, ruthless censorship, to kill off public belief in UFOs."

To this end, CIA officials convened a panel of distinguished scientists to make a secret study of the UFO evidence up to that time. The CIA director in early 1953 was Walter Bedell Smith, another name on the MJ-12 documents. Smith was replaced that same year by CIA Deputy Director Allen Dulles, a former Office of Strategic Services officer under William "Wild Bill" Donovan and one of the men who help create the CIA. Dulles's brother, John Foster Dulles, was Eisenhower's secretary of state. The Dulles brothers would set U.S. foreign policy for almost a decade.

In a 1952 memorandum, CIA director Smith told the National Security Council, "Since 1947, approximately 2,000 official reports of sightings have been received and, of these, about 20 percent are as yet unexplained. It is my view that this situation has possible implications for our national security which transcend the interest of a single service. A broader, coordinated effort should be initiated to develop a firm scientific understanding of the several phenomena which apparently are involved in these reports, and to assure ourselves that the incidents will not hamper our present efforts in the Cold War or confuse our early warning system in case of an attack." In another Smith memo, declassified in 1977, he told the director of the CIA's Psychological Strategy Board that he was sending the NSC a proposal "in which it is concluded that the problems connected with unidentified flying objects appear to have implications for psychological warfare as well as for intelligence and operations."

The CIA scientists—which interestingly included Dr. Lloyd Berkner, another name on the MJ-12 list—began meeting on January 14, 1953, in Washington. The panel was chaired by Dr. H. P. Robertson, a California Institute of Technology physicist tightly connected with U.S. intelligence. In 1943, Robertson had studied the German V-1 program and reported to the government that it was a legitimate threat. One member, Johns Hopkins University astronomer Dr.

Thornton L. Page, set the tone. "At the start I thought it was a lot of nonsense and said so," he recalled. Page was silenced by Robertson, who went to some length to assure everyone present that the CIA-created study was to be serious and open-minded. He and his allies on the panel then set out to debunk every bit of UFO information presented, including a "very hot and very highly controversial study" initiated by Ruppelt and Blue Book government liaison officer Maj. Dewey Fournet. "The study was hot because it wasn't official and the reason it wasn't official was because it was so hot," wrote Ruppelt. "It concluded that the UFOs were interplanetary spaceships."

J. Allen Hynek, who had returned as an adviser to both Blue Book and the Robertson panel, later wrote he was dissatisfied with the panel's cursory examination and lack of curiosity. Furthermore, he stated, "The panel was not given access to many of the truly puzzling cases."

"Supposedly, this was to be a careful, objective examination of the best verified reports," wrote Keyhoe. "Actually, the CIA-selected scientists were known skeptics. Most of them had no real knowledge of UFOs and they considered the subject nonsense." The CIA men in charge of the scientists limited the material and skewed it in such a way that led the willing panelists to a negative view of UFOs. Keyhoe said he was told by one of the AF officers at the meeting, "We were double-crossed. The CIA doesn't want to prepare the public—they're trying to bury the subject. Those agents ran the whole show and the scientists followed their lead. They threw out the Utah film—said the Navy analysts were incompetent. We had over a hundred of the strongest verified reports. The agents bypassed the best ones. The scientists saw just 15 cases, and the CIA men tried to pick holes in them."

Under these circumstances, it was not surprising that the Robertson panel concluded that "evidence presented on Unidentified Flying Objects shows no indication that these phenomena constitute a direct physical threat to national security" but added that "the continued emphasis on the reporting of these phenomena does, in these perilous times, result in a threat to the orderly functioning of the protective organs of the body politic . . . that the national security agencies take immediate steps to strip the Unidentified Flying Objects of the special status they have been given and the aura of mystery they have unfortunately acquired." They were more concerned with public perceptions than with the phenomenon itself.

Al Chop, Project Blue Book's civilian press officer, told Keyhoe, "They killed the whole program. We've been ordered to work up a national debunking campaign, planting articles in magazines and

arranging broadcasts to make UFO reports sound like poppycock."
Keyhoe quoted Ruppelt as adding, "What Al Chop told you isn't the
worst of it. We're ordered to hide sightings when possible, but if a
strong report does get out we have to publish a fast explanation—make
up something to kill the report in a hurry, and also ridicule the witness,
especially if we can't figure out a plausible answer. We even have to
discredit our own pilots. It's a raw deal but we can't buck the CIA. The
whole thing makes me sick—I'm thinking of putting in for inactive."

Substantiation for this policy of secrecy came from none other
than Senator Richard B. Russell of Georgia, who then served as chairman of the Senate Armed Services Committee and later as a member
of the Warren Commission. Russell, after sighting a UFO while in
Europe, declined to speak publicly about his experience, stating, "I
have discussed this with the affected agencies of the government and
they are of the opinion that it is unwise to publicize the matter at this
time."

Deceit also was a part of the secrecy policy. Despite the 1947
Twining memo that concluded UFOs were "something real and not
visionary or fictitious," Air Force Headquarters Lt. Col. L. J. Tacker in
the early 1950s stated emphatically, "There never has been an official
Air Force conclusion that the Flying Saucers are real."

To give some idea of both how long this policy of secrecy and
deceit was maintained and at what levels, it is instructive to consider a
letter to Keyhoe from former House majority leader John McCormack, who said he was unable to gain UFO information even in closed
sessions with top air force officers despite "strong efforts" to learn the
truth. Further substantiation came from Senator Barry Goldwater,
who served as chairman of the Senate Intelligence Committee. In a
letter written on March 28, 1975, Goldwater stated, "The subject of
UFOs is one that has interested me for some long time. About 10 or
12 years ago I made an effort to find out what was in the building at
Wright-Patterson Air Force Base where the information is stored that
has been collected by the Air Force, and I was understandably denied
this request. It is still classified above Top Secret." In 1979, Goldwater,
who for years was a major general in the Air Force Reserve, wrote to
researcher Lee Graham, "This thing has gotten so highly classified . . .
it is just impossible to get anything on it." It seems incredible, but
UFOs—which officially don't exist—are so wrapped in secrecy that
even ranking senators cannot get at information about the subject.

In fact the entire military-UFO issue became a "catch-22" situation. Dr. Robertson, in comparing the UFO investigation to his own
study of German guided missiles at the end of the war, noted, "The
absence of any 'hardware' resulting from unexplained UFO sightings

lends a 'will-o'-the-wisp' nature to the ATIC problem." In other words, only "hardware" could prove the reality of UFOs. But any "hardware" to be had was hidden away by the military.

"The Robertson Panel did get someplace," concluded Hynek later. "They made the subject of UFOs scientifically unrespectable, and for nearly 20 years not enough attention was paid to the subject to acquire the kind of data needed even to decide the nature of the UFO phenomenon."

In this atmosphere, it was no wonder that ranking members of Project Blue Book begin leaving after the Robertson panel dissolved; by 1956 Major Ruppelt was one of these. Later that year, Ruppelt published his authoritative book, *The Report on Unidentified Flying Saucers*, which was critical of the air force's handling of the subject and supportive of the idea of extraterrestrial visitation. According to author Paris Flammonde, "Captain Ruppelt, with Dr. J. Allen Hynek, was probably the best, most honest man the military ever had operating in the area of Unidentified Flying Objects." This assessment has been echoed by many others familiar with the investigation in those days. As the former head of Project Blue Book, Ruppelt lent unquestioned authority to the UFO subject and would have been a person to be stopped by anyone hoping to distract the public from the issue.

His attitude, much to the relief of the debunkers, changed within two years. In May 1958, Ruppelt wrote a letter to a member of the National Investigations Committee on Aerial Phenomena (NICAP) reversing his position. Sounding very much like an official press release, Ruppelt wrote, "I have visited Project Blue Book since 1953 and am now convinced that the reports of UFOs are nothing more than reports of balloons, aircraft, astronomical phenomena, etc. I don't believe they are anything from outer space." Was his conversion real, or had Ruppelt been muzzled in some way? No one can say for certain, since Ruppelt died only two years later.

Reportedly, Ruppelt's widow said his change of mind was due to the continuing lack of physical UFO evidence as well as the introduction of contactees into the issue. Keyhoe had another version. "[Ruppelt] frequently gave me valuable leads, and when I became director of NICAP he steadily cooperated, praising the organization for its struggle against secrecy. But in 1959 this suddenly ended. Ruppelt then was working with an aerospace company with Air Force contracts. Something happened which obviously put him under heavy pressure to stop criticizing AF UFO activities. One explanation—which is unproved—is that the AF implied his company contracts and his job might suffer if he did not cooperate. Perhaps there is another answer, something powerful enough to make him give in. The main target was his revealing book. Somehow, he was forced to repudiate it completely. . . . Like several others who knew Ruppelt well, I have always believed that the enforced retraction and bitter criticism [of his integrity] were partly the cause of his premature death from a heart attack."

After the departure of Ruppelt and others from Blue Book, one thing became very clear, although it was little understood both at the time and even by modern UFO researchers: The CIA, despite their protests, had taken hidden control of the official UFO investigation.

Yet the air force's Blue Book project continued as the visible response of the government. "The Air Force entered upon a long period of unfortunate, amateurish public relations," wrote Hynek, who remained as a consultant. He added, "Some of the Blue Book evaluations of sincere reports were often so transparent and irrelevant that they had later to be retracted." Hynek sensed—or knew but couldn't say—the truth of the situation when he wrote, "Was this all a smoke-screen, a cover-up job for which Project Blue Book was a front, the real work and information being handled by another agency?" Ruppelt stated that an "unpublicized but highly important change took place: another intelligence agency began to take over all field investigations."

The screening of UFO reports began with the 4602nd Air Intelligence Service Squadron, which during another reorganization of Project Blue Book in March 1954 was designated as the group's chief investigators. Only sightings that could not be explained away by the 4602nd would be passed along to the Blue Book offices. Unexplainable reports went to what Ruppelt only called "another intelligence agency." Coral Lorenzen, who would become director of the Aerial Phenomena Research Organization (APRO), had worked at Holloman Air Force Base in New Mexico for several years. She too came to suspect that Blue Book was "nothing more than a public relations front" and "that if a cover-up was in effect, it was being accomplished at CIA level or higher."

Author Peebles explained, "The goal of Blue Book was to lessen public hysteria in order to lower the number of reports and lessen the danger of missing signs of an impending Soviet attack." If this indeed was the goal, it proved to be a dismal failure. In 1962, Edward R. Trapnell, assistant for public relations to the secretary of the air force, was shocked to learn that by that time the rate of UFO sightings was three times higher than in the early days of Project Blue Book.

As the 1960s began, the air force tried several times to rid itself of Project Blue Book. In July 1957, with private UFO groups charging a cover-up, the 4602nd AISS was disbanded and its investigative functions transferred to the 1006th Air Intelligence Service Squadron, which curtailed activities due to limited funding. ATIC first sought to pass Blue Book to the Air Research and Development Command, but the ARDC declined. The AF Office of Public Information also wanted nothing to do with the headaches connected with UFO investigations. It was even suggested that NASA take over the investigation of UFOs. However, this idea was nipped in the bud when it was pointed out that such a move might convince even more people that aliens and their spaceships were something real. In the end, Blue Book remained within the air force, a quiet office where only the most explainable sightings were sent for filing and public dissemination.

But if the air force was quiet, the entire UFO situation was anything but.

Giant Artificial Satellites

Not only did UFO sightings increase, but stories even stranger than simple lights in the sky began to circulate. One of the earliest of these was reported by Maj. Donald Keyhoe, the leading advocate of the theory that the government and military were hiding the truth.

In his book *Aliens from Space*, Keyhoe flatly stated, "Since 1953, [the air force] had known that giant spaceships were operating near our planet." He said it was during that year that the military began experimenting with new long-range radar equipment. "While making the initial tests," Keyhoe wrote, "AF operators were astonished to pick up a gigantic object orbiting near the equator. Its speed was almost 18,000 miles an hour. Repeated checks showed that the tracking was correct. Some huge unknown object was circling the Earth, 600 miles out." According to Keyhoe, shortly after this object was detected, a second large object came into orbit about four hundred miles out and was also tracked on air force radar.

Keyhoe wrote, "Alarmed Defense Department heads hurriedly set up an emergency satellite-detection project at White Sands, New Mexico. The scientist in charge of this secret search was Dr. Clyde Tombaugh, discoverer of the planet Pluto [and] the only noted astronomer who had admitted sighting a UFO. The 'sky sweep' was a combined armed forces project, under Army Ordnance Research."

A serious look at this preposterous-sounding story yielded a good example of the ambiguity and secretiveness associated with the UFO phenomenon.

Keyhoe's story of the detection of two giant satellites was supported by investigative journalist Warren Smith, who stated that a CIA source told him that huge unidentified satellites were picked up on at least thirteen separate occasions in 1953. Dr. Tombaugh indeed was chosen in 1953 to head a satellite search program encompassing the world. And he did have a UFO experience about the same time as Kenneth Arnold.

Shortly before 5:00 P.M. on July 10, 1947, Tombaugh, his wife, and his two daughters were driving down a New Mexico highway when he observed a "curious shiny object" hovering in the air. It was a well-defined elliptical object whose surface appeared polished. The object began rising and accelerated through some cloud cover at a speed estimated by Tombaugh at between six hundred and nine hundred miles per hour. The astronomer concluded, "The remarkably sudden ascent convinced me it was an absolutely novel airborne device."

It is most interesting that a scientist with such an experience was selected to head a satellite search program four years before the Soviets put *Sputnik I* into orbit. It is also interesting to note that in March 1954, after word of Tombaugh's secret satellite search project was published in an article in the newsletter of the Astronomical Society of the Pacific, Army Ordnance officials at White Sands issued a press release stating that the military was searching for small "moonlets" similar to asteroids that had come from space and entered orbit around the earth.

This story was picked up by *Time* magazine, which carried the headline "Second Moon?" in its March 15, 1954, edition. According to this article, "Astronomer Clyde Tombaugh, who spotted the planet Pluto (1930), is looking for a nearer and even more elusive object: a second satellite of the Earth. [Army Ordnance] may merely want to know what opposition from nature their rockets are apt to encounter when they climb deep into space. Or they may have a more ambitious interest: a nearby, natural satellite might be a more convenient base in space than the much-discussed artificial satellite." The article said Dr. Tombaugh refused to give any details of his program, referring all questions to Army Ordnance in Washington. This prompted *Time* writers to comment, "It is fair to assume that the famous rocket men who work for Army Ordnance are interested in the project." The article then discussed the possibility of a new satellite, but in a strange, ambiguous manner: "A small satellite close to the Earth would be hard to spot. It might circle near the Equator, invisible to most of the world's observatories. In any case, it would spend nearly half its time in the shadow of the Earth, where it would be invisible."

Speculative as this sounded, the article then prompted its readers to help look for such an object, stating, "Best time to look for a small satellite would be at dawn or dusk, when it would be shining brightly. . . ."

Further notice of this story came in the March 20, 1954, edition of *Science News Letter*, which noted that "a telescopic search for the circling moonlets is being made for the armed forces by Drs. Clyde Tombaugh and Lincoln La Paz, director of the Institute of Meteoritics of the University of New Mexico, Albuquerque, New Mexico." The article quoted Dr. G. M. Clemence, director of the U.S. Naval Observatory, as saying that chances that one or more small satellites exist between the earth and the moon are "very good" but "spotting them will be difficult." "Such tiny objects, which could serve as ready-made space platforms, might have made Earth-splashing meteorites if they had not been captured by our planet's magnetic field," he added. This article also advised the best way to both observe and photograph the new satellites. "Move the camera at the same speed as the satellite being hunted would flash through the sky," it advised.

Were there satellites there or not? The record remained ambiguous. In its October 1955 edition, a writer for *Popular Mechanics* described Tombaugh's small metal shed on the grounds of the Lowell Observatory in Flagstaff, Arizona, where "a close watch will be kept on the satellite that the United States plans to launch in 1957–58." "From this shed," the article continued, "the United States already is maintaining a surveillance of the space that surrounds the Earth, all the way out to the moon. From here, presumably, regular observations are being made of the Earth's first artificial satellite that is rumored to have been launched into space a year ago. Exclusively reported in the May, 1955, issue of *Popular Mechanics*, the existence of this manmade moon has not yet been officially confirmed. But unofficially it is understood that our first artificial satellite is still sweeping around the Earth. The latest information is that its orbit is slowly changing into an ellipse because of the pull of the moon. Possibly the success of this first experiment lies behind the announcement that we will launch an instrument-carrying satellite two years from now, in connection with the International Geophysical Year, to gather new information about outer space."

The May 1955 *Popular Mechanics* had indeed reported that for some time "persistent" reports from "various independent sources" had described a satellite traveling more than sixteen thousand miles per hour at a distance of eight hundred miles out. The magazine noted, "The implication is that this was an experiment which worked too well. A rocket that was expected to return to Earth inside a certain impact area kept on going . . . at an angle and speed that put it into orbit around the Earth."

Popular Mechanics editors stated that Dr. Tombaugh's satellite search equipment was so sensitive "it could detect a white tennis ball 1,000 miles away." Then they presented a most peculiar quote: "Professor Tombaugh is closed mouth about his results. He won't say whether or not any small natural satellites have been discovered. He does say, however, that newspaper reports of 18 months ago announcing the discovery of natural satellites at 400 and 600 miles out are not correct. He adds that there is no connection between the search program and the reports of so-called flying saucers." Since no one but himself had brought up the subject of flying saucers, Tombaugh obviously knew more than he was saying.

Then came an announcement by astronomer John P. Bagby through the Adler Planetarium in Chicago that "tiny moons" had been discovered orbiting the earth at a distance of 475 miles and traveling about eighteen thousand miles per hour. Bagby, a member of the American Meteor Society and the Royal Astronomical Society of Canada, said he had enlisted the aid of several skilled amateur astronomers to help him track the objects. Bagby, like Tombaugh, never hinted that these "moons" might be artificial.

Cpt. Howard T. Orville, head of the President's Weather Control Commission, was asked during a radio interview if he knew of any conditions under which two objects could have naturally entered orbit around the Earth. "No, not that I know," replied Orville. The captain admitted that the circumstances of the orbiting objects was puzzling, but noted that "military security would prevent discussion."

To compound the mystery, a NASA press release in October 1954 stated that the agency had picked up strange signals from an unknown orbiting object. This announcement was corroborated by a French astronomer who claimed to have also detected indecipherable signals from some unknown source in orbit around the earth. Then in 1955, nationally syndicated newspaper columnist Steward Alsop wrote that he had discovered through insiders within government agencies that the satellite detection program actually was looking for artificial satellites. Well into the 1970s, Dr. Tombaugh still had not published the results of his satellite search.

Keyhoe said such large craft had already been sighted prior to the radar contacts in 1953. He claimed that before the CIA took over the UFO investigation, he saw a 1952 report about an air force bomber crew that tracked a formation of UFOs at more than five thousand miles per hour over the Gulf of Mexico. Suddenly another formation of UFOs came up behind the bomber, slowed down, then raced past it. A large ship had suddenly appeared on the bomber's radar, which showed all the smaller UFOs merging with the larger craft. "Evidently this was a prearranged rendezvous for retrieving the smaller-sized units," surmised Keyhoe. "As soon as they were taken aboard, the huge carrier ship accelerated to a speed of over 9,000 miles per hour and went off the scope."

Keyhoe even had a theory on what had prompted the sudden outbreak of UFO activity in the late 1940s. In his 1955 book, *The Flying Saucer Conspiracy*, Keyhoe related the story of how Swiss physicist and astronomer Dr. Fritz Zwicky participated in a secret Army Ordnance project to bombard the moon, Mars, and other planets with projectiles launched on V-2 rockets in 1946.

Zwicky, who had been director of research at California's Aeroject Engineering Corporation from 1943 to 1946, reportedly developed a plan to carry scores of projectiles high into the ionosphere, where "shaped charges" would blast them into deep space. It was hoped that when these projectiles struck other space bodies at high velocities it would create a huge nuclear-like explosion that might provide important data on the world's makeup to observing Earth scientists.

"Missiles like that could cause real trouble," surmised Keyhoe. "If they hit an inhabited planet—say, Mars—the people would certainly believe we were trying to attack them. I'd think that if they did it to us." He added that the onslaught of UFO activity may have been to ascertain if the missiles being fired from the earth were meant as aggression. Keyhoe said such tests may have been stopped, but noted that the damage had already been done.

Based on all the evidence, it is apparent that something large was orbiting the earth in 1953. But if anyone within or without government knew for certain what it was, they have yet to go public with this knowledge.

According to Keyhoe, the authorities lost contact with both satellites prior to 1955. But prior to that loss, there was an apparent effort to divert public suspicions by terming the satellites natural objects. An Associated Press story stated, "Pentagon scare over the observance of two previously unobserved satellites orbiting the Earth has dissipated with the identification of the objects as natural, not artificial, satellites. Dr. Lincoln La Paz, expert on extraterrestrial bodies, of the University of New Mexico, headed the identification project. One satellite was orbiting at about 400 miles out, while the other was tracked at 600 miles." La Paz later retracted his statement, probably realizing how foolish the idea that natural satellites could simply arrive and orbit the planet sounded.

Something obviously was going on in the years just preceding the successful launch of the Sputnik satellite—but exactly what? There could have been no secret launch of a U.S. satellite, or we certainly would never have long allowed the Russians to claim the distinction of putting up the world's first satellite. It was not a Russian satellite, or they would have gleefully revealed it. The idea that anything natural could come in from space and somehow find just the right speed and trajectory to enter orbit is dubious at best. Since there were no reports of giant meteors falling to Earth, this leaves only the possibility of giant UFOs that entered orbit, then departed.

Whatever was circling the globe did not fall but left orbit before the launching of *Sputnik I*—an impossibility for any natural object. Even odder was the naïveté of the American public in accepting the military's story that two "moonlets" had suddenly moved into orbit around the earth, then disappeared. It was another example of mind-set overcoming critical thinking.

NICAP Fights Secrecy

By the mid-1950s small groups of UFO enthusiasts were gathering across the United States and calling themselves flying saucer clubs. Most fell to internal bickering and did not last long. One of the most successful—and powerful—was the National Investigations Commit-tee on Aerial Phenomena (NICAP), formed in early 1956 and formally incorporated on October 24.

After initial struggles with inadequate funding and personal squabbles, Maj. Donald E. Keyhoe was elected director. He soon assembled an impressive board of governors, which included former CIA director Hillenkoetter, former Blue Book liaison officer Fournet, Aircraft Owners and Pilots Association president J. B. Hartranft, Canadian Department of Transport engineer Wilbert B. Smith, radio commentator Frank Edwards, and a slew of ranking military officers and scientists.

One of Keyhoe's first moves at tearing down the curtain of UFO secrecy seemed reasonable enough. With the clout of NICAP behind him, Keyhoe sought public congressional hearings on the issue. After all, the much publicized army-McCarthy hearings had recently brought down the demagoguery of anti-Communist senator Joseph McCarthy. Keyhoe and NICAP members felt it was time to clear the air about UFOs. Keyhoe's contact with Senator John McClellan's Sen-ate Subcommittee on Investigations was well received and hearings appeared imminent.

However, in January 1958, after meeting with air force officials, McClellan's subcommittee chief counsel, Donald O'Donnell, advised the group to drop the matter—and they did. Keyhoe commented, "They've given in under pressure, obviously."

Meanwhile, Keyhoe had another experience that convinced him—and many others—that free discussion of UFOs was being muz-zled at very high levels. Keyhoe was invited to participate on a live broadcast of the CBS television program *Armstrong Circle Theater*. However, he was required to use a preapproved script. When air force officials objected to Keyhoe reading from government reports, the network cut out the offending statements. Keyhoe cried "censored script," while the network stated it did not want "an open battle with the Air Force." When the show, entitled "UFOs: Enigma of the Skies," was broadcast on January 22, 1958, the frustrated Keyhoe blurted out, "And now I'm going to reveal something that has never been disclosed before. . . . For the last six months, we have been working with a congressional committee investigating official secrecy about UFOs. If all the evidence we have given this committee is made public in open hearings it will absolutely prove that the UFOs are real machines under intelligent control." Before he completed the first sentence, his microphone was turned off. No one in the broadcast audience heard his complete statement. For whatever purpose, it was an obvious move to censor talk about UFOs.

Thwarted in their attempt to initiate hearings before the McClellan subcommittee, Keyhoe and his supporters in NICAP continued to seek an official investigation. Their efforts were rewarded somewhat in February 1958, when a McClellan subcommittee investigator confirmed that the CIA was behind the Robertson panel. This revelation prompted further congressional interest. In June 1958, responding to an inquiry by Ohio representative John E. Henderson, air force officers provided a "special" briefing for congressmen. Whatever was revealed mollified the politicians, who informed the voters that any UFO publicity at that time would be "unwise."

In August, Representative McCormack requested a hearing on UFOs before his House Subcommittee on Atmospheric Phenomena. The weeklong meeting with air force officials was closed to the public and unrecorded. Whatever was said here also "apparently satisfied" the politicians, who discontinued any further hearings. "To close off the possibility that NICAP and Keyhoe might try again," noted author Curtis Peebles, "the Air Force established a new policy in 1959. The policy statement said that the Senate Permanent Subcommittee on Investigations had periodically requested information [on UFOs] and, after preliminary investigation, they indicated that it did not plan to hold hearings."

Keyhoe and NICAP continued to press for public hearings dealing with UFOs, and the air force—which still denied their existence—continued to stall. In 1961, McCormack enlisted the service of Representative Overton Brooks to study UFOs. Brooks, chairman of the House Science and Astronautics Committee, created a Subcommittee on Space Problems and Life Sciences and scheduled hearings for early 1962. But in August 1961, a Brooks assistant, Richard P. Hinds, was given a private tour and briefing by air force intelligence. One week later Hinds reported to the air force that Brooks had decided not to conduct the UFO hearings.

Regardless of Keyhoe's motives or credibility, he was correct in stating that the government in the form of the air force was making extraordinary efforts to prevent any meaningful public debate over UFOs. And obviously something was being said to would-be congressional investigators that convinced them to abandon attempts at finding the truth behind the UFOs. What information could be so powerful that veteran politicians would refrain from conducting highly visible public hearings on a topic of such great concern to so many people? There are no hard-and-fast answers even today, since the curtain of secrecy remains drawn tight.

A Landing at Socorro

One UFO incident that took place during the time that Keyhoe and others were trying to interest Congress in the subject concerned a police officer and a landed UFO. Hynek called it "one of the classics of UFO literature."

About 5:45 P.M. on April 24, 1964, Patrolman Lonnie Zamora, a five-year veteran of the Socorro, New Mexico, police department, was chasing a speeding black Chevrolet north on U.S. 85 when he heard a roaring sound that changed from high frequency to low frequency and then stopped. He then saw a flame in the southwest sky and became concerned that a dynamite shack in that area belonging to the Socorro mayor might have exploded. Abandoning his chase, Zamora turned off the highway and drove over rough gravel road toward the flame, which he described as blue and orange, pointing downward, and narrower at the top.

After being slowed attempting to drive up a steep incline, Zamora reached the top and noticed a shiny object between 150 and 200 yards south of his position. He thought at first glance it was a car turned upside down. Then he saw it was an egg-shaped object that appeared to be made of aluminum or some shiny white metal. He saw two figures in white coveralls standing beside the object. They appeared normal in shape but diminutive, either "small adults or large kids." One of them turned to look at his patrol car and appeared startled, jumping slightly.

Zamora lost sight of the pair and the craft as he maneuvered his car around some low hills toward the site. When he reached the object, it began ascending into the sky with a roar "not like a jet." He noticed a two-and-a-half-foot insignia on the side, which looked like a stick arrow pointing up over a horizontal straight line enclosed in a semicircle. Much later, UFO author Jacques Vallee, who reportedly was portrayed as the French scientist Lacombe in Steven Spielberg's film *Close Encounters of the Third Kind*, would identify this insignia as the Arabic astrological sign for Venus.

Fearful of the noise and the flames now issuing from the craft, Zamora sought protection behind his car but stumbled and lost his prescription glasses. The object, after rising straight up, moved off horizontally, "traveling very fast." Zamora said the craft left behind smoldering plants that were oddly cold to the touch.

Very soon, Sgt. M. S. Chavez of the New Mexico State Police joined Zamora, and they both examined indentations in the earth where Zamora said the UFO had rested. These marks were still there some time later when Hynek arrived to investigate. "I visited the site several days later and verified the landing marks and the charred plants. Chavez had, he told me in a long interview, verified the marks and the burned greasewood plants, which had still been smoldering at the time he first met Zamora at the site."

Although Hynek was unable to interest the air force in making an in-depth investigation of the Socorro incident, he personally continued to look into the affair for nearly a year. "My original investigations, directed toward breaking apart Zamora's account by seeking mutual contradictions in it and also by seeking to establish Zamora as an unreliable witness, were fruitless," wrote Hynek. "I was impressed by the high regard in which Zamora was held by his colleagues, and I personally am willing today to accept his testimony as genuine, particularly since it does fit a global pattern."

Impressive as the Zamora story was, mind-set once again came into play. Dr. Donald Menzel, the longtime UFO debunker whose name was on the infamous MJ-12 list, speculated that Zamora's speeding motorist was a decoy who lured the officer to the remote site, then used a walkie-talkie to signal hoaxers, who released a balloon with a phony flying saucer attached to it. This grasping-for-straws theory was put to rest by Hynek, who noted that a brisk wind was from the south that day and the UFO flew west. Debunker Philip Klass discounts Zamora's accounting of the landing because the marks at Socorro don't correspond to the symmetrical landing legs of NASA spacecraft. Both Klass and, more recently, Peebles take particular note that the landing site was on property owned by the Socorro mayor, who later discussed a tourist attraction. "The implication was the landing was a hoax, to bring in tourist dollars," he wrote.

Neither Peebles nor Klass took note that two days after the

Socorro sighting, the Orlando Gallego family of La Medera, New Mexico—all of whom declared they had heard nothing of the Socorro incident—reported seeing a UFO land that was identical to the one described by Zamora. Police officers found charred vegetation around the La Medera landing site as well as four depressions in the ground, just as at Socorro.

While the hard-nosed debunkers remained unpersuaded, Hynek was slowly changing his mind about the validity of UFOs. One case that helped open his mind was brought to his attention in 1961 while he was on an official Blue Book visit to the British Air Ministry. "I learned at that time that the British military view of the UFO problem was essentially the same as that of Blue Book; indeed, the British—and other governments as well—were looking to the U.S. Air Force to solve the problem," he said, apparently unaware that the CIA was the true authority behind UFO investigations. Hynek also learned of an incredible UFO sighting that occurred during two nights in June 1959, and involved a priest.

Reverend William Bruce Gill, an Anglican priest and graduate of Brisbane University, was in charge of a mission in Boainai, Papua, New Guinea. By June 26, 1959, there had been more than sixty UFO sightings in New Guinea. Reverend Gill was outdoors and observing Venus about 6:45 P.M. when he noticed above the planet a bright, sparkling object that began descending toward him. Several mission members joined him as the craft drew nearer. It was circular with a wide base from which four "legs" protruded. Occasionally a blue shaft of light would project from the object into the sky, and soon four figures were visible on the upper deck of the craft. Shortly after 7:00 P.M. the craft rose through accumulating clouds and disappeared, only to come back in about an hour. This time several smaller circular ships maneuvered around the larger one, their lights reflecting on the clouds.

Despite his experience, Reverend Gill was somewhat skeptical. To a friend he wrote, "I do not doubt the existence of these 'things'— indeed I cannot now that I have seen one for myself—but my simple mind still requires scientific evidence before I can accept the from-outer-space theory. I am inclined to believe that probably many UFOs are more likely some form of electric phenomena or perhaps something brought about by the atom bomb explosions, etc. . . . It is all too difficult to understand for me; I prefer to wait for some bright boy to catch one. . . ." His letter was signed "Doubting William."

The next day the friend received another letter from Reverend Gill, stating, "Life is strange, isn't it? Yesterday I wrote you a letter . . . expressing opinions re the UFOs. Now, less than 24 hours later, I have changed my views somewhat. Last night we at Boainai experienced about four hours of UFO activity, and there is no doubt whatsoever that they are handled by beings of some kind. At times it was absolutely breathtaking. Here is the report. . . ."

Rev. Gill's second report was even more remarkable than the first. On the night of June 27, a mission nurse summoned the reverend to observe a bright, shiny, round object descending toward them. As it approached, figures again could be seen on an upper deck. "And so we waved," reported Reverend Gill, "like that—Hello—and we were a bit surprised now, and the thing waved back. And then Eric, who was with me, my constant companion, waved his two arms, along with another lad, and the figures waved two arms back."

Not only was Reverend Gill's mind changed, but the case hastened along the conversion of Dr. Hynek, who wrote he was "impressed by the quality and number of the witnesses and by the character and demeanor of Reverend Gill as revealed by his report and tapes." Debunker Menzel poo-pooed the whole event, stating that Rev. Gill only saw Venus without his eyeglasses and his congregation all signed statements just to be supportive. Menzel's theory conveniently ignored the fact that the cleric plainly said the episode began as he was watching Venus and that the craft came under cloud cover. His theory regarding Reverend Gill's eyesight was that astigmatism was the "assumed myopic condition of Father Gill" or that "Part of the effect may have been from eyelid defraction apart from irregularities, such as blood cells on the retina." Menzel's myopic arguments were enough to make many researchers think perhaps he was operating on behalf of MJ-12 or something like it.

In 1965, UFOs figured in one of the most publicized events of that year.

The Great Blackout

Over the night of November 9 and 10, 1965, a massive power blackout spread from southern Canada to Pennsylvania, affecting some thirty million people. Nearly one million were left stranded in the New York subway system. It was an event never to be forgotten by those who experienced it. And intriguingly, there were many rumors at the time linking the Great Blackout to UFO activity. Some years later, an abductee named Betty Andreasson claimed aliens admitted to her they had caused the blackout.

Immediately after the blackout, Washington officials and most power grid experts agreed that the problem began near the Clay power substation south of the giant Niagara Falls generating stations. However, no one had an explanation for why the blackout occurred. Charles Pratt, chief of the Niagara-Mohawk generating plant, said, "We have no explanation. There were no severed transmission lines, defective generators or faulty circuit breakers." A Consolidated Edison spokesman commented, "We are at a loss to explain it." Even the chairman of the Federal Power Commission, Joseph C. Swidler, said after a two-day investigation, "The Northeast blackout may never be fully explained. . . ."

Others thought they had an explanation. The Syracuse, New York, *Herald-Journal* reported UFOs were seen near the Clay substation at the time of the blackout. On November 14, NBC newsman Frank McGee reported that a pilot had sighted a UFO near the Niagara Falls power plant just before the blackout. Other media outlets picked up and circulated the UFO connection. Someone within the government must have been concerned that such speculation might lead to in-depth investigations that might crack the secrecy over UFOs.

But all UFO speculation ended on November 15, when it was announced that one broken relay in a Canadian power plant had started the whole thing. Somehow the broken relay had been missed despite an intensive five-day investigation. This explanation seemed to lull both the media and, hence, the public. But serious questions remained.

According to an article in the industry publication *Power* written by Executive Editor J. J. O'Connor, late on the afternoon of November 9, a relay tripped shut in Adam Beck Plant No. 2, disconnecting one of five powers lines to Toronto. The other Toronto lines then tripped shut and within four seconds, the entire grid connecting Canada with the United States collapsed. A large surge of power "cascaded" southward, knocking out the Clay substation and other plants. The power surge knocked out pumps, air compressors, and other auxiliary equipment, preventing immediate restarts. The entire power grid went down, leaving millions with out power for several hours—all because one small relay tripped as though from an unexpected overload.

According to Donald Keyhoe this latest explanation still was not satisfactory. While this account might explain how the collapse occurred, it did not address why.

The *Power* article reported that the errant relay was not broken but tripped shut, a job for which it was designed. The subsequent collapse of the entire electrical grid indicated that the much-vaunted grid safety system was a "dangerous fraud." "But this was preposterous," noted Keyhoe. "It would mean the utility companies had deceived the government, operating under the constant risk of a huge blackout, hoping there would be only minor power failures. The Federal Power Commission almost certainly would have discovered the conspiracy, and company heads would have been exposed to White House and congressional attack, public indignation and probably legal action. . . . Besides this, the grid safeguards had already met the threat of a large power failure. Over several years there had been a few smaller-scale blackouts and the safety devices had kept them from spreading. . . . There was only one true explanation—an unpredictable, overwhelming E[lectro]M[agnetic] interference the safety devices were not built to handle."

If Keyhoe and Andreasson were correct and the Great Blackout was caused by UFOs draining power, it didn't stop there. Through the end of November and into December 1965, there were large-scale blackouts in Minnesota, both East and West Texas, New Mexico, and Mexico.

The blackouts certainly caught the attention of those affected by them, but once a mundane explanation was offered by those in authority, whatever lessons were to be learned were quickly forgotten. Electricity blackouts could be explained in technical language indecipherable to the average citizen. There was no need for extreme explanations like "ball lightning" or "Saint Elmo's fire." In fact, it was rationales such as these that proved the death of Project Blue Book

The Condon Report

On March 20, 1966, residents of Dexter, Michigan, reported seeing a brilliant light in nearby marshland. Sheriff's deputies were summoned and approached the light, which they said was a football-shaped object with a rough, pebbled texture pulsating with light. After hovering for some time, the object shot over the witnesses' heads and disappeared. The next night, a similar object was seen by a Civil Defense director, a college dean, and eighty-seven coeds at Hillsdale College in Hillsdale, Michigan, about forty-five miles southwest of Dexter. This group watched the oval UFO maneuver for four hours and loop around an airport beacon before disappearing into nearby marshes. The number and quality of witnesses prompted Michigan State Police Commissioner Fredrick E. Davids to comment, "I used to discount these reports too but now I'm not so sure."

Dr. J. Allen Hynek was dispatched by Project Blue Book to investigate the Michigan sightings. After a few days of slogging about the marshes, Hynek held a news conference on March 26 to quell what he described as "general bedlam." In consultation with several other scientists, Hynek spoke of the possibility that the lights were caused by marsh gas, swamp lights, will-o'-the-wisp, or fox fire. This tentative explanation was picked up by Blue Book officers, who made it sound like an official position.

The nation's news media convulsed. "Air Force Insults Public with Swamp-Gas Theory" was one typical headline. Particularly incensed were the people of Michigan, who quickly pressured their representatives in Congress to counteract public perceptions of Michigan as the "Swamp Gas State." Responding to this clamor was Representative Gerald R. Ford, who in a letter to Armed Services Committee chairman L. Mendel Rivers wrote, "In the firm belief that the American public deserves a better explanation than that thus far given by the Air Force, I strongly recommend that there be a committee investigation of the UFO phenomena."

Ford's recommendation resulted in a hearing by the Rivers committee on April 5, 1966. Although literally hundreds, if not thousands, of UFO witnesses along with scientists, pilots, and officers of NICAP and APRO conversant with the best UFO cases could have been called to testify, the committee restricted testimony to only three representatives of the air force—Air Force Secretary Harold D. Brown, Blue Book commander Cpt. Hector Quintanilla, and Hynek, none of whom ever claimed to have seen a UFO.

In spite of the obvious attempt to narrow the scope of the hearing, Hynek took the opportunity to voice his changing attitude toward UFOs by stating, "Despite the seeming inanity of the subject, I felt I would be derelict in my scientific responsibility to the Air Force if I did not point out that the whole UFO phenomenon might have aspects to make it worthy of scientific attention. . . . [It] deserves close scrutiny by a civilian panel of physical and social scientists. . . . That would be the gist of my statement. However, I have been scooped by Secretary Brown, who has mentioned that the Scientific Advisory Board has recommended the same thing."

Indeed, just weeks before the hearing, a letter from the air force director of information requesting the formation of a scientific panel to review Project Blue Book had prompted Scientific Advisory Board chairman Dr. Brian O'Brian to appoint an ad hoc committee that included astronomer Carl Sagan. This group recommended that "Contracts be negotiated with a few selected universities to provide scientific teams to investigate promptly and in depth certain selected sightings of UFOs." They also recommended improved Blue Book reports but added that "anything which might suggest that information is being withheld . . . be deleted."

By the summer of 1966, several Ivy League schools had been

contacted with an eye toward conducting the civilian UFO investigation. All, well aware of the public and press clamor as well as the secrecy within the government, declined the honor.

The air force, with the CIA and possibly other intelligence groups in the background, managed to find the right blend of acceptance and credentials. On October 7, 1966, AF officials announced the University of Colorado had accepted the study, which eventually totaled more than $500,000 in government funding.

Most observers—even those who did not especially support the alien visitation theory—saw the study as a clear example of "you get what you pay for." Noted physicist Dr. Edward Uhler Condon was named director of the study, with Colorado assistant dean Robert Low as project coordinator. A former director of the National Bureau of Standards, Dr. Condon had long-standing ties to government secrecy, having worked on the development of the atomic bomb and radar. Less than three months into the study, the tone was set when Dr. Condon was quoted in the media as stating, "It is my inclination right now to recommend that the government get out of this business. My attitude right now is that there is nothing to it." "But I'm not supposed to reach a conclusion for another year," he added with a smile.

With Condon's attitude at the top clashing with the field investigators on the bottom, the study group soon broke into rival factions. Bickering and recriminations, exacerbated by external meddling by UFO organizations, believers, disbelievers, intelligence agents, and newsmen, whether well intentioned or otherwise, brought any meaningful investigation to a near standstill.

This was noted even by outside consultants. Dr. Jacques Vallee, a French-born astrophysicist who was a Department of Defense investigator, in November 1966 was one of the first scientists to be asked to brief the committee. Vallee quickly saw that Coordinator Low was "clearly the key decision maker on the team, although he had no science degree and seemed to have little interest in the matter." "Not surprisingly, a few months later the work of the committee had come to a standstill," Vallee noted.

At one point, almost all of the committee's staff were considering turning in their resignation. One who did was Mary Louise Armstrong, Condon's administrative secretary. In her resignation letter, she accused the study's leadership of foot-dragging, dissembling, and operating from "prejudged opinions." "Bob's [project coordinator Low] attitude from the beginning has been one of negativism. While I doubt that he would agree with this statement, I would expect most of the staff would. Bob showed little interest in keeping current on sightings, either by reading or talking with those that did. . . . To me, too much of his time has been spent in worrying about what kinds of 'language' should be used in the final report so as to most cleverly avoid having to say anything definitive about the UFO problem."

Armstrong alluded to outside control of the study by pointing out that Low had instructed her to send certain UFO cases containing "confidential information" to debunker (and MJ-12 listee) Dr. Donald Menzel. She also remonstrated against inaccurate conclusions, stating, "But to say in our final report, as I believe Bob would like to, that although we can't prove 'E[xtra]T[errestrial]I[ntelligence]' does not exist, we can say that there isn't much evidence to suggest it does, would not be correct. I do not understand how he can make such a statement when those who have done the work of digging into the sighting information do not think this is true."

The credibility of Low and the study suffered a further batter-ing when staffers discovered a 1966 memo from Low to the dean of Colorado University's graduate school. It may have revealed the reality behind the Condon investigation. Low wrote, "Our study would be conducted almost exclusively by nonbelievers who, although they couldn't possibly prove a negative result, could and probably would add an impressive body of evidence that there is no reality to the [UFO] observations. The trick would be, I think, to describe the proj-ect so that, to the public, it would appear a totally objective study but, to the scientific community, would present the image of a group of nonbelievers trying their best to be objective but having an almost zero expectation of finding a saucer. . . . I'm inclined to feel at this early stage that, if we set up the thing right and take pains to get the proper people involved and have success in presenting the image we want to present to the scientific community, we could carry the job off to our benefit." Infuriated that his memo leaked out, Low argued that his comments were misconstrued. The memo speaks for itself. And the Condon study followed Low's line of thinking. Two study staffers who openly criticized Condon and Low's directed verdict were fired for insubordination.

"No critique of the Condon Report can avoid mention of the choice of data for study," wrote Hynek some years later. "By concen-trating largely on current cases—40 of the 90 cases studied were in the year 1967—and also on relatively few cases out of the thousands avail-able to them, they could not pay attention to the worldwide patterns of sightings during the previous 20 years." Hynek also pointed to Con-don's definition of the purpose of his committee: "The problem then becomes that of learning to recognize the various kinds of stimuli that give rise to UFO reports." Hynek commented, "The assumption here is clearly that UFOs are all misperceptions of natural things and that the entire work of the committee was to learn and memorize the varieties of natural stimuli for UFO reports. . . ." Hynek could not restrain himself from adding, "Scientific method! What sort of scientific investigation is it that assumes the answer before starting."

Not unlike the Warren Commission before it, the Condon committee was burdened with predetermined conclusions, selective choice of evidence, and a report that made pronouncements unsupported by—or even in contrast to—its own raw data. Needless to say, no one was satisfied with the result.

In order to forestall dissatisfaction with the committee's report, the air force took steps, including dropping Dr. Hynek as a consultant after twenty years, attacking scientists who questioned the report, and arranging for a secret panel of the National Academy of Science (NAS) to review the report prior to release. In November 1968, the NAS validated the Condon Report, which prompted protests from several quarters, including former Secretary of the Interior Stewart Udall, who characterized the NAS—most of whose members were dependent on grants—as "a virtual puppet of the government."

Dr. Paul Tyler, former director of the Armed Forces Radiobiology Research Laboratory at Bethesda, Maryland, had a long association with both science and the military as both a navy captain and a medical doctor. "My experience with the National Academy of Sciences is, well, you tell me the answer you want and I will give you a committee that will give it to you. I can sandbag a committee any way you want," said Dr. Tyler, adding, "A classic case of having your mind made up before you start was the Condon report. Everybody read the Executive Summary and all everyone got was that there was nothing to it [UFOs]. But you go back and look at the raw data and maybe 15 to 20 percent of the case reports say, 'Hey, there's something here. This one may be real.' Now here's one we know was the northern lights. But this one, we don't know what it is. And Condon picked up the case that was the northern lights and shelved the other, saying, 'There's nothing to it.'"

The Condon Report was officially released on January 9, 1969, with the pompous title "Scientific Study of Unidentified Flying Objects." The report stated, "Our general conclusion is that nothing has come from the study of UFOs in the past 21 years that has added to scientific knowledge. Careful consideration of the record *as it is available to us* [emphasis added] leads us to conclude that further extensive study of UFOs probably cannot be justified in the expectation that science will be advanced thereby." In other words—there's nothing here, folks.

Even debunker Curtis Peebles, who undoubtedly embraced the

report's findings, could not wholeheartedly endorse the committee's study. "The final assessment of the Condon Study is this," he wrote. "It was impossible for the different factions to come together in a common effort. Their views were so divergent they could not understand each other. The Condon Study was a microcosm of the Sixties."

Others were less kind. "[The Condon Report is] one of the most deliberate cover-ups ever perpetrated on the public," said John Northrop, eighty-year-old founder of Northrop Aircraft Company and cofounder of Lockheed Corporation. "The 21st century will die laughing at the Condon Report." University of Arizona physicist Dr. James E. McDonald pointed out that Condon's conclusions were not supported by the full study, which contained many unexplained UFO cases. A review by a subcommittee of the American Institute of Aeronautics and Astronautics (AIAA) agreed and stated, "There are differences in the opinions and conclusions drawn by the authors of the various [report] chapters, and there are the differences between these and Condon's summary. Not all the conclusions contained in the report itself are fully reflected in Condon's summary."

Hynek, growing bolder in his assertions that UFOs were real, also concurred with McDonald regarding good information passed over by Condon, stating, "Several scientists told me that it was a study of the Condon Report that first led them to realize that the UFO problem was one worthy of investigation. The repudiation of its summary conclusions awaits, in my opinion, only a calm and unbiased study of the UFO phenomenon. . . ." Hynek added, "The Condon Report settled nothing. However, carefully read, the report constitutes about as good an argument for the study of the UFO phenomenon as could be made in a short time, and by a group of specialists in their individual disciplines having no prior knowledge of the subject."

Hynek was trying to be kind, as was author Richard L. Thompson, who wrote, "So one way to look at Condon's position is that he recognized that the UFO phenomenon threatened his scientific belief system and he chose instinctively to do what was logically required to keep that system intact."

Others claimed Condon went along with the government cover-up in exchange for exoneration of anti-American charges brought against him during the McCarthy witch-hunt. After Condon's death in 1974, Dr. Paul Santorini, a Greek UFO researcher and former colleague of Albert Einstein, wrote, "It is a pity that an eminent scientist of his level blindly executed orders to back with his name a 'Report' that constitutes a scientific shame. But, I understand, this was done to please some authorities unhappy with his 'securities' affairs."

In 1973, Condon was quoted in the *New York Times* as admitting that "my own study of UFOs was a waste of Government money." It was even worse than that based on what happened to the committee's UFO files. "One would think that they belonged to the scientific fraternity or to the public domain, since American taxpayers paid for the 'research,'" commented Dr. Vallee. "Not so. When the project wrote its report the files were locked up by the University of Colorado in Boulder. They were later transferred to a private home and were burned shortly thereafter."

There is no question that the Condon Committee—the most recent and last official word on UFOs—was superficial as a scientific document and inadequate as a response to a legitimate public concern. Skeptics of officialdom claimed the air force paid for the Condon study simply to avoid any meaningful investigation by Congress. The real question became whether this bungling of an official investigation was purely accidental or by design. Today, only those people who agreed with Condon's conclusions continue to believe that the committee operated by accident.

For example, later in 1969, the members of the prestigious American Association for the Advancement of Science (AAAS), puzzled by the thinly disguised whitewash of the Condon Report, decided to conduct a UFO symposium at the annual meeting in December. Serious efforts were made to halt or at least distract from the symposium. According to author Raymond Fowler, Dr. Condon "was working hard behind the scenes to convince the AAAS to cancel the UFO meetings! He wrote to each board member pleading with him to boycott the meetings. His attempts proved futile, however, and the symposium went on as scheduled."

The idea of internal manipulation is supported by a letter to author Raymond Fowler from an administrative assistant to Dr. Condon during the University of Colorado study. The assistant was responding to Fowler's request for details of a 1954 UFO sighting and wrote, "I am trying to obtain some information on a UFO sighting. . . . There's a good deal of indication of an Air Force 'conspiracy' or foul-up in communications. Frankly, on this case, I suspect the former."

The air force for some time had wanted to dump Project Blue Book, its public UFO investigation, and with the Condon Report stating that there was no scientific justification for such a study, it got its chance—and its timing was perfect.

Although a decision had been made in March, it was not until December 17, 1969, just as the AAAS UFO symposium was about to begin in Boston, that Air Force Secretary Robert C. Seamans Jr. announced the end of Project Blue Book, saying, "The continuation of

Project Blue Book cannot be justified either on the ground of national security or in the interest of science."

"The announcement could not have been timed better for a negative effect," wrote Fowler. "It appeared to be a deliberate attempt to undermine the AAAS Scientific Symposium on UFOs. My suspicions were confirmed shortly thereafter during a telephone call concerning the symposium with Dr. Donald Menzel. Menzel admitted to me that the Air Force announcement at this time was more than a coincidence and coyly suggested that he had been involved in the decision to release it at this time as an Air Force consultant."

The air force announcement further dampened the public's interest by reiterating its long-standing view that "No UFO had given any indication of a threat to national security. . . . There was no evidence any unidentified sightings represent technological developments or principles beyond the range of present-day knowledge. . . . There is no evidence UFOs are extraterrestrial vehicles." After twenty-two years of off-again, on-again public attention to UFOs, the air force closed its Blue Book.

An objective appraisal of Project Blue Book was that there was never a serious, unbiased, and honest study of the UFO phenomenon. Today it is clear that the air force investigation was merely a cover, a whitewash to lull the public while the CIA and perhaps even more secret groups seriously probed the UFO issue.

CHAPTER 6

UFOS UNDERGROUND

While the general public, led by the media, turned away from the topic of UFOs, it is now apparent that behind a curtain of secrecy and professed unconcern, official interest increased over the years.

In the early 1990s a document made its way around the UFO research community that may point to where some of the most secret UFO studies took place. Called the "Pentacle memo" by Dr. Jacques Vallee, the document was found among the papers of the late Dr. J. Allen Hynek. It was stamped "Secret, Security Information" and was dated January 9, 1953—less than a week before the CIA's Robertson panel met—and was written by Howard C. Cross, a senior staff member of Battelle Memorial Institute in Columbus, Ohio. The memo was written to Mr. Miles E. Coll of Wright-Patterson Air Force Base, Ohio, and concerned "a preliminary recommendation to ATIC on future methods of handling the problem of unidentified aerial objects." Cross said the recommendation was based "on our experience to date in analyzing several thousands of reports on this subject" but added "our analysis is not yet complete."

Referring to the upcoming Robertson panel, Cross's memo stated, "Since a meeting of the panel is now definitely scheduled we feel that agreement between Project Stork [a preliminary UFO report for Project Blue Book] and ATIC should be reached as to what can and what cannot be discussed at the meeting. . . ." It is clear that Battelle had much more knowledge of UFOs than any normal private company and that there were matters concerning that subject that "cannot be discussed."

Battelle Memorial Institute began operating in 1929 under the leadership of Horace W. Gillett, who has been called "the Dean of American Metallurgy." The institute began a close relationship with the U.S. military in 1939 when its scientists undertook a study on how to improve armor plating. After World War II, Battelle scientists studied the fabrication of uranium and later produced uranium fuel rods for the world's first nuclear reactor at Oak Ridge, Tennessee.

Ruppelt mentioned in his 1956 book that scientific experts were needed to support Project Blue Book's UFO studies. "It was, of course, impossible to have all of these people on my staff, so I decided to do the next best thing," he wrote. "I would set up a contract with some research organization who already had such people on their staff; then I would call on them whenever their services were needed. . . . Their organization cannot be identified by name because they are doing other highly secret work for the government, I'll call them Project Bear." Ruppelt then identified this project as "a large, well-known research organization in the Midwest" with several hundred engineers and scientists who "run from experts on soils to nuclear physicists."

Researcher Keith Chester, after a detailed study of Battelle, became convinced that Battelle indeed provided the scientists for Project Bear. "If crashed UFOs did exist, and were being hidden from the public eye, then it is logical to assume that the scientific community was involved with the UFO phenomenon from the start. Having craft in government possession meant that it was imperative to ensure that only top scientists and laboratories were handling the material. Battelle was capable of conducting state-of-the-art research on a recovered alien craft, especially one made of unknown metal," Chester noted. "It is highly probable that contributions by Battelle, including laboratory experimentation and extensive study of retrieved UFOs, were ongoing since 1947 and in the years to follow."

Other candidates as a science center secretly dealing with the UFO issue are the Brookhaven National Laboratory on Long Island and the quasi-private Mitre Corporation, headquartered in Boston. Mitre administers the Jason group, an "ultra-elitist organization" of top scientists working on a variety of hush-hush Defense Department projects.

Jason was formed following the Soviet success with Sputnik in the late 1950s and worked on such Cold War problems as turning radios into radiation detectors. *The Pentagon Papers* revealed that Jason developed an acoustical apparatus for detecting human movement along the Ho Chi Minh Trail in Vietnam. Operating in near total secrecy, the Jason group has consistently refused to file reports in compliance with the Federal Advisory Committee Act, according to researcher Vicki Cooper. But true to its charter, the Jason group continues to advise the secretary of defense and the Joint Chiefs of Staff in secret on matters of science and technology.

Early on there may have been a legitimate rationale behind such secrecy. When UFO reports first starting coming in, intelligence officers believed they might represent advanced Soviet technology. Later they surmised that Soviet spies were using UFO investigations as a cover to learn about new U.S. technology. But the continued use of ridicule and deception ultimately convinced many serious researchers that something very deep and mysterious lay behind the government facade of Blue Book.

Blue Book files are missing numerous cases and even one whole report—Report 13. One Blue Book report mentioned that some gun camera film had been sent for analysis, yet the master index listed no such film.

Military officers were chagrined to learn that reports they had filed on UFOs did not show up in Blue Book files. Col. William Coleman was piloting a B-25 Mitchell bomber over the southern United States back in 1955 when he spotted a UFO and gave chase, eventually reaching treetop level. "We were within an eighth of a mile of it and there was this perfect round shadow of this thing, going over the treetops," he recalled. Coleman filed a report of his sighting, yet some years later when he was assigned to Project Blue Book, he failed to find his report or even any record that it had ever arrived. He later indicated to author Timothy Good that he became aware that serious UFO reports were rerouted away from Blue Book.

This, of course, was vehemently denied by the air force. Before a nationwide TV audience in 1958, Air Force Secretary Richard E. Horner proclaimed, "The air force is not hiding any UFO information. And I do not qualify this in any way." This statement was ridiculed by everyone familiar with Project Blue Book, including former CIA director Hillenkoetter, who commented, "The Air Force has constantly misled the American public about UFOs. . . ."

One researcher very familiar with air force secrecy was Leonard H. Stringfield, who was selected in the 1950s for an "off-the-record" role in the official UFO reporting system. "[I] worked cooperatively with the Air Defense Command of the USAF, 1954–1957," he stated.

"On their request, I screened and reported UFO activity occurring, real time, in the tri-state area of southwestern Ohio, northern Kentucky and southeastern Indiana. At that time, many UFO sightings came to my home from police departments, sheriff's offices, state police, the media and citizenry. I was assigned a code number—Fox Trot Kilo 3 Zero Blue—which would identify me at the telephone exchange to report, by phone, to the Air Defense Command Air Filter Center at Lockbourne AFB, in Columbus, Ohio. If my screened UFO report was confirmed by radar, or other means, Air Force interceptors were scrambled. At this point I was told that the resultant actions were classified. The Air Force paid my phone bills."

John L. Acuff, former president of the NICAP, commented, "There is no doubt that the decision was reached by the Air Force to classify most of the case material relating to UFOs. This classification took place throughout the operation of Project Blue Book. The recent decision of the Air Force requiring the deletion of witness names, investigator comments, etc., before UFO records are made available to the public through the National Archives, will make those files almost worthless for research purposes. The real question is not whether secrecy did exist, or still exists; the question is why was it imposed."

William H. Spaulding, a director of Ground Saucer Watch, said over the years he continually heard comments from witnesses and former government officials "that directly infer a UFO conspiracy by our various governmental departments. I have seen repetitive reports citing film confiscation and editing, a landing area being plowed under and the witnesses receiving cruel and unnecessary official ridicule."

"Since 1953, Blue Book had merely served as public-relations diversion," noted James Lorenzen, international director and cofounder of the APRO. "Its purpose was to solve PR problems for the Air Force—relative to UFOs—and it was closed when it began to create more problems than it solved. Recent information has come to my attention which indicates the military establishment, having apparently learned a lesson from Watergate, now rewrites history in connection with UFO incidents to the extent of altering and purging records and framing individuals within their ranks to make sure—apparently— that no telltale material exists for further investigative committees to uncover. Hopefully the purged material is preserved at some higher echelon, as normally happens when classified material is upgraded and called forward; otherwise it is lost to science forever."

Canadian researcher John B. Musgrave, who was affiliated with several UFO groups in the United States, discovered how even foreign governments were constrained by the unwritten UFO secrecy. "With few exceptions, official Canadian policy toward UFO reports and the UFO phenomena consistently reflects official U.S. policy. This is hardly a surprise. Canadian military is subservient to the U.S. military through so-called joint commands such as NORAD and NATO, and police bodies such as the RCMP are closely linked to their U.S. counterparts through networks such as FBI and CIA computer centers. As in the U.S., UFO sightings that have become public are downgraded, and sightings that have come to the private attention of military or police personnel are covered up."

"We have the answer as to why Blue Book failed," wrote researcher Art Crockett. "It was merely a cover for the real investigation going on in secret. The most important cases, undoubtedly, did not go to Blue Book at all, but to the secret agency. This may also explain why so many of Blue Book's files are missing. . . . The most annoying aspect of the whole affair is that the high-ranking Air Force officials who said that they intended to get the subject of UFOs out of the public realm have succeeded!"

Paris Flammonde noted, "As far as the newspapers and the television network news facilities were concerned, at a certain point in the early 1960s UFOs [had] simply ceased to exist." The same could be said today as ongoing UFO reports appear relegated to local media, the tabloids, or "tabloid" TV programming. By the end of 1969, with the public confused and divided by conflicting views and the cancellation of Project Blue Book, the subject ceased to officially exist for the U.S. Air Force as well.

Further confirmation of government deceit was found in the minutes of a meeting of the air force's Scientific Advisory Board on March 17 and 18, 1948. In a transcript obtained in recent years by researcher Bill LaParl, briefing officer Col. Howard McCoy stated, "We have a new project—Project Sign—which may surprise you as a development from the so-called mass hysteria of the past summer when we had all the unidentified flying objects or discs. This can't be laughed off. We have over 300 reports which haven't been publicized in the papers from very competent personnel. . . . We are running down every report. I can't tell you how much we would give to have one of those crash in an area so that we could recover whatever they are." Debunkers pointed to McCoy's statement as proof that the Roswell crash of 1947 did not happen. But, as pointed out by Dr. Bruce Maccabee, who has provided UFO briefings to the CIA, McCoy was not at liberty to mention a crash at Roswell to the advisory board, which was meeting under merely "Secret" security level.

The more important fact of McCoy's statement was the mention of three hundred reports. A review of the master list of Project

Blue Book for this time period showed only about 135 reports cataloged, leaving 165 reports unaccounted for and adding considerable weight to statements that Project Blue Book was kept in the dark about many of the most credible and significant sightings.

At the same time as Project Blue Book was being canceled, NICAP's battle against government secrecy was lost. With a declining membership—some claimed due to Major Keyhoe's obsession with the secrecy issue rather than reporting UFO sightings—and financial problems, the NICAP board of governors ousted Keyhoe as director, in what he termed a "coup." Although the organization lingered for more than a decade, Keyhoe refused to attend any meetings and it was never again a viable force in the UFO controversy. Its place was taken by the Midwest UFO Network, which eventually changed its name to the Mutual UFO Network (MUFON).

Former NSA employee Todd W. Zechel claimed that Keyhoe's removal was orchestrated by the CIA to silence this vocal critic of government secrecy. Pointing out several NICAP officials with links to the agency, Zechel wrote, "Perhaps Keyhoe deserved to be fired from the organization he built with his own sweat, blood and sacrifice. The timing couldn't have been better, in any case. Keyhoe, after all, was beginning to focus on the CIA in 1969, instead of his tunnel-visioned attacks on the Air Force.... If they wanted to destroy the leading anti-secrecy organization of the 1960s, they couldn't have done a better job if they'd tried."

The Bentwaters Case

As time moved on, official secrecy regarding the UFO phenomenon became the order of the day. One classic example of a well-documented but subsequently hushed-up UFO encounter occurred in England in December 1980 and involved U.S. military personnel, radar contact, and was even recorded in official reports.

Just after midnight on December 26–27, 1980, radar installations on the east coast of England began tracking an object that dropped below radar coverage near the East Anglian town of Ipswich. Nearby were the NATO bases of RAF Woodbridge and RAF Bentwaters, both leased by the Royal Air Force to the U.S. Air Force as headquarters for the 81st Tactical Fighter Wing. U.S. Air Force personnel, as well as civilians, saw something descend into Rendlesham Forest, which surrounded the two bases.

One witness was former USAF Sgt. John Burroughs, who had been stationed at Bentwaters since July of that year. Burroughs said both he and his supervisor saw "some strange lights" near the base's east gate. "We decided to go on down off base and kind of check the edge of the woods to see maybe what was going on because it didn't seem right. . . . There was radio traffic back and forth and the decision was made by the shift commander that I should accompany two security guys into the woods," Burroughs recalled. Walking into the woods, Burroughs said he saw "a bank of lights, differently colored lights that threw off an image of like a craft. I never saw anything metallic or hard." One of the security men with Burroughs, identified only as "James Archer," however, later described an object "triangular in shape, with three landing legs . . . about 10 to 12 feet in diameter and eight feet high, with a blue light on top, red lights and a white light in the middle and a brighter white light emanating from the underside." "Archer" was certain he saw something inside the craft. "I don't know what, but the shapes did not look human. Maybe they were like robots," he said.

Another witness, acting security police commander Sgt. Adrian Bustinza, recalled that he too was ordered to check out lights in the forest that night. "When we got to Point A—the sighting of the object—we had trouble turning the light-alls on. Our truck wouldn't run either. It was kind of like all the energy had been drained out of both light-all units," he told researchers in 1984. "We proceeded to look and in the process found kind of like triangular tripods . . . burned into the [ground] at three different standpoints. . . . They were like it was a heavy object. They took radiation readings of the holes, and they got a radiation reading as I recall. Then I recall we were walking through the woods and we came upon the lights again. And that's when I first saw the object. . . ." Bustinza described the object as a circular craft, thicker at the center than the edge, with a red light on top and several blue lights on the bottom. He said it was a "tremendous size" and kept moving about in a large clearing.

Yet another witness, then USAF Sgt. Larry Warren, said that as he approached the woods he saw a strange mist covering the ground. "It looked like a ground fog but was somehow lit up," he recalled. "It glowed very brightly and has the definition of a roughly shaped circle . . . as a small red light . . . made a downward arc and was directly over the fog." Warren said the red light suddenly exploded in a blinding flash and a large "arrowhead" craft appeared. "The main body was pearl white with a rainbow color effect," he said. "It was constantly distorting as I looked at it. At the bottom was a bank of extremely bright cobalt blue lights. Below that, I thought I could make out dark landing gear. Covering the entire surface were what looked like boxes, pipes, and strange extensions."

The witnesses said the craft lingered in the area for more than an hour and that other air force personnel arrived, including the Woodbridge deputy base commander Lt. Col. Charles Halt. Reportedly, both American and British authorities made both film and audiotapes of the astounding event, along with radiation tests.

By 4:00 A.M. on December 27, the giant craft was joined by—or perhaps divided into—at least five smaller glowing objects that, following a moving light display, eventually disappeared into the sky.

The Bentwaters event received little media attention at the time, largely due to denials by the U.S. Air Force. Official spokesmen denied that any audiovisual recordings were made of the event or that any official records existed. This statement was proven false in late 1983 following a Freedom of Information Act inquiry that resulted in the release of a corroborating official report.

The report, entitled "Unexplained Lights," dated January 13, 1981, and signed by Colonel Halt, stated:

1. Early in the morning of 27 Dec 80 (approximately 0300L), two USAF security police patrolmen saw unusual lights outside the back gate at RAF Woodbridge. Thinking an aircraft might have crashed or been forced down, they called for permission to go outside the gate to investigate. . . . The individuals reported seeing a strange glowing object in the forest. The object was described as being metallic in appearance and triangular in shape, approximately two to three meters across the base and approximately two meters high. It illuminated the entire forest with a white light. The object itself had a pulsing red light on top and a bank(s) of blue lights underneath. The object was hovering or on legs. As the patrolmen approached the object, it maneuvered through the trees and disappeared. At this time the animals on a nearby farm went into a frenzy. The object was briefly sighted approximately an hour later near the back gate.

2. The next day, three depressions 1½" deep and 7" in diameter were found where the object had been sighted on the ground. The following night (29 Dec 80) the area was checked for radiation. Beta/Gamma readings of 0.1 milliroentgens were recorded with peak readings in the three depressions and near the center of the triangle formed by the depressions. A nearby tree had moderate (.05–.07) readings on the side of the tree toward the depressions.

3. Later in the night a red sun-like light was seen through the trees. It moved about and pulsed. At one point it appeared to throw off glowing particles and then broke into five separate white objects and then disappeared. Immediately thereafter, three star-like objects were noticed in the sky, two objects to the north and one to the

south, all of which were about 10 degrees off the horizon. The objects moved rapidly in sharp angular movements and displayed red, green and blue lights. The objects to the north appeared to be elliptical through an 8–12 power lens. They then turned to full circles. The objects in the north remained in the sky for an hour or more. The object to the south was visible for two or three hours and beamed down a stream of light from time to time. Numerous individuals, including the undersigned, witnessed the activities in paragraphs 2 and 3.

Astonishing as Colonel Halt's report appeared, in later years he told Timothy Good, "There are a lot of things that are not in my memo. . . ." Halt also confirmed that film of the incident was personally taken by overall base commander Gen. Gordon Williams to a fighter plane at Bentwaters, which delivered the film to USAF European Headquarters at Ramstein AFB, West Germany. The film has never been acknowledged by the air force nor seen publicly.

The official denial that anything out of the ordinary occurred at Bentwaters—one explanation was that all concerned were simply seeing the beam from the Orford Ness lighthouse five miles away—suffered further loss of credibility in 1984 when an edited version of a tape recording made by Colonel Halt at the time of the incident was released by a former Woodbridge base commander. The eighteen-minute tape clearly reveals the excitement and consternation of air force personnel, including Colonel Halt, as they searched the woods. "Straight ahead of my flashlight, there, sir. . . . There it is! . . . Yeah, I see it too. . . . What is it? . . . We don't know, sir. It's a strange, small red light. . . . Everywhere else is just deathly calm. . . . There's no doubt about it—there's some type of strange flashing red light ahead. . . . It appears to be maybe moving a little bit this way? It's brighter than it has been. It's coming this way. It's definitely coming this way! Pieces of it are shooting off. There's no doubt about it—this is weird!"

Despite Halt's official report to the RAF, the tape recording, and the witnesses, nothing has been acknowledged officially about the 1980 incident. But this was not the first—or apparently the last—strange event at the Bentwaters-Woodbridge bases.

During the night of August 13–14, 1956, ground radar operators at Bentwaters recorded a UFO flying directly over the base at speeds exceeding two thousand miles per hour, far beyond any conventional aircraft of the time. The object was seen by both air controllers and pilots as it performed aerobatic maneuvers. Two RAF Venom fighters were scrambled but were outclassed by the UFO's maneuvers and soon lost it. Even the stolid Condon Committee was forced to conclude that "the apparently rational, intelligent behavior of the UFO suggests a mechanical device of unknown origin as the most probable explanation."

In 1988, Bentwaters witness Larry Warren returned to England while preparing a book on his experience. He and researcher Peter Robbins were treated to yet another extraordinary aerial display near the base on February 18. According to Robbins, "Commencing at approximately 9:30 P.M., all hell broke loose in this forested area and above it, and we watched over the next one and a half hours a variety of UFO activity—all soundless—including star-like UFOs, green fireballs flying through the forest and around trees, something which seemed to have white headlights and red tail lights rise on an extreme diagonal in front of an 80- to 100-foot-high stand of evergreens and blink out as it reached the tops.

"Several good-sized, pulsing, disc-shaped things coasted about changing size and color . . . appeared and disappeared, a huge flood of light shined out from the forest floor which gave the impression of being the size of one or two football fields with several hundred floodlights lined up, aimed at the sky, and what I can only describe as what seemed to be something on the ground at the far end of the field which had three rectangular, dark orange—I can only say windows—and possessing an elliptical shape which had articulated movement in front of it. There were no plants, trees, animals between us to create such movement.

"During this time, we observed what we identified as two [U.S.] Air Force security perimeter patrols in jeeps pull up approximately a hundred or so yards in front of us, seemingly to observe these activities."

Warren said that despite honorable service—he was among the military contingent that greeted the returning hostages from Iran in 1981 pictured on the cover of *Time* magazine—when he tried to reenlist, he was informed the air force had no record of him.

It is now obvious to any serious student of the subject that the U.S. government is hiding away information regarding UFOs and has been for many years. Whether or not these hidden secrets pertain to crashed saucers and alien bodies remains to be seen. But something very troubling to someone is being kept under wraps. What exactly this may be remains unproven, but the cumulative evidence strongly suggests it may well pertain to the certain knowledge of intelligent extraterrestrial life by some of the most powerful persons in the world (see Appendix).

UFO Command Flow Chart

If there has been a conscious decision to suppress knowledge of UFO contacts or technology, it undoubtedly has been made at this ruling-class level. This decision, in turn, would become official policy passed down through the ranks of military and government personnel.

Michael Lindemann, president of The 2020 Group, a private organization dedicated to investigating UFOs, stated, "On the available evidence, I consider it likely that the emergence since 1947 of a highly complex, secretive and manipulative intelligence bureaucracy, including the CIA, DIA and NSA, was prompted in part by an urgent need to gather and assess UFO/Alien information while shielding it from public scrutiny. Beyond doubt, today this intelligence bureaucracy is virtually uncontrollable, exercising extra-legal policymaking power and techniques of public deception and manipulation with regard to any issue deemed relevant to national security. Such activities, regardless of their genesis or intent, represent a grave assault upon our democratic institutions, our constitutional rights and even our legitimate national security."

"Socially and psychologically speaking, an operation of this caliber would have been easy enough to secretly implement," stated Anthony Kimery, an award-winning Washington journalist. In a 1989 article, written under the pen name James Neilson, Kimery wrote that information provided to him by several sources who asked to remain anonymous led him to conclude that "policy issuing from the highest levels of U.S. Government, military and intelligence directs a secret, centralized command structure to deal with the UFO situation . . . [and] has been in operation since the mid-to-late 1970s and continues to handle the UFO situation from the ranks of the National Military Command Center, the level at which the Joint Chiefs of Staff in direct link with the White House 'war room' deploy U.S. military forces worldwide and would manage planning and operations in the event of a nuclear war."

Kimery was told by his sources that Project Blue Book was "deliberately disbanded in 1969 to make way for the top-secret government agency to assume centralized control over UFO-related matters."

Kimery concluded, "To be a matter of military preparedness directed at this high command level, the UFO situation is clearly perceived by the government as a threat worthy of continuous, in-depth monitoring and surveillance and, if the need arises, military confrontation."

Evidence collected from the United Nations by Michigan

researcher Tad Sherburn provided confirmation that top military officers in the United States are at "the heart of UFO operations." After repeated Freedom of Information Act requests and negotiations with a source within the State Department, Sherburn obtained documents that refer to a "secret" 1977 UN resolution to create an agency as a "clearinghouse for the exchange of data and coordin[ation of] research on UFOs." This special political UFO group was chaired by the prime minister of Grenada, Sir Eric Matthew Gairy. Sherburn said a study of hundreds of documents show that UFO reports have been gathered from 133 countries. In the United States, UFO data reaches the level of the Joint Chiefs of Staff but includes top civilian authorities.

While actual policy is probably determined by the men and women of the ruling elite, most of whom are largely unknown to the public, overall authority over this UFO command structure, according to Kimery and others, begins with a small high-level group—corresponding to the unproven MJ-12 group. Others have referred to this body as the "UFO Directorate," "The Committee," or "the UFO Working Group." This group reports to the National Security Council (NSC), which obtains legal authority from presidential directives, although it is doubtful that any president's knowledge of UFOs would be extensive. Several UFO researchers claim the president is informed of UFO/alien issues on a "NTKBO" (need-to-know basis only). The president, as usual, would simply be a figurehead, whose orders could be passed along by a senior civilian official such as the National Security Advisor. Another candidate for the decision-making office of a secret UFO command structure is the State Department's Office of Security Assistance, Science and Technology, a nexus of military, intelligence, political, scientific, and corporate authority. Operational orders would then be given to highly compartmentalized secret units staffed by personnel carefully selected for their loyalty and silence within the military and intelligence agencies.

Depending on the individual mission or need, such matters could be handled through the North American Air Defense Command (NORAD), Aerospace Defense Command (ADC), Blue Berets Rapid Deployment Inter-Service Forces, National Reconnaissance Office (NRO), National Reconnaissance Office of Air Force Intelligence (NROAFI), National Photographic Interpretation Center (NPIC), Intelligence Threat Analysis Center (ITAC), or one of the military projects already described such as Aquarius, Sigma, Snowbird, or Garnet, which may or may not be still active. UFO matters handled within the intelligence community could go to one or more of the alphabet groups including the CIA, National Security Agency (NSA), Defense Intelligence Agency (DIA), Air Force Intelligence

Service (AFIS), Air Force Office of Special Investigations (AFOSI), Defense Advanced Research Projects Agency (DARPA), and others.

Lest anyone think that this is all simply a paranoid's nightmare, consider that the *New York Times* reported in early 1996 that the National Reconnaissance Office alone lost track of more than $2 billion. This situation was "created by the extraordinary secrecy under which the reconnaissance office works," explained the newspaper. "The reconnaissance agency is really a set of secret offices—so secret that they have been shielded from each other, like safes locked within safes. Each office, and each program, had separate management and accounting systems."

Meanwhile, media, academic, and other government leaders, jealous of their jobs and positions of authority, would be expected to follow official policy and maintain that there is no evidence of life outside the earth. Most would be sincere in such conservative statements, since direct knowledge of such existence is a closely held secret and not widely available. The public would be aware of the possibility of aliens only through fiction in books and broadcast, by sporadically hearing reports and rumors, and by taking note of the amazing burst of technology in recent years.

And as strong as the desire for power and control is in some people, there is yet a stronger impulse—survival. In past centuries, when warfare or plague threatened a society, the wealthy elite simply moved to safer environs. In Europe during the two world wars, when the going got tough, the tough got going—on extended visits to Africa or the Americas. Once the bombs stopped falling, the powerful families of Europe returned home, picked up the pieces of their commercial empires, and continued business as usual—often with financial aid from their victorious associates in the allied nations.

But the Cold War between the Soviet Union and the United States presented a new problem. With nuclear weapons in the military arsenals, there was no place to run—no haven on earth that could be guaranteed safe from radioactive fallout.

Notes from the Underground

Whether or not it was at the instigation of the ruling clique, it is a fact that beginning in the 1950s and continuing through today, the U.S. government embarked on a massive program to design and construct mammoth underground facilities.

Some of these constructions—such as the famous military command center under Cheyenne Mountain, Colorado—were obviously a necessary component of the nation's postwar defense plans. However, many other similar bases were constructed in secret and could house a much greater population than the small cadre of military and government personnel needed to survive and fight a nuclear war.

Richard Sauder, Ph.D., a financial and military researcher in the Southwest who conducted an in-depth study on the issue of underground bases, concluded, "I consider it an absolute certainty that the military has constructed secret underground facilities in the United States, above and beyond the approximately one dozen 'known' underground facilities. . . ."

Sauder reported such sites at Fort Belvoir, Virginia; West Point, New York; Twentynine Palms Marine Corps Base, California; Groom Lake near Nellis AFB, Nevada; White Sands Missile Range, New Mexico; Table Mountain, near Boulder, Colorado; Mount Blackmore and Pipestone Pass, Montana.

While the existence of many other giant underground bases has not been confirmed, there is absolutely no question that both the U.S. government and private companies have long maintained active plans for their construction. Sauder presented numerous papers, patents, plans, and government contracts to prove not only the interest but also the digging technology to accomplish such an endeavor. This technology ranges from conventional drilling and boring machines to exotic "ground disintegration" devices using microwave, plasma, ultrasonic, electron beam, and laser technology. A 1986 Los Alamos laboratory report and two 1988 reports from NASA researchers at Texas A&M University even detail plans for a "Lunar Tunneler" designed to excavate space for a working colony under the surface of the moon.

Sauder noted, "The first thing to understand is that there are actual tunnelling machines that crawl through the ground like giant mechanical earthworms with huge appetites. These tunnelling machines are used on construction projects all over the world to build perfectly ordinary sewers, subways, utility lines, highways, railroads, aqueducts, hydroelectric projects—as well as jazzy, high-profile projects like the 'Chunnel,' the tunnel underneath the English Channel that now makes it possible to travel on dry ground between England and France."

Some of these underground facilities are not military at all, yet they are still very secret. In addition to a large Federal Reserve facility within Mount Pony near Culpepper, Virginia, there is Mount Weather near Bluemont, Virginia, which was built in the 1950s as a giant government bomb shelter. Today it is under the control of the massive Federal Emergency Management Agency (FEMA), which under a variety of executive orders can assume control of the nation in the event of an "emergency." "Although it is the headquarters for FEMA's far-flung underground empire it does not even appear in the agency's published budget," reported Sauder.

During the Iran-contra scandal in 1987, it was revealed that certain Reagan administration officials, including Marine Lt. Col. Oliver North, drafted a plan to suspend the Constitution and turn over national control to FEMA during an "emergency." Such an "emergency" was defined as "nuclear war, violent and widespread internal dissent or national opposition to a U.S. military invasion abroad." These revelations drew a letter of protest from Attorney General William French Smith and prompted Arthur Liman, chief counsel of the Senate Iran-contra Committee, to declare that such plans grew from a "secret government-within-a-government." Such plans are still abiding in locked government files.

According to Sauder, the FEMA Mount Weather facility is the hub of ninety-six such installations collectively known as Federal Relocation Centers. "Just how many of these secret centers were newly constructed during the 1980s, and how many are older facilities that the Reagan administration merely converted to its purposes—expanded, remodeled and modernized—is not known," he stated.

Even nongovernment organizations have underground facilities. At least one oil giant, Standard Oil Company of New Jersey, maintains an underground center near Hudson, New York. Northrop has a similar facility near the Tehachapi Mountains to the northwest of Lancaster, California, while Lockheed and McDonnell Douglas each operate California facilities near Hellendale and Llano, respectively.

The initial purpose of such facilities apparently was to ensure that the leaders of industry and finance could survive a nuclear war. Some researchers believe this purpose may have been modified in recent years.

As communism collapsed in Russia and Eastern Europe, so did the Cold War. While the threat of mass nuclear destruction appeared over—though not the threat of localized nuclear terrorism—new worries arose. Through their ownership and control over both scientific and social foundations as well as "think tanks," it became clear to many in the ruling elite that an underground bunker may not be adequate protection from widespread natural and environmental disasters. A haven hundreds of feet underground will not help in the event of massive earthquakes or volcanic eruptions. And there is no purpose in surviving if one must exit an underground shelter to find the earth lifeless or radioactive.

The certain knowledge of the existence of a nongovernmental ruling elite coupled with their known resources and their instinct to survive has led some researchers to a chilling conclusion, one that may be the sum total of all the most paranoid suspicions—the ultimate conspiracy.

The Third Alternative

The premise of Alternative 3 is simple. The earth's real rulers—in terms of wealth and power—have long realized that overpopulation and environmental degradation will soon make the planet unable to support human society as we know it. Therefore, a secret plan has been adopted using unpublicized space technology to relocate selected people to colonies on Mars via clandestine bases on the moon. This conspiracy involves cooperation between persons in both the United States and the former Soviet Union and has been in place for many years.

Such a plan is apparently only the latest in survival schemes for the ruling elite, who for some time have realized that mankind's excesses on this planet have passed beyond the point of redemption. According to Jim Keith, a prolific author and researcher into such matters, "Alternative 1 . . . consisted of detonating nuclear bombs in the atmosphere to allow pollution and heat to dissipate into space, whereas Alternative 2 was a plan to construct vast subterranean habitats for the elite to escape into when the going gets tough."

It is obvious why Alternative 1 was discarded. An atmosphere of radiation is hardly an improvement over pollution. Alternative 2 was considered viable for a longer time, considering the massive underground construction that took place during the 1950s and 1960s. But today, knowledgeable eyes look beyond Earth. Only recently have details been made public of the technology required to support a large-scale evacuation of our planet.

In 1996, it was announced that NASA had selected Lockheed Martin to design and build a $941 million X-33 prototype space shuttle scheduled to fly by 1999. Utilizing a "new type of engine potent enough to propel [the shuttle] into orbit without boosters," the cost of sending payloads into space was to be reduced from the current $10,000 per pound to only $1,000. If this technology was being made public by NASA in 1996, it is certain that the U.S. military and perhaps other secret agencies had use of it years earlier.

Most leading scientists do not dispute the idea that the earth is environmentally in trouble. The arguments are simply to what degree. Almost all current world problems stem from one basic issue—human overpopulation.

Warnings about the results of overpopulation have been widely disseminated since the 1960s. Stanford University professor of population studies and author Paul R. Ehrlich warned of the consequences of overpopulation in his popular 1968 book, *The Population Bomb*. It is sobering to know that when Ehrlich was born in the 1930s, the world's population was just two billion. Today, it has almost reached six billion. This explosion of humanity has already begun to strain our social and governmental systems.

As Ehrlich noted, "In the United States, drivers in virtually every large metropolitan area now can encounter gridlock at practically any hour of the day or night. Visitors to our nation's capital find homeless people sleeping in the park opposite the White House, and drug abuse and crime sprees fill the evening news. News about the AIDS epidemic seems to be everywhere, as is talk of global warming, holes in the atmosphere's ozone layer, and acid rain."

Ehrlich's doomsday visions are supported by scientists all over the globe. Famed undersea scientist Jacques-Yves Cousteau in a 1992 lecture said with current trends the earth's population will reach more than sixteen billion within eighty years, bringing about a world where people will be "surviving like rats." World leaders must "realize the urgency of drastic, unconventional decisions," said the explorer. One 1988 statement from the Club of Earth stated, "Arresting global population growth should be second in importance only to avoiding nuclear war on humanity's agenda."

It is inconceivable that people with wealth, power, and authority are as oblivious to this situation as the average citizen. Their positions were not gained through blindness and unconcern. So it is reasonable to conclude that discussions of alternatives to an overpopulated and dying earth surely have been conducted at the highest levels of authority.

The first public presentation of this interplanetary escape plan came on June 20, 1977, with the broadcast in England of a docudrama entitled "Alternative 3." Produced by Anglia TV and written by David Ambrose and Christopher Miles, the show was a compilation of interviews and news footage depicting the worsening conditions on Earth. It outlined the plan to evacuate a number of humans selected for their potential to contribute to a new society—along with a number of brainwashed worker drones described as simply "batch consignments"—to domed bases on the moon and Mars.

The program prompted much outraged in Britain, where it was quickly depicted as mere fiction presented as a documentary. And there were certainly many reasons not to take the program seriously. A key interviewee—a former U.S. astronaut named Bob Grodin—was not a real person, nor was he an American, as evidenced by his British slang such as "We're right out of beer!" and "Have a proper drink." Other participants in the program also were actors.

British author Leslie Watkins, who went beyond the TV show with a 1978 book entitled *Alternative 3*, was very forthright in a letter published by Keith. "This original TV version, which I expanded immensely for the book, was actually a hoax which had been scheduled for transmission on April Fool's Day. Because of certain problems in finding the right network slot, the transmission was delayed."

However, it would be premature to completely write off *Alternative 3* as unworthy of study, as has been the case with many UFO researchers.

Continuing with his letter, Watkins wrote, "I initially took the view that the basic premise was so way-out . . . that no one would regard it as non-fiction. Immediately after publication, I realized I was totally wrong. In fact, the amazing mountains of letters from virtually all parts of the world—including vast numbers from highly intelligent people in positions of authority—convinced me that I had accidentally trespassed into a range of top-secret truths. . . . So, summing up, the book is fiction based on fact. But I now feel that I inadvertently got very close to a secret truth."

Linda Moulton Howe, a respected UFO researcher and author, said she became acquainted with *Alternative 3* as a science and medicine documentary producer for WCVB television in Boston. She recalled questions raised among the staff there as to why the Corporation for Public Broadcasting did not want the docudrama broadcast in the United States.

"I was curious," Howe said, "and I had a discussion with a BBC producer about it. I was told that the program began as a BBC documentary on the so-called British 'brain drain' of the 1970s. You might remember that a large number of British scientists were leaving, reportedly for better paying jobs in America. I was told that the program never came off because the BBC could not locate any of the scientists once they left Britain. It was all very odd. It was like they disappeared."

Howe said writers Ambrose and Miles wrote a script for *Alternative 3* based on real interviews conducted by BBC. And indeed both the TV show and the book made much of the disappearance of scientists. While the scientists mentioned in the show and book appear to have been fictitious, author Keith listed more than thirty scientists from around the world that were connected to the Strategic Defense Initiative (SDI) "Star Wars" program and either committed suicide, disappeared, or died under mysterious circumstances. These deaths and disappearances, along with several bombings of defense installations, were publicly acknowledged during the 1980s. Kurt Rebmann, then federal prosecutor for West Germany, stated in 1986 he believed there was a "coordinated offensive" against the SDI program.

To recap the issue: There just might be a grain of truth somewhere in the *Alternative 3* scenario, since an abundance of documentation has revealed the existence of a wealthy ruling elite interconnected with secret societies, international corporate business, and publicity-shy organizations such as the Council on Foreign Relations and the Trilateral Commission. This elite was surely aware of the many cataclysms—both natural and man-made—that could spell doom for industrialized society. Evidence suggests that this elite, through their hirelings and associates within government, may have instigated massive underground construction projects for survival during the 1950s and 1960s. This same group would be intensely interested in any advanced technology that might help maintain their wealth and position. This group has used the CIA as a covert security arm almost since the agency's inception in 1947 and, as has been shown, the CIA secretly took over matters concerning UFOs in the early 1950s. To this mix must be added the post–World War II fascists, whose survival and power were detailed earlier.

Keith wrote, "It is in this environment of extensive collaboration and infiltration by Nazis and Fascists, a collaboration that involves a long-term continuance of Nazi [racial] goals separated from earlier German territorial goals, and an overall shepherding and betrayal by international monied interests, government and intelligence agencies, that America's descent into totalitarianism, genocide and mind control becomes understandable and the *Alternative 3* template first becomes visible." Keith added that for Alternative 3 to be a viable plan for survival there must be a number of controls set in place. These include mastery of mass populations through a controlled media, television, drugs, religion, or mind-control techniques, control of the military of the major nations possibly through the United Nations, and contingency plans in the event of war, social upheaval, or the "sudden recognition [of such control] by the masses" or natural catastrophes. "This broad outline of controls is a repetition, in almost all specifics, of the details of *Alternative 3*," Keith observed.

If there is any truth to Alternative 3, it might answer many questions raised over the years by various researchers: Why would top leaders in business and banking meet secretly over the years and why would they deal with Nazis? Why has advanced energy and engine technology been repeatedly suppressed over the years? Were Nazi-designed flying saucers actually built, and where on earth have they been used? Could such saucers represent a covert space technology that might then account for the dismissive attitude toward UFOs by the government and military? Could bases on the moon and Mars account for the sightings of numerous anomalous structures on both?

The Alternative 3 concept is intriguing, but hard evidence is difficult to obtain. And the sheer audacity and magnitude of the conspiracy argues against it. But there have been cracks in the protective wall of security thrown around such matters that added support for such speculation. Recent rumors and several articles—mostly outside the mainstream media—have speculated that perhaps the United States is indeed experimenting with clandestine space technology at a top-secret base in Nevada.

What's Going on at Area 51?

At almost 5:00 A.M. on May 16, 1991, a party of UFO researchers, including Norio Hayakawa of the Civilian Intelligence Network and Gary Schultz of Secret Saucer Base Expeditions, sat outdoors in southeast Nevada observing a bright orange and yellowish light hovering overhead. The shiny object then moved to the right and hovered for some time, then appeared and disappeared for approximately fifteen minutes.

In February 1992, six civilian pilots, including Valentino Kent and Ken Brazell, camped out in Lincoln County, Nevada. They had heard stories that strange things had been seen in the skies, and as Kent explained, "Pilots are interested in anything that flies, so we went out there just to see what was going on." The pilots were told to camp on a certain point of high ground by the local sheriff, who examined their identification and wrote down auto license numbers. That night all of the men experienced odd sensations of paralysis and fearfulness, leading them to believe they may have been drugged by a low passing helicopter. "I remember the dusting of Agent Orange in 'Nam, you know," Kent said. "I remember putting my head up, trying to at least keep my head up . . . looking at the moon and it was moving around. . . . I assume because my head was bobbing and I went out." Brazell said, "I literally felt drugged. Who knows?" But before this incident, all of the pilots witnessed a spectacular aerial show involving a large, noiseless, bright gold lighted object along with "red balls flying around with little strobe lights."

These groups were only a few of the hundreds of persons who since 1989 have flocked to the area after hearing stories that the U.S. government was experimenting with "flying saucers" there. While there is yet no hard evidence or official admission that this is the case, something strange definitely is flying in the Nevada skies. "Multiple reports from well-qualified observers lend substantial credence to the existence of numerous secret aircraft flying from remote bases in the southwestern U.S., regardless of the political, funding or technical arguments against that probability," reported the prestigious periodical *Aviation Week & Space Technology*.

One of these remote bases, as mentioned by Sauder, is Groom Lake, Nevada, which has become somewhat of a cause célèbre when news of strange, circular, silent flying craft sighted over this facility leaked out.

Located almost ninety miles northwest of Las Vegas on the northern perimeter of the Nellis Air Force Range, this above-top-secret facility spreads hangers, enormous parabolic antennas, and one of the earth's longest runways across Groom Lake's dry bed. It is popularly known as "Area 51" or "Dreamland" and is the source of much speculation regarding the government and UFOs.

Government actions regarding Area 51 have only added to public interest in the area. "It is a matter of public record that the United States Air Force conducted a blatantly illegal land seizure [in 1984] involving tens of thousands of acres in the vicinity," reported the magazine *UFO*. "When the Air Force was asked by a U.S. Congressman by what authority they acted, the Air Force said that the authority could be revealed, but only behind closed doors." In 1995, agitated air force officials made a successful grab for an additional four thousand acres around Area 51—primarily the high points and mountains from which the curious had been watching for UFOs. As usual the government got what it wanted despite public hearings in 1994 by the Bureau of Land Management, in which ranchers and environmentalists protested this further loss of the desert ecosystem and UFO researchers protested what they saw as unwarranted secretiveness.

This intense secrecy concerning Area 51 has done little to dispel stories of government work on UFOs, whether of new design or as the result of recovered crashes such as the one at Roswell. It was only after the Area 51 expansion hearings in early 1994 that the government even admitted that anything was there, despite the fact that UFO researchers and others had talked about the place for years. "We do have facilities within the complex near the dry lake bed of Groom Lake," the air force admitted in an official statement, adding that the Nellis Range Complex—which includes Area 51—is "used for testing and training technologies, operations and systems critical to the effectiveness of U.S. military forces. Specific activities conducted at Nellis cannot be discussed any further than that."

Abe Dane, senior correspondent for *Popular Mechanics*, wrote, "Groom Lake has been where our government has come when it

wants to be alone. . . . It's a terrestrial black hole into which it's estimated millions of tax dollars disappear each day while hardly a word of
explanation escapes."

Secrecy is nothing new to the Nellis Range. Some of America's
most top-secret aircraft—from spy planes like the U2 and the new
SR-117A to the recent F-117A Stealth Fighter—have rolled from the
hidden hangers of Area 51. But today, craft that break with conventional aviation technology have been sighted in the area. According to
Aviation Week & Space Technology there have been many sightings of
a "triangular-shaped, quiet aircraft seen with a flight of Lockheed
F-117A Stealth Fighters," "a high-speed aircraft characterized by a
very loud, deep rumbling roar reminiscent of heavy-lift rockets . . .
[which] makes a pulsing sound and leaves a thick, segmented smoke
trail or contrail," and "a high-altitude aircraft . . . observed as a single,
bright light—sometimes pulsating—flying at speeds far exceeding other
aircraft in the area, and at altitudes estimated to be above 50,000 ft."
The publication's editors noted, "In addition, there is substantial evidence that another family of craft exists that relies on exotic propulsion and aerodynamic schemes not fully understood at this time."

Another innovation may be the use of private guards to watch
over this government installation. "Five years after the fall of the
Berlin Wall, the lights of Groom Lake burn throughout the night with
wartime urgency," noted Dane, who made a walking trip to the area
along with curious researchers. "And whatever secrets lie there are
guarded with undiminished vigilance. Armed, unidentified men stalk
the sagebrush in camouflage fatigues. Unmarked Black Hawk helicopters sweep the hills. Electronic sensors hidden along the approaching roads report the presence of vehicular traffic. Keep in mind that
you're subject to all this on public land, before you make it to the border marked with signs reading 'use of deadly force authorized.'"

The men in camouflage toting automatic weapons were not
U.S. military personnel but employees of the private security firm
Wackenhut Corporation, whose board of directors is filled with CIA,
FBI, and Pentagon officials such as former FBI director Clarence Kelley, former CIA deputy directors Frank Carlucci and Admiral Bobby
Ray Inman, former DIA director Gen. Joseph Carroll, former Secret
Service director James J. Rowley, and former Marine Corps commandant P. X. Kelley. Before becoming President Ronald Reagan's CIA
director, Wackenhut's outside legal counsel was William Casey,
blamed as the primary mover behind the October Surprise and Iran-
contra scandals.

Wackenhut has a long and dubious history of connections with
some of the government's dirtiest tricks, beginning soon after it was

taken over by George Wackenhut in 1958. A close Wackenhut friend, Senator George Smathers of Florida, helped find a loophole in federal statutes forbidding private detectives from working for the government. Since that time, Wackenhut Corporation grew to include thirty thousand armed employees, an estimated four million files on "suspected dissidents" in the United States, and revenues of $600 million in 1991. According to *Spy* magazine, the company helped supply sophisticated U.S. weaponry to Iraq's Saddam Hussein.

Wackenhut guards zealously protect Area 51, even to the extent of harassing and detaining citizens on nearby public roads and confiscating cameras at gunpoint. Such illegalities prompted investigative reporter Anthony J. Hilder to write an intemperate open letter to Lincoln County, Nevada, district attorney Patty Cafferata requesting a grand jury investigation into Wackenhut's authority at Area 51. "The reason for the urgency of this action," he wrote, "is because of the rapidly increasing number of 'life-threatening' situations created by unidentified paramilitary personnel who operate under the color of law to harass, intimidate and suppress the constitutional rights of many hundreds of American citizens and Japanese nationals who come to view the Unidentified Flying 'Saucer-Shaped Disks' being tested over your county."

Unconventional flying craft and tough private security guards with a company closely connected to the CIA help perpetuate the idea that secret elements within the government may be experimenting with alien technologies. Debunkers cling to the notion that all this simply represents highly secret conventional military aviation development, an outgrowth of the still-classified air force B-2 triangular bomber. Unofficial reports state that a new type or even class of aircraft—designated "Aurora," curiously enough—is under development. No one has denied that new and unusual craft are being tested. The question remains: Did this advanced technology stem from human ingenuity or alien reality?

One man who claims to know the answer has provided an intriguing—and controversial—glimpse of the work being performed at Area 51.

The Scientist and the Saucers

Robert Scott Lazar, better known as Bob, has a boyish smile, thick glasses, and a quiet unassuming demeanor that makes him appear like the computer nerd from next door—a smart guy who can program your VCR. Yet this articulate, educated man has publicly claimed that he worked on alien flying saucers for the U.S. government at Area 51.

Needless to say, Lazar's story has prompted much controversy both within and without the UFO research community.

His story began in June 1982 when the young scientist said he was working as a physicist at Los Alamos National Laboratory in New Mexico. He ran into the famous Dr. Edward Teller prior to a lecture there. Teller was reading a news article about Lazar, who had built his own jet car. "Hi, I'm the one you're reading about there," Lazar said, starting a conversation with the noted physicist. In 1988, after Lazar left Los Alamos, he wrote Teller a letter mentioning their meeting and the fact that he was job hunting. Lazar said he soon received a call from Teller saying he had forwarded Lazar's résumé to a Nevada company with government contracts. "I'd say it was no more than 10 or 15 minutes after he hung up that I got a call to come down for an interview at EG&G [Edgerton, Germeshausen & Grier] Special Projects. So that's how my services were solicited, if you can even call it that," he recalled. Lazar said when he went to EG&G's office, he was interviewed and hired by agents from the Office of Naval Intelligence (ONI).

Gradually, after strenuous security checks including requests for permission to monitor his telephone and search his home, Lazar was recruited to work on what he understood was "an advanced propulsion system" at Groom Lake. "I thought I was going to be at Area 51, where an awful lot of projects are done, including a lot of the black projects such as the SR-71 and so forth. . . . We landed at Area 51, and moments later we got on a bus and started driving and driving. And I realized, gee, I don't work at Area 51. Then, about 15 miles south of there, I was told that S-4 was the destination."

At S-4, sometimes referred to as "Dreamland," the "Ranch," or "Skunk Works," Lazar began to have second thoughts about his new job. He said security was oppressive and that guards even put a gun to his head. "They did that even in the original security briefing," Lazar said. "They did everything but physically hurt me. . . . Guards there with M-16s. Guys were slamming my chest, screaming into my ear. They were pointing weapons at me. Like I said, it's not a good place to work." Lazar began to suspect that there was something very dark and mysterious about this work when he noticed posters all over the place showing a hovering UFO with the caption "They're Here." His apprehension was not eased when he learned that he had been hired to replace a scientist who was one of three killed in April 1987, when an attempt was made to cut into an alien power plant reactor.

Once on the job, Lazar found he was to study and reverse-engineer the power plant from a UFO—a matter/antimatter reactor. He said he discovered the reactor, which was similar to our nuclear reactors but only the size of a soccer ball, produced "waves" nullifying gravity through the use of a superheavy substance he named Element 115 after its theoretical atomic number. "I was the one who identified 115," Lazar said. "That was my only contribution to the project. And I don't stand on the fact that it's 115, but if it's not, it's 114. It's right in there."

During his work at S-4, which lasted from December 1988 to April 1989, Lazar said saw nine alien craft housed in a row of huge hangars. One he was able to touch in passing and another he witnessed taking a short test flight. Intrigued, Lazar said he studied the craft closely. "I gave everything names," he said, "the 'top hat' one, the 'jello mold' and the 'sport model' [which] operated without a hitch. I mean it looked new, if that is what a flying saucer looks like. One of the them looked liked it was hit by some sort of projectile. It had a large hole in the bottom and a large hole in the top with the metal bent out like some sort of large caliber [projectile] had gone through it. . . . I got to look inside, and it had really small chairs. I think that was the first confirmation [of alien technology] I had."

Lazar recalled that one day while walking down a corridor at S-4, he glanced into a room and saw two men in lab coats "looking down and talking to something small, with long arms." Knowing that some people would say he saw a living extraterrestrial, Lazar noted, "They play so many mind games there. Maybe they stuck a doll in front of these guys and made me walk by it and look at it, just to see what my reaction would be. But, when we did turn around to do something, and walk back, it was gone, and the two guys were gone. So, I don't know what I saw."

Interestingly, the idea that aliens may be living at Area 51 was advanced by two unnamed government agents—identified only as "Falcon" and "Condor"—in the 1988 TV documentary *UFO Cover-up? Live!*

While Lazar's exposure to the saucers was short-lived and sporadic, the most astounding information came from more than two hundred pages of "briefing" documents he was required to read to prepare him for his job. Within these blue booklets, which bore no document numbers nor secrecy stamps, Lazar said he learned of other secret projects such as the study of a gravity drive ("Galileo"), looking back in time ("Looking Glass"), and a neutron beam weapon ("Sidekick"), all under a program called "Project Overview." Lazar read that aliens had been visiting Earth—which they called "Sol 3"—for millennia and that mankind was the result of sixty-five genetic "corrections" made over thousands of years. At least one group of small ETs— referred to as "The Kids"—came from a planet in the Zeta Reticuli star system. Lazar also was astounded to learn that the saucers in government hands were not all the result of accidental crashes. "I think . . . that we received those craft more by friendly means than by crash-retrieval or stealing them or however else," he said.

Even after all he had experienced, Lazar said he was still skeptical of statements made in a thick document pertaining to religion. This paper stated that the aliens consider humans as "containers." Asked to clarify this, Lazar replied, "Maybe containers of souls. You can come up with whatever theory you want. But we're containers, and that's how we are mentioned in the documents; that religion was specifically created so we have some rules and regulations for the sole purpose of not damaging the containers. . . ."

One intriguing aspect of Lazar's briefing concerned his description of an apparent battle between aliens and humans at a secret base in 1979. He said he read that a human guard tried to take a weapon into the alien's area, which resulted in fatal head wounds to security personnel. Lazar's description of this incident matches exactly with an account by UFO researcher Paul Bennewitz. In a 1985 letter to author Timothy Good, Bennewitz wrote, "In 1979, something happened. The alien . . . said [there had been] an argument over weapons . . . 66 [security people] were killed, 44 got away." The story has it that the aliens departed, leaving behind equipment, some of which was that studied by Lazar.

Lazar said he was not impressed with the caliber of work taking place at S-4. Only a handful of people were working on the UFO he saw and they seemed more like military people out of their league than world-class scientists. "Everything I saw, every step of the way, just showed me that such an incredible project is being handled not only in an unprofessional manner, but it bordered on the ridiculous." He said he understood that radioactive plutonium had been tried as fuel for the antimatter reactor.

If his account is true, it could explain a mysterious and unsolved UFO case near Houston, Texas. About 9:00 P.M. on December 29, 1980, Betty Cash, Vickie Landrum, and Landrum's young grandson were driving home on when a huge, bright diamond-shaped UFO approached their car spewing sparks. As the craft passed near their car, the light and heat became intense. The women were shocked to see about twenty helicopters—some large, twin-rotor craft along with smaller ones—surrounding the object, as if in escort. Shortly after this bizarre experience, all three witnesses developed headaches, nausea, skin sores, hair loss, and other ailments diagnosed as symptoms of radiation poisoning. Dr. J. Allen Hynek termed the Cash-Landrum experience a "really crucial case" due to the "absolutely unequivocal physical effects" involved. After developing cancer, Cash joined with Landrum in suing the U.S. government in the belief that the incident involved an experimental craft. But in 1986, their case was dismissed after military and NASA officials denied the government was operating any such craft.

Lazar complained that he had no way of obtaining detailed information on the project or the people working there. "You cannot just start a conversation with someone," he said. "They work on the buddy system. You're assigned with one other person, and he is the only person you carry on conversations with, period. As for grabbing someone in the hall, that's out of the question. In fact, even when you go to the bathroom, you're followed by security."

Lazar said he did not work at S-4 for any real length of time or even on a regular basis. According to Lazar, security officials learned from his monitored telephone that Lazar was having marital problems and, while not wanting to confront Lazar with this information, considered him a security risk. "That's why I left S-4," he explained. "I didn't actually leave, they denied my clearance. But that also left them in somewhat of a predicament, because here they had basically told me three-quarters of the story of what's going on, I had hands-on experience with everything, and that's when tensions began to rise, as soon as I got out."

Not helping to ease his security problems was the fact that, prior to leaving his work, Lazar took five of his friends to the mountains surrounding Area 51 to watch lights flying in the sky. After his clearance was denied, Lazar appeared in black silhouette on a Las Vegas TV program. Identified only as Dennis—the name of his work supervisor—Lazar first told his story of alien craft at Area 51 in the spring of 1989. In October, he retold his story using his name and face for a series entitled "UFOs: The Best Evidence" aired on CBS affiliate KLAS-TV.

The show's commentator, newsman George Knapp, attempted to corroborate Lazar's background and found problems. Officials of EG&G, the firm where Lazar claimed he was interviewed by ONI agents for his S-4 job, stated they had never heard of him, as did officials at the Los Alamos National Laboratory.

However, there were problems with the problems. Knapp located a 1982 Los Alamos laboratory internal phone book that listed "Robert Lazar" along with the other scientists. When confronted with the phone book, one official backtracked, admitting that Lazar had worked there but only on "nonsensitive" projects. Knapp also located several Los Alamos employees who confirmed that Lazar had worked with them on top-secret work concerning the SDI "Star Wars" project. Lazar also produced a W-2 Wage and Tax Statement for 1989 that showed his employer as "United States Department of Naval Intelligence, Washington, D.C." and an OMB identification number was listed as "E-6722MAJ." According to researcher Robert Oechsler, a former NASA mission analyst with good intelligence connections, an official with the Department of Energy (DOE) confirmed that the number "E-6722" was an Office of Management and Budget number representing a DOE contract and that the letters "MAJ" represented a "point of contact."

Lazar said while at S-4, he was required to wear a white security badge containing a blue diagonal strip across the top left corner and the letters "MAJ" printed down the right side. He said "MAJ" was "Majestic" and was spelled out on the badge of his supervisor. Lazar admitted that perhaps the "MAJ" designation, which brought to mind the MJ-12 controversy, was merely an inside joke but added that everyone wore an "MAJ" badge. Lazar said before being denied a security clearance, he was given a temporary clearance thirty-eight levels above the top-secret "Q" clearance, which he said was reactivated from his Los Alamos work. One government official denied that any security levels above "Q" exist. However, author Timothy Good determined that special access levels do exist as part of a Sensitive Compartmented Information (SCI) program dating back to World War II. It is used to inform a person only on the details of secret operation he needs to know to deal directly with that project. Author Williams E. Burrows, in his 1988 book, *Deep Black: The Secrets of Space Espionage*, stated there were more than thirty SCI categories in use within U.S. intelligence by 1986.

Dr. Teller did nothing to clarify matters when asked about his knowledge of Lazar by a TV cameraman. Obviously disquieted by the mention of Lazar, Teller vacillated, saying, "Look, I don't know Bob Lazar. . . . I probably met him. I might have said to somebody that I met him and I liked him, after I met him, and if I liked him. But I don't remember him. . . . I mean, you are trying to force questions on me that I simply won't answer."

The contradictions in Lazar's background prompted newsman Knapp to conclude that Lazar's education and work records have been intentionally altered or hidden. More ominously, Lazar said that after his first TV interview someone shot at him from a white car as he left the studio.

Following the shooting incident and death threats, Lazar said his decision to go public with his story was prompted partially by self-preservation and partially by other considerations. "I tried to protect myself in several ways. One of them was going on the air and getting some of the information out. . . . Once that was done—unless they do things for revenge, and I don't believe that they operate that way—there would be no reason to hassle me anymore," he said. "Any action on their part right now would guarantee what I'm saying is true. . . . [Another] of the reasons I'm coming forward with this information is that it's not only a crime against the American people, it's a crime against the scientific community, which I've been part of for some time," he said. "It's just unfair not to put it in the hands of the overall scientific community. There are people who are much more capable of dealing with this information, and by this time, would have got a lot further along than this select group of people working out in the middle of the desert."

Considering the threats involved in Lazar's experiences, it was no surprise when several polygraph (lie detector) tests proved "inconclusive." Initially, polygraph examiner Ron Clay said Lazar showed to be truthful on one test but deceitful on a second. At Clay's request, former Los Angeles policeman and corporate security expert Terry Tavernetti was brought into the case. Tavernetti administered four tests on Lazar and concluded he did not attempt to deceive. His conclusion was supported by a third polygraph test, but a fourth indicated Lazar, while not trying to be deceitful, may have been relating hearsay information, not his own experience. "The difficulty in determining Lazar's truthfulness stems from the fear that was drilled into him," said Tavernetti.

The case for Lazar's veracity was further damaged in 1990 when he pleaded guilty to one count of pandering in connection with a Nevada house of prostitution and was sentenced to three years probation and 150 hours of community service, and advised to get psychological counseling.

Some UFO researchers suspected this brush with the law was a setup to discredit Lazar. However, a close check of the facts indicated that the entire episode was initiated by Lazar himself when he mentioned that he had installed electronic equipment for a Las Vegas brothel during a TV interview. Faced with this public acknowledgment of prostitution, authorities were forced to act, since it was located in one of the three Nevada counties where prostitution remained illegal. The case was a hotbed of unrequited love, youthful naïveté and—at least according to allegations in court papers filed by Lazar—possible police corruption. Although there was some debate over whether or not Lazar knew the operation was illegal, the essence of the case showed that all he did was install some computer and security equipment for a friend. Both the vice squad and the district attorney recommended no jail time. A close friend indicated that further legal action to reverse the guilty plea may be forthcoming.

But the controversy over Lazar and his incredible story concerning Area 51 and its saucers continues unabated. Although several researchers claim to have spoken with other Area 51 workers who confirm Lazar's account, none have agreed to subject themselves to the scrutiny that Lazar has undergone. The TV whistle-blowers "Condor" and "Falcon" corroborated elements of the Lazar story but remain publicly unidentified. Another source has been identified as a former CIA officer who worked for Lockheed named Marion Leo Williams. According to researcher Andrew Basiago, Williams claimed to have been transported to Area 51's Dreamland in the 1970s, where he learned that recovered UFOs were being studied in a supersecret underground government laboratory.

George Knapp, the Las Vegas TV newsman who spent considerable time investigating the Lazar story, said, "We know a lot of secret stuff goes on in Area 51 . . . and there's been this lingering, nagging voice floating around at the test site for many years that something else, something alien, was up there, but no one's ever bothered to check it out. But Bob is the first to come forward to say anything about it—to have inside knowledge. I've spent almost a year on the Lazar story. We've gone over every aspect of the story again and again. Knowing him really sells a lot of it, because he's not out to impress anyone and he's not trying to make a million dollars with this. . . . The story has been consistent again and again." Knapp added he knew of several people who offered to confirm Lazar's story but were warned off by men who said they were government agents.

Timothy Good, who examined the Lazar case in great detail, concluded that "it is my opinion that his story is substantially true" and may be part of a "public indoctrination process" to accustom the public to the concept of extraterrestrial visitation. Knapp harbored similar suspicions. "I sometimes wonder if he wasn't in fact chosen for the release of this information," he said.

Scientist-author Jacques Vallee, while impressed with Lazar's sincerity and scientific knowledge, nevertheless came away from an interview thinking that he had hit a "wall of absurdity." Vallee questioned the lack of scientific equipment at the S-4 site and the casual manner in which he was shown the "briefing" documents. "Robert Lazar's experience had been pure theatre," he wrote in 1991. Vallee indicated his suspicion that the Lazar saucer story may have been used to screen secret nonalien military research.

Don Ecker, who wrote extensively about the case, also believed that Lazar is sincere. "But what's behind all that is the real story. I think he was fed huge amounts of disinformation, but for what reason? Something against the Soviets? Against the people in the UFO field?" he wondered. "I can't believe that if Lazar actually was involved in government saucer research and was telling the truth that they would allow him to live."

Author Curtis Peebles, who dismisses all UFO stories as simply misinterpretations of reality, apparently did not know how to handle the Lazar story. He brushed it off in less than two pages and only stated that "Lazar's story has some holes." Peebles did note Lazar's pandering conviction and took special interest in the fact that Lazar was not listed as a member of the American Physical Society or the American Nuclear Society.

Lazar himself has never flatly denied that he may have been an unknowing participant in some government disinformation scheme, but he declared, "I am telling the truth—I've tried to prove that. What's going on up there could be the most important event in history. You're talking about physical contact and proof from another system—another planet, another intelligence. That's got to be the biggest event in history—period. And it's real, and it's there." In another interview, Lazar was even more emphatic: "I saw what I saw, and you didn't. I don't care who believes me and who doesn't. Screw the rest of you guys."

The truth behind possible government secret space technology, cover-ups, disinformation campaigns, and the military possession of UFOs and aliens remains unproven. If indeed there is development of craft based on alien technology, what is its purpose—to wage war against terrestrial enemies or intergalactic visitors . . . or could it be to provide a means of escape for the world's wealthy elite?

What is clear today is that the UFO phenomenon has spread far beyond mere sightings of unknown craft in the sky. By the 1970s, even stranger ingredients had been added to the mix of UFO lore—animal mutilations, crop circles, and human abductions.

FACE-TO-FACE

Undaunted by ongoing government secrecy and dismissive media reports, UFOs continued to appear in the world's skies. But a new—and more personal—note was added to the mere sightings of flying objects.

Back in the 1950s, nothing so divided the fledgling UFO research community than the idea of physical contact between humans and UFO occupants. To a large extent that division remains today, straining the faith of even the most enthusiastic UFO devotee despite ever-increasing media attention to the subject. Seeing unidentifiable lights and objects in the sky is one thing. But meeting or being abducted by unearthly creatures is quite something else. However, once again history demonstrates that this phenomenon is nothing new.

In the biblical account, Ezekiel not only saw the "wheel" in the air but was taken aboard. After falling prostrate from the sounds and dust cloud signaling the arrival of the "vision of God," Ezekiel was addressed by a man bathed in a brilliant radiance: "Stand up, son of dust, and I will talk to you." "Then the Spirit lifted me up and the glory of the Lord began to move away, accompanied by the sound of a great earthquake," Ezekiel wrote. "The Spirit lifted me up and took me away to Tel Abib, another colony of Jewish exiles beside the Chebar River. I went in bitterness and anger, but the hand of the Lord was strong upon me." To some this sounds like a credible account of an abduction.

Hindu literature scholar Richard Thompson wrote, "There are Vedic accounts in which a human being is abducted for motives of lust by a member of another humanoid race." One such tale comes from the fifth Veda known as the *Ramayana* in which a Raksasa humanoid named Ravana abducted Sita, the wife of the noble Lord Ramacandra. One account of this abduction stated,

> *Unseen dwellers of the woodlands watched the dismal deed of shame,*
> *Marked the mighty-armed Raksasa lift the poor and helpless dame,*
> *Seat her on his car celestial yoked with asses winged with speed,*
> *Golden in its shape and radiance, fleet as Indra's heavenly steed! . . .*
> *Then rose the car celestial o'er the hill and wooded vale.*

As previously related, there were many reports of face-to-face meetings between citizens and the mysterious "airships" of the late 1800s. Typical was the experience of John Barclay, who lived near Houston, Texas. He told the *Houston Post* that on the night of April 21, 1897, he saw an oblong object with lights "much brighter than electric lights" hovering in a pasture near his house. Grabbing his Winchester, Barclay advanced toward the machine when he was met by a man who asked him to lay down his weapon, as no harm to him was intended. Barclay was asked for some lubricating oil, a couple of cold chisels, and some bluestone (stone treated with copper sulfate). Barclay obtained the oil and chisels but could not locate any bluestone. Upon his return, the man offered Barclay a ten-dollar bill for his effort, which he declined. When Barclay ask to see inside the craft, the man refused, saying, "No, we cannot permit you to approach any nearer, but do as we request you and your kindness will be appreciated, and we will call on you some future day and reciprocate your kindness by taking you on a trip." As the encounter was ending, Barclay asked where the man was from and where he was going. The odd reply was, "From anywhere, but we will be in Greece day after tomorrow." With that, the craft shot out of sight.

In the summer of 1947, as the Kenneth Arnold and Maury Island stories were beginning to generate UFO interest in the United States, a strange contact occurred in the Alps north of Venice, Italy. The story, as reported by UFO researcher Jenny Randles, told how geologist Rapuzzi Johannis was searching for rocks near the Italian village of Villa Santina on the morning of August 14, when he discovered an oval craft embedded in the slope of a mountain. Spying what he thought were two boys, he yelled and motioned for them to come see what he had found. As he approached the pair, Johannis was shocked to see two small beings about three feet tall with overlarge heads and huge round eyes. They were wearing close-fitting bluish garments over what appeared to be greenish skin. When Johannis raised his hand containing a rock pick as a friendly salute, one of the creatures, perhaps misinterpreting the gesture as an aggressive move, touched his belt and Johannis was knocked to the ground dazed. While lying help-less, he saw the beings enter the craft, which proceeded to move into the air, shrink in size, and silently disappear.

But such stories were either lost in history or ignored by the media of the time, leaving many to believe that strange contacts with occupants of flying machines began only as the flying saucer era got under way in the late 1940s. The few contact stories that did surface were quickly dismissed by early UFO researchers as too fantastic to even consider. They were having trouble enough dealing with mysteri-ous flying objects.

The Man from Venus

The first well-known UFO contactee was Polish immigrant George Adamski, who early in this century worked at a number of odd jobs and even served with the U.S. Cavalry on the Mexican border between 1913 and 1916. By the 1920s, Adamski began teaching philosophy and by the early 1930s had founded a monastery in California called "the Royal Order of Tibet." Here he acquired a special license to produce wine during Prohibition for "religious purposes." During World War II, Adamski operated a hamburger stand named Palomar Gar-dens, which was located on the slopes of Mount Palomar near the giant Hale telescope. Apparently this proximity to science along with his philosophical teachings prompted him to call himself "professor."

Adamski claimed that nearly two hundred UFOs had passed near the Palomar telescope during the war years. He wrote of these craft in *Fate* magazine in 1950. After taking some photographs of an aerial object, Adamski's reputation as a UFO researcher began to spread, despite the questionable quality of his photos. Adamski voiced the hope that he might one day actually meet the inhabitant of a UFO.

His wish was granted on November 20, 1952, when he, along with six others, saw a silvery, cigar-shaped object floating in the sky near Desert City, California. Driven to a site near the craft, Adamski asked his friends to wait nearby while he approached the object. He later claimed he met a man with shoulder-length hair and a one-piece brown suit and recognized the man as "a human being from another world!"

Using a combination of hand signals and mental telepathy, Adamski claimed he was able to learn that the man's name was Orthon, and that he had come to Earth from the planet Venus to warn humans about the dangers of nuclear bomb tests. Orthon confirmed that ships were visiting the earth from both within our solar system and beyond and that some had crashed as the result of human interference. He said no overt landings would take place since "there would be a tremendous amount of fear on the part of the people, and probably the visitors would be torn to pieces by the Earth people, if such landings were attempted." He also indicated that some Earth people had been taken aboard craft such as his, which he said was simply a "scout" ship ferried to Earth by a large "mothership." When Adamski attempted to take photos, Orthon took his film with a promise to return it.

A few days later, Adamski said the craft returned and dropped his film out of a porthole. When developed, the film was found to contain a series of symbols that have never been deciphered. Adamski wrote a short account of his UFO experience, which was added to a UFO book by British author Desmond Leslie. An astute publisher made Adamski's experience the focal point of Leslie's book and published it in 1953 as *Flying Saucers Have Landed*. It quickly became a best-seller. Over the next decade more books by Adamski—apparently ghostwritten and embellished by others—were published, and his accounts of life in outer space were expanded to include descriptions of trees and rivers on the moon and creatures from most of the planets in the solar system.

"He died in April 1965," wrote author Jenny Randles, "his views having split the UFO community into two camps which still exist today. The occult-oriented Ufologists, fervent believers in friendly extraterrestrials, accept much of what Adamski said as gospel, literally. Most UFO researchers, however, believe his stories were at best hallucinations and perhaps outright fantasies. There is no doubt that Adamski's evidence is barely persuasive. His photographs have convinced few, and many allege analysis shows them to be small, crude fakes. His stories about conditions on other planets in the solar system were found to be scientifically absurd even before he died."

Like so many other aspects of the UFO story, it is tempting to simply write Adamski off as deluded or a hoaxer. Ray Stanford, one of Adamski's most eager followers, later quoted Adamski as saying, "During Prohibition I had the Sacred Order of Tibet. It was a front. Listen, I was able to make wine. . . . Hell, I made enough wine for half of southern California. In fact, I was the biggest bootlegger around. Then that man Roosevelt came along and he knocked out the Prohibition. If hadn't been for that man Roosevelt, I wouldn't have had to get into all this saucer crap." Even Adamski's former publicist, Harold Salkin, noted that in 1963 Adamski's account of a saucer trip to Saturn before a Washington crowd in many ways contradicted the same story he had told earlier in the day to close friends. Salkin also pointed out that at least one of Adamski's UFO photos was proven a "fraud," since the UFO image extended beyond the frame of the film. "He apparently fell into the trap which had snared many of the contactees of the 1950s and 60s," Salkin stated. "In order to whet the appetites of his regular followers, he—like the others—was convinced that he had to come up with some event that was really spectacular. In Adamski's case, it was the trip to Saturn."

But there is some evidence that indicates a possible darker aspect to Adamski's stories. Several UFO researchers have implied that Adamski may have been "set up" in his role as an early contactee celebrity. Randles noted that at the same time Adamski was gaining notoriety, the CIA was convening the Robertson panel in an effort to turn official opinion against UFOs as real objects.

Agency personnel also wanted to deflect serious public attention and noted how the contactees had "reduced the credibility of UFO evidence in the eyes of many people." Adamski himself lent support to the idea that he was used by intelligence when in a 1953 speech he began by saying that his material had been "cleared" by the FBI and air force intelligence. Adamski backed down from this statement a few days later when FBI agents questioned him about such clearance. Author Jacques Vallee noted that Adamski admitted that government scientists from Point Loma Naval Electronics Laboratory near San Diego had asked him to cooperate in studying UFOs, thus helping to launch his career as a contactee. "Adamski's major supporter abroad was a former intelligence officer with the British Army," stated Vallee, adding, "A man who hosted Adamski during his tour of Australia has told me that 'Good old George' was traveling with a passport bearing special privileges." One of the scientists Vallee mentioned, Gene L. Bloom, denied any involvement with Adamski, saying, "Everything Adamski wrote about us was fiction, pure fiction." An associate with Adamski at Palomar Gardens, Jerrold E. Baker, said he overheard a tape recording of Adamski's desert experience before it happened, leading him to write, "I was able to determine that the desert contact was not a mere stab in the dark or a picnic in the desert, but a planned operation."

Another intriguing aspect of the Adamski case came with a 1954 attempt to bring the contactee into federal court. Researcher Thomas Eickoff, incensed that Adamski had written in a later book entitled *Inside the Space Ships* that two government scientists could confirm his out-of-this-world trip, believed Adamski would be forced to produce the scientists in court. Should he fail to produce the pair, Adamski would be subject to fraud charges. Eickoff's plan never got off the ground because his lawyer received a letter from CIA director Allen Dulles stating that, while Eickoff did have a federal case, no one would be permitted to testify regarding Adamski's book because the subject of UFOs was a matter of maximum security. It was unclear if the CIA's position was an attempt to shield Adamski or the UFO subject in general. Such an activity would strongly support the theory that he was somehow connected to a government operation. It was definitely an indication of the intense—and highly secret—interest in the subject within the intelligence community.

There is no doubt that on at least one occasion Adamski was set up as the object of a hoax. Long after his death, two writers—James W. Moseley and Gray Barker—admitted that, as a joke, they had concocted a letter implying an endorsement of Adamski's views on State Department letterhead. Adamski had widely publicized the fraudulent letter from a nonexistent official named "R. E. Straith." The two writers decided not to reveal the joke at the time because federal agents were investigating this apparent misuse of official letterhead stationery.

Then there were some strange bits of information that seemed to lend support to some of Adamski's stories. For example, British author Timothy Good recounted a story of two Yorkshire police constables who in January 1978 encountered an "absolutely, awe-inspiring" glowing object on a country lane. "There were these three great spheres underneath, like huge ball bearings—three of them equally placed around it," said one constable. "There was a hollow area underneath and like a skirting around the bottom, but these things protruded below that." Good noted, "The three spheres seen under the craft have been observed in a number of incidents, most notably by the much vilified George Adamski, whose photographs and film of this type of craft taken in 1952 and 1965 have been ridiculed and denounced as hoaxes."

A 1965 incident concerned an eight-millimeter film Adamski took at the home of Madeleine Rodeffer at Silver Spring, Maryland, on February 26. Both Adamski, Rodeffer, and other witnesses said a UFO maneuvered over the house. It hovered and raised and lowered one of three round "landing pods" on its bottom side. Rodeffer said she could discern human figures in portholes ringing the circular craft. But when the film was returned from developing, Rodeffer claimed, "The film I got back is not the original film at all." However, it was believed that some original frames remained and experts split over its authenticity. Author Good, supported by a former Eastman-Kodak optical physicist, determined that it would have been impossible to produce certain distortion effects seen in the film or to build a small, inexpensive model that could convincingly raise and lower its landing gear. A NASA scientist believed the object in the film was no larger than three to four feet across and considered the film a "fake." The interesting point is that the film depicted a craft identical to Adamski's 1952 photographs. Was this support for his claims or merely support for the idea that he had kept a scale model hidden away for thirteen years?

Adding to the mystery was Stephen Darbishire, who told Good that in February 1954 he took two photographs of a UFO in Lancashire, England, that was identical to those described by Adamski. Unfortunately, both negatives and the prints have since disappeared.

Whether Adamski was sincere but deluded, a hoaxer or a participant—knowingly or otherwise—in an intelligence operation, the results were the same. The work of Keyhoe and NICAP to break government secrecy on UFOs was blunted. "Publicity given personalities such as the late George Adamski, who claimed to have flown in flying saucers, dealt the final death blow to any open scientific discussion on UFOs," noted researcher Raymond E. Fowler.

But if serious scientific interest in UFOs was scotched, the public's appetite for stories of contact was undiminished. Other contactees, following on the heels of Adamski, began coming forward with their own tales of UFO rides, space brothers, and trips to other worlds:

Howard Menger, a U.S. Army veteran who operated a sign-painting business, claimed to have been an alien in a previous life and to have been contacted by "space people" since 1932, when he was a child. He said he had ridden UFOs to most of the major planets in our solar system. In the 1960s, Menger denied his alien contacts, saying the CIA had used him to test public reaction to extraterrestrial encounters. Later he recanted the CIA story and began preaching a message of "love and understanding."

Daniel Fry, the self-proclaimed "best-informed scientist in the world on the subject of space and space travel," first met his space contact, A-lan, when he encountered a saucer near White Sands Proving Ground in July 1950. As he approached the craft, A-lan told him, "Better not touch the hull, pal, it's still hot. Take it easy, pal, you're among friends." Fry said he was offered and accepted a ride on the saucer to New York City and back, a ride he calculated took about thirty minutes. During the trip, A-lan told Fry that his race were descendants of ancient Lemurians who had fled to space following an

SPACEMAN'S HEADSTONE?

This rare photograph shows the partial headstone in Aurora, Texas, marking the place where, according to legend, a small person who was "not of this earth" was buried in 1897. The ballpoint pen at right corner gives perspective. Shortly after this photo was made in the early 1970s, the headstone was stolen and was never recovered.

Photo courtesy of North Texas State University Public Information Office

Photo courtesy of Tom Adams

A PUZZLING FRAGMENT.

Physicist Dr. Tom Gray of the University of North Texas exhibits a fragment found at the site of the alleged 1897 crash of a UFO in Aurora, Texas. In a 1973 study, Gray said the fragment was "puzzling" because it showed no magnetic properties even though it was composed primarily of iron.

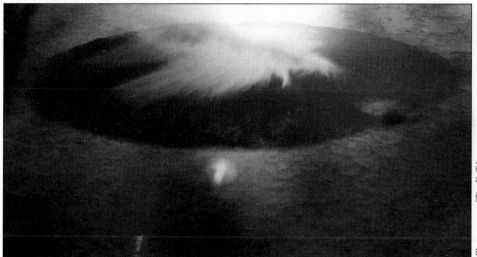

Photo courtesy of Jim Kuffel

THE MOTHERSHIP?
Jim Kuffel took this photo of what appears to be a giant UFO near Antioch, Illinois, on November 10, 1996. Kuffel, intrigued by this aerial apparition, used a 35-mm camera with a 52-mm lens to shoot the thing against the setting sun. In all likelihood, this *Independence Day*-looking "craft" was actually created by temperature inversion caused by layers of warm air mixing with cooler air. But this well illustrates the problem of many misidentifications of normal events as UFOs. However, many sightings are harder to explain.

MJ–12 OPERATIONS MANUAL? This is the reconstructed cover of a document purporting to be a manual issued by the MJ–12 group regarding the recovery and handling of extraterrestrial spacecraft and occupants. The manual covers subjects ranging from the identification of UFO types to maintaining a press blackout. Although controversy still rages over the manual's authenticity, many researchers claim the extent and format of the manual argue against it being a hoax.

Drawings courtesy of David Hatcher Childress

NAZI FLYING DISK. These drawings depict one of the noiseless and exhaust-free "flying disks" developed by Austrian inventor Viktor Schauberger for the Nazis. Schauberger's disks, at least one of which reportedly was test flown, were powered by a rotating water system called liquid vortex propulsion. Some researchers contend that Nazi disk technology was gained through contact with extraterrestrials and that this technology fell into the hands of the Allies after World War II, thus beginning the modern flying saucer era.

FIRST REPORTED
UFOs. Pilot Kenneth Arnold was the first person to receive widespread publicity after reporting UFOs flying near Mount Rainier on June 24, 1947, just prior to the Roswell incident. Arnold reported that the objects acted "like a saucer would if you skipped it across the water," and subsequent reporting put the term *flying saucer* in the public vocabulary.

A CONVERTED
SCIENTIST. The late Dr. J. Allen Hynek was chairman of Northwestern University's Astronomy Department and a longtime consultant on UFOs to the U.S. government. Over the years, Dr. Hynek moved from writing off UFOs as mere swamp gas to calling for a scientific investigation of what he concluded was a genuine and tangible reality.

THE UFO SCIENTIST. Physicist Bob Lazar claims to have participated in the reverse engineering of UFOs in the custody of the U.S. government at a secret base in Nevada known as Area 51. Lazar said the UFOs were powered by gravity wave amplifiers that allowed the craft to travel the vast distances between stars by "folding" space. He also stated that his immediate supervisor during his UFO work wore a badge with the word *Majestic* on it.

ALIENS ARE HERE. Television documentary producer Linda Moulton Howe began her UFO career with her 1980 Emmy Award–winning documentary *A Strange Harvest*, which explored the cattle mutilation mystery. Since then, Howe has explored many other facets of the UFO issue and concluded "that intelligences other than human are forcing glimpses of other realities upon us."

CONTACTEE OR CONMAN? George Adamski, back in the early 1950s, claimed to have been taken on rides in outer space by a Venusian named Orthon. While most people discounted Adamski's stories and crude photographs, more recent study has shown that his popularity may have been engineered by government intelligence agents.

BILLY AND THE PLEIADIANS. No story of alien contact is more bizarre or more well supported than that of Eduard Albert Meier, better known as Billy. Between 1975 and 1978, the one-armed Swiss handyman produced nearly 2,000 pages of notes made from conversations with aliens from the Pleiades star system plus hundreds of astoundingly clear and detailed photographs of the Pleiadian "beam ships." Although laughed off as a hoax, the Meier story had many intriguing aspects.

CROP CIRCLE COMPLEXITY. With the dawn of the 1990s, the complexity of crop circle designs continued to increase as seen in these photographs. Picture A, taken in July 1991 near Barbury Castle in England, displays a working knowledge of Euclidean geometry. Some circles even included one mathematical theorem previously unknown to man. Picture B depicts a design know as an "insectogram" created in a field across a highway from legendary Stonehenge *(top center)*. The sheer number and distances involved in the worldwide crop circle phenomenon conclusively disprove the notion that all are hoaxes.

FATHER OF REMOTE VIEWING. New York artist and scientific researcher Ingo Swann is credited with helping to develop the laboratory methods used in the psychic phenomenon called remote viewing. During the 1970s and '80s, Swann's methods were successfully used by military intelligence officers within the army's Intelligence and Security Command to gather information on the Soviet Union.

AMERICA'S FIRST PSI SPY. Melvin C. Riley was one of the first military men recruited into the army's remote viewing unit. An accomplished remote viewer, Riley was the mentor to several military officers who use the psychic phenomenon to locate hidden enemy military assets. Riley told of viewing both beings and spacecraft from other worlds and commented, "When you can go out and see the universe, who wants to go look at a Russian submarine?"

ONE OF THE LAST VIEWERS. Former Army Major David Morehouse was one of the last persons to be trained in remote viewing by the military. Although regarded as an unusually gifted remote viewer, Morehouse was persecuted by the army after he decided to go public with the remote viewing story. His book *Psychic Warrior* enjoyed popular success after an initial attempt to publish the military remote viewing story was terminated under unusual circumstances.

The American Association of Remote Viewers, Inc.

A GLOWING — THING / FUZZY TO LOOK
NOT AN OBJECT

WORKING — NOT A RESIDENT —
PASSING.

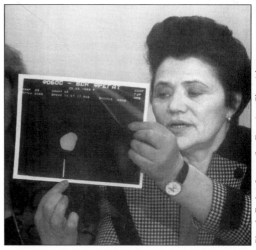

Photo by Frederic Larson, San Francisco Chronicle

AN INTERCEPTOR FROM MARS? The sketch on the left, produced by a military-trained remote viewer, depicts an irregular-shaped object approaching the Russian *Phobos II*, which was lost as it neared Mars in 1989. Months later, visiting Soviet cosmonaut Col. Marina Popovich *(right)* displayed one of the last photographs sent back to earth by *Phobos II*. It showed an irregular-shaped object approaching the space probe and appeared to verify the remote viewing account. Scientists were at a loss to explain the nature of the object with any certainty.

Jim Marrs

REMOTE VIEWING CENTRAL. For nearly two decades these two small wood-frame buildings at Fort Meade, Maryland, were the headquarters of the psychic spy unit known variously as GRILL FLAME, CENTER LANE, and STARGATE. It was here that military intelligence officers, using laboratory-tested methods of psychic remote viewing, furnished information on secret Soviet weapons and installations. Every viewer also encountered UFOs during their searches for foreign technology.

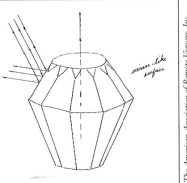

QUARANTINE ENFORCER?

Several remote viewers have seen small objects such as this one hovering in orbit, apparently to enforce a quarantine of earth. About the size of a hand grenade, these multi-faceted objects reportedly are the cause of many space setbacks such as the 1993 *Titan 4* and the *Mars 96* rocket launches, which failed to reach orbit. Some researchers speculate that military and weapons space flights are being blocked by extraterrestrials.

A UFO INVENTORY. Based on remote viewing sessions, various UFO designs such as these have been sketched by the viewers, who claim that various extraterrestrial races are currently visiting the earth for a variety of reasons. Although some alien agendas seem less benevolent than others, none are seen as overtly hostile. Viewers said that aliens interacting with humans are but a very small percentage of races that exist throughout the universe.

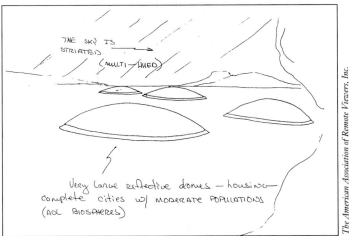

THE SKY IS STRIATED (MULTI-HUED)

Very Large Reflective domes — housing complete cities w/ MODERATE POPULATIONS (A.K. BIOSPHERES)

A BLEAK FUTURE. In a structured remote viewing study, viewers foresaw the earth devastated in the near future by ultraviolet energy due to widening holes in the ozone layer. In their view, humans will be forced underground and into domed cities (depicted above) to survive. Various viewers also foresaw extraterrestrials working side by side to replenish the earth's atmosphere.

atomic cataclysm. He added that mankind needed help because our physical science had far outstripped social science and religion and that man was incapable of dealing with true "understanding."

George Van Tassel, an airline mechanic, who claimed that in 1951 he received telepathic knowledge from a council that ruled our solar system. Van Tassel said humans are a hybrid race created by the inter-marriage of Venusians and Earth apes. He began successful "Giant Rock Saucerian Conventions" between the mid-1950s and 1970 at his airport/café at Giant Rock, California. He also founded the Ministry of Universal Wisdom, Inc. Van Tassel lost influence after authenticating UFO photos sent to him by a New York lawyer, who then exposed them as a hoax.

Truman Bethurum, loudly denounced by Dr. Edward Condon, claimed to have been abducted by eight small beings from a saucer while sleeping in his truck west of Las Vegas in 1952. He developed a relationship with the saucer's captain, a beautiful space woman from the planet Clarion, which is hidden from the earth on the far side of the sun. The woman promised to take him to her misery-free home world but, despite several further contacts, the trip never happened.

Elizabeth Klarer, who claimed to have been taken from her South African home to a planet near Alpha Centauri with a man called Akon in 1954, described the planet Meton as a world of vegetarians free from the problems of humanity. She said she had a child by Akon but had to return to Earth because she was uncomfortable breathing the air of Meton. Akon and her son visited her in 1963, she reported.

Orfeo Angelucci, labeled as sincere in his delusions by psychiatrist Carl Jung, claimed highly mystical and religious experiences through UFO contact. In May 1952, Angelucci got off work at Lockheed and encountered two green glowing balls that spoke to him about man's evolution. Two months later, he boarded a saucer that had landed in a dry riverbed and was taken high above the earth. A "Space Brother" named Neptune told him that man was in danger because his technology was threatening the world. He warned of a global catastrophe in 1986.

All of the Adamski-like contactees exhibited similar attributes—the use of books, newsletters, and lectures to gain money and notoriety, the idea that each was a special contact between humans and benevolent "Space Brothers," a lack of any independent corroboration of their experiences, and ongoing messages of love, peace, and brotherhood. Many contactees formed groups that today would most probably be termed cults.

One exception to such characterization was a twenty-three-year-old Brazilian farmer named Antonio Villas Boas, whose ordeal may have marked the beginning of the modern abduction experience. Although Villas Boas claimed to have been taken on October 16, 1957, due to a lengthy investigation coupled with translation and publication delays, his story was not publicized until late 1964.

Villas Boas, who never profited from his story, told a journalist and a doctor it began about 1:00 A.M. as he was operating a tractor on the family farm near São Francisco de Salles, Brazil. He said he had seen a bright light in the fields the previous night, which returned. Villas Boas described a red light at the front of a circular craft with a rotating cupola on top. The craft dropped three landing legs and landed nearby. When Villas Boas tried to flee on his tractor, the engine failed and it stopped. As he tried to flee on foot, he was grabbed by a humanoid about five feet tall. He pushed the being to the ground and again tried to run but was stopped by three more beings, who dragged him to the landed saucer.

Inside, he was placed in a small, cold, square room with seamless walls. Here he was stripped naked and coated with a gel. Soon he was taken to another room containing a bed with a strange hump in the center. Using tubes, the beings extracted blood and then left Villas Boas alone. After perhaps a half hour, he noticed a noxious odor that made him sick. After another wait, a woman entered the room. She was less than five feet tall and looked human except for an angular face with catlike eyes. Her hair was long and white, but her arm and pubic hair was dark red. Inexplicably, Villas Boas said he became aroused and proceeded to have intercourse with the woman, who appeared relieved when it was over. As she was leaving, she gave Villas Boas a look he thought reflected pity. She then rubbed her belly, pointed to him, then pointed upward. Villas Boas interpreted her signs as a warning she would return, but in light of modern abductions, many researchers believe she meant that she would bear his child in space.

Although angered because he felt "all they wanted [was] a good stallion to improve their stock," Villas Boas was soon given back his clothes and taken on a short tour of the craft before being returned to the field near his home. Upon his arrival, he found that more than four hours had passed.

The young farmer was examined by a doctor in Rio de Janeiro, Olavo Fontes, who found Villas Boas to be rational and unimaginative. The doctor also found the man to be suffering from weakness and nausea. Several small bleeding lesions were found on his body. All this was consistent with mild radiation poisoning, Dr. Fontes concluded. By 1978, Villas Boas had become a lawyer and was the father of four children. In a Brazilian TV appearance, he changed only one portion of his account—he then said the strange woman had taken a sperm sample during the act of intercourse. Interestingly, Villas Boas recalled every detail of his experience without the need for hypnosis.

Fascinating as Villas Boas' abduction was, it was only a precursor to the main event of the 1960s—the abduction of Betty and Barney Hill.

Over the Hills

Although the Hills' case actually began on September 19, 1961, it would not be until 1966 that it reached the public. But when it did—through a book and a film—it set the tone for subsequent abductions with the themes of missing time, claims of medical experimentation, and recollection through hypnosis.

The Hill story most likely would never have occurred but for weather reports of a hurricane off the East Coast. In 1961, Barney Hill, thirty-nine, a black mail sorter, commuted 120 miles each day to Boston from his home in Portsmouth, New Hampshire. Betty, forty-one, was a white social worker with a heavy caseload. Both were active in their church and in the civil rights movement. Pressures were heavy on the interracial couple, and they had visited Montreal, Canada, for a short holiday. Upon hearing the hurricane report, they decided to cut short their visit and return home to Portsmouth.

Driving south on U.S. Highway 3 shortly after 10:00 P.M. on September 19, they both noticed a bright star, which suddenly appeared and seemed to be following them. Barney was skeptical, rationalizing the light as an airplane or satellite. But when the light remained, Betty grabbed some binoculars to view the object. She claimed she could see a double row of windows on the craft. With the object hovering a mere fifty feet away, Barney stopped the car south of Indian Head and took a look for himself. He said it appeared to be a large glowing pancake. Looking closer, Barney thought the object must be some sort of secret military weapon and said to himself, "How interesting, there is the military pilot, and he is looking at me." He saw there were others looking at him through a window in the object and became terrified, convinced somehow that he and Betty were about to be captured. Barney raced back to the car and they drove off, accompanied by a odd "beeping" noise that seemed to come from the car's trunk. The sound made them drowsy. After a second experience with

the beeping sound, they suddenly came fully awake and found themselves a few miles south of where Hill had left the car to view the
object. Unable to recall precisely what had occurred, they drove home.

Expecting to be home by before 3:00 A.M., the Hills noted that
it was 5:30 A.M. when they finally arrived. Puzzled by their experience,
Betty called her sister the next day, who heightened her fear by suggesting that some type of radiation might have been involved.
Wrongly thinking that a compass might register radiation, Betty went
to the car, where she was surprised to discover "a dozen or more shiny
circles scattered on the surface of the trunk, each perfectly circular and
about the size of a silver dollar." The compass never moved when she
placed it on other areas of the car, but when placed on one of the shiny
spots, the compass needle began to spin. Convinced that something
strange had happened to them, the Hills filed a report of the UFO
with Pease Air Force Base in Portsmouth just thirty-six hours after the
incident. In recent years, the Hill story gained some substantiation
when it was learned that, according to Report No. 100-1-61 of the
SAC 100th Bomb Wing, Pease radar registered an "unknown" at the
exact time the Hills encountered their UFO.

In October 1961, the Hills met with investigator Walter Webb,
chief lecturer for the Boston Museum of Science's Charles Hayden
Planetarium and a representative of the UFO group NICAP. Webb,
though highly skeptical, stated, "I was impressed that the Hills under-
played the dramatic aspects of the case. They were not trying to sensa-
tionalize. They did not seek publicity." It was through Webb that the
Hills first realized that more than two hours were unaccounted for in
their story. Something more than a simple UFO sighting must have
occurred.

Shortly after the UFO incident, both Hills began to experience
physical and psychological effects of the experience. Betty had night-
mares in which she found herself taken aboard the UFO and examined
by little humanoid beings. Barney began to suffer from high blood
pressure, exhaustion, ulcers, and a strange ring of warts in his groin
area. Both saw a series of medical specialists during 1962 and eventually met Dr. Benjamin Simon, a respected Boston psychiatrist and neu-
rologist with an extensive background in hypnosis therapy.

Dr. Simon started six months of hypnosis sessions with both
Hills at their own expense beginning in late 1963. Both Betty and Barney told essentially the same story under hypnosis. They now recalled
that their car stalled and stopped in the road near a band of little men
dressed in black uniforms and that they were taken aboard a nearby
landed circular craft. Barney was terrified, saying he felt like a rabbit
before a predator. He described the craft's leader as a "German Nazi"

wearing a shiny black jacket, cap, and scarf. Betty said a long needle was inserted in her stomach as part of a "pregnancy test." Hill said a circular device was attached to his groin. Following Betty's examination, she was given a brief tour of the craft and shown a "star map" when she asked the origin of the UFO. After being told that they would not remember the experience, the Hills were released by their car, and the UFO, appearing like a huge, bright orange ball, departed.

Although the Hill story was circulated among their friends and some UFO publications, it was largely unknown to the general public until 1966, when *Look* magazine publish a two-part excerpt of a book by John G. Fuller entitled *The Interrupted Journey*. Fuller's book soon became a national best-seller, and the story gained even wider notice when it was made into a 1975 NBC-TV movie entitled *The UFO Incident*, starring James Earl Jones as Hill and Estelle Parsons as Betty. Hill died of a cerebral hemorrhage in 1969, while Betty went on to become a celebrity in the UFO community.

Their reported abduction was so similar to that of Antonio Villas Boas, whose story neither of the Hills had heard, that it was considered strong circumstantial evidence for the reality of the experience. With the proliferation of abduction stories resulting from the Hill story publicity, it was a circumstance never to be repeated. Once the general abduction scenario was out in the public, debunkers could always claim ongoing reports were simply copycat accounts. British UFO chronicler John Spencer called the Barney case "one of the most important and significant UFO sightings and abductions in UFO lore."

The credulous saw the Hill story as confirmation of extraterrestrial visitation, while the vast majority of the public was content to be titillated by this new form of science fiction. The Reverend John D. Swanson of Christ Church in Portsmouth wrote, "First let it be said that I do not and cannot doubt the veracity of the Hills' account and I believe in the factual reality of their experience. Anyone who has spoken with them, has heard the recordings made when they were under hypnotic recall, and has examined all the evidence, cannot doubt that what they describe did in actuality happen."

Those with a doubting mind-set were not persuaded by the media hype. Dr. Simon, a professional with understandable hesitation in supporting any outrageous UFO account, gave this caveat in his introduction to Fuller's book: "There is little produced under or by hypnosis that is not possible without. The charisma of hypnosis has tended to foster the belief that hypnosis is the magical and royal road to TRUTH [emphasis in original]. In one sense this is so, but it must be understood that hypnosis is a pathway to the truth as it is felt and understood by the patient. The truth is what he believes to be the truth, and this may or may not be consonant with the ultimate nonpersonal truth. Most frequently it is." Dr. Simon added that the existence of UFOs was of less concern to him than "the experience of these two people showing the cumulative impact of past experiences and fantasies on their present experiences and responses."

Author Curtis Peebles was more to the point when he wrote that while the Hills may have been sincere in their belief of abduction, "The supposed event was only a dream." This assessment eventually was voiced by Dr. Simon, who stated in a letter to UFO debunker Philip Klass, "The abduction did not take place but was a reproduction of Betty's dream which occurred right after the sighting. This was her expression of anxiety as contrasted to Barney's more psychosomatic one."

If it was all just a dream, it was a most unusual one. For one thing, Pease AFB radar tracked an "unknown" at the same time as their dream abduction, and both Hill and Betty gave very similar accounts of the experience down to small details that coincided with the "dream" of Villas Boas, whose story they had never heard. For another, they also must have rubbed a dozen small shiny spots on their car unconsciously to support their shared dream.

Also, Betty claimed to have been given a pregnancy test by her captors, yet some years previously she had had a hysterectomy. During this "test" a long needle was inserted into her navel, an unknown procedure in 1961. Yet, today such a procedure is common in the removal of a woman's eggs for in-vitro fertilization.

Dream or not, the Hill story set the stage for more than two decades of abduction reports.

Nearly ten years after the Hill story was widely publicized, a forty-one-year-old French farmer reported an experience with themes common to that of the Hills and others. On July 1, 1965, Maurice Masse was preparing to work a field near his home in Valensole north of Marseilles when he heard a whistling sound he thought was a military helicopter landing. Walking toward a craft that was standing in his field, Masse was shocked to find an egg-shaped device with two small beings standing beside it. He said they were about three feet tall with large heads, almost no mouth, and large lidless eyes. One of them noticed Masse and pointed a small tube at him, whereupon he was paralyzed, though he remained conscious. Despite this experience, Masse later said he somehow knew the beings meant him no harm. Soon they entered the craft and it vanished from sight. Masse told author Jacques Vallee he was not certain whether the craft moved away so quickly he couldn't follow it or if it actually disappeared. A short time after his experience, UFO researcher Aime Michel showed Masse a photograph of a model made from the description of Policeman Lonnie Zamora, who encountered two beings and a UFO in Socorro, New Mexico, the previous year. The similarities were so great that Masse grew excited, thinking someone had photographed the UFO in his field. Masse claimed no knowledge of the New Mexico sighting.

As the ordeal of the Hills moved alien contact into the arena of unwilling abduction and medical experimentation, the glamour of the contactees dwindled away—except for one fascinating story involving extensive details, clear photographs, and multiple witnesses, which largely remains a mystery to this day.

The Pleiadian Connection

Improbable as it sounds, believers claim that an advanced civilization from the Pleiades—a small cluster of stars in the Taurus constella-tion—selected a Swiss-born, one-armed jack-of-all-trades with only a fifth-grade education to help persuade the people of Earth that they are not alone in the universe.

Selected for this role was Eduard Albert Meier, born on Febru-ary 3, 1937, to farming folk in Bülach, Switzerland. Today he goes by his nickname "Billy" because of his fascination for Billy the Kid and other Bills of Wild West fame.

The story of Billy Meier is another prime example of the clash of mind-sets that appears inevitable around stories of alien contact and interstellar messages. Billy Meier's account of alien visitation has per-haps generated more controversy, contradictory statements, and charges of exploitation and hoax than any other single UFO issue. It is probably one of the most documented and studied cases on record—yet even today there seems to be no clear-cut proof for or against the legitimacy of the Billy Meier story, with its beautiful photos and films of "Pleiadian Beamships" carrying messages of peace and hope.

Most researchers, including some UFO organizations such a MUFON, have branded the entire Meier story a hoax. Others say that while some hoaxing and exploitation may have later become involved, there may be a kernel of truth in the early accounts. Some simply say to listen to Meier's message and intuit for one's self if it rings true or false before attacking the messenger. Both as a well-documented encounter story and a representative view of how such tales are received by the public, it is worth closer study.

One of those intrigued by the Meier story was investigative journalist and attorney Gary Kinder, who spent three years carefully researching the issue. Kinder presented his findings in an 1987 book entitled *Light Years*.

At age five, Meier along with his father had a UFO encounter. The year was 1942, and when young Meier asked his father what it was, he was told, "It's a secret weapon of Adolf Hitler." Disbelieving this explanation, Meier described the sighting to the village minister. "He told me that he knew about these flying objects—back then they were not called UFOs—this was nothing new to him," Meier recalled. "The people who flew in them would come from another world, not from Earth. He told me that he understood this, but that he could not talk about it. He was a priest and he would shock people. He told me to try to learn telepathy, to try to give answers. So I tried as I was told. After a few weeks it worked, and I was able to answer. I remember very well that Father Zimmermann told me not to talk about it to anyone, otherwise everybody would say I was crazy." Meier said he learned that he was receiving telepathic messages from a Pleiadian named Sfath, who informed him that he had been chosen as a contact between the Pleiadians and humans.

If this experience wasn't enough, by the time Meier reached adulthood, he already had lived a lifetime of adventures—not all of them good. At age fourteen, young Meier was placed in a boy's home for being a constant truant from school. He promptly ran away from the home and finally quit school before completing the sixth grade. While working a variety of menial jobs, he was arrested for stealing but ran away from a detention center and joined the French Foreign Legion. Unimpressed with military service, Meier fled back to Switzerland and then, in 1958, began a journey to the Middle East.

On the road, Meier traveled to Jerusalem and Bethlehem, then through Jordan and into Pakistan and on into India, where he studied Buddhist philosophy. All this time, he hitchhiked and worked at a number of odd jobs to survive. In August 1965, he was returning to Europe when the bus he was riding was in a collision near Iskenderun, Turkey. He was thrown through a window, and his left arm was severed just above the elbow. Left for dead for several hours, Meier finally was taken to a hospital, where he recuperated.

Continuing his return home, Meier met a seventeen-year-old Greek girl in Thessaloniki named Kalliope Zafireou. The pair fell in love and were married. Billy and his bride, nicknamed "Popi," traveled to Switzerland and settled in the small town of Hinwel. Meier was employed as a night watchman, and life settled into a peaceful—if impoverished—existence for Billy, Popi, and their three children, Gilgamesha, Atlantis-Sokrates, and Methusalem.

Throughout this time, he claimed to have maintained telepathic contact with the Pleiadians, who counseled him and aided him in his travels. He said he was even forewarned of the loss of his arm, indicating the Pleiadians had some sort of vision into the future. But it was not until January 28, 1975, that physical contact with the Pleiadians was achieved.

That day Meier said he received a telepathic message to take a camera and go to a remote field near Hinwel. When he arrived on his moped, he saw a large, silver, circular craft sail in over the trees and set down nearby. Held immobile by the craft's energy field, Meier could only watch as a slender being stepped out onto the grass. It was a beautiful woman with flowing reddish gold hair and pale blue eyes, wearing a one-piece suit that reminded Meier of elephant skin. The suit had a ring around the neck apparently for connecting a helmet. Through telepathy, Meier said he learned the woman's name was Semjase.

Over a long series of meetings, Meier learned much from Semjase. "Semjase first explained briefly that Pleiadian civilization originated many thousands of years ago, not in the Pleiades, a star system much younger than our own, but in the Constellation Lyra. When war ensued, before the planet was destroyed, much of the population migrated to other star systems—in the Pleiades, the Hyades, and to a planet orbiting a nearby star known as Vega. On one interstellar journey, the new Pleiadians discovered Earth and its early life evolving in an atmosphere hospitable to [them]," Kinder quoted Meier. "Since that time, according to Semjase, Earth had been destroyed twice by its own inhabitants: first by a civilization evolved from early Pleiadians who remained behind and mated with primitive Earth humans; and second when a later generation of Pleiadians colonized Earth and produced advanced technology until war again destroyed the planet. Semjase and the Pleiadians who had chosen to return again to Earth were descendants of a peaceful Lyrian faction that now felt responsible for guiding Earth in its spiritual evolution, so the Earth humans could avoid the setbacks long ago experienced by their Pleiadian ancestors."

Semjase explained that allowing Meier to photograph their saucer ships was part of his mission aimed at alerting humans that they are not alone in the universe. "The Earth human calls us extraterrestrials or star people, or whatever he wants," Semjase explained. "He attributes to us supernatural abilities, yet knows nothing about us. In truth, we are human beings like the Earth human being, but our knowledge and our wisdom and our technical capabilities are very much superior to his.

"We, too, are still far removed from perfection and have to evolve constantly," she also told Meier. "When we choose to come in contact with an Earth human, we do so because we feel an obligation to the developing universe, and to life which is already existing throughout the universe. We are not missionaries or teachers, but we endeavor to keep order throughout all areas of space. Now and then we begin contacts with inhabitants of different worlds by searching out individuals whom we feel can accept our existence. We then impart information to those contacts, but only when their race has developed and begins to think. Then slowly we and others prepare them for the truth—that they are not the only thinking beings in the universe."

According to Meier, Semjase explained that the Pleiadians felt it was inadvisable to make open contact with Earth. "The masses would merely revere us as gods, as in ages past, or go off in hysteria. That is why we regard it as prudent to make contact with individual persons only for the time being, to disseminate, through them, the knowledge concerning our existence and our coming to this planet.

"Furthermore, all Earth governments are made up of human beings for whom power hunger and a thirst for profits are characteristic. They only want, under cover of peace and friendship, to occupy our rayships, to exercise absolute rule over the Earth. But they would not stop there. They would try to capture the cosmos, because they do not know any limits. They, on the other hand, are not even able to create peace and friendship among the nations on Earth, not even in their own countries. How then could they be capable of holding such might in their hands as our rayships? It is for the present advisable to maintain contact only with single Earth humans, and by them to slowly allow the knowledge of our existence and mission to become known, and to prepare others for our coming."

Interestingly, the concept of aliens directing messages to selected humans has been advanced by some thoughtful scientists. James W. Deardorff of Oregon State University in a published paper theorized that an alien communication strategy "might involve their communicating with just one or a very few recipients about the globe. . . . However, in order that scientists in general should not be alerted, only the recipient would be allowed to partake in the communication sessions and to witness the extraterrestrials themselves. The messages might, moreover, contain vague descriptions of extraterrestrial technological achievements that would read like magic or science fiction. They might even contain a few absurdities purposely added; these . . . would help ensure than any scientists who happened to learn about the communications would regard them as hoaxes or fiction. . . . Meanwhile, the messages would get published, translated into various languages, and distributed throughout the world amongst other occult literature." Deardorff's theory compares remarkably well with the Meier story.

After each of his meetings with the alien Semjase, Meier would return home and type out detailed notes of the conversations on an old typewriter. He claimed that Semjase arranged for the conversations to be "played back" in his mind, allowing him to type them up verbatim with his right hand. When the contact with Semjase and the Pleiadians ended in October 1978, Meier had counted 115 face-to-face meetings that produced more than 1,800 pages of notes, hundreds of unusually clear and detailed color photographs and slides, and at least one film of the Pleiadian "beamships." It was "the hands-down greatest UFO case of all time," effused one researcher, "the biggest, most spectacular, longest-running, most productive case in the history of the phenomenon."

But was there proof that any of this was anything other than a brilliant, complex hoax orchestrated by this near-penniless, one-armed Swiss security guard?

The arguments for hoaxing start with the fact that the clear and colorful photos of the "beamships" simply appear to be too good to be true. Large detailed UFOs can be seen in Meier's photos hanging in the clear Swiss alpine air over breathtaking vistas of verdant valleys. "When someone brings you pictures like this your first reaction automatically is, 'This is a lot of crap,'" said Willy Bar, owner of Bar Photo, where Meier brought his photos for developing. "I never saw anything suspicious in the black-and-white film I developed, nor was I ever told to manipulate anything. . . . My personal opinion was always, 'I don't know about UFOs, but the pictures are real.'"

The most damaging evidence against the validity of the Meier photos came from Martin Sorge, one of the hundreds of people who flocked to Meier's farm once his story reached the public. Although Sorge was impressed with Meier and the consistency of his story of Pleiadian contacts, he remained skeptical. One day after he witnessed an argument between Meier and his wife, Popi came to him and gave him several color slides that had been charred by fire. The slides were of a model spaceship in various settings, and Popi admitted that her husband had worked with models. Sorge decided to see if he could also use a model to duplicate Meier's early pictures. He was partially successful. He admitted that his photos were not up to the quality of Meier's, and author Kinder described them as depicting "a crude and somewhat stark beamship frozen in an otherwise familiar setting; but they lacked the feel of Meier's, the natural relationship that appeared to exist between his background and his ships. They had no depth." Nevertheless, since he had found evidence of models, Sorge became convinced that Meier was a fraud.

Supporters of Meier have explained that early in his contacts, Meier decided to build a model to see if his photos of "beamships" could be duplicated but then decided to burn the slides to avoid charges of hoaxing. Popi got hold of the photos and, in a fit of anger, gave them to Sorge. In later years, Sorge himself supported Meier in an oblique way, telling Kinder, "Billy's intellect and his spiritual level are much below the message he preaches, therefore it is not possible that he could have invented this. So this indicates he must have gotten it from some other source. . . . I am certain he has these contacts, but not in the way he's telling us. He may receive them in the form of visions, the way mediums receive things. He may not even know himself if these visions are real. But for him it is reality, and to prove it he has to go out and build these things."

But even Sorge's model story, which appeared to be the basis for subsequent arguments that Meier's photos were fakes, could not fully explain the better shots of craft in the sky. Eric Eliason, a research computer scientist with the U.S. Geological Survey in Flagstaff, Arizona, subjected some of Meier's pictures to computer analysis and concluded that nothing had been added or dubbed into the photograph of the countryside. "And if that dubbing was registered in the film, the computer would have seen it. We didn't see anything," said Eliason. "That doesn't eliminate the idea of somebody taking a little model and throwing it out there. That's a hoax but you couldn't tell that with image processing."

In fact, Meier's photographs could never be properly analyzed because of their treatment. By all accounts, Meier would get his rolls of film processed at Bar Photo, then leave both negatives and prints lying everywhere, sometimes in a shoe box under his bed. Visitors would handle them, "borrow" them, and never return them. Others were given away and some just disappeared. According to Kinder, since no one could determine whether or not a photo was first generation, there was never definitive proof of their validity.

Dr. Michael Malin, a space scientist at Arizona State University, was impressed with Meier's photos. "These pictures are much nicer pictures of UFOs than any I'd seen before in terms of the number and the quality for that number," he said. "You can see they look like real objects. Not just on the impression level, but on a demonstrable level. They glint in the sun, there are distinguishable reflections in the metallic objects, things like that that make them much better pictures. . . . What I found was that the quality of the data . . . was insufficient to do a detailed analysis. . . . But to the level of the quality of the data he gave me, I could not see anything obviously wrong with the images. Couldn't see any hoax to it. There is a proper amount of blurring of edges and distance fading and things like that." Like a true scientist, Malin hedged his bets by adding, "To the level that I saw it, I can say that the thing was not a photographic fake. But that doesn't mean that it wasn't a photographic fake. . . . It could still be an object twenty feet across held up by a helicopter above it on four strings."

The whole problem with Meier using sophisticated equipment and models to fake the photos came back to the fact that there appeared to be no time or privacy for this. During the time of the reputed Pleiadian contacts, Meier became somewhat of a cult figure. His home was constantly filled with visitors, including such notables as actress Shirley MacLaine and author Erich von Däniken. In later years, a group formed around Meier, calling itself the *Freie-Interessen-gemeinschaft für Grenz-und Geisteswissenschaften und Ufologiestudien* (FIGU), the "Free Community of Interest in Border and Spiritual Science and Ufology." More than a dozen members of the FIGU took up residence in the Meier home. Meier was alone only when he left at odd hours of the day and night to meet the Pleiadians. Even then, nosy neighbors watched him closely as he entered the forests and fields. Suspicious farmers would often grant him only a few moments of time in their fields, and the mountain weather was unpredictable and usually windy. Add to this the fact that most of Meier's photos appear to have been shot sequentially, with the "beamship" beginning as a small dot and then growing larger as it approached the camera. Most pictures showed the ships high over a deep mountain valley where there was no place to hang a model, certainly with enough wires to keep it from swinging in the stiff breezes. In some photos it appeared that tree branches were superimposed over a "beamship," indicating that if the craft were a model, it would have to have been more than twenty feet in diameter. And, in an eight-millimeter film shot by Meier, tree leaves swayed in reaction to the passage of one of the circular craft and, under close scrutiny, a red light could be seen flashing along one edge.

Wally Gentleman, an experienced special effects technician, studied the Meier photos for "perspective interlock"—a geometric analysis measuring Meier's "beamships" against known objects in the photo such as tree trunks, houses, and the like. Gentleman found that both the size and location of the "beamships" were exactly as described by Meier.

Dr. Robert Nathan with NASA's Jet Propulsion Laboratory in Pasadena, California, was consulted about Meier's photos. After some study, Nathan said, "If this is a hoax and it looks like it to me but I have no proof, this is very carefully done. Tremendous amount of effort. An awful lot of work for one guy." UFO researcher Lou Zinsstag commented, "Meier's a smart man and he's got a good mind, but he has only one arm, and he's limited in equipment, and he's watched by a lot of people. I don't see how he can do all these things."

Herbert Runkel and Harold Proch were two of Meier's early friends. Both men lived at Meier's home for some time and both searched for evidence that Meier's contacts were a hoax. They even managed to sneak into locked storage rooms and searched through closets and drawers. Nothing was found. "Herbert constantly searched," wrote Kinder, "but found no equipment, rigging or models, not even scientific journals or technical books from which Meier might glean his knowledge of so many things. Meier never left the house unless it was to go on a contact, usually late at night, and no one came to the house to meet with him secretly." Other friends and neighbors did report seeing strange lights and objects in the sky, hearing buzzing or humming noises, and other odd occurrences.

Meier would suddenly arrive home totally dry in the midst of a heavy rain. He explained his condition by saying he had just been materialized from a "beamship." Others saw him suddenly disappear and reappear in a mysterious way. Englebert Wachter, who was helping Meier work on his farm, saw Meier suddenly appear in a nearby field. "I was looking around, looking at the trees, but somehow my glance was pulled back on that meadow," Wachter recalled. "And as soon as I looked back Billy stood in the middle. In the middle of the meadow there are no trees. I looked at that meadow and I could practically see Billy appear out of nothing." Many people felt that if Meier was faking his contacts and photographs, he must have had help. Yet many people, when inspecting contact locations, found only one set of footprints leading in and out.

Hans Schutzbach was with Meier one afternoon when he managed to tape-record what Meier said were the sounds of a "beamship." According to Kinder, it was "an eerie and grating noise, like a high-pitched cross between a jet engine and a chain saw" and seemed to come from a point in midair about thirty feet over Meier's head. Later, a woman named Eva Bieri also taped the sounds of a "beamship" as it hovered invisibly overhead. This tape was subjected to a digital audio analyzer, which determined the sounds were not in the common 50 to 60 hertz line frequencies. Steve Ambrose, an electronics consultant to many rock stars, studied the tape with a spectrum analyzer and concluded they could not have been produced with a synthesizer.

Then there is the matter of the metal triangle. Meier claimed it came from one of the Pleiadian "beamships." In time, it was given to Marcel Vogel, a research chemist for IBM and the holder of thirty-two patents. Studying the small piece of metal under an electron microscope, Vogel was disconcerted to find "the most peculiar maze of elements he had even seen." The triangle contained a combination of "exceeding pure" silver, aluminum, potassium, calcium, chromium, copper, argon, bromium, chorine, iron, sulphur, silicon, and, surprisingly, thulium, which was discovered in two grooves micromachined into the metal. "It is totally unexpected," stated Vogel. "Thulium was only purified during World War II as a by-product of atomic energy work, and only in minute quantities. It is exceedingly expensive, far beyond platinum, and rare to come by. Someone would have to have an extensive metallurgical knowledge even to be aware of a composition of this type."

Vogel found another oddity of the triangle. "It looks like a metal, it has the lustery appearance of metal, but now when you take it and go under the polarized light you find that, yes, it is metal, but at the same time . . . it is crystal!"

Excited, Vogel arranged to meet with another scientist the next day to get his opinion on the odd metal. But—as so often happens in such cases—when he reached into his pocket for the specimen, it was gone. A frantic search failed to find it. According to author Kinder, "Vogel never recovered the lost piece of metal, nor could he explain its disappearance."

Lee Elders and his wife, Brit, spent more than two years and thousands of dollars investigating the Meier story. In 1979, they produced a coffee-table book containing Meier's "beamship" photos entitled *UFO . . . Contact from the Pleiades*. This immediately opened them to the charge that they were in it only for profit. Brit commented, "It took us two years to figure out you're never going to prove [Meier's story] and you're never going to disprove it. It's just there."

The Meier case left author Gary Kinder perplexed. Photoanalysis was inconclusive because the originals could not be studied. The metal triangle had disappeared. The testimony of friends and neighbors was just hearsay. "Almost everyone I interviewed in the UFO community warned that I was wasting my time on an obvious hoax," he wrote. "Having experienced the setting in Switzerland I, like others before me, could not understand how Meier could have created sophisticated special effects in his photography. Then there were the sounds, metal, landing tracks, films, the explanation of the beamship propulsion system, all of which lent credibility to the story."

But Meier's models and some photos found to be copied from a magazine tarnished that credibility. "Meier seemed to possess more evidence than nearly all previous UFO cases combined," stated Kinder. "But that evidence would be seen by few and studied by even fewer, because Meier's preposterous and sometimes misunderstood stories of traveling back in time to see Jesus and photographing the Eye of God would be laughed at and dismissed as nonsense."

Even persons within the UFO research community could not

agree on the merits of Meier's case. One group, Ground Saucer Watch, studied Meier's photos and pronounced that "All of the pictures are hoaxes. . . ." However, sometime later a photo that same group proclaimed "genuine" was found to be a forgery, so a question remained. Others maintained that the Meier story was a total fraud, which prompted one UFO writer, Lucius Farish, to remonstrate with his fellow researchers: "You are free to think anything you wish concerning the Meier case or [the] investigation of it. However, the fact remains that you have no proof that the case is a hoax. I've heard all kinds of accusations, but I have yet to see one iota of real evidence. . . ." Despite the continuing lack of firm evidence of fakery, most ufologists today—not having studied the case closely—accept the idea that it was all an elaborate hoax.

This conclusion vexed Lee Elders, who had spent so much time investigating the case. "I didn't know if we could prove the case to be real, but I knew we had tangible evidence," he lamented. "Not one of these UFO people had ever been to Switzerland. They hadn't spent five minutes with Meier. None of them has been there. So how can they say it's a hoax? That's what frustrated me the most."

Respected British UFO researcher and author Timothy Good followed the Meier case closely beginning in the 1960s. He has noted that Meier's photos bear an uncanny resemblance to UFOs reported in the mysterious Area 51. He nevertheless concluded, "I remain unconvinced by much of Meier's material, but do not doubt that he has had some genuine experiences and that *some* of his photos could be authentic."

Kinder published his research on the Meier case and went on to other things. "Finally I realized, as the Elders had years before, that the truth of the Meier contacts will never be known."

Meier himself downplayed the importance of his material evidence, indicating they were only a means to an end. "The photographs are only to make people think, to show them something," he told a researcher. "People shall come for these pictures, but they shall study the teachings, and they shall come to know."

Know Your Neighbors

Here is a sampling of the "knowledge" as gleaned from the notes of Billy Meier:

The Pleiadians are part of a federation of civilized worlds that live by the words of an advanced race in the Andromeda Galaxy. This race is so spiritually evolved that they no longer require a physical body. They are almost beings of light energy. The Pleiadians occupy four planets around the sun Taygeta, in the star system designated by Earth scientists as M45.

Their home world is the planet Erra, which is very similar to Earth, being only 10 percent smaller. Manufacturing processes are confined to other planets, and the four hundred million Pleiadians on Erra live in a utopian world free of pollution, war, hunger, and disease thanks to advanced technology and spiritual awareness. Because the population communicates by telepathy, there is no dishonesty. All basic necessities are provided freely, and anything beyond that is acquired through individual barter. There is no money and, hence, no irrational grasping for wealth and power.

There are no massive cities. The population is spread out across their world, connected by a series of sentient tubeways that not only transport the population but educate and inform them along the way. What government is necessary is provided by a "High Council" composed of the wisest and most evolved Pleiadians. Any changes to their social order must be approved by a vote of the highest percentage of the population.

According to the Pleiadians, more than three thousand alien craft visit the earth annually. Most have little or no concern with humans and only a very small percentage attempt communication, and this is usually by telepathic means. Due to our common ancestry, the Pleiadians have taken a special interest in Earth. However, they have agreed to abide by federation rules, which state that no race shall be allowed to interfere with the normal evolution of a planet until that world is capable of leaving its solar system. The Pleiadians state that the earth has almost reached this ability and they are concerned that earth humans may reach a point where a hostile alien invasion could occur. Presently, the Pleiadians prevent such a situation by their mere presence around the earth.

During conversations with Meier, the Pleiadian Semjase explained that she was able to travel the five hundred light-years between Earth and her planet Erra in only seven hours because "beamship" technology allowed the Pleiadians to move into "hyperspace" and convert themselves and their ships into "fine-matter particles that can travel faster than the speed of light." The technology involved warping time and space. "I am not allowed to give you any further details," Semjase told Meier back in the 1970s. "But I can tell you that your advanced scientific circles are already working on systems known as light-emitting drives and 'tachyon' drives. The elemental principles are already known to them." Tom Welch, a friend and business associate of Lee Elders, was highly skeptical of Billy Meier. But he was intrigued by Meier's description of the Pleiadian tachyon drive. "We did learn later that for some period of time specialists either connected with NASA or with companies like General Dynamics had been quietly working on that as a propulsion concept. What's interesting is that the man who wrote the notes has a formal education equivalent to the fifth or sixth grade. He does not live near major libraries, he does not live near major scientific centers, he doesn't have immediate contacts in those fields. At the time, we didn't know what 'tachyon' meant. Most physicists didn't know what a tachyon was. And to apply the concept of theoretical tachyon to space propulsion is a huge step to take," said an impressed Welch, adding, "But the thing that was startling to me was that as soon as we started to dig into that, all of a sudden something else would pop up, in the notes or through Billy, that was equally sophisticated, unique, and advanced in a different field. . . . It all seemed out of context with his personality. It seemed as if the man had a tutor in various fields who was one incredible tutor."

Randolph Winters, who claimed that Billy Meier appointed him to write and lecture on the Pleiadian mission, said Meier's work was to prepare mankind for the new major event in history—"open contact with life forms from other worlds and taking our position in the family of man in the universe." Winters said Meier was only one of more than seventeen thousand humans contacted by the Pleiadians, mostly through telepathy, and that, while contact with Meier has ceased, the Pleiadians still man underground bases in Switzerland and Russia where they maintain a mental connection with a number of humans.

Winters produced a book containing a detailed "history" of creation, alien visits to Earth, and a chronology of human progress, including views on spiritual growth, death, and reincarnation—all based on Meier's notes. While some of Winters's writings appear quite rational and well developed—such as his "New Constitution of the People of Earth"—others still seem outlandish to most. Debunkers, of course, consider it all hogwash.

But if the UFO researcher ranks were split by rancor and contention over the ambiguity of the Meier contactee case, it was nothing compared to the next great UFO controversy—one that struck much closer to home.

MISSING TIME

By the late 1960s, the day of the contactees' preaching intergalactic peace and harmony appeared over. Reported contacts with alien beings became terror-filled experiences involving kidnapping, experimentation, and missing time—yet also filled with awe-inspiring revelations and portents.

Somewhat ominously, these contacts no longer happened to people out in the desert or on lonely roads. Now the phenomenon was taking place as people slept or sat in the perceived safety of their homes.

On the night of January 25, 1967, Betty Andreasson (now Betty Luca), described as a "simple, unsophisticated country girl," was in her home at South Ashburnham, Massachusetts, along with her parents and seven children, when the lights flickered and then went out. The family saw a "curious pink light" shining through a kitchen window, which pulsated and grew brighter. Her father, Waino Aho, looked out a window and saw small "Halloween freaks" hopping along in line. All of the family members, except Andreasson, became immobilized and lost consciousness.

Andreasson was shocked to see four small beings advancing in a line through the closed kitchen door. She described them as small creatures with large pear-shaped heads, gray skin, small slits for ears, nose, and mouth, and "large wraparound catlike eyes." She said they looked like "Mongoloid" people and wore dark blue uniforms with eaglelike insignia on the left arm. Her daughter, Becky, later had a conscious memory of the visitors before she too lost consciousness.

Through nonverbal communication—apparently telepathy—Andreasson learned the group's leader was called Quazgaa, who indicated they knew her name and were there for her particularly. After some conversation regarding the safety of her family, Andreasson gave Quazgaa one of the family Bibles, and he presented her with a small, thin blue book filled with symbols. Andreasson was asked if she would go with the creatures. Being a devout Christian, she kept asking if they were men of God. They did not answer this but said they had come to help save the world, which was "trying to destroy itself."

Sensing no hostility, Andreasson allowed herself to be floated inches off the floor, passing through the closed kitchen door along with the group. Outside, she was taken aboard an oval UFO resting on struts. On the underside of the craft were three large balls, similar to those reported by other abductees and depicted in the George Adamski photos. Once inside, Andreasson was asked to disrobe. After donning a white robe, she was given a "medical examination" that included a long needle piercing her navel. When she asked the purpose of the exam, she was told it had to do with creation, but that "there was some parts missing." Interestingly, Andreasson had undergone a hysterectomy some years previously. During the examination, Andreasson was treated very much like a medical patient. One of the creatures told her, "These things won't hurt you. Just lie still—very still." She said that during this ordeal, something was removed from behind her eye with a long flexible needle.

After the exam, Andreasson said she was allowed to dress and then taken down what seemed like an "underground corridor" to a room where she was enshrouded with a "translucent canopy" that soon filled with a thick gray liquid or gel. She was told to keep her eyes closed and breathe through tubes. She then felt she was transported to a different place. Later, under hypnosis, Andreasson declared, "I left this Earth. I believe we were in space, and somehow I believe we were in the center of the Earth. Now how can you be in both?" Author Raymond E. Fowler, who chronicled Betty's saga, noted that during the entire experience "Betty felt somehow under their control." He wrote, "Their polite requests created an illusion of free will, but in reality, she found that her choice always corresponded with their wishes. Her willpower seemed mesmerized by powerful influences beyond her ken."

Andreasson's experiences took a yet stranger turn as she claimed to be escorted into a world where "the atmosphere was a vibrating red color" and strange lemurlike creatures with eyes on stalks climbed around on stucco-type buildings. Next, she passed through a green world with vegetation. Like Ezekiel, Andreasson was unable to identify or even describe some of the sights. Under hypnosis, she said with a sigh, "We are stopping because there is something white there. There is something white. I don't know what it is! It is something like—I can't ever explain it." She said she soon arrived at a city with large crystals hanging in the air. One pyramid-shaped building had a sculpted face at its apex that "looked sort of like an Egyptian head."

She was brought before a large living bird—she could see it breathing—with a bright light behind it. This was to be the high point of her experience. Under hypnosis, she described the scene: "I'm standing before that large bird. It's very warm. . . . And that bird looks like an eagle to me. And it's living. It has a white head and there is light in back of it—real white light. . . . It's very, very hot here. . . . The bird, the feathers are just fluffed out. The light seems so bright in back of it. It's beautiful, bright light." Believing herself in the presence of God, Andreasson was filled with fervent emotions. One of the creatures told her, "Your own fear makes you feel these things. I can release you, but you must release yourself of that fear through my son." Andreasson said she cried out, "Thank you, Lord. . . . I know I am not worthy. Thank you for your Son."

Suddenly the huge bird disappeared. In its place was a fire with heat that hurt Andreasson, and from the ashes of the fire came a large gray worm. This obvious symbolism troubled author Fowler, who wrote that the Phoenix-like bird was not a "readily discernible aspect or symbol of modern Christianity." However, Fowler was surprised to find an encyclopedic notation that "the Phoenix figures prominently in early Christian art and literature as a symbol of immortality and the resurrection."

Andreasson then was taken back to the craft, again immersed in syrupy gel, and transported home. During this time, the leader Quazgaa also told her his group had come to help the human race. "Love is the greatest of all," he told Andreasson, adding that because of love they could not allow man to continue in the way he is going and that it would be better to lose some than to lose all. Quazgaa said it would be easy to hand man the knowledge of life but that he is not yet worthy and must seek such knowledge for himself. He also indicated that Andreasson was only one of many humans his group, or clan, had taken. Finally, she was told, "Child, you must forget for a while."

Under hypnosis, Andreasson was asked if the aliens had any hand in the notorious power blackout of 1965. She indicated they had caused it for the purpose of revealing to man his true nature. "They have powers," she said. "They can control the wind and water and even lightning."

She said the visitors explained that the blackouts were caused to show man his true nature, namely that "Man seeks to destroy himself [through] greed. . . . Everything has been provided for man. Simple things. He could be advanced so far, but greed gets in the way . . . other worlds are involved in man's world. Man is very arrogant and greedy and he thinks that all worlds revolve around him." She claimed to have been given information that seventy different alien races— "Some come from realms where you cannot see their hiding place. Some come from the very Earth"—have been working for the betterment of mankind on Earth "since the beginning of time." These races all work together except for one that is an "enemy."

Once home, Andreasson said she kept the small blue alien book for about ten days but that it then disappeared from her closet. She said she had been told she could not keep it long.

Due to the outlandishness—or "high strangeness," as some call it—of Andreasson's story, a twelve-month investigation was launched by the Center for UFO Studies (CUFOS), which included interviews, hypnosis, background and character checks, and the use of lie detectors and a Physiological Stress Evaluator (PSE). The 1972 PSE analysis report on both Andreasson and Becky concluded, "They were telling the truth with regards to the 1967 incident. . . . In the opinion of this analyst, the results are conclusive."

Betty's story was first published twelve years after the incident, leaving little room for the argument that it was concocted for profit. Andreasson's hypnosis was conducted by Dr. Harold J. Edelstein, director of the New England Institute of Hypnosis. Dr. Edelstein concluded that both Andreasson and her daughter, Becky, truly believed in the truth of their story. "During deep trance hypnotic regression sessions, Andreasson and Becky relived their traumatic experience in great detail," noted Fowler. "They each expressed natural apprehension, fear, wonder, concern, pain and joy. Their facial expressions, voice tones and tears were obviously genuine."

In considering the religious connotations of Andreasson's experience, Fowler considered "that Quazgaa may have paid lip service to Betty's religious convictions simply in order to ensure her compliance." He also mused that if the entire trip was "stage managed" by the aliens as a "reward" for Andreasson, "it's not inconceivable that they might have picked a symbol [the Phoenix] that was obsolete by some 1,500 years!" Such speculation led Fowler to wonder, "Could it be possible that visiting extraterrestrials might in actuality be interstellar missionaries?"

In an introduction to Fowler's book, CUFOS director Dr. J. Allen Hynek wrote that the Andreasson case revealed how "surprisingly complex" the UFO issue had become. "The man on the street's simple opinion that either UFOs are all nonsense or that visitors from outer space do exist is brutally destroyed by close study," he stated, adding, "Those who still hold that the entire subject of UFOs is nonsense will be sorely challenged if they have the courage to take an honest look at the [Andreasson] book. For whatever the UFO phenomenon is—or are—it is not nonsense. It would take an imagination of the highest order to explain the reported happenings described herein as mere misidentifications of balloons, aircraft, meteors, or planets! Neither is there the slightest evidence of hoax or contrivance." Interestingly enough, vocal debunkers Philip Klass and Curtis Peebles failed to address the Andreasson case in their books.

They did give space to a 1973 incident involving two Pascagoula, Mississippi, fisherman who claimed they were abducted and given a physical examination by aliens. Charles Hickson, forty-five, and Calvin Parker, nineteen, both shipyard workers, said that on the evening of October 11, they were fishing on the Pascagoula River when they heard a "zipping" sound, then saw three small beings exit from a glowing UFO hovering nearby. The creatures, described as three feet tall with gray wrinkled skin or covering with slits for eyes and clawlike hands, floated over and took the immobilized men aboard their craft. Inside, both men were scrutinized by a football-shaped device that resembled a large eye. After the exam, which lasted less than an hour, the men were returned to the river dock.

Sheriff Fred Diamond questioned the pair and stated, "They were scared to death and on the verge of a heart attack." A tape recorder was left running while the pair were left alone, yet their demeanor didn't change. One was heard to cry out, "God help me. Don't let me die." They were even examined unsuccessfully for radiation at nearby Kessler AFB. Investigator Dr. James Harder from the Aerial Phenomena Research Organization (APRO) arrived and concluded, "The experience of Hickson and Parker was a real one. It was not a hallucination." With Harder was Dr. J. Allen Hynek, by now head of the Center for UFO Studies (CUFOS), who concluded, "There simply is no question in my mind that these men have had a very real, frightening experience." Hickson and Parker became celebrities, appearing on a number of radio and TV programs.

Debunker Philip Klass soon arrived in Mississippi and the clash of mind-sets began. Klass argued that operators of two nearby toll-booths had not reported any UFOs that night. Next, Klass denigrated the polygraph test that depicted the men as truthful because he claimed the operator was inexperienced and noncertified. Klass noted minute discrepancies in Hickson's story, such as first calling the alien's mouth a "hole" and changing it to a "slit." And, of course, Klass hauled out the old standby charge that the men concocted their story for money. This latter charge was strengthened when local attorney Joe Colingo signed a contract to handle all publicity for the pair. However, in 1987 when the vice chairman of the British UFO Research Association (BUFORA), John Spencer, visited Hickson, he "was instantly impressed by [his] obvious sincerity and honesty." Spencer quoted Hickson as saying, "I was offered all kinds of money to let them do a movie. I declined. I am still declining. Making money is not what this experience is all about."

This same clash of viewpoints—also involving lawmen, lie detectors, psychiatrists, believers, and debunkers—was soon visited on another well-publicized abduction case with predictable results. Unlike other abduction cases, this one had six witnesses, the abductee was reported missing at the time, and no hypnosis was required to bring forth details of the experience.

Walton's Missing Days

Travis Walton was a frisky twenty-two years old on November 5, 1975, when he and six other men were returning home to Snowflake, Arizona, in a large truck following a hard day of clearing brush in the Sitgreaves National Forest. Walton loved adventure. He was a bungee jumper and race car driver. He even once said he would willingly go in a UFO if he got the chance.

He got his chance shortly after 6:00 P.M. that day. As the workers drove down a rough logging road, they said they saw a UFO hovering about a hundred feet away. Walton told his boss, Mike Rogers, to stop the truck and then jumped out and ran toward the glowing golden object.

Suddenly, a bolt of bluish white light flashed from the UFO, knocking Walton back into some brush. His companions raced off in a panic. After about a quarter of a mile, they saw a streak of light in the sky and, believing the UFO had departed, returned to check on Walton. But he could not be found.

Driving to Heber, Arizona, the workers told their story to Navajo county sheriff Marlin Gillespie, who was understandably skeptical. Nevertheless, several fruitless searches for Walton were mounted over the next few days. Suspecting that a homicide may have been committed, the six workers were administered a lie detector test on November 10 by C. E. Gilson of the Arizona Department of Public Safety. The test on one of the workers, Allen Dalis, who first spotted the UFO, was "inconclusive." Dalis said he was too upset by the experience to respond correctly, but author Philip Klass noted that some-time later Dalis was charged with theft and may have flunked his test due to the fear of incriminating himself. As to the other five, Gilson concluded, "These polygraph examinations proved that these five men did see some object that they believe to be a UFO and that Travis Walton was not injured or murdered by any of these men. . . . If an actual UFO did not exist and the UFO is a man-made hoax, five of these men had no prior knowledge of a hoax."

Early on November 11, Walton called home from a telephone booth near Heber and shortly was able to tell his own story. He said the beam of light from the UFO in the woods knocked him out. When he regained consciousness, he found himself in a strange room. In pain, his first thought was, "Thank God, I'm in a hospital." But then he saw around him three small humanoids dressed in one-piece cover-alls. "They had bulging, oversized craniums, a small jaw structure, and an undeveloped appearance to their features that was almost infantile," Walton recalled. "Their thin-lipped mouths were narrow and I never saw them open. Lying close to their heads on either side were the tiny crinkled lobes of their ears. Their miniature rounded noses had small oval nostrils." Later he described these beings as overgrown fetuses with large eyes.

Panicky, Walton picked up a device like a glass rod and was con-sidering attacking the trio when they hurried out of the room as though they could sense his intent. He then made his way though what apparently was a spacecraft. Wandering into a dome-topped room containing a chair and a console of sorts, Walton noticed that as he approached the chair, one wall became increasingly translucent, revealing stars against the blackness of space.

Suddenly he was confronted by a man standing in the doorway. Walton said the man was more than six feet tall, muscular, with coarse, sandy blond hair that covered his ears. The man wore a blue one-piece suit and a transparent helmet. This man, with piercing gold-hazel eyes, did not speak but motioned Walton to follow him. Walton was led through some sort of airlock and into a large hangarlike area that contained three small saucerlike craft. He was taken into a room beside the hangar, which contained two more men and a woman, all dressed identically to his guide. Walton said all four looked "alike in a family sort of way, although they were not identical." Walton lay down on a table, and the woman approached him with what looked like an oxygen mask. The next thing Walton remembered was waking up on the highway outside Heber and seeing a bright circular object rise into the night sky. Exhausted, Walton was fully dressed but discovered he had lost eleven pounds during his five missing days.

While law enforcement officials quickly lost interest in the case, UFO researchers did not. Funded by the tabloid *National Enquirer,* an investigator for the Aerial Phenomena Research Organization (APRO) interviewed Walton and arranged a meeting with two psychiatrists and a polygraph test. Administering the test was veteran examiner John J. McCarthy, who learned that Walton had experimented with drugs and had been convicted of stealing and forging payroll checks four years previously. With this in mind, McCarthy said he believed that Walton was holding his breath, attempting to sabotage the test. McCarthy then concluded, "Based on his reactions on all charts, it is the opinion of this examiner that Walton, in concert with others, is attempting to perpetrate a UFO hoax, and that he has not been on any spacecraft."

Jeff Wells, an *Enquirer* reporter, described Walton during this time as "mute, pale, twitching like a cornered animal." Supporters say Walton, like Dalis, was suffering from shock and failed to respond appropriately on the lie detector test. Others saw his condition as nervousness over a concocted story.

Even doctors differed in their opinions, probably reflecting their respective mind-sets. Lamont McConnell administered a Minnesota Multiphasic Personality Inventory test that showed "no deviations that would point to psychosis." Dr. Jean Rosenbaum, one of the psychiatrists who examined Walton, told ABC News, "Our conclusion, which is absolute, is that this young man is not lying, that there is no collusion involved, and no attempt to hoax." However, psychologist Lester H. Steward, who saw Walton about nine hours after his return, claimed to have seen a fresh puncture mark on the man's arm, which he initially ascribed to his UFO trip. But as Walton returned to normal, Steward became convinced that Walton had been on a drug trip and that the abduction was a hoax. Friends and neighbors, including at least one clergyman, continue to support Walton and say that, for all his foibles, he is telling the truth. None of the other six workers with Walton that day have confessed to a hoax, although the media pressure and payments offered to do so have been significant.

In February 1976, a composed Walton, along with his brother and mother, passed a second lie detector test administered by George J. Pfeifer. Predictably, other polygraph experts differed with Pfeifer's interpretation of the test results, and debunker Klass declared the positive test should be written off, since it indicated a truthful response when Walton declared he was not a UFO "buff," although he had spoken about UFOs at length with his family. Would everyone who simply discussed the Civil War with family members describe themselves as a "buff"? This kind of pettifoggery does little to determine the truth of such situations.

Klass's more serious objection to the Walton story was that Walton may have concocted a hoax to get his employer out from under a Forest Service brush-clearing contract that was already running behind schedule and facing heavy penalties. Klass, who noted that Walton admitted watching the TV movie *The UFO Incident* concerning the Hill abduction, contended that if the contract could not be completed due to outside circumstances, then no penalty would be applied. According to Klass, this is exactly what happened. But while this situation provided a credible explanation for a hoax, it was not proof that such a hoax took place except for those predisposed to the idea.

Travis Walton's ensuing media adventures did not help convince detractors of his veracity. In 1978, his popular autobiographical book, *The Walton Experience*, was published. Then in 1993, his book was turned into the $15.5 million film *Fire in the Sky*, which starred actor D. B. Sweeney as Walton. The movie itself stirred much controversy, particularly among UFO researchers concerned with its sinister scenes of aliens in ooze-covered rooms. "The thing that's disturbing about the movie is that they would take such liberties and still call it a true story," commented Dr. James Harder, the APRO investigator who first obtained the Walton story under hypnosis. "I don't think he'd [Travis] willingly be a party to the distortions." According to writer Quendrith Johnson, the movie's producers, in a deal with Industrial Light and Magic, requested an alien setting that differed from those depicted in the CBS-TV miniseries *Intruders*, which aired about the time of the film's release. The film's scriptwriter, Tracy Tormé, stated, "There is no script that I ever wrote that has that sequence—that you see on the screen—in it. My script was virtually identical to what people read in [Travis's] book."

A new Travis Walton book was published in 1996 to counteract the negative publicity surrounding the film. All this, of course, opened Travis to the charge that he made up his story for profit, the same allegation made against the Pascagoula fishermen. In response Travis commented, "Looking at the positive, I have to say I've learned a lot about people, about humanity. It's given me some real insight into people and the kind of contortions that their reasoning goes through when confronted with something that they cannot accept. This applies to any controversy. When people have an emotional stake in what's going on, it really skews their reasoning. . . . My feeling is that you'll be a much more effective person if you can face the facts as they are. I'd have to say I've learned a lot about some of our institutions and the quote-unquote experts from [my] experience."

In 1977, shortly before Travis Walton published his first book, filmmaker Steven Spielberg released *Close Encounters of the Third Kind*, which set the standard for UFO themes such as government secrecy and strange encounters as well as the appearance of diminutive aliens with oversized heads. From this point on, adding in the TV abduction movies, debunkers would claim that all alien contact stories showed similarities simply because the witnesses shared these common cultural connections. While worth considering, this argument did not address all cases, nor did it explain the reports of alien interest in reproduction that occurred long before any popular presentation of that theme.

Star Children

In 1982, New York artist Budd Hopkins published a book entitled *Missing Time* dealing with abduction cases he had studied since 1975. His book prompted twenty-three-year-old "Kathie Davis" to write and tell of a "missing time" incident involving her sister years before. She also said that on the night of June 30, 1983, she had seen a strange "spotlight" in her backyard, then found a burned area in the grass and the family dog cowering under a car.

After some time, Hopkins met with the woman, and over a course of months, aided by hypnosis, he learned an incredible story he published in a book called *Intruders*. Kathie now has been identified as Debbie Tomey, who lived near Indianapolis, Indiana.

Under hypnosis, Tomey told of multiple contacts beginning as a child in 1966 when she recalled a small creature visiting in her home and leaving her with a small scar on her leg. As a new bride in 1978, she awoke one night to find two small beings with large heads and eyes that were "pitch black in color, liquid-like, shimmering in the dim light" of her bedroom. Over the next few years, Tomey recalled under hypnosis that she was taken aboard a UFO for gynecological studies several times.

On October 3, 1983, following an earlier encounter with a small, gray-skinned creature, Tomey recalled being taken from her home and placed in a UFO. After yet another physical examination, Tomey was shown a small infant and led to believe it was hers, the result on an earlier abduction. In an emotional interview with Hopkins, Tomey described the event: "A little girl came into the room . . . escorted by two more of them [aliens]. . . . She looked to be about four. She looked about [my son's] size. He's four, and she didn't look like them, but she didn't look like us either. She was real pretty. She looked like an elf, or an . . . angel. She had really big blue eyes and little teeny-weeny nose, just so perfect. And her mouth was just so perfect and tiny, and she was pale, except her lips were pink and her eyes were blue. And her hair was white and wispy and thin . . . fine . . . real thin and fine. Her head was a little larger than normal, especially in the forehead . . . the forehead was a little bit bigger . . . but she was just a doll." Tomey said she somehow sensed that the child belonged to her. Later the aliens would tell her that this was one of nine children they had created from tissue taken from her body over the years.

Hopkins believed that the child shown to Tomey was the result of an abduction in 1978, which would have made the child the right age. Hopkins gave descriptions of the UFO medical procedures to Dr. John Burger, director of gynecology and obstetrics at Perth Amboy Hospital in New Jersey. Dr. Burger said they sounded remarkably similar to procedures modern medicine uses to take female reproductive cells for creating "test-tube" babies. Hopkins also compared Debbie's experience with other cases he had studied and commented, "Whether we like it or not the patterns exist—tight, clear patterns which are often buttressed by existing medical evidence."

"So we are left with two possible lines of explanation," wrote Hopkins. "The first requires the existence of a new and heretofore unknown psychological phenomenon, in which women 'hallucinate' nearly identical scenes, involving nearly identical semi-human babies. And this previously unknown psychological phenomenon apparently affects the results of chemical tests for pregnancy, turning negatives into positives. . . . The other remaining explanation is simple but 'untenable': The women [Hopkins cited four separate cases] are actually remembering what they saw. Their experiences were real. Both of these explanations, it is safe to say, violate conventional wisdom."

Author Curtis Peebles raised a valid point by detailing Tomey's medical history, which included obesity due to hormonal imbalance, "having had her gall bladder and appendix removed, and having suffered from hepatitis, Legionnaires' disease, fused vertebrae, an asthmatic attack, years of insomnia and paralyzing anxiety, a collapsed lung, heart arrhythmia, hypoglycemia, hyperadrenism, high blood pressure, chronic allergic reaction to medications, ovarian cysts and kidney failure." Peebles dryly noted that her medical record "makes her an extremely dubious donor for high-quality genetic material. . . ." However, as illustrated by the hysterectomies of Hill and Andreasson, apparently a deficient medical profile is no guarantee against abduction.

Naturally, debunkers of the concept of alien hybrid experimentation claim that all such reports are the result of psychological imbalance aided by reading or hearing of other such stories. Author Peebles pointed to the precedents set by TV shows and movies, including the unemotional Mr. Spock of *Star Trek*. "The abductee myth has numerous similarities with science fiction," Peebles proclaimed. Countering this argument was historian Dr. David Jacobs, who said, "Contactee stories were deeply rooted in a science fiction model of alien behavior [while] abductee stories have a profoundly alien quality to them that are strikingly devoid of cultural programmatic content." British author Jenny Randles noted, "Prior to 1987 at least, this phenomenon [alien abductions involving reproduction] was unknown even to UFO researchers such as myself. We did have a fairly uncontaminated period for case collection. Any sign of such things within the records are very important and it is quite astonishing to see to what extent this does emerge from a study of the evidence. Often these cases had no publicity outside rare sources within Ufology or, indeed, not uncommonly, no publication at all prior to 1987."

Look into My Eyes

"Hopkins' abductees had no overt memories until they were hypnotized. The question becomes whether the abduction story is only a product of being hypnotized," commented author Peebles, joining the chorus of voices who claimed that much—if not all—of abduction recollections stemmed from prompting by their hypnotists. The use of hypnosis has caused considerable controversy both within and without the UFO research community, especially in light of its increasing use in a variety of issues from abductions to child abuse.

Critics of hypnosis were gratified by the results of a test conducted in 1977 by Dr. Alvin H. Lawson, an English professor at California State University and a UFO researcher. Dr. Lawson asked eight hypnotized persons to imagine an abduction experience. With little or no prompting, at least four of the subjects produced an abduction tale remarkably like those of supposed real abductees. Author Peebles claimed the test "shows that nearly anyone can, under hypnosis, provide an abduction story." However, Dr. Lawson's test was roundly criticized by various authorities for using too small a test group, using leading questions rather than the neutral language of most hypnotic regressions, and emphasizing similarities where significant differences abounded.

Researcher Hopkins further pointed out, "We're getting extremely detailed descriptions of abductions from kids six years and under. . . . The child is telling about the little man who stuck a needle in her belly button, and then she hikes up her blouse, and there's a puncture mark and a red spot. . . . The children's memories do not seem adequately blocked and therefore they're coming up with much more detailed memories. Hypnosis is not an issue here."

Even some devout believers in alien abductions question the validity of hypnosis as an investigative tool. "I have seen what I feel are abuses perpetrated by 'investigators' who are really nothing more than part-time, unlicensed and unregulated mental health care counselors," said self-professed abductee and author Whitley Strieber. "They are carrying out their activities in an inappropriate, misguided and dangerous effort to use hypnosis to build a so-called 'credible' case for UFO abduction." Strieber added that he still supports hypnotism as a therapeutic device, "as it is uniquely capable of enabling the subject to break fear-amnesia."

Budd Hopkins, the artist turned abduction researcher, agreed that caution is needed when dealing with hypnosis. "All testimony, hypnotically elicited or otherwise, is affected to some extent by the questioner," he said. "In a court trial, a calm, non-leading judge can elicit one kind of information, a bullying prosecutor another." But Hopkins disputes the contention that all abduction stories are the result of leading questions under hypnosis. "In roughly one-fourth of the abduction cases I've investigated, the subject has recalled virtually all of his or her basic abduction scenario prior to hypnosis," he said. "It should also be mentioned here that in 25 borderline but possible abduction cases, we have used hypnosis with no abduction scenarios coming to light. I am sure that these 25 individuals are not abductees, and their cases attest to the scientific objectivity of our use of the hypnotic process." Hopkins also pointed out that most hypnosis used in his research has been conducted by enlisted professional psychologists and psychiatrists.

Hopkins also said that many abductees experience "screen memories," a cover story or false image implanted in their minds to mask the true abduction experience. "The function of a cover story is to soften a disturbing memory and render it more benign and acceptable," he said. "One never finds a screen memory working the other way—escalating the terror. . . . But more important here is the fact that screen memories clearly establish the need for hypnosis if we are ever to know the whole truth about any abduction experience."

Dr. John E. Mack, professor of psychiatry at the Cambridge Hospital, Harvard Medical School, and founding director of the Center for Psychology and Social Change, has found hypnosis a credible tool in the study of the abduction phenomenon. "My personal experience is that abduction material recovered under hypnosis parallels what has been obtained by conscious reporting," he said, adding in some cases hypnotically retrieved information seemed more accurate because it was less self-serving, more consistent, and more emotional.

Both supporters and critics have been impressed with the raw emotions exhibited by abductees under hypnosis. "It is hard to imagine how the psyche could generate so intense a level of emotion without some kind of exposure to an extraordinary experience as the template for that emotion," noted Dr. Mack. Hopkins likewise wrote, "There is no way for me to convey . . . the emotional authenticity of the hundreds of letters and phone calls I've received and the interviews I've conducted over the . . . years."

Author Raymond Fowler, investigator of the Andreasson mother and daughter, wrote, "We were amazed at how, week after week, the witnesses would pick up their accounts at the precise point where Dr. Edelstein had left off the week before. Deep trance hypnosis, properly administered by a skillful hypnotist, can produce near-total recall of everything a subject has ever experienced. In this trance state, a person must tell the truth, as he or she believes the truth to be."

In the debate over hypnosis, all parties agree that the "truth" revealed by hypnotized persons merely reflects their version of truth, not necessarily an objective truth.

Speaking of details obtained through hypnosis, Hopkins said, "I completely trust the accuracy of these small, highly specific details only when they recur in case after case, but I have no doubt as to the usefulness of hypnosis in unlocking the general abduction scenario. . . . Hypnosis is simply one more investigative tool UFO researchers use to examine our most disturbing modern mystery." His thought was echoed by author Richard Thompson, who probably spoke for the majority of abduction researchers when he stated, "Since the experiences remembered with the aid of hypnosis tend to be much the same as those remembered without it, it would appear that the process of hypnosis itself is not a major cause of abduction accounts. . . . Hypnosis, it seems, is an imperfect and poorly understood tool that can produce useful results but cannot be fully trusted."

Dr. Thomas Bullard of Indiana University undertook an in-depth study of the hypnosis issue in the mid-1980s and found that responses differed widely from hypnotists' expectations. He concluded, "Rather than a full-scale shaping force as postulated by the skeptics, hypnotists appear less the leaders than the led." Flatly declaring that the abduction phenomenon was not the result of hypnosis, Dr. Bullard stated, "The potential for misuse of hypnosis is undeniable, yet an examination of abduction evidence points to a reassuring conclusion: . . . Outcomes in every comparison give little reason to believe that Svengali-like hypnotists lead witnesses or impose standardized abduction stories onto them."

Clearly debunker Peebles did not present an unbiased portrait of the hypnosis issue when he wrote, "Clearly, hypnosis is not the foolproof truth-finding technique the abductionists make it out to be." As Dr. Bullard pointed out, "However rigorous the procedures, however unequivocal the comparative analysis, doubters looking for ways to condemn abduction evidence without facing up to it can always create doubt by questioning hypnosis."

Hypnosis was not the only target of debunkers in the abduction debate.

The Mack Attack

Dr. John Mack, who authored a Pulitzer Prize–winning biography of T. E. Lawrence in addition to his credentials at Harvard, immediately incurred the wrath of those with an antiabduction mind-set with the publication of his book *Abduction: Human Encounters with Aliens* in April 1994. Mack's greatest sin, it appeared, was that he broke ranks with most other credentialed scientists who in the past had maintained a strict "hands-off" attitude toward UFOs in general and abductions in particular.

His book details the accounts of thirteen out of nearly a hundred abductees he studied. Of the hundred abductees, nearly sixty agreed to hypnosis or relaxation sessions. "It is remarkable to me how many people do want to go further [with the study of their experience] . . . even though they know that the recovery of these experiences is going to be disturbing to them. . . ." Mack even had four of the abductees given a battery of psychological tests, "three of whom came out high-functional, healthy, normal range. One young man was quite troubled . . . although those disturbances did not explain his abduction experiences." Mack's study agreed with other abduction researchers, who have found that abductees generally are no different in physiological or psychological makeup than the rest of the population. "None of the efforts to characterize abductees as a group have been successful," Mack stated. "They seem to come, as if at random, from all parts of society."

Addressing those who claim abductee stories may be the result of suppressed sexual abuse, Mack noted that the majority of cases he studied indicated no such abuse was involved. "But it was also clear in the cases where there has been sexual abuse—when they've had both experiences—the abductees are quite able to distinguish the dimensions of trauma that come from sexual abuse versus those which are alien related. The most convincing argument is that some of these people are very solid, healthy, sometimes prominent, well-put-together people, who upon examination do not give evidence of having any other kind of trauma."

Mack, who said he started his abduction work as "an intense skeptic" studying the work of Budd Hopkins, was intrigued with the consistency of the abduction stories and attendant evidence. "In virtually every case there are one or more concrete physical findings that accompany or follow the abduction experience, such as UFO sightings in the community, burned earth where UFOs are said to have landed, and independent corroboration that the abductee's whereabouts are unknown at the time of the reported abduction event," he said. "Seemingly unexplained or missing pregnancies, a variety of minor physical lesions, odd nosebleeds, and the recovery of tiny objects from the bodies of experiencers are also widely seen." While intrigued by reports of unnatural and abortive pregnancies, Mack was quick to point out that "there is not yet a case where a physician has documented that a fetus has disappeared in relation to an abduction."

Still, while striving to maintain an objective approach to this outlandish topic, Mack did bring to the subject his knowledge and acceptance of Eastern spirituality and some tested tools from his experience as a clinical psychologist. When one critic assailed his book as a "subversive assault on psychoanalysis as a science," Mack defended his approach by stating that too many debunkers reject information simply because it conflicts with their mind-set. "To exclude data because it does not fit a particular view of reality can only, in the end, arrest the progress of science and keep us ignorant," he wrote. He also stated that innovative methods must be employed in the study of abductions and the beings behind them because "These entities seem to belong in the parallel universe, but they cross over and manifest in the physical world. They are not of one or the other. The Western Newton-Cartesian paradigm has no way to deal with that."

Mack was viciously attacked for his belief that abductees represent normal humans who have experienced highly abnormal situations, but other less high-profile studies supported his views. Nicholas Spanos and psychologists at Carleton University in Canada studied nearly two hundred persons, some claiming UFO experiences. In their report, the psychologists reported no significant difference between people who have experienced UFOs and others. "These findings clearly contradict the hypothesis that UFO reports—even intense UFO reports characterized by such seemingly bizarre experiences as missing time and communication with aliens—occur primarily in individuals who are highly fantasy prone, given to paranormal beliefs or unusually suggestible," they reported. Other studies, such as those by psychologist Dr. Richard Boylan, also support Mack's research.

But it was Mack who bore the brunt of the debunkers' ire. Shortly after the publication of Mack's book, a woman named Donna

Bessett came forward to announce that she had made up stories of alien abductions that were accepted as truth by Mack. "I faked it, women have been doing it for centuries," she told one audience glibly. She said Mack's abductees were "intelligent, imaginative, but poorly educated" and told the doctor only what he wanted to hear. Bessett's story was widely publicized in such publications as *Time* magazine. She even confronted Mack during the 1994 annual conference of the Committee for the Scientific Investigation of Claims of the Paranormal (CSICOP) as a "surprise speaker," a tactic termed "unconscionable" even by some CSICOP members.

Mack, constrained by patient confidentiality, nevertheless put the matter in perspective by stating, "I saw Donna in good faith several times. If in fact she did fool me, which could happen—it's not impossible—then she was lying to me consistently. That would follow certainly from her claim that she hoaxed me. If, in fact, she has established herself as an effective and thoroughgoing liar, then how can she be considered an authority on matters of integrity regarding my work, methodology, patient-client and physician relationship? The assumption is that she fooled me into using her material as part of my database. The fact is I didn't use one word she had to say in my book."

Mack, like many others in the UFO research community, wondered aloud "why *Time* magazine would go to such lengths to put aside any other positive material [such as interviewing other abductees who have worked with the doctor] to create a story to slander me." Mack said some weeks later *Time* did admit receiving many letters supporting his work but "by that time the damage was done."

The "damage" was a "Special Faculty Committee" formed in 1994 at the Harvard Medical School to assess Mack's work. Attorney Daniel Sheehan, founder of the Christic Institute, which has involved itself in several political causes, argued that Mack's right of due process was violated by the mere act of forming such a committee. Sheehan also stated that the panel wrote a preliminary "Draft Report" criticizing Mack for "affirming the delusions" of his abductee patients and violating Harvard standards without affording Mack any chance to present his side of the issue.

However, in August 1995, after abduction researchers along with Mack's attorney, Eric MacLeish, mobilized widespread support for Mack's work, the committee quietly closed shop without any official censure of Mack or his work. "John Mack is just as he started out—a perfectly full-fledged member of the Harvard faculty with no adverse action taken," stated Anne Taylor, a committee member.

While certainly not a ringing endorsement of Mack's public statements that extraterrestrials have "invaded our physical reality," the committee's decision not to condemn or restrict Mack's work did seem to lend strong support to those who take the abduction phenomenon seriously. Committee chairman Arnold Relman even quipped, "Harvard University isn't going to take action against someone who takes unorthodox views, and with whom it may disagree. John Mack may win the Nobel prize and go down in history as the modern Galileo."

Despite the work of several professionals in the abduction field, perhaps the one person who most popularized the abduction concept was the author of science fiction and horror tales.

A Time of Communion

Already successful as a novelist dealing with issues such as nuclear war and environmental catastrophe, Whitley Strieber launched himself into the maelstrom of the UFO issue in 1987 with the publication of *Communion: A True Story*. The book, which quickly hit number one on the *New York Times* nonfiction best-seller list and went on to become a worldwide success, detailed Strieber's account of his experiences with UFO occupants.

Strieber claimed his experiences ranged over a period of years beginning in childhood and later moved between his New York City apartment and a secluded cabin in upstate New York. It was at the latter residence in December 1985 that Strieber had his first conscious meeting with what he came to call the "visitors," a term deliberately chosen for its vagueness. His account included all the staples of abduction lore, such as feelings of dread and apprehension, strange lights, missing time, abduction, and medical examination. As an articulate person as well as an accomplished author, Strieber was able to convey the subtleties and emotions of the contact experience much better than others.

Following his abduction experience, Strieber visited both his own doctor and psychiatrist Dr. Donald Kline. Both pronounced Strieber entirely normal. Furthermore, a lie detector test administered in February 1987 by Jeremy G. Barrett, managing director of Polygraph Security Services of London, determined Strieber "truthful in response to all questions," including "Are the 'visitors' a physical reality?—Yes." Strieber's experiences were further corroborated by hypnosis.

After the success of a second Strieber book, *Transformation*, investigative journalist Ed Conroy looked in detail at Strieber's story and background. He found childhood friends who confirmed strange events in the author's past, including balls of light in the sky and a charred circle in his backyard—although the latter could have been caused by gasoline balloon bombs the youngsters admittedly made. An interview with film director Philippe Mora revealed that Mora witnessed strange events while staying with Strieber in his remote cabin. Mora said he saw lights moving in the sky. "It looked as if it were a satellite, but I'm calling it space junk. I don't know what it was," he recalled. "Then we all went to bed. . . . I was relaxing. I had the experience of lights blasting through the bedroom window, lights blasting under the crack under the door of the bedroom—I tried to turn the light on in my room, and I couldn't turn it on and I was pushed back into the bed. All the while I was consciously saying to myself, 'This is a hell of a nightmare.' Then I remember being outside the guest room door, in the kitchen area, and the whole cabin lit up—every opening, every exterior opening, the whole thing was lit up with moving lights."

It was Mora who directed *Communion*, an 1989 movie based on Strieber's book, which brought the subject matter to an even wider audience. Actor Christopher Walken reenacted Strieber's confrontations with small gray beings.

By 1996, Strieber claimed to have received more than 165,000 letters from people all over the world, many of whom said they had similar experiences. Because of this plus his own experiences, Strieber is convinced that both UFOs and abductions represent a physical reality. "The game is over," he said of the contest of mind-sets over UFOs. "We've won, thanks to the advent of the camcorder. These things are real!"

However, Strieber does not necessarily believe that aliens from space are conducting the abductions, a position that placed him at odds with other abduction researchers such as his old friend Budd Hopkins. "What is not proved is if there is any connection between the objects and abduction experiences. I feel the phenomena are related," he said. Strieber said that in all his research he knew of only one incident where a human may have died as the result of a UFO encounter. "There was a family living by a lake who saw what they thought were little children playing by the water. The grandfather took a gun and ran down to chase them off. They heard a low boom and found the grandfather dead by the lake. He had not been shot. An autopsy did not reveal the cause of death," he said. Strieber acknowledged that this case was not absolute proof of a UFO-related death, but he said he found nothing enjoyable about his experiences. "The abduction experience is comparable to being run over by a train," he said. "Your whole life changes. But I guess I'd rather have the abduction experience because you can survive that." He compared an abduction to a near death experience and said that the shock is "so deep it threatens more than life."

In 1990, Strieber became so disenchanted with the personality conflicts and squabbles within the UFO community he closed his Communion Foundation abductee support group and withdrew from the UFO scene. He complained that our society is "monstrously inhumane" to persons with UFO encounters and called ufologists "the cruelest, nastiest, craziest people I have ever encountered." But by 1995, he was back with a new book entitled *Breakthrough* espousing new visions and interpretations of his experiences. "I stayed away from all this," he explained, "but the visitors didn't stay away from me and I grew and changed."

Strieber said he continues to bring his story to the public because "If this is 'real,' then it is very important as a testament to this kind of contact. If it is a 'mind thing,' then the book serves notice that something extraordinary is happening to our minds. . . . It has enormously expanded my consciousness. I have gone from a level of about 10 to a level of about 6,000. I have been opened to so many provocative possibilities. I have discovered that this is an extraordinary, quasi-physical reality that somehow emerges out of us. Therefore, the human mind is a bigger, more incredible, and wonderful thing than we have ever dreamed."

Speaking of his new views on the human ability to grow and on visitor benevolence, Strieber wrote, "The message is clear: we are our own greatest resource, and there is someone here willing to take us by the hand—or nudge us or push us or kick us if need be—to help us find that out.

"We can choose to let this experience destroy us through fear and anxiety," Strieber stated. "But I choose to grow from it."

His comment echoes reports from some people who claim to have had pleasant contact experiences.

Midnight Visits

Researcher and California artist Jefferson R. Weekley reported a pleasant visit with unearthly beings as the result of a psychedelic experience in 1992. Although his admitted use of a potent psychedelic may cause many to discount his story as a drug-induced hallucination, it is worth noting the similarity of his account with other descriptions of alien visitation.

Three months after ingesting a mushroom containing psilocybin, Weekley said he awoke in the middle of the night to find three small figures standing by his bed. "They were white with small, frail bodies, large triangular heads and big luminous black eyes," he recalled. "Fear gripped me. I felt helpless. The figures just stood there staring at me. They were really there! They were emanating a feeling of surprise and curiosity. Then somehow I knew that they hadn't come to me but I had entered their world. I decided to treat this as a lucid dream and I willed myself to 'wake up.' I could sense a feeling of bewilderment coming from the three creatures as they receded from me. I returned to my normal state of awareness and I looked around. The room was empty."

Weekley said this and other experiences caused him to take an interest in UFO literature, since the depiction of the popularized "greys" was very similar to the little beings he saw in his home. "The little people were curious and playful beings that were more elf-like than the alien scientists doing frightening genetic experiments on unwilling subjects," he added. "I knew these beings were not from some other planet. They exist in a world that is just next door, and they are waiting with happy expectation for us to come through."

While the frightening alien abduction scenarios grab the public's attention, there are many people not using drugs who also report benign contact.

Charlene Adams is a forty-seven-year-old registered nurse in Dallas, Texas, who is now convinced that she has been the subject of alien visitations all her life. "I've been abducted since a young age," she said. "and it scared me very much. I knew I would die of fright, but I didn't. It was very strange and unreal and I couldn't remember much of what happened. So I didn't tell anybody. But all my adult life I have had the feeling that aliens—the greys—have been around me."

Adams said a late-night visitation in 1995 awakened abduction memories within her and finally convinced her of the reality of her experiences. "One night there was one in my bedroom. I could couch it in terms of a dream, but it wasn't. It was reality. I know because I reached out and touched him. It was real. It felt familiar, loving. I lost all fear. He told me they had been waiting a long time for me to awaken. He said his name was Orion. When I asked where he was from, he replied he was from Waxahatchie [a small community south of Dallas popular for its Indian name, pronounced Wock-se-hatch-ee]. He definitely had a sense of humor. He also said I was part of some 3,000 people on Earth that were part of his network. He said these people were at different levels of consciousness regarding his presence. Some of these people are consciously aware of his involvement, but many others are not. I am now one of the conscious ones. My life is no different now except the fear is gone. Now I'm a volunteer."

With her experience, Adams joined a growing but largely unreported group of people who view the abductions as an ongoing part of alien visitation in connection with the evolution of mankind. They believe they have a role to play in this movement.

Regardless of their view on the issue, abductee self-help groups have sprung up all across the nation, and many mental health professionals have begun taking a serious look at the matter. These professionals along with researchers have logged a number of common aspects to the abduction experience over the years.

A change in the participant's perceptions, such as weakness, drowsiness, or lightheadedness usually at the beginning of an abduction, has been termed the "Oz factor" by British researcher/author Jenny Randles. "It suggests that witnesses are plunged into an altered state of consciousness at the onset of the experience," she stated. Many people noted an eerie stillness or total silence—normal ambient noises from traffic, crickets, birds, or neighbors ceased. Many report that a bright blue or white light permeates their room or car, often accompanied by a buzzing or humming sound. There is usually a sense of apprehension or expectation.

In many abduction cases, there is an attendant power failure. Lights, appliances, vehicles, and other equipment cease to function. Many researchers claim that the closeness of UFOs creates electromagnetic interference, knocking out radios, televisions, and other electronic gear.

Abductees give various descriptions of their captors. The most common is what has come to be termed the "greys," diminutive humanoid beings with hairless, overlarge heads, chalky gray skin usually encased in one-piece coveralls, with large dark eyes and small vestigial ears, nose, and mouth. Occasionally, handsome full-size humans with blond hair are described as well as truly alien beings that resemble reptiles or a praying mantis. While it is argued that popular fiction may account for the similarity of descriptions, it should be noted that the descriptions preceded any widespread media presentation and were derived from UFO witnesses. It is a classic case of what came first—the reality or the publicity?

Many abductees, such as Betty Hill and Betty Andreasson, reported that their abductors had the ability to literally float through solid objects such as doors and walls. This one factor has created much resistance to abduction stories, since the penetration of solid materials goes against our materialistic world-view.

Descriptions of the general configuration of the UFOs involved in abduction cases are remarkably similar, although the craft apparently vary in size. Often the initial UFO joins with a larger one or "mothership." Usually a circular craft, these UFOs contain a control room or deck as well as a small room for medical examinations. Once aboard, many abductees are given brief tours of the craft, and occasionally, as in the case of Andreasson, there is even what seems to be a trip to another world. Researcher Fred Youngren asked Andreasson to make sketches of the interior of the UFO. After studying them, Youngren concluded, "The fact is that the combination of these sketches into a coherent craft has produced a powerful corroboration of the witness's account."

Medical examinations are the most commonly reported experience of abductees, with various instruments used to probe nearly all parts of the body. Special emphasis appears to center on the reproductive system. After being placed in a white, sterile hospital-like room, women report needles being inserted in their navels while men tell of various devices being placed over their genitals. "The purely physical or biological aspect of the abduction phenomenon seems to have to do with some sort of genetic or quasi-genetic engineering for the purpose of creating human/alien hybrid offspring," opined Mack. Many people report being scrutinized by an eyelike ball device on a metal neck or stalk that passes over their body. There is no documented case of any abductee being seriously harmed by these examinations, although the fear and apprehension of many is immense, probably due to feelings that they have no control over the situation.

In cases where there appears to have been a long journey involved, several abductees reported being immersed in a thick liquid similar to that described by Andreasson. Many researchers theorize this is a means of protecting the person against the stresses of deep space travel or rapid acceleration and deceleration.

Abductees often are provided various types of information, which they recall with varying degrees of consciousness. Often it requires hypnosis to bring forth this information. Most often the witnesses are exposed to scenes of nuclear holocaust or environmental degradation resulting in a lifeless and sterile earth. Some researchers believe these scenes are predictions of our future, while others feel such visions are used to generate fear and anxiety in the witnesses, as part of the aliens' studies or agenda. Said Mack, "Some abductees receive information of battles for the fate of the Earth and the control of the human mind, between two or more groups of beings, some of which are more evolved or 'good,' while others are less evolved or 'evil.'"

Abductees are returned home at the end of their experience, usually with far less recollection of the return than of the initial abduction. Vague memories of their experience and resultant messages remain. Occasionally abductees are returned some distance from their point of capture and are dressed differently; some have returned with their clothing on inside out.

Only rarely are abductees seen or found missing during the process of abduction. "Independent witnessing of an abduction does occur," wrote Mack, "but is, in my experience, relatively rare and limited in nature."

Another facet of the abduction experience involves the reported implantation of tiny devices in an abductee's body. This new wrinkle on the abduction theme is only now being studied carefully by a few researchers.

What's Bugging You?

In September 1955, when Richard Price was eight years old, he was playing in some woods near his home in Troy, New York, when he saw a saucer-shaped UFO land nearby. Strange beings took Price up an elevator into the craft to a laboratory-like room.

During a medical examination similar to that related by other abductees, young Price watched a wall view screen as the beings placed a tiny device in his penis.

In 1981, Price showed Dr. Neal Rzepkewski an odd lump on his penis at the exact location he recalled the implant being placed. Rzepkewski, although puzzled by the swelling, recommended doing nothing unless it changed size or became painful. In 1989, Price discovered the object protruding through the skin, and soon, after apparently producing a sensation akin to an electrical shock, it was free. Price showed the small object to David Pritchard, a teacher of physics at the Massachusetts Institute of Technology, who conducted an analysis.

Pritchard, along with Dr. Tom Flotte of Massachusetts General Hospital, tested the object with a light microscope, a scanning electron microscope, and a secondary ion mass spectrometer and determined it to be a collection of organic material suggesting nothing unearthly. Some odd hooklike appendages were found to be cotton fibers apparently from Price's clothing, which penetrated the skin. The bulk of the object consisted of "carbon, oxygen and hydrogen plus substances that looked like collagen, cholesterol, and layers of degenerated cellular matter" consistent with "an old trauma site on the body."

The lack of definitive proof that an alien implant came from Price's body was typical of the problems encountered with this issue, despite the object's sensitive and atypical location.

While this report was disappointing to anyone hoping to find proof of an alien implant, it should be noted that such evidence cannot be regarded as absolute proof that such implants don't exist. Dr. John Mack noted that it would be "extremely difficult to make a positive diagnosis of the nature of any unknown substance without having more information about its origins."

Mack was given a small, wirelike object by one of his clients, who said she took it from her nose following an abduction experience. Analysis showed it was a twisted fiber composed of carbon, silicon, oxygen, and traces of other elements. "A nuclear biologist colleague said the 'specimen' was not a naturally occurring biological object but could be a manufactured fiber of some sort. It seemed difficult to know how to proceed further," he added.

Dr. Richard Neal, a medical doctor who has studied the UFO issue since the early 1960s, is cofounder of the Southern California UFO Research and Abductee Support Group. In an exhaustive study of abduction cases, Dr. Neal wrote, "The nasal cavity, ears, eyes and genitalia appear to be the physical areas of greatest interest to abducting aliens. The umbilical region—navel—is as well, but in females only. Many abductees have described a thin probe with a tiny ball on its end being inserted into the nostril—usually on the right side. They are able to hear a 'crushing' type sound as the bone in this area is apparently being penetrated. Many will have nosebleeds following these examinations. . . . Many researchers believe that alien technology is being used to insert an implant into this area for future tracking of the individual. It is interesting to note that many of the individuals subjected to nasal probing now have a history of chronic sinusitis."

The idea of aliens using devices to trace individuals—much like the electronic tags game wardens place on certain animals to keep track of them—is supported by several abductees, including one of Mack's clients, who claimed her abductors told her an object placed within her body was "to monitor me."

Abductee Betty Andreasson reported that during her examination, her captors removed something from behind her right eye with a long needlelike probe pushed up through her nose. Author Raymond Fowler, who chronicled the Andreasson story, was able to link this extraction to an abduction of Andreasson in 1950 when she was only thirteen years old. Under hypnosis, she recalled that at that time, her abductors removed her eye and inserted a small glass ball about the size of a BB along with one or more small slivers using "two long, glowing needles." "Perhaps the device placed behind Betty's right eye allowed an alien monitoring device thousands of miles away to actually record all that Betty herself sees!" speculated Fowler.

Dr. Neal, Dr. Mack, and others also noted that small scars were often reported on the bodies of abductees, along with the claims of implantation. Mack wrote that abduction experiences "frequently left physical traces on the individuals' bodies, such as cuts and small ulcers that would tend to heal rapidly and followed no apparent psychodynamically identifiable pattern as do, for example, religious stigmata." Neal noted, "Scars have been observed on the calf—including just over the tibia or shin bone—thigh, hip, shoulder, knee, spinal column and on the right sides of the back and forehead." He added that these scars usually included a one- to three-inch-long straight, hairline cut and/or a one-eighth- to three-quarter-inch circular depression as much as a quarter inch in depth.

Researchers see such scars and marks, while not medically significant considered by themselves, as significant corroboration for the abduction experience. A proven implant would be even more significant but, as is the case in the whole UFO issue, firm evidence is elusive.

Two recent researchers—one a California doctor and the other a Texas hypnotherapist—claim they may be on the verge of a breakthrough in the alien implants issue.

In August 1995, Dr. Roger K. Leir, a experienced podiatrist in Ventura, California, assisted by a retired surgeon, removed three objects from a man and a woman, both of whom claimed to have been abducted. Also present was an attorney, a psychologist, two writers, a still photographer, and a video cameraman to document the event. Two objects were taken from the woman's foot, while the other object was removed from the hand of Pat Parrinello. The woman declined to be identified other than as Patricia.

Parrinello, who was not charged for the minor operation, said he had experienced massive headaches prior to the surgery on his hand. The headaches stopped immediately upon removal of the object, which resembled a quarter-inch-diameter fly. "They took something out of me I didn't want in there," he said.

"Surprise number one. The soft tissue surrounding the object, when the report came back, had no inflammatory cells," said Leir, explaining how the human body generates such cells as a defense mechanism against foreign material. He also was surprised when the pathology report indicated the presence of nerve cells in the tissue surrounding the object. "The nerve cells don't belong there," observed Leir, "because anatomically they don't have any position in the soft tissue surrounding the toe, which is mainly fat and fibrous connective tissue. You don't find nerve cells." Noting that the woman patient reacted with pain when his scalpel touched the object, Leir speculated that it may have been designed to transmit messages to the brain. "You want to get in touch with the brain?" he asked rhetorically. "You don't have to go to the brain; you don't have to go to the neck or spinal cord. You can go to any nerve plexus and you've got routing to the brain."

According to the pathology report, the three objects were found to be encased in a tough, black membrane containing hemocyterin, a pigment that aids in oxygenating the blood. "What is hemocyterin doing comprising a membrane wrapped around a foreign body? [It] doesn't belong there!" commented Leir. "I discussed the reports with the pathologists in all cases, trying to get their opinion, and basically they don't have any. Finally, one of them on the phone just said, 'Damned if I know.'"

At the heart of each of the strange objects, Leir found a metallic core with a most unusual property. "These objects are highly magnetic," he said. "They even stuck to the scalpel when we removed them. I went over it with a stud finder and a magnetometer, and they would make the stud finder just stand on end."

Working with Leir on the alien implant issue was Derrel Sims, chief of abduction investigations and director of physical investigations for the Houston UFO Network. Both Sims and Leir cofounded the nonprofit Foundation for Alien-Human Research, dedicated primarily to studying implants. Small sections of the metallic cores of the three objects Leir removed were sent to the private laboratory of a Fortune 500 company but were returned as too small for proper testing. More samples were prepared, but the results were not immediately publicized.

Sims, who proclaimed, "If the evidence is out there, I'm going to find it," said several of the country's top laboratories along with sixteen "top scientists" had agreed to analyze some thirty objects he claimed to have acquired from abductees. However, with the exception of Warren Laboratories near Houston and the University of Houston, Sims declined to name any of them.

Sims said he pledged to protect the identities of the professionals working with him against corporate or government reprisals.

Sims and Leir said they have found keratin, a substance normally found in surface tissues such as hair and nails, in the objects, which gave off an odd green fluorescence when subjected to ultraviolet light. Sims said he suspects that the implants may concern behavior modification. "We have only scant evidence to indicate that might be true," he said, "but there again, scant evidence is better than none."

Author and abduction investigator Budd Hopkins urged extreme caution in dealing with oddities removed from people's bodies. "Mere anomalousness is not enough for the skeptics," he told one reporter. "It must be something we all agree is not something of this Earth. . . . There is sort of an assumption we make that these things will be monitoring or transmitting devices. But they may have different functions than anything we can possibly imagine. And when it comes to non-human or ET technology, we have to assume there will be implant qualities that we can neither measure nor detect."

With hard evidence of alien implants still up in the air and nothing but a multitude of accounts of abductions, UFO researchers continued to seek that one case that would capture the public's attention.

Several thought they may have found it in a recent incident—still under investigation—which involved multiple witnesses, including government agents and a ranking United Nations official. But this case, like the abduction phenomenon in general, is not susceptible to an easy explanation or interpretation.

New York Enigma

In April 1989, Linda Napolitano, publicly identified as Linda Cortile, contacted abduction author Budd Hopkins to say she had experienced abductions since childhood. On November 30, she contacted Hopkins to say that she had been abducted early that morning but could not recall many details. The forty-five-year-old New Yorker stated that as she lay awake in bed at about 3:15 A.M., she felt a paralysis come over her body and saw a gray alien standing by her bed. Resisting the intrusion, she threw a pillow at the creature but then lapsed into unconsciousness and recalled nothing until she came to in bed some time later.

Under hypnosis, Linda recalled being escorted by three creatures as they "floated" her through the closed twelfth-story window of her East Side apartment to a hovering UFO outside. Her husband remained in bed asleep throughout this activity. She said a beam of blue light drew her and the aliens into the UFO, where she was given a medical examination before being returned to her bed. Her experience and subsequent events were chronicled in a 1996 book by Hopkins entitled, *Witnessed: The True Story of the Brooklyn Bridge UFO Abductions.*

This would have been only one more typical abduction experience except for activities that began in February 1991, when Hopkins received a letter from two men claiming to be policemen identified only as "Richard" and "Dan." The pair said they had witnessed Linda's abduction from their car parked a few blocks away. They said they were on duty in Manhattan when they saw a woman being floated from a apartment house into a hovering UFO, which then dived into the East River not far from the Brooklyn Bridge. After the UFO failed to return after more than forty-five minutes, the pair became anxious over the fate of the woman. Hopkins informed Linda of the men's letter and alerted her that they might contact her.

Linda indeed was visited by "Richard" and "Dan" some weeks later. They appeared greatly relieved to find her alive and well and, on her urging, agreed to contact Hopkins again. The author soon received further correspondence from the pair as well as a taped message. They explained that they could not go public because they were really security agents who on the night of Cortile's abduction were transporting an international political figure to a rendezvous with a helicopter. Although Hopkins referred to this person only as "the third man" in his book, several publications identified him as none other than former United Nations secretary-general Javier Pérez de Cuellar. The agents said their car had suddenly stopped and, while waiting, all three men witnessed the abduction. This statement led Hopkins to believe that the entire episode had been a "display" to prove the reality of abductions staged by aliens for the benefit of Cuellar, who reportedly was accompanied by two U.S. government officials and two other statesmen plus several security agents. Some of these witnesses recalled seeing the UFO, while others only remembered that their cars stalled, according to "Richard."

Months later, Hopkins said he was contacted by a retired telephone operator who said her car also stopped while crossing the Brooklyn Bridge in the early-morning hours of November 30, 1989. The woman said she too witnessed the abduction. Drawings made of the event by this woman reportedly closely matched drawings made by one of the security agents. By the publication of his book on the case, Hopkins claimed to have found a total of six separate witnesses to the event.

Many ufologists initially thought the Brooklyn Bridge abduction story to be the "case of the century," the one account that would prove the reality of the abduction experience. But like so much of the whole UFO issue, it too fell into disarray as investigation continued. A government agent unconnected to the case said early-morning rides to helicopters violated normal security protocols, and a spokesman for Cuellar stated that the secretary-general was home in bed at the time of the abduction. Hopkins would not reveal the identity of the telephone operator. Debunkers decried the lack of additional witnesses, pointing out that several people working on a loading dock of the *New York Post*, located across the street from Linda's apartment, saw nothing. Hopkins blunted this attack by noting that in addition to the scarcity of workers at that time of the morning, the dock's door faced away from Linda's building. "The self-styled 'skeptical investigators' circulated a great deal of erroneous information because none of them ever bothered to call me for clarification of any issue about which they were uncertain," he complained.

To increase the confusion, Linda said that on October 15, 1991, she was abducted again—this time by agent "Dan," who took her to a beach house on Long Island and forced her to put on a white nightgown like the one she had worn during her abduction. She said agent "Richard" arrived at the house and sedated "Dan." Linda said she later received a letter from "Dan" written from a mental institution containing an implied threat that he planned to kidnap her—a threat he attempted to carry out, according to "Richard."

Hopkins's investigation revealed the abduction case as one that involved not only repeated abductions of both Linda and her children but also involved the alien abduction of "Richard," "Dan," and the man they were assigned to protect. He also described hypnosis sessions that indicated that there was some sort of interconnection between all of the principals in the case. Hopkins published an X ray of Linda's head showing a small implant in her nose, which later strangely disappeared after all four family members awoke one morning with similar nosebleeds.

While debunkers undoubtedly will continue to dismiss this case, the details Hopkins provided are persuasive. "As for me," he concluded, "it was easier to believe that the unanimity of eyewitness testimony and the existence of many kinds of supporting physical evidence attested to the reality of the event, rather than to believe in the existence of a vastly complex plot ... conceived and orchestrated by a middle-aged housewife of modest means, a mother of two young boys, who would forever be dependent upon—and hostage to—a small army of accomplices." Linda herself added a strong challenge to the debunkers when she asked Hopkins, "If I was only having a hallucination that night in 1989, why not ask a psychiatrist how so many people could have seen my hallucination?"

"This abduction event so drastically alters our knowledge of the alien incursion in our world that it is easily the most important in recorded history," Hopkins wrote. "No previous case has had such a profound effect on so many lives, and none has ever been observed by so many independent witnesses." Hopkins also said this case indicated that the UFO crew attempted to affect global politics by their selective abduction in full view of a world leader.

He added, "It seems obvious that the UFO occupants—whoever or whatever they are—are deeply and intimately involved in the lives of certain human beings. Apparently they can manipulate the behavior of these people, at least temporarily, with near absolute precision.

"Everything I have learned in twenty years of research into the UFO abduction phenomenon leads me to conclude that the aliens' central purpose is not to teach us about taking better care of the environment. Instead, all of the evidence points to their being here to carry out a complex breeding experiment in which they seem to be working to create a hybrid species, a mix of human and alien characteristics."

Although the case is still ongoing and considered by many a strong argument for the abduction experience, it has further split the UFO research community as to its validity.

UFO Pilot Wanted

A most incredible abduction experience was reported by retired military intelligence officer Lyn Buchanan, who said he now has had two recent experiences that convince him that it really happened.

In the mid-1960s prior to joining the army, Buchanan was a young student pastor at the Midway-Elwood Methodist Church near Huntsville, Texas. He had been assigned to a new church and was preparing to move. "My wife and family had already left and I was finishing packing up in the unfurnished parsonage," Buchanan recalled. "It was about 2 A.M. and I had bedded down with some blankets and a pillow when I heard something overhead coming down into the backyard. I suddenly realized that I was wide awake but I couldn't move. I became frightened when I heard some people moving around both sides of the house toward the front window.

"The next thing I knew it was morning and I was standing in the living room, completely disoriented. Then I remembered I was moving, so I packed up and left. That was all I knew at the time, but ever since that time I could never leave home without a compulsion to go back for something, a strong feeling that I had forgotten something. Time and time again I would return home to check on things. It drove my wife crazy. Finally about five or six years ago, I was roaming through the house checking on things I felt I had forgotten. Sarcastically, she said, 'Have you checked the backyard?' and it all came rushing back to me. Over time and using various methods—including remote viewing and hypnosis—I remembered what had happened to me.

"I still don't remember how I got there, but I was in a ship sitting in a row of seats with a scared little old lady beside me. Besides me there were about fifteen people in this room and a large window in the front. A tall person walked by and I asked if I could sit by the window. He seemed shocked and looked at me as if to say, 'Uh-oh, the sharks are loose in the pool.' I think he was surprised that I was conscious and had spoken to him. He ran forward and returned with a little guy with weird eyes who spoke with me. I got the impression he was the pilot. He allowed me to move forward by the window. We were lifting off and setting down, several times.

"Then the pilot came back and said it was time for the 'long trip.' I had watched him at this control panel and I asked if I could fly the ship. He said I couldn't operate the ship because my hands were too small. But I have unusually large hands and held one up. He put his hand on mine, palm to palm, and was impressed that they almost matched. After a while he let me sit at the control panel. It was like I was flying the ship, but I really wasn't. He said he had to take back the controls and soon the ship landed. There were two other saucers sitting there. There was a line of people getting off one and a line getting on the other. We all got out in a line and began to walk up this path to a pavilion-type place on top of a hill. It was dark outside, although it was daytime. And it was real warm and humid. I looked up and the sun was at about the ten o'clock position, but it was a different color than ours and was much dimmer. I knew we were not on Earth.

"The short guy came up and pulled me out of line and we sat on the hillside as the people moved up to this open-sided pavilion. That's when the sounds started. First I heard laughter, like belly laughs, but then also screaming as if in terror. A woman screamed and screamed and everyone else just laughed. But then she started laughing with everyone else and someone else started screaming. I didn't understand what was happening but it scared me and I was glad that I had not gone with the other people.

"The little guy said he wanted to introduce me to someone and soon another guy came up and we compared hand size and talked. For the longest time I could not remember what we talked about but a few years ago I went to a hypnotherapist. I made sure I got one who did not believe in UFOs and I didn't tell him what had happened to me. I only said that I wanted to recover some memories. This hypnotist led me to remember that this second guy was offering me a job flying saucers. I was excited. I said, 'Okay, but I need to go get my family.' He replied that there were no families there and that I could never return if I took the job. So I turned it down. He said I would have to go back with the others. So as the people came back down the hill I rejoined the line back to the ship.

"While waiting there I again talked to the pilot and told him this was a fascinating experience and he replied, 'You won't remember any of it.' I pleaded, 'Please let me remember this,' but it did no good. The next thing I can remember is standing in the living room of that house in East Texas not knowing where I was or what was happening."

Buchanan said that after he finally recalled the experience, he still could not decide if it was real. "But now I know," he said. "I had feedback which allowed me to believe that it was all real."

His "feedback" first came in the form of two men "immaculately" dressed in black who in the late 1980s took him into a small room at the headquarters of the Defense Intelligence Agency for a debriefing. "I think they heard about my experience and wanted to find out if I was crazy because they began to question me about the abduction," Buchanan said. As an E-7 in the service, Buchanan had worked on various classified projects for the U.S. Army before being assigned to a military intelligence unit at Fort Meade in the early 1980s.

He was familiar with interrogation techniques and said one of the men in black asked all the questions while the other sat silently, showing no emotion. "If you react or show emotion, it can influence the answers," he explained. "So, at one point I was describing the control panel in the ship and how it worked. I went through it once but was asked to explain it again, which is another technique to see if you contradict yourself. But this time as I was explaining the function of the control panel, the silent one suddenly asked, 'You mean such and such?' I said, 'No, I mean thus and such.' He slapped his knee and exclaimed, 'So that's it!' I knew right then that they had one of those things but hadn't known how to work it. The other guy, the one who had been asking all the questions, got furious and the two men quickly left.

"About a year later I was on a tour with a group through a building—I'm not allowed to say where or why—to look at some mock-up exhibitions of airplane crash sites. I was looking at one of the exhibitions and there was the control panel like the one on the ship. Without thinking, I turned to this officer and said, 'That's not out of a plane. That's out of a flying saucer!' This officer looked shocked but finally said stiffly, 'It's reported to be.' Within four minutes my group was ushered out of the building and reminded not to talk about our visit. After those two experiences, I became convinced that my abduction experience was real and that the government knows a lot more than it's saying."

Undeniable evidence to support stories like Buchanan's is always elusive, but the sheer number of abduction accounts—as well as their consistency—is overwhelming. A 1991 poll of nearly six thousand Americans by the Roper organization indicated that several hundred thousand—perhaps more than three million—citizens may have had an abduction experience. Respondents answered questions concerning strange encounters, missing time, unusual lights in their room, and puzzling scars on their body. Needless to say, these figures have been sharply criticized by the debunkers, who said if the numbers are valid, the skies would literally be filled night and day with abducting UFOs.

In the words of British author Jenny Randles, "To prove . . . or establish that we really are being visited by strange creatures, requires much more solid evidence than an honest person's self-conviction." Randles then enumerated an extensive list of supportive data, including corroborating witnesses, photographs of UFOs—admittedly some, if not many, are hoaxes or film imperfections—physical evidence such as marks or holes on the ground as well as marks on the body, and anomalous internal "implants" taken from abductees.

Dr. Mack bundled these aspects into one list of "five basic dimensions" that he said must be addressed to ensure a truthful explanation of abductions:

A high level of consistency between the various abduction accounts as well as the reliability of most abductees.

The absence of detectable psychiatric or psychological illness among abductees.

The physical manifestations—bruises, lesions, scars, and the like—found on abductees in many incidences.

The connection between the abductions and UFO activity, often reported independently by witnesses not associated with the abductees.

Abduction reports from children, some as young as age two or three.

"Clearly, no explanation that addresses all of these elements is apparent at the present time," concluded Mack.

Raymond Fowler, who chronicled the Andreasson story and later claimed to have had an abduction experience of his own, also noted the commonality of abduction reports and concluded, "All of these elements provide strong circumstantial evidence that abductions are grounded in reality. Finally, proposed alternative hypotheses for abductions fall short of explaining them in earthly terms."

In studying the many abduction stories, Hopkins too concluded the experience is real. He noted, "These men and women are neither devoured nor saved. They are borrowed, involuntarily. They are used physically and then returned, frightened but not deliberately harmed. And the aliens are described neither as all-powerful, lordly presences, nor as satanic monsters, but instead as complex, controlling, physically frail beings who apparently need something for their very survival that they are forced to search for among their various abductees."

Author Richard Thompson, who also appeared to accept at least some UFO and abduction reports as genuine, stated, "It is possible that actual non-human beings are responsible for many reported UFO communications. These beings may be trying to condition people's thought processes by making use of themes taken, in some cases, from the people's own cultural traditions." After reviewing several theories that suppose the phenomenon to be simply the product of the human imagination, Thompson pondered, "To me, it seems doubtful that ordinary humans have the power to call into being flying objects that can reflect radar, chase jet planes, and interfere with automobiles. If human imagination has so much power, then why don't typical sci-fi movie monsters materialize in American cities?"

Dr. Mack stated the abduction experience is real but admitted that we do not know precisely who is behind it or for what purposes. "UFO abductions have to do, I think, with the evolution of consciousness and the collapse of a world view that has placed humankind at a kind of epicenter of intelligence in a cosmos perceived as largely lifeless and meaningless," he said. "As we, like the abductees, permit ourselves to surrender the illusion of control and mastery of our world, we might discover our place as one species among many whose special gifts include unusual capacities for caring, rational thought, and self-awareness. As we suspend the notion of our preeminent and dominating intelligence, we might open to a universe filled with life-forms different from ourselves to whom we might be connected in ways we do not yet comprehend."

Outlandish as the abduction phenomenon may appear, at least there have been no substantiated deaths connected with it. This is more than can be said for another aspect of the UFO issue—one that concerns death and mutilation.

C H A P T E R   9

DEATH FROM THE SKY

In 1967, a Colorado couple, Berle and Nellie Lewis, decided to ask Nellie's brother to pasture their horse, a three-year-old Appaloosa mare named Lady. The brother, rancher Harry King, had good pastureland in the San Luis Valley of southern Colorado, and it seemed like the obvious solution for where to keep their horse.

Their decision was to have fatal and far-reaching consequences.

For on September 9, rancher King found the body of Lady lying in chico bush not far from his home. The horse's head and part of her neck had been stripped clean of flesh. The remainder of the body was untouched. The skull was so white and clean, it appeared to have been bleached by exposure to sunlight for many days. But King knew that Lady had been alive less than two days earlier. There was no blood and no tracks around the mare's corpse. The cut on her neck was smooth and precise. Rancher King was stunned. "That neck was cut so smooth it couldn't have been done even with a sharp hunting knife," he said later.

The Lewises, too, were impressed by the precision of the neck cut. "It wasn't hacked off—but it was very neat and that was what was so odd," recalled Nellie Lewis after viewing her dead horse on

September 10. She noted a peculiar medicinal odor at the site, something "like incense."

Two weeks after Lady's death, the body was examined by Dr. John Henry Altshuler, then a pathologist at Rose Medical Center in Denver. Dr. Altshuler found the horse had been cut from the neck down to the base of the chest by a "vertical, clean incision." He also discovered that the edge of the cut was firm and of a darker color, as if the flesh had been cauterized with a laser beam. However, as Dr. Altshuler noted, "There was no surgical laser technology like that in 1967." At least there was no such technology as far as the public knew.

The doctor also discovered that some of Lady's internal organs were missing, notably the heart, lungs, and thyroid. "Most amazing was the lack of blood," Dr. Altshuler recalled years later. "I have done hundreds of autopsies. You can't cut into a body without getting some blood. But there was no blood on the skin or on the ground. No blood anywhere. That impressed me the most."

The strangeness of Lady's death increased when it was learned that several people reported seeing a UFO in the area just before the mutilated horse was found. San Luis Valley resident Duane Martin said he had seen several small "jets" zooming around at very high speeds but at very low altitude in the area of Lady's death. Even Harry King's eighty-seven-year-old mother, Agnes King, claimed a "large object" had passed over the King ranch house the night Lady died. Mrs. King said that due to failing eyesight, she could not be sure what the object was. By the first week in October 1967, news articles about the mutilation had been published in nearby Pueblo, Colorado.

In the news reports, Lady was misidentified as "Snippy," the name of her mother corralled near the King ranch. But, mistakes aside, the connection between the horse mutilation and UFOs was too good a story to pass up. Reports were picked up and disseminated by news services. One headline read, "Dead Horse Riddle Sparks UFO Buffs."

It was also the first widely reported animal mutilation case in the United States, and it set the stage for reports of mutilations that continue even today. Much later, various theories were advanced to explain Lady's death. One veterinarian, Dr. Robert O. Adams, postulated that someone found the horse suffering from a severe infection and cut her throat to end the pain. Another, Dr. Wallace Leary, claimed to have found two bullet holes while reconstructing Lady's hindquarters, and Dr. Richard O. Norton, drafting a report for the Desert Research Institute at the University of Nevada, concluded that since there were thunderstorms in the area at the time of death, Lady may have been struck by lightning. "None of these persons, except Dr. Altshuler, examined the horse at the time of death," noted mutilation expert Linda Moulton Howe. "This is just an attempt to reconstruct history."

Since 1967 animal mutilations, mostly of cattle, have been reported in numbers reaching into the thousands. Mutilation reports reached a crescendo in the mid-1970s. However, with the large information-distribution centers like Washington and New York more concerned with conventional news, mutilation stories were largely confined to medium-sized and rural weekly newspapers. When ever-increasing news reports of mutilated cattle began spreading from upper Montana through the Midwest and into South Texas, rural residents of Middle America began to react with fear and anger.

In many cattle mutilation reports, there were attendant sightings of strange lights and objects in the skies as well as military-style helicopters bearing no insignia or lights seen in the vicinity.

A Typical Mutilation

A typical mutilation account can be found in the following March 10, 1975, "Officer's Report" from the Cochran County, Texas, Sheriff's Department, filed by Sheriff C. G. Richards:

> Darwood Marshall came into my office and said he had found a heifer, about 6 miles south of Whiteface, Texas, on his farm, that had been mutilated. I went to the scene and this is what I found.
>
> About two miles over in a field was a perfectly round circle. The heifer was laying in the middle of this circle with the head to the north and it twisted straight up in the air. The bottom jaw was cut back and the tongue was gone. The sex organs were cut off and gone. The navel was cut out in a round circle and the meat inside was not touched. There was no blood on the ground or on the cow. While I was checking this out, Mr. Marshall came up to me and said if you think this is odd, look at that place about a quarter of a mile west. We went over there and found another circle that was the same as the other one. He told me they had drug a steer out of this circle and it was over in the pasture. We looked at the other steer later. This circle was the same as the other one, but the wheat was about four inches tall and it had been burned clean and these circles were about 30 feet across them. I thought, this is a mystery, so I could not get this out of my mind.
>
> I went back to town and got a Geiger counter and checked the circles and it showed that there was radiation present. I called Reese Air Force Base and they sent a team out. . . . They found half of one percent radiation and they told me not to worry about the

radiation. There was not enough to hurt any one or thing, and they left. What I want to know [is] how did it get there in the first place.

I have had reports of UFOs in this area, but have not seen any myself. The people that have been reporting this all tell the same story. It is about as wide as a two-lane highway, round and looks the color of the sun when it is going down and has got a blue glow around it. I have watched the news and the paper and when these people see this thing, in two or three days later, we hear about some cows that have been mutilated. I don't know what is doing this, but it sure has got everyone around here up tight, so who knows. . . .

Reports such as this multiplied all across the United States. From Texas to Montana, heavily armed posses of irate ranchers and friends went on alert for whoever was surgically slaughtering their cattle. They roamed back-country roads for any sign of suspicious behavior.

The prospect of vigilante justice prompted Carl Whiteside, head of the Colorado Bureau of Investigation (CBI), which was coordinating an assessment of the cattle mutilation situation, to state in 1975, "The important thing now is that we deal in fact, not fiction, so that fear doesn't become the victor. And that's what we've got in Colorado now—fear."

In an effort to calm the public clamor, the CBI issued a report concluding that 95 percent of the mutilations were simply the work of predators. The report was jeered by both law enforcement officers and private researchers who had been investigating the mutilation phenomenon. Even the report itself did not accurately reflect the situation. According to the report, out of 206 reported mutilations between May and December 1975, only 35 carcasses had been sent to the Colorado State University veterinary pathology lab. Only nineteen were autopsied due to advanced decomposition. Of the nineteen actually autopsied, fully eleven were confirmed as being cut with sharp instruments. Ignoring the fact that many others may have shown evidence of cuts if they had been studied, Whiteside dismissed the significance of the report's numbers by saying, "That's little more than five percent of all the reported mutilations that were cut by humans."

Ranchers and cattlemen also put little stock in the CBI report. Manuel Gomez, who had raised cattle for more than twenty years near Dulce, New Mexico, set the tone when he said, "I've been ranching my entire life. I know what predators do and this is nothing like it." His tone was echoed by Sheriff Ray Lee of Cheyenne County, Kansas, who commented on the lack of blood at mutilation scenes, "You couldn't cut up an animal like that without it getting nasty."

Sheriff George Yarnell of Elbert County, Colorado, became particularly upset when mutilation hide samples continued to come back to him with the conclusion that predators were the cause. Yarnell knew better. To test his suspicions, Yarnell cut a piece of flesh from a cow with his hunting knife and notched it for identification. The sample was then sent to CBI chief Carl Whiteside, who routinely sent it to Colorado State University's Department of Veterinary Medicine laboratory—where all other CBI mutilation evidence was examined. Sure enough, the specimen came back to Yarnell with the conclusion that the cut was the work of predators. When confronted with the truth, a lab pathologist lamely explained. "We're human. We make mistakes." What was not explained was why the "predator" explanation was offered in every single mutilation case.

The idea that coyotes, vultures, and other animals were responsible for cattle mutilations was firmly put to rest by reporter Dorothy Aldridge of the *Colorado Springs Gazette Telegraph*. In an article, Aldridge noted that a November 1975 blizzard left thousands of cattle dead in the Midwest. Wolves and coyotes immediately moved in for a feast. Yet when reporter Aldridge checked with a rendering plant at Tribune, Kansas, which processed some thirty thousand of the dead cattle, she was told that predators had not touched the cows' eyeballs, ears, or sexual organs, the parts usually taken by the shadowy midnight mutilators.

Veteran ranchers and lawmen never did buy into the predator-did-it theory. Officer Gabe Valdez with the New Mexico State Police summed up their feelings in 1979 when he told this author, "If it is predators, than we have predators with super powers. It is hard to believe that predators can pull a steer's heart out through a small hole in its neck. And I have seen that."

As reports of mutilations grew in mid-1974, rural sections of the nation went to full alert. After a Nebraska pilot checking power lines near Grand Island was shot at by a fearful rancher, the Army National Guard ordered its helicopters to fly at one thousand feet or higher rather than the usual five hundred feet and to report any unauthorized helicopters. Patrols by both armed citizens and local lawmen became a near nightly occurrence.

Reports of strange nocturnal activities grew. The Associated Press reported in 1976 that several persons, including two police officers, saw a huge flying creature in the lower Rio Grande Valley of Texas. Officer Arturo Padilla of San Benito said the creature had a wingspan of more than twelve feet, a batlike face with eyes the size of silver dollars, and a beak three or four feet long. "I've done a lot of bird hunting, but this thing was much bigger," said Padilla. "It scared me for a while but now many people are saying it is a condor from South America. . . . If I get a safe shot at it, I'm going to shoot." Padilla added he thought the big bird might be responsible for recent cattle mutilations in the area.

Another down-to-earth explanation for the animal deaths was that bloodthirsty cults were on a nocturnal prowl.

The Devil Made Me Do It

Dr. Richard Thill, a professor of German at the University of Nebraska at Omaha who also taught noncredit courses on witchcraft, termed the mutilations "ritualistic." "It could be someone setting up a fertility cult of some kind, or it could be someone putting you on. If they are putting you on, they are pretty sick," Thill told a news reporter in 1974.

Persons with a keen interest in Satanism were quick to jump on the bandwagon. A. Kenneth Bankston, who at the time was serving a sentence for bank robbery at the Leavenworth Federal Penitentiary in Kansas, wrote to Kansas state senator Ross Doyen, stating the mutilations were the work of a secret order of devil worshipers called the Sons of Satan. In an exchange of letters with Doyen and UFO researchers, Bankston elaborated, saying that this Satanic cult used hypodermic needles to draw out the animal's blood and that sex organs were used in fertility rites. Bankston continually asked to be transferred from Leavenworth to some small county jail because he feared reprisals due to his snitching. Bankston also implicated another man, Dan Dugan, who was serving time in a Texas prison for crimes related to auto theft, and said that if authorities would transfer both men to a safe place, they would be ready to talk.

After both Bankston and Dugan separately expanded their account of animal mutilations to include plots by Satanists to seize a nuclear missile, steal plutonium, set off terrorist bombs, and assassinate newsmen and members of Congress, including then Minnesota senator Hubert Humphrey, authorities decided to take the tales seriously. Donald E. Flickinger, a special agent with the Bureau of Alcohol, Tobacco and Firearms, was brought in to investigate, and Minnesota federal judge Myles Lord issued an order to bring both Bankston and Dugan to Minnesota for questioning.

In the spring of 1975, the two prisoners told an elaborate story of a widespread "cult of Satan" that included Hell's Angels–like bikers as well as millionaire stockbrokers. This unlikely group, operating in at least twenty-two states, were behind the cattle mutilations, they claimed. Bankston said a potent animal tranquilizer, PCP, was used to sedate the cattle. Then, after amyl nitrite was held to the animal's nose to induce a rapid heartbeat, its blood was withdrawn using a large syringe. Footprints were concealed by wrapping their feet in cardboard, and blowtorches were used to melt snow, obliterating tracks. Round holes were punched in the earth to simulate landing gear in an effort to misdirect investigators. Both Bankston and Dugan claimed the Satanists wanted the mutilations to appear like the result of an extraterrestrial visitation.

The men's allegations stirred up a spate of news stories. The public was alternately calmed by the prospect of a human explanation for the mutilations and horrified at the prospect of rampaging cultists.

But then this fascinating explanation began to fall apart.

Both Bankston and Dugan, in separate incidents, escaped jail. Both were quickly recaptured, but authorities suspected that the men had concocted their stories as part of an elaborate escape plan after reading news accounts of mutilations. Furthermore, an enterprising Texas reporter obtained the criminal record of the man Bankston and Dugan identified as the cult's leader. The man's record showed he had been in jail most of the time Bankston and Dugan claimed he was leading the nightly surgery sessions. Other leaders of the cult the two convicts fingered passed lie detector tests as to their activities at the times in question.

The sheer enormity of the Satan-did-it theory worked against it. For example, in the two years between 1975 and 1977, more than fifteen hundred cattle were killed and mutilated in twenty-two states. This would mean that the cultists had to locate, anesthetize, kill, and butcher more than two cows each day. Counting travel time to each occurrence, the cultists would have had to spend every waking hour slaughtering cattle.

"We ran extensive undercover investigations on cults around that time," recalled Colorado CBI chief Whiteside. "We could prove that these groups existed, but we could never prove that they were involved in any criminal activities, including cattle mutilations. This doesn't mean they weren't responsible for a few of those animals. It just means we were never able to gather any evidence on it.

"It wouldn't have mattered anyway. . . . [Some] people simply will not accept an earthly, normal solution to this thing. They want it to be flying saucers or a government conspiracy. They won't accept anything else. . . ."

No cultist ever broke ranks and talked about this incredible achievement, and various police agencies could find no hard evidence substantiating this possibility. It was all too much to swallow, and the Satanist theory was quickly dropped by the news media.

But by the late 1970s reports of cattle mutilations continued to increase, and western ranchers and lawmen were not accepting glib explanations of predators and Satanist cults. The issue finally reached Senator Harrison Schmitt of New Mexico, the last American astronaut to walk on the moon. Schmitt decided to do something about the mutilation issue.

The Last Roundup

Schmitt scheduled what was to be the first—and last—conference on cattle mutilations in Albuquerque, New Mexico, the last week in April 1979. Opening the conference, Schmitt stated:

> There are few activities more dangerous than an unsolved pattern of crime. There is always the potential for such crimes to escalate in frequency and severity if allowed to go unsolved and unpunished.
>
> Such a dangerous pattern of crime is the mutilation killings of thousands of cattle, horses and other animals over the past several years. These crimes are obviously continuing in spite of the excellent efforts of state and local law enforcement officials and the growing publicity the mutilation incidents have received.
>
> For at least five years, and probably longer, in at least 15 states, animals have been killed and systematically mutilated for no apparent reason by persons unknown.
>
> One of the most extraordinary facts of this problem is that the group or groups responsible for the mutilation killings have shown almost unprecedented discipline. There have been no leaks or informants to assist the state and local law enforcement officials in their investigation efforts.
>
> When I entered politics in 1975, one of the first issues my constituents confronted me with was their loss of cattle and other animals by theft and then mutilation. This has continued to the present. Now the economic losses suffered by individuals probably have reached $2.5 million or more nationally.
>
> In response to these inquiries and my own curiosity, I began to put together a file on the history and nature of mutilation killings in New Mexico.

After learning that some of the mutilations occurred on Indian reservations, which are federal property, and that the illegal use of unmarked helicopters may have been involved, Schmitt was able to have the Justice Department authorize FBI involvement in the mutilation case. This was a step forward, since back in 1975, Senator Floyd K. Haskell of Colorado had asked the bureau to investigate mutilations, but bureau officials declined. Then FBI director Clarence Kelley said that evidence of interstate activities was not strong enough to warrant federal involvement.

Schmitt, in welcoming guests, described the 1979 animal mutilation conference's purpose as one "to further define the scope of the problem, the full basis for federal assistance to state and local authorities and to examine the possible FBI activities which will be of value in solving these crimes."

"Finally, someone is going to do something about this," said one jubilant sheriff's deputy. Cattlemen, ranchers, and lawmen from several states had flocked to Albuquerque, eager to learn what might be responsible for the mysterious mutilation deaths.

They were sorely disappointed.

From the start the one-day conference seemed to pit ranchers, law officers, and private researchers against a host of state and federal officials who were obviously taking a "let's-not-get-excited" attitude. In fact, almost every government official, especially from the federal quarter, showed near hostility toward the whole issue.

Even the experts were divided. Dr. James Prine, a veterinarian pathologist from Los Alamos, New Mexico, said he had examined six cattle carcasses and concluded the "cut wounds" were probably caused by animals. He cited one incidence of a family dog making lesions on a dead horse similar to those in mutilation cases. However, Dr. Clair Hibbs of the New Mexico State Veterinary Diagnostic Laboratory said that while his investigation of Kansas mutilations showed that some apparently were the work of coyotes, several others indicated the use of surgical instruments.

Dozens of law enforcement officers attending the conference planned to share their mutilation evidence but were warned against this at the start of the meeting by New Mexico U.S. attorney R. E. Thompson, who asked the officers "not to bring out any evidentiary material which might be used at a later trial." That meant no statements, no photos, no toxicology reports, no nothing. Although a conciliatory Schmitt later urged the officers "not to shy away from the evidence too much," many of the attending law enforcement personnel privately said they felt "muzzled."

Cpt. Keith Wolverton of the Cascade County Sheriff's Department in Great Falls, Montana, was one of the lawmen expected to present sensational evidence he had gathered during his mutilation investigations. But when requested to present his material, Wolverton merely announced, "I have nothing to offer at this time." Later, when asked if the decision not to present his material was entirely his own, Wolverton replied, "No."

So, with law enforcement officials effectively silenced, the conference quickly degenerated into spiteful arguments between irate ranchers and mutilation researchers versus government experts and spokesmen who offered various explanations, most of which centered on the discredited idea that predators were mostly behind the mutilations.

Apparently even Senator Schmitt began to have second thoughts on his crusade to learn the truth about mutilations. At the end of the mutilation conference, Schmitt urged that a multidisciplinary scientific task force be created to study the phenomenon, then added, "That's all I have to say."

No such task force was ever forthcoming. However, four days after the ill-fated conference, the Law Enforcement Assistance Administration (LEAA) announced the awarding of a $50,000 grant to investigate cattle mutilations. Former FBI agent Ken Rommel, who had displayed skepticism at the Schmitt conference, was placed in charge.

After a year studying only fifteen of the twenty-nine mutilations reported to him, Rommel issued a 297-page report entitled "Operation Animal Mutilation" in May 1980. Since prior to the release of his official report Rommel had stated he was convinced there was nothing unnatural going on, it was no surprise when his report concluded, "There is simply no concrete evidence to support the theory that mutilations are being conducted as experiments by highly skilled individuals using precision instruments. The facts cited to support this belief are at best questionable, and in many cases involve incredible flights of fantasy." It appeared that mind-sets were again clashing.

But if nothing else, the New Mexico conference was an excellent opportunity for persons from several different states interested in mutilations to compare notes.

Mutilation Traits

Researchers and lawmen discovered that there were certain factors common to classic mutilation cases. Among these were:

The absence of blood. Mutilated cattle were systematically drained of blood, often through small holes punched in their jugular vein. Much evidence indicated that the cattle were still alive, if unconscious, when the blood was taken.

Cuts on mutilated animals displayed sophisticated anatomical knowledge as well as the use of surgical instruments. In some cases, cuts were found to include heat searing to seal surrounding tissue and blood vessels preventing blood loss. In cases where jaws and other bones have been cut through there is no bone debris or dust, indicating some sort of high-pressure vacuum system may have been used.

In most cases, internal organs—especially the sex organs—were removed from the animals.

In some mutilations, evidence of residual radiation or tranquilizing chemicals were found.

Increased numbers of UFO sightings were common in the areas where the mutilations occurred. Physical evidence was cited in a number of cases, such as circular depressions in the ground and flattened circles in crops or grass. One physical oddity involved a small blue plastic valise or satchel found on the property of a Colorado rancher in the late summer of 1975. According to a CBI report, the valise "contained a scalpel, part of a cow's tongue, an ear, and several plastic—arm's length—artificial insemination gloves." This discovery prompted lawmen to speculate that someone might be producing copycat mutilations. Since the contents of the valise could not be connected to any local mutilation, CBI Chief Whiteside said the issue was passed to another jurisdiction with no investigation.

Along with the UFO accounts were numerous reports of blacked-out helicopters with neither insignia nor identification numbers seen in the vicinity of cattle mutilations. There were also reports of large white vanlike trucks with government license plates seen in the same areas. Some researchers theorized that the vans were used to transport the black helicopters from one state to another.

Some mutilated animals were found with broken legs and backs, even horns pushed into the ground, as if they had been dropped to the ground from a significant height.

With no immediate official explanation for the phenomenon forthcoming, coverage of the mutilation issue in the mainstream media dwindled away, leaving only the smaller papers and rural weeklies to report on nearby mutilations.

Though it was clear that the mutilations were continuing, only a handful of dedicated private researchers continued to compile ongoing developments. On August 20, 1994, the Associated Press noted, "Reports of mutilated cattle, suggestive of cases around the nation 20 years ago, are on the rise again in New Mexico. In the past 16 months, nine ranchers reported 27 cattle mutilated, the largest number near Eagle Nest. . . ."

A classic case was reported in May 1995, in Carroll County, Tennessee, when Jerry Chandler of the J. B. Simmons farm near McKenzie discovered a mutilated newborn calf as he was searching for a missing bull. According to news accounts, "The calf was missing its reproductive and alimentary organs, lower lip, tongue and left eye. In addition, a semicircle section of the left ear approximately an inch and a half wide had been removed. . . . The area around the missing half-moon section of ear tissue appeared to be very smooth and with a fine brown beading covering it, as though it might have been subjected to heat. . . . Also unusual was the condition of the animal's hoofs. The bottom of all four hoofs had apparently been subjected to some kind of grinding process, leaving deep serrated marks. Hoof material had been removed from the left front appendage to a depth that almost eroded into the bed beneath. There was no blood visible around any of the spots where specimens had been removed from the animal—not even a large and near perfectly round hole about five inches in diameter in the animal's hindquarters where the vagina and anus, and connected interior organs, had been removed. . . . One strange thing was the lack of stiffness in the animal. Although the animal was found dead several hours before, it was still totally free of rigor mortis and extremely limber. The small pool of blood inside the body cavity also appeared very fluid and showed no signs of clotting." Sgt. Randall Dunn of the county sheriff's department initially speculated the calf was killed by "Devil worshippers" but after studying the animal at the scene, commented, "I've read about it, but I've never seen anything like it. . . . I don't see how it was done without any blood anywhere." A local newspaper said several persons, including two attorneys, reported black, unmarked helicopters in the vicinity prior to the mutilation.

According to law enforcement officials, more than sixty cattle mutilations were reported during 1995 in southeast Oklahoma alone. Undersheriff Kenny McKee of the McCurtain County Sheriff's Department reported, "Right off the top of my head, we had two cattle mutilations in the last half of 1995 and I believe we've already had one in 1996."

One of those who continued to investigate the mutilation phenomenon was Linda Moulton Howe, who in 1979 was director of special projects for the CBS television affiliate station in Denver. Holding a master's degree in communications from Stanford University, Howe had already received several local, national, and international awards for her newswork, gaining a reputation for producing timely and incisive documentaries.

"On September 1, 1979, I began researching bizarre animal deaths," she recalled. "Much of my television work . . . involved stories about environmental issues. I thought perhaps I was dealing with a contamination story—maybe the government had accidentally released some kind of poison into the land and was randomly spot-checking tissue from grazing animals to monitor the contamination's spread." But after pouring through newspaper files, Howe learned that animal mutilations had been reported worldwide, with some reports dating back to the 1700s.

Yellowed news clippings and books showed the mutilation phenomenon was nothing new. There were accounts of sheep mutilations in Great Britain and Australia in the 1800s, some in connection with UFO sightings. One of the earliest accounts linking an animal mutilation to UFOs came from the April 23, 1897, edition of the *Farmer's Advocate* of Yates Center, Kansas.

In a sworn statement, Yates Center farmer Alexander Hamilton said he was awakened at about 10:30 P.M. on April 19 by the bawling of his cattle. Leaving his home to investigate, Hamilton saw "an airship slowly descending upon my cow lot about 40 rods from the house."

He described the craft as cigar-shaped, approximately three hundred feet long with a transparent, brilliantly lit undercarriage. Inside the ship were "six of the strangest beings he ever saw" who turned a beam of light on him. Hamilton said the ship began to make a buzzing sound and rose to a height of about three hundred feet from where a two-year-old heifer was drawn aboard by means of a thick cable. The craft then flew off, leaving Hamilton staring in amazement.

The next day Hamilton was having trouble believing what had happened until he learned from a neighboring farmer that the hide, head, and legs of his stolen heifer had been found.

Hamilton, a former member of the U.S. House of Representatives and a respected member of his community, stated, "I don't know whether they are devils or angels, or what, but we all saw them, and my whole family saw the ship, and I don't want any more to do with them." Local people who signed an affidavit attesting that Hamilton's story was "true and correct" included the local sheriff, deputy sheriff, justice of the peace, postmaster, registrar of deeds, a banker, an attorney, and the druggist. However, author Jerome Clark said that in the mid-1970s an elderly woman claimed Hamilton was a member of a local Liar's Club and had concocted the story as a prank.

Be that as it may, Hamilton's account matches those of other reports of the period concerning livestock found slaughtered with medical precision. Some reports, dating back into the 1800s, came from Canada, Mexico, Central and South America, Australia, Europe, and even the Canary Islands off the west coast of Africa.

Howe About Those Mutes?

Intrigued by her research into the mutilation mystery, Howe produced an Emmy Award–winning 1980 documentary entitled *A Strange Harvest*, which linked cattle mutilations to UFOs. In 1989, Howe published her ongoing research in a book entitled *An Alien Harvest: Further Evidence Linking Animal Mutilations and Human Abductions to Alien Life Forms*.

Her careful and well-documented investigation eventually moved Howe to conclude that two separate forces appear involved in mutilations within the United States: unidentified flying objects of unknown origin and unmarked helicopters, apparently of government origin.

She was intrigued by official government reports indicating intelligent guidance of UFOs.

One such report from the Air Force Aerospace Defense Command headquarters included a section of the North American Air Defense (NORAD) Command director's log dated November 8, 1975. The report stated that two F-106 fighters were scrambled from Malstrom Air Force Base in Montana to chase as many as seven UFOs traveling at twelve thousand feet. The document further stated that "[Air force observers] reported that when the F-106s were in the area, targets would turn out lights, and when the F-106s left, targets would turn lights on. F-106s never gained visual or radar contact at any time due to terrain clearance. This same type of activity has been reported in the Malstrom area for several days. . . ." Howe and other researchers saw this report as firm evidence that these UFOs were under intelligent control.

Howe continued to follow the cattle mutilation story into the 1990s, and reports became even stranger, such as the case of Bill and Linda Dzuris. The couple had worked around cattle their entire lives. On September 9, 1982, the couple found a six-year-old pregnant cow mutilated in a field less than a half mile from their home. In the official sheriff's report it stated that there was a hole about two feet in diameter where the rectum had been, most of the udder was missing, and it appeared "these areas were cut by some type of instrument rather than being torn away by some type of animal."

It was a typical cattle mutilation except for one thing—this cow was killed and mutilated in broad daylight.

The Dzurises reported they had checked on the cow at noon. "Everything was okay. So we went back to the house and had lunch," Linda Dzuris later recalled. "We worked outside on the truck all afternoon. It was a pretty day and we hadn't seen or heard anything." At 5:00 P.M. when Bill Dzuris drove off for a load of hay, he say the cow lying in the field dead.

An even stranger account came from a rancher near Waco, Texas, who asked not to be identified. He told of stumbling upon two four-foot-high "creatures" while out searching for a missing cow. In an interview with Howe, the rancher related how he saw the pair carrying a calf between them. He described the calfnappers as looking like small adults, neither fat nor skinny but slightly muscular. Their heads were shaped like eggs with the smaller end down. There was no hair or nose. Their eyes were angled upward and came to a point. "They were sloe-eyed," he said, "like big, dark almonds. I was afraid of them seeing me. I've read all about them abductions and I didn't want them taking me away in some flying saucer! I took off down the hill pretty fast to my truck."

The rancher said that two days after his encounter, he returned to the scene with his wife and son. They found the calf's hide turned inside out lying on the ground. Nearby was a calf's backbone, but with no ribs to be found. There was no signs of blood or predators.

With stories like this, it was obvious that the need to calm the public was as strong as ever. Four years after Rommel's report that nothing was really happening, public concern over the mutilations was further mollified with the 1984 publication of *Mute Evidence*, written by Daniel Kagan and Ian Summers. Kagan, a New York City resident who had been a rock singer, a correctional officer, and manager of a traveling theater as well as a magazine and book editor, and Summers, a book illustrator and science fiction writer, claimed to have solved the mutilation problem that had vexed professional animal experts and law enforcement officials for years. Leaning largely to the belief that cults were behind a paltry few cattle mutilations and the remaining reports the result of hysteria, Kagan and Summers proclaimed, "The mutes are for the most part nonexistent." Their bias was obvious from the start when, in reporting the words of Senator Schmitt, they wrote, "This was a senator talking, not some flying-saucer nut." They also seemed to uncritically accept the word of "official" spokesmen, as though the concept that government officials might—out of perceived necessity—hide the truth had never occurred to them.

They did find plenty of space to attack the private researchers. Although grudgingly admitting that Linda Howe's film *Strange Har-*

vest "came across like a documentary—with narration, on-camera interviews with lawmen, ranchers and scientists, captioned frames indicating the dates and places where these people had been interviewed, and practical demonstrations," they insisted it was "entirely a product of Linda Howe's singular vision of the cattle mutilation phenomenon." Later they stated, "Her real goal was showing quite blatantly. It did not matter whether her 'investigating' produced reliable information. What mattered was how Linda Howe would benefit from cattle mutilations and UFOs." Apparently they never intended to profit from their own book.

"There is nothing in my professional life to suggest that my investigations were motivated by profit," responded Howe in a recent interview. "In my time as a staff employee for KMEH-TV, the CBS affiliate in Denver, Colorado, I was paid a weekly salary as director of special projects which included many documentaries other than cattle mutilations. Kagan and Summers only proved what an obnoxious and incompetent research team they are. From what I could tell, they never intended to do a meaningful report in their book. Early on they came to the TV station, screened my documentary with me. Then Daniel Kagan proceeded to lecture me that there was nothing to the animal mutilations except predators and that they would prove that in their book. So you can see there was nothing about their so-called investigation that was objective."

Kagan and Summers trivialized the numerous mutilation accounts as hearsay, yet accepted police accounts of widespread cult activity despite the fact that these reports were largely hearsay themselves and stories from paid informants, who are disposed to tell the authorities whatever they want to hear. They were forced to note that there were never any arrests or convictions of cultists in connection with the cattle mutilations, a decidedly odd circumstance if the grisly killings had indeed been perpetrated by large-scale cult activity over many states.

Another researcher targeted by Kagan and Summers was Tom Adams, who in 1978 began publication of a newsletter entitled *Stigmata* to disseminate information about the mutilations. Adams, still active in UFO research circles, made it a point to maintain an objective attitude in his public statements. Kagan and Summers were disappointed when they were unable to force Adams into making a statement they could use against him in their book. "He avoided the dilemma by simply refusing to answer the question. He tried to turn it around on us. 'Well, that depends on how you define objectivity. How do you define it?' he asked. We were at an impasse. Tom Adams would never throw off his mask," they wrote, apparently unable to accept that Adams's attempt to be objective was sincere. Today, Adams said he still does not voice an opinion because "I have no opinion. I am still trying to remain objective and let the evidence lead to its own conclusion." He added, "But I defy any rational, objective person to look at the evidence, the whole evidence, and say that there's nothing to it."

The perspective of sophisticates Kagan and Summers once again reflected mind-set. They chose to believe official hearsay rather than eyewitness hearsay and they dismissed the very idea that officialdom might cover up mutilation evidence. So, unable to prove the nonexistence of the mutilations—after all, there were plenty of dead cows—Kagan and Summers fell back to offering some questionable psychological opinions on the phenomenon. While they admitted that the "little tribe of mutologists" did not start the whole thing, they concluded that such researchers, with profit as a motive, did provide a susceptible news media with horror stories that, in turn, caused well-meaning people to simply see a mutilation where none existed.

"Once people had made the assumption that there were cattle mutilations and that there was something bizarre about them, their perceptions followed their beliefs. They began to see 'evidence' where there was none, because they had assumed evidence would be there. They began to read meaning into meaningless events," they wrote. To Kagan and Summers, the cattle mutilations were simply an outgrowth of the times—the disillusionment of the Vietnam War, shaken confidence in government thanks to Watergate and the CIA scandals. It was all in our heads. Debunker Curtis Peebles echoed this refrain when he wrote, "The image one gets [of the cattle mutilations] in retrospect was of the development of a parallel myth—connected to the flying saucer myth, but still apart, existing outside it."

This was the same psychobabble and unproven theory used to deny the existence of UFOs in the first place. But unlike the sparseness of physical evidence in the case of the UFOs, there still remained the problem of explaining all the mutilated cows and attendant strange stories such as those of two Colorado ranchers.

On December 23, 1985, Denver's *Rocky Mountain News* carried a mutilation story that seemed to have involved a UFO. Myron Scott, a young rancher near Trinidad, Colorado, saw lights hovering above a nearby pasture. The next day Scott found a dead steer at the site.

According to the news clipping, "Scott said he is used to death. He loses a few head to lightning and disease each year. But he said he had never seen anything like this. The six hundred pound steer's hide was pulled up over its body 'like you'd roll a cigarette paper'; its tongue was cut out and its horns and spine were broken as if it had fallen from a considerable height. Yet there was not trace of blood, no footprints. Coyote tracks stopped about 30 feet from the body." Scott's experience, multiplied by hundreds more, clearly showed that a genuine phenomenon was taking place, not just overheated imaginations due to media reports.

A former U.S. marshal turned cattle rancher may have gotten a look at one of the mysterious craft. Late one afternoon in August 1993, Leslie D. Weisenhorn was irrigating fields on his ranch near Holly, Colorado, when he saw a large silver "dome" squatting on the ground in a pasture. Based on the distance between fence posts, Weisenhorn estimated the object as fifty feet wide and about twelve feet high. "It was almost glowing," he recalled, "and at first I thought it was a great big old stock trailer. I figured someone was stealing cattle. So I ran back to the house to get my guns. I was going to shoot them and then call the sheriff to come pick up the bodies."

Weisenhorn raced back to his house, donned a bulletproof vest, and grabbed two guns. Returning to the field, he found the object was gone. He was puzzled that he could find no tracks—neither tires not footprints—in the muddy field. However, in checking the field early the next morning, he discovered one of his calves dead from precise but bloodless incisions. "It was strange," said Weisenhorn. "You could tell this 350- to 400-pound calf had been spun in almost a perfect circle by the marks in the mud, yet there was no footprints or tire marks anywhere. None of the other cows would come to that section of the field and even the calf's own mother wouldn't come close." Weisenhorn, who retired as a supervisor of marshals after seventeen years of federal service, said the government knows much more than it admits about these things. "They don't want the people to know that on the evolutionary scale, we're not much more evolved than the ordinary pissant," he commented.

In August 1995, Weisenhorn found another mutilated steer in the same location. "This is the same kind of substantial link between mutilations and UFOs that has been going on for forty years," commented Howe.

Howe said the one case that most persuaded her that extraterrestrials were behind the mutilations involved a woman named Judy Doraty, who may have been one of the only persons to actually witness an animal mutilation in progress.

The woman suffered from headaches and anxiety for several years until in 1978 she underwent hypnosis, which revealed memories of an abduction.

An Abduction Remembered

On March 13, 1980, at the urging of Linda Howe, Judy Doraty underwent hypnosis by Dr. Leo Sprinkle, then director of the Division of Counseling and Testing at the University of Wyoming in Laramie. It was then that her entire ordeal came out.

It was a late evening in May 1973 as Doraty, her teenage daughter, her mother, her sister-in-law, and her brother-in-law drove home from playing bingo in Houston, Texas.

"What's that light?" asked her mother, pointing out of the car window. "I think it's a helicopter," said the brother-in-law. "See that big spotlight. They must be looking for something."

"But it's not moving," commented Doraty.

After several miles the light was still hanging in the night sky.

"It's a helicopter, I tell you. It's probably heading for Galveston Airport. It's heading away from us and that's why it doesn't appear to move," offered the brother-in-law. The light didn't change in size. The whole episode was beginning to puzzle Doraty, so she pulled the car to the side of the road and listened for the sound of helicopter rotors. There was no sound on the night air. She stepped out of the car and could see that there was something of substance behind the bright light. Walking to the rear of the car, she saw a pale yellow light extending to the ground from the hovering craft. It was a light that appeared to have substance to it, like dust particles in a swirling motion.

Looking up, she saw a calf in the light, looking quite small as it was drawn up toward the light. She immediately had a feeling that she should not have been seeing this. "I'm not suppose to talk about this," she thought. "It is an accident that I am seeing this."

Suddenly Doraty felt as though she was in two separate places at once. Part of her was still standing by the side of the road while another part was inside the hovering craft.

The part in the craft was aware of two little humanoids standing beside her. They had long clawlike hands and large heads. They were only about three feet tall. They wore gray body suits, and the skin of their hands and heads appeared white and somewhat translucent. Their eyes were large with no eyelids. They were piercing and frightening.

The "men" were talking to her in English, the voices high-pitched, as though someone were holding his nose while he talked. She could not see them talking with a mouth, but she heard them distinctly nevertheless. She came to feel their communication was mental.

"You're not suppose to be here," was the message. She somehow knew she was in a laboratory where the pair conducted tests. But the time was not right to explain what the tests were about. The pair indicated they were stationed here on earth and were only doing a job. They indicated their work was necessary and for the betterment of mankind—that mankind could destroy itself through pollution. Though she listened attentively, the men said she probably wouldn't understand their explanation.

The problem apparently involves man-made toxins working their way through the food chain. It has something to do with chemicals and chemical changes. It has to do somehow with nuclear testing or wastes, which are causing a change in certain chemical compositions. Much more is involved than simple pollution.

She understood that the problem has already passed a certain state. It has moved from water to vegetation onto animals. She was told the situation can still be reversed but there will still be loss of life because it has gotten to the point where there is so much poison in the water that people are going to die from it. The extent of contamination was being determined by studying the reproduction system of animals.

Doraty decided she was being treated like a child by the pair. If they felt a need to respond to her questions, they would. Otherwise they ignored her or made her feel stupid for asking questions.

She asked the pair about God and they responded, "He's the same to us as He is to you."

All the while the pair continued to work on the calf that had been lifted into the craft. It was in a tiny round room. Moving quickly, the two excised parts from the calf. For some reason the calf's heart was not removed and it did not die immediately. Probes were inserting in various parts of the calf. There were examinations of the teeth, tongue, eyes, ears, and reproductive organs. They were particularly interested in the reproductive organs because they said that with each generation, the poison becomes more pronounced.

Doraty understood that these tests were not confined to cattle, but done on almost every animal imaginable. She watched as the calf was dropped to the ground near where it had been taken. It was dead, and she was sickened by what she had witnessed. She heard the two beings laughing and saying that she would not remember any of what happened anyway. "It's like they are busy doing whatever they are doing and just don't want to bother to take the time to make me go away," she thought to herself.

Then came the most horrible experience of all.

Doraty saw her daughter Cindy stretched out on a table in the craft. She was afraid they would do to her what they had done to the calf. The men examined Cindy, taking tissue scrapings from the inside of her mouth.

But presently Doraty and her daughter were back in their car. No one in the car remembered the encounter with the craft. But the strange light in the sky followed them home and was seen by relatives and neighbors. Several children chased the light into a nearby pasture, where it suddenly shot straight up and disappeared into the night sky.

This and many other similar reports created a sense of awe in Howe, the veteran documentary maker. The mutilations obviously represented a phenomenon that persists right up to today. "There has never been a year since 1967 when mutilations have not been reported, so it's not as if they got what they needed and went away," she said. "It's an ongoing situation."

Over her years of research, Howe has met and talked with many people in the government and military. She is convinced that there is some connection between the government and the cattle mutilations. Her best guess is that the government—in the form of black helicopters with no insignia and unmarked trucks with official license plates—is tracking the mutilations, which are being committed by someone—or something—else.

She cited one documented case in the 1970s when a sheriff and his deputies joined some fearful ranchers to stake out a pasture where mutilations had occurred repeatedly. Nothing was seen or heard, and when dawn came, the sheriff returned to his office to drop off some things before heading home for some sleep. No sooner had he arrived at his office than his phone rang. It was the rancher he had spent the night with informing him that a mutilated cow had been found right in the middle of the pasture they had watched all night. This was not the only such report.

"Whatever the phenomenon is, it is able to cloak itself," commented Howe. This assessment is supported by retired Sandia Laboratories physicist Dr. Henry Monteith. After studying mutilations at length, Dr. Monteith concluded nonhumans who were able to make themselves invisible were conducting an "environmental testing program." He found that Southwest Indians were particularly terrified of the phenomenon, burying carcasses as soon as they were found. Nevertheless, the Indians advised him not to probe the issue, saying, "The 'star people' know what they're doing and should be trusted."

"Overall," Howe wrote, "the strange characteristics of these mutilations suggest that human technology is not involved, and natural causes definitely can't account for it, so that begs the question, How does it occur? Alien activity has to be considered. . . . I am convinced that one or more alien intelligences are affecting this planet. I would like to know what they are, what they want and why the government is so silent. Deception marks the behavior of both."

Howe is convinced of the government's knowledge of the reality of UFOs because of something that happened to her in the early 1980s.

"On April 9, 1983, I was taken onto Kirtland Air Force Base in Albuquerque, into an office where an Air Force Office of Special Investigations agent pulled out an envelope and said his superiors had asked him to show these pages to me. They contained a summary of this government's retrieval of several crashed disks and alien bodies, including a live alien from a second crash near Roswell in 1949. The paper said this extraterrestrial had been taken to Los Alamos National Laboratory, where it had been kept until it died of unknown causes on June 18, 1952. Then the paper summarized some of the information that had been learned from this distinctly alien life form about our planet and its civilization's involvement with this planet. One of the paragraphs said, 'All questions and mysteries about the evolution of *Homo sapiens* on this planet have been answered and this project is closed.'

"I remember reading those words, and reading them a second time, and reading them a third time as the implications of such a startling sentence washed over me. Because the paper was implying that this gray alien life form had been able to answer all of the government's questions about the evolution of *Homo sapiens*. Further, it stated that these gray extraterrestrials had been personally involved in the genetic manipulations of already evolving primates on this planet, suggesting that Cro-Magnon was the result of genetic manipulation by the gray extraterrestrials. Well, if any or all of that is true, then what we are coming up to, after decades of animal mutilations and human abductions and UFO flaps and all of the drama associated with the phenomenon over the last four or five decades, might be some kind of an introduction between them and us."

But Howe, as everyone who has researched the cattle mutilation phenomenon, was still puzzled. Why were the mutilations mostly performed on cows?

The answer to the latter question may have come from a United Press International story that was carried on the news wires in February 1984: "A scientist has discovered than humans share many of their innermost genetic secrets, represented by 'perfect match' chromosomes, with another mammal—cows," UPI reported.

"The discovery was unexpected and just developed in recent months," said James Womack, an animal geneticist at Texas A&M University. "What we are finding are big chunks of cattle chromosomes identical to large regions of human chromosomes. These are big blocks of homologous material, perfect matches. The genes fall in the same sequence. We must have more in common [with other mammals] than previously believed."

Researchers have speculated that perhaps UFO occupants are studying cows to determine how man-produced radiation, both atomic and electromagnetic, and environmental pollution are affecting humans. After all, they say we are what we eat. And obviously no one has gotten as upset over some mutilated cows as they might over a similar number of mutilated humans. Howe speculated that "ET's are harvesting deoxyribonucleic acid (the building blocks of life known as DNA) to create biological clones, robots or something unimaginable."

In recent years, many researchers have come to the firm belief that the mutilation phenomenon is clearly connected somehow to the issue of human abductions. "Most accounts by persons who believe themselves to be abductees involve emphasis on human sexuality, procreation and medical experimentation. And, of course, the connecting point is UFOs," said Howe. "I think the most important and definite parallel between the animal mutilations and the human abductions is this. In the human abduction cases, pieces of tissue from various parts of the body are often taken. In women, there are often reports of vaginal exams of some sort and the removal of ova or eggs from the ovaries. In men, it is common to have a description that sperm is somehow removed. In both cases, you have a focus on the reproductive organs. . . .

"When you go over to the animal mutilations, you've got a parallel in the sense that tissue is excised. Great quantities of fluid are removed. The genitals are taken, for the most part. There's a parallel there, but the difference is that the animals are returned to pastures dead and mutilated, while humans for the most part are returned with these odd excisions, or burns, or various things done to their bodies; but they are alive."

Attack of the Goat Sucker

Beginning in March 1995, a new wrinkle appeared in the animal mutilation story—reports of strange bloodless animal deaths in Puerto Rico that spread to Mexico and into Texas. Unlike the classic cattle mutilations, these deaths were attributed to a creature, or creatures, frequently seen by residents.

Many animals, ranging from chickens and pet birds to cows and horses, were found drained of blood and with unusual puncture marks and a unknown viscous substance on their bodies.

Large circular puncture marks were found on haunches, necks, and even in the top of the head.

Superstitious islanders immediately branded the killer a *Chupacabra* (goat sucker) and tried to connect the beast with ancient Indian legends. Police and government authorities were less creative. They attributed the animals' deaths to packs of wild dogs or monkeys escaped from some laboratory. Neither explanation was acceptable to the frightened citizens. Dog packs had presented no problem in the past, and the idea that a small monkey could kill and drain a large cow or horse seemed preposterous.

Besides, several people reported seeing the culprit, and their descriptions were consistent. It was described as a four-foot-tall creature with powerful hind legs, thin forearms ending in three-fingered hands with long claws, a pear-shaped torso covered with fine gray hair with dark spots, and topped by a large oval head with small slits for nostrils and mouth. The most noticeable thing about the *Chupacabra* was its large, slanted red eyes, which, according to some reports, actually gave off light.

As in the cattle mutilations, there seemed to be a connection between the *Chupacabras* and UFOs. Most reports of animal attacks came from areas with a large number of UFO sightings. José Soto, the mayor of Canvanas, Puerto Rico, said more than 150 animal deaths had been blamed on the *Chupacabras* and added he believed the creature could be from outer space.

Despite appeals from those affected by the *Chupacabra* attacks, Puerto Rican authorities reacted the way the U.S. government has officially reacted to UFOs—they did nothing, apparently in the hope that the reports would go away. They didn't. Through 1996, the reports continued to come in and various grassroots attempts to kill or capture a *Chupacabra* proved fruitless.

Late in the spring of 1996, reports of *Chupacabras* had spread to Mexico with an ominous addition—the victim list now included humans. An unidentified farm worker in the Mexican state of Jalisco were treated at a village clinic for bite wounds. He claimed to have been attacked by "a beast three feet tall with a huge snout and dark, velvety skin." According to a news report, "It has the fangs of a vampire, the wings of a bat and the personality of an extraterrestrial."

Chupacabra reports poured in from the countryside, prompting the *Mexico City Times* to proclaim, "Goat-Sucker Fever Sweeps the Nation." The state of Sinaloa even created a task force to deal with the problem. This group concluded that no goat sucker exists but that pollution has gotten so bad that it's driving ordinary animals—wild dogs and wolves—to crazed behavior. Ernesto Enkerlin, a wildlife biologist at the Technological Institute of Monterrey, stated, "This is a sign of collective psychosis. I don't know if it's the [economic] crisis or what, but this is an exaggerated amount of noise about a fairly common occurrence."

By summer, reports of the *Chupacabra* were coming from Miami, where Dade County officials dismissed the death of forty animals in three days as wild dog attacks. Then came a report from the far South Texas town of Donna, interestingly enough, not far from the town of Puerto Rico. It was here that Sylvia Ybarra discovered her pet goat, Nena, dead from three puncture wounds in the neck in early May 1996. "I'm scared," her mother, Maria, told news reporters. "I have a lot of grandchildren around here. We've always had a lot of animals and we never had this happen before." Steve Edelstein, a local veterinarian, said Nena probably was attacked by a dog and the bites became infected.

With Spanish-language radio and TV stations carrying lurid accounts of the attacks, word of the *Chupacabra* grew to include a song and a video game. But legend, song, games, and "collective psychosis" aside, authorities are still left with hundreds of animals dead from strange puncture wounds, killed by a creature that witnesses have linked to UFOs. Theories on the *Chupacabras* range from hungry space aliens to CIA genetic experiments gone awry.

But if researchers thought cattle mutilations and *Chupacabras* had them running in circles, another mystifying UFO field began gaining public notoriety—the mystifying patterns in crops.

CHAPTER 10

GOING IN CIRCLES

On November 14, 1976, Joyce Bowles and a friend, Ted Pratt, were driving on Chilcomb Lane near Winchester in Hampshire, England, when the car's engine suddenly stopped. The pair watched in amazement as a large UFO landed nearby and a tall being in a silver suit approached their car.

Mrs. Bowles and Pratt were subsequently taken to a room—presumably inside the UFO—where they were met by three tall beings. Later, after reporting her experience, Mrs. Bowles said she received telephone calls from someone who said the British government was annoyed with the publicity given to her story and warned her to keep quiet. She reportedly replied to the caller, "This is a free country and I shall talk to whom I please, and neither you nor the government will stop me."

The Bowles experience would have simply been another in the long line of UFO sighting and contact stories except for one thing: Seven weeks after the encounter and some twelve hundred yards along Chilcomb Lane was discovered one of the first publicized crop circles.

Crop circles are quite simply circles that increasingly have been discovered in fields of cereal grains such as wheat, rye, barley oats, and rapeseed (a European cabbagelike herb fed to sheep and hogs). Other crops such as corn also have been affected. Beginning in the late 1970s, crop circles have appeared regularly throughout southern England, with the highest concentration in the large grain-growing counties of Wiltshire and Hampshire. Many crop circles in this region have been found near some of the world's most mysterious structures—the giant stone circles of Avebury and Stonehenge and legendary man-made Silbury Hill. Some researchers have wondered if the circle makers are drawn to these places or if these ancient circular structures were built in reverence to the mystifying circles.

Though largely ignored at first, crop circles eventually grew into a popular subdivision of the UFO field. Like mutilated cattle, the evidence remained in place for some time, available for measurement and study. But unlike the animal mutilations, which involved unnatural death and destruction, the crop circle phenomenon involved visions of natural beauty and the awe-inspiring appearance of intelligent design.

As with other UFO-related issues, a close study revealed that crop circles were not a recent phenomenon—only the widespread reporting of them. One account dated back to 1633, when a Mr. Hart walking at night in a Wiltshire field encountered "greene circles" with "an innumerable quantitie of pigmies or very small people dancing rounde and rounde." He reported that the little creatures "pinch'd him all over, and made a sorte of quick humming noyse all the time."

Another account from 1678 referred to the "mowing devil" of Hartfordshire, which both impressed and frightened a farmer by mysteriously cutting his field of oats overnight. The devil "cut them in round circles, and plac't every straw with that exactness that it would have taken up above an age for any man to perform what he did in that one night."

Of course these old accounts are open to various interpretations. So while some researchers claim they may refer to crop circles, no clear-cut proof of such has been offered. However, it is clear that the phenomenon began before the 1970s. When Simon Brown, a veteran farmer near Winchester, was told in August 1986 that a classic crop circle had been discovered in one of his fields, he replied with equanimity, "Oh, it's in that field this year, is it? My father used to point those circles out to me when I was a lad. They have appeared in one of my fields almost every year for the last 28 years that I can remember." Another farmer near Whiteparish, Gordon Sparkes, said he had found several such circles during his twenty-nine years of farming in the area. Area resident Evan Scurclock told researchers, "We used to find them close to Pepperbox Hill, near the spot where an aeroplane crashed, around 1936 to 1940."

Whether or not these reported circles represent genuine modern crop circles or something else, it is apparent that the mysterious circles have increased in number only since the late 1970s. The Royal Commission on the Historical Monuments of England possesses a collection of aerial photographs going back more than fifty years known as "Greater Wessex from the air." None show classic crop circle formations, an argument against the theory that the circles are a natural and regular atmospheric occurrence.

In mid-1965, two separate incidents highlighted a crop circle found just off the Warminster-Westbury Road in Wiltshire, England. On August 10, truck driver Tim Simpson encountered a large red ball of light that gave off "enormous vibrations" before spinning out of sight. On September 7, British army major William Hill also experienced serious vibrations after his car stalled on the same stretch of road. Hill described a noise like "the sounds of high-powered refrigeration units or deep-freeze equipment, but . . . magnified many times." Soon after these incidents, crop circles were discovered in nearby fields.

The connection between the circles and the UFO incidents was so obvious that many researchers and newsmen immediately labeled the depressions in the fields "UFO nests." To most observers it appeared as if some spinning craft had descended close to the earth or landed, creating the swirled patterns in the crushed crop. Thus, the crop circle and UFO phenomena became intertwined right from the start.

As the 1980s progressed, so did reports of crop circles. In 1988, three circles forming a triangle were found in a field near Cheesefoot Head. By 1990, circle formations had grown from small, simple circular depressions to large, elaborate designs involving straight lines, rings, rays, bars, circles within circles, spurs or serifs, and other geometric figures such as triangles and rectangles. Some formations even had rectangular areas with protruding spikes reminiscent of the human hand. Such complicated designs came to be known as "pictograms" or "agriglyphs." Reports of such circles spread from England to include Spain, France, Switzerland, Germany, Austria, Sweden, Russia, Japan, Australia, New Zealand, South Africa, Brazil, Mexico, Canada, and the United States.

As the circles took on more complicated designs, more researchers were drawn to the phenomenon, all seeking an explanation of how such circles might have been created. They began to call themselves cerealogists after Ceres, the Roman goddess of agriculture. All researchers attempted to deal with the first and most obvious question of the crop circles: How were they formed? Later, they would ask who formed them and why.

Anatomy of a Circle

Three basic theories regarding the creation of crop circles were advanced, based on the mind-set of the person offering them. For debunkers, the circles were obviously hoaxes perpetrated by humans fueled by mischief, alcohol, or both. The skeptics, which included many UFO researchers, regarded the circles as the result of some previously unknown atmospheric phenomenon. The mystically credulous saw in the intricate designs a new form of communication by nonhuman intelligences.

As these theories clashed in the arena of public opinion, serious researchers of all stripes worked hard to document the factual evidence. It was found that crop circles generally encompassed the following characteristics:

Very few of the circles—perhaps only 2 percent—are perfectly round. Many are elliptical and others oblate. Researchers saw this fact as a strong argument against the circles being a creation of nature, which generally acts with strict geometrical precision.

The crop is generally swirled outward from the center. Most go in a clockwise pattern, although once this was publicly noted, many counterclockwise patterns were discovered.

The crop is pressed down in different layers, with some layers swirling in a direction opposite to the layer above or below.

The crop stalks are pressed to the ground, many at a ninety-degree angle, yet are not damaged or broken.

Often the stalks are interwoven, braided like hair.

The crop remains alive, yet will not grow upwards again following a circle formation. Instead the crop grows horizontally.

Recent scientific studies show changes in the molecular structure of the affected plants, consistent with the application of intense heat for a short duration.

Straight paths of flattened crop have been found both within circles and connecting circles. Yet these paths show no sign of human footprints, nor can they be traced to the edge of the field.

Atmospheric conditions appear to play no part in the phenomenon. Crop circles have been formed in all types of weather. There are even reports of circles formed during daylight, although the vast majority are formed at night.

Topographical features also seem not to affect the creation of a circle. It is as if a giant cookie cutter has been pressed to the earth, making a circle regardless of the contours or features of the landscape.

Circles never overlap the borders of the fields and appear to take into account existing features such as tractor tracks and pathways, adding to the idea of intelligent control.

The boundary edge of circles between the flattened and standing crop is always clearly defined. The edge is sometimes abrupt and sharp and, at other times, serrated, notched, or even interlaced—a further argument against hoaxing. Boundaries appeared "mechanically precise," noted researcher Pat Delgado, who added, "It is an astounding and unnaturally instant cut-off point."

Circles apparently are created in a matter of seconds, since the longer it would take to press stems to a horizontal position, the more the likelihood of damage. "From the evidence we have," wrote Delgado, "it would seem that the flattening, swirling, whorling and swathing takes place over the whole of the circular area at the same time. This unknown force creates all the various circle floor details in less than a half minute but probably more than five seconds. We conclude this because to achieve a swirled, flattened condition pressed hard to the ground, the stems must have a maximum vertical to horizontal transformation time, above which they would be damaged by whiplash. Once all the stems had started moving in a steady manner, the whole circle, whatever its size, would be formed in possibly 20 seconds."

Despite the fact that the crop in most circles is undamaged, there is evidence that a violent force has been at work. "Some plants are pulled up randomly or ejected from the soil and thrown into the peripheral standing crop," observed author Pat Delgado, a retired British electromechanical engineer who spent seven years in Australia working for the British military and NASA. He also said there is evidence that one circle has been superimposed on another. "We know some circles have been re-affected later because the stems have a completely different lay to the lay recorded on our first visit," he wrote.

"Despite this double exposure, the crop usually continues to ripen normally and the head remains intact."

Another curious effect is "combing." Researcher Vince Migliore explained: "When a rectangle is seen from the air, there appear to be distinct edges to the design. But if all the crop inside the rectangle is laid down bending north, then you would expect at the north end of the formation that the erect standing stalks would interfere with bent stalks, creating a tangled confusion of erect and flattened plants. This is not the case. Instead, the bent stalks are neatly combed and interleaved between the standing plants."

Delgado noted that in a few circles, "Bundles of stems lie one over the other to form a typical plait or braid, the stems remaining straight in all cases. Some of the bundles have had two or more bundles laid at differing angles over and under them, so they are actually intertwined. The force field that produced this would have to be operating like a knitting machine. On two occasions, in two different circles, some bundles of these braids have been laid in opposition to each other. There seems to be no limit to the complication of lay that this extraordinary unknown force cannot [*sic*] produce."

In addition to the circles themselves, a variety of other effects have been noted in connection with the phenomenon, such as luminous balls, flashing lights, colors, knocking, whining or humming sounds, as well as subtle energy fields detected by both humans and animals.

Theories as to how the circles and their effects were achieved are as varied as the researchers themselves. However, the more prevalent theories tend to fall into one of two broad categories—intelligent or nonintelligent design.

One of the leading proponents of nonintelligent design is Dr. Terence Meaden, editor of Britain's *Journal of Meteorology* and founder of Britain's Tornado and Storm Research Organization. Meaden opined that the circles are formed by an atmospheric anomaly he called "plasma vortex." According to this theory, wind currents are broken up as they pass hills or other obstructions, and when they rejoin, a vortex of air, similar to a whirlwind or dust devil, is created, which can dip down and form a circle in the crop. He speculated that the swirling vortex might separate and concentrate electric energy in the air, thus creating both visible fireballs and humming sounds. While this idea sounds perfectly plausible, it describes an exceedingly rare phenomenon and fails to account for the lack of damage to the plants or explain the complex noncircular patterns.

In the early 1990s, researcher Donald L. Cyr found supporters for his technically detailed theory that crop circles were caused by "whistlers," very low frequency radio waves accompanied by charged particles produced by lightning bolts. These charged particle waves, which produce a whistling sound, then ricochet off the Van Allen belt in the upper atmosphere back to Earth in set trajectories, creating swirled circles in southern England. "All the favorable factors have to line up, like the 'go' conditions in a computer program," Cyr explained. "Maybe only one lightning stroke [*sic*] from Marion Island [near Prince Edward Island off the southern tip of Africa] per storm is powerful enough to penetrate to the ground in the Wiltshire region, producing a crop circle, or what I prefer to call a 'whistlegram.'" The whistler theory, in addition to being based on several highly technical controversies and dubious assumptions, does not account for the fact that the fields of southern England have been well surveyed and photographed for many years, yet the large and complex crop circles have appeared only recently.

Other nonintelligence explanations include:

Electromagnetism. While experiments showed that electromagnetic force could bend plants, it required an immense amount of force to flatten them. This kind of force would require a large amount of heavy equipment, including generators.

Piezoelectric energy. Here the same problem comes up: How can a person or a group of people move the equipment necessary to produce energy into and out of fields without detection? And how could they produce such complex patterns without intricate guides and assistance in use over a lengthy period of time?

Subterranean gas or energy pressure. While there is some scientific basis for this conjecture, it remains to be explained how such a natural phenomenon could produce such regular and repetitive patterns.

Even more earthly theories have been offered by debunkers seeking a rational explanation. Some claimed the circles were caused by rutting deer, hedgehogs in heat, or swarms of hungry crows—none of which could possibly have flattened circles of grain without damage.

None of the strictly earthbound explanations adequately address all the mystifying evidence found in the crop circles. Despite this, many skeptics—including some ufologists—lean toward the natural explanations. John Spencer, Paul Fuller, and author Jenny Randles worked with Britain's National Farmers Union and concluded that "there was a high probability that the cornfield circles were a natural phenomenon, the result of hurricane vortex action."

In the mid-1980s, several scientists in Britain formed Circle Effects Research (CERES) to study the issue, and by 1989 they had categorized twenty-four common circle patterns. But after eight years of research the CERES scientists still could find no adequate theory to explain the phenomenon.

The fact that natural explanations cannot reconcile all of the facts known about crop circles has led many people to speculate on the possibility that the circles are artificially created—by humans or otherwise.

One fascinating theory involving humans is that the crop circles are produced by lasers or energy beam weapons that constitute America's Strategic Defense Initiative (SDI), or "Star Wars" satellite program. If this is the case, it is small wonder that the U.S. military would maintain secrecy over millions of tax dollars being wasted just to create beautiful patterns in English crops a few months out of the year. Why not melt elaborate holes in Antarctic ice shelves, where their work would be unobserved?

It should be noted here that circle researchers have indeed long noted a very obvious military presence in the areas of crop circles. Southern England has many military installations, which could account for some of the activity. Military helicopters and troops equipped with infrared and other monitoring devices have been seen near crop circles. Most researchers believe that the authorities are taking a much greater interest in the phenomenon than is generally believed. Why such interest if ranking military officers knew that the circles are the result of military tests or experiments? Again, wouldn't such activities be conducted in more secluded areas?

Such speculation added to the mystery of the crop circles, as did the ever more complex and compelling designs found as the 1990s began. "The circles and rings present numerous inconsistencies," noted Delgado. "As soon as we think we have solved one peculiarity, the next circle displays an inexplicable variation, as if to say, 'What do you make of it now?'"

Another example of apparently intelligent teasing came when about fifty scientists in the spring of 1991 prepared to keep watch on a field where crop circles had regularly appeared. The day before they set up a variety of monitoring equipment, a classic circle appeared. Yet during the eight days they watched the field, nothing happened. Disgusted and bored, the scientists packed up and left the field only to discover that a new circle had appeared in an adjoining field.

In his fact-filled 1989 book, *Circular Evidence*, written with Colin Andrews, Delgado wrote, "It is very sobering to stand in one of these circles and ponder what force could have arrived and departed, leaving behind this beautiful record of its visit with no clue how it was achieved." But if Delgado and others didn't have a clue in 1989, they certainly got one in 1991. Then the entire world learned of the simplest explanation of all—the mysterious crop circles were merely the creations of very human hoaxers.

The Saga of Doug 'n' Dave

It is most probably no coincidence that with the arrival of even more wondrously elaborate crop circle designs in the early 1990s came Doug and Dave—by now arguably the world's most famous hoaxers. After all, the new complex circles drew ever-increasing worldwide media and public attention. Officialdom could no longer ignore the phenomenon, nor could they offer any satisfactory conventional explanation.

In England, authorities met the situation with a quiet conference of high officials.

According to George Wingfield, a lecturer with Britain's Centre for Crop Circle Studies, the meeting was held in September 1990 in London and included the Ministries of Defense, Agriculture, and Environment. Wingfield, who claimed to have obtained information on the meeting from a person who attended, stated, "The meeting lasted long and the conclusion was that the cause of the crop circles was completely unknown. Stationary whirlwinds were ruled out and it was stated that hoaxing only accounted for an insignificant percentage of the circles. Responsibility for keeping track of what was happening was left firmly with the Ministry of Defense, who had for some years used Army helicopters to photograph new circles."

It was decided that should the need arise, the Ministry of Defense might take "appropriate measures" to quell public excitement, including the possibility of "disinformation," Wingfield learned.

Exactly one year later the British tabloid *Today* published an exposé with the headline, "Men Who Conned the World." "The mysterious corn circles that baffled scientists around the world are a gigantic hoax, *Today* can reveal," crowed the tabloid's copy.

The hoaxers were identified as two Southampton men in their sixties named Doug Bower and Dave Chorley. The pair claimed they had created "no less than two hundred corn circles" in the Hampshire area over a period of thirteen years beginning in 1978. Doug said he decided to confess to the hoax after his wife, Ilene, became suspicious of his nightly absences. "It started to cross my mind that he might be seeing another woman," quipped Ilene. The *Today* story was accompanied by photographs of Doug and Dave pressing down corn with wooden planks guided by a length of rope. In one fell swoop, a growing mystery with definite UFO connections was dispensed with—it was all a hoax perpetrated by Doug and Dave and a few copycats.

It was not the first attempt to discredit crop circles as hoaxes. In 1990, BBC-TV along with Nippon TV had engaged Pat Delgado and Colin Andrews to participate in a program called Operation Blackbird designed to keep watch over a crop field in an attempt to photograph a forming circle. Some hoaxed circles initially fooled the Blackbird observers. An amateurish attempt—artifacts such as horoscope charts and crosses were left in the circles—it was soon judged to be a hoax designed to implicate "New Age" groups. The Blackbird hoax story was not widely known. "I certainly don't have any doubts that the hoax was perpetrated by the British Army, and also that other maneuverings that I'm aware of at Blackbird were also played by the Army's hand," stated Andrews. In the 1980s, a man named Francis Shepherd claimed to have hoaxed several circles but later admitted that a newspaper had paid him to confess so as to discredit circle stories in a rival publication.

The Doug and Dave story, on the other hand, was immediately picked up by America's Associated Press and distributed widely. "Most British newspapers ignored the story," commented Wingfield, "but many U.S. ones seemed prepared to accept it at face value."

Not one news organization seemed capable of simply taking a look at the crop circle statistics for the previous two years. Dr. Terence Meaden, a proponent of natural causation, reported some four hundred circles were documented in 1989. In 1990, this number rose to nearly a thousand with more than three hundred new formations in the first few crop months of 1991 in Britain alone. Considering that the British growing season is five months long, this means that Doug and Dave would have had to somehow trample down more than fifteen hundred crop circles within a period of fifteen months. This would mean the pair would have had to create nearly four circles every night—a patently impossible task especially in view of the distances between discovered circles. And this calculation does not even take into account the hundreds of crop circles that by the mid-1990s were reported in remote parts of Canada, Australia, Russia, Japan, and the United States, nor the fact that circles were reported years before 1978.

As if to give particular lie to the hoax story, researcher Michael Strainic reported more than twenty crop circles in Canada within a ten-week period at about the same time that the Doug and Dave story was being circulated worldwide. "It was as if we had been assaulted by a circle-making SWAT team," commented Strainic. Likewise a classic crop circle with undamaged stalks laid over in a swirl pattern was discovered in September 1990 by Roger and Lynda Lowe in a sorghum field south of their home in Osceola, Missouri.

Furthermore, there is evidence that Doug and Dave gleaned information used in their story from some young crop circle researchers. Julie Varden and three companions were watching crops overnight a few weeks before the *Today* story broke. "These men are liars," she told Wingfield adamantly, "and we can prove that they are liars. We met them at Cheesefoot Head on August 20th and they have taken things we spoke about and rehashed them in the *Today* story."

Varden said at their meeting she mentioned some jellylike substance found at several circle sites and was told by Doug, "I know what that was. It's the discharge from an aircraft toilet." In the *Today* story, Doug indeed tells of being knocked unconscious by "something which fell from space" while creating a crop circle. "But when we got into the light I saw the mess on my head was the frozen discharge from an aircraft toilet," he recounted blandly, apparently repeating his previous conjecture to Varden unaware that he most probably could not have survived such an event.

Another of the researchers who met Doug and Dave at Cheesefoot Head, Nick Riley, said he showed the pair some ore he had found near a crop circle. Despite Riley's insistence that it was simply iron, Doug declared it to be a meteorite. In the *Today* story, Doug claimed that he and Dave had collected some meteorites and placed them in one of their circles near Stonehenge. "They did indeed leave stones there, not that that proves they made the Stonehenge circle," said Wingfield. "But I also met the man who found these 'meteorites' and they were, of course, just the sort of stones described by Nick Riley. . . . Local knowledge and a close study of the various books on the Circles has given a veneer of authenticity to what then seemed plausible claims."

In short, Doug and Dave's hoax proved to be a hoax itself. Yet the public—particularly in the United States—is only aware that there was a brief crop circle craze that turned out to be merely the work of pranksters.

Is this erroneous view simply a creation of a lazy and inattentive media, or is it the result of something more sinister? Several crop circle researchers, including Colin Andrews, George Wingfield, and others, have publicly accused the British government of perpetrating a "disinformation" campaign using Doug and Dave. And there is circumstantial evidence to support this charge.

First is the way that writers at the tabloid *Today* ambushed researcher Pat Delgado. These tactics may have simply been normal procedure for circulation-seeking tabloids or they may reflect a conscious effort to discredit circle researchers. Tabloid writers took Delgado to Sevenoaks in Kent one week before publication of the Doug and Dave article and asked his opinion of a new crop pictogram later referred to as an "insectogram" because of its resemblance to some sort of insect. Delgado was amazed at the sight of a formation that previously had only been found in Hampshire and Stonehenge. Although it did not exactly match previous such circles, Delgado initially confirmed it as a genuine crop circle. He was asked to keep quiet about this circle and he did. A few days later, *Today* staffers brought Doug and Dave to Delgado's home. "In quick-fire succession they confronted him with proof that they had made the Kent formation, then laid claim to this circle and that circle and so on until he was literally reeling on the ropes," commented Wingfield. "The *Today* reporter, Graham Brough, then wrung all sorts of unwise concessions from his hapless victim, which were subsequently printed in the paper."

Soon fellow circle researcher Colin Andrews arrived at Delgado's home and began questioning Doug and Dave. He quickly found that "when they were asked how they could have made such precise circles which have appeared by the thousands, accurate within three millimeters and up to 700 yards in diameter, these guys couldn't come up with the answers." Andrews said Doug and Dave, unable to answer pertinent questions, were quickly whisked away by Brough and others.

When the well-orchestrated *Today* story broke, Doug and Dave demonstrated their circle-making ability for the news media in a Sussex wheat field. "Photographs clearly show that this was nothing like a genuine crop formation," said Wingfield. "The laid crop is all over the place and there is no swirl pattern. The edge of these circles is rough and bears no resemblance to the precise cutoff which many of us have become so used to. . . . *Today* excused this shortcoming by saying that this was caused by the trampling of the TV crew."

But there were deeper mysteries than Doug and Dave's inability to duplicate a genuine crop circle. Researchers noted that while the tabloid story noted "*Today* has paid no money" for the Doug and Dave account, it was copyrighted by something called "MBF Services." A *Today* editor identified MBF only as a freelance press agency that "put us in touch with these people [Doug and Dave] so they own the copyright" and declined to say more. Doug and Dave both denied any knowledge of MBF Services.

Researcher Wingfield discovered that no press agency with the name "MBF Services" was listed in England, but did find a "MBF Consultancy" described as a "scientific research and development company." One of the company's directors was Dr. Andrew Beech

Clifford, owner of Maiden Beech Farm (MBF) in Somerset. Dr. Clifford was a scientist who admitted doing confidential work for the Ministry of Defense, some of which involved America's Star Wars program. He denied any connection between MBF Consultancy and MBF Services.

Another MBF company, Macfarlane Business Forms in Scotland, also performed confidential work for the British government. But again no connection could be made with MBF Services.

Wingfield then made contact with sources inside Britain's MI5, their equivalent to the CIA, and discovered some interesting information regarding "disinformation." He was told that one method used by MI5 in a Northern Ireland antiterrorist campaign was to "set up a bogus private news agency and supply the disinformation story to a selected newspaper."

Pat Delgado, who was so effectively ambushed by Doug, Dave, and the *Today* staff, studied the matter and concluded, "Investigations so far have brought to light a well-orchestrated misinformation and debunking campaign that was initiated last year by 'official departments.' There are at least two other countries involved in this network of intrigue, the USA and France. The two men, Bower and Chorley, who claimed hoaxed all the crop circles, are but pawns in a plan to discredit me and the crop circle subject. . . . Neither the two men nor anyone else have offered me a shred of evidence, either photographs, video or anything else, to substantiate their claims. . . . I feel the reason for 'departments' concern is the enormous surge of interest in crop circles by the whole spectrum of mankind throughout the world, including professional, scientific and people in so-called high places who are now seen to be heavily associated and involved in the manifestation of a subject that cannot be officially controlled. The fact that the subject carries very significant spiritual connotations, by opening up people's awareness and unifying them beyond belief, may also be very worrying, or even seen as some kind of threat."

Delgado went on to recount an incident on September 26, 1991, when a "strip of shapes" was discovered in a cornfield near Highland, Kansas. He said men in dark suits soon arrived, secured the field, and then questioned nearby residents. "It was obvious there had been an attempt to destroy the 'pictogram.' A new hot wire fence had been placed round the site. Photos and diagrams are available to confirm all this. It has been confirmed the vehicles and men were from the government and the CIA. You have not heard the last of crop circles by any means and the subject is far more significant now than it ever was. Why are the 'official departments' running scared?"

Following publication of their story, Doug and Dave went on an extensive tour of Europe, where they freely talked to any media that would listen. "One can't help wondering who finances these trips?" questioned Wingfield. "It's obvious they're backed by a lot of money," noted researcher Andrews. "But it's not traceable."

"What we have here are perhaps the early signs of a major disinformation campaign," he added, "because the governments of the world do not know what is going on. They feel they must deactivate the level of public interest in the situation."

Wingfield agreed. "There seems little doubt now that the *Today* story is part of a deliberate campaign of disinformation to persuade people that the circles phenomenon is just an illusion—a trick perpetrated by two old jokers and by others who have copied them."

Whether or not a "disinformation campaign" truly existed, the Doug and Dave story—and more particularly the major media's uncritical dissemination of it—has indeed blunted general interest in the crop circles.

The Doug and Dave explanation was invoked as recently as December 1995, when astronomer Carl Sagan produced an article for the widely distributed *Parade* magazine using the pair to debunk UFOs in general and the crop circles in particular. "They dreamed it up over stout one evening in their regular pub, the Percy Hobbs. They had been amused by UFO reports and thought it might be fun to spoof the UFO gullibles," Sagan explained. "At first they flattened the wheat with the heavy steel bar that Bower used as a security device on the back door of his picture-framing shop. Later on, they used planks and ropes. Their first efforts took only a few minutes. But, being inveterate pranksters as well as serious artists, the challenge began to grow on them. Gradually, they designed and executed more and more demanding figures. . . . Bower and Chorley were delighted [with the subsequent publicity], especially when scientists and others began to announce their considered judgment that no merely human intelligence could be responsible."

In an odd kind of reverse argument, considering how much the Doug and Dave hoax story turned public interest away from the subject of crop circles, Sagan concluded, "Those who have something to sell, those who wish to influence public opinion, those in power, a skeptic might suggest, have a vested interest in discouraging skepticism." Addressing the crop circle phenomenon in a mass-audience article without mentioning the anomalous nature of the circles struck many researchers as joining the effort to discourage any public interest.

John Mitchell, editor of the *Cerealogist*, noted, "The common-sense belief, that the crop circle phenomenon is nothing but an elaborate hoax, is now established as the official doctrine."

But while the media and the general public seem to have lost interest in the circles thanks to the Doug and Dave publicity, this has not stopped new circles from being formed each year, nor has it stopped a growing legion of researchers studying the phenomenon—with more surprising results.

Science Takes a Look

Analyses ranging from simple compass readings to elaborate laboratory tests confirm that something very strange separates the vegetation within crop circles from surrounding plants.

Researcher Charles Thomas, using a 1944 type P11 boxed aircraft compass such as used in World War II bombers, documented magnetic disturbances that resulted in the compass needle swinging from five to ten degrees off true north within crop circles. After some careful study, Thomas concluded that "the process of crop-circle formation in these cases appears to have produced a local magnetic anomaly detectable with a reliable instrument. . . . The anomaly appears to be linked to the direction in which stalks are flattened and that the strength of the anomaly appears to vary with the distance from ground level—or possibly proximity to crop-ear level. There may be a suspicion that the magnetic field is created at the time of formation and decreases through time. . . . I have no idea what this means, nor which of the many alternative hypotheses—if any—it supports."

Dr. W. C. Levengood holds degrees in both physics and bioscience, seven patents including a seed analyzer, and is owner of Agro Sciences, Inc., and Pinelandia Biophysics Laboratory in Michigan. After lengthy study, Dr. Levengood found evidence of consistent changes in cell structure, seeds, and growth within circle plants.

For example, within the cells of circle plants, he found a 21 percent average increase in the diameter of pits, microscopic cavities that allow organic compounds and gases to pass through the cellular structure. Levengood also found that cell pit size consistently grew larger from the outer edges of the plant into the center, indicating the effect was caused by some outside agency. The only way he was able to duplicate such cell pit changes in control plants was to place them in a microwave oven. After heating the plants for thirty seconds on one side, he found cell pits were enlarged 14 percent. Further heating caused dehydration. Since crop circle plants were still alive, Levengood came to the same conclusion as researcher Pat Delgado—the heat applied to circle plants must be intense but brief, no more than thirty seconds in duration. "There is no way a hoaxer can do this by simply tromping on the plants," noted Levengood. Similar changes in the molecular structure of circle plants were detected by chemist Kenneth Spelman of Signalysis Laboratories in Rodborough, England.

Further evidence of heating came from a flat porcupine. On August 29, 1992, Canadian farmer Joe Rennick discovered a circle in his Saskatchewan wheat field. In the center was a dead porcupine pressed flat with its four appendages splayed outward. Although the animal apparently had been dead for several days, there was no odor nor evidence of decay. The body was desiccated, dried up, and the ground within the circle was hard and dry while the rest of the field was soggy. "That ground was hard as cement, like someone put it inside an oven and baked it," said Rennick. Canadian researcher Chad Deetken speculated the porcupine, rather than running away as most animals, may have rolled itself into a ball for protection and was sucked into the circle at the time of its formation. "Its quills lay in the same direction as the swirl of the wheat," he noted. Unlike those in the surrounding field, wheat seeds taken from the crop circle were dried and shriveled like many found in the British circles.

Studying seeds, Levengood was surprised to find a complete lack of development in early-season crop circle plants. But an even bigger surprise came when he found that more mature plants—from July onward—not only produced normal-appearing seeds but germinated faster than control plants, sometimes as much as 45 percent. Researcher Linda Howe noted that agriculture seed experts say a 5 percent increase in growth rate is considered quite successful. "Forty-five percent is astonishing," commented Levengood.

Professor Bruce Rideout of Ursinus College in Collegeville, Pennsylvania, discovered that plants taken from some Pennsylvania crop circles also exhibited cell pit diameter enlargement as well as growth nodes—the bulges on a plant stem where the leaf or bud is attached—which were split or cracked along with some that were mysteriously bent. His findings were confirmed by Levengood, who stated, "There was a pronounced elongation and lateral twist of the growth nodes anywhere from 30 to 90 degrees from the vertical." Both scientists found lateral cracks across the outside of the bent nodes. "This lateral splitting was observed in all four sets of circle samples," noted Levengood, "and was not seen in the four sets of control samples. The formation of this type of fissure would require complex stresses in order to rupture the semi-rigid longitudinal fibers in the epidermal tissue. For example, it would require the node to be weakened and expanded from an internal force such as might be caused by transient heat energy. This would be followed by a longitudinal extension or tension stress. That combination of forces is unlikely to be generated by a windstorm."

Yet another anomaly was discovered by Marshall Dudley, a designer of radiation detection equipment in Oak Ridge, Tennessee, who, along with researcher Michael Chorost, found evidence of unnatural radioactive isotopes in crop circle specimens. They found eleven such isotopes that were not present in control plants taken just several feet from a circle. "None appear to be residues from Chernobyl or atmospheric nuclear tests, not do they appear to have any other mundane origin. . . . The authors believe this finding definitively rules out hoaxers for that particular formation."

After three years of study including the discovery of disturbances in the cell walls of crop circle plants, Levengood concluded, "Whatever is doing these formations, is affecting the fundamental biophysics and biochemistry of the plants. . . . The consistent pattern of conductivity measurements in some formations compared to controls indicates that the basic micro fibril structures of the plants have been altered. Such cellular changes cannot be hoaxed."

So something in motion seems to be applying intense heat of a short duration to fields in order to form the genuine crop circles—but what? Although it appears to be the official position of governments and the news media and other public authorities, hoaxing of all the circles is out of the question. Likewise, no solid evidence of a natural phenomenon has been forthcoming. Once again, UFOs must be considered.

Residents of Bristol, England, reported seeing flashing lights and one large dark object in the night skies on July 16–17, 1991. About 3:30 A.M. the warden of nearby Barbury Castle heard a pulsating humming roar like hundreds of airplanes passing overhead for a few minutes. At 6:00 A.M. a crop pictogram composed of a 177-foot triangle enclosing a circle with three circles at each apex was discovered near the castle. The formation "embodies geometry of the very highest order," commented researcher Wingfield.

Pat Delgado told of several circles being formed near Westbury, England, in 1989 following the sighting of a large UFO ringed by orange lights in the vicinity. "UFOs are claimed to be capable of producing the most extraordinary behavior and phenomena," commented Delgado. "The control of force fields unknown to us may well result in rings and circles. It may well be within the capability of a UFO to manipulate a rotary force field which is enclosed in a sharp cut-off electro-magnetic shield. It is also possible that UFOs are only visible when they wish to be in our light spectrum, so the forces they may control could be demonstrated with or without their presence."

There does appear to be significant differences, however, in classic UFO sightings and reports of objects near crop circles. Many people, including author Whitley Strieber, have reported circles near the scenes of UFO sightings. These tend to be circular areas that give evidence of a crushing weight with occasional signs of charring or smoldering such as experienced by New Mexico patrolman Lonnie Zamora. UFO sightings usually involve sizable craft in a variety of shapes, whereas crop circle sightings mostly have been of small balls of light or spinning globes. It may be that two distinct phenomena are at work here with one having little or no relation to the other.

Misunderstood Messages

Many researchers, after studying the geometry, complicated swirls and braiding, cellular changes, and their undetectable creation, have concluded that crop circles must involve nonhuman intelligence. Physicist and astronomer Archie Roy of Glasgow University is convinced mankind is encountering an advanced intelligence.

Are there indications of intelligent thought behind the circles? The answer appears to be yes, especially in light of the work of scientist Gerald S. Hawkins, already well known for his studies of Stonehenge as an ancient observatory. Hawkins, retired chairman of Boston University's Astronomy Department and a science adviser to the director of the U.S. Information Agency, became intrigued by the crop circles while visiting England in 1990. He discovered geometric relationships in several circles that matched the diatonic ratios of the musical scale.

Hawkins explained, "A ratio in the diatonic scale is the step up in pitch from one note to another. It can be measured exactly. From C to G is an increase of 1.5 times, or the ratio of 3 over 2. The whole set makes an octave of eight white notes on the piano.

"As a careful scientist, I'm not saying the patterns are musical, only that the sizes follow the same mathematical law as the intervals in western music. The creators [of crop circles] seemed to know of these fractions, taking care to encode them in the shapes so that they could be retrieved by somebody studying aerial photographs. The accuracy required in a typical 20-meter circle is about 15 centimeters, or six inches. Without the precisely-made edges, my analysis would not have been possible."

Studying the precise measurements of eighteen crop circle patterns, Hawkins was able to find an exact match of geometric ratios in eleven of them. His findings seemed to exclude the idea of natural causes such as whirlwinds. Hawkins knew these measurements involved more than blind luck, so he began studying geometric relationships within other circles.

According to writer Ivars Peterson, Hawkins discovered five separate geometric theorems concealed in crop circle geometry. "It was the approach I had taken at Stonehenge. It wasn't just one alignment here and nothing there. That would have had no significance," explained Hawkins. "It was the whole pattern of alignments with the sun and moon over a long period that made it ring true to me. Once you get a pattern, you know it probably won't go away."

Peterson wrote, "Remarkably, he could find none of these theorems in the works of Euclid, the ancient Greek geometer who established the basic techniques and rules of what is known as Euclidean geometry. He was also surprised at his failure to find the crop circle theorems in any of the mathematics textbooks and references, ancient and modern, that he consulted. . . . The hoaxers apparently had the requisite knowledge not only to prove a Euclidean theorem but also to conceive of an original theorem in the first place—a far more challenging task." Following his discoveries, Hawkins sent a letter to confessed hoaxers Doug and Dave asking how they were able to produce "ingenious, previously unknown geometric theorems" in their circles. No satisfactory answer was forthcoming.

Hawkins continued to seek the intelligence behind the circles despite the scientific community's willful indifference. "My scientific colleagues have checked out the mathematics and they confirm what I have discovered, but usually their interest stops there," he said. "Unless I can tell them how the circle makers have entered the fields undetected, managing to bend living plants without cracking the stalks, they regard the events as a problem of no scientific interest. I suppose in our modern academic climate, it would be difficult for them to get a grant for crop circle research. For me, I do not need a grant, and I look beyond the circle makers' new communication technology to the intricate information conveyed."

But at least one man didn't have to rely on mathematical theorems to obtain a message. Bryce Bond was walking in an English wheat field after dark in the spring of 1991 when he suddenly found himself paralyzed. He tried to scream but couldn't find his voice. "Seconds later," he later recounted, "another voice . . . low and gentle was heard in my head. It said, 'Be at peace. We mean no harm. You are standing in the middle of our craft. We are not of your dimension.' When the paralysis wore off, Bond found himself in the middle of a crop circle.

Others without such direct experience have offered much speculation as to the meaning of the crop circles. As writer Vince Migliore noted, "The crop circle problem is inextricably tangled with UFOs, psychic readings, ancient history, religious monuments, ley lines, mythology, occult Earth sciences, metaphysics and spirituality. This 'borderland' can be viewed as a quagmire or the mother lode, depending on your point of view."

One idea finding currency in both Britain and the United States is that the circles are the manifestation of energy from the living Earth, sometimes referred to as Gaia. Several researchers have reported their recording equipment registering audible oddities within crop circles, such as noises, static, and humming. "This suggests that there are transients present all across the electromagnetic spectrum— from DC to daylight, as technicians would call it," noted Migliore. "Whether the medium is microwaves, radio waves or audio frequency radiation, the point is that some sentient mind is responsible for it." Mother Earth or Gaia is crying out against man's misuse and abuse of her natural resources, so the idea goes.

The concept of organic energy is quite similar to the idea of a primal life-giving force called "orgone energy" by psychoanalyst Dr. Wilhelm Reich, who died while imprisoned by U.S. authorities in 1956 for selling "orgone" boxes for personal therapeutic use, despite the support of Albert Einstein and others.

Such beliefs have led some circle researchers to the use of dowsing rods in an effort to determine if energy, or ley, lines play a part in the phenomenon. Interestingly enough, while conventional science discounts the validity of dowsing, some researchers claimed to have found consistent energy lines within circles, especially along a major axis and at ninety-degree tangents to the edge of rectangles. Psychics also have been used to study the crop circles, and several report they are the product of an energy flow toward the earth that is spiritual in nature.

One researcher, Jon Erik Beckjord, claimed "it is simply invisible UFOs that are using force-beams to 'write' the crop circle pictograms, in all countries they occur" in a four-thousand-year-old Norse language called Tifinag. Beckjord said it was highly unlikely that "a crew of Tifinag-knowledgeable hoaxers were cruising around, making 30–50 crop forms per day during the season. . . ." He added that "Alien logic is not human logic" and that the aliens don't like world leaders, so they bypass them. "The vibes are wrong," he explained, "so they—illogically to us—approach simple people, good people, nice people, psychic people—people with little or no power" with their crop messages. While admitting his translations are "speculative" and "more like an art or craft than science," Beckjord claimed to perceive such crop messages as "This is the place of the Serpent or devil, an evil place" and "This is a dangerous place to camp."

Researcher Dennis Stacy criticized Beckjord, asking, "Which of the world's many anomalous phenomena *couldn't* be explained by the introduction of invisible UFOs. Why stop at crop circles . . . ?" Pointing out numerous flaws in Beckjord's theory, Stacy noted, "Trying to make sense of the symbolic meaning of the circles has resulted already in interpretations based on ancient Sumerian and Semitic languages, as well as modern weather chart symbology! Tifinag . . . is only the latest such fruitless search."

Stacy and many other UFO researchers have expressed the difficulty they have in believing that space aliens who have the knowledge to travel to Earth from light-years away couldn't devise a better means of communication than etching out incomprehensible symbols in some grain field. This rational thought argues well for the idea that if indeed the crop circles are communications, they may not be intended for us.

Author Peter Hewitt, who has written about the supernatural within a scientific framework, suggested that the circle messages may come from earthly intelligences long mentioned in legends and myths as fairies, pixies, dryads, satyrs, and elves. "No one any longer believes in or attends to the nature spirits. But they want recognition," explained Hewitt. "The circles are their graffiti."

Some researchers with an even more mystical bent, such as George Wingfield, see the crop circles as messages aimed at the human subconscious, signaling a new step in the evolution of human consciousness. Pragmatists like Dennis Stacy see them as meaningless expressions of nature like rainbows and waterspouts. "The Circles are saying nothing more than we humans force them to say," commented Stacy. "We don't argue, for the most part, that a sunbeam is sending us a particular message."

Vince Migliore, on the other hand, sees just such a message. "One view is that [the subject of crop circles] should simply be appreciated for its beauty and mystery. For instance, are the northern lights or the dance-language of the bumblebee any less awe-inspiring now that scientists can explain the phenomena?" he wrote. "Aren't they still beautiful and astounding? And, aren't these same documented wonders still studied because the observer is forced to decide whether this is just some quirk of Nature, or is it, like the rainbow, a sign, a promise from God, that he is loved?"

Hewitt speculated that once the novelty of the circles has worn off—for both us and the makers—they will cease.

Events proved otherwise. Classic crop circles of even more elaborate and complex designs were reported during the 1996 crop season in England. According to circle researcher Andy Thomas, one intricate design composed of more than 140 circles of various sizes apparently was created within a half hour in July 1996 in a field adjoining Stonehenge. "A pilot flew over the field at around 5:30 P.M. and there was no formation," reported Thomas. "When he returned shortly before 6 P.M., there it was."

Hoaxing can account for only a small percentage of the world's mysterious crop circles, and natural phenomena have been pretty well ruled out, especially in light of the latest scientific findings. Other than to ignore the subject, one is compelled to begin thinking of the circles in terms of signs from a nonhuman intelligence—whether from Earth or elsewhere. Many researchers, such as Michael M. Chorost, who has studied crop circles firsthand since 1990, claim there are two possibilities if the circles are communications: Either humans have failed to interpret them or their content is not meant for us. The question as to why an advanced intelligence could create these mysterious circles but can't seem to find a way to communicate with us lends support to the latter possibility.

The arguments over the meaning of such messages will undoubtedly continue for some time. One thing is certain: Attempts to understand nonhuman or alien intelligence has caused many thoughtful people to search deep within the mental and spiritual nature of humanity for insights and answers. Some of these people were in the U.S. military, and what they discovered was almost as unbelievable as the UFO phenomenon itself.

CHAPTER 11

IN THE MIND'S EYE

One day in the fall of 1985, according to author and Pulitzer Prize nominee Howard Blum, a collection of ranking military officers met in a lead-lined conference hall on the third floor of the Old Executive Office Building across from the White House to watch a psychic in action.

Seated in front of the officers and the president's science adviser were two Stanford Research Institute (SRI) scientists and a man known for his psychic abilities.

The occasion was a demonstration of the phenomenon known as remote viewing (RV)—the ability to mentally perceive a person, place, or thing from any distance by other than the normal five senses. It was a psychic ability that had been studied and developed by U.S. intelligence and the military for more than a decade at that point. But on this day, what to most people was extraordinary moved into the fantastic.

After the psychic successfully described the country dacha of Mikhail Gorbachev by coordinate remote viewing, a second test was begun. This one was designed to demonstrate the use of RV against submarines. A series of photographs depicting various submarines were shown to the viewer. He calmly gave their current locations: One Soviet sub was off the coast of Iceland, another located in international waters off the coast of South Carolina.

But the last photo—that of a Soviet Delta-class submarine—caused the viewer some consternation. He hesitated as though he had seen something unexpected.

The viewer announced that the sub was patrolling a sector of ocean between Maine and Nova Scotia. But he hesitated again. There was more, but he appeared uncomfortable in saying so. More than one member of the audience thought the viewer appeared frightened.

"What is it?" asked one of the scientists.

The viewer explained that while searching for the submarine he had seen something else at the same coordinates, something that hovered above the submarine.

"Was it an airplane?" queried the scientist. The remote viewer would only shrug his shoulders.

The viewer was asked to sketch what he saw. He rapidly began drawing circles; one was elongated, apparently the submarine. But above this was a circle with no wings.

Asked if he saw a rocket, the remote viewer again would only shrug. Finally, expressing the hopes or fears of many in the room, the scientist said, "Well, what else could it be? I mean, you're not going to tell me it's a flying saucer."

"Yes," replied the viewer, "that's it exactly."

Despite this brush with the fantastic, Naval Intelligence and the Defense Intelligence Agency (DIA) accepted the legitimacy of the demonstration and within six months launched a classified operation using remote viewers to seek Soviet submarines called Project Aquarius. "Over the next 14 months there were at least 17 recorded sightings of 'hovering unidentified flying objects' by the scanning participants in Project Aquarius," reported Blum. It is unclear if this was the same Project Aquarius mentioned in the MJ-12 briefing documents.

The 1985 demonstration and its acceptance by high-ranking military, intelligence, and science officials was just one more episode in a long history of Washington duplicity. While officially scoffing at any publicized report on UFOs, various government agencies quietly continued to give serious attention to such matters, even to the extent of using psychic remote viewers.

And why not? After all, nearly all modern UFO close encounters appear to involve some form of telepathy or mind-to-mind communication. Many abductees report that their captors communicate by mental means. They "hear" alien voices inside their own head. Abductees Betty and Barney Hill, Betty Andreasson, and Travis Walton, among many others, all said they never saw their captors' mouths move but instead "felt" their thoughts.

If alien visitors are using mental or psychic powers to communicate with humans, perhaps humans could use those same powers to penetrate the alien agenda. In fact, many people familiar with remote viewing believe this process may be the best method yet available to penetrate the UFO enigma. If this is so, the question becomes, do humans indeed have such a psychic capability and can it be proven reliable?

The U.S. government, based on the fact of continued funding and study by both the military and intelligence agencies, obviously believes the answers to these questions are in the affirmative. To understand how they arrived at such a controversial conclusion, one must study the history of psychic phenomena.

The Bible Tells Me So

All of the world's great religious texts, from the Bible to the Koran to those of Oriental mysticism, contain a wealth of stories involving prophecy, visions, and spiritual instruction. And all seem to involve visual input. The biblical book of Isaiah opens with the statement "These are the messages that came to Isaiah, son of Amoz, in the visions he saw during the reigns of King Uzziah, King Jotham, King Ahaz and King Hezakiah—all kings of Judah."

According to the *Holman Bible Dictionary*, early biblical prophets influenced almost every institution of Israel, despite the fact that they often were viewed with contempt, locked up, ignored, and persecuted. Prophets formed guilds or schools and their assistants recorded their words for posterity.

Biblical prophecy was not limited to men. In the Old Testament book of Judges, we find that a "prophetess" named Deborah provided the Israelite leader Barak with information about the military disposition of Sisera, the commander of the forces of the King of Canaan. Sisera's forces were routed and thus Deborah, using psychic intelligence, played a pivotal role in the conquest of the Promised Land.

Even in the New Testament, prophecy and visions played an important role as the messianic plan unfolded. Saint Paul offered some advice on prophecy that modern people might well take to heart. "Do not scoff at those who prophesy, but test everything that is said to be sure if it is true, and if it is, then accept it," he advised church members in Thessalonica.

Prophecy also figured largely in ancient Greek literature from Homer to Aristophanes—and in Greek history as well. According to the Greek historian Herodotus, King Croesus desired to learn strategic military information from the available prophets and oracles. But he was skeptical and wanted to assure himself of their accuracy. So about the year 550 B.C., Croesus conducted the first recorded test of psychic abilities. He sent messengers to the top seven oracles of his day with instructions to approach the oracles exactly one hundred days after their departure. They were to ask the oracles to describe what the king was doing on that day. On the appointed day, Croesus chose an unkingly activity—he cooked up a stew of lamb and tortoise using a bronze kettle.

Only the oracle at Delphi correctly reported the king's activity, stating,

> *"Can I not number all the grains of sand, and measure all the water*
>   *in the sea?*
> *Tho' a man speak not I can understand;*
> *Nor are the thoughts of dumb men hid from me.*
> *A tortoise boiling with a lamb I smell:*
> *Bronze underlies and covers them as well."*

King Croesus, having satisfied himself of the Delphic oracle's accuracy, asked if he should cross the Halys mountains and attack Cyrus of Persia. The oracle replied, "When Croesus has the Halys crossed, a mighty empire will be lost." Croesus, thinking his plans were promised success, attacked Cyrus. But Croesus was defeated and it was his "mighty empire" that was lost. This experience attests to both the problem of correctly interpreting psychic information and correctly relaying that information.

Such accounts continued throughout history. Joan of Arc was a visionary and diviner who used her power of supernatural sight to great advantage during her battles to liberate France from the English.

But the visions of Saint Joan pale when compared to the most famous of medieval seers—Michel de Nostredame, better known to history as Nostradamus. Nostradamus, already well respected in his own time as a physician and scientist, assured his place in history as a prophet by the publication of his book *Centuries* in 1555, which included accurate predictions even to naming future leaders such as "PAU, NAY, LORON"—a fairly obvious anagram for NAPAULON ROY, Napoleon the King—Franco as a leader of Spain, and a Germanic tyrant Nostradamus called HISTER.

There was a legitimate reason for such word games. Due to the zeal of the Inquisition, Nostradamus was forced to use a skillful combination of puns, anagrams, and scientific and astrological jargon to prevent his arrest as a practitioner of witchcraft. Actually, Nostradamus, whose family included men educated in both the Christian and Jewish traditions, became a devout Christian and always attributed his prophetic insight to powers given by God.

While admittedly there is no certain interpretation of all of Nostradamus's writings, his predictions have been uncannily correct in many instances, enough so that everyone who has studied the French seer at any length has realized that his accuracy rating went far beyond any simple trick or ingenious interpretation.

In *Centuries*, Nostradamus described how he gained his prophetic insights. He would closet himself at night in a secret study and place a cup of water on a brass tripod. After quieting his mind, Nostradamus would stare into the water until, acquiring a meditative state, he would see visions of the future. This method is strikingly similar to that devised for remote viewing.

A more modern parapsychological researcher was Charles Richet, a member of the Society for Psychical Research founded in 1882. A professor of physiology at the University of Paris medical school and a Nobel Prize winner, Richet studied clairvoyance by having subjects identify playing cards placed in opaque envelopes, thus pioneering the methods later used by the well-known psychic researcher J. B. Rhine.

Joseph Banks Rhine and his wife, Louisa, both became heavily involved in psychic research at Duke University in Durham, North Carolina. The thrust of the Rhines' experimentation was initially statistical. Using specially designed cards, hundreds of subjects would try to guess which card would come up next. The Rhines and their associates had by 1932 clearly demonstrated the existence of psychic phenomena. Rhine applied the term "extrasensory perception" (ESP) to his findings. But, perhaps more importantly, he had demonstrated that ESP involved natural relationships in the same manner as ordinary psychological phenomena.

From 1927 until J. B. Rhine's death in 1970, the husband-and-wife team produced a prodigious quantity of scientific papers demonstrating the existence of both ESP and psychokinesis (PK), the ability to move physical objects. This exciting research into psychic phenomena was presented in dry papers with titles such as "Experiments Bearing on the Precognition Hypothesis: Pre-shuffling Card Calling" and "A Review of the Pearce-Pratt Distance Series of ESP Tests."

The Rhines did have their fair share of critics. Yet over the years they quietly, yet steadfastly, answered every criticism that came up. In 1940, the Rhines, along with other parapsychologists, produced a book entitled *Extra-Sensory Perception After Sixty Years*, a compendium of psychical research up to that time. The research in this book was so careful and scientific that the book became assigned reading for introductory psychology classes at Harvard for the 1940–41 academic year.

Even the most cursory look back over the historical record of psychic phenomena should convince the most ardent skeptic that there is definitely something beyond the five human senses at work. Louisa Rhine wrote in 1967, "The ESP process has revealed itself, or enough of itself, in the studies of parapsychology so far made, that a consistent outline of it can now be seen. Naturally, because parapsychology as a science is very young, knowledge about this process is still far from being complete. No doubt it will be a long time before many of the puzzles it presents can be fully resolved. Even so, there is little question that the outline of its progress as traced from the deep unconscious into the consciousness is a true one. . . ."

Psychic research continued despite objections within the orthodox scientific community, and much headway was made. Techniques such as "ganzfield" sensory deprivation experiments and "meta-analysis" or an all-inclusive study of psychic experiments proved successful in proving the existence of psychic phenomena. "Several lines of parapsychological research are undoubtedly producing consistent, reliable effects that cannot be attributed to chance, poor methodology, or the vagaries of a few experimenters or unusual studies," noted Dr. Richard S. Broughton, a former president of the International Parapsychological Association.

One of those researchers who produced consistent and reliable effects was New York artist/scientist Ingo Swann, who had experienced psychic incidents since childhood. In the early 1970s, Swann met with Cleve Backster, a New York polygraph operator who in 1966 had made the amazing discovery that plants hooked up to the polygraph machine registered responses to outside stimuli just like humans.

His finding—now termed the "Backster effect"—was the object of an immensely popular 1973 book entitled *The Secret Life of Plants*. After finding that any living tissue, including even the bacilli of yogurt, exhibited reactions on his graphs, Backster concluded, "Sentience does not seem to stop at the cellular level. It may go down to the molecular, the atomic and even the subatomic. All sorts of things which have been conventionally considered to be inanimate may have to be re-evaluated."

Swann worked in Backster's lab for about a year. Backster's work, verified and augmented by other scientists around the world, convinced Swann that something very real was transpiring on a psychic or subconscious level.

By the end of 1971, Swann was engaged in psychic experimentation with Dr. Karlis Osis and his assistant Janet Mitchell at the

American Society for Psychical Research (ASPR) in New York. This work was done under the auspices of Dr. Gertrude Schmeidler with the Department of Psychology at the City College of the City University of New York and a board member of ASPR. The results of this experimentation were generally good, with more "hits" than "misses."

But, on at least two occasions, the tests resulted in something quite extraordinary. On March 3, 1972, the target box had been lined with white paper and Swann reported that there was printing on a portion of the paper. The tester commented that this test was a "miss" because there was no printing on the paper. "To everyone's chagrin, when the box was taken down and inspected, there was the printing just as I felt I had seen," recalled Swann. It seems the person lining the box had missed the printing.

In another instance, Swann was valiantly trying to view the inside of a lighted box, but all he perceived was darkness. "The goddamned light is out over the target," he shouted to the testers, who replied, "Impossible!" However, when one of the monitors climbed a tall ladder to reach the target box, it was discovered that the light had indeed gone out, just as Swann had perceived. With results like this, Swann's psychic ability began to flower and the concept of remote viewing drew nearer.

Viewing Remotely

It was during this work for Dr. Schmeidler and Dr. Osis that Swann and Mitchell first used the term "remote viewing." "It was coined to identify a particular kind of experiment—not a particular kind of psi ability," Swann later wrote. "I suggested that we call [these experiments] 'remote-sensing.' Shortly, though, it became clear that I didn't just sense the sites, but experienced mental-image pictures of them in a visualizing kind of way. Without at all thinking much about it, and before the end of 1971, we began referring to the long-distance experiments as remote-viewing ones, since this term seemed the most suitable."

During this time Swann learned of a proposal from Dr. Harold E. Puthoff, a physicist at Stanford Research Institute (SRI)—now called SRI International—in Menlo Park, California. Puthoff wanted to study basic research into quantum biology and had no interest in psychic phenomena. But, after several conversations with Swann, both men agreed to test remote viewing, but only under the strictest scientific protocols. This began nearly twenty years of remote viewing study at SRI. It was "the most severely monitored scientific experiment in history," according to Jack Anderson investigator Ron McRae.

During his time at SRI, Swann devised a method of using coordinates to determine a remote viewing target without telling the viewer what was at the location in advance. By giving a viewer the name of a target—such as the Eiffel Tower—the viewer automatically could draw on memory and his own imagination to produce a picture of the target.

"I did some experiments at the ASPR in which I moved my viewpoint to some remote location and described what was there. That was fun to do and the studies were statistically significant," Swann recalled. "I said I think I could look anywhere in the world if you just gave me some coordinates like latitude and longitude. Let's design an experiment around that!"

And with that suggestion, coordinate remote viewing moved into the SRI laboratory. At first it was hit and miss. But in a final run of ten coordinate remote viewing tests, Swann was given seven "hits" by independent judges and only one clear "miss" indicating that, like his experience at the ASPR, his ability improved as he went along.

Swann would simply be presented a set of coordinates and he would describe what he "saw" at those coordinates. A world atlas would be consulted—*National Geographic* was found to be an excellent reference source—and the researchers would get immediate feedback. The Australian desert, Madagascar, Hong Kong, Borneo, the Great Salt Lake, Mount Shasta, the Yukon, and the Indian Ocean were just a few of the sites given to Swann only as coordinates.

In a 1993 interview, Swann said there was one particular remote viewing session that convinced him of the reality of the phenomenon. "They were using a wall map to get their coordinates," he recalled. "Now this map had a picture of Lake Victoria in Africa, so they plunked a coordinate down right in the middle of the lake. I reported a land-water interface, a peninsula getting narrow here, etc. They said, 'Well, that's not correct,' and I said, 'It has to be correct, I mean that's what I saw.' I told them that the wall map ratio was pretty small and suggested that we consult a bigger map of Lake Victoria.

"So away we went and jumped in the car. We went over to a bookstore and Hal had to plunk down $110 for this huge atlas. We opened it right away, right there in the store, and there in Lake Victoria, on this larger-scale map, was a land peninsula sticking out with a narrow point. Bingo! There was the coordinate right over it. They didn't know that—nobody knew that. I said, 'Okay, Hal, this is what I'm going to offer the client as a repeatable experiment. Believe me, it is repeatable.' So that is how it got started."

Their chief "client" proved to be the Central Intelligence Agency. CIA officers were responding to the public's reaction to a 1970 book entitled *Psychic Discoveries Behind the Iron Curtain* by Shiela Ostrander and Lynn Schroeder. This books postulated that the United

States was lagging behind the Soviets in psychic research based on the authors' tour of the Soviet Union and Eastern Europe.

According to Puthoff, two CIA men approached him at SRI in 1972. "They knew of my previous background as a Naval Intelligence Officer and then civilian employee at the National Security Agency several years earlier, and felt they could discuss their concerns with me openly," Puthoff recalled. "There was, they told me, increasing concern in the intelligence community about the level of effort in Soviet parapsychology being funded by the Soviet security forces; by Western scientific standards the field was considered nonsense by most working scientists. As a result they had been on the lookout for a research laboratory outside of academia that could handle a quiet, low-profile classified investigation, and SRI appeared to fit the bill. They asked me if I could arrange an opportunity for them to carry out some simple experiments with Swann, and, if the tests proved satisfactory, would I consider a pilot program along these lines? I agreed. . . ."

This remote viewing study—dubbed Project SCANATE (SCANning by coordinATE)—proved so successful that CIA funding continued until 1976, when the psychic program was taken up by the U.S. Army's Intelligence and Security Command (INSCOM). More than a dozen military intelligence officers were trained using protocols developed at SRI and, in 1976, were formed into Detachment G, also known as Project GRILL FLAME, located at Fort Meade, Maryland. Over the years, the project was variously known as CENTER LANE, SUN STREAK, and STARGATE.

This unorthodox military unit of psychic operatives—or psi spies—was the creation of Maj. Gen. Ed Thompson, then the army's assistant chief of staff for intelligence. "I became convinced that remote viewing was a real phenomenon, that it wasn't a hoax," recalled Thompson. "We didn't know how to explain it, but we weren't so much interested in explaining it as in determining whether there was any practical use to it."

Although apparently never utilized as a primary intelligence source—prejudice among ranking officers against anything psychic remained strong—remote viewing was used to locate enemy military installations, rocket-launching sites, and submarines. In the Gulf War, it was used in an attempt to locate Saddam Hussein's biochemical weapon stockpiles.

It was learned that multiple viewers strengthened the accuracy of any remote viewing. The more viewers involved, the more reliable the information, just as at an auto accident scene where a synthesis of eyewitness testimony generally produces near 100 percent accuracy.

That the army, and later the DIA, believed there were credible and practical benefits to be gained from remote viewing is attested to by the fact that both RV studies and the operational psi spies unit were continued until mid-1995. Then, following the abrupt and unusual cancellation of a major book on the subject, the CIA first admitted its role in psychic research. Although the story was covered on ABC-TV's *Nightline* and the Washington newspapers, little or no coverage of the remote viewing story made it into local media. The American public remains largely ignorant of the intense and lengthy government study of this psychic phenomenon and its use as an intelligence tool.

A CIA-commissioned report issued on September 29, 1995, by the American Institutes for Research tried to downplay the issue. While admitting that "a statistically significant effect has been observed in the recent laboratory experiences of remote viewing," the report writers nevertheless concluded that "continued support for the operational component of the current program is not justified." Echoing the position of the mainstream scientific community, the report stated, "To say a phenomenon has been demonstrated, we must know the reasons for its existence." In other words, if we don't know how something works, it must not be truly working. It was the old conflict of mind-sets all over again.

An official CIA statement swept the issue even further under the rug by claiming that the remote viewing program, "always considered speculative and controversial—was determined to be unpromising." What was not explained to the public was why this "unpromising" psychic program had continued under at least three separate government organizations and four presidents for more than a quarter of a century. The reason, quite simply, was that remote viewing works. Or as Puthoff stiffly put it in a formal report, "The integrated results [of the RV studies] appear to provide unequivocal evidence of a human capacity to access events remote in space and time, however falteringly, by some cognitive process not yet understood."

Another aspect of the psi spies program conspicuously absent from the media stories was that every remote viewer had, at one time or another, encountered UFOs in their mental searches. Initially ordered to locate high-flying, high-performance aircraft in order to view new Soviet technology, the psi spies were amazed to discover craft that did not originate on Earth.

The laboratory studies of remote viewing had demonstrated that the phenomenon is not limited by time or space. Some viewers were able to perceive persons at a specific location even before they arrived. And no amount of distance seemed to diminish the viewer's insights. It has been speculated that space exploration may be one of the most important and cost-effective applications of remote viewing.

A View from Space

The use of remote viewing in space exploration was confirmed in the early 1970s, when Ingo Swann recorded his impressions of various bodies in our solar system. His visions were taken lightly at the time, but later confirmed by various NASA deep space missions.

While undergoing endless tests with the SRI scientists, Swann grew eager for some diversion. "In the midst of this desperation during March, 1973, I noted with growing interest the approaching bypass of NASA's *Pioneer 10* spacecraft with the distant planet Jupiter. *Pioneer 10* would begin to send back data about Jupiter approximately December 3, nine months away. Wouldn't it be interesting if a psychic probe of Jupiter could be compared to the eventual feedback from *Pioneer 10*?" Swann mused.

Swann, in conjunction with another psychic, Harold Sherman, conducted a remote viewing of Jupiter on April 27, 1973. The recorded impressions of both Swann and Sherman were virtually identical.

Swann's description stated, "There's a planet with stripes. I hope it's Jupiter. I think that it must have an extremely large hydrogen mantle. If a space probe made contact with that, it would be maybe 80,000–120,000 miles out from the planet's surface. . . . Very high in the atmosphere there are crystals, they glitter, maybe the stripes are like bands of crystals, maybe like the rings of Saturn, though not far out like that, very close to the atmosphere. . . . Now, I'll go down through. . . . Inside those cloud layers, those crystal layers, they look beautiful from the outside. From the inside they look like rolling gas clouds—eerie yellow light, rainbows. I get the impression, though I don't see, that it's liquid. Then I came though the cloud cover, the surface looks like sand dunes. They're made of very large grade crystals so they slide. Tremendous winds sort of like maybe the prevailing winds of Earth but very close to the surface of Jupiter. From that view the horizon looks orangish or rose colored but overhead it's kind of greenish-yellow. If I look to the right, there is an enormous mountain range. . . . Those mountains are huge but they still don't poke up through the crystal cloud cover. . . . I see something that looks like a tornado. Is there a thermal inversion here? I bet there is. . . . I'll move more towards the equator. I get the impression that there must be a band of crystals similar to the outer ones, kind of bluish. They seem to be sort of in orbit, permanent orbit down through another layer farther down which are like our clouds but moving fast. . . . Tremendous wind. It's colder here. Maybe it's because there's not a thermal inversion there. . . . The atmosphere of Jupiter is very thick."

Crystal rings? An atmosphere? These were ridiculous concepts at the time. Even after the passage of *Pioneer 10*, there was not enough data to substantiate Swann's descriptions. SRI scientist Puthoff said, "In post-experiment discussions with astronomers, the consensus was that the results of our experiment were not at odds with either what was already known or what additional data were radioed back by the flyby, but no definite evaluation could be made either."

Full confirmation of Swann's descriptions did not come until six years later with the 1979 *Voyager 1* and *2* space probes.

Time magazine reported, "The most unexpected phenomenon, however, occurred when *Voyager* began detecting a stream of matter inside the orbit of Amalthea [one of Jupiter's satellites]. Fortunately, mission controllers had programmed the camera shutter to remain open for 11.2 minutes on the remote chance—no one took the possibility very seriously—that Jupiter had some kind of ring. To everyone's amazement, *Voyager's* time exposure produced a streaky image that the scientists could explain only as a ring of boulder-sized debris. The findings seemed so unlikely that the NASA team delayed making the information public for several days while the data were checked and rechecked. Saturn was long the only planet known to have rings and considered to be the only one that could have them. In 1977 that theory was shattered with the discovery of rings around the planet Uranus. Jupiter itself was surveyed earlier by the *Pioneer 10* and *11* spacecraft, but it is easy to see why no Jovian ring was found. Jupiter's is almost paper thin, perhaps 1 km (0.6 miles) high and impossible to view from earth."

But not impossible for Ingo Swann to have remote-viewed six years earlier. Many other Jovian features described by Swann were confirmed by the later NASA missions: the high winds, towering mountain ranges, and thick cloud cover.

On March 11, 1974, Swann made a mental trip to the planet Mercury in anticipation of the upcoming *Mariner 10* flyby. This remote viewing session was monitored by Dr. Janet Mitchell. Swann's comments were recorded, transcribed, notarized, and deposited by noon, March 13, with various parties, including the Central Premonitions Registry in New York.

He stated, "I guess I have to go in the direction of the Sun, so I can see the Moon in back of me. There we go. Do you suppose Mercury has—what shall we call it?—a magnetosphere. Like a circular sphere of magnetism, of magnetic belts around it, except with Mercury, they are not a sphere but on the sun side of Mercury, it is set closer to the planet's surface and on the far side of the planet, it is sort of pushed out into space. . . . Everything seems very clear. Oh, I don't know why! There seems to be a thin atmosphere, but it is not enough to—it doesn't make a blue sky like on earth, so you see blackness except where the sun is, maybe it is purple, I guess. There is not much haze. I get the impression of humidity—water. And tides, huge tides; liquid tides . . . as the planet turns, the sun creates waves of earth tides, so that the surface has lots of cracks and fissures. The gravity must be uneven, pulling more towards the sun at all times. I see clouds—electrical storms now. These clouds come and go very fast and they form sort of on the day side of the planet, on the two peripheries of the day side. I see rainbows that seem to leap up. They arch—they are more like auroras, I guess. On the surface there is both a liquid—it seems heavier than water—but liquid. It's water of some sort and land tides, both water tides and land tides and a fast condensation cycle. I guess that is what you would call it. This creates the leaping rainbows in all directions sometimes. It must have different gravities, depending upon which side you are on. It's beautiful—God, it's beautiful. . . . I see land masses, but they look waterwashed, as if the water just twirls around the planet all the time. . . . It seems a lovely little planet. There are differences in land masses, in a way mountainous, but not too mountainous. Everything looks chewed down, I guess because of the land tides. I'd say that the planet is characterized by sort of a low-keyed electric magnetic splendor. That's all."

Swann's detailed description of Mercury was thought to be a novel oddity by those few astronomers who read the report. After all, it was established dogma in scientific circles that Mercury had no atmosphere, no magnetic field, and no ionosphere.

The established view of the planet was overturned less than a month later when the *Mariner 10* flyby began producing man's first close-up photographic view of Mercury.

Science News reported, "Until last week, the majority of planetologists felt, with good reason, that Mercury was a pretty nothing planet. No atmosphere—the solar wind would blow it away—no magnetic field—the planet's slow rotation would not create the dynamo effect necessary to sustain one—no ionosphere—no magnetic field to trap the ionized particles—no moons. All in all a dull world. Now it is 'strange,' 'startling,' 'spooky,' and 'fascinating,' all thanks to a few days of observations by *Mariner 10*. The first spacecraft ever to fly by Mercury has taken close-up photos which reveal a heavily cratered surface and transmitted reams of surprising data that invalidates many of the theories about the sun's nearest and smallest planet."

One by one, Swann's remote viewing observations about Mercury were proven correct as the data from *Mariner 10* continued to come in. *Science News* reported, "A major surprise was the discovery that the supposedly airless world has an atmosphere. . . . The atmosphere is extremely thin, less than one hundred-billionth as dense as earth's . . . but is indisputably there. . . . The most significant discovery about the atmosphere . . . was the existence of a helium 'tail' streaming out from Mercury in a direction away from the sun. It was significant because shaping the tail was another unexpected Mercury feature, a magnetic field. . . . About 20 minutes before the spacecraft reached its closest distance to Mercury—about 466 miles—there were very clear signs of a bow shock, a shock front formed by the solar wind ricocheting off the planet's enveloping magnetic field, of which the moon has little or none. . . . There are definite signs of lava flows suggesting volcanic activity and long, not-too-twisted cliffs and fissures pointing to a planet with at least a somewhat active history."

A year later, Mercury's magnetic field was confirmed as *Mariner 10* again swung close to the planet. *Science News* reported, "Surviving a knuckle-whitening last-minute cliffhanger, the crippled *Mariner 10* spacecraft this week revealed that the magnetic field of Mercury, a complete surprise when the probe first detected it a year ago, is definitely the planet's own, intrinsic to Mercury, rather than something generated from outside by some complex interaction with the solar wind."

Swann had correctly identified Mercury's thin atmosphere, magnetic field, and the helium trail streaming out from the planet away from the sun. These observations were in direct contradiction to the scientific thinking of the time. Swann certainly didn't read about such planetary attributes beforehand.

Since the credibility of remote viewing in space appeared established by the Swann experiments coupled with scientific feedback, serious consideration must be given to the off-planet experiences reported by trained remote viewers. What sounds like the wildest fantasy to most of the public became the norm for these government-trained remote viewers. Knowing their superiors did not want to hear discomforting reports of UFOs and alien races, the psi spies created "Enigma Files" in which they accumulated their most extraordinary cases. It was a real-life forerunner of *The X-Files*. These cases involved remote viewing sorties that went far beyond Earth.

Their work continued even after leaving the military. In 1989, several of the military-trained viewers formed a private company named PSI TECH Inc. They planned to offer their remote viewing expertise to organizations and business. For several reasons—not the least of which was lack of capital—all but one of the military remote viewers had left PSI TECH by 1996.

One of PSI TECH's clients was the short-lived Center for

North American Crop Circle Studies in New Canaan, Connecticut, which was studying the crop circle phenomenon.

How to Make a Circle

In June 1992, five experienced remote viewers made a study of the mysterious crop circles, concentrating on a well-documented case at Barbury Castle near Marlborough, England. It was considered a particularly good case because the circles were outstanding in their geometric complexity and because witnesses heard pulsing hums in the air and saw flashing lights in the sky.

In a final report, their "Key Assessments" were that the crop circles are not symbols intended as a message to man, but rather signposts or reference marks produced by aliens moving in both space and time. "At least 12 different species of extraterrestrials, all from different points of origin, use and recognize these crop circles. Apparently a great deal of importance is attached to these pictographs because these vehicles often change direction after a flyby. Some stop in the vicinity of the circles for what appears to be communications checks," stated the report, adding that crop fields are selected as the medium for their messages because they are temporary. Apparently, the aliens don't want permanent marks that would draw the attention of scientists and the authorities. "This is not in the 'game plan' of these visitors, who are attempting to maintain a covert presence, as much as operationally possible."

According to the RV report, these circular marks, or similar ones, have been made for centuries, and their presence has been reflected in man's stories of the supernatural, like the idea of elves and their green rings, Navajo sand paintings showing sky "gods and circles, and the figures on the plain of Nazca. Strongly associated with these observing missions are indications that an intelligent agency is/has been intervening in human affairs at critical junctures," the report noted. "Certain key historic events seem to have been manipulated . . . [although it] is not determined whether the agencies responsible for producing the circles are themselves involved in this intervention, or are acting merely as observers/recorders."

However, at least one of the remote viewers who participated in the circle study said he got a different picture of the phenomenon than was reflected in the report. Lyn Buchanan said he had no idea he was supposed to be viewing the formation of crop circles. "Basically, I got the impression of a teacher and some students sitting at desks which moved in different patterns around the teacher. It was some type of flight school and they were doing touch-and-goes, but not on an airfield. Instead it was in tall grass. They would swoop down and stop at certain points which would leave these patterns in the grass. The circles were not messages, but simply the result of their maneuvers."

The report stated that to produce the crop circles, the aliens use two different devices, which may have been used separately or in conjunction with each other. One produces both heat and pressure waves that bend and twist plant stalks in different directions. It also produces a bursting effect within the plant's cells. The other is a rotating glowing globe, about fifteen inches in diameter, that produces a ray somewhat like a laser, but there is no transmission of energy. There are only energetic effects at the ray's target. This device disrupts and disables the molecular structure of the plant, which collapses and falls over. It accomplishes this with surgical, programmed precision, creating intricate designs in the crop. It is interesting to note that the description of these molecular changes perfectly matched recently published scientific studies indicating just such effects.

By the time of the crop circle report, the concept of aliens visiting the earth was nothing shocking to the military-trained remote viewers. All had experiences that took them far beyond our world.

"During early training sessions, I was aware that there was some sort of noise or interference—something outside the realm of my reality," recalled former army major David Morehouse, who entered the remote viewing unit in 1988. "I was told, 'You'll find out all about that later.'" Morehouse went on to have a wide variety of experiences beyond Earth. He described other planets in other solar systems as well as dimensions close to ours, all filled with beings both strange and wonderful.

Computer expert Lyn Buchanan said he was "blown away" by his first remote viewing attempt. "What I got was a tall flagpole with a large American flag on it," he recalled. "I saw it from the vantage point of standing on the wooden front porch of an abandoned dirty white house nearby. The windows had no curtains and I described a table with a gingham tablecloth I saw through the kitchen window. But then I was told that I had missed it—that the target had been a water tower.

"But when we drove out to the water tower to get my feedback, we found the water tower was blue with red and white stripes. I had viewed my feedback, not the target. And then we found nearby an abandoned dirty white house with a wooden front porch and no curtains on the windows and we could see a gingham tablecloth on a table in the kitchen. I was just overwhelmed by the experience but the most surprising thing was that I was the only one surprised by it. Everyone else—who had been remote viewing for some time—took it in stride."

Buchanan recalled the first time he remote-viewed into space. "It's just like viewing things on Earth," he said. "The first time I was given an ET [extraterrestrial] target I experienced bilocation—I call it perfect site integration—where the mind is so absorbed that the viewing experience seems real. I looked up and I was not in the room anymore but in the mouth of a cave looking out on a desert with mountains in the background. But the sky was too dark and the sun was too small. I realized that I was not on Earth. It dawned on me that only a second or two before I was in a remote viewing session. It scared me, and suddenly I was back in the room at Fort Meade."

Mel Riley, who was among the first members of the Grill Flame unit, also claimed to have visited other worlds and dimensions via remote viewing. To him, it's no big deal.

"It's interesting that a bunch of soldiers, GIs, started out with the skills to look inside of things and ended up doing these kinds of things," said Riley. "But all this has been such a part of my life for so long that it's just part of my life."

Linda Anderson, another experienced remote viewer who was trained by Buchanan, agreed. "There's no doubt in my mind that it works. But it took a while for me to think that I could really do it. I don't think of myself as a psychic. Now when strange things happen, I'm not surprised anymore," she said. "You want to say, 'Yep, it just works that way,' but it's still amazing. I thought it was amazing that you can be trained to do this." Anderson too said she has remote-viewed beyond Earth. "I did that in training sessions," she said, "but I never knew where I was until after the session. We just seem so small. There is so much out there in the universe."

The psi spies said it is difficult to concentrate on the day-to-day problems of Earth, once a person has traveled to other realms. "When you can go out and see the universe, who wants to go look at a Russian submarine?" quipped Riley.

"As remote viewers we went to places that were so beautiful. And that's about where your ability to describe it ends," Morehouse explained. "I guess one of the hardest things to fathom is that we are all so insignificant. We're just a small part of one dimension. And there are other dimensions, dimensions with countless worlds in them. Countless, I know that now. I've seen them. Our world is like one page—one thin page in a thick encyclopedia, an encyclopedia with volumes which stretch on forever. No beginning, no end. Worlds within worlds. Places so beautiful that we don't have the ability to describe them. You just can't imagine what it's like out there! We just don't have the ability to come back and describe to people what we've seen."

But Morehouse did describe one visit to an extraordinary place. It occurred during a remote viewing session in his home. Stretching out on his couch, he began the process of allowing his mind to relax and clear. "This is going to be an open search," he thought to himself. "I'm just going to let my mind go and see what's out there." Morehouse said he closed his eyes and felt his mind drifting on its own.

Suddenly he felt a faint yet familiar tearing. He had experienced this before during out-of-body sessions. It was the onset of bilocation. Opening his eyes, Morehouse found himself in a large chamber of light. He was standing directly behind three huge golden thronelike chairs covered with strange hieroglyphics. But what really caught his attention was the three giant beings that occupied the chairs. They wore great golden beards that flowed to their chests. They each wore large golden helmets. They looked to him like Greek gods.

One of the beings turned and looked right at him. He was petrified. He had no idea of where he was or if these beings were friendly. He wanted to run but had no idea where to go. The great golden man, for they all had the appearance of humans, looked at him, and Morehouse felt as though feelings were being projected into him. Without knowing why, he suddenly felt safe and secure. He somehow knew that these three creatures meant him no harm.

The one who had acknowledged his presence returned to his activity. "He knows I'm here, but he has nothing to say to me," Morehouse recalled thinking. "It would be like me noticing a fly on the wall and then going back to work on my computer. I'm not mad at the fly. I don't mean it any harm. I'm just indifferent to it."

Meeting no opposition, Morehouse slowly began shifting his attention to his right. Passing the end figure, he notice a great golden wall in front of the trio. The wall was filled with carvings in high relief, and there were humanlike creatures standing in front of it. The carvings or impressions were many and varied. Most were incomprehensible to Morehouse. But one looked like a depiction of a sun, a circle with stylized flames radiating out from it. The entire wall was radiant and golden.

After a short time, Morehouse noticed that the three golden men on the chairs seemed to be directing the people before them to touch certain portions of the wall. He decided the wall must be some sort of control panel, one that he couldn't come close to explaining or even understanding. But he was convinced that these people were running something by their work on this wall. As he stood in that strange place and tried to make sense of his surroundings, he was suddenly pulled away. Morehouse realized that his consciousness had returned to his body lying on the couch in the living room of his home.

He said he lay still for a long time, thinking about his experience. He had experienced many dreams and this definitely was not a dream. "I knew it. I felt it. My visit to the golden hall was as real as anything I had ever experienced in my life," he said.

One of the sights most fascinating to remote viewers who have soared through space is not the vehicles flying around with living beings inside, but towers located on airless worlds throughout the galaxy. They seem to be sort of relay towers. They claim these towers appear to fling vehicles beyond light-speed from one part of the galaxy to another, bypassing time and space. "There are technologies far ahead of us out there," commented Morehouse.

All of the psi spies said such wondrous visions only strengthened their religious beliefs. "Once you know, really know, that death is not the end of your existence, then you are truly liberated, truly free," said Morehouse. "The only thing I can imagine it being like is going into the presence of God and standing there in a four-dimensional world where you can go forward in time and backwards in time—everything at any given distance. Omniscient, omnipotent, that's how you become. That is the realm of God.

"We hear people stand in a pulpit and read words, saying God is omniscient, omnipotent and all knowing. And we sit back and say how the hell can you be that? But if you've been to a fourth dimensional world, then you see how that can be. I've seen it. Mel and the others have seen it."

Morehouse and Riley recounted an incident when the psi spies made an attempt to describe their experiences in the fourth dimension: "There was this funny time in the office one time. Mel and myself sat down with a block of butcher paper. We decided that we were going to describe a four-dimensional world. It didn't work," Morehouse recalled. "We tried to draw pictures. Then we tried to draw pictures on top of the pictures. Because in a fourth-dimensional world, every-thing is translucent, you can see inside everything. I could see inside my coffee cup in the fourth-dimensional world. We all had coffee in our hands. I was sitting right next to my familiar desk trying to describe this fourth-dimensional world where we had all been. Mel had a black marker in his hand, standing in front of the butcher paper. He was saying, 'Well, it sorta looks like . . . maybe try this . . . perhaps I could draw it this way. . . . Oh, screw it, let's go drink some beer.' It was hilarious. It just can't be done."

He added that the psi spies have learned that other dimensions apparently intersect with our own, so it is often unnecessary to "go out there" to experience these worlds.

A Dark Future

Unfortunately, all of the remote viewing experiences have not been as uplifting as Morehouse's visit to the golden room. Within the "Enigma

Files" are reports laden with foreboding. One of these has to do with the continuing problem with our ozone layer.

In March 1992, five remote viewers agreed to explore the ramifications of the ozone problem. Their contract came from the Institute for Human Potential, a think tank formed in honor of Senator Claiborne Pell, chairman of the Senate Foreign Relations Committee. Funding for the institute comes primarily from grants by Laurance Rockefeller.

"The outlook is grim," succinctly stated a cover letter with the final project report, which stated, "Atmospheric ozone depletion/replenishment was perceived to be driven by a natural ebb and flow process—a geophysical cycle. But this process has become overwhelmed by manmade activity. . . . The complex natural ozone cycles/patterns, in combination with the manmade alterations, make it extremely difficult for present scientists to figure out just what is happening. A long series of tests, research and small-scale experiments, using several types of chemicals, will be undertaken . . . but these efforts to stop the ozone decay will have little or no impact—they are only 'Band-Aid' approaches. A critical point is reached, circa 2005–2012, where the destruction will begin a runaway course, in a fashion analogous to metastasis—the transfer of malignant cells from one location to another. During this period, the problem—and its potential consequences—will no longer be subject to question. . . . The ozone decay will not necessarily be slowed down, but its effects temporarily ameliorated by coincidental volcanic activity, possibly as early as 1996. One such related event will be the explosion of an 'extinct' volcano in the North American Cascade chain. . . . The volcanic activity will literally and figuratively eclipse the ozone problem, but decreased sunlight will wreak havoc with crop production in many places. Chaotic weather patterns in combination with decreased sunlight will necessitate the construction of huge environmentally-controlled greenhouses, so that food production can carry on without being subject to vicissitudes of climate/weather. Unwittingly, these structures form the templates for technologies which will become increasingly critical to sustaining human life. They will begin to be seen as sanctuaries—then habitats, as society begins to 'migrate' into them. . . . A point is reached where very little life is seen outside of the artificial structures. The atmosphere outside these 'biospheres' is almost antiseptic. The sky is striated and multi-hued. Earth's remaining (surviving) inhabitants have either been driven underground or into these very large, climate-controlled domes which now house complete medium-sized cities. Our children's children are residents there.

There is no perceivable violence. Most creative energy is directed to questions of survival."

But the report goes farther into the future, indicating that humankind is not doomed.

According to the report, the human race will adapt to the new conditions and to living in domed cities. Although our bodies will become less attractive, they will be more durable. And there will be efforts to return plants and animals to the earth.

Lyn Buchanan was one of the viewers who worked on the ozone report. "I was tasked to find out what was needed to help the Earth recover," he recalled. "What I saw was there were far-sighted people who had taken samples of materials later killed by the ultra-violet rays. After the ozone was in recuperation, they reintroduced them into the environment. They had cultivated microbes—especially mosses and lichen—away from the harmful UV. This is something someone should be doing right now. As far as I know, no one is doing this."

Furthermore, the viewers foresee another race—not from Earth—joining us in the near future. "They were once endangered also and suffered similarly, but now serve as 'consultants,' friends, brothers from another place," stated the report, adding, "Eventually, the inhabitants jointly build very large generators which will produce molecules, not oxygen, that rise to 'seal' and form a protective layer, artificially restoring the Earth's atmosphere."

The truth of these dire predictions probably won't be known for several years, but the negativity of their view of the future did not deter the viewers from continuing to probe "Enigma" targets.

They claim to have answers where other researchers have only offered theories or raised questions because their remote viewing brings "direct knowledge," or as the old adage goes, "Seeing is believing." They also state that they are close to learning some long-sought answers regarding life beyond earth. They base these answers on continuing studies of UFOs, which they refer to as "aerospace anomalies."

Their quest began with NORAD (the North American Aerospace Defense Command), which has a number of satellites called DSPs (deep space platforms) more than five hundred miles out in space that monitor missile launches on earth. Using "over-the-horizon" radar technology, these deep space satellites can pick up the launch signal of any missile fired on the planet.

What the DSPs were not programmed to monitor were high-performance craft approaching the earth from deep space. These fast-moving objects became known as "fast walkers." NASA claimed they are merely small meteors called "boloids." But some of these "boloids" possessed characteristics suggesting they were of artificial origin. They accelerated, decelerated, and changed course. So the psi spies began taking a special interest.

Late in 1988, Riley recalled that their superiors brought them a satellite photograph to study. The photograph showed simply a glowing object. But remote viewing sessions indicated the object had humanoid people in it and it was hovering above a nuclear storage facility. Their impression was that these visitors were taking inventory of the number of armed warheads at this depot.

It didn't take long for the psi spies to realize that these "fast walkers" contained technology that was neither American nor Soviet. "We found they were 'man made' but not by anyone from around here," Morehouse said.

When the psi spies remote-viewed and tracked these objects back to their point of origin, they found they came from subsurface locations on our moon and from Mars and that they would come to rest in subsurface locations on Earth.

The psi spies did not tell anyone—even their own superiors— about their "Enigma" sessions because "everyone would think we had gone nuts, and because none of the intelligence services, particularly DIA, had any charter to study such things," said Morehouse.

He explained that initially the psi spies applied remote viewing against almost everything, willy-nilly, one target to the next—an abduction here, a sighting there, next a photograph of a moving object. Due to lack of systematic work, they were not able to form a broader understanding of the UFO phenomenon.

"We only now have some inklings into the agenda, but this is largely personal opinion, based on individual interpretation," said Morehouse.

Intergalactic Boat People

The psi spies then began to systematically study these visiting vehicles. As they continued to work with the "Enigma Files," their fascination increased. Remote viewers had to learn how to distinguish man-made objects from those of nature. Morehouse said man-made objects almost always deal with combustion technology and were easily distinguished by the viewers. On closer examination they began to classify other types of flying vehicles as alien in nature. Morehouse added that the psi spies were not able to closely study all of the vehicles they encountered in their psychic travels because there were just too many of them. "Many of these craft are just passing through," he said. "You might say they're just intergalactic boat people. We would probably be better off working on the problems of this world instead of making a big deal out of extraterrestrials."

Morehouse described remote viewing as very hard work. You look at one thing at a time. You don't get interested in the surroundings. Like a pilot on a bombing mission, the viewer is intensely thinking about the target. He said the entire subject of these vehicles and their occupants is much more complex and subtle than first thought and is very sensitive, as it has to do with potential contact between species.

Eventually, the psi spies accepted the idea of alien cultures and other dimensions as a matter of fact. "This is just part of the overall cosmos. They've always been here, before humans, and they will be there after we've gone," said Mel Riley. Lyn Buchanan concurred, pointing out that there are different confederations of aliens with many different agendas.

Amazing and unbelievable as all this must seem to many, there is now feedback on at least one of the psi spies' "Enigma" cases that strongly corroborates their claims.

This case concerned the Mars *Observer*, which vanished August 20, 1993, just as it was about to go into orbit around Mars. Both scientists and laymen had high hopes that the Mars *Observer* would transmit photographs back to Earth that might solve some of the Martian mysteries—such as the human "face on Mars" and the three symmetrical pyramids seen in NASA photographs.

The 5,672-pound Mars *Observer* spent eleven months traveling to our neighboring planet and was scheduled to go into orbit around Mars on August 24. The $980 million satellite was to begin a two- to six-year mission to map the planet in greater detail than ever before. It was to be the vanguard of several spacecraft not only from the United States but from Russia and Japan.

But contact was broken and the craft hasn't been heard from since. What happened?

NASA officials initially theorized that the probe's timing clock malfunctioned, making the onboard computer unable to process commands being radioed from the Jet Propulsion Lab. But as days passed and communication was never resumed with the craft, hopes dimmed of ever knowing precisely what happened to the Mars *Observer*.

But the psi spies knew.

Less than a week after the Mars probe was lost, remote viewers reported that the fate of the Mars *Observer* was identical to that of the Soviet *Phobos II*. In March 1989, the unmanned probe was lost just as it too was about to move into orbit around Mars. Communication was lost as *Phobos II* passed into the vicinity of Phobos, one of the two Martian moons. The Soviets issued a communiqué suggesting that the craft had spun out of control due to an erroneous ground command.

There the matter rested until mid-1991, when remote viewers formerly with the GRILL FLAME unit were commissioned by officials within the Russian space program to study the cause of *Phobos II's* disappearance. Six remote viewers were asked to view what really happened in the space near Mars in March 1989.

Their final report, entitled "Enigma Penetration: Soviet Phobos II Space Craft Imaged Anomaly," was issued on September 29, 1991. The report stated:

> Sometime after entering Martian orbit, the *Phobos II* space craft appears to have entered an "ADIZ" [Air Defense Interrogation Zone, an electronic zone which protects national boundaries] of sorts, triggering an ensemble of actions in response to its presence: A disc-shaped object, Object 1, arose from the planet's surface to meet the probe, briefly perused it, then returned to the surface. Another object, already in space, was also attracted. Object 2 moved into close proximity and, in an act having some similarity to an "IFF" [Interrogation, Friend or Foe aircraft transponder] query, directed a very powerful, wide, penetrating particle beam into the interior of the space craft. Shortly afterwards, Object 2 departed. The directed energy was neither reflected nor absorbed by the probe's skin. However, the beam inflicted serious damage upon the space craft's electronic components, altering or rearranging their material structure at the molecular level to such a degree that circuits became paralyzed, in turn rendering many systems dysfunctional. *Phobos II* attempted to "fix itself" but became even more paralyzed in the process, creating short circuits and locking up servo mechanisms. Continued ground commands caused chaos, exacerbating the already hopeless situation. Subsequently, *Phobos II* underwent a radical course change, *after* [emphasis in the original] which—in a totally random event—a small meteoroid administered the *coup de grace*, effecting catastrophic damage to the space craft. At no time did the viewers detect hostile intent in connection with the [re]actions of Objects 1 and 2. Moreover, unintentional damage notwithstanding, *Phobos II*—an "alien" object—seems to have merited merely passing interest and cursory inspection. There are certain perceptions attendant with viewing Objects 1 and 2 that persuade one to label them as "escort vehicle" and "navigational buoy" respectively. A parallel idea is connected with yet another object that viewers detected on the Martian surface during this project. This takes the form of a tall,

pyramid-shaped edifice which serves as a type of "corner reflector" or "glide path homing transponder," a passive navigational aid. It designates a site around which much or all of this activity seems to focus. In the vicinity of this marker, beneath the Martian surface, something is existing—something living—that is periodically visited by "others" on "caretaking" missions. Perceptions that are strongly connected with this resident life form include: ancient, marooned and desperation combined with associated ideas of tremendous tragedy, grief and pathos.

Once again the psi spies had produced a report that read like a science fiction story. And again, the question of feedback arose. Was there anything to prove the validity of what the viewers saw?

Ingo Swann, the father of remote viewing, urged caution when he stated, "In the case of the ET [extraterrestrial] thing, there may never be feedback. 'The public gets very excited. . . .' 'Oh gee, a highly-trained remote viewer is going to try to view the extraterrestrials.' I mean, there's a lot of sensational interest in that!" he commented. "But there is a bottom line. The bottom line says 'feedback,' and without that [the whole thing] could be a waste of time."

Swann's caution is well advised, but in this instance there was feedback—astounding feedback from the Soviets themselves. It first came from Alexander Dunayev, chairman of the Soviet space organization responsible for the *Phobos II* project. Dunayev announced that the doomed probe had photographed the image of a small odd-shaped object between itself and Mars. He suggested the object might have been "debris in the orbit of [Mars moon] Phobos" or even jettisoned parts from the spacecraft. His tone was anything but certain.

More detailed—and exciting—news came in December 1991, when Soviet cosmonauts visited the United States. Retired Soviet air force colonel and cosmonaut trainee Marina Popovich displayed to newsmen in San Francisco one of the last photographs received from the *Phobos II*. She said the photo was given to her by cosmonaut Alexei Leonov, a high official in the Soviet space program.

The photo showed the silhouette of an odd-shaped object approaching the spacecraft. Popovich said the picture was taken on March 25, 1989, in deep space near the Martian moon Phobos shortly before contact with the craft was lost. She said the object very well may have been an alien spacecraft but would not say so. "The reasons for its disappearance are unknown," commented Popovich. "The photo is only information for thinking . . . information for all kinds of decisions."

Several theories about the object in the photo were advanced; some thought it might be a small undiscovered Martian moonlet or simply a product of a *Phobos II* camera malfunction. Professor Emeritus James Harder of the University of California at Berkeley and former director of research for the Aerial Phenomena Research Organization, stated, "No one can answer precisely what it is."

The photographed object bore an uncanny resemblance to the object drawn in the remote viewer's *Phobos II* sketches. The remote viewers of PSI TECH saw the photo and its similarity to their vision as confirmation—feedback—of what they viewed months earlier. And if their account of the demise of *Phobos II* is correct, then serious attention must be given their statement that the same fate befell the Mars *Observer*.

"It appears that whoever is up there does not want us to know about them," commented Morehouse.

A "micrometeorite" was described by two separate remote viewers as delivering a *coup de grâce* to the *Phobos II*. This may have been no accident. The psi spies said it seems like all of the technology we put into space is scrutinized closely. If it would reveal alien activities, then it is decommissioned. They noted the similarity of fates between the *Phobos II* and the Mars *Observer* and the Titan 4 rocket, which blew up carrying a supersecret spy satellite in August of 1993.

That same month, we lost our newest weather satellite. The weather satellite, NOAA-13, was lost shortly after its launch on August 9, 1993, according to the Associated Press. The polar-orbiting satellite, designed to permit a view of the entire Earth during the course of one day, had been operating successfully until contact was suddenly lost, said officials of the National Oceanic and Atmospheric Administration. Later in 1993, on October 5, a new *Landsat 6* satellite was lost after being released 180 nautical miles from Earth from a Titan 2 rocket launched from Vandenberg Air Force Base. No once knows what happened to it.

An article in *Science News* said the loss of the *Landsat 6* would force both private companies and government agencies to rely on the *Landsat 5* satellite for images of Earth. The *Landsat 5*, which lost part of its ability to transmit data, was launched in 1984.

The Titan 4 rocket, carrying a top-secret military cargo, exploded moments after takeoff on August 2, 1993. According to *Space News*, the cause of the explosion was thought to have been linked to a solid rocket motor segment that had undergone repairs by the manufacturer.

A less mundane cause was cited in the same article. It stated, "But in a strange twist, [U.S. Air Force colonel and the Titan 4 program manager Frank] Stirling said he has been told that the Air Force video of the launch shows an unidentified object apparently striking the Titan at an altitude of about 110,000 feet, shortly before the rocket blew up. Stirling is not a member of the Air Force investigation team and has not seen the official Air Force video of the launch and the explosion. His office, however, is conducting its own investigation."

Remote viewers believe all of these mysterious space losses may be attributable to the same cause: small, faceted objects that remote viewers have seen dipping out of an earth orbit and striking man-made spacecraft.

These objects are described as "little multifaceted devices whose facets look like shiny, polished graphite." These devices, according to some viewers, measure eight inches wide by about twelve inches tall. They said there appears to be about fifty or sixty up there at any given time. Several military remote viewers who were familiar with top-secret projects contend these objects are not the "brilliant pebbles" of our Star Wars system. They are alien. They are hollow inside, and the faceted surface comes apart upon striking something, very similar to a fragmentation hand grenade.

One remote viewer who has seen these small objects is George Byers, a public affairs officer for a large corporation in the Southwest. Byers studied RV under a former military remote viewer.

In December 1993, four months after the Titan 4 disaster, Byers took a mental look at that event. "I ended up identifying what destroyed the missile," he said. "It was something like a small projectile, about fist sized. It was shiny and hit the missile. It was definitely not a natural object. It hit and burst apart like a grenade. I did get the very distinct impression that it was not made on earth and that it was directed at the Titan 4 for the purpose of destroying it. Whoever made this thing knew what they were doing. In other words, it accomplished the job for which it was intended."

The viewers saw that something illuminated the Titan 4, and one of these little devices detected that illumination. It then swung down out of orbit, accelerated, and punched through the Titan 4. There was no sign of a propulsion system. Some viewers said it certainly appears as if this planet is being kept in quarantine for some reason.

The concept of a quarantine, or embargo, of Earth is not limited to science fiction writers and remote viewers. Many reputable scientists such as James W. Deardorff with the Department of Atmospheric Sciences at Oregon State University have theorized about the possibility. In one scholarly article, Deardorff mused, "The arguments are . . . that our Galaxy is nearly saturated with extraterrestrial life forms, that our existence requires in hindsight that they were and are benevolent toward us, and that our lack of detection of them or communications from them implies that an embargo is established against us to prevent any premature knowledge of them.... Any sudden lifting of the embargo in a manner obvious to the public would cause societal chaos and possibly touch off a nuclear exchange, while any communications received via radio telescope would likely be either quickly confiscated by government agencies and not revealed to the public, or heavily censored.... It follows that any embargo not involving alien force must be a leaky one designed to allow a gradual disclosure of the alien message and its gradual acceptance on the part of the general public over a very long time-scale."

    Time senior writer Lance Morrow mused publicly, "Perhaps a master system of intergalactic ethics dictates that no planet may have contact with another until it has subdued its own self-destructive violence. Maybe the Earth is under a sort of quarantine."

    As if the idea of an imposed quarantine of Earth was not hard enough to swallow, some remote viewers have also talked about the Martians.

Men from Mars

Since its inception, members of the psi spies unit had come into mental contact with extraterrestrial vehicles and their occupants. On occasion they passed along information to various government intelligence and scientific agencies. These agencies challenged the viewers to locate some "ground truth," some tangible "alien" person or device that could be studied or a place where nonhuman activities could repeatedly be observed. Thus began a lengthy search that continued even after most of the psi spies left the military.

    Over time they began to differentiate between the various types of beings they encountered. They said many alien cultures had been noted but that there appeared to be three prominent groups involved with humanity. One was survivors of a calamity on Mars. They were material beings, humanoid in appearance, who worked with a second group—small gray creatures with large, luminous eyes who originally came from outside our solar system. Both used exotic technology in their activities.

    These "greys" were living creatures but without the ego-centered consciousness of humans. They related more to whales and dolphins than humans. There was a sense that these creatures were somehow artificially produced. There were indications that these "greys" may have played a role in the rescue and preservation of the Martian race.

The actual Martians were also material beings. They were glimpsed infrequently and seemed to include the pilots of the visiting craft. They were very interesting to the remote viewers because they could relate to them as soldiers. These beings had feelings similar to soldiers in an underdeveloped country. They had an attitude of smugness, being superior to the natives. Yet, there was no sense of hostility. They were on a peaceful mission.

A third group involved energy beings—termed "Transcendentals" by some of the remote viewers. Although energy beings with only the "idea" of form, these shapeless, phantomlike entities appeared able to manifest themselves in any way, shape, or form. They exist in other dimensions and therefore outside of our time. They can apparently "pop" into time at any point they choose, often carrying out operations in different times concurrently.

Unlike the humanoid aliens, these beings can perceive remote viewers looking at them. Further, they can affect the viewing to the point of editing the process. There appeared to be a tremendous amount of religious symbolism connected to the Transcendentals. For all intents and purposes, the descriptions, activities, nature, and capabilities of these beings matched the characteristics that Church fathers have attributed to "angels."

The Transcendentals often appeared to be teasing the remote viewers. They seemed to have access to all levels of human consciousness and appeared willing to reveal some details of their operations when confronted by human researchers who displayed an objective and open-minded attempt at understanding.

Morehouse said two separate reports from a Canadian consulting firm concerned "anomalous phenomena" in New Mexico, where some viewers thought they had located an underground Martian base as far back as 1984.

The first report, dated November 30, 1991, told of a trip to New Mexico by researchers, including at least one remote viewer. This was just one of more than a dozen visits to the site since its discovery through remote viewing. Various types of scientific equipment were used to study the area, including a very sensitive portable spectrum analyzer, two battery-powered, twelve-channel strip chart recorders, a portable scintillometer, and a portable broad-beam microwave peak detector. These instruments were set up and monitored over the course of one night.

"Main tests were halted at 06:30," stated the report. "Although this was deemed to be well outside the normal optimal viewing time for the phenomena, it is believed that significant observations were recorded."

According to the report, the monitoring equipment recorded short bursts of high-amplitude microwave signals that may have been the residue from some sort of propulsion process. Investigators heard a high-frequency squeal that they could not pin down and saw an extremely bright white object low in the western sky about 3:30 in the morning. It winked off and on several times before disappearing. They felt it was an artifact of some sort of propulsion process. "The data presented above support the contention that an unusual but discernible and measurable phenomenon is manifest at the site in question," concluded the report.

Investigators found further strange events taking place at the site during another visit on June 26, 1992. A report on this visit again noted various anomalies and concluded, "The observations present a continually challenging enigma. . . . Each trip to the site appears to supply us with more pieces to the puzzle. It's as if we are being shown just enough to keep us interested in the site."

According to remote viewers, this issue has been studied since 1984. Since that time they developed enough data to formulate an astounding, but incomplete, picture of an ancient Martian civilization—one that predates ours by millions of years. They claim to have seen their structures on the surface of Mars. They also knew that the Russians have had a continued interest in this matter.

An account of Mars's history, based on remote viewing sessions by multiple viewers and public statements, indicated that in the far distant past—about sixty-five million years ago—a passing body in space, perhaps a meteor or small moon, caused a cataclysm on both Mars and the earth. This object struck the earth and the resulting devastation apparently caused the extinction of the dinosaurs.

This same object sideswiped Mars, ripping away most of its atmosphere. The resulting atmospheric disturbance produced tremendous storms and volcanic eruptions on the planet's surface for many years and eventually caused a complete loss of the atmosphere. As conditions worsened, Mars's humanoid inhabitants were forced to build increasingly stronger communal shelters, first on the surface and then later underground. When it became apparent that their atmosphere had deteriorated beyond the point of regeneration, the surviving Martians began working with small "grey" aliens, who helped place them in hibernation using technology far beyond what we have developed. It was similar to people today who have themselves placed in cryogenic suspended animation to await new technologies that may cure their health problems.

One group of Martians managed to leave their planet in search of sanctuary. It appears they came to Earth during prehistoric times.

They found that Earth's surface conditions were not hospitable, but food was available and survival was possible. This group went deep underground, where conditions were similar to those they had become accustomed to on Mars.

There are continuing visits here by Martian space vehicles that come from deep space and vanish, only to reappear on landing pads within these subsurface bases. These bases appear to be standby shelters, storage sites, and operations centers located mostly in caverns, although some are under the sea. These shelters exist on both planets and are mostly insurance against another planetwide catastrophe.

These Martians are angry at us right now, according to one report. They've been waiting centuries for human civilization to advance to the point where our technology might be able to help them in their plight. They hoped to join with us in inhabiting the earth. But, today, while both our technology and our consciousness have risen to a point where the two races might work together, we humans have almost wrecked this world through pollution and deforestation. The Martians see no humor in the irony of being forced to abandon their planet due to cosmic accident, and now seeing their hopes for Earth being dashed due to our primitive ignorance.

This situation may explain why the remote viewers say the Martians consider humans to be inferior to themselves, much as most adults tend to discount the worth of children. But they also realize that mutual cooperation between the races might vastly improve both's survival prospects. They are also well aware that man's technology has reached the capability to categorically detect their activity. They are taking steps to postpone this eventuality.

Asked if these Martians are trying to take over the earth, Morehouse replied, "We don't think so. If that was their purpose, they could have done it years ago, before we developed the technology to resist. I think they are biding their time, hoping that human consciousness will evolve enough to accept the idea of sharing the planet with them. I mean, look how the races of man can't get along. What would happened if everyone suddenly became aware that Martians were among us? No, I think we still have further to travel on the evolutionary scale."

Some of the viewers believe that, for now, the Martians are simply using the earth for necessary raw materials. That's where the UFOs come in. Many are shuttle craft used to transport certain chemical fertilizers—especially potash—plasticizers, milk, and other natural resources back to the survivors on Mars. This work is being done with the assistance of specialized organic beings that have become known as the "greys."

Several remote viewers claim the Martians are not responsible for human abductions. They state that Martian activity on Earth is not connected with the abductions, which appear to be a much more esoteric—even metaphysical—experience involving the Transcendentals.

However, the greys do seem to be somewhat involved in abductions. They appear to be assisting the Martians, yet are also responsible for certain human abductions. The impression received by some viewers is that they may be members of some sort of intergalactic Red Cross—or, more correctly, they seem to be conducting something akin to an oversight role, like a United Nations peacekeeping force.

According to some remote viewers, the greys are working to save the Martians, who have underground bases on Mars and Earth and who are being monitored by the Transcendental energy beings. They all apparently interact. But there's little doubt that the Transcendentals are the ones in charge—at least on Earth missions. They, in turn, seem to be carrying out orders from some controlling authority located at a distant point beyond our own galaxy. It's as if they have a job to do and they are doing it with scant regard to our presence or desires. They seem very professional.

The theme of this synthesis of remote viewing reports was echoed in 1996 with the publication of *Cosmic Voyage* by Dr. Courtney Brown, an associate professor of political science at Emory University in Atlanta, who studied remote viewing under a former member of the army's psi spies unit. After several RV sessions, Brown wrote, "There *are* [emphasis in the original] Martians on Earth, but one must think clearly about the implications of this before ringing the alarm bell. These Martians are desperate. Apparently they have very crude living quarters on Mars. They cannot live on the surface. Their children have no future on their homeworld. Their home is destroyed; it is a planet of dust."

George Byers also came face-to-face with Martians during his remote viewing training. "I was a total skeptic," Byers recalled. "I remember thinking, 'Why am I doing this? I'm wasting my time. I could be out mowing the yard.' But then, real late in my training, I was put in front of a Martian. He was stocky with a sunken, wizened face, dark complexion and Mongoloid or Indian features—a Fu Manchu type of face. I didn't know who this was. I just kept describing him until the session ended. Then I learned my target—'Martians—present survivors.' I was confident enough [in my remote viewing] by this time to just accept what I saw. I was eye-to-eye with a Martian high priest. It's hard to sell others on this, but I'm sold on it myself. There's no longer any doubt in my mind."

Interestingly enough, new thinking in science appeared to support the remote viewers' incredible claims of Martian life. Christopher P. McKay, a planetary astronomer in the Space Sciences Division of NASA's Ames Research Center in Moffett Field, California, wrote, "Results from recent studies point more and more toward an early Mars that was astonishingly like the early Earth when life gained foothold here. . . . The *Viking* results strongly suggest that no life exists on the surface of Mars today; it is too dry, too cold, and too oxidizing. But the *Viking* landers only scratched the surface—both literally and figuratively—in their search for life on Mars. Underneath the surface it may be possible for liquid water to exist and persist for long periods of time. After all, the outflow channels offer direct evidence that liquid water has been present in subsurface aquifers on Mars throughout most of its history. . . . To get to the evidence for life on Mars we will have to dig deep into the surface. This is true whether we search for fossil evidence of past life or try to reach present forms in their subsurface habitats."

In mid-1996 the study of a four-billion-year-old rock believed to have originated on Mars revealed microscopic forms providing compelling evidence to support the concept of life on the red planet. NASA administrator Daniel S. Goldin announced that a team of scientists "made a startling discovery that points to the possibility that a primitive form of microscopic life may have existed on Mars more than three billion years ago." Goldin, well aware of the current clash of mind-sets regarding extraterrestrial life, quickly added, "These are extremely small, single-cell structures that somewhat resemble bacteria on Earth. There is no evidence or suggestion that any higher life form ever existed on Mars."

Despite at least one scientist calling this proof of life "unequivocal," the debunkers responded appropriately. As NASA announced plans to launch further missions to Mars in an effort to validate the findings, a spokesman for Taxpayers for Common Sense said, "Here come the space spin doctors with a billion-dollar bacteria boondoggle."

Some mainstream scientists were typically hesitant to embrace the concept of Martian life but clearly understood the significance of the issue. "If the results are verified, it is a turning point in human history," said astronomer Carl Sagan. Others were more casual. Harvard paleontologist Stephen Jay Gould commented, "E.T. is a 12. A bacterium is a 1.7. It's so unsurprising. It's not evoking in me and most paleontologists any wondrous new thoughts because we've been well aware of the likelihood that Mars was inhabitable for at least a billion years of its history."

Religious leaders fell into predictable camps concerning the discovery of bacteria fossils in the Martian rock, which was discovered in 1986 by a scientific expedition to Antarctica. "I don't see it as a big obstacle to religious thought," said Minnesota theologian and physicist Ian Barbour. "To be sure it's a further displacement of humanity from a unique status, but we've been facing that for a long time." Speaking on behalf of Christian fundamentalism, Jerry Falwell pronounced, "They can spend a trillion dollars looking for it [intelligent life] but they'll never find it. The Bible makes clear that Jesus Christ is the only mediator between God and Man."

Author Kim Stanley Robinson, who has written extensively about the possible colonization of Mars, said, "It might take a few days, a few weeks, even a few decades for this to sink into the popular culture. But when this sinks in, anyone who believes in the scientific method will see the thousands of stars in the night sky in a whole new way. They'll be looking at a universe just stuffed with life. If it happened two times in this one solar system, it means life is very common in the universe."

The evidence for previous life on Mars was hailed as a "stunning" discovery by the mainstream media. But for the many people who have claimed this for years—including the remote viewers—it was just further scientific substantiation for what they have known all along.

The Trouble with Remote Viewing

However, none of this means that government-developed remote viewing can be considered 100 percent reliable. From a scientific point of view, the technology is just too new. And individual beliefs and interpretations can cloud perceptions.

One problem with the remote viewing of Courtney Brown, for example, is that he was tutored by Maj. Edward Dames (U.S. Army, Ret.), a former member of the army's GRILL FLAME unit. Dames provoked controversy within the UFO research community after publicly stating his views on UFOs, which included the idea that Martians are a dying race, some of whom are hibernating in a New Mexico cavern. At a 1992 conference in Atlanta, Dames shocked his audience by stating that the 1947 Roswell incident never happened. According to Dames, it was actually "brain wave entrainment—something akin to electromagnetically-induced mass hypnosis" that aliens generated as an experience that seemed 'real' to the human participants." Dames did admit that this was his personal opinion based on "a cursory probe." Later, other military-trained remote viewers disputed this claim, stating that based on their experiences, the Roswell incident appeared to have been based on real events.

Amid this dissent, further credibility was lost in early 1993 when Dames publicly stated his hopes that he might facilitate a meeting with the Martians in New Mexico. "We want the face to face," he told UFO writer Antonio Huneeus. "If we don't have it by the end of August, we're getting out of the UFO game." It didn't happen.

Ingo Swann continued to express reservations about placing undue emphasis on the results of RV sessions, particularly when it involved UFOs. "If parapsychology is the illusive science, then clearly UFOlogy is virtually the 'Feedbackless Science'—with the true exception so far of the hundreds of camcorders that have filmed UFOs," he wrote. "To my knowledge, UFOs and ETs do not cooperate with humans regarding our efforts to substantiate anything about them.

"Those alleging themselves to be remote viewers, then, cannot simply 'remote view,' but are obligated also to show positive evidence of the 'viewings'—e.g. positive feedback. Without the feedback, such 'viewers' are merely offering unsupported accounts that may or may not be of psychic origin," he added.

In 1996, writer Michael Miley spent considerable effort researching the remote viewing story. After studying remote viewing literature, Miley attacked the claims of both Dames and his pupil, Courtney Brown. He reported that Joe McMoneagle, one of the original psi spies, had contradicted many of Dames's statements regarding his remote viewing experience. McMoneagle stated that Dames was never commander of the psi spies unit and, in fact, was simply a monitor, never a remote viewer, and had no connection with the research portion of the program.

Miley concluded that the Martian story from Dames and Brown was "scientifically dubious" and was the result of "front-loading"— where the biases and knowledge of the monitor are passed along consciously or unconsciously to the viewer. "Ed Dames, a monitor and trainer with publicly professed views on aliens and UFOs, trains Courtney Brown on a pool of targets that they both select beforehand," he explained. "Brown, while still in training and with no publicly documented profile of accuracy on mundane 'real' targets, turns his brand-new skills to metaphysical, unverifiable ones. Together, they gather their 'data.' After initial sessions, they have lunch together and worry over the fate of the aliens, based solely on the result of their RV findings—despite the lack of concrete feedback."

"My conclusion is a sad one," Miley wrote. "I began this project in search of a new paradigm for researching UFOs and aliens—and I found it. It had been carefully developed over 24 years by a group of dedicated people—though it wasn't used primarily on anomalous targets. What I then found was a couple of space cowboys, drunk in the heart of the temple, destroying the covenant."

Perhaps lost in the controversy and contradictions in this issue is the fact that no one with direct knowledge of the CIA/army/DIA remote viewing program has denied that UFOs and aliens were perceived by all concerned. It seemed that only Dames and Brown had the intemperance to speak about it openly. Others have been more circumspect.

But the consistency of descriptions of remote-viewed life on other worlds and the UFOs visiting Earth passed far beyond the possibility of simple coincidence. It created the appearance of factual reporting. For example, in 1988 Mel Riley gave a description of what he termed "Galactic Headquarters" that eerily matched a description from an unconnected source given years later.

Galactic Federation Headquarters

Riley said one of the factors that prevented the remote viewers from understanding the agenda behind their off-world experiences was the inability to relate them. "It all sounds far-fetched because none of us has the ability to describe the things we've seen beyond Earth. We just don't have the words," he explained. "But we did get the definite feeling that all is not chaos. There is a method to what is going on.

"We thought that we might better understand by going straight to the controlling authority, you know, going from the top down rather than the other way. The complexity is just too great at our level, the bottom levels. We already had done considerable remote viewing, backtracking spacecraft and such. We knew that the controllers were outside our galaxy. We also knew there was many types of races out there and that there was some sort of federation. So, just for lack of a better word, I tagged on the term 'galactic,' meaning that it encompassed all the nearby galaxies. It was just a concept. We wanted to see this controlling authority, so we simply termed it 'galactic federation headquarters.'"

Riley recalled his experience, which was recorded in a report dated January 13, 1988. "Well, after starting my remote viewing, I began to bilocate, to really experience it," he said. "Soon I was sailing along, not really knowing where I was. I began describing terrain and then a structure. This was definitely a physical place in whatever dimension I was in. From one mile overhead, the view was dark, black and empty—a feeling of nothingness. Upon descending, I got the impression of very high, very rugged peaks. There was a flat, plateau-like area and below this, a blue body of water that seemed to be surrounded by a flat, open, grassy plain. It reminded me of pictures of Lake Titicaca.

"Then I got the impression of a round structure located on the flat top of what seemed to be something like a mesa. There were streaking rays, like sun streaks, emanating from, or going into, this structure. I wound up going into this structure through some sort of inclined passageway, like a causeway. And I was moving forward through this place. It was dark and cool and seemed to be made of rough stone, like a cavern. At the end of the causeway was a long, dimly-lit, rectangular corridor constructed of smooth, dressed stone on all sides.

"At the end of the corridor was a steep incline with a very high ceiling. This corridor ended in a large room with a very high, vaulted ceiling. It appeared man-made because it was squared off—you know, corners and angles and things of that nature. Now I've never been in a pyramid, but it reminded me of that kind of thing.

"There was a polished-stone platform in this room, like a slab or altar. And, for some reason, I had the urge to walk up there and lie down on this slab. There were these white-robed people—entities, that is—standing in a semicircle to one side. Some of them were in a line, but one was behind me. A female, I think. The room was dimly lit and there was a feeling of something sacred, or holy, there. It was like this was a religious place. It also felt familiar, as if I been there before.

"And as I was lying on this slab or whatever, one of these entities walked up to my side. Suddenly I was illuminated by a shaft of white light—some type of beam—from head to toe. It was coming from overhead. And as this was going on, the individual who had walked to my side held his hands out over my abdomen, my solar plexus. And that's when it started fading out and the session was over.

"It was a very beautiful experience. I felt very calm and secure. I've always had a feeling that there was something I should have remembered about that. That something should come back to me, something relating to that experience. It's almost as if I had been to that place before. It's like I should have remembered that place."

In 1996, Ray Bordon, a Dallas-area linguist, began organizing remote viewers with an eye toward promoting further public study of the phenomenon. Bordon learned remote viewing in the 1970s while working for a military contractor. But his education was unofficial and he had no contact with the military-trained viewers. Although sensitive about the reaction to his statements, Bordon too spoke privately about alien life-forms—he called them "biokinds"—UFOs, and a catastrophe on Mars millions of years ago. He too claimed to have seen the transcendental energy beings, which he called the "disincorporates." Bordon said that in the 1980s, he remote-viewed the GRILL FLAME viewers at Fort Meade because "they were making bubbles in the ether."

During a 1996 interview, Bordon mentioned that our galaxy is controlled by one of seven "Confederation Headquarters" scattered throughout the universe. He gave this description of this headquarters: "It is reminiscent of a Sumerian temple with obelisks similar to the Washington monument standing before a long inclined entrance ramp. It was made of white, polished stone, like Italian marble, and surrounded by sand on a plateau. Inside is a room with a high vaulted ceiling covered with ornate carvings, pictures, signs and letters. The center of the ceiling is light which can change color depending on who is in the room, kind of like the old mood rings. On the floor in the center is a raised platform or offering place, though not really an altar. I knew I had been there before. This was not a feeling. I had been there before."

As can be seen, the similarities in Bordon's and Riley's descriptions are uncanny. Either they have been reading from the same script, which seems unlikely since both claim no contact with the other, or they are both describing the same place—a place far outside our solar system. It is highly intriguing, but certainly not the kind of concrete feedback that debunkers would demand.

Nevertheless, it would appear that remote viewing may provide real insights into the alien agenda if the scientifically developed protocols are rigorously applied by serious researchers.

What the Seers See

Just such an effort was organized by the American Association of Remote Viewers, Inc., in mid-1996. Seven experienced remote viewers, whose level of performance was known based on prior testing, were commissioned to look at the UFO issue.

Their raw input—the results of their individual RV sessions—was sent to a judge termed "process control" who analyzed the material, matching responses to the five original questions. It was a "double-blind" study in that none of the participants, including the process control judge who assigned each viewer their numbers, knew the object of their viewing. Randomly chosen numbers represented each question. The individual responses as well as drawings produced by the viewers were passed along to the "target officer"—the person who knew which number represented which question. This person checked the analysis against the raw data, then sent the viewers "second-order" questions based on their initial responses. A "project officer" studied the analyses and compiled a final report.

The report was issued on September 4, 1996. "Due to the nature of the subject of the study, all research remote viewers have opted to remain anonymous; each is identified by a randomly assigned set of four numbers," stated a cover letter.

Despite being unaware of the object of their search, five of the seven viewers immediately realized that they were looking at nonhuman beings and craft. Their realization of the UFO target prompted the intrigued viewers to add several questions of their own to the study. Over a two-month period—July and August 1996—these viewers conducted remote viewing sessions using number coordinates representing the questions. Their responses follow.

What are UFOs?

While five of the seven viewers quickly and correctly identified their target as UFOs, all said that UFOs represent a physical object that can fly. Descriptions included "bright lights," "vehicles, like buses," objects "like pebbles, hopping and skipping over . . . water," "objects, but flying in the air . . . very bright, like a light," and one even described "plumed serpents," a possible reference to the Aztec god Quetzalcoatl. Two viewers reported seeing unmanned or "drone" craft belonging to small alien "greys."

What technologies are in use?

As only one of the viewers had a technical background—as a pilot and software engineer—answers to this question were limited to descriptions of effects. Some of the descriptions included "very high electrical voltage, humming, weird material [that] changes shape like rubber but is strong and light"; "vertical takeoff like a chopper, but silent . . . must be a weird vehicle because it's shaped like an egg and its got like wings"; "many-sided, like polygons, tetrahedrons, things like that . . . uses streams of . . . energy, radiation energy"; "geometric shapes acting like dynamos of some kind," "lots of electromagnetic fields around." One viewer described a round undercarriage at the base of a craft that drops down and gives off a white light. Another described "a dome-like structure on the top part of the ship [with] eight windows set into it, the bottom part giving off orange-colored light." Yet another viewer was astounded and reported, "Interesting craft. It can travel in time and in space. Good God! This was built about 200 years in the future. And it is here now. It's already been in service for about as long." Another stated, "The technology is about 2,000 to 3,000 years ahead of ours, but there are others that are less advanced than that—about 300 to 500 years, that's all."

Is this technology on Earth today?

The viewers agreed that UFO technology is indeed operating widely around the world. "Yes, it's here all right," one reported. "I see bases of theirs, not one race, but several. These are living quarters and craft bases for people. I see them inside mountains, at the bottom of the ocean, on the floors of lakes in both northern and southern hemispheres of the Earth." "Oh, yes, they are everywhere actually," reported another. "I see them in the skies, inside mountains, under water . . . more than one . . . kind." A third said, "Oh yeah, I've seen them . . . not the greys, but human-looking ones. They—and there's more than one kind—are here. Bases in the ocean, inside mountains in what looks like caves, but they are man-made, or alien-made." "Yes, this technology is definitely on the planet," reported a fourth, "been here for millennia, I sense, for a long, long time. They have brought this technology with them. They are everywhere." A fifth stated, "There are like bases in environments that are ocean-like, large caves in mountains, even desert-like conditions and forests and jungles. On Earth? Could be, but I don't want to commit to anything on this one just yet."

Is UFO technology in government hands?

This question split the viewers in half: "Three of them saw it in official hands, while three others did not see anything that would indicate to them any sort of government involvement." The seventh had no opinion, saying, "[It's] hard to see on this one." One viewer saw what appeared to be a hangar with men in blue military uniforms inside while another sensed a "cave-type of setting" complete with air filtration system. Another said, "To have it in hand is one thing and I sense there are craft in vaults underground in two different places. But it's quite another [thing] to know how to work it. I sense whoever is going through the craft and other artifacts in their possession doesn't understand it all just yet. The physics is partly understood in theory, but the technology is not there yet—at least what we can produce. They—especially grey ones—will share things with human counterparts; I take these presences to be formal, which to me means government types, but there are things they will not [share] particularly what we know as engines—a weird-looking contraption . . . looks like small ball and you hold it between your legs. . . . You put your hand on it . . . and you move it and the thing flies." This viewer began to bilocate, due to the intensity of his experience. "Jeez, this thing's completely wired to my brain; it'll do what I think as I think it. Nice piece of work, this thing," the viewer continued. "I'm seated on a chair-like contraption that molds to me. I hear a soft hum coming from every-where. Good God! We've taken off! There are greys—little ones—three of them and two humans, soldier types. The greys know I'm here and don't seem to mind. One of the humans has a box-like thing on his lap, larger than a laptop. The grey one I'm in is letting me steer this thing. He—this one feels male—is quiet, almost sad inside, even bored. This is a job for him. Hey, wait a sec! The soldier-boy just found out I'm here. He doesn't like it [and] is telling the grey to let me go. He's entering something into this box-like thing on his lap. He's seated close by. . . . These guys—the humans—are learning about the craft. This is a crew. Wait! He's doing something to me, this soldier-boy. What is that? Feels like I'm on fire, like a thousand ants are biting me all at once. Uhuh . . . I just lost it."

How many contacts and how often with nonhumans?

This question—one of those generated by the remote viewers themselves—revealed that at least three of the viewers had experienced alien abductions in the past. "[I] lost count on both number and fre-quency," stated one. "When I was a child, I used to get picked up every other month. This went on for several years." Another reported, "My sense is that I've been in touch with them. Yes, ever since my teen years, I've participated in their campaign. They are getting something from us. Greys, I mean. They certainly were from me. I don't know to this day what it was. I don't know how often. And I don't know about anybody else. I don't think I want to know." A third reported contacts "in the hundreds ever since I was a child." This viewer saw the con-tacts as benevolent. "I mean that I got traumatized, but then got past it and began to see what was really going on. I could then dialogue with them without having to be consciously suppressed. Now it's like old friends. They still come and they still visit," added the viewer. A fourth viewer reported no physical contact but did disclose numerous dreams, daydreams, and meditations involving "grey beings with great big eyes." Another viewer indicated that contact has been numerous over time. "It would be very hard to tap into the experience of every single person that's been in contact with them," said this viewer. Yet another viewer reported being in a well-lit room with an assembly of greys. "I'm asking them this question," the viewer said. "Millions, says one. Many millions, says another. All the time, since the beginning, says another. What's the beginning, I ask. When you were created, says one of the tall ones. You were not supposed to have been created for the reasons you were, said the same tall one. What do you mean, I ask. You are the product of your kind and our forefathers, whom we also uphold because they are like us and like you. We are caretakers and we host advancement of your kind. Your forefathers are divided and you are the prize. This does not uphold life and we preserve and protect life. But you are not yet ready to face this and it is coming."

What is the current level of human adoption or duplication of UFO technology?

Although there were differences in the responses to this question, all the viewers indicated that work connected to alien technology is being done on Earth today. One saw a huge hangar where a half-dozen humans in flight or pressure suits were working to install a black, football-shaped device into "one of those sleek, black planes you see in the movies." Another envisioned what appeared to be an underground laboratory. One viewer seemed to witness a demonstration of exotic technology for President Bill Clinton in the Oval Office. This viewer reported a round room filled with furniture, with a round design "like a bird of some kind" on the floor. "I'm in the middle of some kind of meeting here. . . . I can't tell what's going on, except I could swear I'm looking at [President Clinton].. . . There are two uniformed guys with a little black case of some kind. These guys are setting up whatever's in this case. Well, I'll be . . . It looks like a rectangular doughnut of some kind and there are two inverted either conical or pyramidal shaped objects inside, tip to tip so to speak, but the tips don't quite touch. On the upper side . . . is a flat cone of sorts that points upward, with a pin-like thing sticking out from its center. There are a couple of rows of switches inside this case and one of the two uniformed guys is switching the top row of switches. Then each of the other rows." This reporter said remote viewing was suddenly cut off at this point as though blocked in some way.

Yet another viewer gave a report that sounded very much as though exotic technology had been used as a weapon. "I'm at a seashore of some kind and there are guys there. It's totally dark and deserted. No one else around. I see eight of them. Way yonder's a truck of some kind, box-like and black. It's got a small dish on top and there are cables, thick ones going from the truck to the group of guys on the beach. . . . I also see . . . that one of the guys has a contraption on his head, like head-gear of some kind, with a dark visor. It's a man, human definitely, and he's holding some kind of pole-like thing that has a handle of some kind that sticks downward at one end. He's got great big hands and he's dressed in a cowboy shirt, plaid, and I think blue jeans. There is a kind of needle that sticks out of this tube thing, on the opposite side of the handle, and there is a circle at the tip of this needle. This is some sort of weapon. I say that because he's holding it like you would hold a rifle and he's aiming it upward. This is strange. It's night time, I can see the stars and clouds and a rising half moon. Oh, he's also got some sort of earpiece on. He's about to fire this thing. . . . I am seeing a yellow-green something come out of the end of this thing and going upwards. It's going up into the night sky. Inside this light-like stream coming out of this thing, there is a streak of light that extends forever upwards. It looks like a wave of some kind, but it's real intense. I sense a great deal of heat and some kind of field coming off this stream. The target is something up there, but I can't tell. This thing lasts for a very short while and then the whole thing is repeated. There is a whirring sound around as this thing . . . powers up? I can't tell what the sound is, or where it comes from, but it's all over this place."

Who is currently visiting Earth?

Another "blind" question, it provoked varied responses—yet all were in agreement that various nonhuman beings are presently operating on and around our planet. One viewer saw a parade of alien beings. "I see your standard big-eyed greys, both tall ones and short ones. I also see the reptilian type, with leathery skin and eyes larger than humans," said this viewer. "Here come the blond ones, tall ones. This is weird. I'm seeing albinos now, but one has black eyes and the other has glowing red eyes. . . . They are like floating past my field of vision. Like they are saying hello."

Another viewer stated, "There is this entity right in front of me. It's like he's—yes, it's a male all right—it's like he's making it possible for me to see him. He's telling me something . . . that he will see me soon . . . that he's related to me, to all humans. This is one humungous dude. He's a lot taller than I am and I'm not exactly short. What is so striking about him is that he is a complete albino, in the true sense of the word. And what I sense about him right now is a profound kindness, as if his whole body permeated this feeling and exuded it like a field."

A third viewer saw the albinos and greys together on a world other than Earth. "It's like the greys are helping these albinos," said the viewer. "Oh, God, these greys are bringing these other ones, the albinos, here. But why? Good Lord, there are others like them here already. They are all over . . . hidden." Another viewer saw little greys and albinos working with humans. Yet another saw various races of beings at a structure on another world, strangely similar to the one Riley and Bordon described. "This is an entrance to a beautiful, white pyramid-type structure on a rocky promontory. . . . There is a whole city behind me. . . . There is like a platform that goes up to this big opening. The door is interesting. There isn't one! But you can't go inside unless invited. There are two Indian files of people dressed in what I would call ancient dresses. Long flowing gown-like things. One of the Indian files is made up of men, males, I mean. . . . Blond, all of them, about the same height, can't tell size. Their robes are a beautiful gold color and have hoods, and they have hair, beautiful golden hair. . . . They are walking slowly toward the entrance. I'm not allowed to go past the portal, I've been told. But I'm welcome to be there with them." One of the viewers who had indicated being an abductee witnessed nothing but the grey aliens in the context of a consensual work program on Earth, while another former abductee said the viewing was somehow being blocked. "Someone or something was not wanting me to see anything, hear anything, say anything about anything," this viewer reported. "I'm feeling like I'm being shut out of the loop, so to speak."

What is the aliens' purpose here?

Another "blind" question, it produced varied responses. One viewer said he spoke directly with grey aliens and was not afraid or angry. "They are here to help us," this viewer explained. The greys said a planet is about to make an appearance in our solar system within the next sixty years and will "wreak havoc here" because "this time this thing is going to pass on the side of the sun facing us and the sun won't be there to protect us." The viewer added that the greys are concerned about the survival of the human species and that they want nothing "except that we remain alive" because we are related to them. Another viewer offered the same theme, stating, "This is a high-risk planet . . . and that their perspective is much longer, in terms of time, than ours. These people are worried about us and yet they know that we could conceivably make it. It will be rough for a while, but it won't kill us all. There are people who will be taken aloft before the trouble begins down here. . . . This sort of thing happens every so often that it isn't the first nor the last time this will happen." The viewer who saw a tall albino said, "This tall dude . . . with a kind face and red eyes, keeps telling me that they don't have a choice about the visits, that every so often, the planet on which they live comes this way and they get to visit what I take to be their old stomping grounds, so to speak. He also says that they colonized Earth a long time ago and that they are responsible for the human race, just as the blonds are responsible for them. The blond with this guy is a little smaller in size but he is still big by human standards. . . . He says that everything is being done to preserve and protect the human race and all other forms of life on this planet from extinction. He says that there are differences of method and reality in the approach to things ... between the tall ones he is with right now and the tall ones who are already in this solar system. He says we will have a choice as to who we want to believe in and go with."

One viewer reported observing the "grey" aliens. "I am sensing a lot of ships—UFOs—like in the atmosphere above. I am on one of them and there are little greys on board. There are also two humans on board. This is like a training exercise of some kind," reported this one. According to the report, there are at least two kinds of "greys" and perhaps more. "I'm in what looks like a city," reported another. "There are lots of people around. There are some that have very dark, black eyes. [They] look like black contact lens. These people are fairly tall. When I'm around them, I close up. I don't want them to know me. Just a hunch. These guys are not ... these people are not exactly good. They are misguided. They do things for their own people and be damned with everybody else. I see them clear as day now."

One viewer saw a variety of alien life-forms—"greys, reptilians, blonds, albinos and several variations of human-like forms"—moving through "subspace or hyperspace" to appear in Earth's atmosphere. One viewer described some visitors as disincorporated energy beings. "I'm not sure that I can say they have a body like we do. But whatever or whoever is 'they,' they exist nonetheless. I feel them. I sense them, more than see them or can touch them in the physical sense. However, I can see something of what they are. Some are like dissipated, but brilliant at the center. Others are like the outlines or forms of bodies that they must have had, but no longer are. ... Then there are those ... who cannot live like that and wish to get back into this world and those who are quite well adjusted to where they are now. Golly! These things, especially the ones who aren't well adjusted, feed on fear. To them it's like food. But their real aim is to get back in here any way they can. Jeez Louise, this is getting weirder by the minute. Where am I? There are all kinds of remnant energy beings here. They come from all the worlds that exist, I can sense. That they want to come back into the world is not wishful thinking; it's a plan of some kind. They are being kept there somehow ... it is their will not to be there, but they are there by someone else's will, something or someone very powerful. These guys also communicate with people here. One of them tells me that they can interpenetrate ... this reality. They can't affect it or act in it, but they sure can influence it by influencing the folks who are in the world through our minds. But there is a problem with that, too. Some will listen but not act as these guys want them to act and others will act on their behalf, unconsciously of course, but cannot be kept under control for very long periods. ... And there is some sort of gate or place they can go through but only with willing people in the world calling for them. God, this gets complicated . . . I'm going to terminate this session now."

Describe any interaction between Earth governments and visitors beginning one hundred years in the past and moving two hundred years into the future.

This question provoked some of the most fascinating answers in the report. Although only three of the seven remote viewers offered a time line with their reports, it seemed like there was unofficial contact up until the 1950s. One viewer told of speaking with a grey alien as a writer/storyteller in the 1890s. The viewer gave that time frame because sailing ships and horse-drawn carriages were seen. The alien told him of "submarines and airplane, wonder drugs and new medical procedures" in English. This viewer was told that preferred means of communication during this time period was through "dreams and waking-state reverie."

Another viewer indicated that mental contact with aliens may have taken place early in this century by one or more persons in Germany. "I have never been in Germany and I've had no interest in German since I can remember," stated this viewer. "But I speak German somehow because I can understand what's being said around me. . . . I can understand this very complicated calculus and all these equations. I'm in what feels like an island, but it's an island in a river, not the sea. We're talking about . . . high physics here. There are people here that I only recognize by name. This is some kind of symposium . . . sometime during the 1920s. . . . This place is like some sort of castle or something. There's a man called Heidel . . . something, that everyone's talking about. There is also talk of splitting the atom and the harnessing of energy. But I don't understand the explanation. . . . There are people from America here. No, from England. I can hear the British accent. They are all talking about physics and tensor . . . and what the hell's a quantum field? . . . There are people here who look human but they are not. I can see this guy, this blond guy, . . . and from time to time I get a flash of . . . I don't know . . . something that looks like a praying mantis. Small head, tallish, skinny, that sort of thing. But only for a split second."

One viewer gave an intriguing account of a meeting between aliens and President Dwight Eisenhower in what seemed like the early 1950s. "What I hear right now is a band playing 'Hail to the Chief' like they do on political conventions when the President comes into the hall. But this is not this time. . . . I see a highway sign on what looks like a two-lane road, but it's desert-like in this place. This is sometime during the day. I feel the heat of the sun. There is some sort of airstrip, like an airport around here, close by I can tell. I'm hearing the sound of aircraft, like jet planes. This is some sort of restricted area, though. I see some guard or observation towers. . . . There is a convoy of cars, dark cars, coming down this blacktop road where I was. No, wait a minute! This is a base, a military base. An Air Force base. People get out of the car and go inside this building. They are all dressed in suits, dark suits. . . . Now this is interesting! There are two, no, three saucer-shaped craft approaching. One of them lands while the other two stay up. Another lands and the third lands. Then the third lands. The first that landed opens up. One of the black cars and a couple of jeeps go out to it. Two, no three, greys appear and descend from the craft. They are not walking. They, like, are floating to the ground. The door of the car opens and this tall, older man steps out, then a couple of military guys and one other civilian type. This is a hot place, the temperature is desert-like. . . . Two of these greys are small, one is tall, but not as tall as the older human. Something funny about this guy. Wait a sec! Holy shit! It's one of our past presidents." (The viewer later acknowledged it was Eisenhower.) This viewer said the group got in a big black Cadillac that took them to a nearby building. "They are scooted in quickly by some people in blue and white helmets, big guys. The President and his party and the greys go into a room, conference room it looks like. Just a minute! I'm sensing this whole thing to be preplanned. This thing was supposed to happen. Both sides feel anticipation, but the feeling tone is low-key, almost muted. The greys are interested in opening and maintaining communication. This civilian type asks how this can be done. The tall grey responds that they will provide them with the means to communicate with them locally and at a distance. This tall one also asks that they (the humans) not fear them. The President asks why are they here and the tall one replies that they are here in anticipation of future changes and that they will help accelerate the rate of development. Not for war purposes, says one of the little ones. They want an understanding with them, says the tall grey, but not an alliance. The President wants to know how long they have been around. The short one replies, a long time. He says longer than your recorded history. He says we were abandoned by our forefathers, our makers. . . . The civilian type is visibly upset, like he's about to have a heart attack. The three greys turn and look at this guy. Wow! He calmed down almost immediately. They like the President. They feel he is steady. They don't like the civilian type with him, no, actually, they feel sorry for him. The President says he wants friendship and cooperation with the aliens and the tall grey says they too want the same. He also says they will continue to observe and wait to see what we do, how we act towards them. But, he says, they will continue to be active here. The civilian type wants to know what changes are coming. One of the small greys says they will tell us more when it is the right time. Soon, he says. The tall grey turns toward me now. Whoaa! He knows I'm here. One of the military guys kinda wakes up and wants to know what's wrong. Nothing, says the tall grey, just that we have a visitor. How can that be possible, asks the military guy. It is not yet time [to explain], says the small one." This viewer said his RV session ended abruptly after this incident, as though his thoughts were being blocked "as though there were still things to talk about in private, without eavesdroppers around like me."

Another viewer added details to the idea of coming changes when he remote-viewed a meeting between yet another American president and greys "sometime in the future from where we started [the mid-1950s])." "Can't tell you when this happened but I'll venture to say a little before the year 2000," reported the viewer. "There are four greys here, two tall ones and two short ones. Besides the two men in dark suits, there are others around in military suits and regular suits. I don't see a ship or anything like that, just some chairs . . . [which look like they are] made out of grayish gum-like substance. When you sit down on it, it molds around you and holds you very well. But it doesn't constrain your movements. These greys are sitting on them, one to each of them. So they are talking. The greys are telling about the orbit of something. They say it's an anomaly, but it's something that was done to preserve life. It required a lot of energy, the tall one that looks like a praying mantis says. He says they and others are going to do everything to help avoid catastrophe on the surface. . . . He's speaking of models. He says the way it looks now is that they will have to wait until the values can be entered when this thing gets nearer because the gravitation of this thing is so disruptive that every time it comes, it affects everything else differently each time. . . . He's also telling the guys in suits that they are staying out of the squabble. He's not specifying what this is. He's also recommending that they—the guys in suits—stay out of it. One of the men—the tall one, I think— says that we will have to defend ourselves if any one of the parties involved tries to enter secured zones. It is necessary, he says, to protect our own development and it is in our best interest. [But he] does not specify what development he's talking about. But he also says we are not taking sides and your vessels . . . will be respected under the maritime and space human laws and treaties."

Yet another viewer also envisioned a meeting between aliens and human leaders in which coming geophysical changes were discussed. "The changes, is saying the tall skinny grey, are going to affect the planet. He says that every 25,000 revolutions around the sun, the Earth is pelted by large stones from the sky. He must be talking about meteors or asteroids. There is also a planet that crosses the orbits of planets in this solar system and that, this grey says, causes a lot of problems for Earth and the other planets. This thing's apparently big or at least bigger than Earth. . . . He just produced like a hologram of the orbit of this thing cutting across the plane of the orbits of the planets in our solar system. That's neat! He's showing the guys in suits that this planet is going to be close to Earth as it begins to accelerate in its own orbit going out of our solar system. This hologram also shows them that there are asteroids from the asteroid belt that get dislodged from their orbits and decay. Some get pulled in by the Earth and miss it barely, others hit it head on. . . . He tells them to get people involved in putting up a—the best I can come up with here is 'shield' because he's talking about protection. He tells the honchos that there is not much they can do now, meaning at this time. . . . The guys in suits have questions—how many will die? What can they do to plan for this event? That sort of thing. The tall skinny grey speaks to them again. He says they must build underground facilities for themselves and their people—not just where they are but in other places where there are mountains and bedrock. What about the rest of the people, asks the guys in suits. The grey replies that there are humans who will die because they are not prepared. He says that the job of the guys in suits is to prepare the people for this event and to tell them how to prepare themselves. Panic, he says, is inevitable but there are means of keeping problems to a minimum and we will give you those means." This viewer went on to describe how humans in orange jumpsuits left with the greys after a "ceremony of departure."

What are the ambassadors, technicians, and police?

This question was asked by the remote viewers themselves after all but one saw references to these types in their sessions. Two saw alien beings in the role of ambassadors, two saw unearthly technicians working on and near Earth, while two more envisioned alien policemen involved. One saw ambassadors representing many alien races conducting a meeting in "a grand meeting place. Are they like ambassadors of some kind? I can't think of any other way of looking at them. They are not blocking anything from me. They know I'm here," stated this viewer. Another viewer saw what was described as an alien technician of sorts. "There's this robed guy, tall and he's like shimmering all over. . . . He is telling these others that it is very important to have the energizer working properly and tested soon. He's also saying that the amount of energy must be modulated carefully so as not to harm life forms. There's no mention of where or what kind of 'energizer' was spoken about." Yet another viewer saw one bunch of aliens protecting "two guys who knew how to do or perform something technical." One viewer who saw these guards referred to them as police. "These guys are funny to me because they don't have any sense of humor at all," reported this viewer. "They are as serious as the plague and they take their jobs very seriously. They work in pairs, just like cops on the beat, you know. But there's a reason for that. It's got to do with protection. One of them tells me that if they are in danger, they can together call for help and it is instantly given. Whereas when you ask for help alone, you have to go through like a central switchboard of some kind, but together with someone else, you get instant resonance—whatever that means about this? Makes no sense to me. . . . These guys say they have a hierarchy and they work in groups of twelve, six pairs. He says there are thousands and thousands of them in pairs all over the galaxy. They just work this galaxy, says one. He says until I understand what life really is, I won't understand fully what it is that they do. He also says their primary duty is to uphold life, whatever that means"

Why is there a quiet war going on right now?

This is another question asked by the viewers after several got the definite impression that some sort of secret conflict is taking place around the earth today. Five of the seven remote viewers provided some insight into the situation. "There is a guerrilla war going on, I'm sensing," reported one. Another added it was more like "a lot of hit-and-runs between two groups. They don't like each other. We are in the middle of it. It's like we're one pawn in this war." Another view was even more ominous. This viewer saw "a whole armada of very large ships just outside our solar system, like they're waiting for something or someone to come. Kinda reminds me of that movie with Luke Sky-walker and the bad guys." One viewer described the conflict as "between two factions of the same party." "They don't see things eye to eye and one side feels very responsible for Earth, while the other side wants to use Earth, wants to rule it and take things from there. There is a larger group of many kinds of beings that don't like what's going on but won't do anything about it. They just try to keep the peace and prevent . . . these guys from hurting us or anyone else."

Another viewer explained, "It's not as simple as it all appears to be. This is not a hatred war, where one side hates the other. No, this has been going on for a long time. This thing's about survival of one of the two sides. This side wants to live here and the other side says no, it belongs to us. This is what I'm getting. It feels like a 'Star Wars' kind of situation, like science fiction, but I can't shake the feelings and impression." Yet another viewer said, "This war, if it is a war, is like two dogs fighting. They are not out to kill each other but rather to have one expose the neck to the other so they can get back to being peaceful. But one side doesn't like that approach, I sense. This thing's not over yet by far." None of the viewers got any sense on when this conflict began nor when it might be ended.

Does the UFO issue involve matters usually thought to be of a spiritual, religious or metaphysical nature?

This was another "blind" question that produced truly intriguing responses. Several questions regarding this topic were added by the viewers. All got various visions, but all indicated that intelligent life does not end at the boundaries of Earth. "As best I can, I'd call it the feel of a mantle of some kind," responded one, "like being covered by a bed cover when it's cold or being inside a cocoon of a kind that's everywhere and I mean everywhere. Like this whole universe was full of life just waiting to happen. . . . It's like everything is a humungous pattern and there isn't really one person but rather it's one whole cloth. I'm a seamstress and I can only think of the whole thing as if I were making a gown and the extent of this thing is, well, you can make billions and billions of gowns from it and it would still be endless."

Another viewer said, "I'm sensing that there is what we call God but it's not like we think of God at all. It's more impersonal. It's not a personal thing at all. What is personal is that, well, as best as I can say, it's like people who have gone before us, who are now serving as role models and guides to how things are and how we're supposed to do it while we're here. I'm gonna call them 'people' because they are like me in every conceivable sense of the word, 'cause I don't feel different from them and that's weird in itself. The way I'm getting this is that we are actually all the same, just different casings. The pattern is the same. It's like a conspiracy for life, all kinds of lifeforms, that is. The little guys [greys] know and understand all this and so do most of the others. I don't see them having a religion like we do. They experience the force field of what we would call the Creator, with a capital C. Oh, but they do have their ceremonies. They are not like our masses [this viewer is a Catholic], quite different in spirit. That's it! When they do things like that, like a ceremony of something, spirit is there. I can feel it and it feels good, like an embracing cocoon, it kinda envelops you. I've never been in a tub of warm molasses, but I wouldn't bet it's much different. Maybe it would be. At any rate, it feels good. I'm there now! . . . It's like a raised plateau. There's a . . . Good grief! It looks like one of those Mexican pyramids except it has a door at the bottom and some kind of entrance mall leading up to it."

Another viewer also mentioned a "temple" where hooded beings met for worship. "It's very bright in there," said this viewer. "There is a low humming sound and the color of light changes with the intensity of the sound. It feels really good. I can't quite go inside this temple because I'm not allowed to go inside the main room where everybody is. But I'm in like an anteroom. There is like a monolith in the middle of this room and there is a reddish, eight-sided stone, large, about halfway up this thing. Looks like onyx or black granite . . . Well, I'll be damned! This humming is the prayer! That's how these guys pray. But to whom or what? Everybody, comes the answer."

One viewer witnessed another ceremony involving water—"the water of life, they call it." Perhaps a hundred hooded beings participated in the ceremony in a large rectangular room with the walls covered by hieroglyphics. "Everybody is praying and giving thanks to the One. Maybe this One should be capitalized. Maybe this is God to them. No, this is a little different, feels a little different. This is a form of what I would call God but it's like the whole lot of them and everybody who is alive. I mean the sum total of our spirits . . . God Almighty! Could it be that they are praying to all of us put together? Is that what One is?"

One possible answer came from another viewer who told of a conversation with a hooded being who patiently tried to explain that each individual being is the eyes and ears of the Creator. "When one forgets that, there is separation and separation is unnatural," this viewer was told. "He says that regardless of what body form we have, we are also made of something that interfaces with body form. He says we call this the mind, but it's more than that. . . . He says mind and feelings go together and have always gone together, but that emotions, strong emotions cloud awareness. He's also telling me that to really live simply means to live without fear. Everything is energy, he says, and that I must try to understand things in terms of energy exchanged, shared and not to steal energy from another. He says this is what reality really is—energy and energy exchanges. He's now telling me that what I think the world—no, the universe—is really like, isn't. He says I am relying too much on what others tell me and what I and others agree is. He says for me to go on a discovery. Find out things, he says. And now he takes off his hood. It's a guy with shoulder-length light brown hair and light eyes, hazel, I think." One amazing aspect to this portion of the remote viewing report was that two viewers separately provided sketches of the site on another world where they saw the One worshiped—and they are virtually identical.

The conclusion of the remote viewing report was that multiple species of extraterrestrials—including variations of the familiar greys as well as energy beings—are visiting Earth. While no incontrovertible evidence was offered, several sessions strongly suggested that there is interaction between some of the ETs and representatives of government, both former and present, to include recovered or donated craft. It was apparent that the technologies in use with UFOs far exceed those of present-day humans, but no clear definition of such technology was given. It was suggested that this may be due to the lack of knowledge on the part of the remote viewers—as only one had any scientific training. It appeared from the reports that Earth is caught in the middle of a conflict between factions of the same race. A good part of the secrecy concerning UFOs may be due to national leaders seeking more time to determine which side—if either—they might want to align with. Finally, the experiences of the viewers when dealing with the metaphysical aspects of the UFO phenomenon are most compelling in their similarities and consistencies. It lends considerable weight to the argument that remote viewing, done properly with established protocols, may well prove to be an effective tool for determining the alien agenda.

A METAPHYSICAL EXAM

The year was 1917, and the seventy thousand people gathered near a small Portuguese town all saw the UFO. The rain, which had continued all morning, suddenly stopped about noon. The clouds parted, and the sun appeared to throw out shafts of colored light in hues of violet, blue, and yellow.

There was a strange fragrance in the air, and some heard a soft humming sound. Then came the revolving flat disk, spinning down toward the earth in a zigzag pattern before reversing its course and disappearing into the sun. The crowd—many of whom thought the object was the sun—was shocked to realize that their rain-soaked clothing was now completely dry.

Although fully documented by attending journalists and investigated thoroughly by the Catholic Church, this case is rarely acknowledged in the UFO literature. It is reserved for the religion shelf. It has become known as the miracle of Fatima, a small hamlet located about seventy miles north of Lisbon. According to believers, it represented an earthly visit by the Blessed Virgin Mary, who brought messages of love and prophecies of coming cataclysms.

But others, such as longtime researcher and author Dr. Jacques Vallee, saw a definite connection with the UFO experience. "The famous apparitions at Fatima offer a historical example of the religious dimension of UFO encounters," wrote Vallee.

The last apparition appeared on October 13, 1917, and ended six months of sightings, each of which occurred on the thirteenth day of the month. The only persons to actually claim to have seen and heard the Virgin Mary were three young children who said they were first approached by a beautiful lady surrounded by brilliant light on May 13, 1917, while tending a flock of sheep.

"The final 'miracle' had come at the culmination of a precise series of apparitions combined with contacts and messages that place it very clearly, in my opinion, in the perspective of UFO phenomena," stated Vallee. "Not only was a flying disk or globe consistently involved, but its motion, its falling-leaf trajectory, its light effects, the thunderclaps, the buzzing sounds, the strange fragrance, the fall of 'angel hair' that dissolves upon reaching the ground, the heat wave associated with the close approach of the disk—all of these are frequent parameters of UFO sightings everywhere. And so are the paralysis, the amnesia, the conversions, and the healings."

Retired U.S. Air Force lieutenant colonel Dr. Nelson S. Pacheco has made an in-depth study of Marian phenomena, while Tommy R. Blann, a former researcher to the late Dr. J. Allen Hynek, has studied UFOs since the early 1960s. In their self-published book *Unmasking the Enemy*, both men argue that religious apparitions exhibit some major differences from UFO encounters.

"First, the Fatima message is the traditional Judeo-Christian call to return to God," they wrote. "As with prophets of old, the Virgin Mary linked the establishment of peace in the world not to geopolitical considerations, but to the cessation of sinfulness ... [while] UFO manifestations' ... appeal is amoral—having more to do with our own human potential, the destruction of the environment, government secrecy, and so forth.

"Second, the imagery of Fatima fits traditional Catholic archetypes, and the feeling reported by the visionaries is one of peace—except for the vision of hell—quite different from the typical imagery and emotions typically reported by UFO visionaries. . . . Finally, the miracle of the sun at Fatima stands by itself in its magnitude. It is paralleled only by Old Testament miracles and makes even the most magnificent UFO display seem minuscule in comparison."

All three authors do share a common belief—that the UFO

phenomenon involves nonhuman intelligences that are not necessarily aliens from another planet.

"I believe that the UFO phenomenon is one of the ways through which an alien form of intelligence of incredible complexity is communicating with us symbolically," stated Vallee. "There is no indication that it is extraterrestrial. Instead, there is mounting evidence that it has access to psychic processes we have not yet mastered or even researched."

Today, there is a growing belief among UFO researchers that the issue involves much more than simple flying machines from outer space. There appears to be an interconnection between sightings, contacts, and abductions that involves matters previously thought to be the sole province of parapsychology, anthropology, and even religion. For many this is a troubling thought.

As author Whitley Strieber noted, "Any explanation of the phenomenon that is not prosaic must inevitably lead to a profound challenge to cherished theories about the nature of mind and universe and man's place in the cosmos."

The Wee Folk

Once again, a search of both UFO and mythology literature indicates that various phenomena involving both can be traced back to man's prehistory. It is nothing new.

Vallee, who has made an extensive study of folklore, observed, "It is difficult to find a culture on Earth that does not have an ancient tradition of little people that fly through the sky and abduct humans." Vallee also stated that, based on his studies, he has been tempted to hypothesize "that in times remote contact occurred between human consciousness and another consciousness, variously described as demonic, angelic, or simply alien."

These "little people" went under a variety of names: the Scandinavian *trolls*, the *ihkals* of Mexico, and the Malaysian *bunians*. The British Isles provide a wealth of such legends, from the Celtic stories of babies abducted by elves to Irish *leprechauns* and Scottish *sleagh maith* [good people]. In France, these legends concern *fees*, or fairies, and a diminutive race known as the *fions*. Interestingly, these wee folk, like the Christian stories of angels and demons, are said to form two basic groups—the good and the evil. "Such elemental beings have formed a backdrop to the religion and folklore of all nations for some millennia," stated author Jenny Randles. "The consistency between belief in such entities is truly remarkable."

"It would be a grave mistake to believe that we, in the late twentieth century, are the first people smart enough to recognize that this phenomenon is worthy of investigation and obeys certain fixed patterns," commented Vallee. "Priests and scholars left books about the legends of their time concerning these beings. These books had to be found, collected, and studied. Together, these stories presented a coherent picture of the appearance, the organization, and the methods of our strange visitors. The appearance was—does this surprise you?—exactly that of today's UFO pilots. The methods were the same. There was the sudden vision of brilliant 'houses' at night, houses that could fly, that contained peculiar lamps, radiant lights that needed no fuel. The creatures could paralyze their witnesses and translate them through time. They hunted animals and took away people."

Richard L. Thompson, the former NASA scientist who has connected UFOs to the ancient Vedic literature of India, urged more openness to the legends of other peoples. He suggested that a massive cross-cultural study "would result in a unified picture of human cultures that attributes much greater reality to each culture's world view than modern science allows."

To Vallee, the commonality of the world's legends goes far beyond mere coincidence of some ancient stories. "This is not simply a case of a few tales relating encounters between a few humans and strange creatures from the sky," he wrote. "This is an age-old and worldwide myth that has shaped our belief structures, our scientific expectations, and our view of ourselves. I do not use the word myth here to mean something that is imaginary, but on the contrary something that is true at such a deep level that it influences the very basic elements of our thoughts."

He even postulated that the intense interest in UFOs may presage a new mythological movement. "Through the UFO phenomenon, we have the unique opportunities to observe folklore in the making and to gather scientific material at the deepest source of human imagination. We will be the object of much contempt by future students of our civilization if we allow this material to be lost."

Much to the chagrin of some within the UFO research community, Vallee pointed out that he sees no unquestioned proof that UFOs are extraterrestrial spacecraft. The phenomenon may, he asserted, represent "something even more interesting: a window toward undiscovered dimensions of our own environment.

"Although I am among those who believe that UFOs are real physical objects, I do not think they are extraterrestrial in the ordinary sense of the term. In my view they present an exciting challenge to our concept of reality itself," he wrote. "I believe that a UFO is both a physical entity with mass, inertia, volume, and physical parameters that we can measure, and a window into another reality."

To support this thesis, Vallee noted several UFO traits that indicate that something other than simple space travel is involved:

UFOs not only travel through the air, often violating the laws of motion as we understand them, but according to many accounts, they can materialize and dematerialize—wink in and out of existence.

UFOs have been sighted throughout history and always within the context of the time period. Ancient peoples regarded them as gods. In the Middle Ages, they were manifestations of magic. During the Great Airship Mystery of the late 1800s, they were believed the work of scientific geniuses. Today, they are believed to be visitors from another planet. Of course, this could be the result of human interpretation rather than any conscious effort on the part of aliens.

Many abductees claimed to have experienced loss of time and to have been transported to worlds similar to, but not, our own. With recent developments in physics, the nature of the UFOs has to be expanded to include the possibility of origins outside of our normal time and/or dimension.

Although most abductees and contactees remain silent about this aspect of their experience, many report that their perceptions of themselves and the universe undergo a drastic change following a UFO experience. Some even claim to have developed increased psychic powers.

Whatever the experience, UFO contacts appear to always occur under conditions controlled by the UFO operators. One such underlying condition seems to be a factor of absurdity, such as the pancakes left behind in one case. Such absurdity, reasoned Vallee, "leads to a rejection of the story by the upper levels of the target society and an absorption at a deep unconscious level of the symbols conveyed by the encounter."

Vallee claimed the idea that UFOs are simply spaceships from another planet is naive. "The explanation is too simple-minded to account for the diversity of the reported behavior of the occupants and their perceived interactions with human beings," he explained.

New Yorker John Keel, a longtime student of UFOs who has authored several books on the subject, reached similar conclusions. In *UFOs: Operation Trojan Horse*, Keel stated, "Thus, by all the standards of our sciences—and our common sense—the UFOs do not really exist as solid objects. They may be a constant part of our environment, but they are not an actual part of our reality. We cannot, therefore, catalog them as manufactured products of some extraterrestrial civilization sharing our own dimensions of time and space. They are extra dimensional, able to move through our spatial coordinates at will but also able to enter and leave our three-dimensional world. If this is a true hypothesis, then they may also be operating beyond the limitations of our time coordinates. Our years may be minutes to them. Our future may be their past, and thus they have total knowledge of the things in store for us."

Referring to the conditioned-response studies of behaviorists such as B. F. Skinner, Vallee drew a comparison with UFO activity. "I suggest that it is human belief that is being controlled and conditioned," he stated. "When I speak of a spiritual control system I do not mean that some higher super civilization has locked us inside the constraints of a space-bound jail, closely monitored by entities we might call angels or demons. What I do mean is that mythology rules at a level of our social reality over which normal political and intellectual trends have no real power."

Vallee noted that the most effective form of reinforcement is one that combines regularity with unpredictability, he said, "Learning is then slow but continuous. It leads to the highest level of adaptation. And it is irreversible. It is interesting to observe that the pattern of UFO waves has the same structure as a schedule of reinforcement."

Considering the past fifty years of UFO history, there seems little doubt that a conditioning process has been taking place—whether intentional or not. Polls taken in the 1950s indicated that very few people believed there was any form of life outside the earth. Today's polls show the opposite. A Roper poll in 1987 indicated that slightly more than 50 percent of those questioned believed that UFOs are real. Interestingly, that figure jumped to 65 percent among people with college degrees. The December 1996 edition of *George* magazine quoted from a Luntz Research poll of more than eight hundred Americans that indicated that respondents who believed that there is life on other worlds had increased to 55 percent. Of this number, 53 percent believe that aliens have visited the earth within the past hundred years and 70 percent believe the government has covered up the fact.

It stands to reason that if an alien civilization is advanced enough to reach Earth in flying craft, it would be advanced enough socially to realize the disruption a public appearance would cause in our planet's evolution.

A clear example of such enlightened concern can be found in the story of the Tasaday Indians, a primitive Filipino tribe first discovered in 1966. Although questions have arisen about the authenticity of this "Stone Age" tribe, it is nevertheless instructive to note how modern science reacted to its discovery. In past history, many indigenous peoples—American Indians among them—were literally destroyed by the advent of Western European culture with its guns, Bibles, and disease.

In the early 1970s, it was decided that direct confrontation with the Tasadays would occur only after a period of acclimation. Slowly, over the course of months, anthropologists would allow the Tasadays to view them at a distance. Finally, a face-to-face meeting was arranged. Even then, only a few metal knives were given as presents. This prevented a total disruption of the Tasaday culture, giving scientists an opportunity to study what was hailed as "one of the most intriguing anthropological finds of the century."

Some thoughtful UFO researchers have wondered if perhaps the earth's population is experiencing a similar type of conditioning, in preparation for a face-to-face meeting with extraterrestrial neighbors.

Others see a more sinister form of conditioning in the UFO phenomenon.

The Gods of War

When researcher-author William Bramley began a seven-year investigation into the causes of war, he fully expected to find profit as the prime motivating factor behind mankind's turbulent history. After all, as Bramley discovered, war is not only very profitable to those who lend money or sell arms but it is an excellent means of social and political control. War can be used to "encourage populations to think in ways they would not otherwise do, and to accept the formation of institutions that they would normally reject. The longer a nation involves itself in wars, the more entrenched those institutions and ways of thinking will become," he noted.

Studying man's history of warfare, Bramley found abundant evidence of third-party manipulation. "It is no secret, for example, that prior to the American Revolution, France had sent intelligence agents to America to stir up colonial discontent against the British Crown," he wrote. "It is also no secret that the German military had aided Lenin and the Bolsheviks in the Russian revolution of 1917. Throughout all of history, people and nations have benefited from, and have contributed to, the existence of other people's conflicts."

What Bramley was unprepared for was the discovery of UFOs as a continuous influence in history. From the concept of "ancient astronauts" to the modern flying saucer phenomenon, he found the traces of UFO manipulation—whether as space beings or spiritual entities—well documented throughout the ages. "As I probed deeper . . . I was compelled to face the possibility that some human problems may be rooted in some of the most utterly bizarre realities imaginable," Bramley wrote in his well-researched and documented 1990 book, *The Gods of Eden*. "Because such realities are rarely acknowledged, let alone understood, they are not dealt with. As a result, the problems those realities generate are rarely resolved, and so the world seems to shamble from one calamity to the next."

According to Bramley, the earth's population remains under the hidden control of an alien race of "Custodians" that use war as an effective means of control. "Human beings appear to be a slave race languishing on an isolated planet in a small galaxy," he concluded. "As such, the human race was once a source of labor for an extraterrestrial civilization and still remains a possession today. To keep control over its possession and to maintain Earth as something of a prison, that other civilization has bred never-ending conflict between human beings, has promoted human spiritual decay, and has erected on Earth conditions of unremitting physical hardship. This situation has existed for thousands of years and it continues today."

Bramley's thesis echoes that of Charles H. Fort, a writer and researcher whose interest in obscure and bizarre facts led to the formation of the Fortean Society in 1931, the year before Fort's death. Following a lifetime of collecting strange and little-known information, Fort concluded, "I think we're property. I should say we belong to something: that once upon a time, this Earth was No-man's Land, that other worlds explored and colonized here, and fought among themselves for possession, but that now it's owned by something. That something owns this Earth—all others warned off."

If Bramley and Fort sound preposterous, it should be noted that their ideas are supported by none other than Dr. Fred Hoyle, one of the world's foremost astrophysicists. In a 1971 news conference, Hoyle stated, "Human beings are simply pawns in the games of alien minds that control our every move. They are everywhere, in the sky, on the sea, and on the Earth. . . . It is not an alien intelligence from another planet. It is actually from another universe which entered ours at the very beginning and has been controlling all that happened since." Hoyle added that many of his scientific peers believed in the existence of such nonhuman entities, but declined to say so publicly.

Students of a controlling alien presence, such as Bramley, Fort, and Hoyle, relied on research and documentation to provide the foundation for their beliefs. Others were more fortunate. They simply received messages from the aliens themselves.

Voices from the Ether

Richard T. Miller, a participant in the famous Mantell UFO case, left the air force in 1949 but served as an undercover civilian UFO investigator for ATIC [Air Technical Intelligence Center] until 1952 on a part-time basis. Full-time he worked as a television repairman.

In the summer of 1954, Miller met George Hunt Williamson, one of the early contactees, who claimed to have received alien transmissions using ham radio equipment. Williamson gave Miller a list of radio frequencies that he said carried the transmissions, and on September 10, 1954, Miller and some friends did indeed hear a strange broadcast in English. Thinking some fellow ham operators might be pulling a joke, Miller and others used direction-finding equipment to trace the powerful signal but failed to locate the source. The Federal Communications Commission was called in, but agents also failed to locate the signal's source. After one of the ham operators accidentally broke his antenna, it was discovered that the signal was being beamed straight down on the earth from the direction of the North Star. Shortly after beginning to receive these strange signals, Miller and some friends had another startling experience at his home.

"A glowing UFO came down to treetop height, jockeyed back and forth and lined itself up beautifully with our little [radio] unit, sat there, and then did the next most impossible thing electronically we could think of—it modulated the glowing force field around the craft at an audio rate, and sent us a message." The message, among other things, advised the listeners to contact none other than contactee George Adamski at Mount Palomar and warn him of a coming earthquake. Although Miller failed to reach Adamski, he learned from newspapers that a mild earthquake had indeed struck Mount Palomar on the designated date. "That was all the verification we needed," said Miller, who went on to record dozens of transmissions from "our friends from outer space."

Some time later, Miller claimed to have been taken aboard a UFO for a lengthy conversation with a human-appearing alien named Soltec. Following this experience, Miller said he was able to converse with the space beings by telepathy alone. By this means, he was able to accumulate much information.

Miller said he was told the UFO that took him was a "Galactic Survey scientific ship" named the "Phoenix" measuring "magnetic field anomalies" and cosmic radiation around the earth as well as on the moon. He learned the craft represented a Galactic Confederation that had been studying and observing the earth for millions of years. Miller was told that the earth was somewhat "unique" from other worlds due to the "crudeness and ferocity" of its life-forms and that the planet was "approaching the end of a cosmic cycle and there was going to be a form of transition into a new state."

"He said they were primarily attempting to reach as many people as they could," Miller recalled. "They had instrumentation on board their ships, that as they flew around the planet, they could pick up on individuals who had telepathic potential. The main reason they were here was to help raise the general level of awareness of all life forms on the planet Earth."

Miller learned that, unlike the newborn of other worlds, humans were born with no memory of past lives or conscious telepathic powers. This deficiency was one of the basic causes of human strife. "As a result of all this, they quarantined the planet Earth and it has been quarantined ever since," Miller stated in a compilation of his communications published in 1979. In these detailed and intricate messages, an astounding history of the earth was revealed, including references to ancient civilizations such as Atlantis and Lumeria. One part dealt with the Great Pyramids of Egypt, which, according to Miller's notes, were built by aliens as giant "motion stabilizers for the planet," eliminating a dangerous wobble in its rotation about forty-five thousand years ago. In this account, the pyramids originally were built on the earth's equator but ended up on the thirtieth degree of north latitude following a prehistoric axis tilt. This shift resulted in the Great Flood of Noah, which nearly exterminated mankind.

According to Miller, these aliens used a form of energy surrounding them even in deep space. "[Soltec] described it as being the electromagnetic and electrostatic lines of force that they twisted or bent parallel for a fraction of a moment. This provided them with all the energy they needed," he wrote. "Aboard this particular space ship, they did have a small fusion generator, an atomic generator which was like a starter motor. It generated the power to create a force field, which in turn, could bend the lines of force and release the energy they needed." Interestingly enough, there has been productive modern research into just such energy—called zero point energy. Research at the Institute for Advanced Studies in Austin, Texas, has determined that the vacuum of outer space is neither empty nor tranquil, but filled with phantom particles of energy and fluctuations only now being discovered. According to physicists John Wheeler and Richard Feynman, there is enough energy in the vacuum of a solitary lightbulb to boil all the earth's seas. It has been speculated that zero point energy may be "the Rosetta stone of physics, explaining everything from gravity to atoms to the origin of the cosmos itself."

Through telepathic communication, Miller recorded a variety of messages from nonhuman beings with names like Hatonn, Korton, Voltra, Ashtar, Mon-Ka and Lalur, who spoke on everything from a prehuman history of Earth to giant spacecraft production plants under the surface of Mars to a tour of "Galactic Central."

One of Mon-Ka's messages stated that many world leaders, including President Dwight Eisenhower, were contacted prior to 1956 regarding the aliens' presence. "Some choose to listen to our statements and believe," related Mon-Ka. "Others, unfortunately, choose to circumvent our offers by not informing their people of these contacts. Mankind on your planet is eager to know the truth. It is a pity that a few would decide that the majority should remain ignorant." Mon-Ka went on to indicate that the U.S. government had several alien craft in its possession.

Mon-Ka, as recorded by Miller, also dealt with the metaphysical, stating that the universe consists of both many worlds and dimensions, all under a force he called "the thought of Our Divine One." "All consists of energy, matter and thought," he explained. "Three manifestations of that which is known as original with our Creator— all existing [as different forms of energy] upon planes of reference known as vibration, or more commonly, frequency."

Miller was only one of a long list of people who claimed to have made contact with nonhuman intelligences through various means, primarily telepathy.

One of the most notable of such persons was Edgar Cayce, a Kentucky farm boy who dropped out of school in the ninth grade but became world famous as a prophet and psychic healer while in a trance. This quiet, unassuming man, widely known as "the sleeping prophet," recommended psychically received treatments for more than fourteen thousand patients who sought him out until his death in 1945. According to authors David Wallechinsky and Irving and Amy Wallace, "Unlike most psychics, Cayce kept complete transcripts of his trance-induced utterings. These transcripts, together with the follow-up research done on his patients, proved that Cayce's methods had an amazingly high success rate. Cayce's prophecies have also been uncannily accurate."

Cayce alluded to visitations by alien beings, said Rob Grant, a researcher with the Association for Research and Enlightenment, Inc., a group devoted to the study of Cayce's words. In Reading 1616–1:27, Cayce said one patient was once "among the priestesses of the Mayan experience." "It was just before that period when those as from the east had come, and there were the beginnings of the unfoldments of the understanding that there were other portions of the same land, or those that were visiting from other worlds or planets," he added.

Cayce also saw human experience on Earth as only a small portion of sentient life in the universe. "For, the Earth is only an atom in the universe of worlds," he wrote. Cayce explained, "Man's origin was as a spirit, not a physical body. These souls projected themselves into matter, probably for their own diversion, interrupting an evolutionary pattern then going on in the Earth. Through the use of his creative powers for selfish purposes man became entangled in matter or materiality to such an extent that he nearly forgot his divine origin and nature."

Jane Roberts, a poet from Elmira, New York, claimed to have encountered a disincorporated entity named Seth, described as an "energy personality essence." She said Seth spelled out messages while she experimented with a Ouija board in late 1963. "Not long after, however, I felt impelled to say the words aloud, and within a month I was speaking for Seth while in a trance state," she recalled. Over time, the entity Seth, speaking through Roberts, dictated the book *Seth Speaks*, which enjoyed some popularity in the early 1970s.

Seth claimed to have consciously entered our three-dimensional reality to educate humans to their inherent potential. "You are truly multidimensional personalities," he explained through Roberts. "The entire personality structure dwells in many dimensions, and simultaneously.

"Your concept of reality as seen through your physical senses, scientific instruments, or arrived at through deduction, bears little resemblance to the facts—and the facts are difficult to explain. . . . Your planetary systems exist at once, simultaneously, both in time and space. The universe that you seem to perceive, either visually or through instruments, appears to be composed of galaxies, stars, and planets, at various distances from you. Basically, however, this is an illusion. Your senses and your very existence as physical creatures program you to perceive the universe in such a way. The universe as you know it is your interpretation of events as they intrude upon your three-dimensional reality. The events are mental. This does not mean that you cannot travel to other planets. . . ."

According to Seth, "The self that you know is but one fragment of your entire identity. These fragment selves are not strung together, however, like beads on a string. They are more like the various skins of an onion, or segments of an orange, all connected through the one vitality and growing out into various realities while springing from the one source."

Seth offered this analogy to explain why humans seem to have blocked any remembrance of their multidimensional selves from memory: "A rich man who tries to be poor for a day to learn what poverty is learns little, because he cannot forget that wealth that is available to him. Though he eats the same poor fare as the poor man, and lives in the same poor house for a day—or for a year or five years—he knows he has his mansion to return to. So you hide these things from yourself so that you can relate. You forget your home so that you can return to it enriched."

He said scientists are only just now learning what some philosophers have espoused for centuries—that the mind can influence matter. "Consciousness creates form. It is not the other way around. All personalities are not physical. It is only because you are so busily concerned with daily matters that you do not realize that there is a portion of you who knows that its own powers are far superior to those shown by the ordinary self. You have lived other existences, and that knowledge is within you though you are not consciously aware of it.

"You may think of your soul or entity . . . as some conscious and living, divinely-inspired computer who programs its own existences and lifetimes. But this computer is so highly endowed with creativity that each of the various personalities it programs spring into consciousness and song, and in turn create realities that may have been undreamed of by the computer itself.

"The fact is that each of you create your own physical reality; en masse, you create both the glories and the terrors that exist within your earthly experience. Until you realize that you are the creators, you will refuse to accept this responsibility. Nor can you blame a devil for the world's misfortunes. You have grown sophisticated enough to realize that the Devil is a projection of your own psyche, but you have not grown wise enough to learn how to use your creativity constructively."

Seth said some UFO sightings are instances where human and nonhuman thought projections touch and represent only our perceptions of "visitors from other realities." "What happens is that you have an attempt to exchange camouflage realities," he explained. "The beings entering your plane cannot appear within it as themselves. Since their atomic structure is not the same as yours, distortions must occur in order to make any contact possible. Thus you are greeted with a certain set of sense data. You then try to figure out what is happening but the sense data, you see, means that the event is already distorted to some degree. The physical vehicles that are often perceived are your interpretation of the event that is actually occurring."

A Ouija board also figured into another successful book based on channeled information, this time from a collection of soul entities claiming to bring messages from a higher plane of existence under the name Michael. Michael's messages were compiled into a popular 1980 book by Chelsea Quinn Yarbro entitled simply *Messages from Michael*.

Michael, like Roberts's Seth and Miller's space friends, acknowledged one supreme force but refused to call it God. "We prefer not to use the word God in speaking of the ultimate creative force of the universe," Michael explained, speaking through an unidentified California woman. "Primarily because the word God in your society has become masculinized and requires the use of the masculine pronoun, thus perpetuating the personification of the universal creative force. . . . Unfortunately the word God gives rise to anthropomorphic fantasies that have no place in this teaching. For our purposes we shall call this constant creative force the Tao, for it is impossible for the Western mind to construct any visual image around this word."

Michael also stated that we are all parts of a greater whole, living in a "pandimensional universe." The Michael entity explained that each individual is a bit of sentient energy or soul that is separate from the personality. This soul is "trapped" in a series of physical bodies "for as long as it is necessary for them to experience all of life through the cycles. . . . There is growth on the higher planes as well, very like those of the physical plane, and as the soul grows older on the physical plane it becomes more aware of this higher evolution. . . . The continuous creative force that is universal casts out entities into physical lifetimes. These entities fragment and become many different personalities. Their integration is the evolutionary pattern for all souls. You do not feel the desire to seek the remaining fragments of your entity until the last physical cycle. Then, at that time, there is almost a compulsion."

"Let us use an analogy," Michael explained. "Imagine the Atlantic Ocean as the whole; imagine filling 10 test tubes, then sealing them so that they are both airtight and watertight, then imagine dropping them back into the ocean. They are part of the whole, yes, but unless some outside force liberates them, they are remote from the source and trapped in an effective prison. This same way the soul is trapped in the body. The body is very limited in what it can do. The soul in its true spiritual state has no limitations or handicaps."

Like Seth, Michael warned against creating a new religion around such messages, stating, "It is too easy for you to be lured by your expectations into making this a new faith, which is in complete opposition to our intention. Blind faith eliminates understanding, and without understanding there can be no growth or agape, which is the goal."

When asked if humans are the only ones to have souls that grow through reincarnation, Michael replied, "There are two such species on this planet. Human beings and cetaceans. This is, whales and dolphins. However, we think you should know that there are over 10 million ensouled species in this galaxy alone."

Aliens Save the Earth

Another recent self-proclaimed representative of disembodied beings was a personable man calling himself Drunvalo Melchizedek. This person, whose human name was never publicized, reportedly volunteered to leave his body in 1972 in exchange for an unspecified "gift." His absence allowed the personality of Drunvalo Melchizedek to enter this dimension for educational purposes.

Interestingly, the Bible mentions in Hebrews 6:20 that Jesus himself was "a high priest forever, in the order of Melchizedek" (New International). Hebrews 7:1–5 states that Melchizedek had no mother or father nor any ancestral record; was never born and never died, but was like the "Son of God," a priest forever who was given a tenth of all he possessed by the Old Testament patriarch Abraham and praised by the author of Psalms. Obviously this strange and mysterious Melchizedek was a powerful authority in the eyes of the biblical authors.

A Melchizedek was said to be someone who can consciously traveled through dimensions. Drunvalo reportedly traveled through many levels of both physical and spiritual existence to reach Earth. On this journey, he visited advanced civilizations in the star systems of Orion, Sirius B, and the Pleiades.

"Drunvalo doesn't tell these stories about himself to prove that he is anyone special," reported Drunvalo student Bob Frissell in his 1994 work, *Nothing in This Book Is True, But It's Exactly How Things Are*. "To the contrary, it is to serve as a reminder to you, to show how special you are. Consider, for example, the possibility that you too are a higher-dimensional master here on special assignment. Consider also that in order for you to properly do your job, it is necessary to become as human as possible; that is, to go to sleep and forget, and at the proper time you would be reminded of your true nature. You have done the first part perfectly. Now it is time for phase II. Drunvalo does remember and that is the difference."

Drunvalo weaves celestial mechanics, ancient alien visitations, spiritualism, multidimensionalism, and religion into one grand unified explanation. He stated that we have all entered a new age of enlightenment. Author Frissell explained, "As a civilization we gathered a certain amount of information since the days of Sumeria 6,000 years ago until 1900. Between 1900 and around 1950 we doubled that amount of information. Then from approximately 1950 to 1970, we doubled it again, from 1970 to 1980 again. Information now is doubling so fast that NASA is about eight years behind in getting some things into its computers so they can even use them. We are so far from catching up with ourselves that we have already entered a new phase of history while pretending that everything is the same way it's always been. Not so."

According to Drunvalo, humans are multidimensional beings unaware that we share this planet with others. "Dimensions are separated from one another by wavelength much as the notes are on a musical scale," explained Frissell. "Each tone on the scale sounds different because of its wavelength. The piano has eight white keys and five black keys, which together give its player the chromatic scale. In between each key and the next are 12 harmonic points; in dimensional terms these are the overtones. It is also the same as changing channels on a TV set. When you operate the channel control, you are turning to different wavelengths. . . . This planet has many different worlds; they are all right here, but our consciousness is tuned to one particular wavelength. Meanwhile, we literally exist on all dimensional levels and our experience on each level is completely different." Frissell said that archeologists are working in the wrong vibration, which explained the lack of evidence proving the existence of early civilizations such as Atlantis and Lemuria.

Drunvalo also dismissed the idea that man is at the top of the intellectual heap. "We think that we are the most advanced, but the whales and dolphins are far, far beyond us," wrote Frissell. "We think we are the most advanced because we can create external things. . . . The most advanced life forms do not create externally. They create everything they need internally."

Referring to a variety of concepts such as "sacred geometry," Eastern mysticism, meditative breathing, the internal "chakra"—or the basic vibration centers of the body—system, and the merging of mind, spirit and body into one "Christ-Consciousness," Drunvalo asserted that the human purpose is to evolve into a higher dimensional plane. "According to Drunvalo we have already reached the point where 1½ billion people will definitely make the conscious shift, and the 'masters' [inter-dimensional light beings here to assist] are projecting that everyone or almost everyone will make it into the next dimension," wrote Frissell.

Drunvalo claimed it is extremely important to perfect the quality of our thoughts here on the third dimension because in higher dimensions, mere thought will create our reality. "This is what Jesus meant when he stressed the purity of thoughts," Frissell stated. "Love and peace and unity and being kind to your neighbors are ultimately very practical because they work reciprocally. These things are important on the third dimension also, but, because of the time delay in manifestation, we get away with playing dumb and not seeing cause and effect. The third dimension seems to be a realm for mastering limitations or victim consciousness. In victim consciousness, the ultimate victim is one who doesn't know that he or she is creating reality, and believes than things just happen to them."

An interesting twist to Drunvalo's teachings is the idea that aliens altered this planet's predicted doom in 1972. According to this story, Earth was subjected to a gigantic solar flare on August 7, 1972, which would have destroyed all life on the planet, since we had not yet achieved the higher consciousness or vibration necessary to shift into a higher and safer plane of existence. According to Drunvalo, intelligent beings from Sirius, assisted by about a hundred other races, were given permission by "Galactic Command" to experiment and try to avert this disaster. They established a holographic energy field around the earth and everything on it that not only protected life against the solar flare but made everyone blissfully unaware of the event.

Indeed, in 1972 *Science News* noted, "The early days of August saw a severe disturbance on the sun that produced four major flares between August 2 and August 7 . . . among the most major ever recorded. . . . The August 7 flare ran the X-ray sensors off the scale."

This event caused unforeseen results, according to Drunvalo, who claimed all previous predictions regarding the future of Earth—such as those of Edgar Cayce and Nostradamus—are no longer valid due to the change of 1972.

"According to Drunvalo," Frissell wrote, "extraterrestrials regularly visit a planet like ours. But it is against universal law for them to interfere with us. For this reason they enter one overtone higher than the one the planet sits on so that they are invisible to us. But they can monitor us very clearly from this higher overtone. In fact, the next higher overtone on our planet is right now so full of vehicles filled with curious occupants that more recently arriving visitors have had to go into the second overtone, and they have now almost completely filled that one. There are even beings from distance galaxies here to watch."

One alien race now on Earth that is mentioned frequently by Drunvalo is the familiar "greys." By his account, the greys are distant ancestors of Martians, who are even now struggling with the loss of atmosphere and environment on their own planet. Both the Martians and the greys tried to cope with their realities by external intellect. They built spaceships and other devices to help them in their evolution, but lost the internal energy of love and emotion—the so-called Christ-Consciousness—that allows all sentient beings to connect with the universal whole.

"The Greys now realize that to get out of the trap they created for themselves by separating themselves from the source of life, they have to get back their emotional bodies. Unfortunately, the only way they know how to do this is by studying us intellectually, which, of course, will never work," explained Frissell.

However, according to Drunvalo, the greys made contact with a "secret government" on Earth prior to World War II and have traded their advanced technology for the right to experiment on the earth, which included animal mutilations and human abductions. "Whether you call them the secret government, the Illuminati, the Bilderbergers, the Trilateral Commission, or the Council on Foreign Relations, the name is irrelevant," Frissell noted, echoing the statements of Bramley and others. "The 'secret government' is basically made up of the richest people in the world. There are about 2,000 of them and they have been controlling our so-called governments for a long time. They control who gets elected, when, and where; they control when there is a war and when there isn't. They control planetary food shortages and whether a country's currency is inflated or deflated. All these things are dominated completely by these people. They can't control natural disasters, of course, but they can and do control a lot."

Drunvalo said that by the late 1960s, this "secret government" learned from scientists that a planetary disaster was imminent and began to join their assets in both the United States and the former Soviet Union in an effort to design an escape plan for themselves. He said that both nations secretly used grey technology to build their own saucers and that "about 50 percent of the UFOs sighted are our own." He added that this "secret government" has built secret bases on both the moon and Mars, explaining some of the anomalies on both.

However, in basically supporting this Alternative 3 scenario, Drunvalo said that the people within the "secret government" have become like the greys and are in danger of losing their emotional bodies to sheer intellect. According to Drunvalo, the greys are on the way out, not having learned enough regarding inner growth to survive on their physical plane. And members of the "secret government" have begun to realize that they cannot survive on their own. They need love and "unity consciousness" too and so are allowing more and more material to be made available to a wider public audience in opposition to their previous policy of maintaining strict secrecy.

Unbelievable as all this sounds to most people, it echoes the basic message of a book first published back in 1955, which has attracted a small but loyal following. *The Urantia Book* is nearly three thousand pages of an obtuse and overly detailed description of the nature of God and the creation and structure of both Earth and the universe reportedly channeled from a variety of nonhuman entities, including an entity also named Melchizedek. According to *The Urantia Book*, the original Melchizedek was a direct creation of God who, along with another direct creation, Gabriel, administers our known universe, referred to as Nebadon, which contains ten thousand inhabited systems. Urantia is this book's name for Earth.

The book's authors made it clear that sentient life exits both on other physical worlds as well as other dimensions. They also stated that humans are spiritual beings living simultaneous existences on many different levels but that most people have lost this knowledge except in regard to religious matters. "We worship God, first, because he is," wrote the authors, "then, because he is in us, and last, because we are in him."

This book agreed with other researchers in stating that a wide variety of nonhuman life-forms, many of them energy beings, visit and work on the earth for the purpose of assisting in the planet's evolutionary growth toward God. It stated that Lucifer, once a distinguished administrator of God, fell from grace by thinking that his own intellect was the same as God's—the same mistake attributed by others to the grey aliens. The struggle between good and evil on this world is a physical manifestation of the struggle between those beings who chose to follow their own desires and intellect and those who would follow the sum total of creative energy—God.

While such words of love and immortality, whether channeled or otherwise, are written off by most people as some sort of "New Age" balderdash, there is an intriguing consistency to these messages. Whether this is due to some cosmic truth or simply the result of an evolving mythology among writers of such material who read each other and then add their own interpretation appears a matter of individual belief.

What is certain is that once again, the clash of individual mindsets enters the picture, particularly in considering the religious implications of the UFO phenomenon. And while individual belief and faith are matters far beyond the scope of this work, it is instructive to note the various positions advanced by the voices of those speaking for religion.

An Alien by Any Other Name

A diminutive being with large, hypnotic eyes is encountered during a walk in the woods. Should he/she/it be regarded as an angel, a devil, an elf, or an alien? It would appear to depend upon the observer's perspective.

A pragmatic debunker such as Curtis Peebles would probably

deny the whole encounter, chalking it up to some passing psychological anomaly or badly digested food. A peaceful person oriented toward New Age philosophy might believe she had encountered a "space brother" working for man's enlightenment. A person with a mythical bent might believe he had met an elf or wood faerie. For the suspicious fundamentalist, fearful of damnation and the erosion of his tightly constructed world, it would be a disciple of the devil. For the more positive-thinking religious person, the figure would be an angel. After all, there are currently numerous books, records, and videos concerned with angels. In fact, there's almost a whole subculture of those intrigued by angels. How are we expected to determine whether a manifestation is an angel, devil, or alien?

Authors Pacheco and Blann concluded that since deceit and misrepresentation are so prevalent in the UFO field, entities relating with humans must be evil. "As difficult as it may be to accept in our materialistic society, the real answer behind the paranormal might not lie in science, but in the occult," they wrote. Stating that society's attempts to separate the physical from the spiritual are doomed to failure, they said, "Discussion of metaphysical entities such as 'angels' or 'demons' infer the existence of a moral code which our society is gradually jettisoning. If instead of 'angels and demons' we used such words as 'Jungian archetypes' or 'interdimensional realities' then this would be more acceptable, since it would not imply a conflict of 'good versus evil' and certainly would not suggest the existence of either a God or Satan."

Similar arguments have been raised by researchers who point to the reported behavior of aliens, particularly those blamed for abductions. They intrude into people's homes, incapacitate their victims, take them by force, and then subject them to unwanted and frightening medical examinations and procedures. Many people ask how anyone could call such behavior benevolent.

Others argue that it could well be a situation comparable to a small child being grabbed up and taken to a hospital, where efficient medical personnel operate on her in a coolly professional manner. The child is terrified and does not understand what is happening, while the ones operating treat her as a patient to be processed. Such an attitude, born of repetition and weariness, can be found in emergency rooms all over the country.

Pacheco and Blann claimed that due to the combination of "widespread paranormal phenomena" with current geophysical and political events, mankind must be entering the biblical "end times": "Perhaps not the 'end of the world' in a physical sense, but at least the end of the current phase of human existence."

They went on to conclude that "our society is in the midst of a concerted campaign of deception being promoted by certain individuals who are themselves under deception by 'consciousness' that inhabits the twilight world between the real and the surreal—similar to what Carl Jung called 'archetypes of a collective consciousness,' and what religions call angelic beings." In other words, we are all involved in the age-old battle between good and evil, God versus Satan.

"Some of these manifestations are constructive, respect our free will, and assist us in our path toward ultimate good, or God. These are the angelic phenomena typified by 'messengers of God' and true apparitions of the Virgin Mary," they wrote. "Others are summarily evil, and attempt either to seduce us through seemingly 'good' manifestations, or force us to adopt a false belief, while undermining our rational thought processes and our human spirit. These are primarily the manifestations reported as UFOs."

This summation is supported by many religious writers, including John Weldon, who, along with Hebrew Christian author and lecturer Zola Levitt, warned, "It is perfectly reasonable, from a Biblical point of view, to expect that the UFOs represent demon activity. Contact with them will grieve God . . . and He will remonstrate with man in a disastrous way."

Author Dr. Clifford Wilson, who attacked the ancient astronaut theories of von Däniken on biblical grounds, made clear his belief that UFOs have no connection to God. He wrote, "To argue that God's heavenly messengers need UFOs to achieve His purposes is to limit God's powers, and his thoughts, to those of men. Much of the modern writing about UFOs and the Bible tends to think of God as little more than a glorified astronaut. . . . The physical principles by which UFOs operate might well be utilized for the purposes of God, but the Bible certainly does not confine Almighty God to a heavenly 'super-car.'

"The fact is, this is serious. The aliens are here," he added. "We say, not from other planets. Not from outer space. Not just from the innermost depths of human reality. We say the answer is paraphysical and that the author of terror (Satan) is himself the perpetrator of these phenomena."

Paul Davies, author of *The Mind of God* and *Are We Alone?*, explained the anxiety of religious fundamentalism concerning nonhuman intelligent life thusly: "Belief that mankind has a special relationship with God is central to the monotheistic religions. The existence of alien beings, especially if they were further advanced than humans intellectually and spiritually, would disrupt this cozy view."

Pacheco and Blann offered this formula for dealing with nonhuman intelligences. "Although we claim that there are both good and evil manifestations, we are not able to tell the difference in any systematic or definitive way. . . . Therefore, one could argue that the best approach is to avoid any such manifestations."

As every Christian fundamentalist has been taught, Satan is the Great Deceiver. The New Testament book 2 Corinthians 11:14 (Revised Standard) states, ". . . for even Satan disguises himself as an angel of light." "Those who look upon such phenomena as the UFOs, contactees and the occult as benevolent are playing into his hands," wrote Weldon and Levitt.

Since the UFO researcher is told that from the human perspective he cannot separate angels from demons posing as helpers, he is trapped in a spiritual "hall of mirrors" just as confusing as the one erected about UFOs by government deceit and disinformation. Small wonder that so many people choose to ignore the UFO phenomenon rather than deal with all its ramifications.

The problem is even more acute for those who have experienced a UFO sighting or an abduction firsthand. Some are awed and excited by their experience, such as Lyn Buchanan, who said he almost accepted an offer to become a UFO pilot. Others are frightened and disoriented, such as Travis Walton.

"They [UFO visitors] respond to what you give out to them," explained author and abductee Whitley Strieber in a recent interview. "If you look at the experience with fear, it will be fearful. They are projecting their subjective reality to us and we are projecting our subjective reality to them. They spent ten years playing games with my fears." Strieber said he has noticed that negative UFO experiences tend to increase around military bases, where fear of attack and infiltration is most intense.

This thesis seems to have been true for the military-trained remote viewers, who voluntarily chose to take a mental look at UFO occupants and had confidence in their RV expertise. None of them apparently have suffered any ill effects simply from viewing what they perceived as alien races.

But while religious fundamentalists may have trouble dealing with the concept of aliens as opposed to angels and demons, many clerics voice a certain equanimity when it comes to the idea of life outside the earth.

Speaking in reaction to the discovery of the meteorite said to contain fossils of ancient Martian life, the Reverend James A. Wiseman, chairman of the Department of Theology at Catholic University, said, "Personally, I've always believed we will find life on other planets." He said those whose faith might be shaken by aliens are those who believe "God created life on Earth and Earth alone." He added that changing such an "egocentric and ethnocentric mind-set" might require a massive shift in beliefs comparable to Copernicus persuading the public that the earth actually revolved around the sun.

"What this challenges, interestingly enough, is not classical Christian and Jewish theism, which has always known that everything that is, is God's creation," stated Stanley Hauerwas, professor of theological ethics at Duke University Divinity School. "It challenges the high humanism that has been characteristic of our lives since the 17th century, namely that the human species is what it's all about, that everything exists to serve us."

James Leo Garrett, a professor at the conservative Southwestern Baptist Theological Seminary in Fort Worth, Texas, did not exclude the possibility of extraterrestrial life. "We need to be cautious saying that life on other planets is precluded, because [the Bible] also says that God is the creator of all," he said.

New York's Jewish Theological Seminary professor Burton Visotzky remarked that the stories of creatures, spirits, demons, and angels down through history suggests that nonhuman beings might exist. He indicated that rabbinical tradition has accepted such a possibility since the fourth century. Fathi Osman, a retired professor of Islamic studies at the University of Southern California, provided a quote from the Koran that seems to indicate that God created life outside of Earth. He pointed to Surah 42:29, which reads, "And among His signs is the creation of the heavens and the Earth. And the living creatures that He has scattered through them. And He has power to gather them together when He wills."

While the debate over the existence of intelligent extraterrestrial life continues, more and more people are claiming to have made contact with beings from beyond, and recent scientific discoveries have brought new knowledge that lends support to the concepts offered in metaphysical messages.

Contactees, remote viewers, and spiritualists have all spoken of visiting planets outside our solar system for many years. Yet it was only in April 1994 that Penn State astrophysicist Alexander Wolszczan published convincing data proving what until then had been only speculation: that planets do exist outside our solar system. Wolszczan confirmed the presence of three planets circling a pulsar star in the constellation Virgo. His discovery was quickly followed in 1996, when San Francisco State University astronomers Geoffrey Marcy and Paul Butler announced the discovery of two planets—one in the Ursae Majoris system and the other in the Virgo constellation—which appeared to be temperate enough for water to exist in liquid form, a presumed prerequisite for life as we know it.

As noted by *U.S. News & World Report* writer Traci Watson, "The discovery that other planets exist boosts the chances that somewhere aliens do, too." The 1996 discovery of what appear to be Martian fossils in a meteorite only increased the chances further.

When the military-trained remote viewers returned from their mental voyages and described multiple dimensions, distance planets, and stars and travel through time, their own bosses were so skeptical of their claims that they refused to pass such information along to higher authorities.

But in a series of recent books, sober-minded physicists are now claiming to have found evidence of a "top quark," which they take to be a key element in their current view of our physical universe. According to some scientists, "It is a universe where space exists in 10 dimensions, where one can travel through time into the past, where holes in the fabric of space and time pop up and serve as shortcuts to other parts of the universe, and where the visible universe may be only one of myriad mini-universes that coexist like so many soap bubbles in a cosmic froth."

But no hard-and-fast answers are available to the objective researcher as yet, for such answers transcend the material world. They cannot be answered with a computer, slide rule, microscope, or telescope. They can only be addressed by each individual as his or her mind-set allows.

NEW REALITIES

As the twentieth century draws to a close, cattle mutilations continue, crop circles are more elaborate than in the past, and the abduction experience appears to be more widespread than ever, in spite of the debunkers and media-supported public disbelief.

The UFO issue appears to be coming to head. New realities are impinging upon our collective consciousness.

Two concepts increasingly accepted by all but the most intransigent skeptic are that there is much more to life than our own brief material existence on Earth and that we are not alone on our world.

The concept that we are not alone is supported by overwhelming evidence, including multitudinous sightings, photographs, films and video, radar contacts, personal confrontations, abduction reports, crop circles, animal mutilations, channeled messages, multiple-witness reports, and physical evidence such as indented landing sites, holes in the ground, burned vegetation, human scars, and implants. Some of the human reports and photographic evidence undoubtedly are the product of misinterpretation or hoaxers, but the sheer number and consistency of descriptions argues against all of them being mistakes or fakes.

Another argument supporting the idea of nonhuman visitors is the longevity of the reports. If sightings had occurred only in recent times, they might be attributable to some passing mass psychosis, an aberrant copycat function of minds frightened by the onrush of modern technology. But reports of flying machines and unearthly visitors predate man's history. And the evidence of technology superior to ours in the distant past is particularly compelling. Although there is no clear indication that such technology was the product of alien visitation rather than some lost civilization of man, the many ancient tales of sky-gods and their flying craft tip the scales in favor of alien contact.

The possibility of ancient astronauts provides not only a credible explanation for legends and strange artifacts in man's history but also for the documented anomalies on the moon and Mars—some of which appear strikingly similar to our own mysterious Great Pyramid.

It would seem that early UFOs were viewed and reported through the perspective of the times in which they were observed. Thus, it was only near mid-twentieth century that UFOs began to take the form of flying machines. In view of the sum total of evidence available today, it would appear that the earth is being visited by a wide variety of craft bearing many different species. This created confusion in the past because most people had trouble conceiving of even one type of visitor to Earth.

There can be no doubt that beginning at least with World War II, military and government authorities in the United States took a keen interest in reports of flying craft and the glowing orbs that chased warplanes. Much material exists to suggest that the leaders of Nazi Germany may have developed a flying saucer based on advanced technology, which ended up in the hands of another nation. Whether this saucer was the result of human ingenuity or perhaps alien contact has yet to be been determined.

The year 1947 marked an obvious turning point in the government's attitude toward the subject, adding considerable weight to speculation that something unearthly was recovered near Roswell, New Mexico, and perhaps other locations. Where the government had acknowledged the possibility of extraterrestrial craft and beings prior to 1947, a new attitude of dismissal and ridicule was instituted. Right up to today, official denial has effectively blocked any public consideration of the phenomenon. Yet consistent internal reports and testimony from a variety of people showed that official interest in UFOs at the highest levels of government never diminished—only went deep undercover.

The Brookings report coupled with numerous public statements by several different officials indicated that leaders were fearful of the knowledge they had concerning UFOs. They feared disruption of public institutions and panic. Military officers, as always, viewed exotic technology as potential weapon systems to be kept secret from any potential enemy. Other leaders may have been less concerned about the public's state of mind or military security than about their own interests in maintaining control over public institutions, technologies, and profits.

It is clear from the record that beginning in 1952, government intelligence, initially the CIA, began to assume control over the UFO issue. U.S. Air Force Project Blue Book became merely a public relations front with a twofold purpose: to quiet the public clamor by dismissing as many UFO reports as possible and yet at the same time quietly collecting serious UFO information that was passed along to higher authorities.

It appears highly plausible that about this same time, a top-level, highly secret group of military officers, scientists, and other leaders was established to study the UFO issue—an MJ-12 group in effect if not in name. According to a wide variety of sources, such a group still operates today. Such a group would clearly more represent the wealthy top 2 percent of the United States population than the bottom 98 percent, and it is fair to assume that their interests—particularly from the standpoint of self-survival—might not coincide with the best interests of the general public. Then there are the bizarre stories—too many from too many different sources to ignore—that at some point representatives of the government may have in fact made contact with aliens.

All of this would presuppose the tightest secrecy possible by government—exactly the situation discerned by a study of the historical record. However, this wall of silence may have developed some cracks in recent years. It may be that our leaders are making sporadic efforts to condition the public to the idea of alien visitation. Strange alien creatures have been showing up in everything from expensive Super Bowl TV ads and children's cartoons to series such as *The X-Files* and *Dark Skies*, not to mention blockbuster movies. While the profit motive undoubtedly plays a large part, that such airings are allowed indicates to many that such concepts are being encouraged by the leadership of the tightly controlled mass media.

A truly free and democratic people—such as we like to think of ourselves being—should assert their right to the same knowledge as the wealthiest members of society. After all, we will all share equally in the future of Earth. It could very well be that the reason so many ordinary people claim to have had contact with alien beings is that those human leaders who have sought to keep the public ignorant of the alien presence are being bypassed.

Despite what appears to be a concerted effort by government and others to hide away this alien presence, an ever-growing number of people are becoming conscious of this new reality through a variety of means, including personal contact, channeled messages, the wider dissemination of news and information through computer networks, books, movies, TV, videos, a growing number of public speakers, plain old intuition, and military-developed remote viewing.

A consistent message is becoming clear—we are all free-willed multidimensional beings composed of both the physical and the spiritual. Our individual bodies are made up of physical matter that must conform to physical laws. But our bodies are energized by a thinking form of energy—the soul, if you prefer—which, like all energy, can neither be created nor destroyed, only change form. Many researchers into our spiritual side believe that mankind is in the process of shifting into a higher plane of existence—one that deals from the heart, not the intellect.

Our multidimensional side has blocked conscious memory of our true nature because of the lessons to be learned during our physical existence on Earth. At the level of this sentient and creative energy, we are all—humans as well as all other life-forms in the universe— connected in some type of comprehensive energy grid, akin to Einstein's unified field theory. This appears to operate at the submolecular level or beyond, which our science is only just now discovering. It is at this level that man's intuitive and psychic abilities come into play. According to nearly all personal reports, most alien beings are more aware of this reality than ourselves, which may explain their apparent delicate handling of the contact between us.

This could also explain why there has been no direct *Independence Day*–type attack or physical attempt to subjugate humanity. After all, if their intentions were hostile, common sense dictates that they would have moved against us much earlier than today when they would face our deep space platforms and "Star Wars" weaponry.

This may also explain misconceptions regarding the abductions. Many believers in this all-are-one concept contend that abductees have agreed to work with the alien greys at one of the basic unconscious levels. Yet, when contact is made, the conscious mind is terrified at the experience. "Besides," commented one metaphysical student, "the greys have no bedside manner." The greys are trying to learn to deal with humans. They are probably puzzled that abductees feel abused by their medical experiments. Additionally, according to some researchers, the greys are living in a state of fear, and that fear is often reflected by the humans they contact.

It has been said that they must learn to reach higher levels of consciousness through the heart, not through the mind. It is ironic that apparently the only way they know how to learn about love and emotion is through cold, intellectual study. It's a bit like trying to teach someone to dance—you can explain about steps and count all you want but unless they have rhythm, forget it.

The alien agenda obviously encompasses much more than one race seeking to enslave or exploit the earth. Considering all accounts, there are many different races visiting us today, apparently for many different reasons—some benign and helpful, others perhaps more selfish. No one motive can be established any more than a Fiji Islander could ascribe one motive to the many travelers daily flying high over his head on trans-Pacific jetliners.

Whatever the motivations and whatever the technology in use, this agenda involves all concerned, human and otherwise, and it involves the prime creative force in the universe—the creator of all. As abductee Judy Doraty was told by an alien grey when she asked about God, "He's the same to us as He is to you."

It would appear that religion—or more specifically spiritualism—is interconnected with the alien agenda. While most religions address facets of spiritual truth, none can claim exclusive knowledge. The world's religions can be compared to the story of the blind men and the elephant. They all have a piece of the truth, but their interpretations may not be on the mark. Today, many feel that organized religion is about the control of understanding. It is the mind of man trying to interpret the heart of God—and not doing a very good job of it.

It has been said that every human feeling originates from only two basic emotions—love or fear. Love, the basis of compassion, sympathy, and understanding, stems from man's highest energy level, while fear, the producer of intolerance, hatred, and violence, comes from our basest energy level. Love, said to flow from God, is of the heart. Fear is a product of the mind. Unfortunately, too many religions focus on fear—fear of Satan, fear of death, and fear of the afterlife—to control members.

All of humanity may be moving into a higher consciousness. Some call it "Christ-Consciousness." There is no question that the old order—the old systems, the old ways of doing things—is crumbling. New dimensions, new realities are on the horizon. And each of us has a role to play. Mankind is only as strong as its weakest link. There are no victims or castaways. Everyone is involved. Each of us is like a tuning fork. When one resonates with the higher frequency of heartfelt love and understanding, others follow.

Many feel that the aliens of energy and light, called the Transcendentals by the remote viewers, are here to witness—and perhaps help—our shift to new realities. It is literally a rebirth and, like any birth, there will be pain as we all move through the physical transitions. Fear will only make it worse. Yet, fear will continue to be a large part of our experience until we are able to break through the government secrecy and media-driven illusion of life to gain full knowledge of our world, our true history, our future, and our relationship with others in the universe.

The advent of the UFO phenomenon on our collective consciousness in recent years may well be a wake-up call—a not-so-subtle message that human intellectual knowledge is not the end-all of existence or any assurance of peace and tranquillity. It won't be proven with a slide rule nor seen in a telescope. For true love and understanding, the basis for everything good and desirable, we must look inward. We all know truth when we hear it. It resonates deep within the individual being. We will know it by the subtle signals from the heart.

Mankind in its present growth phase might be compared to the college student, who as a freshman believes she knows everything but as a senior realizes she knows very little. Our adolescence is coming to an end and it is time to break free from Mommy and Daddy—all dogmatic authority figures—and begin to take our rightful place as free-thinking and responsible members of a universal public.

After all, to anyone not from Earth, we are the aliens—and fearsome ones at that with our primitive and destructive ways. Perhaps we are the focus of universal concern and are all being guided by a host of nonhuman life-forms.

To paraphrase that great possum philosopher Pogo, "We have found the alien agenda and it is about us."

TAKE ME TO YOUR LEADER

The sleek silvery saucer-shaped UFO glided silently over the country-side, finally coming to rest in a field near a farmer who stood transfixed in awe and wonder. Out stepped a diminutive emerald-hued figure who approached the farmer with one hand held aloft in a universal sign of friendship.

"Take me to your leader," intoned the little green man.

This scene has become a cliché in popular science fiction litera-ture. But while depictions of alien visitors has evolved from the blood-thirsty monsters of the 1950s and 1960s to the strange but often kindly creatures of *E.T.* and *Close Encounters of the Third Kind*, the question of leadership has acquired new significance.

Who is our leader? Who speaks for Earth? Clearly, neither the American nor the Russian president speaks for Earth. Many question if they even speak for their respective nations. Certainly, at this time no single individual or group appears to speak on behalf of Earth as a whole. Many UFO researchers believe that no public contact with unearthly intelligences can take place until a representative can speak for the planet. If this is so, it becomes incumbent upon us to determine who—if anyone—is in charge on this world. This section will address this question.

To begin, one must address the two basic theories of history—accidental and conspiratorial. The former idea was summed up by Zbigniew Brzezinski, President Jimmy Carter's National Security Advisor and a former director of the Trilateral Commission. "History is much more the product of chaos than of conspiracy . . . increasingly, policy makers are overwhelmed by events and information."

The idea of conspiracy in history has been largely dismissed by American politicians and the media. However, while *Webster's Third New International Dictionary* defines *conspire*—literally "to breathe together"—as a secret agreement between two or more people to commit a criminal or treasonous act, it also means "to concur or work to one end: act in harmony."

In today's business-oriented society, a company owner or manager who would admit to not having any business plan would be laughed out of the room as a soon-to-be-bankrupt loser. Yet, a business plan, while not necessarily criminal, is usually secret, at least from the competition. It is a form of conspiracy.

The act of conspiring is an ancient and well-documented part of human history. From the brothers of the biblical Joseph to Watergate, the record is replete with conspiracies. The assassinations of Julius Caesar and Abraham Lincoln, the American Revolution, the Spanish-American War, and World War I were all the results of human conspiracies. That master politician Franklin D. Roosevelt was quoted as saying, "In politics, nothing happens by accident. If it happens, it was planned that way."

The Attempted Coup of 1934

A classic but little-known example of conspiracy within the United States can be found in the attempted overthrow of Roosevelt early in his presidency. It is not only an example of hidden U.S. history—you didn't hear this story in high school—but also the lengths to which powerful persons will go to exert their will.

Only a year after Hitler came to power in Germany, many wealthy Americans looked with favor on a fascist system to act as a shield against socialism and communism. Many were disgruntled with President Roosevelt's social policies and felt he was secretly a communist.

"Early in 1934, Irénée du Pont and [General Motors president William S.] Knudsen reached their explosion point over President Roosevelt," reported author Charles Higham. "Along with friends of the Morgan Bank and General Motors, certain Du Pont backers financed a coup d'etat that would overthrow the President with the aid of a $3 million-funded army of terrorists, modeled on the fascist movement in Paris known as the Croix de Feu."

The undoing of this scheme was Marine Corps commandant Gen. Smedley Butler, who was approached by the plotters and urged to head the new military-based government. Butler, who had openly attacked Roosevelt's New Deal programs, however, proved to be a loyal citizen and immediately informed Roosevelt of the treasonous conspiracy.

"Roosevelt . . . knew that if he were to arrest the leaders of the houses of Morgan and Du Pont, it would create an unthinkable national crisis in the midst of a depression and perhaps another Wall Street crash. Not for the first or last time in his career, he was aware that there were powers greater than he in the United States," noted Higham.

Roosevelt decided to leak the story to the press, which generally downplayed it as a "ridiculous" rumor. Nevertheless, some of the primary plotters skipped the country until the furor died down, and the story prompted Congress to appoint a special committee to look into the matter. Yielding to the powerful interests involved, the committee dragged its feet for four years before finally publishing a report marked for "restricted circulation." Although downplaying the significance of this attempted coup, the committee's report did state that "certain persons made an attempt to establish a fascist organization in this country" and that the committee "was able to verify all the pertinent statements made by General Butler."

This was the last overt move against an American president by powerful business interests until 1963. However, it revealed that America's hidden rulers were not always content to operate within the confines of the U.S. Constitution. The fact that this attempted overthrow of the government is not mentioned in history texts illustrates the deficiency of this nation's public education in such matters, thanks to a mass media more concerned with "Mickey Mouse" topics than investigative news. It is ironic that today the Disney empire includes many news media organizations.

In the preface to their book *Fifty Greatest Conspiracies of All Time*, authors Jonathan Vankin and John Whalen point out, "The 'Disney' version of history could just as easily be called the '*New York Times* version' or the 'TV news version' or the 'college textbook version.' The main resistance to conspiracy theories comes not from the people on the street, but from the media, academia, and government— people who manage the national and global economy of information."

Mankind's history has indeed proven to be one long evolutionary movement into larger and more complex communities built upon one conspiracy after another. From tribes to city-states to nations to economic communities, the world has continued to move toward unified, planetwide rule. While this movement may be inevitable, many people today fear becoming a mere cog in some centrally controlled "New World Order" machine. Many fear that the people most likely to represent Earth—due to their power and wealth—may not represent the best interests of the average person. Many question whether this fear is valid. Is there evidence of a history of conspiracies by elitist individuals and groups?

The record is clear—the answer is yes. And it is in this record of conspiracies that the answer to who rules Earth may be found.

Pass the Buck

Power and wealth go hand in hand. To determine who has the power, one must look at who has the money. For this, one must gain a basic understanding of money itself.

Early man had no need for money. He hunted when he was hungry and farmed to stockpile food for the winter. But as civilization progressed, work became more specialized. The chicken farmer would barter a hen for some tomatoes. This soon proved impractical, especially for those like the sheepherder who could not always take his herd to the marketplace. Humans soon turned to coins as a measure of wealth. Precious metal, especially gold, was limited in supply, always desirable, and easily transported as small coins imprinted with words or pictures to guarantee purity. But heavy, bulging sacks of gold were burdensome, not to mention a tempting target for thieves and robbers.

So paper currency came into being. A paper bill was simply a promissory note to be exchanged for specified goods or services. This method worked well for a time, but then certain individuals learned that paper money could be much more than simply a means to an end; if loaned at interest, money could be used to earn more money. Early goldsmiths who warehoused gold coins used this stockpiled wealth as the basis for issuing paper money. Since it was highly unlikely that everyone would ask for their gold back at the same time, the smiths became bankers, loaning a portion of their stockpile to others for interest or profit. This has become known as fractional-reserve banking—loaning out more money than is actually kept in the bank. This system worked well unless everyone suddenly wanted their deposits back and started a "run" on the bank.

Added to fractional banking was the concept of "fiat" money, intrinsically worthless paper money made acceptable by law or decree of government. An early example of this system was described by Marco Polo during his trip to China in 1275. Polo noted that the emperor forced his subjects to accept black pieces of paper with an official seal on them as legal money under pain of imprisonment or death. The emperor then used this fiat money to pay all his own debts. "One is tempted to marvel at the [emperor's] audacious power and the subservience of his subjects who endured such an outrage," wrote author G. Edward Griffin, "but our smugness rapidly vanishes when we consider the similarity to our own Federal Reserve Notes. They are adorned with signatures and seals; counterfeiters are severely punished; the government pays its expenses with them; the population is forced to accept them; they—and the 'invisible' checkbook money into which they can be converted—are made in such vast quantity that it must equal in amount to all the treasures of the world. And yet they cost nothing to make. In truth, our present monetary system is an almost exact replica of that which supported the warlords of seven centuries ago."

Author William Greider, former assistant managing editor of the *Washington Post*, wrote, "The money illusion was transferred to a new object with the rise of demand deposits, better known as checking accounts. . . . It took generations for the public to overcome its natural distrust of checks, but by 1900 most people were persuaded. Personal checks, written by the buyers themselves, were accepted as just as valuable as dollar bills. The nationalization of currency issuance, completed with the creation of the Federal Reserve in 1913, simply continued this arrangement. A new dimension of trust had added to the illusion. Finally, the last prop for the money illusion was kicked away in this century: the gold standard was abandoned." Today, money is increasingly only numbers in a computer accessed by plastic cards at ATMs. There is nothing to back it up. Yet as this illusionary money is loaned by institutions, interest is added. As the total amount grows, the value of the money decreases. This is called inflation, in effect a built-in tax on the use of money.

In the Great Depression of the 1930s, money retained its value. It was simply hard to come by and prices were depressed to reflect its scarcity. Today, America is experiencing an inflationary depression—prices continue to increase because of an inflated money supply.

The answer to what controls this money supply is the central bank of the United States, better known as the Federal Reserve System, or "the Fed"—a collection of twelve large regional banks described as an "independent department" of the federal government. Its connection to government is tenuous at best. The twelve Fed banks are owned and controlled by commercial banks, which, in turn, are owned and controlled by private investors.

Arguments over the need of a central bank have raged since before the framing of the U.S. Constitution. "I sincerely believe," wrote Thomas Jefferson, a leading opponent of a central bank, "that banking establishments are more dangerous than standing armies; and that the principle of spending money to be paid by posterity, under the name of funding, is but swindling futurity on a large scale." On the other side was Alexander Hamilton, George Washington's treasury secretary. "Hamilton, believing that government must ally itself with the richest elements of society to make itself strong, proposed to Congress a series of laws, which it enacted, expressing this philosophy," wrote historian Howard Zinn. "A Bank of the United States was set up as a partnership between the government and certain banking interests."

A quick look at the fate of the first two central banks of the United States is instructive. The first, the Bank of North America, was chartered by the Continental Congress in 1781 and was modeled after the Bank of England. Due to the expediencies of the Revolutionary War, the bank was granted a government-sanctioned monopoly to create and issue paper money. Before the end of three years, runaway inflation quickly prompted the desire for hard specie money. This resulted in the end of the bank.

The Bank of the United States fared little better. Granted a twenty-year charter in 1791, it was a near duplicate of the failed Bank of North America. This bank too was given a monopoly to issue banknotes as well as serve as the official repository for all government funds. This bank too created inflation by the issuance of fractional-reserve notes. Money merchants prospered but the average citizen suffered. A vote to renew its charter was defeated by one vote in both the Senate and House in 1811. It was the end of a central bank for a time.

Although the names of the prominent Americans who profited from this bank have been lost to history, one name pointed to an international arrangement. Author Gustavus Myers wrote in 1936, "Under the surface, the Rothschilds [the famous European banking family] long had a powerful influence in dictating American financial laws. The law records show that they were the power in the old Bank of the United States." It is clear that conspiring European bankers and their New World associates were trying to gain control over America's money supply.

Despite ongoing public opposition to a central bank, international banking interests never gave up. After the turn of this century, there were a series of bank panics caused not by consumers or lack of money, but by internal banking problems such as currency drains. In November 1910, Senator Nelson Aldrich—father-in-law of John D.

Rockefeller Jr.—convened a secret meeting between top executives of the Morgan and Rockefeller interests at the hunting lodge of financier J. P. Morgan on Jekyll Island off the coast of Georgia. Here plans were laid to create a central bank for the United States.

Griffen noted, "What emerged [from the Jekyll Island meeting] was a cartel agreement with five objectives: stop the growing competition from the nation's newer banks; obtain a franchise to create money out of nothing for the purpose of lending; get control of the reserves of all banks so that the more reckless ones would not be exposed to currency drains and bank runs; get the taxpayer to pick up the cartel's inevitable losses; and convince Congress that the purpose was to protect the public."

Following this meeting, Aldrich introduced appropriate legislation in Congress, but it was defeated because of deep suspicions about his international banking connections. Aldrich, a Republican, was too closely identified with Wall Street bankers. Cloaked in a new wrapping, the legislation was finally pushed through Congress in 1913 by the chairman of the House Banking and Currency Committee, Virginia's Carter Glass—a Democrat. Twenty-two years after the fact, Frank Vanderlip, president of the Rockefeller National City Bank and an attendee at the Jekyll Island meeting, wrote, "Although the Aldrich Federal Reserve Plan was defeated when it bore the name Aldrich, nevertheless its essential points were all contained in the plan that finally was adopted."

The Fed—only today publicly acknowledged as a central bank—controls the economy of the United States through the use of three main tools: setting the reserve requirements of all depository institutions (what fraction of wealth they must keep on hand; raising requirements reduces loans and slows the economy), setting the discount rate the Fed charges commercial banks to borrow money, and open market operations in which the Fed directly buys and sells government securities. Additionally, the Fed controls other banks through the Federal Deposit Insurance Corporation. Also, through the buying and selling of foreign currencies, it influences the exchange rate and coordinates international financial policy.

"The Federal Reserve governors also made prophecy," added Greider, "but they had the ability to make their own predictions come true."

In other words, the Fed controls the economy and hence, the very life of the United States. Greider wrote that the Federal Reserve System "coexisted with the elected one, shared power with Congress and the President, and collaborated with them. In some circumstances, it opposed them and thwarted them." He added that the Fed was "the crucial anomaly at the very core of representative democracy, an uncomfortable contradiction with the civic mythology of self-government."

Other observers were less kind. Wright Patman, the longtime Texas congressman who headed the House Banking and Currency Committee, stated, "In the United States today, we have in effect two governments. We have the duly constituted government. Then we have an independent, uncontrolled and un-coordinated government in the Federal Reserve System, operating the money powers which are reserved to Congress by the Constitution."

In 1913, Congressman Charles Lindbergh Sr. warned that creation of the Fed "established the most gigantic trust on Earth. When the President signs this act, the invisible government by the money power . . . will be legitimized. The new law will create inflation whenever the trusts want inflation." Representative Louis McFadden, a successor to Glass as chairman of the Banking and Currency Committee, stated, "When the Federal Reserve Act was passed, the people of these United States did not perceive that a world banking system was being set up here—a super-state controlled by international bankers and international industrialists acting together to enslave the world for their own pleasure. Every effort has been made by the Fed to conceal its powers but the truth is—the Fed has usurped the government."

In a 1963 publication, Fed officials explained, "The function of the Federal Reserve is to foster a flow of money and credit that will facilitate orderly economic growth, a stable dollar, and long-run balance in our international payments." If indeed this is the Fed's function, it has failed miserably. Author Epperson evoked a conspiratorial view by wryly suggesting that perhaps the "system was created to do exactly the opposite of what it tells the American people!"

Griffin called for abolition of the Federal Reserve because it is incapable of accomplishing its stated objectives, it is a cartel operating against the public interest, it is the "supreme instrument of usury," it is our "most unfair tax," it encourages war and destabilizes the economy, and it is "an instrument of totalitarianism."

Every schoolkid knows that much of each year's revenues to the United States goes to "retire the national debt"—which today is nearing six trillion dollars, a totally unimaginable figure. In 1994, according to the Treasury Department, $296.3 billion, or more than 20 percent of total federal outlays, went to pay interest on a public debt of $4.6 trillion. What this means is that nearly a quarter of our tax dollars go to pay interest on the money borrowed in the past to run the government. Since it was the Federal Reserve banks that loaned the money in the first place—with the authorization of a cash-strapped Congress—they get the interest payments. They are paid to create our money, which decreases in value as the supply grows ever larger, requiring ever more loans.

Usury is a term that has all but disappeared from the language. Once the word was defined as any interest charged for a loan. But today dictionaries define it as "excessive" interest. The Texas Constitution once defined "usury" as any interest in excess of 6 percent. This ceiling was increased over the years until the whole concept was deleted from the document. Critics have noted that even the Bible only required 10 percent for God.

"Charging interest on pretended loans is usury, and that has become institutionalized under the Federal Reserve System," argued Griffin. "The . . . mechanism by which the Fed converts debt into money may seem complicated at first, but it is simple if one remembers that the process is not intended to be logical but to confuse and deceive." Greider noted, "The details of [the Fed's] actions were presumed to be too esoteric for ordinary citizens to understand."

According to Greider, the money dealers designed such intricate and esoteric details about their financial operations that it assumed the proportions of a cult. "To modern minds, it seemed bizarre to think of the Federal Reserve as a religious institution," he wrote. "Yet the conspiracy theorists, in their own demented way, were on to something real and significant. . . . [The Fed] did also function in the realm of religion. Its mysterious powers of money creation, inherited from priestly forebears, shielded a complex bundle of social and psychological meanings. With its own form of secret incantation, the Federal Reserve presided over awesome social ritual, transactions so powerful and frightening they seemed to lie beyond common understanding. . . . After all, money was a function of faith. It required an implicit and universal social consent that was indeed mysterious. To create money and use it, each one must believe and everyone must believe. Only then did worthless pieces of paper take on value."

Throughout the years of its existence, the Fed has rebuffed every attempt at a meaningful independent audit.

"The result of this whole system is massive debt at every level of society," wrote William Bramley, who began his research studying the underlying causes of war. "The banks are in debt to the depositors, and the depositors' money is loaned out and creates indebtedness to the banks. Making this system even more akin to something out of a maniac's delirium is the fact that banks, like other lenders, often have the right to seize physical property if its paper money is not repaid. At the national and international levels, we read today of Third World nations staggering under huge debts. Most of these debts are 'illusionary' in the sense that the bulk of the loans come from banks which generate or channel 'created-out-of-nothing' money. Some of these banks, such as some represented by the International Monetary Fund (IMF), have the right to dictate economic policies and demand austerity measures within the indebted nations to get the loans repaid." This type of control represents real and significant power.

Rule by the Few

There is no doubt that the incomprehensible and unauditable Fed is our most powerful institution, but does it always act in the best interest of the citizens of the United States?

Greider emphasized the unequal distribution of the wealth of America's families as reported in a study by the Federal Reserve Board: "54 percent of the total net financial assets were held by the two percent of families with the greatest amount of such assets and 86 percent by the top 10 percent; 55 percent of the families in the sample had 0 or negative net worth."

This cycle of the rich getting richer while the poor get poorer has been growing since 1968. It gained added momentum in the 1990s, according to the U.S. Census Bureau. From 1992 to 1994, the wealthiest 5 percent's share of the national income rose 14 percent, nearly twice that of everyone else's gain during the past twenty-five years. It was this richest percent that Hamilton wanted to ally with government, and this group can be counted on to act in its own self-interest. It's the "Golden Rule"—those that own the gold make the rules—as some humorists have put it. Obviously it is this oligarchy—this 2 percent—that represents the true rulers of our nation.

David Wallechinsky, who along with Irving Wallace produced the popular *The People's Almanac*, wrote, "There are many forces at work in U.S. society, but the most powerful by far are the interlocking directorates of the major banks, corporations, and insurance companies, with the backing of the leaders of the military."

This interconnectedness of the top banks and corporations was confirmed in 1978 by a Subcommittee on Reports, Accounting and Management of the Senate Committee on Governmental Affairs. "Chaired by a western Democrat senator, Lee Metcalf of Montana, the subcommittee asks who controls American business, and it comes up with the answer: Eastern monied interests," reported journalist Milton Moskowitz. "New York City banks, through their trust departments, exercise a huge chunk of control by the shareholder votes they cast. Even though they may be holding these shares for the real owners, such as pension trusts, they have the voting rights. . . . Since the banks are such heavies, who owns the banks? The answer, wouldn't you know, is that the big banks are controlled by other big banks. For example, the largest voter of stock in J. P. Morgan & Co., the parent of Morgan Guaranty, is Citibank, which has 2.6 percent of the votes. And the largest stock voter in Citicorp, the parent of Citibank, is Morgan Guaranty, which holds 3.2 percent of the votes.

"Morgan is also the largest voter of stock in three other giant New York City banks, Manufacturers Hanover, Chemical and Bankers Trust. Chase Manhattan is the largest voter of stock in one of Chicago's banking giants, First Chicago. And between them, Morgan Guaranty and Citibank vote more than five percent of the shares in the nation's largest bank, the Bank of America, based in San Francisco. Getting to the bottom of who controls is a little like a scene from 'Alice in Wonderland' or an Abbott and Costello comedy routine." While Moskowitz's data is somewhat outdated today—Manufacturers Hanover no longer exists, having first merged with Chemical in 1992, which in turn merged with Chase Manhattan in 1996—the system has only become more concentrated.

For the average citizen it is often difficult to conceive how a handful of people could control a large nation or the whole world. Yet, anyone who has lived in a small town easily understands that in each community of people there exists a pecking order of power. In any given city or town, a few individuals are the acknowledged decision makers. These individuals may include the local politician, banker, police chief, or maybe even the undertaker. But usually the person at the top of the pecking order represents wealth and long standing in the community. Sometimes this person makes the decisions, sometimes he merely guides others to a consensus. But make no mistake about it, the pyramid of command exists.

Every adult can understand this fact of life. We also understand that sometimes, those decision makers can be criminals. Many recall in the old grade-B westerns, it was the kindly banker who turned out to be boss of the rustlers driving the settlers off their land so it could be bought by the bank and sold to the railroad at great profit. Researchers of this issue are puzzled that so many people cannot seem to extrapolate this understanding to national and international politics. Of course, the corporate media tell us daily that everything is really okay and disparage any talk from "conspiracy theorists."

The ruling elite makes its will felt in a variety of ways, not the least of which is ownership control over the major media of nations such as the United States, which today is becoming concentrated in fewer and fewer hands. No wonder six of the top ten "censored stories" of 1995 as determined by Alternet involved business issues such as the monopolization of telecommunications, the worsening child labor situation, increased government spending on nuclear arms, medical industry fraud, the chemical industry's battle to subvert environmental laws, and the broken promises of the North American Free Trade Agreement (NAFTA).

Like media ownership, the Federal Reserve System is run by men and women beholden to the oligarchy. Greider, who basically favors the Fed, explained, "With only scattered exceptions, the Fed governors were drawn from two disciplines—financial economics and banking. In the case of the Federal Reserve Board, the American meritocracy allowed capable people to rise to the top, but it also screened them carefully. There were no radical thinkers or original theorists among them. No one with unorthodox opinions would be chosen." This portrait appeared identical to that of many corporations today. Obviously, there was no room for anyone who might consider questioning the need for the Fed or a banking system based on paper money and credit. The connection between business and the Fed was explained by Greider as a "revolving door" that "created an unofficial fraternity of industry insiders, men who spoke the same language and traded gossip, not unlike the military officers who left the Pentagon to work for defense contractors. Indeed, the professional esprit at the Fed resembled the professional officers' corps of the armed forces. 'You almost don't have to give orders,' one former economist said, 'because the troops already know what the orders will be.'"

That both present and former officials of the Federal Reserve System are members of this "fraternity" is undeniable. In addition to their business contacts, these officials are members of organizations with international connections such as the Trilateral Commission and the Council on Foreign Relations (CFR). Such officials include Fed chairman Alan Greenspan, former Chairman Paul Volcker (who went on to become North American chairman of the notorious Trilateral Commission), Cyrus R. Vance, Bobby Ray Inman, E. Gerald Corrigan, Robert P. Forrestal, Anthony M. Solomon, and many other prominent men.

Media members of the CFR read like a "Who's Who" of the industry. They include CBS chief Laurence A. Tisch, anchorman Dan Rather, NBC chief John F. Welch Jr., anchormen Tom Brokaw and David Brinkley, ABC chief Thomas S. Murphy and anchor Diane Sawyer, PBS's Robert MacNeil and Jim Lehrer, the *Washington Post*'s Katharine Graham, CNN's Daniel Schorr, *U.S. News*'s David Gergen, the *New York Times*'s Harrison Salisbury, columnists George Will, Meg Greenfield, William F. Buckley Jr., Georgie Ann Geyer, Ben J. Wattenberg, and many others.

The CFR is the American branch of the British Round Table

groups founded by Cecil Rhodes, who in the late 1800s grew wealthy from his monopoly on South African diamonds thanks to the cooperation of the Bank of England and Rothschild banking interests. Carroll Quigley, professor of history at the Foreign Service School of Georgetown University, wrote, "The Rhodes Scholarships ... are known to everyone. What is not so widely known is that Rhodes in five previous wills left his fortune to form a secret society, which was to devote itself to the preservation and expansion of the British Empire. And what does not seem to be known to anyone is that this secret society ... continues to exist to this day."

In his 1966 book *Tragedy and Hope: A History of the World in Our Time*, Quigley addressed the question of historical conspiracy by writing, "There does exist, and has existed for a generation, an international Anglophile network which operates, to some extent, in the way the radical Right believes the Communists act. In fact, this network, which we may identify as the Round Table Groups, has no aversion to cooperating with the Communists, or any other groups, and frequently does so. I know of the operations of this network because I have studied it for 20 years and was permitted for two years, in the early 1960s, to examine its papers and secret records. I have no aversion to it or to most of its aims and have, for much of my life, been close to it and to many of its instruments. I have objected, both in the past and recently, to a few of its policies—notably to its belief that England was an Atlantic rather than a European Power and must be allied, or even federated, with the United States and must remain isolated from Europe—but in general my chief difference of opinion is that it wishes to remain unknown, and I believe its role in history is significant enough to be known."

Quigley added, "Since 1925 there have been substantial contributions from wealthy individuals and from foundations and firms associated with the international banking fraternity, especially the Carnegie United Kingdom Trust, and other organizations associated with J. P. Morgan, the Rockefeller and Whitney families. . . . The chief backbone of this organization grew up along the already existing financial cooperation running from the Morgan Bank in New York to a group of international financiers in London led by Lazard Brothers. . . . At the end of the war of 1914 [World War I], it became clear that the organization of this system had to be greatly extended."

Quigley explained that "front organizations" were created for the Round Table Group. In London, this was called the Royal Institute of International Affairs. In America, it was the Council on Foreign Relations, a "front for J. P. Morgan and Company in association with the very small American Round Table Group."

It should be noted that Quigley is not a "conspiracy theorist" but a respected historian, and the acknowledged mentor of President Bill Clinton, himself a Rhodes scholar. But the mainstream media consistently fails to mention the connections between America's leaders and the organizations to which they belong. Other CFR members of the first Clinton administration included, but were not limited to: Vice President Al Gore, National Security Advisor Anthony Lake, Secretary of State Warren Christopher, Secretary of Defense Les Aspin, Secretary of the Interior Bruce Babbitt, Secretary of Housing and Urban Development Henry Cisneros, and Secretary of Health and Human Services Donna Shalala.

Conspiracy-minded researchers have been concerned for years that these government officials along with their media associates rarely mention their own membership in such groups, nor do they break silence and report on these activities.

One recent example involved the 1996 meeting of the Bilderbergers, a shadowy group of internationalists and CFR members named after the Bilderberg Hotel in Oosterbeek, Holland, where they were first discovered in 1954. Their secret conferences are attended by world leaders in government, finance, business, media, and labor. Although the Bilderbergers are pledged to silence about the subjects of their meetings, the group's first chairman, Prince Bernhard of the Netherlands, gave a good indication of what they're about in 1964 when he wrote, "It is difficult to re-educate the people who have been brought up on nationalism to the idea of relinquishing part of their sovereignty to a supernational body. . . ."

Between May 30 and June 2, 1996, the Bilderberger group met in King City near Toronto, Canada. Attendees included President Clinton's senior adviser George Stephanopolous, Defense Secretary William Perry, Henry Kissinger, Lloyd Bentsen, and David Rockefeller. At least some of the current government officials attending the meeting traveled at taxpayer expense. The Canadian media was filled with what news it could gather, carrying headlines such as "[Canadian prime minister Jean] Chrétien to speak at secret world meeting," "[Canadian publisher Conrad] Black plays host to world leaders," and "World Domination or a round of golf?" The American media, as usual, was mum on the subject.

Bilderberg officials have long tried to picture this gathering of the wealthy and powerful as just an informal discussion group. This image was shattered by one outspoken member, Jack Sheinkman, chairman of Amalgamated Bank, who told reporter Trisha Katson he had attended ten Bilderberg annual meetings. Sheinkman said, "In some cases discussions do have an impact and become [official] policy.

The idea of a common European currency was discussed several years back before it became policy. We had a discussion about the U.S. establishing formal relations with China before Nixon actually did it."

If future public policy is being discussed at these meetings, why are they not reported by America's "watchdog" media? A secretary for attendee William F. Buckley Jr. replied, "I don't think that is the nature of the meeting, is it?" Paul Gigot of *The Wall Street Journal* was more explicit when he explained, "The rules of the conference, which we all adhere to, are that we don't talk about what is said. It is all off the record. The fact that I attended is no secret."

Based on the evidence available today, there can be little doubt that a small clique of the wealthy elite exercise unprecedented conspiratorial control over much of the world's business and government, despite denials from the very media they own. But would this group take any interest in extraterrestrial life?

The answer would have to be yes because of the possible impact of any alien energy technology alone. But this is a highly speculative area, with but a small amount of evidence available.

What is clear and undeniable is that through calculated and aggressive government and corporate planning/conspiracies, our world has been made totally dependent on two major forms of energy: petroleum and nuclear. Activist Barry Commoner wrote that developing an inexpensive, abundant, and nonpolluting energy source is a "social need, and it is hopeless to expect to build it on the basis of production decisions that yield commodities rather than solutions to essential tasks; that produce goods which are maximally profitable rather than maximally useful; that accept as their final test private profit rather than social value."

Don Kelly, a design engineer and author of *The Free Energy Manual*, stated, "Both the oil and nuclear options have brought about the rise of monopolies which have functioned at the expense of the planet's environment. It's no wonder that the reported extraterrestrial visitors must consider our planet a wide open insane asylum when we consent to the adoption of dubious energy sources which have the clear potential of destroying the planet and all its inhabitants."

More than a few conspiracy researchers see this undeniable energy monopoly—supported by massive government subsidies and protections—as further proof of a plan to suppress any uncontrolled energy source, whether from UFOs or innovative human inventors like Nikola Tesla. A study of possible alternative energy sources led magazine editor Vicki Cooper to conclude that "the real energy solution lies not in a change of politics or government priorities, but in a change of consciousness."

Certain members of the world's wealthy elite have expressed a more than casual interest in UFOs and their occupants. Laurance S. Rockefeller, for example, sponsored a UFO project within the non-profit foundation BSW, Inc. A recent BSW report said preliminary results of the UFO project—which is both multidisciplinary and multinational—have been presented to government leaders. Limited to only one thousand copies, the 1995 report, entitled *Unidentified Flying Objects: The Best Available Evidence*, noted, "But if UFOs are real, as the information in this report strongly suggests, the issue in this case is access to knowledge of potentially profound significance with regard to man's place in the universe, to human society, and to science." The report also stated, "We believe this material has made a substantial impression on the present [U.S.] government and that there is an interest now to gradually open the door on UFO information." How quickly that door opens remains to be seen.

Since the wealthy elite—through mechanisms such as the Federal Reserve System, the World Bank, and the International Monetary Fund along with private groups such as the Council on Foreign Relations and the Trilateral Commission—exert a substantial degree of control over the world's governments, it would stand to reason that they would be very concerned with UFOs and life in space. Such a group would desire to be foremost in any alien contact so as to gain control of or suppress any alien technology that might unbalance the status quo. Any technology that might unseat the monopolies of energy, communication, or health care would be viewed as dangerous to a position of power. After all, would the long-suffering public continue to pay ever-increasing prices for ever-decreasing reserves of gas and oil if they knew for certain that fuel-free, nonpolluting electromagnetic or antigravity technology existed? Would the public remain passive with the certain knowledge that there were cures for AIDS, cancer, and perhaps even old age?

Viewed from this perspective, the cause for secrecy concerning extraterrestrial contact becomes abundantly clear.

SOURCES

Introduction

Page

xii   "my long investigation": Maj. Donald E. Keyhoe, *Aliens from Space: The Real Story of Unidentified Flying Saucers* (New York: Doubleday & Company, 1973), p. x.

xii   Dr. James E. McDonald: Ibid., p. xi.

xii   represents Smithsonian views: Author's telephone interview with Smithsonian Institution Press editor in chief Alex Doster, February 12, 1996.

xii   Peebles on Keyhoe: Curtis Peebles, *Watch the Skies! A Chronicle of the Flying Saucer Myth* (New York: Berkley Books by arrangement with Smithsonian Institution Press, 1995), pp. 44–45.

xiii "I am a skeptic": Ibid., p. xii.

xiv   Astronaut John W. Young: David Wallechinsky and Irving Wallace, "It's a Bird, It's a Plane—What Is It?" In *The People's Almanac #2*, ed. Roy Sorrels (New York: Bantam Books, 1978), p. 596.

xiv   Hermann Oberth: Antonio Huneeus, "Prof. Hermann Oberth: Confirmed UFO Believer!" *Unsolved UFO Sightings* 4, no. 2 (summer 1996), p. 66.

xiv   Wernher von Braun: Ibid., p. 67.

xvi   Kennedy quote: LeRoi Smith, ed., *We Came in Peace: The Story of Man in Space* (Chicago: Classic Press and Professional Press, 1969), p. 18.

xviii Lake Worth Monster: Jim Marrs, "Fishy Man-Goat Terrifies Couples Parked at Lake Worth," *Fort Worth Star-Telegram*, July 10, 1969, p. 2-A.

xviii "Some believe": Mark Chorvinsky, "Our Strange World," *Fate*, October 1992, pp. 31–35.

xxi   tens of thousands viewed the light: Paris Flammonde, *UFO Exist!* (New York: Ballantine Books, 1976), p. 97.

xxi   First "saucer" report: Jacques Vallee, *UFO's in Space* (New York: Ballantine Books, 1965), p. 1.

xxi   first dirigible flight: Peter Brookesmith, *UFO: The Complete Sightings* (New York: Barnes & Noble Books, 1995), p. 23.

xxi   continued news reports: Philip J. Klass, *UFOs Explained* (New York: Random House, 1974), p. 259.

xxii public conditioned by media: Ibid., p. 255.

xxii Aurora residents: personal interviews and media reports.

xxiv Dr. Tom Gray: Paula Doyle, Press Release, Public Information Office, North Texas State University, May 29, 1973.

xxiv "Subsequent analysis": Klass, op. cit., p. 263.

xxv Peebles summation: Peebles, op. cit., pp. 240–241.

xxvi AP wire stories: Original wire transmissions in author's files.

xxvi Wakefield accounts: Jim Marrs, "A Black Object Fell Into a Pond—Yes or No?" *Fort Worth Star-Telegram*, January 18, 1977, p. 1-B and original notes in author's files.

Chapter One: The Greatest UFO?

1   "Rosetta stone": Robert Jastrow, *Red Giants and White Dwarfs* (New York: W.W. Norton, 1990), p. 115.

2   "spawned a score of mysteries": Earl Ubell, "The Moon Is More of a Mystery Than Ever," *The New York Times Magazine*, April 16, 1972, p. 32.

2   "nearly as old as solar system": Jastrow, op. cit., p. 108.

2   *Sky and Telescope*: Don Wilson, *Secrets of Our Spaceship Moon* (New York: Dell, 1979), p. 166.

2   "refractory elements": Ibid., pp. 173–74.

3   layer description: Ubell, op. cit., p. 32.

3   "why . . . all the iron": Ibid., p. 33.

3   "wind" of water: Ibid., p. 50.

4   craters of internal origin: *The New Encyclopedia Britannica*, Vol. 27, p. 538.

4   "The relative cool": Ibid., p. 51.

4   scientists misled: Jastrow, op. cit., p. 114.

4   mascons: Ubell, op. cit., pp. 50–51.

4   internal heat: *The New Encyclopedia Britannica*, Vol. 27, p. 541.

5   "artificial construction": Wilson, op. cit., p. 156.

5   "moonquakes": *The New Encyclopedia Britannica*, Vol. 17, p. 662.

5   Nikolay A. Kozyrev: *Encyclopedia Britannica*, Vol. 1, p. 294; Vol. 27, p. 546.

5   glow moved: Wilson, op. cit., p. 18.

5   reddish glows: *Encyclopedia Britannica*, Vol. 27, p. 546.

5   like stock market: Walter Sullivan, "Seismic Net Set to Find Source of Tremors as Moon Nears," *New York Times*, August 4, 1972, p. 1.

5   artificial construction: Wilson, op. cit., p. 159.

6   small or no core: Editors, *The New Encyclopedia Britannica*, Vol. 27, p. 534.

6   MacDonald: Dr. Gordon MacDonald, report, *Astronautics*, February 1962, p. 225.

6   "negative mascons": Wilson (1979), p. 97.

6   Solomon: Ibid.

6   Sagan quote: Ibid., p. 94.

6   moon reverberated: Ibid., p. 100.

6   Ewing and Press: Ibid., pp. 101–02.

7   "reacted like a gong": Ibid., p. 104.

7   large meteor: Ibid., p. 106.

7   Dr. Farouk El Baz: Ibid., p. 107.

7   uranium 236: Ibid., p. 171.

7   rustproof iron: Ibid., p. 124.

8   magmatic processes: *Encyclopedia Britannica*, Vol. 27, p. 549.

8   Asimov: Wilson, op. cit., p. 85.

9   give moon the velocity: William R. Shelton, *Winning the Moon* (New York: Little, Brown, 1970), p. 58.

9   "no astronomical reason": Wilson, op. cit., p. 87.

9   Vasin and Shcherbakov: Ibid., p. 75.

10   not completely natural: Wilson (1975), pp. 11–12.

10   "world . . . not be entirely natural": Ibid., p. 161.

11   Arcadians: Ibid., p. 120.

12   *Gondwana*: Peter Kolosimo, *Timeless Earth* (New York: Bantam Books, 1975), p. 49.

12   moon placed in orbit: Immanuel Velikovsky, *Worlds in Collision* (New York: Doubleday & Company, 1950), p. 359.

12   closer moon: Maurice Chatelain, *Our Ancestors Came from Outer Space*, trans. Orest Berlings (New York: Doubleday & Company, 1978), p. 158.

12   Coral reef study: John D. Barron, *The Artful Universe* (Oxford: Oxford University Press, 1995), p. 116.

12   the Kalasasaya: Graham Hancock, *Fingerprints of the Gods* (New York: Crown Publishers, 1995), p. 77.

12   the Great Idol: Erich von Däniken, *Chariots of the Gods?* (New York: Bantam Books, 1971), p. 19.

12   symbols on idol: H. S. Bellamy and P. Allen, *The Calendar of Tiahuanaco* (London: Faber & Faber, 1956), p. 21.

13   NASA moon event study: Ibid., pp. 25–30.

14   Operation Moon Blink: Ibid., pp. 28–29.

14   "bridge": Don Ecker, "Long Saga of Lunar Anomalies," *UFO* 10, no. 2 (March/April, 1995), p. 23.

14   "It looks artificial": Wilson (1975), p. 151.

15   "Shard": Ecker, op. cit., p. 24.

15   "Tower": Ibid.

15   moon "occupants": George Leonard, *Somebody Else Is on the Moon* (New York: Pocket Books, 1977), p. 23.

15   professionals ignore signs: Ibid., p. 27.

16   statuesque shadows photographed: Wilson (1979), p. 23.

16   Blair and Abramov: Ibid., pp. 20–21.

16   "eerie similarity": Richard C. Hoagland, *The Monuments of Mars* (Berkley, CA: North Atlantic Books, 1987), pp. 267–268.

17   Barney's planet of origin: George Rodrigue, "Lunar-Tic Fringe," *The Dallas Morning News*, April 1, 1996, p. 7C.

17   "This is science?": Leonard, op. cit., p. 199.

18   Alan Bean and Brian Welch, "Claims of Ruins on Moon Just Not True, Says NASA," *Houston Chronicle*, March 22, 1996, p. 6A.

18   Armstrong: Timothy Good, *Above Top Secret: The Worldwide UFO Cover-up* (New York: William Morrow, 1988), p. 387.

18   cylindrical UFO: Wilson (1979), pp. 44–45.

18   Edgar Mitchell: Timothy Good, *Alien Contact* (New York: William Morrow, 1993), pp. 206–07.

19   "evidence is very strong": Transcript of *Dateline NBC* aired April 19, 1996.

19   Cooper letter: Good (1988), pp. 379–80.

19   ambassador letter from Cooper: J. Antonio Huneeus, "UFO Chronicle," *Fate* 48, no. 7 (July 1995), p. 21.

19   Michael Hesemann: Ibid., p. 18.

20   Gordon Cooper's thoughts: Robert T. Leach, "Col. L. Gordon Cooper Speaks Out," *UFO* 11, no. 4 (July/August 1996), p. 28.

20   "they're . . . watching us": Good (1988), p. 384.

20   Armstrong and UFOs: Chatelain, op. cit., p. 17.

20   NASA "strict control": Ibid., p. 16.

20   Chatelain background: Ibid., pp. 1–7.

21   "great number of channels": Ibid., p. 10.

21   Rep. Howard Wolpe: Don Ecker, "Superpower Problems in Getting to Mars," *UFO* 8, no. 6 (November/December 1993), p. 35.

21   Dr. Garry Henderson: Good (1988), p. 381.

21   National Security Agency: Ecker, op. cit., p. 25.

21   astronaut was evasive: Brian O'Leary, *Exploring Inner and Outer Space* (Berkeley, CA: North Atlantic Books, 1989), p. 92.

22   Brookings report: United Press International, "Mankind Is Warned to Prepare for Discovery of Life in Space," *New York Times*, December 15, 1960.

23   Dr. Jack Kasher and STS-48 tape: Dr. Jack Kasher interview, AFS/Dialogue, Minneapolis, MN, 1994.

24   Apollo and Gemini flights followed: Chatelain, op. cit., pp. 16–17.

24   Apollo program ended: Ibid., p. 13.

24   "like . . . Rolls-Royce": Ubell, op. cit., p. 56.

24   "we were 'asked' to leave": Ecker, op. cit., p. 25.

24   "we were warned off": Good (1988), p. 386.

25   "like a hot potato": Leonard, op. cit., p. 215.

25   Dr. Robert Jacobs and Atlas rocket: Ibid., pp. 292–93.

25   *Clementine*: Sean Casteel, "NASA and DoD Share Clementine Data," *UFO* 10, no. 2 (March/April 1995), p. 26.

Chapter Two: Ancient Astronauts

27   Velikovsky: David Wallechinsky and Irving Wallace, "Famous and Infamous Scientists," in *The People's Almanac*, ed. Arthur Bloch (Garden City, NY: Doubleday & Company, 1975), pp. 929–31.

28   von Däniken quote: Von Däniken (1970), p. viii.

28   von Däniken chastised: Colin Wilson, *The Mammoth Book of the Supernatural* (New York: Carroll & Graf, 1991), p. 505.

29   "von Däniken not the first": Clifford Wilson, *Crash Go the Chariots* (New York: Lancer Books, 1972), p. 51.

29   von Däniken discredited: Colin Wilson, op. cit., pp. 505–6.

29   "no way around von Däniken": Hoagland, op. cit., pp. 266–67.

29   Chinese characters on Olmec figures: Charles Fenyvesi, "A Tale of Two Cultures," *U.S. News & World Report*, November 4, 1996, pp. 46–48.

29   various beliefs: Erich von Däniken, *Gods from Outer Space* (New York: Bantam Books, 1972), pp. 161–62.

30   "accuracy of biblical references": Zecharia Sitchen, *The 12th Planet* (New York: Avon Books, 1976), p. vii.

30   *vimanas*: Richard L. Thompson, *Alien Identities* (Alachua, FL: Govardhan Hill Publishing, 1993), p. 201.

31   parallels with UFOs: Ibid., p. 211.

31   context dictated by conditioning: Ibid., p. 388.

31   King Salva's attack: Ibid., pp. 213–14.

31 One description of machines: Zecharia Sitchen, *The Wars of Gods and Men* (New York: Avon Books, 1985), p. 67.

32 "admirable men": Graham Hancock, *Fingerprints of the Gods* (New York: Crown Publishers, 1995), p. 156.

32 return to stars: Ibid., p. 141.

32 Quetzalcoatl legend: Kolosimo, op. cit., p. 163.

32 "strange craft in the skies": T. Lobsang Rampa, *The Third Eye: The Autobiography of a Tibetan Lama* (London: Martin Secker & Warburg Ltd., 1958), p. 140.

33 Tibetan kings: Andrew Tomas, *We Are Not the First* (New York: Bantam Books, 1973), p. 117.

33 "Flight of Etana": Ibid., p. 113.

33 cave graves: von Däniken (1972), pp. 96–99.

33 "imprint of a shoe sole": Serge Hutin, *Alien Races and Fantastic Civilizations* (New York: Berkeley Medallion Books, 1970), p. 5.

33 "five-toed llamas": Kolosimo, op. cit., p. 207.

34 vertical landing technology and "genuine mystery": Hancock, op. cit., p. 38.

34 J. Alden Mason and navigation guides: Kolosimo, op. cit., p. 206.

34 Landing at Nazca: von Däniken (1972), p. 105.

35 "folk memory": Tomas, op. cit., p. 121.

35 Maltese cross: Chatelain, op. cit., pp. 72–74.

35 Jacob's story: *The Holy Bible*, Authorized King James Version (London: Collins' Clear-Type Press, 1948), Genesis 28:11–14.

37 "Escape for thy life": Ibid., Genesis 19:17.

37 "brimstone and fire": Ibid., Genesis 19:24–26.

37 "pillar of vapor": Sitchen (1985), pp. 313–14.

37 "columns of smoke": *The New Layman's Parallel Bible* (Living Bible) (Grand Rapids, MI: Zondervan Bible Publishers, 1981), p. 45.

37 communities abandoned and radioactivity: Sitchen (1985), p. 315.

38 "visions of God": *The Holy Bible* (King James Version), Ezekiel 1:1.

38 Ezekiel's description: *The New Layman's Parallel Bible* (New International Version), pp. 2108–10.

39 NASA official: Josef F. Blumrich, *The Spaceships of Ezekiel* (New York: Bantam Books, Inc., 1974), foreword.

39 "technically feasible": Ibid., p. 3.

39 "distinct from prophetic content": Ibid., p. 7.

39 "does not interpret": Ibid., p. 13.

39 phases of the landing: Ibid., p. 63.

40 visions not literal: Wilson, op. cit., p. 59.

40 Hou Yih's moon travel: Tomas, op. cit., pp. 114–15.

41 past is a vacuum: Ibid., pp. 8–9.

42 "a computing machine": Ibid., p. 127.

42 "device could not exist": Simon Welfare and John Fairly, *Arthur C. Clarke's Mysterious World* (New York: A&W Publishers, 1980), pp. 65–66.

42 jet plane in tomb: Tomas, op. cit., p. 128.

43 Clarke's comments: Welfare and Fairly, op. cit., p. 67.

43 Wilhelm König: Ibid., p. 62.

43 Dr. Arne Eggebrecht: Ibid., p. 63.

44 "same human skull": Ibid., p. 54.

44 "perfect skull emerged": Ibid., p. 53.

44 screw and pavements: Frank Edwards, *Strangest of All* (New York: Ace Books, Inc., 1956), pp. 100–01.

45 "intriguing items": Alan and Sally Landsburg, *In Search of Ancient Mysteries* (New York: Bantam Books, 1974), pp. 20–22.

46 Strabo and Senaca: Tomas, op. cit., pp. 84–85.

46 *Vishnu-Purana*: Ibid., pp. 85–86.

46 Bronislav Kouznetsov: Ibid.

46 Chinese map: Hancock, op. cit., p. 32.

46 Col. Harold Z. Ohlmeyer: Ibid., p. 3.

47 Charles Hapgood: Ibid., p. 10.

47 Columbus's map: Tomas, op. cit., pp. 87–88.

47 "20 old charts": Ibid., p. 89.

48 Mercator, Oronteus Finaeus and Buache: Hancock, op. cit., pp. 18–22.

48 "worldwide culture": Tomas, op. cit., p. 90.

48 aerial photographs: von Däniken (1971), p. 15.

48 Voynich manuscript: Ibid., p. 91.

49 steel cables: Welfare and Fairly, op. cit., p. 87.

49 "liked a hard life?": von Däniken (1971), p. 94.

49 Gerald Hawkins: Tomas, op. cit., p. 128.

49 "calculator": Chatelain, op. cit., p. 150.

50 Newgrange and Maes Howe: Welfare and Fairly, op. cit., pp. 91–93.

50 Magnus Spence: Ibid.

50 energy pulses: Ibid., p. 96.

50 following historian's footsteps: Hancock, op. cit., p. 294.

50 John Anthony West: Hancock, Ibid., pp. 418–19.

51 "ironclad evidence": Ibid.

51 land-based cranes: Ibid., p. 342.

51 I. E. S. Edwards: O'Leary, op. cit., p. 100.

51 Col. Howard Vyse: Hancock, op. cit., pp. 302–3.

52 "archeological fraud": Stichen (1985), p. 136.

52 no signs of burial: Hancock, op. cit., p. 313.

52 Kane, Edwards, Isler, and Faulkner: Robert Bauval and Adrian Gilbert, *The Orion Mystery: Unlocking the Secrets of the Pyramids* (New York: Crown Publishers, 1994), pp. 50–51.

53 British inches: Peter Lemesurier, *The Great Pyramid Decoded* (New York: Avon Books, 1977), p. 299.

53 "architectural symbol": Ibid., p. 8.

53 pyramid as navigation tool: William Bramley, *The Gods of Eden* (San Jose, CA: Dahlin Family Press, 1990), p. 64.

53 pyramid as time keeper: Chatelain, op. cit., p. 57.

54 Pyramids are Osiris: Bauval and Gilbert, op. cit., p. 122.

54 "air shaft": Ibid., p. 173.

54 10,450 B.C.: Ibid., pp. 192–93.

54 "garbled nonsense": Chatelain, op. cit., p. 64.

54 "radiation barriers": Ibid.

55 "global influence": Bramley, op. cit., pp. 188–89.

55 "global legacy": Hancock, op. cit., p. 32.

55 Japanese earthen statutes: Jacques Vallee, *Dimensions: A Casebook of Alien Contact* (New York: Ballantine Books, 1988), pp. 9–10.

56 story of Nibiru: Sitchen (1985), pp. 345–50.

56 "A heavenly body": Thomas O'Toole, Washington Post News Service, "'Mystery' Body Found in Space," *Detroit News*, December 30, 1983, p. 4-A.

56 Thomas Van Flandern: Hugh McCann, "10th Planet? Pluto's Orbit Says 'Yes,'" *Detroit News*, January 16, 1981, p. 1.

56 Sumerians "far ahead": Ibid.

57 Nephilim "heroes": Trent C. Butler, ed., *Holman Bible Dictionary* (Nashville, TN: Holman Bible Publishers, 1991), p. 1017.

58 Robert Morning Sky and Star Beings: Karen Degenhart, "Robert Morning Sky and the Extraterrestrial Connection," *Fate* 49, no. 9 (September 1996), p. 48.

58 "the extent of alien influence": Ibid., p. 49.

59 no material . . . can last: Chatelain, op. cit., p. 185.

CHAPTER THREE: Military Observers

60 Floyd Thompson: Raymond E. Fowler, *UFOs: Interplanetary Visitors* (New York: Bantam Books, 1974), p. 226.

61 Thutmose III: Jacques Vallee, *UFOs in Space* (New York: Ballantine Books, 1965), pp. 5–6.

61 Roman sightings: Brookesmith, op. cit., p. 15.

61 ships from "Magonia": Jerome Clark, *UFO Encounters & Beyond* (Lincolnwood, IL: Publications International, Ltd., 1993), pp. 12–13.

61 "two large shields": Vallee (1965), p. 9.

61 "dragon," large ship and battles: Brookesmith, op. cit., pp. 16–17.

62 "ghost aircraft" characteristics: Ibid., p. 32.

62 Los Angeles raid: Good (1988), p. 15.

63 Navy Secretary Frank Knox: Terrenz Sword, "The Battle of Los Angeles, 1942," *UFO Sightings* 4, no. 1 (spring 1996), p. 61.

63 Peter Jenkins and Chief J. H. McClelland: Ibid.

63 Paul T. Collins: Good (1988), p. 16.

64 "censorship": Ibid.

64 balloon theory: Sword, loc. cit., p. 62.

64 commentator: Ibid., p. 63.

64 Lt. Donald Meiers: Flammonde, op. cit., p. 135.

64 Smokey Stover: Ibid., p. 136.

65 *Herald Tribune* report: W. A. Harbinson, *Inception* (New York: Dell Publishing, 1991), p. viii.

65 three kinds: Flammonde, op. cit., p. 134.

65 Japanese searchlight plane: Klass, op. cit., pp. 90–91.

65 Lt. David McFalls: Brookesmith, op. cit., p. 35.

65 *Daily Telegraph*: Harbinson, op. cit.

65 Harbinson: Ibid.

66 Captain Alvah Reida: Good (1988), p. 19.

66 enemy airmen followed: Brookesmith, op. cit., p. 35.

66 "discussions of flying saucers": Brian Ford, *German Secret Weapons: Blueprint for Mars* (New York: Ballantine Books, 1969), p. 6.

66 Pitt: Ibid., p. 7.

67 *Feuerball* description: Renato Vesco and David Hatcher Childress, *Man-Made UFOs: 1944–1994. 50 Years of Suppression* (Stelle, IL: Adventures Unlimited Press, 1994), pp. 85–86.

67 *Kugelblitz*: Ibid., pp. 156–57.

67   Rudolph Schriever's saucer: Harbinson, op. cit., p. ix.

68   "designs mislaid or stolen": Ibid.

68   Schriever's death and plans: W. A. Harbinson, *Genesis* (New York: Dell, 1982), p. 590.

68   "flying saucers" in final stages of development: Ford, op. cit., pp. 34–35.

68   Viktor Schauberger: Vesco and Childress, op. cit., p. 243–45.

68   Himmler's letter: Albert Speer, *Infiltration: How Heinrich Himmler Schemed to Build An SS Industrial Empire* (New York: Macmillan, 1981), pp. 207–8.

69   Kammler as commissioner general: Ibid., p. 209.

69   facilities moved: Ford, op. cit., p. 22.

69   Blizna, Poland: Mark Birdsall, "Nazi Secret Weapon: 'Foo Fighters' of WW II," *UFO* 7, no. 4 (July/August 1992), p. 32.

69   "Himmler's proposal": Speer, op. cit., p. 3.

70   secret weapon plant concealed from Speer: Ibid., p. 179.

70   Kammler to "bargain": Jean Michel, *Dora* (New York: Holt, Rinehart and Winston, 1980), p. 290.

70   "disappeared without a trace": Ibid., pp. 296–97.

71   Bishop Johannes Neuhausler: Paul Manning, *Martin Bormann: Nazi in Exile* (Secaucus, NJ: Lyle Stuart, 1981), p. 15.

71   Dr. Hugo Blaschke and Fritz Echtmann: Ibid., p. 16.

72   SS General Heinrich Mueller: Ibid., p. 17.

72   Simon Wiesenthal: Louis L. Snyder, *Encyclopedia of the Third Reich* (New York: McGraw-Hill, 1976), p. 37.

72   "postwar commercial campaign": Manning, op. cit., p. 24.

73   750 front corporations: Ibid., p. 136.

73   ITT: Charles Higham, *Trading with the Enemy: An Exposé of the Nazi-American Money Plot 1933–1949* (New York: Delacorte Press, 1983), p. 99.

73   Gerhardt Westrick: Ibid., p. 95

73   Schroder and Schellenberg: Ibid., p. 93.

73   oil to Spain: Ibid., p. 59.

73   changed registry/close associates: Ibid., p. 35.

73   banking connections: Ibid., p. 22.

74   Chase and Schmitz: Manning, op. cit., p. 159.

74   "Schmitz's wealth": Ibid., p. 280.

74   Martin Walker, "Banking on Nazi Crimes," *The Guardian*, reprinted in *World Press Review*, vol. 41, no. 11, November 1996, p. 31.

75   Nazis did not die: Jim Keith, *Casebook on Alternative 3: UFOs, Secret Societies and World Control* (Lilburn, GA: IllumiNet Press, 1994), p. 148.

75   Orvis A. Schmidt: Manning, op. cit., p. 146.

75   Admiral Karl Doenitz: Editors, "Hitler Vanishes—Where Did Der Führer Go?" *The National Police Gazette*, January 1977, p. 32.

75   Admiral Richard Byrd: Harbinson (1982), p. 594.

76   "underground research factories": Ibid., p. 599.

76   Swedish statement: Flammonde, op. cit., p. 139.

76   80 percent identified: Peebles, op. cit., p. 4.

76   Foo-Fighters "advanced technology": Birdsall, loc. cit., p. 32.

77   BBC report: Vesco and Childress, op. cit., p. 225.

77   *Toronto Star* report: Ibid., pp. 252–53.

77   Americans shown saucer: Ibid., p. 255.

77   Donald Quarles: Ibid., p. 259.

78   V-173 "Flying Flapjack": David C. Knight, *UFOs: A Pictorial History from Antiquity to the Present* (New York: McGraw-Hill, 1979), p. 34.

78   governments are lying: Harbinson (1991), p. xi.

78   CIA memo: Good (1993), p. 143.

78   Lt. Col. George Edwards: John Spencer, ed., *The UFO Encyclopedia* (New York: Avon Books, 1991), p. 103.

78   Robert Dorr: Good (1993), p. 144.

79   Richard S. Shaver: Peebles, op. cit., pp. 4–7; Flammonde, op. cit., pp. 174–80.

79   "concise summary of flying saucer myth": Peebles, op. cit., p. 7.

80   "Silence is the best thing": Brookesmith, op. cit., p. 38.

80   "tremendously bright flash": Flammonde, op. cit., p. 163.

80   Chinese kite tail: Brookesmith, op. cit., p. 45.

81   speed calculated: Peebles, op. cit., p. 10.

81   "guided missiles": Flammonde, op. cit., p. 166.

81   "significance of this": Spencer, op. cit., p. 25.

82   Davidson and Brown: Flammonde, op. cit., pp. 184–85.

82   Palmer and Crisman letter: Peebles, op. cit., p. 14.

82   Arnold's second encounter: Flammonde, op. cit., pp. 185–86; Good (1988), p. 571.

82   hotel room, volcanic rock, and anonymous letter: Flammonde, op. cit., pp. 186–89.

83   hoax or espionage: Ibid., p. 190.

83   "secrete a listening device": Ibid., p. 191.

83   "fake" stuff: Ibid., p. 192.

84   "more rocky and less metallic": Ibid., p. 197.

84   B-25 crash and cause: Ibid., pp. 200–2; Peebles, op. cit., p. 16.

85   Harold Wilkins: Roger Ford, "A Secret Never to Be Told?" in *UFOs: The Final Answer*, ed. David Barclay and Therese Marie Barclay (London: Blandford Press, 1993), p. 110.

85   Crisman and "hardware": Anthony L. Kimery, "The Secret Life of Fred L. Crisman," *UFO* 8, no. 5 (September–October 1993), p. 35.

85   first man called: Ibid., p. 36.

86   Permindex and CMC: Jim Marrs, *Crossfire: The Plot That Killed Kennedy* (New York: Carroll & Graf, 1989), p. 499.

86   Crisman as "extended agent": Extractions from CIA file: CRISMAN, Fred Lee, Number OSS/CIA 4250ece, located at Control Records Dispatch, Davenport, Iowa.

86   John Keel theory: Brookesmith, op. cit., p. 39.

87   air force report: Peebles, op. cit., p. 16.

87   "still . . . a mystery": Flammonde, op. cit., p. 206.

87   "intelligence . . . deeply immersed": Kimery, loc. cit., p. 38.

87   first mention of outer space: Peebles, op. cit., p. 28.

CHAPTER FOUR: The Road to Recovery

88   Project 1947: Jan L. Alrich, "1947: A Progress Report." *UFO* 11, no. 2 (March/April 1996), pp. 22–25.

91   Barney Barnett discounted: Peebles, op. cit., p. 298.

91   "fragments in a field": Ibid., p. 302.

91   additional witnesses: Kevin D. Randle and Donald R. Schmitt, *The Truth About the UFO Crash at Roswell* (New York: Avon Books, 1994). These witnesses are only a partial listing taken from a cursory study of this well-documented book.

92 "not anything from this Earth": Ibid., p. 155.

97 Frank Press regarding Roswell: Author's conversation with William Pitts, April 12, 1996.

97 GAO report: Editors, "NEWS: GAO Comes Up Empty Handed on Roswell," *UFO* 10, no. 5 (September/October 1995), p. 5.

98 FBI teletype: Peebles, op. cit., p. 300.

98 other crashes: Good (1988), pp. 388–98.

98 Dr. Chris Stringer: "Autopsy of the Third Kind," *World Press Review*, October 1995, p. 38.

100 "secret" letter: Art Crockett, "The 'Project Blue Book' Cover-up," in *The Total UFO Story*, ed. Milt Machlin (New York: Dale Books, 1979), p. 147.

100 Gen. Nathan Twining's report: Peebles, op. cit., pp. 17–18.

101 Randle and Schmitt suggested: Randle and Schmitt, op. cit., p. 109.

101 Schulgen memo: Good (1988), p. 262.

101 2A priority: J. Allen Hynek, *The UFO Experience: A Scientific Inquiry* (Chicago: Henry Regnery Company, 1972), p. 174.

101 "division grew greater": Ibid., p. 170.

101 reports not too convincing: Ibid., p. 172.

101 a dozen reports "unidentified": Peebles, op. cit., p. 19.

101 Hynek's "sense of sport": Hynek, op. cit., p. 2.

102 "phenomenon . . . being proved": Ibid., p. 171.

102 Mantell's comments: Official Air Intelligence report reproduced in Good (1988), p. 481; amplified in Peebles, op. cit., p. 23.

103 *Times* headlines: Flammonde, op. cit., p. 218.

103 Glen Mays: Ibid., p. 219.

103 "no one could account for this": Richard T. Miller, *Star Wards: Welcome Home Earthman* (Middletown, CA: The Solar Cross Foundation, 1979), p. 3.

103 "Some mysterious force": Ibid.

104 Captain James F. Duesler: Tony Dodd, "The Fatal Flight of Captain Thomas Mantell," *UFO Magazine*, July/August 1996, p. 29.

105 "he was after something": Ruppelt, op. cit., p. 37.

105 Venus nearly invisible: Peebles, op. cit., pp. 24–25.

105 "Skyhook" balloons: Klass, op. cit., p. 34.

105 no records located: Flammonde, op. cit., p. 232.

105 Cabell's memo: Good (1988), p. 263.

105 other 1948 UFOs: Vallee (1965), pp. 72–73.

106 Gorman statements: Flammonde, op. cit., pp. 259–260.

106 Pentagon's "subtle ridicule": Hynek, op. cit., p. 2.

107 public relations effort: Peebles, op. cit., p. 40.

107 "brush-off attitude" in releases: Hynek, op. cit., p. 174.

107 "change . . . difficult to explain": Ibid., p. 175.

107 Jaime Shandera finds film: Howard Blum, *Out There* (New York: Simon and Schuster, 1990), pp. 239–41; author's interview with Jaime Shandera, September 7, 1996.

107 MJ-12 briefing papers: Copies in author's files; Good (1988), pp. 545–51; Blum, Ibid., pp. 282–89.

108 Hillenkoetter quote: Good (1988), p. 259.

109 Twining trip canceled and William Moore: Ibid., p. 260.

110 Gray and psychological strategy board: Ibid., p. 259.

110 Menzel quote: Blum, op. cit., p. 247.

110 "biggest cons": Ibid., p. 219.

111 "systematically confuse . . . ": Editors, "Disinformation Ploy Revealed," *UFO* 4, no. 4 (September/October 1989), p. 4.

111 "Aquarius Telex": Peebles, op. cit., pp. 310–11; reproduction of telex, Good (1988), p. 528.

112 Project Aquarius briefing papers: Don Ecker, "The Aquarius Document," *UFO* 7, no. 1 (January/February 1992), pp. 8–10.

114 "skillfully doctored": Good (1988), p. 234.

114 Menzel's double life: Ibid., pp. 249–50.

115 paper maker checked: Ralph Steiner, "Stanton Friedman: The Case for UFOs as Alien Spacecraft and the Government UFO Cover-up," in *UFOs and the Alien Presence: Six Viewpoints*, ed. Michael Lindemann (Santa Barbara, CA: The 2020 Group, 1991), p. 45.

115 Classification not used until Nixon: Randle and Schmitt, op. cit., pp. 230–31.

116 identical signatures and 1963 typewriter: Peebles, op. cit., p. 321.

116 MJ-12 Operations Manual: Copy provided by GAO to Rep. Deborah Pryce, 15th District, Ohio, copy in author's files.

116 "a great deal of work": Kevin D. Randle, "The MJ-12 Operations Manual: Another Forgery?" *International UFO Reporter* (spring 1996), p. 9.

116 Manual a "fake": Ibid., p. 10.

116 Richard Davis: Letter to Rep. Deborah Pryce, September 12, 1995.

117 "document seems authentic": Good (1988), p. 260.

117 "essentially factual": Good (1993), p. 123.

117 Lee Graham and DIS: Lee Graham and Ron Regehr, "One Man's Journey to Verification: Going by the Rules," *UFO* 10, no. 1 (January/February 1995), pp. 25–27.

118 FBI probe and quote: Blum, op. cit., pp. 263–67.

119 Dr. Eric Walker: Letter from T. Scott Crain Jr., *UFO* 7, no. 1 (January/February 1992), p. 5.

119 Tommy Bland on Mrs. Margaret Fuller: Author's interview, June 28, 1996.

120 FBI memo: Good (1988), p. 541.

121 Washington SAC memo: Ibid., p. 527.

121 Smith memo and report: Good (1988), pp. 183–85.

121 Dr. Sarbacher's letter: Ibid., pp. 525–26.

122 Gen. George C. Marshall: Ibid., p. 414.

122 Gleason story: Good (1993), pp. 104–5.

122 Larry Warren: Timothy Green Beckley, "UFOs Among the Stars," *UFO Sightings*, 3, no. 4 (winter 1996), pp. 27–28.

122 Milo Spiriglio: Vicki Ecker, "UFOs Linked to 'Marilyn' Conspiracy," *UFO* 10, no. 2 (March/April 1995), pp. 19–20.

123 Vic Golubic and CIA report: Author's interview, June 25, 1996.

123 Briton tells of UFO crash: Dorothy Kilgallen, "'Flying Saucer' Wreckage Assures Britons of Reality," *Fort Worth Star-Telegram*, May 23, 1955.

124 Air Chief Marshal Lord Dowding: Good (1988), pp. 47–48.

124 "my hands are tied": Author's interview with Bill Holden, May 14, 1996.

125 NSA and Project Aquarius: Good (1988), p. 425.

CHAPTER FIVE: Plausible Deniability

126 "Dark Ages": Ruppelt, op. cit., p. 63.

126 "cover up the real story": Ibid., p. 67.

126 "schizophrenic approach": Ibid., p. 86.

127 CIRVIS and airline meeting: Raymond E. Fowler, *UFOs: Interplanetary Visitors* (New York: Bantam Books, 1979), pp. 234–35.

127 "Big Brother" attitude: Ibid.

127 Keyhoe on regulations: Peebles, op. cit., p. 134.

128 "interplanetary spaceships": Ruppelt, op. cit., p. 109.

128 "natural phenomenon": Ibid., p. 110.

128 General Mills witnesses: Ibid., p. 120.

129 personal opinion at the Pentagon: Ibid., p. 132; Peebles, op. cit., p. 70.

129 20 reports a day: Ruppelt, op. cit., p. 154.

129 "fantastically high speeds": Ibid., p. 158.

130 "media were ordered out": Ibid., p. 164.

130 headlines: Ibid., p. 166.

130 press conference and resulting headline: Ibid., pp. 168–69.

130 "temperature inversion . . . indicated": Peebles, op. cit., p. 79.

130 Ruppelt's findings: Ruppelt, op. cit., p. 170.

131 Dan Kimball: Donald E. Keyhoe, *Aliens from Space* (New York: Doubleday and Company, 1973), pp. 79–80.

131 "two pie pans": Ruppelt, op. cit., p. 224.

131 "under intelligent control": Keyhoe (1973), p. 82.

132 Admiral Hillenkoetter: Ibid.

132 Smith memo: Good (1988), p. 511.

133 "study was hot": Ruppelt, op. cit., p. 218.

133 Hynek on panel: Hynek, op. cit., p. 169.

133 scientists "known skeptics": Ibid., p. 83.

133 "double-crossed": Ibid., p. 85.

133 Robertson panel conclusions: Peebles, op. cit., p. 102.

133 Al Chop: Keyhoe, op. cit., p. 85.

134 Ruppelt quote: Ibid., p. 86.

134 Sen. Richard B. Russell: Ibid., p. 89.

134 Lt. Col. L. J. Tacker: Ibid., p. 9.

134 majority leader John McCormack: Ibid.

134 Sen. Barry Goldwater: Good (1988), p. 405.

135 UFOs "scientifically unrespectable": Hynek, op. cit., p. 169.

135 assessment of Ruppelt: Flammonde, op. cit., p. 173.

135 Ruppelt's widow: Peebles, op. cit., p. 168.

136 Ruppelt forced to repudiate book: Keyhoe (1973), pp. 90–91.

136 Hynek quotes: Hynek, op. cit., p. 173.

136 "another intelligence agency": Ruppelt, op. cit., p. 231.

136 Coral Lorenzen: Peebles, op. cit., p. 168.

136 "The goal of Blue Book": Ibid., p. 132.

136 rate of UFO sightings: Ibid., p. 172.

137 Keyhoe on giant satellites: Keyhoe (1973), p. 157.

138 Tombaugh sighting: Flammonde, op. cit., p. 171.

138 "second satellite": Editors, "Second Moon?" *Time*, March 15, 1954, p. 83.

138 search for "moonlets": Editors, "Tiny Earth Satellites," *Science News Letter* 65, no. 12 (March 20, 1954), p. 80.

139 "first artificial satellite": Editors, "He Spies on Satellites," *Popular Mechanics* 104, no. 4 (October 1955), p. 106.

139 rocket kept going: Editors, "Have We Sent a Rocket into Space?" *Popular Mechanics* 103, no. 5 (May 1955), p. 112.

139 "Tombaugh is closed mouth": *Popular Mechanics* (October 1955), p. 334.

140 John P. Bagby: Maj. Donald E. Keyhoe, *The Flying Saucer Conspiracy* (New York: Henry Holt and Company, 1955), pp. 260–61.

140 Captain Howard T. Orville: Ibid., p. 198.

140 NASA release, Stewart Alsop: Keyhoe (1973), pp. 161–62.

140 Tombaugh not published: Carl Sagan and Thornton Page, eds., *UFOs–A Scientific Debate* (Ithaca, NY: Cornell University Press, 1972), p. 29.

140 bomber crew experience: Keyhoe, op. cit., p. 164.

141 Dr. Fritz Zwicky and rockets: Keyhoe (1955), pp. 105–7.

141 satellites as natural objects: Ibid., pp. 194–95.

142 NICAP members: Peebles, op. cit., p. 139.

142 Keyhoe comment: Ibid., p. 157.

143 CBS censors Keyhoe's statement: Ibid., pp. 154–55.

143 AF "special" briefing: Ibid., p. 157.

143 McCormack hearing and Peebles quote: Ibid., p. 158.

144 "one of the classics": Hynek, op. cit., p. 144.

144 Zamora account: Brad Steiger, ed., *Project Blue Book: The Top Secret UFO Findings Revealed* (New York: Ballantine Books, 1976), pp. 115–21.

145 insignia as sign for Venus: Vallee (1988), p. 33.

145 "verified the marks and . . . plants": Hynek, op. cit., p. 145.

145 attempts to break story "fruitless": Ibid.

145 Hynek and Menzel's theory: Steiger, op. cit., p. 134.

145 "landing was a hoax": Peebles, op. cit., p. 185.

146 La Medera landing: Brookesmith, op. cit., p. 81.

146 Rev. Gill letters and report: Hynek, op. cit., pp. 147–49.

147 Menzel's theories: Ibid., p. 242.

148 no blackout explanation quotes: Keyhoe (1973), pp. 213–14.

148 news reports on UFOs: Ibid., p. 215.

148 *Power* article: Ibid., p. 216.

148 fraud "preposterous": Ibid., p. 217.

149 blackouts in Texas, New Mexico: Spencer, op. cit., p. 44

149 Fredrick E. Davids: Flammonde, op. cit., p. 357.

150 typical headline: Peebles, op. cit., p. 205.

150 Gerald R. Ford letter: Flammonde, op. cit., p. 360.

150 "worthy of scientific attention": Hynek, op. cit., pp. 196–97.

150 ad hoc committee: Thompson, op. cit., p. 92.

151 "there is nothing to it": Peebles, op. cit., p. 217.

151 "committee had come to a standstill": Dr. Jacques Vallee, *Dimensions: A Casebook of Alien Contact* (New York: Ballantine Books, 1988), p. 211.

151 Armstrong resignation letter: Hynek, op. cit., p. 244.

152 "confidential information" to Menzel: Ibid., p. 249.

152 "ETI" does not exist: Ibid., p. 246.

152 Low's memo: Peebles, op. cit., p. 211.

152 "choice of data": Hynek, op. cit., p. 195.

152 "problem" defined: Ibid., pp. 203–4.

153 Stewart Udall: Keyhoe (1973), p. 282.

153 Dr. Paul Tyler: Author's interview, August 16, 1993.

153 Condon conclusion: Peebles, op. cit., p. 225.

154 "final assessment" of Condon Study: Ibid., p. 229.

154 John Northrop quote: Fowler (1979), p. 159.

154 Dr. James E. McDonald: Ibid., p. 238.

154 AIAA review: Thompson, op. cit., pp. 95–96.

154 "worthy of investigation": Hynek, op. cit., p. 230.

154 "Report settled nothing": Ibid., p. 195.

154 "scientific belief system" threatened: Thompson, op. cit., p. 95.

154 Dr. Paul Santorini: Raymond E. Fowler, *The Watchers* (New York: Bantam Books, 1990), pp. 335–36.

155 "waste of Government money": Flammonde, op. cit., p. 16.

155 UFO files burned: Vallee (1988), p. 211.

155 Condon tries to halt AAAS: Fowler, op. cit., p. 166.

155 air force "conspiracy": Fowler, op. cit., p. 284.

155 Robert C. Seamans Jr. statement: Peebles, op. cit., p. 229.

156 Menzel's admission: Fowler, op. cit., pp. 165–66.

156 AF reiterates views: Peebles, op. cit., p. 230.

CHAPTER SIX: UFOs Underground

157 Howard C. Cross memo: Vicki Cooper, "'Pentacle' Controversy," *UFO* 8, no. 3 (May/June 1993), pp. 6–7.

158 Battelle background: Keith Chester, "Blue Book's 'Institute of Choice,'" Ibid., pp. 8–11.

158 "Project Bear": Ruppelt, op. cit., p. 118.

158 "contributions by Battelle": Chester, loc. cit., p. 8.

158 Jason group: Vicki Cooper, "Jason Group: DOD's Secretive, Scientific 'Elite,'" *UFO* 7, no. 6 (November/December 1992), pp. 7–8.

159 Col. William Coleman: Good (1993), pp. 128–129.

159 AF Sec. Richard E. Horner: Keyhoe (1973), p. 9.

159 Hillenkoetter: Ibid., p. 12.

159 Stringfield as UFO spotter: Leonard H. Stringfield, *UFO Crash Retrievals: The Inner Sanctum–Status Report VI* (Cincinnati, OH: Leonard H. Stringfield, 1991), p. 141.

160 John L. Acuff: Leonard H. Stringfield, *Situation Red, the UFO Siege!* (Garden City, NY: Doubleday & Company, 1977), p. 155.

160 William H. Spaulding: Ibid.

160 James Lorenzen: Ibid., p. 156.

160 John B. Musgrave: Ibid., p. 160.

161 "why Blue Book failed": Crockett, loc. cit., p. 158.

161 "UFOs simply ceased to exist": Flammonde, op. cit., p. 353.

161 Scientific Advisory Board: Bruce Maccabee, Report on America Online: TEwa 70220, May 6, 1996, p. 1.

162 Todd Zechel: Good (1988), p. 349.

162 John Burroughs: Antonio Huneeus, "Two Points of View–The Bentwaters UFO 'Crash': Friend or Foe?" *UFO Universe* 1, no. 4 (August/September 1991), p. 20.

163 "James Archer": Good (1988), p. 83.

163 Sgt. Adrian Bustinza: Ibid., pp. 85–86.

163 Sgt. Larry Warren: Huneeus, loc. cit., p. 22.

164 Col. Halt's report: Ibid., p. 25.

165 "lot of things that are not in my memo": Good (1988), p. 96.

165 film delivered to HQ: Ibid., p. 93.

165 tape transcript: Ibid., pp. 89–90.

166 "a mechanical device of unknown origin": Brookesmith, op. cit., p. 61.

166 Peter Robbins and lights: Terry Ecker, "UFOs Still Cavorting Around Bentwaters AFB," *UFO* 6, no. 2 (March/April 1991), pp. 6–7.

166 no records on Warren: Ibid.

167 "a grave assault": Michael Lindemann, "UFOs and the Alien Presence: Time for the Truth," Summary Report I, Visitors Investigation Project of the Democracy and Security Conference, a division of The 2020 Group, March 1990, pp. 13–14.

167 Neilson per name for Kimery: Author's interview, 1997.

167 "secret, centralized command structure": James Neilson, "High-Level Disclosures: 'Secret' U.S./UFO Structure," *UFO* 4, no. 1 (March/April 1989), p. 4.

168 Tad Sherburn: Editors, "U.N. Runs UFO Agency, Says Researcher," *UFO* 10, no. 3 (May/June 1995), p. 10.

168 UFO chain of command: Neilson, op. cit., p. 5, plus several sources who requested anonymity.

169 NRO loses $2 billion: *New York Times*, "Secretive Agency Misplaces $2 Billion," *Portland Press Herald*, January 30, 1996, p. 5A.

169 secret underground facilities and locations: Richard Sauder, *Underground Bases and Tunnels: What Is the Government Trying to Hide?* (Abingdon, VA: Dracon Press, 1995), p. 11.

170 "Lunar Tunneler": Ibid., p. 101.

170 projects like the "Chunnel": Ibid., p. 84.

171 FEMA installation not in budget: Ibid., p. 49–50.

171 Oliver North, Arthur Liman, and FEMA plan: Alfonso Chardy, "Plan Called for Martial Law in U.S.," *Fort Worth Star-Telegram*, July 5, 1987, section 1, p. 9.

171 how many not known: Sauder, op. cit., p. 52.

172 Alternatives 1 and 2: Keith, op. cit., p. 7.

172 X-33 space shuttle: Editors, "The Shuttle That May Put You in Space," *U.S. New & World Report*, July 22, 1996, p. 13.

173 gridlock and homeless people: Paul R. Ehrlich & Anne H. Ehrlich, *The Population Explosion* (New York: Simon and Schuster, 1990), p. 11.

173 Jacques-Yves Cousteau: Associated Press, "As Population Grows, People Will Live 'Like Rats,' Cousteau Says," *Los Angeles Times*, June 6, 1992, p. A17.

173 second only to nuclear war: Ehrlich, op. cit., p. 18.

174 "actually a hoax": Keith, op. cit., p. 14.

174 "very close to a secret truth": Ibid.

174 Linda Howe and BBC producer: Author's interview, July 8, 1996.

175 Kurt Rebmann: Keith, op. cit., p. 56.

175 "infiltration by Nazis": Ibid., p. 41.

175 "broad outline of controls": Ibid., p. 159.

176 Norio Hayakawa and Gary Schultz: Don Ecker, "Dark Chopper Tries to Crash S-4 'UFO Party,'" *UFO* 6, no. 4 (July/August 1991), p. 10.

176 Valentino Kent and Ken Brazell: Don Ecker, "Strange Camp-out at Area 51," *UFO* 8, no. 3 (May/June 1993), pp. 12–15.

177 "numerous secret aircraft": Editors, "Multiple Sightings of Secret Aircraft Hint at New Propulsion, Airframe Designs," *Aviation Week & Space Technology*, October 1, 1990, p. 22.

177 "illegal land seizure": Don Ecker, "Strange Camp-out at Area 51," *UFO* 8, no. 3 (May/June 1993), p. 12.

177 air force statement: Abe Dane, "Flying Saucers: The Real Story," *Popular Mechanics* 172, no. 1 (January 1995), p. 50.

177 Abe Dane: Dane, loc. cit.

178 sightings described: Editors, "Secret Advanced Vehicles Demonstrate Technologies for Future Military Use," *Aviation Week & Space Technology*, October 1, 1990, p. 20.

178 "guarded with undiminished vigilance": Ibid.

178 Intelligence chiefs at Wackenhut: John Connolly, "Inside America's Secret Secret Police," *Spy*, September 1992, p. 49.

179 armed employees, files and revenues: Don Ecker, "Corporate Spooks Ride High at Wackenhut," *UFO* 8, no. 1 (January/February 1992), pp. 9–10.

179 Anthony J. Hilder letter: Copy dated July 30, 1992, in author's files.

179 Bob Lazar and Dr. Edward Teller: Lindemann, op. cit., pp. 89–90.

180 S-4 destination: Ibid.

180 gun to head: Don Ecker, "The Saucers and the Scientist," *UFO* 5, no. 6 (November/December 1990), p. 17.

181 Element 115: Lindemann, op. cit., p. 106.

181 nine UFOs: Ibid., p. 18.

181 small "doll": Good (1993), p. 208.

181 briefing papers and "containers": Ibid., pp. 210–12.

182 UFOs gained by "friendly means": Lindemann, op. cit., p. 105.

182 Paul Bennewitz letter: Good (1993), p. 210.

182 "unprofessional manner" and "buddy system": Lindemann, op. cit., p. 108.

182 Betty Cash and Vickie Landrum: Thomas R. Adams, *The Choppers—and the Choppers*, rev. ed. (Paris, TX: Project Stigma, 1991), p. 36.

183 "why I left S-4": Ibid., p. 92.

183 Los Alamos phone listing: Ecker (1990), loc. cit., p. 16.

184 W-2 form and "E-6722MAJ": Good (1993), p. 202.

184 "MAJ" and SCI clearance: Ibid., pp. 172–73.

184 Dr. Teller vacillated: Ibid., pp. 171–72.

185 "crime against the American people": Ibid., pp. 194–95.

185 polygraph tests: Ecker (1990), loc. cit., pp. 17–18.

185 legal action: Author's interview with Gene Huff, July 16, 1996.

186 Marion Leo Williams: Good (1993), p. 207.

186 George Knapp: Ibid., pp. 198–99.

186 "public indoctrination process": Ibid., p. 212.

186 "chosen for release of this information": George Knapp, "Lazar's Story Unchanged," *UFO* 5, no. 6 (November/December 1990), p. 19.

186 "wall of absurdity" and "theatre": Vallee (1991), p. 227.

187 "huge amounts of disinformation": Author's interview with Don Ecker, July 16, 1996.

187 "story has some holes": Peebles, op. cit., p. 329.

187 "I am telling the truth": Good (1993), p. 213.

187 "I don't care who believes me": Ecker (1990), loc. cit., p. 19.

CHAPTER SEVEN: Face-to-Face

188 Ezekiel's account: *The New Layman's Parallel Bible* (Living Bible), p. 2113.

189 "vedic accounts": Thompson, op. cit., p. 226.

189 Ravana abducts Sita: Flammonde, op. cit., p. 48.

189 John Barclay: Vallee (1988), pp. 42–43.

189 Rapuzzi Johannis: Jenny Randles, *Alien Contacts & Abductions* (New York: Sterling Publishing Co., 1994), pp. 16–17.

190 George Adamski: Peebles, op. cit., p. 115.

191 "torn to pieces": Peebles, op. cit., p. 116.

191 "embellished by others": Randles, op. cit., p. 19

191 "hallucinations . . . fantasies": Ibid.

192 "saucer crap": Peter A. Jordan, "The Early Days," *UFO* 10, no. 3 (May/June 1995), p. 34.

192 Adamski a "fraud": Harold D. Salkin, "George Adamski—Cosmic Saint or Sinner?" *UFO Universe* 2, no. 4 (winter 1993), pp. 22–23.

192 "reduced the credibility": Ibid., p. 20.

192 scientists and "Good old George": Vallee (1988), p. 223.

192 Gene L. Bloom: Peebles, op. cit., p. 114.

192 Jerrold E. Baker: Ibid., p. 119.

192 Thomas Eickoff: Good (1988), pp. 341–42.

193 joke letterhead: Peebles, op. cit., p. 160.

193 two constables: Good (1988), p. 117.

193 Silver Spring film: Ibid., pp. 374–77.

194 Stephen Darbishire: Ibid., p. 377.

194 "final death blow": Fowler, op. cit., p. 40.

194 contactees: Thompson, op. cit., pp. 172–73; Brookesmith, op. cit., pp. 65–67; Peebles, op. cit., pp. 113–25.

196 Antonio Villas Boas account: Randles, op. cit., pp. 24–27; Brookesmith, pp. 61–63.

197 Betty and Barney Hill account: Ibid., pp. 27–32; pp. 74–75; Peebles, op. cit., pp. 193–99.

197 "military pilot": John G. Fuller, *The Interrupted Journey* (New York: Dell Publishing Co., 1966), p. 145.

198 "shiny circles": Ibid., pp. 38–39.

198 Pease radar "unknown": Vallee (1988), p. 103; Brookesmith, op. cit., p. 75; Spencer, op. cit., p. 145.

198 Walter Webb: Fuller, op. cit., p. 53.

198 "German Nazi": Ibid., p. 115.

199 Rev. John D. Swanson: Fowler (1979), p. 297.

199 Dr. Simon's caveat: Fuller, op. cit., p. 9.

200 "cumulative impact": Ibid., p. 10.

200 "only a dream": Peebles, op. cit., p. 200.

200 "abduction did not take place": Ibid., p. 273.

200 Maurice Masse account: Ibid., pp. 24–25; Brookesmith, op. cit., p. 83; Randles, op. cit., pp. 36–38.

202 "secret weapon": Gary Kinder, *Light Years* (New York: Pocket Books, 1987), p. 89.

202 Father Zimmermann: Ibid., p. 90.

202 Meier background: Ibid., pp. 92–96.

203 Semjase and Pleiadians: Ibid., pp. 98–99.

203 "still far removed from perfection": Ibid., p. 17.

204 no open contact: Ibid., p. 65.

204 "one or a very few recipients": James W. Deardorff, "Possible Extraterrestrial Strategy for Earth," *Quarterly Journal of the Royal Astronomy Society* 27 (1986), p. 99.

205 Willy Bar: Kinder, op. cit., p. 207.
205 Martin Sorge: Ibid., pp. 260–63.
206 Eric Eliason: Ibid., pp. 273–74.
206 Dr. Michael Malin: Ibid., pp. 275–78.
207 Wally Gentleman: Ibid., p. 283.
207 Dr. Robert Nathan: Ibid., p. 281.
207 Lou Zinsstag: Ibid., p. 105.
208 Herbert Runkel and Harold Proch: Ibid., p. 42 and p. 49.
208 Englebert Wachter: Ibid., p. 70.
208 "eerie and grating noise": Ibid., p. 21.
208 Steve Ambrose: Ibid., p. 240.
208 Marcel Vogel and triangle: Ibid., pp. 290–91.
209 "Vogel never recovered" triangle: Ibid., p. 292.
209 Brit Elders: Ibid., pp. 303–4.
209 "wasting my time": Ibid., p. 305.
209 "evidence would be seen by few": Ibid., p. 220.
210 Ground Saucer Watch: Ibid., pp. 229–30.
210 Lucius Farish: Ibid., pp. 235–36.
210 Lee Elders: Ibid., p. 237.
210 "genuine experiences": Good (1993), p. 256.
210 "Finally I realized": Kinder, op. cit., p. 306.
210 "they shall come to know": Ibid., p. 215.
210 Meier's "knowledge": Randolph Winters, *The Pleiadian Mission: A Time of Awareness* (Yorba Linda, CA: The Pleiades Project, 1994), pp. 64–74.
211 "beamship" technology: Kinder, op. cit., pp. 216–17.
211 Tom Welch: Ibid., pp. 217–18.
212 new major event in history: Winters, op. cit., p. vii.

CHAPTER EIGHT: Missing Time

213 "Mongoloid" people": Raymond E. Fowler, *The Andreasson Affair* (New York: Bantam Books, 1980), p. 13.
214 help save the world: Ibid., p. 22.
214 "some parts missing": Ibid., p. 43.
214 "lie very still": Ibid., p. 52.
214 "I left this Earth": Ibid., p. 80.
214 "powerful influences beyond her ken": Ibid., p. 59.
215 "something white": Ibid., p. 73.
215 "real white light": Ibid., p. 83.
215 "Thank you for your Son": Ibid., p. 87.
215 no symbol of modern Christianity: Ibid., p. 91.
215 "symbol of immortality": Ibid., p. 93.
216 Man and greed: Fowler (1980), pp. 132–33.
216 seventy alien races: Ibid., pp. 137–38.
216 PSE results "conclusive": Ibid., p. 211.
216 "hypnotic regression sessions": Ibid., p. 9.
216 "interstellar missionaries": Ibid., pp. 201–3.
216 Hynek quote: Ibid., p. ix.
217 UFO phenomenon is "not nonsense": Ibid., p. x.
217 Charles Hickson and Calvin Parker account: Fowler (1979), pp. 307–8.

217 Sheriff Fred Diamond and tape recorder: Ibid., pp. 40–41.

217 Dr. James Harder: Peebles, op. cit., p. 242.

217 "very real, frightening experience": Randles, op. cit., p. 41.

217 Klass argued: Peebles, op. cit., pp. 243–44.

218 Hickson declined money: Spencer, op. cit., p. 240.

218 Travis Walton account: Travis Walton, *The Walton Experience* (New York: Berkley Books, 1978); Randles, op. cit., pp. 44–46; Brookesmith, op. cit., pp. 111–12.

218 C. E. Gilson and polygraph test: Peebles, op. cit., p. 275.

219 Dalis feared self-incrimination: Randles, op. cit., p. 45.

219 humanoids description: Walton, op. cit., p. 106.

220 John J. McCarthy: Peebles, op. cit., p. 276.

220 Jeff Wells: Ibid., pp. 276–77.

220 Travis and lie detector: Quendrith Johnson, "'Fire in the Sky' Inquiry," *UFO* 8, no. 3 (May/June 1993), p. 21.

220 Lamont McConnell and test: Good (1993), p. 85.

220 Dr. Jean Rosenbaum: Ibid.

220 Lester H. Steward: Peebles, op. cit., p. 387.

221 Klass and Forest Service contract: Ibid., pp. 279–80.

221 Dr. James Harder: Johnson, loc. cit., p. 21.

221 Tracy Tormé: Ibid., p. 22.

221 "some real insight": Ibid., p. 23.

222 "pitch black" eyes: Budd Hopkins, *Intruders: The Incredible Visitations at Copley Woods* (New York: Ballantine Books, 1987), p. 17.

222 description of child: Ibid., p. 223.

223 "the patterns exist": Ibid., p. 235.

223 Dr. John Burger: Ibid., pp. 253–54.

223 two possible lines of explanations: Ibid., pp. 267–68.

223 Tomey medical history and comment: Peebles, op. cit., p. 388.

224 "similarities with science fiction": Ibid., p. 287.

224 "profoundly alien quality": Ibid., p. 286.

224 unknown prior to 1987: Randles, op. cit., p. 162.

224 "no overt memories": Peebles, op. cit., p. 288.

224 anyone can provide a story: Ibid., p. 289.

224 abduction stories from kids: Vicki Cooper, "Studying 'Anomalous Experiences,'" *UFO* 6, no. 4 (July/August 1991), p. 16.

225 "abuses perpetrated": Whitley Strieber, "Technique Out-of-Control," *UFO* 2, no. 4 (May/June 1989), p. 22.

225 "break fear-amnesia": Ibid., p. 23.

225 "All testimony . . . affected": Budd Hopkins, "One UFOlogist's Methodology," *UFO* 2, no. 4 (May/June 1989), p. 27.

225 "borderline . . . abduction cases": Ibid.

225 "screen memories": Ibid., p. 28.

225 "hypnosis parallels . . . reporting": John E. Mack, *Abduction: Human Encounters with Aliens* (New York: Ballantine Books, 1994), p. 430.

226 "extraordinary experience" as template: Ibid.

226 no way to convey emotional authenticity: Hopkins, *Intruders*, p. 176.

226 "We were amazed": Fowler (1980), p. 32.

226 one more investigative tool: Ibid., p. 304.

226 Thompson on hypnosis: Thompson, op. cit., pp. 152–53.

226 hypnotists are led: Dr. Thomas Bullard, "Hypnosis No 'Truth Serum,'" *UFO* 4, no. 4 (May/June 1989), p. 34.

226 potential for misuse undeniable: Ibid., p. 35.

226 "Clearly, hypnosis is not . . . foolproof": Peebles, op. cit., p. 290.

227 "doubters . . . create doubt": Bullard, loc. cit., p. 35.

227 "it's remarkable to me . . . ": Richard Cutting, "Q&A: John Mack, M.D.," *UFO* 9, no. 5 (September/October 1994), p. 26.

227 one young man troubled: Ibid.

227 They come . . . "at random": Mack, op. cit., p. 4.

227 sexual abuse vs. . . . alien-related: Cutting, loc. cit., p. 28.

228 "concrete physical findings": Mack, op. cit., p. 389–90.

228 no fetus disappeared: Ibid., p. 27.

228 "keep us ignorant": Ibid., p. x.

228 entities from parallel universe: Cutting, loc. cit., p. 27.

228 Nicholas Spanos study: Thompson, op. cit., pp. 157–58.

229 Donna Bessett at CSICOP: Geoff Olson, "'PSI-COPS' Bite into Abduction Claims," *UFO* 9, no. 5 (September/October 1994), pp. 14–15.

229 Mack on Bessett: Cutting, loc. cit., p. 31.

229 Mack on *Time*: Ibid.

229 Daniel Sheehan on committee: Vicki Cooper, "Point Piece: Committee Targets John Mack's Work with Abductees," *UFO* 10, no. 3 (May/June 1995), pp. 6 and 46.

229 Anne Taylor: Alex Beam, "Harvard Takes 'No Adverse Action' on UFO Researcher," *Boston Globe*, August 3, 1995, p. 1.

230 Arnold Relman: Ibid., p. 22.

230 Strieber's lie detector test: Ed Conroy, *Report on Communion* (New York: William Morrow, 1989), p. 61.

231 Philippe Mora's experience: Ibid., p. 210.

231 "We've won": Author's interview, Dallas, Texas, January 13, 1996.

231 family living by lake: Ibid.

232 "the cruelest, nastiest": Sean Casteel, "Q&A: Strieber Sounds Off," *UFO* 8, no. 5 (September/October 1993), p. 21.

232 "I stayed away from all this": Whitley Strieber talk, Unity Church, Dallas, Texas, January 13, 1996.

232 "If this is 'real'": Djuna Wojton, "Whitley Strieber's Journey Beyond Communion," *UFO Universe* 1, no. 1 (July 1988), p. 66.

232 "The message is clear": Whitley Strieber, *Breakthrough: The Next Step* (New York: HarperCollins, 1995), p. 281.

232 "We can choose": Strieber talk.

232 psychedelic visitors: Jefferson R. Weekley, "Denizens of the Psychedelic," *UFO* 8, no. 4 (July/August 1993), pp. 33–34.

233 "I reached out and touched him": Author's interview with Charlene Adams, August 11, 1996.

234 "Oz factor": Randles, op. cit., p. 16.

235 Fred Youngren: Fowler (1980), p. 225.

235 "human/alien hybrid offspring": Mack, op. cit., p. 24.

236 battles between "good" and "evil": Ibid., p. 26.

236 Independent witnessing "rare": Ibid., p. 20.

236 Richard Price account: Vicki Cooper Ecker, "Alien Implants, Part I: State of the Evidence," *UFO* 11, no. 2 (March/April 1996), p. 18.

237 substances from "old trauma site": Ibid., p. 21.

237 Dr. Mack and twisted fiber: Mack, op. cit., p. 27.

237 Dr. Richard Neal's study: Fowler (1990), p. 232.

237 "to monitor me": Mack, op. cit., p. 111.

238 "alien monitoring device": Fowler (1990), p. 55.

238 "cuts and small ulcers": Mack, op. cit., p. 7.

238 "Scars have been observed": Fowler (1990), p. 233.

238 no inflammatory cells and nerve cells: Vicki Ecker, loc. cit., p. 20.

239 "routing to the brain": Ibid.

239 hemocyterin in membrane: Ibid.

239 stud finder stood on end: Ibid.

239 Derrel Sims and objects returned: Vicki Cooper Ecker, "Alien Implants, Part II: Fate of the Evidence," *UFO* 11, no. 3 (May/June 1996), p. 24.

239 keratin, green color, and "scant evidence": Ibid., p. 26.

240 Budd Hopkins quotes: Ibid., pp. 27–28.

240 Linda Cortile account: Budd Hopkins, *Witnessed* (New York: Pocket Books, 1996); Randles, op. cit., pp. 132–35; Brookesmith, op. cit., pp. 136–37; "News Notes: UFOologists Take Sides on Volatile 'Linda Case,'" *UFO* 8, no. 1 (January/February 1993), p. 13.

242 "a geat deal of erroneous information": Hopkins (1996), p. 389.

242 ". . . as for me": Ibid., p. 389.

242 Linda's retort to debunkers: Ibid., p. 381.

242 "most important in recorded history": Ibid., p. xiii.

243 "manipulate the behavior": Ibid., p. 376.

243 "complex breeding experiment": Ibid., p. 378.

243 UFO pilot recruited: Author's interview with Lyn Buchanan, August 9, 1996.

246 1991 Roper poll: Mack, op. cit., p. 448; Dennis Stacy, "Millions of Americans Abducted?" *Fate* 45, no. 9 (September 1992), pp. 60–61.

246 "more solid evidence": Randles, op. cit., p. 104.

246 "five basic dimensions": Mack, op. cit., pp. 28–29.

247 "All of these elements": Fowler (1990), p. 353.

247 "These men and women are neither devoured": Hopkins, op. cit., p. 277.

247 "It is possible": Thompson, op. cit., p. 196.

247 "To me, it seems doubtful": Ibid., p. 168.

247 "UFO abductions have to do . . . ": Mack, op. cit., p. 420.

CHAPTER NINE: Death from the Sky

248 Account of Lady's death: Linda Moulton Howe, *An Alien Harvest: Further Evidence Linking Animal Mutilations and Human Abductions to Alien Life Forms* (Littleton, CO: Linda Moulton Howe Productions, 1989), pp. 1–2.

249 Dr. John Altshuler: Ibid., pp. 3–4.

250 "an attempt to reconstruct history": Author's interview with Linda Howe, August 7, 1996.

250 Sheriff C. G. Richards's account: Cochran County Sheriff's Department Officer's Report, March 10, 1975, copy in author's files.

251 Carl Whiteside on fear: Bella Stumbo, "Cattle," *Los Angeles Times*, wire report LBYLOYYFRYYR (1975), p. 7.

251 CSU veterinary pathology lab: Daniel Kagan and Ian Summers, *Mute Evidence* (New York: Bantam Books, 1983), pp. 78–79.

251 "little more than 5 percent": Ibid.

251 Manuel Gomez: Jim Marrs, "Conference on Cattle Mutilations Gives No Answers," *Fort Worth Star-Telegram*, April 26, 1979, p. 1-B.

251 Sheriff Ray Lee: Dorothy Aldridge, "Are Satan's Phantom Killers Mutilating Cattle?" *Colorado Springs Gazette Telegraph*, June 13, 1975, p. 3-B.

252 Sheriff George Yarnell: Howe interview, August 7, 1996.

252 Dorothy Aldridge: Dorothy Aldridge, "Do UFOs Fly in Colorado?" *Colorado Springs Gazette Telegraph*, April 24, 1977.

252 Gabe Valdez: Marrs (1979), loc. cit., p. 1-B.

252 Arturo Padilla and creature: Associated Press wire story, "Night-Flying Creature Is Sighted in Valley," *Fort Worth Star-Telegram*, January 10, 1976, p. 1-A.

253 Dr. Richard Thill: Jim Ivey, "Ranchers Fear Devil Cultists in Mutilations," *Fort Worth Star-Telegram*, September 8, 1974.

253 Kenneth Bankston: Ed Sanders, "The Mutilation Mystery," *Oui*, September 1976, pp. 52 and 92.

254 Carl Whiteside on cultists: Kagan and Summers, op. cit., pp. 322–23.

255 Sen. Harrison Schmitt: Marrs (1979), loc. cit., p. 1-B.

256 Dr. James Prine and Dr. Clair Hibbs: Ibid.

256 U.S. Attorney R. E. Thompson: Ibid.

256 Capt. Keith Wolverton's decision: Ibid.

257 Ken Rommel's conclusion: Peebles, op. cit., pp. 264–65.

258 Carl Whiteside and valise: Kagan and Summers, op. cit., pp. 324–25.

259 1994 mutilations: Richard Benke, "Cattle Mutilations on Rise in Northern New Mexico," *Albuquerque Journal*, August 14, 1994, p. 4-G.

259 McKenzie mute: Jim Chandler, "Strange Case of Cattle Mutilation Discovered Near McKenzie," *The McKenzie Banner*, May 17, 1995, p. 3.

259 Undersheriff Kenny McKee: Telephone interview, May 30, 1996.

260 Alexander Hamilton: Flammonde, op. cit., pp. 113–14.

260 Hamilton and Liar's Club: Clark, op. cit., p. 31.

261 Bill and Linda Dzuris: Howe (1989), pp. 72–73.

262 rancher sees calfnappers: Ibid., pp. 83–84.

262 "mutes . . . nonexistent": Kagan and Summers, op. cit., p. 490.

262 "flying-saucer nut": Ibid., p. 10.

262 Howe's film: Ibid., p. 124.

263 Howe's "real goal": Ibid., p. 482.

263 Howe's response: Author's telephone interview, May 31, 1996.

263 Tom Adams: Kagan and Summers, op. cit., p. 405.

264 Adams still has no opinion: Author's telephone interview, May 30, 1996.

264 "Once people had made the assumption": Kagan and Summers, op. cit., p. 491.

264 "The image one gets": Peebles, op. cit., p. 269.

264 Myron Scott: Howe (1989), op cit., p. 85.

265 Leslie Weisenhorn and Howe's comment: Author's interviews, May 31, 1996.

266 Judy Doraty account: Howe (1989), pp. 48–58.

268 phenomenon is cloaked: Ralph Steiner, "Linda Moulton Howe: The 'Alien Harvest' and Beyond," ed. Lindemann, op. cit., p. 67.

268 Dr. Henry Monteith: Good (1993), p. 55.

268 "Overall, the strange characteristics": Steiner, loc. cit., p. 63.

268 "I am convinced": Howe (1989), op. cit., p. 224.

269 taken to Kirtland AFB: Ibid., pp. 80–81.

269 James Womack and cow chromosomes: United Press International wire story, "Bovine Beasts, Humans Share 'Perfect Match' Chromosomes," *Texarkana Gazette*, February 27, 1984.

270 parallel between mutilations and abductions: Steiner, loc. cit., p. 69.
270 Puerto Rico deaths: Scott Corrales, "Close Encounters with Puerto Rico's Chu-pacabras," *UFO Sightings* 4, no. 2 (summer 1996), pp. 24–26.
271 Mayor José Soto: Fernando Del Valle, "'Goat Sucker' Fears Sweep South Texas," *Dallas Morning News*, May 7, 1996, p. 13A.
271 Mexico fear: Washington Post, "Blood-Sucking Goat Killer Has All of Mexico Talking," *Des Moines Register*, May 13, 1996, p.1.
272 "collective psychosis": Ibid.
272 Sylvia Ybarra, Maria and Steve Edelstein: Del Valle, loc. cit.

CHAPTER TEN: Going in Circles

273 Joyce Bowles quote: Good (1988), p. 71.
274 Mr. Hart and pigmies: R. M. Skinner, "A Seventeenth-Century Report of an Encounter with an Ionized Vortex?" *Journal of Meteorology*, November 1990, p. 346.
274 Simon Brown: Pat Delgado and Colin Andrews, *Circular Evidence: A Detailed Investigation of the Flattened Swirled Crops Phenomenon* (Grand Rapids, MI: Phanes Press, 1989), p. 37.
274 Gordon Sparkes and Evan Scurclock: Delgado and Andrews, op. cit., pp. 55–56.
275 "Greater Wessex from the air": Charles Thomas, "Magnetic Anomalies," *The Cerealogist*, no. 5 (Winter 1991/2), p. 10.
275 Tim Simpson and Maj. William Hill: Brookesmith, op. cit., p. 160.
275 "UFO nests": Ibid.
277 "mechanically precise": Delgado and Andrew, op. cit., p. 132.
277 "From the evidence we have": Ibid., p. 156.
277 ". . . some plants are pulled up": Ibid., p. 158.
277 ". . . we know some circles": Ibid., p. 121.
278 combing: Vince Migliore, "Crop Circle 'Evolution,'" *UFO* 6, no. 5 (September/October 1991), p. 18.
278 "no limit to the complication": Delgado and Andrews, op. cit., pp. 127–28.
278 Donald Cyr and "whistlegram": ed. Donald L. Cyr, *Crop Circle Secrets–Part Two: America's First Crop Circle* (Santa Barbara, CA: Stonehenge Viewpoint, 1992), p. 7.
279 "hurricane vortex action": Spencer, op. cit., p. 73.
280 "numerous inconsistencies": Delgado and Andrews, op. cit., p. 12.
280 intelligent teasing: Sean Devney, "The Circles: England's Greatest Unsolved Mystery," *UFO Universe* 1, no. 5 (July 1990), p. 32.
280 "It is very sobering": Ibid., p. 158.
281 "appropriate measures" and "disinformation": George Wingfield, "The Doug 'N' Dave Scam," *The Cerealogist*, no. 5 (winter 1991/2), p. 5.
281 *Today* headline and copy: Ibid., p. 3.
282 Blackbird hoax: Howe (1993), p. 27.
282 "accepted at face value": Ibid.
282 four hundred in 1989: Jon Erik Beckjord, "The English 'Circles' Mystery," *UFO* 5, no. 6 (November/December 1990), p. 10.
282 "nearly a thousand": Migliore, loc. cit., p. 21.
282 "circle-making SWAT team": Michael Strainic, "Canada's Wave of Circles," *UFO* 6, no. 6 (November/December 1991), p. 7.
283 Julie Varden and toilet discharge: Wingfield, loc. cit., p. 6.
283 "meteorites": Ibid.
284 "reeling on the ropes": Ibid., p. 5.

284 guys couldn't come up with the answers: Vicki Cooper, "NEWS: Experts Assail Brits' Hoax Claims," *UFO* 6, no. 6 (November/December 1991), p. 6.

284 MBF owns copyright: Wingfield, loc. cit., p. 5.

285 "bogus private news agency": Ibid.

285 "debunking campaign" and CIA: Pat Delgado, "LETTERS: Claimed Hoaxing of Crop Circles," *The Cerealogist*, no. 5 (winter 1991/2), p. 24.

286 "who finances these trips?": Wingfield, loc. cit., p. 6.

286 a trick by two old jokers: Ibid.

286 major disinformation campaign: Cooper, loc. cit., p. 7.

286 Doug and Dave in Percy Hobbs Pub: Carl Sagan, "Crop Circles and Aliens: What's the Evidence?" *Parade* (December 3, 1995), p. 12–13.

287 "official doctrine": John Michell, "Editorial Notes," *The Cerealogist*, no. 5 (Winter 1991/2), p. 2.

287 magnetic disturbances: Charles Thomas, loc. cit.

287 cell pit changes: Howe (1993), p. 45.

288 "no way a hoxer can do this": Ibid., p. 47.

288 Joe Rennick, Chad Deetken and porcupine: Ibid., pp. 67–68.

288 "Forty-five percent is astonishing": Ibid., p. 49.

288 Bruce Rideout and splitting: Ibid., pp. 50–51.

289 unnatural radioactive isotopes: Marshall Dudley and Michael Chorost, "The Discovery of Thirteen Short-lived Radionuclides in Soil Samples in an English Crop Circle," *The Cerealogist*, no. 5 (winter 1991/2), p. 25.

289 biochemistry of plants affected: Ibid., pp. 51 and 83.

289 George Wingfield and Barbury Castle: Ibid., pp. 4–5.

289 UFOs manipulate rotary force field: Delgado and Andrews, op. cit., p. 168.

290 Archie Roy: Howe (1993), p. 4.

290 "A ratio in the diatonic scale": Howe (1993), p. 54; Editors, "Crop Circles: Theorems in Wheat Fields," *Science News* 150, no. 15 (October 12, 1996), p. 239.

290 "accuracy required": Ibid., p. 55.

291 Stonehenge approach: Ivars Peterson, "Euclid's Crop Circles," *Science News* 141, no. 5 (February 1992), p. 77.

291 Euclidean geometry and letter: Ibid. and p. 76.

291 "intricate information conveyed": Howe (1993), p. 58.

291 Bryce Bond: Migliore, loc. cit., p. 24.

292 "borderland" quagmire or mother lode: Ibid., p. 22.

292 audible oddities: Ibid.

292 Dr. Wilhelm Reich: David Wallechinsky and Irving Wallace, "Gallery of Important Persons in the History of Sex," *The People's Almanac*, ed. Ed Rehmus (Garden City, NY: Doubleday, 1975), pp. 1002–3.

292 Tifinag Norse messages: Jon Erik Beckjord, "UFOs Did It: 'Decoding' the Agriglyphs," *UFO* 6, no. 5 (September/October 1991), p. 26.

293 "the latest such fruitless effort": Dennis Stacy, "Counterpoint: A Faulty Translation," *UFO* 6, no. 5 (September/October 1991), pp. 27–28.

293 fairies, pixies, and elves: Peter Hewitt, "A 'Question of Psychology': Cosmic Graffiti," *UFO* 6, no. 5 (September/October 1991), pp. 31–33.

293 "The Circles are saying": Dennis Stacy, "Crop Circles: Brief History and Overview," *MUFON 1991 International UFO Symposium Proceedings* (Versailles, MO: 1991), p. 290.

293 "a promise from God": Migliore, loc. cit., p. 24.

294 circle done in half hour: Andy Thomas, "Fields of Dreams: A Breathtaking Phenomenon," *Sightings*, no. 5 (fall 1996), p. 17.

CHAPTER ELEVEN: In the Mind's Eye

296 "it's a flying saucer": Blum, op. cit., pp. 37–38.

296 Project Aquarius: Ibid., p. 39.

297 "Prophets formed guilds": Trent C. Butler, gen. ed., *Holman Bible Dictionary* (Nashville, TN: Holman Bible Publishers, 1991), p. 1142.

297 Deborah: Judges 4:4–16.

297 Saint Paul: 1 Thessalonians 5:20–21 (Living Bible edition).

298 Croesus: Richard S. Broughton, *Parapsychology: The Controversial Science* (New York: Ballantine Books, 1991), pp. 50–51.

298 Joan of Arc: Justine Glass, *They Foresaw the Future: The Story of Fulfilled Prophecy* (New York: G. P. Putnam's Sons, 1969), p. 96–98.

299 Nostradamus's method: Centuries: Erika Cheetham, *The Prophecies of Nostradamus* (New York: G. P. Putnam's Sons, 1974), pp. 20–21.

299 Charles Richet: Broughton, op. cit., pp. 64–65.

299 J. B. and Louisa Rhine: Ibid., pp. 66–68.

299 Harvard textbook: Ibid., p. 72.

300 "a consistent outline": Louisa E. Rhine, *ESP in Life and Lab: Tracing Hidden Channels* (New York: Macmillan, 1967), p. 267.

300 "consistent, reliable effects": Broughton, op. cit., p. 296.

300 Backster's conclusion: Backster: Peter Tomkins and Christopher Bird, *The Secret Life of Plants* (New York: Avon Books, 1973), p. 27.

301 Printing on paper and light out: Ingo Swann, *To Kiss Earth Goodbye* (New York: Dell Publishing, 1975), pp. 135–36.

301 "remote viewing" term coined: Author's interviews with Ingo Swann, August 27–28, 1993; Ingo Swann, "On Remote-Viewing, UFOs, and Extraterrestrials," *Fate* 46, no. 9 (September 1993), p. 75.

302 "most severely monitored . . . experiment": Ronald M. McRae, *Mind Wars: The True Story of Government Research into the Military Potential of Psychic Weapons* (New York: St. Martin's Press, 1984), p. 99.

302 Lake Victoria: Swann interviews.

303 CIA wants experiments: H. E. Puthoff, "CIA-Initiated Remote Viewing Program at Stanford Research Institute," *Journal of Scientific Exploration* 10, no. 1 (1996), p. 65.

303 Gen. Edmund Thompson: Jim Schnabel, "Tinker, Tailor, Soldier, Psi," *Independent on Sunday*, August 27, 1995, p. 11.

304 CIA-commissioned report: Michael D. Mumford, Andrew M. Rose and David A. Goslin, "An Evaluation of Remote Viewing: Research and Applications," prepared by the American Institutes for Research, September 29, 1995, pp. 5-1, 5-4, and 5-3.

304 "unequivocal evidence": Puthoff (1996), loc. cit., p. 76.

305 *Pioneer 10* bypass noted: Swann, op. cit., p. 149.

305 Swann's description of Jupiter: B. Humphrey, "Swann's Remote Viewing Probe of Jupiter," *SRI International Report* (Menlo Park, CA, March 17, 1980).

306 "no definite evaluation": Targ and Puthoff, op. cit., pp. 210–11.

306 "The most unexpected phenomenon": *Time*, March 19, 1979, p. 87.

306 Ingo to Mercury: Targ and Puthoff, op. cit., p. 211; Swann interviews.

307 "a dull world": "Science News of the Week: The Strange and Cratered World of Mercury," *Science News* 105 (April 6, 1974), p. 220.

308 ". . . world has an atmosphere": Ibid., pp. 221–22.

308 "a complete surprise": "Science News of the Week: Mercury's Magnetism Is Its Own," *Science News* 107 (March 29, 1975), p. 188.

309 12 species of extraterrestrials: PSI TECH report entitled, "Final Project Report: Enigma Penetration: Crop Circles," June 1992, p. 2.

309 "flight school": Author's interview with Lyn Buchanan, August 9, 1996.

310 "Two different devices": PSI TECH report, loc. cit., pp. 3–6.

310 David Morehouse: Author's interviews, 1993 and 1996.

310 Lyn Buchanan: Author's interviews, 1993 and 1996.

311 Mel Riley: Author's interview, 1993 and 1996.

311 "It just works that way": Author's interview with Linda Anderson, December 3, 1993.

312 golden giants on thrones: Morehouse interview, August 29, 1993.

314 ozone: PSI TECH report entitled "Atmospheric Ozone Depletion—Projected Consequences and Remedial Technologies," February 24, 1992; viewer's notes including sketches.

315 reintroduce life to environment: Buchanan interviews.

316 "intergalactic boat people": Morehouse interviews.

317 "part of the overall cosmos": Riley interviews.

317 Mars *Observer:* William J. Cook, "The Invasion of Mars," *U.S. News & World Report,* August 23, 1993, pp. 50–59.

318 *Phobos II*: Final Report, "Enigma Penetration: Soviet Phobos II Space Craft Imaged Anomaly," PSI TECH (September 29, 1991), pp. 1–2.

319 Swann cautions: Vicki Cooper, "The Business of Remote Viewing," *UFO* 8, no. 3 (1993) p. 27.

319 Dunayev: Patrick Huyghe, "Martian Mystery: Is the Red Planet Host to a Third Lunar Body or UFOs?" *Omni,* May 1993, p. 79.

319 Marina Popovich: Jack Vlots, "Soviet Photo of a UFO Near Mars," *San Francisco Chronicle,* December 7, 1991.

320 "Several theories": Huyghe, loc. cit.

320 Weather satellite missing: Associated Press, "New Weather Satellite Lost," *Los Angeles Times,* August 23, 1993.

321 Col. Frank Stirling: Ben Iannotta, "Titan 4 Motor Is Prime Suspect," *Space News,* August 23–29, 1993, p. 1.

321 orbiting devices: Author's interview with George G. Byers, May 19, 1994, and September 12, 1996.

321 Earth embargo: James W. Deardorff, "Possible Extraterrestrial Strategy for Earth," *Quarterly Journal of the Royal Astronomy Society* 27 (1986), p. 94.

322 "system of intergalactic ethics": Lance Morrow, "Is There Life in Outer Space?" *Time,* February 5, 1996, p. 51.

323 New Mexico site: George D. Hathaway, "Report on Preliminary Invesigations of Anomalous Phenomena in Western New Mexico," prepared by Hathaway Consulting Services, Toronto, Canada, November 30, 1991, p. 10.

324 Second visit: George D. Hathaway, "MJ5 Trip Summary Report Western New Mexico Site #1: May 12, 13 & 14, 1992," prepared by Hathaway Consulting Services, Toronto, Canada, June 26, 1992, p. 13.

325 Martians on Earth: Internal correspondence, PSI TECH, Inc., "Long-term Study: A Martian Civilization," September 23, 1991, pp. 1–2; author's interviews.

326 "There *are* Martians on Earth": Courtney Brown, *Cosmic Voyage: A Scientific Discovery of Extraterrestrials Visiting Earth* (New York: Dutton, 1996), pp. 68–69.

326 Face-to-face with Martian: George Byers interviews.

327 "subsurface habitats": Christopher P. McKay, "Did Mars Once Have Martians?" *Astronomy*, September 1993, pp. 28 and 33.

327 NASA's Daniel S. Goldin: John Noble Wilford, "Clues in Meteorite Seem to Show Signs of Life on Mars Long Ago," *New York Times*, August 7, 1996, p. 1.

327 "bacteria boondoggle": Traci Watson, "The Martian Chronicles," *U.S. News & World Report*, August 19, 1996, p. 48.

327 Carl Sagan and Stephen Jay Gould: David Colton, "Discovery Would Equal Finding the New World," *USA Today*, August 7, 1996, p. 1A.

328 Ian Barbour, Jerry Falwell, and Kim Stanley Robinson: Ibid.

329 "We want the face to face": J. Antonio Huneeus, "UFO Chronicle," *Fate* 46, no. 9 (September 1993), p. 32.

329 "Feedbackless Science": Ingo Swann, "On Remote-Viewing, UFOs and Extraterrestrials," *Fate* 46, no. 9 (September 1993), p. 80.

329 the need for feedback: Ibid., p. 79.

329 Joe McMoneagle on Dames: Michael Miley, "Remote Viewing and Alien Targets: Room with an (Alien) View," *UFO* 11, no. 3 (May/June 1996), p. 40.

329 Miley's summation: Ibid., p. 41.

330 "space cowboys": Ibid., p. 42.

330 "Galactic Federation Headquarters": Mel Riley, "Remote Viewing Session Summary," January 13, 1988; author's interviews.

332 "Confederation Headquarters": Author's interview with Ray Bordon, April 17, 1996.

333 "opted to remain anonymous": Letter of Transmittal from American Association of Remote Viewers, September 4, 1996.

333 UFO descriptions: A. R. Bordon, Project Officer, *UFOs and Alien Agenda* (Dallas: American Association of Remote Viewers, Inc., 1996), p. 6.

334 technology: Ibid., pp. 6–7.

334 technology in government hands: Ibid., pp. 7–8.

335 box-like laptop: Ibid., p. 8.

335 numerous alien contacts: Ibid., pp. 9–10.

335 three abductees: Ibid., p. 9.

335 "millions": Ibid., p. 10.

336 adoption of technology: Ibid., pp. 12–13.

336 craft in hangar and cave: Ibid., p. 7.

336 President Clinton: Ibid., p. 12.

336 weapon on seashore: Ibid., p. 13.

337 "parade of aliens": Ibid.

337 "humungous dude": Ibid.

337 "white pyramid": Ibid., p. 14.

338 "shut out of the loop": Ibid., p. 15.

338 planet "wreaks havoc": Ibid.

338 "training exercise": Ibid., p. 17.

339 "not exactly good": Ibid.

339 "remnant energy beings": Ibid.

340 1890s writer: Ibid., pp. 21–22.

340 Germans: Ibid., p. 22.

340 one "like praying mantis": Ibid., p. 25.

340 Eisenhower meeting: Ibid., pp. 20–21.

343 hologram: Ibid., p. 23.

343 "grand meeting place": Ibid., p. 26.

343 "energizer": Ibid., p. 27.

344 "just like cops": Ibid., pp. 27–28.

344 "guerrilla war": Ibid., p. 28.

344 "a whole armada": Ibid.

345 "two dogs fighting": Ibid., p. 29.

345 "billions of gowns": Ibid.

346 "low humming sound": Ibid., p. 30.

346 "separation is unnatural": Ibid., p. 31.

CHAPTER TWELVE: A Metaphysical Exam

349 "a historical example": Dr. Jacques Vallee, *Dimensions: A Casebook of Alien Contact* (New York: Ballantine Books, 1988), p. 173.

349 "The final 'miracle'": Ibid., p. 178.

349 major differences with UFOs: Nelson S. Pacheco and Tommy R. Blann, *Unmasking the Enemy: Visions and Deception in the End Times* (Arlington, VA: Bendan Press, 1994), p. 103.

350 "communicating . . . symbolically": Vallee (1988), p. 257.

350 "a profound challenge": Ibid., p. x.

350 "ancient tradition of little people": Jacques Vallee, *Revelations: Alien Contact and Human Deception* (New York: Ballantine Books, 1991), p. 275.

350 "demonic, angelic or simply alien": Vallee (1988), p. 32.

350 "a backdrop to the religion": Randles, op. cit., p. 7.

350 "a grave mistake": Vallee (1988), p. 65.

351 "scholars left books": Ibid., p. 64.

351 "cross-cultural study": Thompson, op. cit., p. 12.

351 "worldwide myth": Vallee (1988), p. 99.

351 "folklore in the making": Ibid., p. 146.

351 "undiscovered dimensions": Ibid., p. 203.

351 "real physical objects": Ibid., pp. xiii–xiv.

352 "mass, inertia, volume": Ibid., p. 202.

352 UFO traits: Ibid., pp. 159–60.

352 "too simple-minded": Ibid., p. 158.

352 John Keel: Clifford Wilson, *The Alien Agenda* (New York: Signet Books, 1988), p. 159.

353 "spiritual control system": Ibid., pp. 246–47.

353 "schedule of reinforcement": Ibid., p. 245.

353 Luntz Research poll: Editors, "What Does America Believe?" *George*, December 1996, pp. 114–17.

354 "intriguing anthropological finds": Editors, *The New Encyclopedia Britannica*, vol. 11, 15th ed. (Chicago: Encyclopedia Britannica, Inc., 1991), p. 569.

354 war as social control: Bramley, op. cit., p. 3.

354 third-party manipulation: Ibid.

355 "utterly bizarre realities": Ibid., p. 4.

355 humans as "slave race": Ibid., p. 37.

355 "we're property": Charles Fort, *The Books of Charles Fort* (New York: Henry Holt, 1941), p. 163.

355 Dr. Fred Hoyle: Otto O. Binder, "UFO's 'Own' Earth and All Mankind!" *Saga*, December 1971, p. 36.

356 "A glowing UFO": Miller, op. cit., Prologue, p. 8.

357 "attempting to reach as many people as they could": Ibid., p. 15.

357 energy in space: Ibid., p. 22.

357 one bulb boils seas: Owen Davies, "Volatile Vacuums," *OMNI* (February 1991), p. 54.

357 "Rosetta stone": Ibid., p. 50.

358 world leaders informed: Miller, op. cit., p. 6.

358 "the thought of our Divine One": Ibid., p. 78.

358 Cayce uncannily accurate: David Wallechinsky, Amy Wallace, and Irving Wallace, *The Book of Predictions* (New York: Bantam Books, 1981), p. 371.

358 "Mayan experience": Author's interview with Rob Grant, Research and Development, Association for Research and Enlightenment, September 3, 1996.

359 Man's origin as spirit: Edgar Evans Cayce, *Edgar Cayce on Atlantis* (New York: Paperback Library, 1968), p. 82.

359 "speaking for Seth": Jane Roberts, *Seth Speaks* (New York: Bantam Books, 1972), p. vii.

359 "multidimensional personalities": Ibid., p. 459.

359 "an illusion": Ibid., p. 41.

359 like an onion or orange: Ibid., p. 13.

359 "poor for a day": Ibid., p. 485.

360 "Consciousness creates form": Ibid., p. 5.

360 "divinely-inspired computer": Ibid., p. 40.

360 "visitors from other realities": Ibid., p. 473.

360 God as Tao: Chelsea Quinn Yarbro, *Messages from Michael* (New York: Berkley Books, 1980), p. 23.

361 "pandimensional universe": Ibid., p. 208.

361 entities fragment: Ibid., p. 65.

361 test tubes in ocean: Ibid., p. 64.

361 "Blind faith eliminates understanding": Ibid., p. 51.

361 "two such species": Ibid., p. 268.

362 information doubles: Bob Frissell, *Nothing in This Book Is True, But It's Exactly How Things Are* (Berkeley, CA: Frog, Ltd., 1994), p. 10.

363 "musical scale": Ibid., pp. 21–22.

363 whales and dolphins: Ibid., p. 46.

363 "everyone will make it": Ibid., p. 171.

363 "what Jesus meant": Ibid., p. 173.

364 "X-ray sensors off the scale": Editors, *Science News* 102, no. 8 (August 19, 1972), p. 119.

364 "extraterrestrials regularly visit": Ibid., pp. 19–20.

365 "secret government": Ibid., p. 165.

365 they need love: Ibid., p. 168.

366 the local universe of Nebadon: *The Urantia Book* (Chicago, IL: Urantia Foundation, 1955), p. 1.

366 "we are in him": Ibid., p. 196.

367 "the occult": Pacheco and Blann, op. cit., p. 28.

367 separate physical from spiritual: Ibid., p. 39.

367 "end of world": Ibid., p. 364.

368 "campaign of deception": Ibid., p. 9.

368 "UFOs represent demon activity": John Weldon with Zola Levitt, *UFOs: What on Earth Is Happening?* (Irvine, CA: Harvest House Publishers, 1975), p. 23.

368 "heavenly super-car": Clifford Wilson, op. cit., pp. 208–9.

368 "author of terror": Ibid., p. 227.

368 "special relationship with God": Paul Davies, "The Harmony of the Spheres," *Time*, February 5, 1996, p. 58.

368 "both good and evil manifestations": Pacheco and Blann, op. cit., p. 63.

369 "the best approach": Pacheco and Blann, op. cit., p. 63.

369 "playing into his hands": Weldon and Levitt, op. cit., p. 15.

369 projecting subjective reality: Author's interview with Whitley Strieber, January 13, 1996.

369 Rev. James A. Wiseman: Bill Broadway, "What Life on Mars Could Mean," *Portland Press Herald*, August 17, 1996, p. 1C.

370 Stanley Hauerwas: Ibid.

370 James Leo Garrett: Ibid.

370 Burton Visotzky and Fathi Osman: Ibid., p. 2C.

370 Alexander Wolszczan: Traci Watson, "Astronomy: A Big Find, No Kidding," *U.S. News & World Report*, May 2, 1994, p. 12.

370 Geoffrey Marcy and Paul Butler: Michael D. Lemonick, "Astronomers Have Detected Water-Bearing Planets Around Nearby Stars," *Time*, February 5, 1996, p. 53.

371 "aliens": Watson, loc. cit., p. 12.

371 "bubbles in a cosmic froth": William F. Allman, "Alternative Realities: Beyond the Top Quark Lies a Bizarre New Realm of Theoretical Physics," *U.S. News & World Report*, May 9, 1994, p. 59.

APPENDIX: Take Me to Your Leader

380 Zbigniew Brzezinski: Hedrick P. Smith, "Brzezinski Says Critics Are Irked by His Accuracy," *New York Times*, January 18, 1981, p. L3.

380 Franklin D. Roosevelt: A. Ralph Epperson, *The Unseen Hand: An Introduction to the Conspiratorial View of History* (Tucson, AZ: Publius Press, 1985), p. 7.

380 The coup of 1934: Higham, op. cit., pp. 163–64; also see Jules Archer, *The Plot to Seize the White House* (New York: Hawthorne Books, 1973).

381 "Disney" version: Jonathan Vankin and John Whalen, *Fifty Greatest Conspiracies of All Time* (New York: Citadel Press, 1995), p. xii.

382 Marco Polo and fiat money: G. Edward Griffin, *The Creature from Jekyll Island: A Second Look at the Federal Reserve* (Westlake Village, CA: American Media, 1994), p. 156.

383 "money illusion": William Greider, *Secrets of the Temple: How the Federal Reserve Runs the Country* (New York: Simon & Schuster, 1987), p. 228.

383 "independent department": Ibid., p. 49.

384 Thomas Jefferson: Martin A. Larson, *The Essence of Jefferson* (New York: Joseph J. Binns, 1977), p. 196.

384 Alexander Hamilton: Howard Zinn, *A People's History of the United States* (New York: Harper & Row, 1980), p. 100.

384 Rothschilds' power: Griffin, op. cit., p. 331.

385 "five objectives": Ibid., p. 23.

385 Frank Vanderlip: Ibid., p. 464.

385 prophecy: Ibid., p. 60.

385 "opposed them and thwarted them": Greider, op. cit., p. 11.

386 "crucial anomaly": Ibid., p. 12.

386 Wright Patman: Epperson, op. cit., p. 174.

386 Charles Lindbergh: Ibid., p. 173.

386 Louis McFadden: James Perloff, *The Shadows of Power: The Council on Foreign Relations and the American Decline* (Appleton, WS: Western Islands, 1988), pp. 23–24.

386 1963 publication and Epperson's comment: Epperson, op. cit., p. 173.

386 abolition of the Fed: Griffin, op. cit., p. iii.

387 "The . . . mechanism": Ibid., p. 207.

387 "too esoteric for ordinary citizens": Greider, op. cit., p. 12.

387 Fed as religious institution: Ibid., p. 53.

387 the result is massive debt: William Bramley, *The Gods of Eden* (San Jose, CA: Dahlin Family Press, 1989), p. 432.

388 unequal distribution of wealth: Ibid., p. 39.

388 Census Bureau statistics: Editors, "Inequality: Still on the Rise," *U.S. News & World Report*, July 1, 1996, p. 15.

388 "interlocking directorates": Wallechinsky and Wallace (1975), p. 464.

388 interconnected stock: Milton Moskowitz, "If Banks Own It All, Who Owns the Banks?" *Fort Worth Star-Telegram*, August 28, 1978, p. 5b.

389 top ten censored stories: Editors, "Unfit to Print," *Utne Reader* (July–August 1996), p. 22.

390 "no radical thinkers": Greider, op. cit., p. 73.

390 unofficial "fraternity": Ibid.

391 "secret society": Carroll Quigley, *The Anglo-American Establishment: From Rhodes to Cliveden* (New York: Books in Focus, 1981), p. ix.

391 "international Anglophile network": Carroll Quigley, *The World Since 1939: A History* (New York: Macmillan, 1968), p. 290.

391 "The chief backbone": Ibid., p. 291–92.

392 first Clinton administration and CFR: Annual Report, 1991–91, Council on Foreign Relations, New York City.

392 Prince Bernhard: Epperson, op. cit., p. 206.

392 Jack Sheinkman: Trisha Katson, "Some U.S. Bilderbergs Break Silence," *The Spotlight* 22, no. 25 (June 24, 1996), p. 1.

393 William F. Buckley Jr. and Paul Gigot: Ibid., p. 4.

393 energy as "social need": Barry Commoner, *The Poverty of Power: Energy and the Economic Crisis* (New York: Alfred A. Knopf, 1976), p. 238.

393 "wide open insane asylum": Don Kelly, "Successful Devices at Hand: Update on 'Free Energy,'" *UFO* 6, no. 3 (May/June 1991), p. 27.

394 Laurance Rockefeller and BSW: Editors, "Point Piece: 'Elite' Foundation Launches UFO Project," *UFO* 10, no. 1 (January/February 1995), p. 6.

INDEX